THE EXECUTIVE BRANCH OF FEDERAL GOVERNMENT

Other Titles in ABC-CLIO's

ABOUT
FEDERAL GOVERNMENT
Set

Charles L. Zelden, set editor

The Judicial Branch of Federal Government: People, Process, and Politics, Charles L. Zelden

The Legislative Branch of Federal Government: People, Process, and Politics, Gary P. Gershman

THE EXECUTIVE BRANCH OF FEDERAL GOVERNMENT

People, Process, and Politics

Brian R. Dirck

A B C **CLIO**

Santa Barbara, California   Denver, Colorado   Oxford, England

Library of Congress Cataloging-in-Publication Data
Dirck, Brian R., 1965–
   The executive branch of federal government : people, process, and politics / Brian R. Dirck.
      p. cm. — (ABC-CLIO's about federal government)
   Includes bibliographical and references and index.
   ISBN 978-1-85109-791-3 (hard copy : alk. paper) -- ISBN 978-1-85109-796-8 (ebook)
1. Presidents—United States. 2. United States—Politics and government. I. Title.
JK516.D57 2007
351.73--dc22
                           2007010753

11   10   09   08   07   10 9 8 7 6 5 4 3 2 1

Senior Production Editor: Cami Cacciatore
Editorial Assistant: Sara Springer
Production Manager: Don Schmidt
Media Editor: Karen Koppel
Media Resources Coordinator: Ellen Brenna Dougherty
Media Resources Manager: Caroline Price
File Management Coordinator: Paula Gerard

ABC-CLIO, Inc.
130 Cremona Drive, P.O. Box 1911
Santa Barbara, California 93116–1911
This book is also available on the World Wide Web as an eBook. Visit abc-clio.com for details.

This book is printed on acid-free paper ∞ .
Manufactured in the United States of America

CONTENTS

Foreword, vii
Preface, xi
History of the Executive Office, xiii

1 Roles, Functions, and Powers of Presidents, 1

2 The People Who Serve: Seeking, Winning, and Holding the White House, 39

3 The Role of the Presidency in American Politics, 77

4 The Politics of the Presidency, 129

5 The White House's Relations with Other Branches, 187

Glossary of Concepts and People, 237
Inaugural Addresses (edited highlights), 247
   Inaugural Addresses 1789–1865, 249
   Inaugural Addresses 1869–1933, 305
   Inaugural Addresses 1949–2005, 353
State of the Union Addresses (edited highlights), 395
   State of the Union Addresses 1790–1862, 397
   State of the Union Addresses 1865–1930, 427
   State of the Union Addresses 1934–2002, 449
Annotated Bibliography, 481
Index, 495
About the Author, 511

FOREWORD

Most of us know something about the federal government. At the very least, we can name its three branches—executive, legislative, and judicial—and discuss the differences between them. At an early age, we are taught in school about the president of the United States and his official roles and responsibilities; we learn about Congress and the courts and their place in our government. In civics classes, we often get a skeletal picture of how the nation's government works; we are told that Congress writes the laws, the president executes them, and the Supreme Court acts as the interpreter of the U.S. Constitution. News reports, blogs, and editorials we read as adults add to this knowledge. Many of us can go further and explain some of the basic interactions among the branches. We know that the laws Congress passes are subject to the president's veto power and the Supreme Court's powers of judicial review; we understand that the president names the members of his cabinet and nominates justices to the Supreme Court, but that the Senate has to confirm these nominations; and we can discuss how the Supreme Court, as the "caretaker" of the Constitution, can declare laws unconstitutional, but that it is up to the legislative and executive branches to enforce these rulings. We bandy around such terms as *checks and balances* and *separation of powers.* We talk about majority votes and filibusters in the Senate.

For most of us, however, this is about as far as our knowledge goes. According to newspaper accounts spanning decades, most Americans have trouble naming members of the Supreme Court, or key figures in the congressional leadership, or the members of the president's cabinet. Still fewer of us can explain in detail how a bill becomes a law, or the president's authority in foreign affairs, or how the Supreme Court decides a case. If we ask about the historical development of these institutions and officials and their powers, the numbers of those who understand how our federal government works drop even further.

It is not surprising that most of us do not know a lot about the workings of our government. Government is a large and complex enterprise. It includes thousands of people working on subjects ranging from tax reform to national security, from voting rights to defining and enforcing environmental standards. Much of the work of government, although technically open to the public, is done out of sight and hence out of mind. We may know about those parts of the government that affect us directly—the Social Security Administration for the elderly, the Defense Department for those with family members in the military, or the Supreme Court when the news is filled with such controversial topics as abortion or the right to die or prayer in schools—but our understandings are generally limited to only those parts that directly affect us. Although this state of affairs is understandable, it is also dangerous. Our form of government is a demo-cratic republic. This means that, although elected or appointed officials carry out the duties of government, "We the People of the United States" are the ultimate authority, and not just because we choose those who run the government (or those who appoint the men and women who run the day-to-day business of government). In the end, it is our choices that shape (or, at least, should shape) the scope and function of the federal government. As Abraham Lincoln gracefully put it, ours is a government "of the peo-ple, by the people, for the people."

Yet what sort of choices can we make if we do not understand the structures, work-ings, and powers of the federal government? Choices made in ignorance are dangerous choices. When a president goes on TV and claims a power not granted by the Constitu-tion, we need to know that this claim is something new. It might be that what the pres-ident is asking for is a reasonable and necessary extension of the powers already held by the executive branch—but it might, on the other hand, be a radical expansion of his powers based on nothing more than his say-so. If we do not understand what is normal, how can we judge whether abnormal and exceptional proposals are necessary or proper? The same is true when pundits and politicians rant on about the dangers of "activist judges." How can we know what an "activist judge" is if we do not even understand a "normal" judge's job? What one person calls dangerous activism could be courageous defense of constitutional rights in other people's eyes—or what one person praises as a creative reading of the Constitution, another person might denounce as an irresponsi-ble and unwise judicial experiment.

This is the point: without knowledge of the way things are supposed to be, how can we judge when the powers of government are being underused, misused, or even abused? The need for this knowledge is the root from which the three volumes of the About Federal Government series have grown. Our goal is to present the federal govern-ment as a living, working system made up of real people doing jobs of real importance—not just in the abstract, but for all of us in our daily lives. Knowledge is power, and this is as true today as when Lord Francis Bacon wrote it about four hundred years ago. Un-derstanding how our government works, and how each of its institutions works, and how they interact with one another and with "We the People" is not just something we might need to pass a civics test or a citizenship exam—it is a source of power for us as citizens. Knowing how a bill becomes a law and the many ways that a good idea can be derailed by the process of lawmaking is a source of power—for some day, there may be a bill that you want to see enacted into law, or that you want to prevent being made a law. Knowing the stress points at which a bill is most vulnerable to defeat can give you the opportunity to put pressure where it would do the most good. We can find similar examples for the other two branches as well.

One way of showing the living and evolving nature of the federal government is to place it into its historical context. Our government did not just come into being fully formed. The government we have today is the result of over two hundred years of growth and change, of choices made and laws passed. Much of what we hold to be gospel today, when it comes to the goals and methods and powers of the national government, resulted from our experiences—good and bad—in the past. How can one understand today's civil rights laws, for example, without first understanding the impact of slavery, the Civil War, and Reconstruction on the structure of our government? Forgetting the past leaves us powerless to deal with the present and the future. A second way to bring our government to life is to focus on the interactions among the three branches of the federal government, as well as between these three branches and the states. Most of the controversy shaping our governing structures grew out of conflicts among the various branches of the federal government, or between the federal government and the states. When Congress fights with the president over budgets or the Supreme Court overturns a popular law passed by Congress and signed by the president, or when a state defies a mandate issued by the U.S. Supreme Court and the president must put that state's National Guard under his authority to enforce the Court's decision, those crises clarify the actual working structures of our government. Like flexing a muscle to make it strong, these interactions define the actual impact of our government—not only today, but in the future as well. Finally, we can understand the living nature of the federal government by examining the people who make up that government. Government is not an abstract idea: it is people doing their jobs as best they can. If government can be said to have a personality, it is the direct reflection of the collective personalities of those who work in our government. Hence, when we talk about Congress, we are talking about the people who are elected to the House of Representatives and the Senate and whose values, views, beliefs, and prejudices shape the output of the national legislature. The About Federal Government series integrates all three of these approaches as it sets out the workings and structures of our national government. Written by historians with a keen understanding of the workings of government past and present, these volumes stress the ways in which each of the branches helps form part of a whole system—and the ways that each branch is unique as an institution. Finally, we have given special stress to bringing the people and the history of these branches to life, in the process making clear just how open to our own intervention our government really is. This is our government, and the more we understand how it works, the more real our "ownership" of it will be.

Charles L. Zelden, Set Editor
Nova Southeastern University

PREFACE

Like most Americans, I have never been particularly close to a president. In 1990 I lived in Houston and was occasionally on the periphery of a George Bush Sr. visit to his adopted hometown. His presence wasn't exactly subtle. When the presidential motorcade arrived, policemen were posted on every overpass along his route, and traffic was redirected in various creative and inconvenient ways. I can recall seeing his limousine flash by a couple of blocks away from the traffic jam in which I found myself, flanked by police cars and Secret Service vehicles.

Bush also chose Houston's Rice University to host a worldwide economic summit, and the preparations for that high-profile event were massive. Getting around campus that summer suddenly became difficult, and students were informed that there would be several days during which we would not be allowed to enter under any circumstances. Several classrooms were rebuilt to accommodate the summit's security concerns, and an entirely new wall was added to the front entrance of the library. (The rationale for this was never clear.) I again saw the presidential motorcade from a distance when it roared onto campus the day of his speech.

I came just a bit closer to a president two years later, during the 1992 campaign, when candidate Bill Clinton visited Independence, Missouri, Harry Truman's adopted hometown. I had moved to nearby Lawrence, Kansas, at the time and attended the speech he delivered in front of Truman's bronze statue during a Labor Day rally. I don't remember much about what he said. He touted his health care reform program and tried to claim the Truman mantle of representing small town America's midwestern values. But I do recall the massive crowd, turned out in a pouring rainstorm to see and shake hands with the Democratic candidate.

Clinton wasn't even a president (yet), but the presence of a man who could someday occupy the Oval Office was enough to inspire an almost rockstar presence. I only managed to get within about one hundred feet from him before he was engulfed by a sea of outstretched hands, as many of which he shook as was possible. At one point he had both arms completely outstretched, straining the seams of his suit and bending close to the speaker platform's edge as scores of people reached up and out—he wasn't so much shaking hands as slapping at them.

It's an apt little symbol, in its way: a president—or in this case, a president-to-be—both touching and separated from the people who elect him. A cynic might observe that this was faux democracy—the appearance of connecting with "the people," when in fact presidents are walled off from their constituents by ranks of plexiglass, body guards, and all the insignia and trappings of the most powerful office in the world.

An optimist, on the other hand, might point out that the mere fact that an individual with such power should feel compelled to at least try touching the masses of American voters suggests something unusual and unique in human history. Few kings ever did so, and even fewer dictators or strongmen. Granted that presidents are not nearly so directly and innocently hooked into the lives of ordinary Americans as they would have us believe. In one famous recent instance during the 1992 presidential campaign George Bush Sr. couldn't name the price of a loaf of bread because the man rarely if ever did his own shopping. After he left the White House, Harry Truman was in the bad habit of running stoplights, because for years his motorcade had stopped traffic, not vice versa. Even the most unassuming presidents receive special treatment. Still, as world leaders go, presidents are remarkably accessible.

It is an uneasy alliance, democracy and power. It always has been, ever since the days of the ancient Greeks. Over the last two hundred plus years, the American presidency has on occasion tipped itself toward one or the other side of that alliance, sometimes excessively so. But on the whole, presidents and the people who elect them have walked the tightrope pretty well. No, I never got the chance to meet or shake hands with a once or future occupant of the White House. But the fact that I might reasonably expect to someday do so speaks volumes about the fundamentally democratic nature of the office.

HISTORY OF THE EXECUTIVE OFFICE

1787   The United States Constitution is drafted, establishing the office of president.

1789   George Washington defeats John Adams in the first presidential election in American history.

1792   George Washington defeats John Adams to win his second and last presidential election.

1796   John Adams narrowly defeats Thomas Jefferson.

1800   Thomas Jefferson narrowly defeats John Adams in one of the most bitterly contested elections in American presidential history.

1804   Thomas Jefferson wins reelection handily over Federalist opponent Charles Cotesworth Pinckney.

1808   James Madison defeats Federalist candidate Charles Cotesworth Pinckney.

1812   James Madison wins reelection over Federalist DeWitt Clinton; President Madison asks for and receives a declaration of war from Congress against Great Britain.

1816   James Monroe defeats the last Federalist candidate, Rufus King.

1820   James Monroe overwhelmingly defeats independent candidate John Quincy Adams to win a second presidential term.

1824   John Quincy Adams defeats Andrew Jackson to win election; Jackson's supporters cry foul over the so-called corrupt bargain between Adams and Henry Clay.

1828   Andrew Jackson defeats John Quincy Adams, ushering in the creation of the Democratic and Whig parties.

1832   Andrew Jackson wins reelection to a second term by defeating Whig Henry Clay.

1836   Martin Van Buren wins election by defeating William Henry Harrison.

1840   William Henry Harrison wins the presidency, using the famous slogan "Tippecanoe and Tyler too."

1841   President Harrison suddenly dies in office, elevating Vice President John Tyler to the presidency.

1844   Democrat James K. Polk wins the presidency on a strongly expansionist platform.

1846   President Polk asks for and receives a declaration of war against Mexico.

1848   Mexican War hero and Whig Zachary Taylor wins election to the White House, defeating Lewis Cass.

1850   Vice President Millard Fillmore becomes president when Zachary Taylor dies in office.

1852   Democrat Franklin Pierce is elected to the presidency over military hero Winfield Scott.

1856   Democrat James Buchanan defeats the Pathfinder, Republican John C. Fremont.

1860   Abraham Lincoln defeats Stephen Douglas and John C. Breckinridge, candidates of a broken Democratic Party, and Constitutional Union candidate John Bell.

1864   Abraham Lincoln defeats Democrat and military general George B. McClellan.

1865   Vice President Andrew Johnson becomes president when Abraham Lincoln is assassinated by John Wilkes Booth in Ford's Theatre, Washington D.C.

1868   Andrew Johnson becomes the first president in American history to be impeached, the reasons being violation of the Tenure of Office Act and his Reconstruction policies; he escapes conviction by one vote. Civil War icon Ulysses S. Grant wins election to the White House as a Republican.

1872   Despite a scandal-ridden administration, President Grant wins reelection, defeating New York newspaperman Horace Greeley.

1876   Rutherford B. Hayes wins the White House after a compromise between his Republican Party and Democrats, in which he promises to bring Reconstruction to a close.

1880   Republican James Garfield defeats fellow Civil War general Winfield Scott Hancock.

1881   Vice President Chester A. Arthur becomes president when James Garfield is assassinated at a Washington, D.C., train station.

1884   Grover Cleveland defeats James G. Blaine to become the first Democratic president since James Buchanan.

1888   Republican Benjamin Harrison defeats Grover Cleveland.

1892   Grover Cleveland regains the White House for a second term by defeating his 1888 opponent and Republican incumbent Benjamin Harrison.

1896   William McKinley becomes the last Civil War veteran to serve in the White House by defeating populist Democrat William Jennings Bryan.

1898   President William McKinley asks for and receives a declaration of war against Spain.

1900   President McKinley wins a second term by again defeating William Jennings Bryan.

1901   Vice President Theodore Roosevelt becomes president after William McKinley is assassinated in Buffalo, New York.

1904   President Roosevelt wins reelection to a second term by defeating Democrat Alton B. Parker.

1908   William H. Taft defeats perennial Democratic candidate William Jennings Bryan.

1912   Woodrow Wilson defeats incumbent Taft and Progressive (Bull Moose) Party candidate Theodore Roosevelt.

1916   Woodrow Wilson wins reelection with the slogan "He Kept Us out of War," referring to America's reluctance to involve itself in Europe's World War I.

1917   Despite his campaign pledges, President Wilson reacts to Germany's targeting of American shipping by asking for and receiving a declaration of war and entering World War I.

1920   Warren G. Harding defeats Democrat James M. Cox.

1923   Vice President Calvin Coolidge becomes president after Harding dies in office.

1924   President Coolidge defeats Democrat John W. Davis.

1928   Republican Herbert Hoover defeats Democrat Alfred E. Smith.

1932   Democrat Franklin D. Roosevelt defeats incumbent Herbert Hoover.

1936   President Franklin D. Roosevelt wins reelection in a landslide over Republican Alf Landon.

1940   Franklin Roosevelt wins an unprecedented third term by handily defeating Republican Wendell Wilkie.

1941   Following the Japanese assault on Pearl Harbor, President Franklin Roosevelt asks for and receives a declaration of war against Japan, Germany, and Italy.

1944   Franklin Roosevelt wins a fourth term in office, defeating Thomas Dewey.

1945   Vice President Harry S. Truman becomes president when Franklin Roosevelt dies of heart failure at Warm Springs, Georgia.

1948   President Harry Truman stuns many political observers by defeating Republican Thomas Dewey and winning election to the White House in his own right.

1952   World War II general Dwight D. Eisenhower defeats Democrat Adlai Stevenson.

1956   President Dwight Eisenhower wins reelection by again defeating Adlai Stevenson.

1960   Democrat John F. Kennedy narrowly defeats Richard M. Nixon in one of the closest elections in American presidential history.

1963   Vice President Lyndon B. Johnson becomes president when John F. Kennedy is assassinated in Dallas, Texas.

1964   Lyndon Johnson wins election to office in his own right by easily defeating Republican Barry Goldwater.

1968   Richard M. Nixon defeats Democrat Hubert Humphrey.

1972   President Richard Nixon wins reelection by easily defeating Democrat George McGovern.

1972   Vice President Gerald Ford becomes president when Richard Nixon resigns from office under threat of impeachment for his role in the Watergate scandal.

1976   Democrat Jimmy Carter defeats incumbent Republican Gerald Ford.

1980   Former California governor Ronald Reagan defeats Jimmy Carter.

1984   President Ronald Reagan wins reelection by defeating Democrat Walter Mondale in a landslide.

1988   Vice President George Bush Sr. defeats Democrat Michael Dukakis.

1992   Democrat William J. Clinton defeats Republican incumbent George Bush.

1996   President Clinton wins reelection by defeating Senator Robert J. Dole.

1998   President Clinton becomes the second president in American history to be impeached, in his case for his role in the Monica Lewinsky scandal, but is not convicted.

2000   George Bush Jr. defeats Vice President Albert A. Gore in a disputed election that is eventually decided by the U.S. Supreme Court.

2004   President George Bush is reelected, defeating Democratic challenger John F. Kerry.

1

ROLES, FUNCTIONS, AND POWERS OF PRESIDENTS

"The thought of being president frightens me," Ronald Reagan once admitted, "I do not think I want the job." It was an astonishing admission, coming as it did from a man who seemed entirely at ease during his time in office—sometimes too much so. Rumor had it he slept during Cabinet meetings, played with a jar of jelly beans on his desk while listening to policy briefings, and was rather lax in his attention to presidential detail. Some people thought he did not take the job seriously. "My fellow Americans, I am pleased to tell you I just signed legislation which outlaws Russia forever," he once quipped while testing a supposedly dead microphone, "The bombing begins in five minutes" (www.quotationspage.com/quote/129.html). Few presidents were more genial, comfortable, or easygoing than "the Gipper," whose acting background seemed to have perfectly equipped him to handle the fishbowl life of the nation's chief executive.

But he was right; the presidency is, in fact, a scary job. Look at any photograph of a president taken at the beginning of his term in office and another at the end, and signs of aging will be evident, far beyond the amount of time the man actually spent in office. Reagan's eight years in the White House—and they were by most standards successful years—left him noticeably less hale and hearty. Bill Clinton's hair was much grayer in 1998 than it had been in 1992. Lyndon Johnson's weather-beaten face was pocked with worry lines and wrinkles—many placed there by the morass in Vietnam—when he chose not to run for reelection in 1968. Nor were the pressures merely the product of modern times. "Had I been chosen President again," John Adams remarked after his defeat in 1800, "I am certain I could not have lived another year" (www.quotedb.com/quotes/3726).

Small wonder that presidents have been prone to crack wry, gallows-humor jokes. "Being president is like being a jackass in a hailstorm," Johnson once observed, with his trademark Texas wit. "There's nothing to do but stand there and take it" (www.quotedb.com/quotes/3716). Of course, all these men wanted the job, some very badly. The presidency ground them down, but it also lifted them up to heights few can equal. They crack jokes about that, too. "There is one thing about being President," Dwight Eisenhower observed, "no one can tell you when to sit down" (www.quotedb.com/quotes/3725).

THE POWER OF THE PRESIDENCY

Ultimately, the presidency's appeal and burden are about power: its responsible exercise, its restriction, its expansion and limitations. It is the power that frightens and engenders respect, that prematurely ages the men who have wielded it, and that has sometimes motivated men to do and say things they might not otherwise have said and done in order to attain it. The president's ultimate function in the American system, the foundation of all his many roles, is his ability to successfully wield the power of his office.

From where does that power originate? On the most visible level, there is the Constitution. It spells out in black and white the shape, duties, and responsibilities of the office. Most of this information can be found in Article II, with other relevant language scattered throughout the document (including the seven amendments added since 1787 that pertain directly to the presidency).

Article II creates a skeletal framework for the presidency's basic mechanics, the operative word being "skeletal." The Framers left much unsaid and undone. In the spare language of the document, they spelled out the precise mechanism by which a president may stand for and achieve election and enter office. Article II likewise describes the president's basic powers duties, namely, commanding the military forces of the nation, directing the actions of the various executive departments, appointing federal judges and other officers; his veto over congressional legislation; and ways in which he may be hemmed in by impeachment and removal from office. In every case, these various facets of the executive branch are merely sketched out by the Framers; time and experience would fill in the details.

Today, the mechanics of the presidency are almost indescribably complicated. If a president transmits an order to the military, for example, his decision filters down through a flow chart that may include briefings with his National Security Adviser (an office not mentioned in the Constitution), members of the National Security Council (created in 1947), the Joint Chiefs of Staff (representing, in turn, the four major branches of the nation's armed forces), and his secretary of defense—none of which was mentioned in the Constitution or apparently contemplated by the Framers) before ever reaching the actual men and women who will carry out his wishes. Depending upon the president, his needs, and the context of the times, a single order from the commander in chief to his troops might therefore be analyzed and filtered through the eyes and ears of dozens of people.

This maze of executive power has its origin in the Constitution, so at first glance the Constitution would appear to be the foundation upon which a mighty presidential edifice has been constructed, an edifice of enormous power and prestige through which all the president says or does must flow. But it would be almost silly to suggest that the Constitution is the ultimate authority of presi-

The U.S. Constitution is signed on September 17, 1787, at the Constitutional Convention in Philadelphia. The Constitution was drafted by legislators in Philadelphia between July and September 1787. (Library of Congress)

dential power: it is, after all, just a piece of paper. It possesses only the authority we choose to give it.

There is also the power of the institutions under the president's direct command: the employees of the executive department, various federal law enforcement agencies, and the army. At one time, this did not amount to much. Thomas Jefferson had one secretary, a Virginia friend and neighbor named Meriwether Lewis, whom he eventually dispatched to lead the most famous exploration in American history. Sixty years later, the executive branch had doubled: Abraham Lincoln managed the entire Civil War with two private secretaries, John Hay and John Nicolay. Even then, the federal budget provided the president with enough money for only one assistant. Hay's uncle Milton, and then Lincoln himself, had to seriously consider paying the young man's salary out of their own pockets until the Interior Department came to the rescue and appointed him as a clerk.

One hundred and forty years later, times have changed. Where Nicolay and Hay were able to do their jobs working in one cramped White House office, the president's employees now occupy entire buildings in Washington, D.C. By the twenty-first century, the White House had become a complex and sophisticated bureaucratic and administrative structure that is an integral part of the executive branch's capacity to function.

At the top of the White House's flow chart are those men and women who function as direct advisers and support personnel. Their numbers have steadily grown, so that, by the time George Bush Jr. took office in 2000, they included nearly eighty people: a chief of staff and his or her two deputies; sixteen assistants to the president, whose duties can range from speechwriting to advice on homeland security issues; two dozen deputy assistants, considered to be second-level advisers on a variety of political, economic, military, and social issues; and three dozen special assistants, who likewise advise the president on a variety of issues, but whose tenure tends to be briefer and more specialized. The White House also includes the Executive Office of the President (EOP), an amorphous collection of offices and agencies that together constitute the president's policymaking capacity. Originally created in 1939 to help manage the ballooning bureaucracy of Franklin Roosevelt's presidency, the EOP encompasses nearly every executive function: budget making, communications, national security, homeland security, domestic policy, military affairs, and so on. The larger and more permanent EOP offices—the Office of Management and Budget, for example—are accompanied by scores of smaller, shorter-term agencies created to reflect a particular president's concerns: drug abuse prevention,

space exploration, and so forth (Pfiffner, 2005, 100).

The White House's reach expands still further than the EOP, though the precise lines of organization and control become increasingly murky, mixing with civil service and legislative prerogatives. In fact, the presidency's legislative relations apparatus has become a bureaucratic kingdom unto itself, encompassing elements of the Office of Management and Budget, the Defense Department, the Council of Economic Advisers, and any number of other offices. Executive-legislative relations have become so large and complex (and important) that the Eisenhower administration saw fit to create an Office of Congressional Relations, which coordinates the various contact points between the White House and Capitol Hill.

As impressive as all of this sounds, however, there are definite limitations on the president's power to command the resources of his own departments. Their salaries are not paid by the president, but by Congress. A maze of laws and regulations govern exactly what they can and cannot be ordered to do, and even the executive branch's size limits the president's ability to affect directly its employees' activities.

More generally, there is the power of what might be called presidential legitimacy. The sheer weight of the institution, accumulated by decades of history, politics, and social perceptions gives it a heavy gravitational pull in American political life. Americans afford the presidency respect and deference because it is the office once held by the likes of

George Washington, Abraham Lincoln, and Franklin Roosevelt, men who most agree are the best leaders America has produced. While presidents incur their share of disdain, mockery, and criticism, this is tempered by the shared belief that a fool cannot rise to the highest political office in the land. "It will not be too strong to say, that there will be a constant probability of seeing the station filled by characters pre-eminent for ability and virtue," Alexander Hamilton observed in 1787 (Rossiter, 1961, 320). The office itself is larger than any one man, and that fact in itself gives the person temporarily living in the White House authority he would not otherwise enjoy. "When you get to be President, there are all those things, the honors, the twenty-one gun salutes, all those things," Harry Truman observed, but "you have to remember it isn't for you. It's for the Presidency" (McCullough, 1992, 519).

But there are limits to the power of legitimacy. Hamilton was correct; in the last two centuries, Americans have yet to live under the yoke of a president who was truly an idiot or a reprobate. Even presidents whose reputations were tarnished by the partisanship and political wrangling of their own time (deservedly or not) tend to find that history almost always vindicates them in some way and in some quarters. Few presidents left office with a lower standing in the public eye than, for example, Truman. His approval ratings in polls bottomed out at twenty-six percent; Republican critics called him "a stooge of Wall Street" and a "traitor to the high principles in which

many of the nation's Democrats believe" (McCullough, 1992, 837, 909). Some believed he would go down in history as one of the worst presidents America had ever put into office. But perspectives softened in hindsight. A bumper sticker produced during the politically tumultuous 1960s read "I Miss Ike [Eisenhower]: Hell, I Even Miss Harry." In 1992 Truman was the subject of a flattering popular biography by David McCullough that eventually became a best seller, and he began creeping up the lists of chief executives who were well-regarded by the general public. "Remembering him reminds people what a man in that office ought to be like," observed journalist Eric Sevareid. "It's character, just character. He stands like a rock in memory now" (McCullough, 1992, 992).

That said, it is certainly not beyond the realm of possibility that Americans could someday choose an incompetent or dangerous person to run the executive branch of their government. If that day ever came, presidents would quickly find that the legitimacy of their office was a transient thing, its power reduced by bad decision making. For brief periods of time this has occurred. Andrew Johnson brought the presidency into such disrepute with his Reconstruction policies and general ineptitude (leading eventually to the nation's first presidential impeachment in 1868) that for three decades after he left the office, Congress was the dominant branch of the federal government. One hundred years later Richard Nixon nearly became the second president to undergo impeachment for his attempts to hide the presidency's role in the Watergate political scandal. When Nixon resigned in disgrace, polls showed that a majority of Americans did not trust the presidency, damaging the ability of Nixon's successors to use the office in a robust way and emboldening Congress and the Supreme Court to create a variety of new restrictions on the president's power to curb freedom of the press, initiate a war, use new intelligence-gathering technology like wiretaps, and impound money appropriated by Congress that a president might feel would be better spent elsewhere (a tactic Nixon perfected).

On a still broader level, presidents derive their power from the people. They are directly elected (more or less) by millions of ordinary Americans who go to the polls every four years and cast their ballots. But even that relatively simple process has been greatly complicated by the passage of time. Prospective chief executives are vetted by a party primary system that weeds out weak candidates long before they ever get within hailing distance of the White House. Any serious candidate must garner the support of key operatives and fund-raising sources within his own party, often spending months and even years prior to the election working behind the scenes in various party forums—fund-raising dinners, think-tank meetings, and so on—laboriously building what has been sometimes termed a "war chest" of the vast sums of money required to mount a national political campaign.

Having done so, the presidential wannabe must then negotiate the murky and sometimes treacherous shoals of our national party primary and caucus system—a series of polls conducted by both parties in all fifty states to determine who will be awarded the states' delegate votes to the parties' national conventions. Size matters, of course, with populous states like California wielding a heavy influence because of their large blocs of delegates and votes. But for the candidates the calendar is just as important, if not more so—the earlier one can score a primary or caucus victory in the campaign season, the more likely a candidate can build momentum heading into his party's national convention. Thus have early states like Iowa and New Hampshire wielded a disproportionate influence on presidential politicking, despite their small size, because they hold their polls so early and thus serve as a bellwether for a candidate's future success or failure.

The power conferred by the presidency's democratic roots is strong. It gives authority to the president as the mouthpiece of the people—"the people," all of them, in their collective whole as Americans. No other political office can do this. State and local officeholders speak for their towns, cities, counties, and states. Members of Congress speak for their states or regions; and while they can and often do try to keep the entire nation's best interests at heart when writing legislation, more often they look after their constituents first. Nobody blames them for this. Supreme Court justices are guardians of the Constitution; a national responsibility, surely, but one which does not carry quite the same direct conduit to the people, given that they are appointed rather than elected, and that they are not subject to the periodic reexamination of elections or to term limits.

Democracy gives presidents a tremendous trump card when they engage in politics. Moreover, it is a power conveyed by Americans even when the machinery of democracy itself suffers an occasional breakdown. This was manifestly the case during the presidential election of 2000, when contested election results in the state of Florida threw the contest between George Bush Jr. and Al Gore into disarray. Partisans on both sides lobbed charges of voter fraud, intimidation, and corruption, and Florida's election process was so compromised that no one was sure who would become the forty-third president. In the end, the Supreme Court intervened, declaring Bush the winner. In any other nation, Bush's leadership capacity would have been compromised by this sort of mess; and yet opinion polls showed that, despite it all, a majority of the American people agreed with the Court's decision and wanted the matter settled. The American people as a whole gave their approval to George Bush Jr., contested election and Supreme Court intervention notwithstanding. The machinery of democracy groaned and creaked loudly under the strain, but it somehow worked.

But here we arrive at that which is at once the most uniquely American and most maddeningly vague aspect of presidential authority. The concept of "the people" is far and away the presidency's most powerful source of authority, and yet it is a less tangible and measurable source than the Constitution's words or the various trappings of the office itself. In fact, it is hard to describe exactly what the power of the people is, or when it is conferred.

Moreover, the president has a lot of competition. He is the only directly elected national official, yes, but Congress can claim to be speaking for "the people" in its own way, as well. The Supreme Court, which is not an elective branch and has at best a distant tie to the democratic process, could plausibly argue that, in its capacity as the Constitution's guardian, it represents the spirit of American democracy through the ages. Even those thousands and thousands of executive branch workers might justifiably suggest that they too have a certain indirect relationship with the American people as their employees. The Web site for the office of the U.S. trade representative, for example, claims to speak for the economic interests of American "families, farmers, manufacturers, workers, consumers, and business" (ustr.gov/Who_We_Are/Mission _of_the_USTR.html).

Presidents also find their connections with the people filtered through a variety of institutions, people, and circumstances over which they have little control. The national news media have often proven to be a feisty and unforgiving avenue of exchange between presidents and the electorate. Talented communicators like Ronald Reagan or Bill Clinton have proven capable of using the presidency's "bully pulpit" to shape national debates on various issues, but just as often presidents have been frustrated by an inability to "get the message out" because reporters intervene instead with uncomfortable or embarrassing questions. Nixon was dogged by questions concerning Watergate in 1972, despite his repeated attempts to get reporters refocused on accomplishments more flattering to his image. Fuming about the "nattering nabobs of negativism" (as his Vice President Spiro Agnew put it), Nixon could only stand by helplessly as the scandal slowly engulfed his presidency with a deluge of searching and ultimately fatal questions from the media. Nixon thought he deserved better. "The whole hopes of the whole goddamned world of peace, you know . . . you know where they rest, they rest right here in this damned chair," he stormed to an aide. "The press has got to realize that." But they—along with Congress and the people themselves—would come to feel that Watergate outweighed Nixon's usefulness as savior of the planet. "You can't have damaged goods in the White House," Nixon himself would ruefully observe (Reeves, 2001, 598).

Presidential power is, then, hardly a simple matter. It is multifaceted and complex, probably more so than the power of most chief executives in other systems. Kings traced their authority directly to God—a brash yet simple approach. Leaders of various totalitarian regimes, whatever their outward justifications, have held power based upon their ability to bring direct, naked coercion to bear on their detractors through command of a nation's army, for example, or the ability to manipulate police and court systems.

Virginia governor Edmund Randolph, a delegate to the Constitutional Convention, initially refused to sign the U.S. Constitution, fearing that it gave the executive too much power. However, he pressed for ratification when he realized that Virginia needed the stability and resources that accompanied membership in the burgeoning nation. Randolph joined the administration of George Washington, where he served as the nation's first attorney general and later succeeded Thomas Jefferson as secretary of state. (Library of Congress)

Americans have seen fit to obfuscate presidential authority, giving their presidents' multiple and competing roles and functions. The Revolutionary generation that created the presidency for the most part wanted it that way. They worried that a president who was too directly powerful, perhaps even too efficient in

his exercise of power, would be dangerous, providing what Edmund Randolph
called "the fetus of monarchy" (Madison, 2005, 46). So they gave him a variety
of different hats to wear—chief law enforcement officer, commander of the
army, head diplomat, occasional monitor
of congressional deliberations via the
veto—and they also made sure that, in
every case, other members of the federal
government wore similar hats, the better
to keep his head from growing too large
to fit inside of any them.

In trying to understand the basic roles
and functions of the presidency, we will
focus our attention on the Framers in
this chapter. Think of it as examining
the basic superstructure of the presidential edifice, the beams and crossbars put
in place by the Revolutionary generation—a structure that has since been
crusted over by over two centuries of traditions, politics, people, and process. It is
a structure that has remained, for the
most part, surprisingly unchanged.

THE REQUIREMENTS
FOR OFFICE

If power was the primary concern of the
Revolutionary generation, then character, particularly that of the nation's political leaders, came a close second. "In all
Governments, *Magistrates* are *God's
Ministers*," wrote an eighteenth-century
observer, "designed *for Good to the People*. The End of their Institution, is to be
Instruments of Divine Providence . . . to
secure Men from all Injustice, Violence
and Rapine . . . [and] that the Unjust and
Rapacious may be restrained, the ill Ef-

fects of their Wickedness be prevented,
the secular Welfare of all be secured and
promoted" (Hyneman and Lutz, 1983, 7).
People defined leadership in moral
terms, and they worried that heads of
state who were not possessed of sterling
virtue would become a threat to the nation. Indeed, it was almost to be expected. "The notion of a perpetual danger to liberty is inseparable from the very
notion of government," wrote one political theorist (Banning, 1980, 58).

These worries were all the more intense when it came to individuals holding executive authority. America had
just gotten itself out from under a king.
It did not want another one, or a leader
by some other name who nevertheless
possessed monarchical powers. Some
people gloomily thought that an American king was all but inevitable. Any national chief executive "will be an elective king, and feel the spirit of one,"
mused Hugh Williamson of North Carolina, "He will spare no pains to keep
himself in for life, and will then lay a
train for the succession of his children"
(Madison, 2005, 357).

Many of the men who met in Philadelphia to draft the Constitution, however,
were of quite the opposite opinion. Conservative in their tastes and habits, they
had been appalled by the mob violence
and rampant lawlessness pervading the
countryside in the years immediately
after the war. George Washington, for
one, was stunned by news of an armed
rebellion led by one of his former soldiers, Daniel Shays, in rural Massachusetts during the fall of 1786. "For God's
sake tell me what is the cause of all these

commotions," he wrote to a friend. "Do they proceed from licentiousness . . . or real grievances which admit of redress? . . . If the former, why are not the powers of government tried at once?" (Flexner, 1974, 98). If some Americans worried about a lack of virtue in their leaders, many others fretted about an evident lack of virtue in the people themselves and shied away from an excessive amount of democracy. "It is become a received opinion," noted the pamphleteer Philodemus in 1784, "that a Commonwealth, in proportion as it approaches to Democracy, wants those springs of efficacious authority which are necessary to the production of regularity and good order, and degenerates into anarchy and confusion. This is commonly imputed to the capricious humor of the people, who are said to run riot with too much liberty, to be always unreasonable in their demands, and never satisfied but when ruled with a rod of iron" (Hyneman and Lutz, 1983, 616).

Probably most of the Framers fell somewhere between the two extremes. They wanted a vigorous executive, but they also wanted limits on that vigor. They needed to write a Constitution that could function without republican virtue, if necessary. As James Madison famously observed, "If men were angels, no government would be necessary. If angels were to govern men, neither external nor internal controls on government would be necessary. In framing a government which is to be administered by men over men, the great difficulty lies in this: you must first enable the government to control the governed; and

in the next place oblige it to control itself" (Rossiter, 1961, 269). Madison and others like him wanted a chief executive who would restrain himself, by dint of his personal values and principles: his integrity, honor, self-discipline and patriotism. But they were not especially optimistic about their chances, and so they needed the next best thing: a government structured in such a way that even a given president's lack of virtue would not be an insuperable harm to the Republic.

As they wrote and then defended the Constitution, the Framers tried to reassure Americans on this score. "The process of election affords a moral certainty, that the office of President will never fall to the lot of any man who is not in an eminent degree endowed with the requisite qualifications," noted Alexander Hamilton, who had urged the creation of a strong executive. "Talents for low intrigue, and the little arts of popularity, may alone suffice to elevate a man to the first honors in a single State; but it will require other talents, and a different kind of merit, to establish him in the esteem and confidence of the whole Union, or of so considerable a portion of it as would be necessary to make him a successful candidate for the distinguished office of President of the United States." Hamilton believed that the sheer size of the Union alone made it likely that capable men would be elected president. "It will not be too strong to say, that there will be a constant probability of seeing the station filled by characters pre-eminent for ability and virtue" (Rossiter, 1961, 320–322).

James Wilson was one of the primary architects of the U.S. Constitution and one of the first associate justices of the U.S. Supreme Court, serving from 1789 to 1798. (Associate Justice James Wilson by Robert S. Susan, Collection of the Supreme Court of the United States)

Others were not so sure. James Wilson, a delegate from Pennsylvania, argued that "it had been observed that in all countries the Executive power is in a constant course of increase." He was surprised to note that there were delegates who "seemed to think that we had nothing to apprehend from an abuse of Executive power. But why not a Cataline or a Cromwell arise in this Country as well as in others[?]" George Mason of Virginia agreed. "Do gentlemen mean to pave the way to hereditary monarchy?" he asked. "Do they flatter themselves that the people will never consent to such an innovation? If they do, I venture to tell them, they are mistaken" (Madison, 2005, 63–64).

Those delegates who wanted strong leadership in the new government knew better than to ignore these concerns.

What worried delegates like Mason and Wilson behind the closed doors of Independence Hall would surely be echoed and magnified many times over in the streets of America by those same Americans who not so long ago had railed against the excesses of George III. "As to the Executive, it seemed to be admitted that no good one could be established on Republican principles," Hamilton lamented in a long speech before the Constitutional Convention. Still, he argued, "was this not giving up the merits of the question [?]" (Madison, 2005, 135).

As a result, they placed in the Constitution the most specific jobholding requirements for any federal elected official. Only the president has a constitutionally prescribed oath of office, written out, word for word, for generations to follow: "I do solemnly swear (or affirm) that I will faithfully execute the Office of President of the United States, and will to the best of my Ability, preserve, protect and defend the Constitution of the United States." The president has a specific age limit (he must be over thirty-five), and he must be a natural-born citizen of the United States.

The delegates also required the president to have resided in the United States for at least fourteen years; time enough, they reasoned, to have hopefully sloughed away any sinister influences from abroad. "One of the weak sides of Republics was their being liable to foreign influence and corruption," argued one delegate. "Men of little character, acquiring great power become easily the tools of intermeddling Neibours [sic]." (Madison, 2005, 136). In fact, an early draft of the document would have put the residence requirement at twenty-one years, but it was later scaled back, probably because the delegates felt that fourteen years was more realistic in a new nation swimming with immigrants. While anti-immigrant sentiment was alive and well in parts of the nation, the provision was also part of a general scheme to create a set of qualifications, a mold for future presidents, that would guarantee the man holding the highest political office in the land would be mature, bound by the rule of law, and lack any suspicious ties to foreign governments or interests. At the same time, however, the Framers wanted the president to have a certain degree of independence and an ability to act from a sense of right and justice rather than the shifting currents of democratic politics.

A key issue here was the presidential salary. Since our presidents have historically been rich men, modern Americans tend to overlook the fact that they are paid a salary: they are employees of the people, making (as of the last pay increase, in 2001) $400,000. Recent presidents have normally donated their salaries to charity; but in the Founders' time they could not afford to be quite so cavalier on the matter. Washington would be paid $25,000 in 1789; a very handsome sum in those days. Moreover, colonial-era Americans had witnessed several ugly and contentious political episodes involving royal governors whose salaries had been reduced or withheld entirely by colonial legislatures as a means of forcing the governors to toe the line on various legislative policies. In fact, many Americans felt that the legislatures' ability to reach into governors' pockets had been a bulwark against royal tyranny before the war. They had written language into their own state constitutions giving them the power to do so and would be suspicious of attempts to make the salary of the president independent from the legislative will.

As a result, the Philadelphia delegates devoted a great deal of time to this seemingly trivial issue. It was among the first matters discussed during the Convention. Some delegates—for example, Benjamin Franklin—believed the executive ought to receive no pay at all. Wilson heartily agreed, telling the delegates that "there are two passions which have a powerful influence on the affairs of men. These are ambition and avarice." The presidency by its very nature fed the

Benjamin Franklin's ingenuity earned him worldwide acclaim as a writer, scientist, statesman, and diplomat during the eighteenth century. Among other numerous accomplishments, Franklin negotiated crucial French aid during the American Revolution, signed the Declaration of Independence, and attended the Constitutional Convention. (National Archives)

first; pay the president a salary, Wilson declared, and the effect would be doubly destructive. "Place before the eyes of such men, a post of *honour* that shall be at the same time a place of *profit,* and they will move heaven and earth to obtain it." Furthermore, Wilson declared, he did not for a moment think that presidential salaries could be limited enough to make it a nonfactor in national politics. "Tho' we may set out in the beginning with moderate salaries, we shall find that such will not be of long continuance," he believed. "Reasons will never be wanting for proposed augmentations" (Madison, 2005, 52–53).

From there, Wilson painted an overwrought picture of the slippery slope a presidential salary would create, from good intentions all the way to dictatorship and slavery. "There is scarce a king in a hundred who would not, if he could, follow the example of Pharaoh, get first all the people's money, then all their lands, and then make them and their children servants for ever." Wilson then pointed to the Convention's president as a model of patriotic altruism. "Have we not seen, the great and most important of our offices, that of General of our armies executed for eight years together without the smallest salary, by a Patriot whom I will not now offend by any other praise" (Madison, 2005, 55). If such altruism was good enough for George Washington, then why not for future presidents?

Proponents of a presidential salary allayed Wilson's concerns by freezing the president's pay at a fixed rate for the duration of his time in office, "which shall neither be increased or diminished" (Madison, 2005, 392). For good measure, they also banned the president from receiving, in the Constitution's words, "any other Emolument from the United States, or any of them."

The salary debate neatly encapsulates the delicate balance the Framers tried to achieve as they laid out the basic qualifications for those who would someday hold the office of the presidency. They wanted independence without arrogance, accountability to the people without the sort of demagoguery that would make the president a mere sailor on the shifting waves of public opinion. They wanted maturity, stability, and a more rigid sort of accountability than might otherwise be expected from a legislator or judge, as embodied in their drafting of a carefully worded oath of office. It was a tall order. "It is the most difficult of all rightly to balance the Executive," one frustrated Framer pointed out (Madison, 2005, 361).

CHOOSING THE PRESIDENT: THE ELECTORAL COLLEGE

By the time they finished addressing the presidential salary, oath, and general qualifications for office, the Framers had painted a reasonably clear picture of what they wanted in a chief executive. The question then became, how would they go about getting such a leader?

What exactly would be the machinery for finding and selecting a president?

The states offered different precedents for choosing an executive. Constitutions framed early during the Revolution allowed governors to be elected by state legislators, rather than the people themselves, the idea being that the people's representatives could better identify and select a governor of worth and ability than the people. But as the war progressed and Americans became increasingly radical in their opinions, many adopted more democratic methods. A few states mandated yearly elections as a way of keeping governors closely accountable. Virginia and Maryland forbade governors who had won election three years in a row from running again for another fourth year. Pennsylvania got rid of its governor entirely, replacing him with an Executive Council of twelve members who were elected directly by the people.

Those who sought a strong chief executive, one above the vicissitudes of democratic mood swings, wanted the president's choice to be removed as much as possible from direct choice by the people. "An Election by the people being liable to the most obvious and striking objections," believed South Carolina's Charles Pinckney, "they will be led by a few active and designing men" (Madison, 2005, 307). George Mason of Virginia agreed: "It would be as unnatural to refer the choice of a proper character for chief Magistrate to the people, as it would, to refer a trial of colours to a blind man" (Madison, 2005, 308).

One of the first blueprints for the Constitution, the Virginia Plan put forth by conservative Edmund Randolph, would have had the "National Executive" chosen by Congress, and therefore possessing only an indirect connection to the people as a whole. Randolph, and those who supported the plan, had a variety of reasons for doing so. They feared that the nation was too sprawling to conduct a proper election (and this in an era when the United States was only thirteen former colonies), and they worried that it would be impossible for any one man to command majority support from such a diverse pool of voters. People would instead unite behind someone from their own state or region, and the result would be a destructive factionalism in which whatever president commanded the resources to win a presidential election could then dictate policy to the rest of the nation. "The sense of the Nation would be better expressed by the Legislature [Congress], than by the people at large," declared Roger Sherman of Connecticut (Madison, 2005, 306).

Just as predictably, those Framers who wanted an accountable, democratic president demanded the most direct connection possible between the presidency and the people. In attacking Randolph's plan, Gouverneur Morris of Pennsylvania argued that the president "ought to be elected by the people at large, by the freeholders of the Country." He believed that, "if the people should elect, they will never fail to prefer some man of distinguished character, or services; some man, if [I] may so speak, of continental reputation" (Madison, 2005, 306).

As usual, the mass of delegates—and likely most of the American people—

fell somewhere between the two extremes. During their deliberations throughout the summer of 1787, delegates floated various schemes to address the perspectives of all concerned: multiple chief executives; selection of presidents by state governors; and one proposal that would have had the president chosen by fifteen congressmen, who were in turn themselves selected by lot, rather like some high stakes presidential lottery.

The idea of sandwiching a group of electors between the people and the president was a classic American political compromise. In a long speech on the executive, James Madison, with characteristic intellectual clarity, considered and disregarded the various schemes for election until he was left with two: "an appointment by Electors chosen by the people—and an immediate appointment by the people" (Madison, 2005, 365). Madison preferred the latter idea, and yet he admitted that there were two problems: "the disposition in the people to prefer a Citizen of their own State," which Madison believed would exacerbate the already severe tensions between big and small states, and "the disproportion of qualified voters in the N[orthern] and S[outhern] States, and the disadvantages which this mode would throw on the latter." A congressional selection, involving as it would a carefully balanced Congress, would solve these problems, but open a host of new ones, chief among these being Congress's tendency toward creating its own intrigues and factions. In the end Madison, and the Convention as a whole, opted for an electoral college

James Madison, fourth president of the United States, dedicated his life to public service. Often called the "Father of the Constitution" for his critical role in drafting the document, he also served as secretary of state for eight years and was elected to four terms in the House of Representatives. (Library of Congress)

which "would be chosen for the occasion, would meet at once, and proceed immediately to an appointment, [so] there would be very little opportunity for cabal, or corruption" (Madison, 2005, 365).

Modern Americans read of the Framers' ongoing controversies about the College and its electors and shake their heads: why such angst over what has become a mostly invisible American institution, populated by electors whom virtually no one could name? But in 1787 matters looked much different. The Framers expected the College to act as a bulwark against, to put it bluntly, the occasional twitch of democratic stupidity. They were far too realistic (or jaded, depending upon one's point of view) to believe that the people were incapable of error in choosing their leaders. A poor choice for representative or senator was bad enough; a poor choice for the presidency, with all of the latent powers they were pouring into that office, might be disastrous.

In the end, the College did not function as the Framers expected. It had the effect of limiting the number of viable candidates for the office, since each state (except Maine and Nebraska) apportions its electors entirely for one individual in a winner-take-all system. This means that only candidates who have a realistic shot at capturing an entire slate of electoral votes in a given state will tend to appear on the nation's radar screen. The Framers probably would have appreciated the value of this, as so many were afraid a marginal candidate could manipulate local factions in such a way as to capture the office without representing a truly national vision. The Electoral College makes this difficult.

But the College has never been used to overturn an election result. Electors have on rare occasions cast their votes for a candidate other than the one chosen by their state as a way to make a political point, and the Electoral College has collectively elected presidents who failed to win the majority of a popular vote. Abraham Lincoln received votes from only 39 percent of the electorate. (The rest were divided among three other candidates.)

But he gained 180 Electoral College votes; his opponents garnered 123 college votes combined. On three other occasions in American history (most recently in 2000), a candidate who failed to win a popular majority nevertheless ascended to the White House because he won the Electoral College vote.

The fact that a person can be elected president without a majority mandate due to the Electoral College's peculiar structure leaves some critics fuming that the institution is an undemocratic dinosaur. The College has sometimes been seen as the American body politic's appendix: an organ meant to do something useful at one time but which has become an anachronism. "The Electoral College is a weird mechanism for choosing the American president," argued a recent editorial. It is "as zany as a Marx Brothers movie, but not funny. To paraphrase a Groucho song, 'Hello, I Must Be Going,' it has outlived its original shaky rationale, and it's time for it to go" (*Newsday*, October 31, 2004).

But while there are occasional rumblings about reforming or even abolishing the Electoral College, few of the attempts to do so have gotten far. In 1968, for example, a constitutional amendment designed to substitute a direct popular vote for the Electoral College system failed to win approval, despite the endorsement of President Nixon and a substantial majority of congressional representatives. Americans were in the end unwilling to take such a big step into the legal and political unknown. Thirty-two-years later a commission headed by former president Jimmy Carter, which

met to investigate possible changes in presidential elections following the Bush-Gore mess in 2000, refused seriously to consider the issue because there seemed to be no hope that Americans would countenance such a fundamental change to their election system. "I think it is a waste of time to talk about changing the Electoral College," Carter claimed. "I would predict that 200 years from now, we will still have [it]" (*Boston Globe*, October 17, 2004).

REMOVING THE PRESIDENT

The oath, age, and residency requirements tell us what sort of president the Framers wanted. The Electoral College tells us how they wanted to get such presidents. Assuming all went according to plan, the next logical question was this: once we get the right person for the presidency, how do we eventually get rid of him?

In a way, the question itself was revolutionary. In most monarchies, there was no fixed procedure for deposing a king. He either died or was deposed by methods that were treasonous and were therefore highly irregular. Severely authoritarian regimes likewise rarely provide mechanisms for their dictators' retirement, and even the many other democracies created since 1787 have often been destabilized by controversies surrounding presidential succession.

The Framers knew their history. They had read the accounts of Rome's decline from democracy into tyranny, in large part because military strongmen seized the reins of power at propitious moments and then refused to step down. "Every man the least conversant in Roman story, knows how often that republic was obliged to take refuge in the absolute power of a single man, under the formidable title of Dictator," noted Alexander Hamilton, "as well against the intrigues of ambitious individuals who aspired to the tyranny, and the seditions of whole classes of the community whose conduct threatened the existence of all government, as against the invasions of external enemies who menaced the conquest and destruction of Rome" (Rossiter, 1961, 356–357).

The Framers' generation also knew the sordid history of Europe's various machinations and scandals involving executive succession. English history alone carried with it tales of betrayals, civil war, and the beheading of a king. So when the time came to design their own chief executive, the Framers wanted a structure that compelled presidents to step down. Or if they could not put into place a formal legal mechanism to do this, they wanted to at least foster a set of social and political expectations that the president would step aside when the proper time arrived, whatever and whenever that circumstance might be.

To do this, the Framers gave their president what no king had faced: a fixed term of office. Just how long this should be was a matter of conjecture. Ideas ranged from two to seven years, with those Framers favoring a more strict accountability for the president generally favoring the shorter periods. Those who were more intensely worried about a

president's virtue, or possible lack thereof, wanted a short term as well, the better for the nation to rid itself of "unfit characters." On the other hand, some of the Framers worried that overly frequent elections would pose difficulties in such a large nation, including excessive time used and the expense involved. Various limits to a president's reelection were also tossed about. Gunning Bedford wanted a president to be ineligible for reelection after nine years; others thought seven years might be better. Some wanted no fixed number of years, but preferred to insert language in the Constitution allowing a president to seek reelection upon his continued "good behavior." George Mason, for one, was bothered by this suggestion, as the omnipresent fear of an incipient American king again reared its head. Mason "considered an Executive during good behavior as a softer name only for an Executive for life. And that the next would be an easy step to hereditary Monarchy" (Madison, 2005, 58).

At the end of the day, the Framers opted for striking out all formal limitations on a president's ability to run for reelection. The chief reason was another ongoing fear that beset the Framers throughout their debates on the presidency: the fear that a president might become too subservient to Congress. "Experience had proved a tendency in our governments to throw all power into the Legislative vortex," Madison declared. "The Executives of the States are in general little more than Cyphers, the legislatures omnipotent" (Madison, 2005, 312). To him, this was more worrisome than a tendency to monarchy (which Madison did not believe was terribly prevalent in the proposed document, anyway). Leaving the ultimate end of a given president's term open was a way to preserve his political clout and therefore a degree of political independence.

But even if the final draft of the Constitution contained no term limit for the president as such, the idea persisted that a president should in some way be limited in the amount of time spent in office, for the good of the country. In particular, that idea took root in the back of George Washington's mind, possibly as he sat witnessing the long arguments on the issue from his place as head of the Convention. He said nothing at the time, but when he eventually became the nation's first chief executive he limited himself to serve only two terms—yet another extraordinary act of self-discipline from that supremely disciplined man— establishing a long, unwritten tradition that would bind every president save one (Franklin Roosevelt) and would eventually be encoded in the Twenty-second Amendment.

Americans could expect to face a turnover in the office of their president every eight years, at the most, and four-year elections would in the meantime hold presidents accountable to the people. Still, four years is a long time. If he chose to do so, if he were greedy, reckless, or incompetent, a president could do a great deal of damage in that time frame. "The duration of our president is neither perpetual or for life; it is only for four years," John Adams noted, and yet he cautioned that the president's "power

during those four years is much greater than that of an avoyer, a consul, a podesta, a doge, a stadtholder, nay, than a king of Poland; nay, than a king of Sparta" (Wood, 1969, 586).

The Framers understood that some sort of mechanism was necessary for the removal of a president under extraordinary circumstances, a mechanism that did not involve the unwieldy and time-consuming device of a special general election to oust him from office. Nor was it enough to wait for the next four-year election cycle to come around before a bad president could be removed. "The limitation of the period of his service, was not a sufficient security," Madison argued, for "he might lose his capacity after his appointment. He might pervert his administration into a scheme of peculation or oppression. He might betray his trust to foreign powers." Any of these events, he warned, "might be fatal to the Republic" (Madison, 2005, 333).

An impeachment process was the answer; that is, a legal proceeding whereby a president could be brought before some sort of tribunal and either made to answer for his wrongdoing or have his character publicly exonerated. It would need to be relatively speedy, so a president could be removed before wreaking real devastation. On the other hand, the Framers did not want impeachment to become a political weapon whereby a president's detractors in Congress could blackmail political concessions from him, and in the process set the legislature to rule over the executive. In fact, some were so worried about this possibility that they wanted to make the president subject to impeachment only after he left office.

Most did not want to go this far, rightly thinking that such a provision would render impeachment all but useless. "Shall any man be above Justice?" asked George Mason, and "above all shall that man be above it, who can commit the most extensive injustice?" Ben Franklin pointed out that, in other systems lacking an impeachment process, the only other resort for a people oppressed by a corrupt leader was assassination, "in which he was not only deprived of his life but of the opportunity of vindicating his character" (Madison, 2005, 331, 332). Presidents had to be held directly accountable in some way for their actions. But the Framers wanted this accountability to be narrowly tailored, covering, as Gunning Bedford of Delaware put it, "misfeasance only, not incapacity" (Madison, 2005, 49). The impeachment process, it was thought, should only be used to punish a president's criminal conduct.

How exactly might this be done? A whole host of problems presented themselves. Gouverneur Morris astutely laid these out before the Convention. "Who is to impeach?" he asked, and "is the impeachment to suspend [the president's] functions[?] If it is not the mischief will go on. If it is the impeachment will be nearly equivalent to a displacement, and will render the Executive dependent on those who are to impeach" (Madison, 2005, 331, 334, 535). The Framers bandied about various ideas. Hamilton and Edmund Randolph thought a tribunal might be formed, consisting of state

At the U.S. Constitutional Convention of 1787, George Mason framed the Declaration of Rights, which then served as the basis for the Bill of Rights. (Library of Congress)

judges who could render a verdict in a grand national trial. Others thought the House of Representatives or Senate might conduct such a trial, or perhaps the Supreme Court.

The final draft of the Constitution offered an amalgam of the various impeachment ideas. It held the president accountable (along with the vice president and other federal "civil officers") for "Treason, Bribery, or other high crimes and misdemeanors," the latter a phrase lifted from the English common law and covering a variety of offenses. It made the Senate the forum for an impeachment trial, presided over by the chief justice of the Supreme Court. To underscore the gravity—and hopefully relative rarity—of impeachment trials, the Framers required a two-thirds majority for conviction, and held that impeachment "shall not extend further than to removal from Office, and disqualification to hold and enjoy any Office of honor, Trust or Profit under the United States."

Generally speaking, this system has worked pretty well, albeit not without some unforeseen complications and difficulties. The Framers wanted impeachment to be a last resort, a rarity, and in this they got their wish. Only two presidents, Andrew Johnson and Bill Clinton, have ever been impeached (neither was convicted), while a third, Richard Nixon, was dragged to the edge of impeachment before he resigned from office. Critics of a given administration sometimes threaten to begin impeachment proceedings as a way of signaling their displeasure with the White House. Democratic representative Henry B. Gonzalez of Texas talked darkly of impeaching both George Bush Jr. in 2002 and his father, George Bush Sr., ten years earlier because Gonzalez disagreed with the their policies toward the regime of Saddam Hussein in Iraq. He even introduced resolutions to this effect, but neither got very far, a fact which no doubt would have pleased those Framers who worried about the possibility that dissenting congressmen could use impeachment as a way of browbeating a president into submission.

The Framers wanted impeachment to be more of a legal than a political proceeding. But in this they would have been disappointed, for in the impeachment trials of both Johnson and Clinton, politics played a central role, and not always for the better. Johnson was brought up on impeachment charges in 1868 as much for his disagreements with Congress over Reconstruction policies as anything else, and Bill Clinton's trial in 1998—focusing on his commission of perjury and obstruction of justice during an investigation of Clinton's sexual misconduct with a White House employee—was likewise colored by the extraordinary animosity some Republicans felt toward the president. In both trials the presidents' defenders charged that impeachment was being used as an overt political tool, in direct contravention of the Framers' intent; and in both trials, they had a point.

But what if a president was not guilty of "high crimes and misdemeanors" and was instead ill or incapacitated in some other way for a lengthy amount of time? The Framers devoted surprisingly little time or effort to this issue. Given that their ongoing model for future chief executives was the Convention president, George Washington, who was an impressive physical specimen, even at the then-ripe age of fifty-five, perhaps the notion of a physically debilitated president never occurred to them.

Generally speaking, America's presidents have been a healthy bunch; remarkably so, given that we have tended to draw our presidents from the older segments of the population. In two hundred years, only three presidents—William Henry Harrison, Zachary Taylor, and Warren G. Harding—have died from illness while in office. Presidents have historically enjoyed a high standard of medical care, and in recent years a number of them have been highly visible practitioners of various healthy activities like jogging, as well as promoters of public exercise programs via the President's Council on Physical Fitness and Sports (yet another of those presidential institutions the Framers never foresaw).

That said, illness has been a fact of presidential life from the very beginning. Washington may have seemed a hearty and robust man to the Framers, but early in his tenure he had to have a painful tumor removed from his thigh, and later he was stricken with a case of pneumonia so severe that Secretary of State Thomas Jefferson confided to a friend, "We have been very near losing the president" (Flexner, 1974, 246). Older chief executives like Andrew Jackson suffered from a variety of ailments: in Jackson's case, everything from chronic toothaches to internal bleeding caused by the two bullets he carried in his body from past duels. Even younger men faced occasional health lapses. Abraham Lincoln was sometimes laid low by colds, and Teddy Roosevelt—whose mania for the "strenuous life" and exercise was world famous—could find ways to hurt himself. He was sometimes bothered by rheumatism, swollen ankles, "infernal leg troubles" with an abscess, and a cataract so severe that, during his last year in the White House he was completely blind in his left eye" (Dalton, 2002, 295).

There have also been much more serious presidential health concerns. Grover Cleveland had a cancerous growth removed from his jaw during an operation held in great secrecy aboard the presidential yacht in 1893; advisers feared that public knowledge of the operation might damage the nation's economy. Cleveland was fitted with a special rubber plate to mask the operation's effects, and a cover story was spread that he had merely had a sore tooth removed. Twenty-six years later Woodrow Wilson suffered a massive stroke while touring the country to drum up support for his foreign policy initiatives; for weeks he saw no visitors at all, not even his Cabinet, while his wife Edith smoothed over the crisis by telling people that the president was suffering from "a nervous breakdown, indigestion, and a depleted nervous system" (Clements, 1992, 196). In 1944 Franklin Roosevelt pursued an unprecedented fourth term in office, despite the fact that he was slowly dying from a variety of ailments, most related to a degenerating heart condition. "I cannot live out a normal life span," he groaned to Eleanor, "I can't even walk across the room to get my circulation going" (Goodwin, 1994, 516). But he pursued reelection nonetheless, concealing the seriousness of his situation from all but his family and closest advisers.

The Wilson and Roosevelt illnesses raised fears of what might happen if a president did not die in office, but instead lingered in a protracted health crisis that might conceivably paralyze the federal government. And those two men were wartime leaders, war being a time when the president's leadership is most keenly and directly felt by the nation at large. The Wilson matter was particularly disturbing, for during his long illness the First Lady conspired with doctors to keep the situation a closely guarded secret. She managed the day-to-day affairs of the White House while failing even to inform the president's immediate successor, Vice President Thomas Marshall, of the situation. She refused to allow the president's chief physician to sign a certificate of disability. "I am not thinking of my country now," she declared, "I am thinking of my husband" (Clements, 1992, 198).

The Constitution left some blank areas when it came to the succession of presidential authority. Section 1 of Article II stated that "in Case of the Removal of the President from Office, or of his Death, Resignation, or Inability to discharge the Powers and Duties of the said Office, the same shall devolve on the Vice President." In most cases this seemed fairly straightforward: vice presidents directly assumed the powers of an incapacitated president. Why else, really, did the office of vice president exist? But some wondered if this meant that the vice president was merely an acting president until his boss returned to health, or whether he became the nation's chief executive until the next general election.

In 1967 the states ratified the Twenty-fifth Amendment, which tried to put these doubts to rest. It stated that, when the heads of the Senate and the House of Representatives received a letter from the president indicating he could no longer fulfill his duties, the vice president would become acting president. The vice president himself could also write a letter stating the president was incapacitated, provided that this was agreed to by "a majority of either the principal officers of the executive departments or of such other body as Congress may by law provide." Once he was able to resume the duties of his office, the president would again inform Congress via a written declaration. If for some reason the vice president disagreed, he would have four days to state his reasons, after which Congress would be called into a special session to deliberate upon the matter and then decide (by two-thirds majority vote of both houses) whether the vice president should continue to act as the nation's chief executive or whether the president was fit enough to return to power.

Despite these efforts to spell out clearly when and how an incapacitated president should be replaced, confusion is still possible. In March 1981 Ronald Reagan was nearly assassinated by a lone gunman named John Hinckley. During the tense hours immediately following the shooting, Reagan clung to life on an operating table with a bullet lodged near his heart while Vice President George Bush flew back to Washington, D.C., from his home in Texas. In the meantime, Secretary of State Alexander Haig took it upon himself to announce to a stunned press corps that, "as of now, I am in control here, in the White House pending return of the Vice President." Haig hastily added, "If something came up, I would check with him of course" (Cannon, 2000, 198). He had a disheveled and rather wild-eyed look when he said this, and in those overwrought moments, some wondered if the man was trying to stage a kind of palace coup. Bush's return and Reagan's recovery made the point moot, and Haig had nothing of the sort in mind; but the incident wrecked his political future: "I am in control here" became a running joke in the Reagan White House as a sarcastic reference to any situation that was in fact out of control.

COMMANDER IN CHIEF AND HEAD DIPLOMAT

Having found ways to vet a president's character, place him in office and, then dispose of him when need be, what did the Framers intend a president to do in the meantime?

Alexander Hamilton was a strong proponent of presidential prerogatives. Like everyone else, he probably had George Washington foremost in mind when he discussed the new chief executive's office. And like everyone else, Hamilton thought of Washington with his most recent and most prominent public service foremost in mind: general and chief military hero of the Revolutionary war. In fact, Hamilton may have been more inclined than most to imagine Washington the future president in his military uniform; he had served as Washington's aide during the war and endured many of the Continental Army's privations along with his commander.

He therefore had no problem at all with the language in the Constitution's final draft that put the president squarely in

Nineteenth-century painting of George Washington receiving a salute on the field of Trenton in 1776. (National Archives)

charge of the armed forces. This included not just the national army but also, in time of war, the militia organizations of the various states—which, in 1787 at least, constituted more men and matériel than the tiny regular army and nearly nonexistent navy. "The President shall be Commander in Chief of the Army and Navy of the United States, and of the Militia of the several States, when called into the actual Service of the United States," reads Article II, Section 2.

When it came time for Hamilton to offer his defense of the Constitution in the *Federalist Papers*, he devoted relatively little space to the president's status as commander in chief. To him, this power was practically self-explanatory. "The propriety of this provision is so evident in itself, and it is, at the same time, so consonant to the precedents of the State constitutions in general, that little need be said to explain or enforce it," he wrote in *Federalist* No. 74. Hamilton stated that "of all the cares or concerns of government, the direction of war most peculiarly demands those qualities which distinguish the exercise of power by a single hand. The direction of war implies the direction of the common strength; and the power of directing and employing the common strength, forms a usual and essential part in the definition of the executive authority" (Rossiter, 1961, 376).

There had been considerable debate over whether America even needed professional, full-time soldiers. Many Americans believed their nation could get along just fine with the militia and without a standing army of military professionals. These were also by and large the same individuals who thought the nation could get along well with a weak chief executive—or no chief executive at all. The fears of kings and fears of professional soldiers shared a common frontier in the minds of radical Americans, who thought soldiers in a standing army were nothing more than a willing tool for the tyrant kings who paid their salaries. "A *military king*, with a *standing army* devoted to his will, are to have an uncontrouled power over our lives, our liberties, and property, in all cases whatsoever," fumed one writer, and

"none but a sycophant or a slave should submit to it" (Kenyon, 1966, 72).

To Alexander Hamilton, however—who had frozen half to death at Valley Forge and watched Washington literally begging the Continental Congress and the states for money to feed and clothe his ragged troops—such arguments smacked of an unhealthy parsimony and an unrealistic belief that the nation could function in a hostile world without a decent military establishment or a strong military leader. But even he realized that the final say in American military matters must be from a civilian, not a soldier, and he tried to soothe fears of a possible military takeover led from the top, remarking that "the President will have only the occasional command of such part of the militia of the nation as by legislative provision may be called into the actual service of the Union." Comparing this power to that of a monarch or even a state governor, Hamilton pointed out that the "king of Great Britain and the governor of New York have at all times the entire command of all the militia within their several jurisdictions. In this article, therefore, the power of the President would be inferior to that of either the monarch or the governor" (Rossiter, 1961, 364).

"Commander in chief" is a somewhat vague phrase, however. Did it mean that presidents should be expected to actually take the field and personally lead American soldiers into battle? Critics of a strong executive feared this possibility, to the point that one early proposal in the Philadelphia Convention (a draft that envisioned a committee of executives) would only have placed those executives in charge of the military "provided that none of the persons composing the federal Executive shall on any occasion take command of any troops, so as personally to conduct any enterprise as General or in [any] other capacity" (Madison, 2005, 120).

No such restriction reached the final draft, and the possibility still exists that a president might take direct command of the armed forces should he choose to do so. George Washington called upon the Pennsylvania militia in 1794 to suppress what would come to be known as the Whiskey Rebellion in the western marches of that state; he then donned his old Revolutionary war uniform, mounted a horse, and led these troops into the field. Before he actually came under fire, however, the rebellion collapsed. Other presidents have occasionally toyed with the idea. Abraham Lincoln once wrote the notoriously plodding commanding general, George B. McClellan, "My dear McClellan: if you don't want to use the army I should like to borrow it for a while" It is hard to say whether or not Lincoln was joking. But otherwise no sitting president since Washington has actually "borrowed" the army and gone looking for a fight.

Instead, presidents and their administrations see "commander in chief" as an administrative title. Presidents construct hierarchies of command, with themselves at the top, consisting of proven experts in a given area of military operations. A secretary of defense represents the armed forces in the Cabinet; the Joint Chiefs of Staff gather representatives of the four major military branches—army, navy, air force, and marines—under one umbrella organization, the better to coordinate their efforts.

The president is also served by various military and national security advisers, all of whom presumably possess the requisite knowledge to administer their particular corner of America's military establishment. Since 2003, for example, the Office of Homeland Security has functioned as a Cabinet-level department designed to coordinate the efforts by various federal intelligence and security agencies to protect the nation from terrorist attack. It comprises nearly 17,000 employees and oversees the activities of twenty-two separate agencies, utilizing a budget of over $40 billion.

The president can call upon many such experts, each of whom is usually more involved in day-to-day military operations than their commander in chief. Still, it is the president who makes the big decisions setting the massive American military machine in motion and pointing it in one direction or another. Those decisions are, of course, strategic, reflecting military goals and operations. But the president must defend his actions before Congress and the American people, and in that sense his commander in chief role is political as well as military.

It is also diplomatic. The president's military function is naturally connected to his status as the nation's head diplomat, its chief face to the outside world. Immediately following the section making him commander of the armed forces (the first enumerated power of the president listed in the Constitution), the Framers declared that the chief executive "shall have Power, by and with the Advice and Consent of the Senate, to make Treaties, provided two thirds of the Senators present concur; and he shall nominate, and by and with the Advice and Consent of the Senate, shall appoint Ambassadors, other public Ministers and Consuls."

Post–Revolutionary war Americans had learned the hard way that foreign nations needed a single leader to represent the nation's interests abroad. In the years immediately following the war, when the Articles of Confederation provided no head of state who could speak for all of the states, hostile nations like England felt free to violate America's international rights—blocking the nation's shipping on the high seas, for example, or enacting ruinous trade barriers—with the excuse that they did not know with whom they could negotiate in arriving at some sort of mutually satisfactory arrangement. "There is a strong propensity in this people," wrote John Adams, America's chief representative in England, "to believe that America is weary of her independence; that she wishes to come back; that the states are in confusion; Congress has lost its authority; the governments of the states have no influence [and that] no navigation acts we can make will be obeyed [and] no duties we lay on can be collected" (McCullough, 2001, 348).

Without a single head of state to reassure foreign countries on all these points, America was vulnerable. The Framers knew this, and yet they were still unwill-

ing to entrust treaty-making power solely to one man, a setup that looked a bit too much like the British king's power to conduct foreign relations with little direct input from Parliament. While some felt that Congress should not be involved in diplomacy much at all—Madison argued that for "obvious reasons it was proper that the President should be an agent in Treaties"—most of the delegates believed the Senate should be given the power of ratifying any international agreement negotiated by the president (Madison, 2005, 520). Even then, some radical Americans felt this was too dangerous, since the Senate (at that time) was not directly elected by the people. "The Senate, by making treaties, may destroy your liberty and laws for want of responsibility," warned one critic (Kenyon, 1966, 260). The president's combined power to command the nation's soldiers and negotiate settlements with foreign authorities was probably the biggest cause for worry among Americans who were generally indisposed to grant their new federal government much authority.

Today, the president—like so much else in the executive branch—is not a single actor on the diplomatic front, but rather the coordinator of a vast diplomatic system of experts, agencies, and departments. He still makes the most important foreign policy decisions, of course, but only while accessing the resources of the State Department, any of a number of national intelligence services—the Central Intelligence Agency, for example—and any relevant branch of the armed forces. He might also, if he chooses to do so, make use of a variety of independent agencies and think tanks that study various aspects of America's foreign policy and can be called upon to offer advice or analysis.

DOMESTIC FRONTS

Richard Nixon once pungently dismissed making domestic policy as "building outhouses in Peoria" (Reeves, 2001, 33). He much preferred international politics to the home front. While there have been presidents who felt quite the opposite— Bill Clinton, for example—probably most presidents most of the time preferred the foreign policy arena. In that area their leadership is relatively unchallenged.

Domestic policy is a messier, more difficult proposition. When a president tries his hand at workplace regulation, medical care, labor relations, and so forth, he is not dealing with just one head of state, but rather a plethora of competing, jostling, and sometimes angry interest groups. Congress is institutionally designed to deal with this; it has a variety of elected officials, their staffs, and numerous committees and task forces that mirror the complex interests of American society and do a fairly good job of channeling those interests into areas where they can best be served in proportion to their relative importance. The presidency, on the other hand, can prove inadequate to this task.

Clinton's attempt to reform health care early in his first term furnishes an excellent illustration of the problems involved when a president tries to carry out ambitious domestic reforms. During his 1992 campaign, Clinton made health care reform a top priority, declaring that "the American health-care system costs too much and does not work. It leaves 60 million Americans without adequate health insurance and bankrupts our families, our businesses and our federal budget." He and running mate Al Gore promised that "in the first year of a Clinton-Gore Administration, that will change. We will send a national healthcare plan to Congress, and we will fight to pass it" (Clinton, 1992, 108). Clinton produced a plan that was remarkably detailed for a campaign document. It described spending caps on medical procedures, prescription drug industry reforms, insurance reforms, a guaranteed basic health benefits package, small business reforms, various cost control devices—a smorgasbord of policy initiatives that would have been the envy of any congressional staff.

When the time came to act on these promises, President Clinton placed his wife Hillary in charge of a large task force of experts whose job was to translate his campaign plan into a doable reality, and here the entire program quickly came unglued. Trying to perform the job of perhaps a dozen or so legislative committees, the health care task force crammed nearly every available reform initiative into a behemoth legislative proposal that would have been one of the largest, costliest, and most complex domestic programs in American history. Had it originated in Congress, the various initiatives in the plan could have been vetted through the slow but valuable percolation of the many interest groups and factions that meet in legislative halls, hammer out compromises, and move on. Or, more likely, it would have been broken up into several different plans, each one streamlined by the legislative process with its all-knowing art of the possible.

As it was, the Clinton plan was a huge and unswallowable lump that had something in it to choke almost everyone. When the various naysayers gathered to kill the proposal, the presidency proved structurally incapable of rising to the occasion. "The White House failed to bring together political alliances capable of supporting specific legislation," observed one journalist. "Instead, special interests drifted away quickly and hardened into adamantine opposition" (Hayden, 2002, 33). The health reform plan died unceremoniously in Congress. Clinton himself later observed, "We had taken a good shellacking" (Clinton, 2004, 621).

The truth is that the Framers never intended presidents to wade through thorny domestic policy thickets like health care reform; they wanted Congress to take the lead in such matters. "What are to be the objects of federal legislation?" Madison asked in *Federalist* No. 56. "Those which are of most importance, and which seem most to require local knowledge, are commerce, taxation, and the militia" (Rossiter, 1961, 315). A very short list, but suggestive of the Framers' views on Congress's proper sphere: even the militia, while of course part of the nation's overall military defense system, was in late-eighteenth-century terms primarily a domestic institution.

Accordingly, the Framers gave presidents very few tools to use for influencing domestic policy debates. Their concern for separation of powers meant that they created no institutional means by which presidents could regularly engage in the legislative process. There is no constitutionally created presidential presence during the drafting of legislation. Article II does provide that the president "may, on extraordinary Occasions, convene both Houses, or either of them." Presidents have done so twenty-seven times, dating back to John Adams's call in 1797 for Congress to deliberate on the nation's contentious relations with France. But once he calls Congress into such a special session, the president's influence is limited. The members of Congress themselves decide what they will actually do—or if they will do anything at all.

Unlike the British foreign minister, presidents are not expected to frequently address the nation's legislators. In fact, the Constitution provides for only one address by presidents to the people: the State of the Union Address. Article II states: "He shall from time to time give to the Congress Information of the State of the Union, and recommend to their Consideration such Measures as he shall judge necessary and expedient."

Most presidents have interpreted "from time to time" as an annual affair, a yearly laundry list of what has been occurring throughout the land. This has often been presented merely as statements of fact, not policy guidelines for the legislation a given president wants from Congress. "There was reason to hope, the pacifick [sic] measures adopted with regard to certain hostile tribes of Indians, would have relieved the inhabitants of our southern and western frontiers from their depredations," reads a typical passage, taken from George Washington's first State of the Union Address. "But you will perceive, from the information contained in the papers, which I shall direct to be laid before you, (comprehending a communication from the Commonwealth of Virginia) that we ought to be prepared to afford protection to those parts of the Union; and, if necessary, to punish aggressors" (www.law.ou .edu/hist/washsu.html). Presidents also use a State of the Union Address to indicate subtly their wishes in regard to domestic policy measures. These occasions have become much more frequent in recent years as the presidency has grown in size and complexity, and as Americans have come to expect comprehensive legislative agendas from their presidents. "I outlined my plan for the future," Bill Clinton wrote of his 1998 State of the Union Address, "I proposed that before spending the coming [budget] surpluses on new programs or tax cuts, we should save Social Security for the baby boomers' retirement. In education, I recommended funding to hire 100,000 new teachers and to cut class size to eighteen in the first three grades; a plan to help communities modernize or build five thousand schools," and so on (Clinton, 2004, 777).

In 1787 the Framers never thought a president would even have much of an opinion on school class sizes and the like, let alone that he would seek to translate those opinions into law. They were worried enough about congressional interference with the president's prerogatives—George Mason, for example, fretted about the potential for "making the Executive the mere creature of the Legislature" should Congress gain too much say in presidential decision making—but they were just as concerned about the prospect of presidential meddling in the everyday affairs of Congress. Separation of powers cut both ways. "If it be essential to the preservation of liberty that the Legislative: Executive: and Judiciary powers be separate," Madison noted, "it is essential to a maintenance of the separation, that they should be independent of each other" (Madison, 2005, 311).

The Framers accordingly allowed the president only one formal role in congressional deliberations, and a decidedly negative role at that. Article I, Section 7 gave the president veto power over national legislation. The Framers granted this boon with a fair amount of hand-wringing. Some wanted to leaven the veto power by having him share it with the judiciary as part of a Counsel of Revision that would collectively review congressional legislation. Benjamin Franklin feared that a president who exercised veto power by himself would be liable to commit all sorts of abuses. "If a negative should be given as proposed" to the president alone, Franklin argued, "more power and money would be demanded [by him] till at last eno[ugh] would be gotten to influence and bribe the Legislature into a compleat subjection to the will of the Executive." Others took quite the opposite view, seeing the veto as a presidential shield against congressional slings and arrows. "Without such a self-defense the Legislature can at any moment sink [the Executive] into non-existence," Mason declared (Madison, 2005, 61–62).

The Framers wrangled back and forth on this matter for a long time; some even threatened to withdraw their support for a national chief executive entirely should he be given a veto power over Congress. Pierce Butler of South Carolina "had been in favor of a single Executive Magistrate; but could he have entertained an idea that a compleat negative on the laws was to be given him he certainly should have acted very differently." But those Framers who generally supported a stronger executive branch replied that it was unlikely a president would actually use the veto very often. In the end, supporters of the veto won their case. But the general nervousness with which the Framers collectively supported the idea is plain in the complex architecture of Article 7 itself. It declared that "Every Bill which shall have passed the House of Representatives and the Senate, shall, before it become a Law, be presented to the President of the United States; If he approve he shall sign it, but if not he shall return it, with his Objections to that House in which it shall have originated." The Framers required those objections to be openly recorded in the congressional journal, for all to see, after which Congress would revisit the matter. "If after such Reconsideration two thirds of that House shall agree to pass the Bill, it shall

be sent, together with the Objections, to the other House, by which it shall likewise be reconsidered, and if approved by two thirds of that House, it shall become a Law." The Framers wanted this to be as transparent a process as possible, to forestall any accusations—real or imagined—of backroom bribery or wheeling and dealing. "In all such Cases the Votes of both Houses shall be determined by Yeas and Nays, and the Names of the Persons voting for and against the Bill shall be entered on the Journal of each House respectively." Nor was the president allowed to sit on a bill indefinitely. "If any Bill shall not be returned by the President within ten Days (Sundays excepted) after it shall have been presented to him, the Same shall be a Law, in like Manner as if he had signed it, unless the Congress by their Adjournment prevent its Return, in which Case it shall not be a Law" (U.S. Constitution, Article I, Section 7).

The Framers' nervousness about a presidential veto might have paled in comparison to their reaction regarding the vast bureaucratic and regulatory apparatus that is currently at a modern president's disposal. The veto is a blunt and rather ham-handed instrument, high profile and drastic; in fact, a president can affect domestic policy in a myriad of far more subtle ways, because at his disposal is a large federal regulatory bureaucracy that oversees everything from tax regulations to food and drug safety. These agencies are created by Congress, but presidents often possess appointing power for the higher-ranking bureaucratic positions, and they can use this power to affect policymaking on a micro level. Who a president appoints as chairman of the Federal Reserve, for example, can have a drastic effect on the nation's monetary policy and hence its economy. Congress has much to say about these matters as well, but presidents can bring their enormous media and political powers to bear on bureaucratic initiatives they find important.

There are, however, limits to what a president might accomplish through the modern Washington bureaucracy. Presidents and their political supporters have a relatively short shelf life, following the Constitution's restrictions on holding office—the two-term limit—and the naturally short election cycles of a vibrant democratic system. Moreover, agency heads' terms of office are staggered (deliberately so), making it difficult for a president to implement truly sweeping changes within a given four-year term. And career bureaucrats, often resistant to sudden and dramatic change, know that they may need only to outlast a president.

Over the years various attempts to reform the federal bureaucracy by simplifying procedures, holding federal employees more accountable for their mistakes, or using the bureaucratic structure to effect policy changes have met with limited success, at best. Quite a few modern presidents have entered office pledging to "clean up" the "bureaucratic mess" in Washington, responding during their campaigns to constituents' frustration at the ever-increasing maze of federal rules and regulations. But various

protections enacted by civil service reform laws, bureaucratic inertia, and (to be fair) the necessity for national oversight of complex national domestic problems like poor relief or health care have limited such presidential initiatives.

HEAD OF LAW ENFORCEMENT

Beyond the veto and the war-making and treaty-signing powers invested in the presidency, there is the somewhat more vaguely defined notion that he is the nation's chief law enforcement officer. Article II, Section 3 states the matter succinctly: "He shall take Care that the Laws be faithfully executed, and shall Commission all the Officers of the United States." Alexander Hamilton put it this way in *Federalist* No. 75: "The essence of the legislative authority is to enact laws, or, in other words, to prescribe rules for the regulation of the society; while the execution of the laws, and the employment of the common strength, either for this purpose or for the common defense, seem to comprise all the functions of the executive magistrate" (Rossiter, 1961, 422).

"Take care that the laws be faithfully executed" and "execution of the laws"—this sounds simple enough. But what does it really mean?

In the early years of the nation, it meant rather little. Law enforcement was a local affair, carried on by state and county officials. The federal government did not create that many laws to enforce, or at least few that had an impact on the daily lives of most Americans. There was, consequently, little reason to put a large federal law enforcement establishment at the president's disposal.

In 1789 Congress authorized the United States Marshal's Service (as part of the Judiciary Act of that year), consisting of men who were charged with carrying out the everyday, tedious work of the federal court system: issuing warrants, paying court clerk salaries, renting jail space and courtrooms, and the like. They also acted as the representatives of the federal government, distributing presidential proclamations, taking the federal census (until 1870), and gathering statistical data for Congress to use when needed. As the nation's head law enforcement officers, they were, on a purely theoretical level, the president's employees. In reality, they acted as agents for the will of both Congress and the president, and on the whole did so quite well during most of the nineteenth and early twentieth centuries. As the federal government expanded in size and scope during the twentieth century, so did the various tools the president possessed to enforce laws. In 1865, the United States Secret Service was formed as the Treasury Department's enforcement arm in its efforts to track down counterfeiters. Later the service began its more famous task as the president's bodyguard, when it began to act in that capacity for Grover Cleveland. In 1908 Attorney General Charles Bonaparte assigned a small number of detectives and office employees to investigate various crimes that fell within his office's purview. The little group eventu-

ally grew into the modern Federal Bureau of Investigation (FBI). Forty years later Congress created the Central Intelligence Agency (CIA) to coordinate the various agencies involved in gathering information on national security.

The Secret Service, FBI, and CIA became the nucleus for what has become a sprawling law enforcement establishment, authorized and funded by Congress but run by the executive department. The president is now at least the titular boss of thousands of federal law enforcement operatives, overseeing everything from counter-espionage to anti-drug-trafficking operations. As new problems arise, the general trend has been to concentrate still more police power in the president's hands. In the wake of September 11 and the war on terror, the president and Congress created a new Cabinet-level Office of Homeland Security, designed to coordinate the many antiterrorism and internal security efforts around the country. In 2004 Congress also gave the president a director of national intelligence, or "intelligence czar," whose job is to pool the myriad intelligence-gathering resources of the federal government and make their insights more readily available to the president and other national policymakers.

In addition to catching those who commit crimes against the United States, the president also has the authority to absolve Americans of crimes. The Constitution holds that the chief executive "shall have Power to Grant Reprieves and Pardons for Offenses against the United States, except in Cases of Impeachment." Given that an executive's pardoning power had traditionally been controversial—English monarch James II, for example, used his pardoning powers to benefit Roman Catholics, to the chagrin of English Protestants—it is surprising how little debate the subject provoked in the Philadelphia Convention. This was perhaps because the Framers saw it not so much as a power to be wielded by the president, but rather as a brake against excessive or arbitrary powers wielded by others in the judicial system—capricious juries, perhaps, or malicious judges who might inflict unduly harsh sentences. "The criminal code of every country partakes so much of necessary severity, that without an easy access to exceptions in favor of unfortunate guilt, justice would wear a countenance too sanguinary and cruel," Alexander Hamilton wrote in *Federalist* No. 74, and "it may be inferred that a single man would be most ready to attend to the force of those motives which might plead for a mitigation of the rigor of the law, and least apt to yield to considerations which were calculated to shelter a fit object of its vengeance. . . . One man appears to be a more eligible dispenser of the mercy of government, than a body of men" (Rossiter, 1961, 415–416).

The pardon is an odd little corner of presidential power, normally exercised in ways quiet and unobtrusive. Over the years, presidents have received thousands of pardon requests; the numbers granted vary widely, from 16 issued by George Washington to over 3,000 by Franklin Roosevelt. The individuals and their offenses likewise run the gamut of major and minor wrongdoings: NASCAR legend Junior Johnson was pardoned by Reagan in 1985 for bootlegging (an offense that would have applied to many early stock car drivers); Jimmy Carter pardoned celebrity bank robber and erstwhile hippie cult member Patricia Hearst; Gerald Ford pardoned Tokyo Rose, who acted as a Japanese propaganda spokesperson during World War II. Since the Truman Administration, presidents have traditionally pardoned a turkey scheduled for execution and the subsequent repast of someone's Thanksgiving banquet. The lucky bird is code named "Biscuits," and "Gravy" is the backup turkey.

Sometimes presidential pardons make national headlines for more serious reasons. This was true in 1974, when President Ford pardoned his predecessor, Richard Nixon, for any crimes Nixon may have committed during the Watergate scandal. Ford's motives in doing so were patriotic. "I was very sure of what would happen if I let the charges against Nixon run their legal course," he recalled. "Months were sure to elapse between an indictment and trial. . . . A period of such prolonged vituperation and recrimination would be disastrous for the nation. America needed recovery, not revenge" (Ford, 1979, 161). But many Americans thought a backroom deal had been struck, whereby Nixon resigned and spared the nation the ordeal of impeachment only when guaranteed that he would later receive Ford's pardon.

Ford always denied this, but he observed that, his good intentions aside, the perception of a corrupt bargain between Nixon and himself probably cost him the 1976 election.

THE UNFORESEEN INSTITUTIONS

In a variety of ways, the presidency presents a case study in the law of unintended consequences. However farsighted and admirable the Framers' original blueprint for the presidency, it was impossible for those men, sitting in a room in Philadelphia in 1787, to squeeze every conceivable contingency into the slightly-over-1,000-word section of the Constitution that addresses presidential authority. "The office was created at a specific historical moment out of materials and in circumstances that cannot be replicated," historian Forrest McDonald has observed, "and it has evolved along lines peculiarly American" (McDonald, 1995, 479). As we have seen, those lines were not always predictable or even desirable, according to the Framers' lights.

Perhaps the most important unforeseen presidential happenstance was the presidential Cabinet. The Framers did predict the need for presidents to have advisers who could give them guidance in running the executive branch's various departments. Section 2 of Article II declared that the president "may require the Opinion, in writing, of the principal Officer in each of the executive Departments, upon any subject relating to the

Duties of their respective Offices." The Constitution gave the Senate an "advice and consent" role in the executive's appointment of advisers (along with other executive department officers). But the Framers did not quite envision these presidential advisers as constituting a formal cabinet, possibly because the idea carried dark overtones reminiscent of the English king's Privy Council, a body that many felt was responsible for George III's disastrous and oppressive policies toward the colonies. This fear had killed various proposals to create a presidential council with actual governing powers, leaving only Article II's rather vague provision for "principal Officers."

Early in his presidency, however, George Washington discovered the need for something more formal and organized than merely a cadre of advisers. Congress approved the creation of the core executive departments—State, War, and Treasury—and Washington appointed appropriate men to head the departments. Over the years the Cabinet has undergone a variety of changes in size and composition, reflecting the needs of different presidents and circumstances. It grew to encompass twelve more departments: agriculture, commerce, interior, justice, labor, education, energy, transportation, health and human services, homeland security, veterans affairs, and housing and urban development. In Washington's time, Cabinet members often met with Washington during his regular visitor hour (three o'clock in the afternoon), and later presidents held meetings in the White

President George Washington (right) with members of his first Cabinet: (from left) Secretary of War Henry Knox, Secretary of State Thomas Jefferson, and Attorney General Edmund Randolph. (Library of Congress)

House's East Room. In 1902 Theodore Roosevelt gave the Cabinet its own room in the White House, and in that room presidents have since discussed innumerable weighty matters, from wars to presidential scandals.

Traditional Cabinet officials have been joined by others whose usefulness became apparent as the nation grew larger and more complex. By 2005 the presidential flow chart included the Office of National AIDS Policy, the Office of Science and Technology Policy, the President's Critical Infrastructure Protection Board, the USA Freedom Corps—the list could go on and on. The Framers never foresaw this phalanx of executive department officials, located somewhere between Cabinet-level department heads and lower-level administrators, who have become a familiar part of presidential life.

Most of these positions were created to meet immediate circumstances, as presidents discovered that their times brought with them new administrative needs. The office of presidential chief of staff, for example, grew out of the twentieth century's increasingly complex presidential bureaucracy, and was created as an office to act as a sort of jack-of-all-trades, handling everything from the transition for an incoming president to firing members of the presidential retinue when necessary. "Andrew Card is chronically there," noted an observer about President George Bush Jr.'s chief of staff, "as in *there* in the room, in the meeting, in the photo, on the Sunday [talk] shows" (*Washington Post,* January 5, 2005).

The chief of staff is also an apt example of the presidency's tendency toward exponential growth during the modern age. It was technically authorized in 1939, when a congressional committee recommended expansion of the executive branch to keep pace with Franklin Roosevelt's rapidly expanding presidency. However, neither FDR nor his successor, Harry Truman, created such a post. But Dwight Eisenhower did (reflecting perhaps Ike's military experience with a similar staff organization), and from that point on—with the exception of Presidents Kennedy and Johnson, who for various reasons did not appoint chiefs of staff—the office has become its own multifaceted growth industry. There has been a deputy chief of staff, deputy chief of staff for policy and political activity, deputy chief of staff for White House operations, counselor to the chief of staff, and special counselor to the chief of staff. In the Clinton White House, Victoria Radd served as the chief of staff to the chief of staff.

CONCLUSION: THAT "SCARY" PRESIDENCY

Ronald Reagan had every right to be frightened at the prospect of such an administrative behemoth. The various hats a modern president must wear are enough to intimidate any sensible person. But even when the presidency was far smaller, the office still had the power to daunt. A Renaissance man like Thomas Jefferson, able to do so many things so well, breathed an audible sigh of relief when he neared completion of his second term and the prospect of replacement by James Madison. "I am now

leaving to be settled by my friend Mr. Madison," he wrote in March 1809. "Never did a prisoner, released from his chains, feel such relief as I shall on shaking off the shackles of power" (Peterson, 1984, 1203).

The "shackles of power"—that phrase cut through the details and captured with typical Jeffersonian precision the heart of the matter. The American presidency intimidates not so much because of its enormous complexity, its many ambiguities, or its prominent place in American public life. No, the source of its awe is the stark fact that it concentrates power, of whatever amount, in the hands of a single lone individual; and however alluring that power may be, sooner or later every man who has held the office comes to understand that it is also a weary burden. At the very least, it is not a thing to be taken lightly. One of Mr. Reagan's biographers called the presidency the "role of a lifetime." Indeed.

FURTHER READING

Banning, Lance, *The Jeffersonian Persuasion: Evolution of a Party Ideology* (Ithaca, NY: Cornell University Press, 1980).

Belz, Herman, Alfred H. Kelly, and Winfred Harbison, *The American Constitution: Its Origins and Development*, 2 vols., 7th ed. (New York: W.W. Norton, 1990).

Boritt, Gabor, ed., *The Lincoln Enigma: The Changing Faces of an American Icon* (New York: Oxford University Press, 2001).

Brookhiser, Richard, *Founding Father: Rediscovering George Washington* (New York: Free Press, 1996).

Cannon, Lou, *President Reagan: The Role of a Lifetime* (New York: Public Affairs, 2000).

Clements, Kendrick A., *The Presidency of Woodrow Wilson* (Lawrence: University Press of Kansas, 1992).

Clinton, William J., Jr., *Putting People First: How We Can All Change America* (New York: Times Books, 1992).

Clinton, William J., Jr., *My Life* (New York: Alfred A. Knopf, 2004).

Dalton, Kathleen, *Theodore Roosevelt: A Strenuous Life* (New York: Alfred A. Knopf, 2002).

Flexner, James, *Washington: The Indispensable Man* (Boston: Little, Brown, 1974).

Ford, Gerald R., *A Time to Heal: The Autobiography of Gerald R. Ford* (New York: Harper and Row, 1979).

Goodwin, Doris Kearns, *No Ordinary Time: Franklin and Eleanor Roosevelt—The Home Front in World War II* (New York: Simon and Schuster, 1994).

Hayden, Joseph, *Covering Clinton: The President and the Press in the 1990s* (Westport, CT: Praeger, 2002).

Hyneman, Charles S., and Donald S. Lutz, *American Political Writing during the Founding Era, 1760–1805*, 2 vols. (Indianapolis, IN: Liberty Press, 1983).

Kenyon, Cecelia, The *Antifederalists* (Indianapolis, IN: Bobbs-Merrill, 1966).

Madison, James, *The Constitutional Convention: A Narrative History from the Notes of James Madison* (New York: Modern Library, 2005).

McCullough, David, *Truman* (New York: Simon and Schuster, 1992).

McCullough, David, *John Adams* (New York: Simon and Schuster, 2001).

McDonald, Forrest, *The American Presidency: An Intellectual History* (Lawrence: University Press of Kansas, 1995).

Pfiffner, James A., *The Modern Presidency* (New York: Wadsworth, 2005).

Peterson, Merrill D., ed., *Thomas Jefferson: Writings* (New York: Library of America, 1984).

Reeves, Richard, *President Nixon: Alone in the White House* (New York: Simon and Schuster, 2001).

Rossiter, Clinton, ed., *The Federalist Papers* (New York: Signet, 1961).

Wood, Gordon, S., *The Creation of the American Republic, 1776–1787* (Chapel Hill: University of North Carolina Press, 1969).

2

THE PEOPLE WHO SERVE: SEEKING, WINNING, AND HOLDING THE WHITE HOUSE

"None of my friends ever thought he should be president—much less that he could be," journalist Richard Ben Cramer observed. "Of course, we were all taught that it was possible (in America, God bless her). But our lives separated us from that notion by the time we left our teens. A President—*the* President—was someone altogether larger, and more extraordinary, than we." Looking at the various presidents and presidential candidates he had covered during his years as a reporter for the *Philadelphia Inquirer* and other publications, Cramer boiled it all down to some simple questions: "Who are these guys? What are they like?" (Cramer, 1993, vii).

THE POWER OF PRESIDENTIAL PERSONALITIES

Who, indeed? People everywhere around the world are fascinated by the individuals who have held the office of president. More has been written about one of them, Abraham Lincoln, in the English language than any other individual except Jesus Christ. George Washington and Thomas Jefferson have been icons in faraway places like France and China.

Germans cheered John F. Kennedy wildly during his 1963 visit and were not even much offended when JFK mangled the phrase "Ich bin ein Berliner" (I am a Berliner) so badly that it came out technically as "I am a jelly doughnut."

Even less-famous presidents garner an unusual amount of public attention. John Tyler, an obscure Virginia politician who was nicknamed "His Accidency" because he was elevated to the White House from the vice presidency after William Henry Harrison died suddenly in 1841, has been the subject of at least a half dozen books. Harrison, who was president for all of thirty days, garners twenty four hits in an amazon.com book search. Some political scientists claim that Martin Van Buren's contributions to American politics are underrated (not to mention his contributions to American slang; one theory has Van Buren inventing the word "okay"). Every year some of the locals in Greeneville, Tennessee, hold a ceremony marking the birth of one of their favorite sons, Andrew Johnson.

Presidential trivia is an American art form; even the most inconsequential of presidential quirks and pronouncements can become national events. Teddy Roosevelt's sparing of a bear cub that had been brought to him caged for execution during a hunting trip in 1902 gave birth to the "Teddy Bear." George Bush Sr.'s offhand remark that he did not like broccoli sparked a protest by broccoli farmers in front of the White House and the brief celebrity of "broccoli man," whose perambulations in a large plastic broccoli mask and yellow tuxedo at baseball games and conventions earned him headlines as far away as Germany and England. Presidents' children become frontpage news, as do their pets. Barbara Bush wrote a book from the point of view of the family's springer spaniel; there is an entire Web site devoted to FDR's dog, Fala.

Presidents become the butt of endless jokes, from wisecracks about William Howard Taft's girth to *Saturday Night Live* comedy sketches concerning Bill Clinton's various sexual peccadilloes. Presidents are Hail to the Chief and Mr. President, but they are also more affectionately FDR, Ike, JFK, LBJ, and Dubya. Of course, other nicknames are less kind: Americans called Richard Nixon Tricky Dick and Bill Clinton Slick Willie. During the Depression they hung Herbert Hoover's last name on the various problems of the time: shantytowns became Hoovervilles, newspapers used for cover by the poor became Hoover blankets, and empty pockets were Hoover flags.

Presidents are easily available targets of the vital criticism democracies can produce. John Quincy Adams's opponents during the 1828 campaign accused him in all seriousness of running a whorehouse in Paris while acting as the

U.S. ambassador to France; his supporters in turn accused his opponent, Andrew Jackson, of bigamy. In 1860 Democrats spread rumors that Republican candidate Abraham Lincoln had an African American mistress and was perhaps of mixed-race descent himself (a serious charge during that race-conscious era). During the 2004 election, columnist Charlie Booker referred to George Bush Jr. as a "lying, sniggering, drink-driving, selfish, reckless, ignorant, dangerous, backward, drooling, twitching, blinking, mouse-faced little cheat" (*Washington Post*, October 25, 2004).

Presidents can get sucked into the darker side of the American psyche. In 1960 Republicans spread stories that John F. Kennedy's Catholicism would have him taking orders directly from the pope (another damaging allegation in a country where Catholics have sometimes been mistrusted and persecuted). Anti-Clinton extremists spread absurd rumors that he dealt drugs and had one of his own advisers murdered, while extremist critics of George Bush Jr. spread rumors that he engineered the Iraqi war at the behest of Saudi Arabian oil interests, or that he had notorious terrorist Osama bin Laden locked away in a secret CIA prison cell, saving the news of his capture until the political timing was right.

Assassinated presidents spawn their own cottage industries of dubious conspiracy theorizing. Lincoln's secretary of war, Edwin Stanton, was said by some to have engineered the president's murder for his own political purposes. The list of shadowy suspects in the Kennedy assassination is large, ranging from the Mafia to Vice President Lyndon Johnson. One theory holds that Kennedy was killed by a shotgun blast from a CIA midget hiding in a storm drain along Dallas's Dealey Plaza.

Silly these theories may be, but their very existence underscores the fact that presidential personalities have been almost seamlessly woven into the larger fabric of American culture. We think they are funny, dangerous, tragic, goofy, weird, noble, admirable, and lovable—but we are not indifferent. Americans are not just entranced by the presidency as an office; we are entranced by the presidents themselves, as people who live in the very public fishbowl that is the White House.

During the first one hundred years or so of America's history, interest in the presidents stemmed from the novelty of the office itself. People who lived their lives ruled by kings were fascinated by the fact that America's presidents were not to the manor born. What sort of a man, people wondered, could make this new political office, with its odd mixture of power and democratic accountability, work?

Since World War II people have shifted their perspective somewhat, from regarding presidents as novelties to seeing them as world leaders possessing unprecedented power. To those living in the eighteenth and nineteenth centuries, presidents looked rather like big fish in a small pond—they mattered a lot in the United States, but not so much elsewhere. After World War II, however, presidents could quite literally destroy the world, with large nuclear arsenals at their beck and call.

Whether drawn by presidents' novelty or their power, people have long asked some variation of Cramer's basic question: just who are these guys? While a diverse group, it is possible to sketch some broad characteristics shared by most of the men who have served as America's chief executive over the years.

First, they have all been men. No woman has served as president, nor have any of the handful of women who received party primary votes (Eleanor Roosevelt in 1952, for example) stood a realistic chance of capturing the office. This is not say that women have had no influence on the presidency; quite the contrary. Numerous First Ladies have exerted power behind the scenes. Mary Todd Lincoln, for example, frequently gave her husband advice concerning Cabinet appointments and bills he should (or should not) sign into law. Her forthright love of politics caused a few tongues to click in disapproval. "Mrs. Lincoln is making and unmaking the political fortunes of men," complained a New York journalist, "and [she] is similar to Queen Elizabeth in her statesmanlike tastes" (Baker, 1987, 181).

Many modern First Ladies have been more open in their public and political activities. The watershed figure in this regard was Eleanor Roosevelt, Franklin's brilliant and outspoken wife. She redefined the role of First Lady as a public figure by holding her own press conferences, employing her own retinue and press secretary, writing regular newspaper columns, and touring the country as the Roosevelt Administration's goodwill ambassador to the victims of the Great Depression. Her tours served a less widely known but still more vital service as well; she gave him access to the countryside he would otherwise never have been able to achieve, given his wheelchair-bound state (he was stricken with polio in 1921) and his desire to keep his handicap a secret. "It was Franklin who had encouraged her to become his 'eyes and ears,' to gather the grass-roots knowledge he needed to understand the people he governed," according to historian Doris Kearns Goodwin (1994, 27).

Some subsequent First Ladies have chosen to follow Eleanor's example, while others have not. Bess Truman, Eleanor's direct successor, canceled the press conferences Eleanor had routinely held, and once told her husband that, should he ever again refer to her jokingly as "the boss" in public, she would go home to Missouri and never return. On the other hand, Hillary Rodham Clinton consciously emulated Mrs. Roosevelt, whom she referred to as a "guiding spirit" and reportedly held séances to contact—and in 2007 declared her candidacy for president, becoming the first woman with a serious chance of winning the office.

Nevertheless, the presidency has so far been a men-only club; and the men have always been white. For the first 150 years of the office's history, this was a more or less accurate reflection, unfortunately, of the nation's overall racial mores. Presidents have not been, on the whole, either more or less racially enlightened or bigoted than their neigh-

bors. At one extreme Abraham Lincoln freed several million African American slaves and was the first president to meet with and consult African American leaders like Frederick Douglass. Douglass (who was not always so well disposed toward Lincoln) later observed that the president was "the first great man I talked with in the United States freely who in no single instance reminded me of the difference between himself and myself, of the difference of color" (Oates, 1984, 118). At the other extreme stood Lincoln's successor, Andrew Johnson, who after an icily hostile 1866 visit by Douglass and other black leaders turned to his secretary and remarked, "I know that d—d Douglass; he's just like any nigger, and he would sooner cut a white man's throat than not" (McPherson, 1982, 498).

Black members of presidential administrations have been few and far between. Robert Clifton Weaver, who served as the secretary of housing and urban development in Lyndon Johnson's administration, was the first African American member of a presidential Cabinet. Colin Powell, who served as George Bush Jr.'s secretary of state, was the first high-profile black Cabinet officer (along with Condoleezza Rice, Bush's National Security Adviser and later Powell's successor as secretary of state). African Americans have been scarce even on the margins of the presidency. Despite the existence of a vigorous African American press dating back to the earliest days of the Republic, for example, no African American was admitted to the White House press corps until Harry S. McAlpin of the National

Negro Press Association was allowed in during 1944.

Black presidential candidates have been even more scarce. In 1972 Shirley Chisholm became the first African American to run for the office, knowing as she did so that she stood no chance of capturing the Democratic Party's nomination. In the 1980s and 1990s, some prominent African American leaders generated intense but short-lived groundswells of support. Civil rights leader Jesse Jackson probably came closest to a bona fide run at the Democratic Party nomination in 1988, generating a brief surge of public interest (including a *Time* magazine cover story) before fading. Periodic media speculation focuses on high-profile African Americans— Colin Powell, for example—who might someday have a realistic chance at the presidency or vice presidency, although to date this has not resulted in an actual nomination. However, in 2007, African American U.S. senator Barack Obama threw his hat in the presidential ring and was given a real chance of winning the Democratic nomination. There have been almost no serious attempts at the presidency by a Hispanic American or Asian American.

While things may change in the near future, presidents have so far been men, they have been white, and most of them have been rich—in some cases extraordinarily so. Even those with genuinely humble roots overcame their poverty long before reaching the White House. Benjamin Harrison may have been born a farmer's son in rural Ohio, but by the time he ran for governor of Indiana in

1876 (and president twelve years later), he was rich enough that his opponents effectively taunted him with the label "kid gloves Harrison." Andrew Jackson came from such an impoverished background that he was not quite sure whether the cabin in which he was born was located in North or South Carolina, but when he became president in 1828, he was a wealthy Tennessee slaveholder. Even Abraham Lincoln, whose self-education by the light of a pioneer fireplace and rail-splitting manual labor have become the stuff of American legend, had by 1860 built a prosperous law practice and lived in a comfortable upper-middle-class home.

Forty-three presidents, forty-three rich white boys—it would be easy to become cynical about the presidency as an historical expression of diversity. Still, there have been quite a few variations in the personalities, intellects, and characters of the presidents, variations that in turn reflected changing times, circumstances, and the vicissitudes of mere human nature. The more democratically minded Founding Fathers wanted the presidency to reflect America's population and the president to be a man of "the people" in all their diverse glory. In many ways, the Founders' wishes have been satisfied.

But beyond their diversity, such as it was, presidents contributed a certain broad set of overarching values and characteristics, passed along to each of their successors. There have been forty-three presidents, plural, but there is also a presidency, singular—a mosaic of ideas each president brought to the office concerning what a president should be and do. Each president has placed his special tile in the presidential mosaic. Some of the contributions have been rather small—as with William Henry Harrison and Zachary Taylor, for example, each of whom died in office after only a few months—while others, of course, have been extraordinarily large and dominant: Washington, Lincoln, and the two Roosevelts.

In this chapter it has been necessary to focus on those larger presidential tiles, on the presidents who effected truly momentous changes in the presidency's 200-year development. The goal here has been to identify those presidents who contributed most significantly—in ways good and bad—to the general development of the office as we know it today.

George Washington played an indispensable role in the founding of the United States, leading the Continental Army to victory in the American Revolution and becoming the country's first president. (Library of Congress)

GEORGE WASHINGTON AND THE PRESIDENTIAL BALANCING ACT

As the Framers wrote the Constitution's provisions for a chief executive, they were quite literally looking at fifty-five-year-old George Washington for their guide. He was the overwhelming consensus choice for president of the Convention, the man who "having conducted these states to independence and peace [now] appears to assist in framing a Government to make the People happy," an observer said (Brookhiser, 1996, 59). Throughout those long hot days in Philadelphia, as the Framers wrangled and fought behind locked doors, Washington presided with a quiet but firm hand in moving the Convention along to a successful conclusion. The association

of his name to the entire affair as president of the Convention helped ease public acceptance of what was otherwise a divisive new Constitution.

The nearly universal assumption that Washington would be the nation's first president also helped Revolutionary-era Americans accept that controversial office. "Had any character of less popularity and celebrity been designated to this high trust," noted one Antifederalist, "it might at this period have endangered, if not proved fatal to the peace of the Union" (McDonald, 1994, 209). A people who had just emerged from under a monarchy were understandably anxious that their new chief executive—the closest thing to a ruler the new nation would have—be not just an officer tied down by legal and constitutional checks and balances. They also needed him to be, in their estimation, a good man, and they needed a high degree of unanimity in that estimation.

Washington fit the bill as no other man could. Conservative or radical, Northerner or Southerner, denizen of the coastlands or the frontier, farmer, merchant, or lawyer—everyone loved George. He was "the closest approximation to a self-evident truth in American politics," wrote historian Joseph Ellis (2001, 120). When the time came, Washington was not elected the nation's first president; he ascended to the post by nearly universal acclaim. No future president would enjoy Washington's unanimous approval by the American people.

Why? After all, he did not possess a unique intellect (like Thomas Jefferson), a unique temperament (like John Adams), or a unique skill in some obviously relevant discipline (like Alexander Hamilton). His political résumé was not terribly impressive, either: he had been a delegate to the Second Continental Congress but had no previous experience as a political executive. He was a famous general, of course. But even so, it was hard to pinpoint exactly what made him a great military leader, aside from the fact that he had led the winning side. At a time when Americans were blessed with a galaxy of extraordinarily talented and capable political leaders, Washington can seem rather pedestrian.

But perhaps it was not a matter of uniqueness, at least not where the presidency was concerned. Indeed, Washington's chief virtue lay in his lack of uniqueness. He embodied what his generation considered to be the most important virtues necessary for a public figure. He was in some ways extraordinarily typical.

His chief virtue in the eyes of his admirers was his restrained exercise of power. Americans of the age feared what we would today call the charismatic leader, the dynamic individual who could parlay his personality and resources into despotism. They did not yet have the modern model of a Hitler or a Stalin for such a man, but they had seen what ruthless, powerful monarchs could do, particularly when blessed to have a rapport with ordinary people. This was one of the chief problems with a democracy in the eyes of critics: the notion that "the people," allegedly not possessed of much intelligence or education, would not be able to tell when they were being duped by a leader who knew how to play the common man's game to advance a dubious agenda.

Washington was one of those critics. He was himself rather suspicious of democracy, fearing the power of the people in the streets when improperly led. "Cool reason . . . is as little to be expected in the tumults of popular commotion as an attention to the liberties of the people is to be expected in the dark divan of a desperate tyrant," he believed (Flexner, 1965, 174). Moreover, he was an aristocrat. He was wealthy, owned slaves, and moved in the circles of Tidewater Virginia, the closest thing America had to nobility. Politically, he was no leveler, no social or economic radical along the lines of a Samuel Adams or a Thomas Paine.

But if he did not quite trust democracy, he understood its powerful appeal in the new nation; and he knew that, where "the people" were concerned, he had better tread carefully. He must not appear avaricious or grasping for power. He could so easily have acquired power, a great deal of it, in post-Revolutionary America. He could have been a king had he chosen to pursue such ambitions. Yet he did not do so, rejecting suggestions from monarchy-minded Americans that he found a Washington dynasty capable of carrying an American crown. During the war he was informed by one of his officers that calls for his kingship were rampant in the army's ranks; Washington's response was swift and unequivocal. "No occurrence in the course of the war has given me more painful sensations than your information of there being such ideas existing in the army," he wrote, ideas that were "big with the greatest mischiefs that can befall my country" (Flexner, 1965, 170).

This sense of restraint remained with him even as he was called out of retirement in 1787 to preside over the creation of a new constitution. His name rarely appears in the Constitution's minutes, leading some people to suggest that he did not really do much in Philadelphia. Actually, it would be more accurate to say that he understood the value of re-

straint, that reticence was a necessary virtue for a man in his position. Awarded the presidency of the Convention, Washington gave a little speech in which he "reminded [the Framers] of the novelty of the scene of business in which he was to act, lamented his want of better qualifications, and claimed the indulgence of the House towards the involuntary errors which his inexperience might occasion" (Madison, 2005, 45).

That was the longest speech he gave at the Convention. Was it merely false modesty? Maybe. But if it was an affectation, it was a very effective one, for moments like this cemented Washington's status in the minds of his countrymen as a careful individual, someone who could surely control his impulses toward acquisition of power when bestowed with the presidency. It went a long way toward alleviating the fears of those Americans who felt there should be no such office.

Restraint in the exercise of power was part and parcel of Washington's other great virtue: self-discipline. Few Americans were as reserved as George Washington. He seemed forever able to exercise the most rigid and inflexible control over his own emotions. "Never exceed a decent warmth," he advised his nephew, "and submit your sentiments with diffidence" (Brookhiser, 1996, 65–66). There was much to control, for Washington possessed a fiery temper, and he was internally roiled by insecurities he allowed no one to see. Many who knew him sensed this, at least on a visceral level— there was a fire behind those eyes and a potential volcanic eruption of passion

Nineteenth-century lithograph based on Junius Brutus Stearns' Washington as a Farmer at Mount Vernon, *1851. The painting depicts George Washington, surrounded by slaves who are harvesting hay on his Mount Vernon estate. Washington was passionate about farming and devoted considerable time to developing his plantation. (Library of Congress)*

beneath that marble exterior. People admired Washington all the more because he was able to control himself so carefully. "Thousands have learned to restrain their passions," observed a colleague, "though few among them had to contend with passions so violent" (Brookhiser, 1996, 6).

Restraint, self-discipline, austere simplicity—Washington brought these qual-ities to the presidency. But this should not imply languor. One of the less-appreciated aspects of Washington's life was his underlying reserve of energy. He was an enormous man for his time, tall, robust, and possessed of remarkable stamina. His appearance matched his character, for he put in long, hard days farming, riding, administering the thousand and one details of Mount Vernon's little world and exhorting yet one more effort from his battered little Continental Army. As an ambitious Virginia planter, Washington's energy was invaluable; as a political leader, it was almost priceless, for it meant that even at the relatively advanced age of fifty-six, when he ascended to the presidency, he would bring to the office a keen edge and a certain presence. "He has so much martial energy in his deportment," marveled one observer, "that there is not a king in Europe but would look like a valet de chamber beside him" (Ellis, 2001, 124).

It all added up to one overarching value, one that defined him as president and would become a primary value, pursued with greater or lesser degrees of success, by presidents thereafter: the value of balance. As president, Washington stood not so much on a throne of power, but on a tightrope, precariously balancing power with liberty, energy with restraint, and authority with democracy. But unlike the presidents who came after him, Washington had no guidelines, no blueprints from which to work. He was aware, painfully so, that every single thing he did as president would set precedents, creating the tone for this brand new, untried political office. "So much is expected, so many untoward circumstances may intervene, in such a new and critical situation," he privately worried (Flexner, 1965, 215).

Washington's inauguration typified the pressures under which he functioned, and his success in doing so. There were those who thought the presidential swearing-in ceremony should closely resemble a coronation, so as to awe the people and foreign observers with the power latent in the new office. Others wanted to go to the opposite extreme and create a ceremony with as little ceremony as possible, speaking to the democratic spirit of a nation founded upon government by the people.

Taking these views into account, Washington as always acted the part of the balancer. Parts of the ceremony were indeed regal in flavor. He arrived in a splendidly adorned carriage drawn by six white horses and guarded by a spit-and-polish contingent of New York militiamen. As he entered the legislative chamber of New York's City Hall, the audience stood in respect and reverence. But the ceremony itself was simple. The new president placed his hand on the Bible, repeated the oath, then kissed the book; the man presiding over the oath, New York chancellor Robert R. Livingston, said simply "It is done. Long live George Washington, President of the United States" (McCullough, 2001, 402). It seemed a fitting mix of executive power and democratic humility. Even Washington's dress was carefully balanced; he wore his ceremonial dress sword, but with a suit of plain brown broadcloth.

As his inauguration went, so did his behavior during eight years in office. He carefully juggled the prerogatives of the presidency with those of the other branches, particularly Congress. Privately, he had his doubts about some of the people's representatives—just as he harbored worries about the people themselves—but publicly he deferred to the legislative branch as the chief governing body for the new nation. He stayed out of Congress's day-to-day operations, proposing no legislative programs and remaining publicly silent on the policy debates that roiled Congress. He was likewise restrained in his attitude toward the president's chief political weapon, the veto, which he used only two times (both for minor procedural matters) in eight years.

Washington also tried to bring a sense of balance to the embryonic political parties that were born during his administration. He did not want parties. "The alternate domination of one faction over another, sharpened by the spirit of revenge, natural to party dissension, which in different ages and countries has perpetrated the most horrid enormities, is itself a frightful despotism," he declared (www.yale.edu/lawweb/avalon/washing.htm). But parties Washington had, whether he liked it or not. The Cabinet squabbling between his secretary of state, Thomas Jefferson, and his secretary of the Treasury, Alexander Hamilton, slowly took a more organized form during his administration. By the beginning of his second term, Hamiltonian (Federalist) and Jeffersonian (Republican) factions were well on their way to becoming permanent features of American political life.

While in so many ways Washington was a resounding success in his balancing act, here he was far less so. He could not prevent the creation of parties, nor could he stem his own increasingly pro-Federalist tendencies. He simply agreed more often with Hamilton than Jefferson, and toward the end of his second term, this pro-Federalist perspective earned him the distrust and even enmity of some Republicans. Washington found himself in the uncomfortable position of being pilloried in the Republican press, and he was stunned to find that, in the heat of party battles, "every act of my administration would be tortured, and the grossest and most insidious misrepresentations of them made (by giving one side *only* of a subject, and that too in such exaggerated and indecent terms as could scarcely be applied to a Nero, a notorious defaulter, or a common pickpocket)" (Flexner, 1965, 346).

These attacks contributed to his final balancing act as president, one that would have important ramifications for future chief executives: he decided not to seek a third term. Again, he was, wittingly or not in this case, juggling the competing interests of power and restraint in the presidency, of staying around long enough to do the job, but not so long as to create the opportunity for a debilitating entrenchment that could either sap the office of its power or, worse, create opportunities for a dynastic-type despotism. Washington thus set in motion what would for the first century and a half of American history be a time-honored tradition, broken only once, and in the last fifty years mandated by constitutional amendment: a two-term limitation on the presidency.

The next five presidents all lived, to a greater or lesser degree, within Washington's immediate shadow. Like Washington, three of them were powerful figures in their time, leading lights of the Founding generation: Thomas Jefferson; John

Adams; and James Madison, the "father of the Constitution." Even James Monroe—whose chief claim to fame was his stint as minister to France—and John Quincy Adams—just barely on the edge of the Revolutionary generation by virtue of being John Adams's son—were widely admired as embodying the spirit of a legendary age.

But none so much as Washington, and none with more relevance to the office of the presidency. Washington *was* the presidency to Americans living in the first fifty years of the nation's life. Of all the things he contributed to the office, none was more important than the fundamental value of balance, of carefully juggling the competing concerns of power and restraint, decisive leadership and responsiveness to democracy, and executive prerogatives and the wishes of Congress. On a more subtle level, Washington balanced the competing tones of the presidential character: distance from and closeness to "the people," ceremony but also simplicity, and the desire to serve but the willingness to step aside. It was a lasting legacy.

ABRAHAM LINCOLN AND THE PRESIDENT'S WORDS

By modern standards the first fifteen presidents were a hands-off group. Following Washington's lead, they deferred to Congress as the primary branch of national government. Their purview (as they saw it) lay in negotiating treaties, commanding the army and navy, enforcing federal law, and running the execu-

tive department. Given the fact that most nations considered the United States a backwater nation with low diplomatic priority, that the army had only a few thousand men and the navy pitifully few ships, that there was very little federal regulation of national life, and that the executive branch was smaller than the operations of any medium-sized bank, the job description of the presidency did not actually amount to much. Occasionally, a stronger-than-average president like Andrew Jackson would bare his teeth, but such episodes were few and far between.

Presidents did not see their job as providing the broad moral guidance to the nation that we now take for granted. They did not speak to the national conscience, as modern presidents often do when addressing abortion rights, affirmative action, stem cell research, and other sensitive issues. Early chief executives avoided such topics, and the media was so truncated (again, by modern standards) that they would have found it very difficult to try to shape public opinion on a national scale.

In fact, they did not deliver many speeches at all, not even in their own behalf. Public opinion considered it gauche for a presidential candidate to campaign for himself; the office should seek the man and not vice versa, it was felt. Once in power, a president had little to say in public. His annual State of the Union Address, required by the Constitution, was actually a message sent to Congress, not a speech. Even in times of relative crisis, like a war, presidents did not mold public opinion directly. James K. Polk's assertion in 1846 that "the cup of forebearance has been exhausted" with Mexico, and his subsequent call for a declaration of war, came in the usual message to Congress, not from a speaker's platform of a press conference (Bergeron, 1987, 76).

During the 1840s and 1850s, presidents tried even harder to avoid speaking to the pressing domestic issues of the day. There were no presidential pronouncements on the evils of alcohol, for example, even as the temperance movement roiled American society. The first major meeting of women's rights activists at Seneca Falls, New York, in 1848 produced no reaction from President Polk. The murder of abolitionist Elijah Lovejoy at the hands of an angry mob in Alton, Illinois, shocked the nation in 1837, but newly elected president Martin Van Buren said nothing publicly about the incident.

Slavery was a problem that antebellum presidents absolutely wished to avoid: it was a no-win situation for them politically, and involving the presidency in what was fast becoming an intractable national problem would do the office no good. Agitation of the slavery problem also threatened to splinter the major political parties of the day along sectional lines. Democrats in particular—who dominated the White House during the era—had to avoid putting a man in charge who was too northern for Southerners and too southern for Northerners. The press called these nominees "doughfaces," usually bland Northerners with southern friends and sympathies who could be expected to stay quiet about the ever-deepening moral,

political, and sectional morass that American slavery created.

James Buchanan was the premier doughface of his day, symbolizing the get-along-to-go-along leadership model of the antebellum presidency. An affable but nondescript Pennsylvanian who sympathized with white southerners and their problems, Buchanan was a U.S. representative, U.S. senator, and diplomat who owed his election in 1856 largely to the fact that, having been out of the country serving as the nation's ambassador to Great Britain, he had not alienated anyone by expressing an opinion on anything that really mattered. His idea of leadership was to pull the presidency out of slavery's firing line entirely. He strongly hoped the Supreme Court might solve the slavery dispute, and told Americans in his Inaugural Address that, "to their decision, in common with all good citizens, I shall cheerfully submit, whatever this may be" (www.bartleby.com/124/pres30.html). Hardly the sort of man to turn the presidency into a moral beacon of national leadership, Buchanan was by turns shocked, then confused, then resigned to the fact of the secession of most southern states in 1860 and 1861.

When elected Buchanan's successor, there was reason to believe that Abraham Lincoln would be yet another in a long line of presidents who ducked the big moral questions of his day. Nothing in his background suggested that he had the wherewithal to effect revolutionary changes in the White House. Lincoln was a self-educated Illinois lawyer whose only exposure to national political service was a single term in the House of

Abraham Lincoln served as president of the United States during the turbulent years of the American Civil War. Lincoln's crucial role in abolishing slavery in the U.S. in 1863 has earned him the informal title of Great Emancipator. (Library of Congress)

Representatives. He became president with the backing of less than 50 percent of the popular vote in an odd four-way election during which his name did not even appear on most southern ballots. Before he could take the oath of office, a large chunk of the South left the Union to form its own nation. It was a time that called for treading very carefully. To many Americans, it was most certainly not the time for an embattled minority president to suddenly try acting as the nation's moral mouthpiece.

There was no doubt about Lincoln's personal conviction concerning what he called the "monstrous injustice of slavery." "I hate it," he declared, "because it deprives our republican example of its just influence in the world—enables the enemies of free institutions, with plausibility, to taunt us as hypocrites—causes the real friends of freedom to doubt our sincerity, and especially because it forces so many really good men amongst ourselves into an open war with the very fundamental principles of civil liberty" (Basler, 1953–1955, 2: 255). But as a politician he often felt constrained to temper his antislavery convictions, and as president he was under even greater pressure not to exceed the constitutional mandate of his office. "If slavery is not wrong, nothing is wrong," he wrote, "and yet I have never understood that the Presidency conferred upon me an unrestricted right to act officially upon this judgment and feeling" (Basler, 1953–1955, 7: 281).

He inherited a situation in 1861 that called for a further dissembling on these matters. Traveling eastward to Washington, D.C., as the nation's president-elect, he begged white Southerners not to do anything intemperate, even as they were in the process of wrecking the Union. During his Inaugural Address, he appealed to Southerners' sense of national fraternity. "We are not enemies, but friends," he told them. "We must not be enemies. Though passion may have strained, it must not break our bonds of affection" (Basler, 1953–1955, 4: 271). And he reiterated his promise not to touch slavery in the states where it already existed.

Lincoln did not seem poised to open a new moral dimension for the American presidency—not in 1861 at least. But as he himself later admitted, "I claim not to have controlled events, but confess plainly that events have controlled me" (Basler, 1953–1955, 7: 281). This was true in a multitude of ways. The war turned him into an effective military strategist despite his lack of military experience. It also turned him into the Great Emancipator, despite his early promises to leave slavery alone. But perhaps most of all, the war turned Abraham Lincoln into an enormously effective spokesman for the moral heart of America, despite the long precedent of presidents staying out of moral matters.

In an era before television, radio, and the Internet gave presidents direct outlets to the American people, newspapers were Lincoln's best tools for opening a direct moral dialogue with his constituents. Press conferences were unheard of, and people were still wary of presidents who too actively propagandized, so Lincoln honed a different communications tool: an ostensibly private letter, written in response to a critic, that Lincoln knew would be widely disseminated in print.

The best example of this approach was Lincoln's famous response to the *New York Tribune*'s Horace Greeley, a fiery antislavery editor who in August 1862 had raked Lincoln over the coals for not having the courage or leadership acumen to free the slaves. Lincoln responded with a letter indicating that to him, the Union was paramount. "My paramount object in this struggle *is* to save the Union, and is *not* either to save or to destroy slavery," he wrote. "If I could save the Union without freeing *any* slave I would do it, and if I could save it by freeing *all* the slaves I would do it; and if I could save it by freeing some and leaving others alone I would also do that. . . . I have here stated my purpose according to my view of *official* duty; and I intend no modification of my oft-expressed *personal* wish that all men every where could be free" (Basler, 1953–1955, 5: 388).

At the time he wrote this, Lincoln had already secretly decided to free those slaves living behind Confederate lines: the Emancipation Proclamation was lying in his desk, waiting for a Union battlefield victory. Lincoln knew emancipation would soon become a reality, and he knew that it would arouse fear in many quarters that he had exceeded his lawful authority as president. The Greeley letter was an effective method of calming those fears, but it also kept the president in charge of the moral dialogue about emancipation and the higher meaning of the war. The impact of that last little phrase—Lincoln's "wish that all men every where could be free"—is perhaps difficult to understand today. But in the era of the doughfaces, it signaled a bold new direction for a presidency that had previously been structured to avoid nearly any expression of a sentiment concerning right or wrong, particularly in the context of slavery.

Lincoln also used his speechmaking skills to place his presidency at the center of the Civil War's moral drama. Again, the context was much different than modern Americans might expect. His great moment at Gettysburg was almost an afterthought. Incredibly, Lincoln's speech was supposed to be an anticlimax, a "few fitting remarks" tacked onto the back end of the dedication ceremonies for the new national cemetery at Gettysburg, Pennsylvania, in November 1863. No one expected the president to make a speech for the ages.

The Gettysburg Address was a succinct, powerful evocation of battlefield death and its meaning for a nation wracked by civil war. "We are met on a great battle field of that war," he noted, "We have come to dedicate a portion of it, as a final resting place for those who died here, that the nation might live." Lincoln never mentioned the South or slavery; indeed, his words could have been reasonably interpreted as a benediction upon all the young men slain in the war, North and South. "We can not dedicate—we can not consecrate—we can not hallow, this ground," he told the audience, "The brave men, living and dead, who struggled here, have hallowed it, far above our poor power to add or detract."

And then he reached that familiar climax: "we here highly resolve these dead shall not have died in vain; that the nation, shall have a new birth of freedom, and that government of the people by the people for the people, shall not perish from the earth" (Basler, 1953–1955, 7: 17–18).

Fifteen months later Lincoln made another speech for the ages. His second Inaugural Address was the shortest in American presidential history, yet it was a tour de force. As at Gettysburg, Lincoln spoke to the higher meaning of the war; but where his underlying theme in Pennsylvania had been the patriotic meaning of death, in his second Inaugural he spoke of the more complicated moral issues of retribution, guilt, and reconciliation. He told Northerners that they too were culpable for the national sin of slavery, and he warned against any overly simplistic interpretation of God's will in the war's results. "Both [sides] read the same Bible, and pray to the same God; and each invokes His aid against the other," he pointed out. "It may seem strange that any men should dare to ask a just God's assistance in wringing their bread from the sweat of other men's faces; but let us judge not that we be not judged." At the end of the day, Lincoln believed, the only viable future direction would be the pursuit of national healing: "with malice toward none; with charity for all; with firmness in the right, as God gives us to see the right, let us strive on to finish the work we are in; to bind up the nation's wounds; to care for him who shall have borne the battle, and for his widow, and his orphan—to do all which may achieve and cherish a just, and a lasting peace, among ourselves, and with all nations" (Basler, 1953–1955, 8: 332–333).

No other president had presumed to speak of such matters. Context was a big reason why, of course, for no previous president had been compelled to guide the United States through such an awful crisis. But character was just as important as context. Lincoln possessed the personal capacity to rise and meet the challenges of his day. Events had controlled him, as he observed; but through his use of presidential word craft, he had shaped and directed those events, as well.

His successor was a far less capable man who squandered the opportunities Lincoln created for presidential influence. Ascending to the presidency after Lincoln's assassination, Andrew Johnson had little sympathy for the plight of African Americans in the postwar South, and he was ill-disposed to do anything much about the wave of racial violence sweeping the region. His vetoes of congressional civil rights laws and other Reconstruction measures precipitated a series of running feuds with Congress that culminated in his 1868 impeachment trial, during which Johnson escaped conviction and removal from office by merely one vote.

When Johnson tried his hand at presidential communication by embarking on a whistle-stop speaking tour in 1866, dubbed the "swing around the circle" in the press, the results were ugly. Where Lincoln ascended to the heights of eloquence, Johnson plumbed the depths of ineptitude. He shocked audiences by comparing his congressional critics to Confederate traitors, and he offended others by overtly comparing himself to Jesus Christ. "If more blood is needed, erect an altar, and upon it your humble speaker will pour out the last drop of his blood as a libation for his country's salvation," he declared (McPherson, 1982, 562). Hecklers tormented him with abuse, and he stooped to name-calling matches with them that struck many as entirely unpresidential. "Is that dignified?" asked an incredulous onlooker during one such exchange. "I care not a fig for dignity!" Johnson roared back (McKitrick, 1960, 322). During some stops the engineer left the station early, while Johnson was still speaking from the rear railroad car, fearing that angry mobs might storm the train.

In the wake of the Johnson debacle—he arguably had the worst term in the presidency's history—Congress became the dominant branch of the federal government. Presidents feared taking bold action that might precipitate another impeachment crisis, and no one wanted to repeat the "swing around the circle." There is a reason why few Americans today remember Rutherford B. Hayes, Chester Arthur, James Garfield, and other Gilded Age chief executives. They were competent men—even Ulysses S. Grant, whose administration was rocked with corruption scandals, had his good points—but they usually deferred to Congress on major policymaking matters. It would be a long time before any occupant of the White House approached Lincoln's level of communication or influence.

TEDDY ROOSEVELT AND THE VIGOROUS PRESIDENCY

William McKinley was the last Civil War veteran to serve as president. Elected in 1896, he had risen from the ranks, enlisting as a private in 1861 and ending his military service as a brevet major. He was not a violent man, however. He cared far more about fostering a friendly environment for America's booming industries than he did for taking up arms. "I have been through one war," he said. "I have seen the dead piled up, and I do not want to see another" (Linderman, 1974, 28).

But Americans were clamoring for a showdown with Spain to avenge the destruction of the USS *Maine* (supposedly sunk by Spanish saboteurs) and carve a new American empire out of Spain's overseas possessions, especially Cuba and the Philippines. McKinley dragged his feet, presenting the curious spectacle of a president who needed to be pushed into war by Congress. In April 1898 the president gave in to political pressure and popular opinion and requested a declaration of war from Congress.

The "splendid little war" with Spain turned out well, at least in the eyes of those who supported American imperialism. The U.S. Navy demolished the Spanish fleet in Manila Bay, while the army conquered Cuba and occupied the Philippines and Puerto Rico. More troops died from disease than Spanish bullets. America had its empire.

McKinley now needed to get on the right side of public opinion; he needed to appear more aggressive and robust in this age of American imperialism. For the 1900 election, his party gave him a genuine war hero, Theodore Roosevelt, whose leadership of a cavalry charge up San Juan Hill had earned him nationwide acclaim. Privately, McKinley had misgivings, calling Roosevelt a "damned cowboy" (Gould, 1980, 149). Teddy was not much enamored of his new boss, either, telling people that the president had "the backbone of a chocolate éclair" (Pringle, 1995, 45). Personal disdain aside, the pairing was successful, as McKinley won his reelection bid.

Ten months later an assassin's bullet put the "damned cowboy" in the White House. McKinley was murdered by a mentally suspect anarchist named Leon Czolgosz while attending the Pan-American Exposition in Buffalo, New York, making Roosevelt, at age forty-two, the youngest man ever to become president. "It is a dreadful thing to come into the Presidency this way," he said, but "here is the task, and I have got to do it to the best of my ability; and that is all there is to it" (Brands, 1997, 418).

It was typical Roosevelt: blunt, passionate, a bit blustery, and above all self-confident. He fairly oozed self-confidence—or, rather, a carefully cultivated image of such. Beneath his facade of exuberant, manly optimism lay a host of insecurities, rooted in physical problems (Roosevelt was born so sickly that doctors believed he could never make it to adulthood) and an abiding sense of shame that his father had avoided military service during the Civil War. But through hard work and sheer willpower, he managed to shove these problems

Colonel Theodore Roosevelt and his Rough Riders pose victorious following the Battle of San Juan Hill near Santiago de Cuba, on July 1, 1898. The Spanish-American War ended Spanish colonial rule in the Americas and resulted in U.S. acquisition of territories in the western Pacific and Latin America. (Library of Congress)

deep down inside himself. He lifted weights, boxed, and wrestled to overcome his physical frailty, and he rode up San Juan Hill to give himself the military pedigree his father lacked. Along the way he wrangled cows on a ranch in the Dakota Badlands, traveled in Europe and Africa, read voraciously ("With me, reading is a disease," he once confessed), and wrote an astonishing thirty-five books,

on everything from military history to foreign policy (Brands, 1997, 49). There was a lot to admire in TR.

He also had a lot of faults. He could be unforgiving and even nasty toward his detractors, he had a tendency toward self-absorption, and he had a temper that sometimes clouded his judgment. Roosevelt also sometimes substituted bullying for leadership, particularly in foreign policy, where he used some very heavy-handed tactics to get what he wanted. Nor was he overly tolerant toward people whose skin was not as white as his own. He consented to a dinner with African American leader Booker T. Washington—the first time a black man was a guest for dinner at the White House—but he held racial views that were not on the enlightened side. "Negroes are a perfectly stupid race," he once said (Pringle, 1995, 110). A champion of conservation, he did far more to protect the moose and bears at Yellowstone National Park than he did to protect African Americans from waves of racist lynchings and violence.

That said, Teddy Roosevelt breathed fresh life into the presidency. Under his direction, the office took large strides toward recovering from the damage Andrew Johnson had wrought. "I did and caused to be done many things not previously done by the President," he claimed, "I did greatly broaden the use of executive power" (www.nvr.org/pres/doc/pres_essay1.pdf). Teddy was bragging, but he was also right.

This was especially true where presidential communication was concerned. Roosevelt is famous for having said that, in the realm of foreign policy, America should "speak softly, but carry a big stick." In reality, Roosevelt was hardly a soft speaker. He relished use of what he termed the "bully pulpit" of the presidency; that is, the president's power to shape public opinion with well-targeted speeches. And Roosevelt gave a lot of speeches. In addition to being a very effective stump speaker on

the campaign trail, he composed long and exuberant State of the Union Addresses, filled with exhortations to Congress and the nation to improve employer-employee relationships, encourage immigration ("We can not have too much immigration of the right kind, and we should have none of the wrong kind"), conserve natural resources, curb excessive labor unrest, and strengthen child labor and minimum wage laws—laundry lists of Roosevelt's projects, dreams, and priorities. His first address was 20,000 words long. "Never have I seen an annual Message followed with so much interest and attention," wrote a senator (Brands, 1997, 425).

But TR used more than just words; he wielded a big stick of presidential authority in areas where no previous president had tread. When the nation was nearly paralyzed by a crippling coal workers' strike in 1902, he took the unprecedented step of intervening directly in the dispute. "It was essential that organized capital and organized labor should thoroughly understand that the third party, the great public, had vital interests and overshadowing rights in such a crisis," he declared, and he understood the presidency as the "great public's" primary spokesman in such matters (Brands, 1997, 462). Where business and corporations were concerned, TR not only pressed Congress for various workplace reforms; he also picked up long dormant federal regulatory weapons to strike at corporations he deemed to have grown too large for the public good. The president used the Sherman Antitrust

Act to bring lawsuits against the American steel, oil, tobacco, and railroad industries in an attempt to break up their monopolies on key sectors of the American economy.

For the first time a president became consistently and actively involved in pressing for initiatives in Congress. Roosevelt had a long history as a reformer, dating back to his days as New York's police commissioner, and unlike his predecessors, he was quite willing to bring this perspective to the White House. He corresponded frequently with congressional allies, followed closely the track of favored bills, and made known his wishes in a direct, forthright way that would have stunned hands-off predecessors like George Washington. When Congress dragged its feet, sometimes Roosevelt simply went ahead without it, consequences be damned. Contemplating a landing of U.S. troops in Cuba to deal with that country's internal problems in 1903, he observed, "if it becomes necessary to intervene I intend to establish a precedent for good by refusing to wait for a long wrangle with Congress" (Brands, 1997, 573).

This was not your great-great-grandfather's chief executive; Washington would have been shocked, and probably dismayed, by Roosevelt's frank, high-spirited flexing of presidential muscle. He was the most active president Americans had ever seen, and the office would never quite be the same. Some of his immediate successors, including Woodrow Wilson, directly followed in his activist path, while others explicitly rejected the TR model. These included Calvin Coolidge, whose reticence and laid-back ways became the stuff of presidential legend. But whether they loved or hated, emulated or rejected TR, future presidents could not ignore him.

FRANKLIN ROOSEVELT AND THE MEDIA PRESIDENCY

Modern Americans are accustomed to the idea of a president as a constant factor in their lives. Not even movie stars have quite the media presence of a sitting president. There are daily press examination and commentary upon nearly his every word and deed (and often those of his family members, as well), along with extensive coverage on television, radio, and the Internet. Everyone knows what America's president looks like and how he talks, moves, gesticulates, smiles, or scowls. If he cracks a joke, lapses into profanity, or trips down the stairs, the whole world will soon know about it.

But until the antebellum era, presidents existed only in Americans' everyday lives via the written words in newspapers and perhaps an occasional lithographic print or painting. Few Americans could travel to the nation's capital to see the chief executive in person, and fewer still were privy to a president's personal whims, jokes, or idiosyncrasies. During a campaign, a presidential candidate might engage in a bit of what we would call media marketing—Martin Van Buren had his likeness placed on snuffboxes, for example, during the 1836 election. But once in office, presidents devoted very little time to shaping their media image. There was no image to shape.

Things began to change slowly during the mid- and late nineteenth century. In 1841 William Henry Harrison became the first American president to have his image recorded by the new technology of photography. Fifty years later, Benjamin Harrison had his voice preserved on a wax cylinder, probably the first such recording. (Though rumor has it that someone once recorded Abraham Lincoln's voice, no such recording has ever been found.) At about the same time, Grover Cleveland became the first American president to be filmed.

The American presidency made its way into the media age in fits and starts as the development of technology progressed. Photographs, an occasional voice recording, some scratchy films of a president on the campaign trail or boarding a train, mention of a president during a news broadcast on a new invention called radio—the pieces were all there by 1930 for a president to construct a truly comprehensive media presence. What was now required was a president with the intelligence to grasp the opportunities presented by these new technologies, and a time period, a context, in which media marketing of the presidency would assume major importance.

Franklin Delano Roosevelt possessed intelligence in abundance. Scion of a wealthy New York family (he was Teddy's fifth cousin), Roosevelt was a graduate of Harvard University and Columbia Law School. As a New York State senator and later assistant secretary of

the navy under Woodrow Wilson, he acquired a reputation for energy, intelligence, and an amazing grasp of detail. While serving as assistant secretary of the navy, wrote a captain, Roosevelt would "come aboard a new ship and say to me, 'See that electric clock there? That takes exactly so much money and so much feet of wire and so many man hours to build and install.'" He was also known as a man with unusual political gifts. "He was in a high-level political sense a planner, always looking forward, always calculating the future," noted one observer, and "it was this quality that enabled him to encourage different men along somewhat different or competitive lines. . . . He was a pluralistic leader of a pluralistic people" (Morgan, 1985, 182, 530).

Roosevelt was astute enough to understand the possibilities offered by film, radio, and the modern media. He also functioned within the right contexts. One was personal: Roosevelt needed to control carefully his image, because unbeknownst to most people, he had polio. Stricken with the disease while on vacation in July 1921, he could not walk unassisted, requiring either heavy metal leg braces (they weighed seven pounds each) and a helping hand, or alternatively, a wheelchair. In early-twentieth-century America, such a disability would have quickly ended his career. People who needed braces and wheelchairs should not, it was thought, assume leadership positions. So he carefully hid his condition, wearing the braces under his suit and seeing to it that no one ever witnessed him being assisted while he either walked or rode in his wheelchair. It was not easy. "When he had to stand up, his jaws went absolutely rigid," remembered a journalist, "the effort of getting what was left of his body up was so great his face changed dramatically. It was as if he braced his body for a bullet" (Goodwin, 1994, 17).

The other context was national. When FDR entered office in 1932, the United States was in the third year of the Great Depression, the most disastrous economic crisis in its history. For a variety of reasons, ranging from reckless stock market speculation to drought conditions in the West, 13 million Americans were unemployed, and billions of dollars in savings and assets were wiped out. Farm incomes were cut in half; the New York Stock Exchange was worth only one-fifth of what it had once been.

Roosevelt's predecessor, Herbert Hoover, was not a bad man or a bad president. He simply did not grasp the magnitude of the nation's economic disaster or the need for a creative response from the White House. He did not understand that the eyes of the nation were on him, and that by 1929 there were several different kinds of "eyes": newspapers, photographers, filmmakers, and radio broadcasters, the caretakers of the new media age. Hoover managed to trip constantly over his own feet, making one embarrassing gaffe after another. "Prosperity is just around the corner," he jubilantly asserted. The phrase grated on the ears of the 12 million Americans on the unemployment lines; they thought the president was utterly out of touch with reality. On the other hand, his belief that the

only real solution lay in appealing to private businessmen and organizations, rather than creating new government agencies, had the contradictory effect of putting the worst aspects of the Depression constantly before the public eye. "Hoover's repeated appeals to the nation's charitable instincts kept the consciousness of privation always to the fore," observed one historian (Lyons, 1964, 290). Even when Hoover did take positive steps to address the crisis, appealing for stricter regulations on the stock market or stiffer trade laws to bolster American manufacturing, he seemed to have no idea how to market those initiatives in such a way that people would give him the credit.

FDR knew better. He intuitively understood that the American people needed not only greater government intervention to stem the crisis; they also needed the appearance of energy, the lifting of a foreboding sense of gloom that hovered over the heads of destitute families and displaced workers. They needed hope for a better future and someone in the White House who could articulate that hope. "The leader in a democracy has to keep the people entertained," observed Roosevelt's chief of staff, George Marshall. "That may sound like the wrong word but it conveys the thought" (Goodwin, 1994, 349).

Roosevelt knew how to do presidential "entertainment." He had a gift for catchphrases. When campaigning for the presidency he dubbed Republican opponents as being afflicted by the "Four Horsemen": "Destruction, Delay, Deceit, and Despair." As president he declared that "we have nothing to fear but fear itself," and "this generation of Americans has a rendezvous with destiny." He described his foreign policy as a "good neighbor" approach and his peacetime buildup of the armed forces the "arsenal of democracy." In 1941 he spelled out the "Four Freedoms" that would guide his approach to diplomacy. He pitched the whirlwind legislative blitz with which he began his presidency as the "First One Hundred Days" initiative, a concept that has remained lodged in Americans' minds ever since. Using the term *New Deal* was an effective way to easily summarize his ongoing blizzard of reform programs in an easily remembered, easily repeated phrase. Critics sneered that the New Deal did little more than put a few people to work raking leaves and digging ditches, but Roosevelt knew that the press would take pictures of all those ditchdiggers and leaf rakers, projecting an aura of boundless energy for his administration and perhaps turning the camera lenses away from the breadlines (Morgan, 1985, 363).

Hoover had seemed constantly caught off guard by the Depression, but for Roosevelt there were no unguarded moments. He worried constantly about the image his presidency evoked in the minds of the press and the American people. When someone sent him a newspaper clipping about a WPA worker who had broken his wrist while resting on his shovel, FDR half-jokingly called for introducing a "nonskid shovel handle" (Morgan, 1985, 417). He carefully screened every photograph made of him,

weeding out any that might reveal his polio condition or project an image other than the forthright optimism and boyish enthusiasm he wished to convey. Approved images of FDR had him constantly smiling, an ever-present cigarette holder angled jauntily from his lips and an air of serene confidence that everything would be all right.

Roosevelt was one of the first presidents to cultivate a positive relationship with the Washington press corps. While Hoover created the office of White House press secretary in 1929, it was Roosevelt who three years later greatly expanded the role of a permanent liaison between the administration and the media. His press secretary held press conferences with unprecedented frequency: twice a week for seven years and only a bit less frequently thereafter. He talked with, cajoled, and schmoozed reporters, got to know them personally, and extended various little acts of kindness that helped cement a generally positive relationship between them and his office. One journalist called him "the best newspaperman who has ever been president of the United States" (Goodwin, 1994, 26).

FDR's most innovative public relations measure came in the new arena of radio broadcasts. Beginning in 1933, the president initiated a series of radio addresses, which his press secretary said was intended to convey an image of his audience being "a few people around his fireside" (Goodwin, 1995, 57). The press latched onto this characterization, and FDR's "fireside chats" became a regular feature of his administration. It was a

Treasury secretary Henry Morgenthau Jr. (left) with President Franklin D. Roosevelt during a visit to Warm Springs, Georgia, on November 25, 1933. (Library of Congress)

simple yet extraordinary tool: by using pithy phrases, straightforward logic, and a conversational tone, Roosevelt could project the image of an everyday man, sympathetic with Americans' everyday problems, in a way for which no previous president could have hoped.

When Roosevelt suddenly became a war president in December 1941, his communication skills stood him in good stead. Circumstances forced him to limit his press conferences, and the number of fireside chats dropped off sharply as FDR was forced to turn his attention to the mammoth job of directing the war effort. But he never quite forgot the importance of media manipulation. His administration oversaw the creation of a government propaganda and censorship machine the likes of which Americans had never seen. Roosevelt himself personally saw to it, for example, that stories of the devastating U-boat attacks on American shipping in 1942 never made it into the newspapers. And he never forgot the importance of maintaining a positive public image of his presidency as a way to sustain wartime morale. Though it was a strain on his increasingly frail health, he undertook highly publicized tours of war factories and military bases, always trying to project the same jaunty optimism that helped see the United States through the Depression. "With the help of God we are going to see this thing through together!" he exclaimed to a crowd of workers at the Kaiser shipyard in Portland, Oregon (Goodwin, 1994, 361).

FDR revolutionized the office of the presidency in a variety of ways. He built the chief executive's office into a modern, multifaceted dynamo. Gone were the days when presidents saw their jobs as merely enforcing the laws and passing down an occasional veto. Now every president would be judged by what he did during his first hundred days, and every president would be expected to provide detailed and ambitious legislative programs to Congress. Every president would have to appear cognizant of major foreign and domestic issues and well-versed in the policy debates of his day. Presidents were now "the central focus of political emotion," according to historian Arthur Schlesinger Jr. (1973, 4).

This was so not just because of the enormous political, economic, and military power modern presidents wielded. It was also due to FDR's insistence that a president must be media savvy. No pres-

ident after Roosevelt could afford to let down his guard for very long. Some did, and the results were usually disastrous. Roosevelt's successor, Harry S. Truman, had a habit of speaking first and thinking later, and it got him into trouble. In one of his more famous public gaffes, Truman wrote a public letter to a *New York Times* music critic who had disparaged the singing abilities of Truman's daughter. "I've never met you, but if I do you'll need a new nose and a supporter below," the president stormed, thus scandalizing the nation and damaging his prestige (McCullough, 349). FDR would have winced mightily; not perhaps from Truman's sentiments, but from his carelessness in voicing them so publicly.

Other presidents had a better grasp of what Roosevelt had wrought. John F. Kennedy was a brilliant manipulator of his media image (perhaps in part because, like Roosevelt, JFK had extensive health problems he wished to conceal), projecting a vigorous, youthful image of his administration and what was dubbed a Camelot atmosphere of high society and intellectual sophistication in his White House. Ronald Reagan—for whom, as an actor, media exposure was second nature—possessed a Roosevelt-style aptitude for catchphrases, with his "Morning in America" sloganeering and his ready wit.

For better or worse, Roosevelt put the presidency squarely in the middle of America's modern media revolution. Presidents would now be required to administer more than just the laws. They would be required to administer their public personas, as well.

RICHARD NIXON AND THE SCARRED PRESIDENCY

Americans have always believed they were good at two things: war and politics. Until 1975, the nation had never lost a war, had triumphed in fact during the great cataclysm of the twentieth century, World War II. Battlefield heroes were household names, adorned with the sort of nicknames a proud nation could bestow: "Stonewall" Jackson, "Unconditional Surrender" Grant, and George "Blood and Guts" Patton, for example. War movies inaugurated Hollywood's ascendancy during the 1920s and 1930s, military books were routinely best sellers. General Douglas MacArthur's pipe was the stuff of American legend.

Where politics was concerned, as the nation approached the end of its second century of existence, it could point to its Constitution as a jewel of national civic pride. It had proven to be a remarkably durable document, equally amenable to both stability and change. The basic structure remained intact from 1787, but it had also undergone important amendments that reflected the changing needs of a growing nation. "We must never forget, that it is a constitution we are expounding," wrote Supreme Court chief justice John Marshall in *McCulloch v. Maryland* (1819), and it is "a constitution intended to endure for ages to come, and, consequently, to be adopted to the various crises of human affairs" (*McCulloch v. Maryland*, 17 U.S. 316). Twentieth-century Americans could justifiably claim to have fulfilled Marshall's vision.

In America's pride over its record of success in war and politics, the presidency loomed large. Presidents are, after all, commanders in chief. For several presidents—Washington, Grant, Eisenhower—success on the battlefield led directly to the White House. Others—Lincoln, Roosevelt—made their way into the nation's highest circles of hero worship based largely upon how they had conducted themselves as wartime leaders. And it did not hurt for still other presidents to put some act of battlefield heroism on their résumé from their younger days; John F. Kennedy, for example, whose exploits as commander of a patrol boat in the Pacific during World War II added a dash of adventure to his public image.

If presidents were symbols of America's successful war making, they were also symbols of the nation's political sagacity. By the 1970s the presidency was one of the oldest political offices in the world. It was now hard to remember the time when many people believed it to be a newfangled and even silly office. In Washington's day, kings laughingly predicted that no executive could function under the restraints and contradictions imposed upon it by the U.S. Constitution. The kings were now dust, gone or reduced to figureheads in countries that often looked to the presidency as a model for their replacement. Washington and his successors had the last laugh, after all.

Perhaps most importantly, presidents symbolized America's collective self-restraint, its ability to create a powerful position of power without simultaneously sowing the seeds of authoritarianism. In the twentieth century this was especially remarkable, for that century was in many ways defined by despots. It witnessed the awful consequences of executive power run utterly amok in the guise of a Hitler or a Stalin, with millions of people paying with their lives. With germ warfare and chemical and nuclear weapons a frightful reality after 1945, people worried what might happen the next time a dictator seized power. The potential damage wrought by a rogue leader with access to modern technology was almost unimaginable.

American presidents in particular had access to destructive power on a global scale. But most people could live with this uncomfortable fact because in an age peppered with leaders who were zealots and megalomaniacs, Americans presidents were models of political decency and restraint. In 200 years no president had ever attempted anything like a coup or a military takeover of government. No president had ever started a major war without some form of approval from Congress, the people's branch of government. Those rare occasions during which a president had exercised extraordinary authority—Lincoln's 1861 declarations of martial law and use of military arrests to quell Confederate sympathizers, for example—had been short-lived and nearly always enjoyed the eventual approval of Congress, the Supreme Court, and the American people.

Presidents made mistakes, of course. They took wrong turns, they sometimes were ham-handed in their use of power, and they occasionally initiated or endorsed bad ideas and policies. But on the whole, Americans looked back on the nearly 200 years of presidential history with a collective shrug of their shoulders at such incidents. They had a quiet, almost serene confidence that, whatever the situation, a given president would surely possess the requisite qualities of character and judgment to avoid making serious errors of judgment of the kind that would lose a war or jeopardize the Constitution. America was still the best when it came to war and politics; we played those games better than anyone else, and the presidency was our nation's quarterback. Or so Americans thought, circa 1970.

In 1976 the nation celebrated its bicentennial with fanfare. There were larger than usual parades, parties, and fireworks shows and a veritable blizzard of red-white-and-blue marketing campaigns incorporating stamps, license plates, toys, and even a special edition bicentennial Cadillac convertible sporting patriotic upholstery. Television networks ran "bicentennial minutes," little infomercials that detailed what had been taking place that day in American history two centuries previously. Celebrities from various walks of American life narrated the series: movie stars, sports heroes, politicians. The honor on July 4 was reserved for President Gerald Ford.

On the surface, all seemed well. But underneath, the nation was experiencing a wrenching crisis of self-confidence about itself, its place in the world, and perhaps most of all, its ability to perform those two tasks, war and politics, which had been America's defining hallmark of excellence for so long. Presidents were at the very center of this crisis. Their character and judgment were called into question as never before, as commanders in chief, as politicians, and as safe guardians of the most powerful political office on earth. Even as Ford pleasantly intoned the stock opening phrase of his bicentennial minute—"two hundred years ago today"—polls showed that many of his listeners were not entirely sure they could trust presidents anymore; or at least, that trust did not come reflexively or without some measure of doubt. Every man who has since served in the White House has been affected, sometimes profoundly so. One could argue that the office has never really recovered.

Americans' sudden self-doubt about their war-making skills, and the efficacy of their presidents as commanders in chief, had its roots in a backwater corner of Southeast Asia. There, in a tiny country called Vietnam, pro-Communist forces in the North stared down pro-democracy forces in the South, with an uneasy, porous border stretched between them across the country's midsection. American policymakers wanted to maintain that border, keeping democratic South Vietnam from "going Communist," which many saw as the first step in the domination of Southeast Asia by Communist China and Russia.

If there was ever a president's war, defined and guided by the focused, at times almost obsessive attention of the presidency, it was Vietnam. Harry Truman and Dwight Eisenhower oversaw the quiet buildup of America's presence in South Vietnam during the 1950s, and in the early 1960s John F. Kennedy greatly expanded the number of American military advisers in the area, laying the foundation for direct military intervention in the future. "Vietnam represents the cornerstone of the Free World in Southeast Asia, the keystone to the arch, the finger in the dike," Kennedy declared; and while historians have ever since debated whether or not Kennedy intended to eventually pull out of Vietnam, the fact remains that, at the time of his assassination in 1963, America was more involved than ever in propping up—with money, soldiers, and political support—South Vietnam's precarious government (Fishel, 1968, 144).

Perhaps most of all, Vietnam was Lyndon Johnson's war. It was not a war he wanted to fight. A hard-fisted, profane, rawboned man who grew up dirt poor in Texas's hill country, LBJ wanted more than anything to be remembered as the president who eradicated poverty once and for all in America. His Great Society program of immense government expenditures to educate, feed, house, and care for Americans in need was even more ambitious than the New Deal. Johnson wanted to focus his considerable energy and negotiating talent (he was one of the most effective members of Congress in American history) on these domestic matters, not Southeast Asia. His political enemies wanted "to use this war as a way of opposing my Great Society legislation," Johnson grumbled; they "don't want to help the poor and the Negroes but they're afraid to be against it at a time like this when there's been all this prosperity. But the war, oh, they'll like the war" (Dallek, 1998, 244).

Johnson did not like the war, but he hated Communism almost as much as he hated poverty. Believing he could not afford to let South Vietnam fall under the pressures brought to bear by North Vietnam's military and guerrilla forces, LBJ began a massive buildup of American military force in Vietnam. By 1968, over half a million American soldiers were serving there. But nothing Johnson tried—more soldiers, more guns, more money—seemed to make much of a difference. Four years after he began America's large-scale commitment to South Vietnam, the government there remained weak, corrupt, and susceptible to guerrilla assaults from the North. Americans were dying daily in the Vietnamese jungles, yet there seemed to be no feasible end in sight. Johnson grew increasingly disillusioned. He told Senate leaders that "he personally wished he had never heard of South Vietnam" (Dallek, 1998, 443).

Vietnam destroyed Johnson, both politically and personally. "He had no stomach for it," his wife Ladybird believed, "it wasn't the war he wanted" (Dallek, 1998, 249). As the morass deepened, LBJ found his frustration mounting, to the point that, in March 1968, he announced he would not seek reelection that fall. Ostensibly, his reason was that he did not want the "presidency to become involved in partisan divisions that are developing in this political year. . . . I do not believe that I should devote an hour or a day of my time to any personal partisan causes or to any duties other

than the awesome duties of this office." In reality, Vietnam colored everything. "I want my hands free to do what is necessary to end this thing," he told advisers (Dallek, 1998, 529).

When Johnson announced his retirement, Richard Nixon, like everyone else, was flabbergasted. Conventional wisdom held that Johnson's reelection in 1968 was, if not inevitable, at least probable. Now, the door was open for Nixon to make the latest in a series of political comebacks, one that this time would finally put him in the White House.

Whatever his faults—and there were many—Richard Nixon was without a doubt the most resilient man ever to serve as president. To hear him tell it, life itself had smacked him around, time and again, only to have him rise above adversity and fight back. He came, he said, from a working-class background of hardscrabble and hard luck. His father was "sort of a little man, common man. . . . He was a streetcar motorman first, and then he was a farmer, and then he had a lemon ranch. It was the poorest lemon ranch in California, I can assure you. He sold it before they found oil on it" (Ambrose, 1991, 441–442). Nixon saw himself as rising from this humble background one difficult step at a time, fighting the condescension of the "Harvard elites," the Eastern intellectuals, and the snobbish media, battling back time and again from their backroom snubs and their blue-blooded disdain to attain political power through his sheer willpower and drive. It was his mantra, this story, repeated tirelessly to anyone who would listen. It was his greatest personal

Secretary of State Dean Rusk (left), President Lyndon B. Johnson (center), and Secretary of Defense Robert McNamara (right) meet on February 9, 1968, at the height of the Vietnam War. (National Archives)

strength, and at the same time his most glaring and personal weakness, for if it made him tough and resourceful, the story also made him a twitchy bundle of unforgiving resentments and insecurities. "In politics the normal reactions are to have strong hatreds," he claimed (Reeves, 2001, 64). No one hated better than Richard Nixon.

After losing to John F. Kennedy by a razor-thin margin in the presidential election of 1960, political experts everywhere declared that Nixon was finished as a politician of national stature. His loss to Edmund G. Brown in the race for California's governor two years later put an exclamation point on the matter. If the man could not be governor of a state, how could he be taken seriously as a presidential aspirant? Even Nixon seemed to think so, holding a memorable press conference in the wake of his defeat in which he announced his retirement from public life and growled to the reporters present, "As I leave you I want you to know—just think how much you're going to be missing. You won't have Nixon to kick around anymore."

An ABC television broadcast that aired a week later spoke for most observers when it termed this "the political obituary of Richard Nixon" (Ambrose, 1987, 671, 673).

But the resiliency story kicked in again when Johnson retired. Nixon seized the nomination of the Republican Party, exploited the divisions between the antiwar extremists and moderates in the Democratic Party, and beat Hubert Humphrey to win the presidency in 1968. In his Inaugural Address, Nixon appealed to America's need for a happy ending in Vietnam and for peace in general. "Where peace is unknown, make it welcome," he declared, "where peace is fragile, make it strong; where peace is temporary, make it permanent. After a period of confrontation, we are entering an era of negotiation" (www.yale.edu/lawweb/avalon/presiden/inaug/nixon1.htm).

Part of Nixon's appeal to the American electorate was his campaign declaration that he could find a way to win such a peace in Vietnam. Once in office, his plan turned out to be a tremendous escalation in bombing attacks on the North Vietnamese. This, coupled with a rapprochement with Vietnam's Communist ally, China, and a slow takeover of the war effort by South Vietnamese forces (called Vietnamization by Nixon), would bring the North Vietnamese to the negotiating table; or so Nixon hoped.

The plan had the desired effect, in the sense that serious negotiations were underway with the North Vietnamese by 1970. American troop levels also began to slowly decline. By 1971 there were less than 160,000 U.S. soldiers still "in country." But the costs of Nixon's plan were tremendous. American bombs rained down indiscriminately on North Vietnamese men, women, and children, causing horrendous casualties. Many foreign observers were appalled, and the antiwar movement at home was galvanized into action, holding rallies and protests across the nation. And there were still darker repercussions. The Nixon Administration saw fit to secretly authorize an American invasion of Cambodia, Vietnam's neighbor to the west, as a way of neutralizing North Vietnamese supply routes and base camps in the area. Some in the administration even spoke quietly of using nuclear weapons, should all else fail.

The Cambodia affair illustrated a disturbing tendency in the Nixon Administration—its obsessive quest for secrecy, and in particular Richard Nixon's paranoia about his enemies, real and imagined. Even after winning a landslide reelection in 1972, Nixon could not relax. Indeed, his victory—the very pinnacle of political achievement, the ultimate comeback for the grocer's son—only seemed to exacerbate these tendencies. He and his staff prepared "enemies lists" of politicians, journalists, activists, writers, and actors who had in some manner, however small, expressed criticism of Nixon or his policies. After his reelection, he wanted ruthlessly to weed out of the executive department anyone who did not profess absolute allegiance to him. This included his Cabinet, from whom he solicited resignations—all of them, after which he would invite back whomever he thought met his standards of loyalty. "You've got one week," he told his advisers, "and that's the time to get all those resignations in and say 'Look you're out, you're out, you're finished, you're done, done, finished.' Knock them the hell out of there" (Reeves, 2001, 544).

Nixon's hatreds, paranoia, and resentment permeated his entire administration, as did his relentless quest for secrecy. He and his advisers created a shadow organization of security and intelligence operatives whose job was to plug security leaks—hence their name, the Plumbers—and create mayhem among Nixon's political opponents. They tapped telephone lines, concocted phony documents to implicate South Vietnamese president Diem in the assassination of John F. Kennedy, and spread nasty rumors about Democratic politicians. In 1971 they broke into the offices of a psychiatrist, seeking damaging information on a man named Daniel Ellsberg, who had leaked top-secret documents about the Vietnam War to the press.

Ellsberg's Pentagon Papers did not even concern Nixon. They were an exposé of the various lies and misinformation on the war given by previous administrations. Nevertheless, Nixon was apoplectic at the security breach, and he wanted whatever dirt he could get on Ellsberg. "Just get everything out," he fumed to his advisers, "Try him in the press . . . leak it out. We want to destroy him in the press." For Nixon, it was all one large conspiracy: Ellsberg, Democrats, liberals, the antiwar movement, the press, everybody. "Those sons of bitches are killing me. . . . We're up against an enemy, a conspiracy. They're using any means. We are going to use any means" (Reeves, 2001, 337–338). In such a superheated atmosphere, the Plumbers seemed like a very handy tool.

On the evening of June 17, 1972, five Plumbers broke into the headquarters of the Democratic National Committee, located in the Watergate complex in Washington, D.C. This time, however, they were caught and jailed. At first the scandal seemed minor; Nixon was reelected five months after the break-in by one of the largest popular majorities in American history. But soon after, driblets of incriminating information began to leak out, helped along by the investigation of two *Washington Post* reporters, Bob Woodward and Carl Bernstein. They discovered ties between the Watergate burglars and the White House and evidence of a conspiracy to silence the Watergate burglars using bribery and intimidation. In May 1973 Congress began conducting hearings into the matter and eventually discovered an angry beehive of illegal and quasi-legal White House activities: the Plumbers and all their works, along with allegations of corruption and wrongdoing that reached right to the door of the Oval Office itself.

To the door, but not quite inside—until Congress stumbled upon the fact that the Nixon Administration routinely taped conversations between the president and his advisers. (Lyndon Johnson had begun the general practice of taping presidential conversations as a way of recording what he said for posterity's

Richard Nixon delivers a farewell speech to his White House staff on August 9, 1974. Nixon is the only president to have resigned from office. (National Archives)

sake and perhaps for future use in writing presidential memoirs.) Now the tapes became something far less benign; they were a noose fastened around Richard Nixon's neck. Congress demanded that the president turn over the tapes. He refused, citing executive privilege. Eventually, under enormous pressure from the public and politicians alike—including some members of his own party—Nixon turned over heavily edited transcripts, and eventually some of the tapes themselves, albeit with gaps in key areas (the administration claimed they were created by accidental erasures). Eventually,

the Supreme Court itself ruled that Nixon must hand over all of the tapes. Congress began drawing up articles of impeachment, with bipartisan support.

Cornered, Nixon had few options. He could endure impeachment and almost certain conviction, thus going down in history as the first president to be forcibly removed from office. Or he could resign, save something of his dignity, and fight the battle of the tapes in court (where he could argue that, as a private citizen, they were his personal property). He resigned on August 8, 1974. Even to the very end, Nixon was unapologetic. "Whatever mistakes I made in the handling of Watergate, the basic truth remains that when all the facts were brought to my attention I insisted on a full investigation and prosecution of those guilty," he claimed. "I am firmly convinced that the record, in its entirety, does not justify the extreme step of impeachment and removal of a president" (Reeves, 2001, 609).

The Watergate scandal did nearly incalculable damage to America's perception of itself and the presidency. In 1966, 65 percent of Americans in one poll said they could trust their government. By 1974, that number had plummeted to 36 percent, where it has more or less remained ever since. "Americans saw a presidency disintegrate before their very eyes," wrote CNN commentator William Schneider. "The effect on public trust was immediate and dramatic. Watergate crushed the public's faith in government" (cnn.com/ALLPOLITICS/1997/gen/resources/watergate/trust.schneider/).

Optimists might argue that the system worked: a free press caught the president, despite his best efforts at secrecy, and the indignation of the people's representatives—the people themselves, in fact—brought him down. But it had been a near thing. If the Plumbers had been a bit less incompetent in their activities, and if Richard Nixon had been just a bit more adroit in his orchestration of the cover-up, the whole thing might have gone unnoticed. A sitting president could easily have gotten away with conspiracies, blackmail, bribery, and burglary. Certainly, it was only a "third-rate burglary," as some of the president's men claimed; but what if the same arrogance of power and disregard for the Constitution were someday to be applied by a like-minded president to, say, the conduct of a war, or the rigging of an election? How much damage could a Nixonian president do in the nuclear age and with unprecedented power at his disposal? Suddenly the idea of an American chief executive turning into a dictator did not seem so farfetched. At the very least, future presidents would no longer be given the benefit of the doubt.

Watergate also shook Americans' warmaking ideals to their very core, for the scandal also indirectly scuttled the fragile progress made in Vietnam. By 1973 there were only a few American soldiers remaining there; Nixon had gotten his negotiated peace with North Vietnam. The peace settlement was the classic velvet glove over the mailed fist. There was peace, yes, and Americans were no longer on the front lines. But everyone knew that only the threat of America's return kept the North Vietnamese from overwhelming the much weaker South Vietnamese government. When Watergate consumed Nixon he no longer had the political capital to reignite the war; and the American people were so wearied by the scandals and Nixon's wrongdoing that they had no stomach for renewing the conflict. Thus, in early 1975 North Vietnamese forces rolled through South Vietnam, crushing everything in their path. President Gerald Ford did not dare ask Congress for the money and troops to prop the South up once again and so had to stand by helplessly as

Communist forces prevailed. America had finally lost a war.

Watergate became the template of choice for future descriptions of even minor presidential wrongdoing, and Vietnam became the standard of measurement for future president's war-making initiatives. From 1972 on, any presidential scandal, however minor, had the "-gate" suffix attached to it: "travel-gate," for example, described a small tempest concerning the firing of employees in the White House travel office by Bill Clinton in 1994, and "Monica-gate" stuck to the protracted scandal involving Clinton's liaison with a White House intern named Monica Lewinsky in 1997.

Vietnam likewise became the dismal yardstick by which any American military action was measured. The nation would not attempt another major military operation for fifteen years, until in 1991 President George Bush Sr. sent American troops rolling into Kuwait to liberate that nation after it was invaded by neighboring Iraq and its brutal dictator, Saddam Hussein. When American forces enjoyed a quick and relatively painless victory in the first Gulf War, politicians everywhere proclaimed that the demons of Vietnam had finally been exorcised. An American president could order troops into harm's way again and be confident of victory.

Or could he? Following the September 11 terrorist assault in 2001, George Bush's son sent troops into Afghanistan—and again, the ghosts of Vietnam surfaced, as critics everywhere decried the possibility of another Vietnam-like morass. Vietnam loomed as an even larger presence when President George Bush Jr. chose to wage war against Iraq a second time, this time to depose Saddam Hussein and to bring some measure of democracy to Iraq. The war's inevitable ups and downs provoked comparisons with Vietnam at every turn, and an American president again proved vulnerable to charges that he had recklessly endangered American lives.

In some ways Nixon proved to be more resilient than the presidency. He was gone by the time George Bush Jr. began his war with Iraq. He never knew about the Lewinsky scandal, either, having died of a stroke in the spring of 1994. At the funeral, five presidents—Clinton, Ford, Carter, Reagan, and Bush Sr.—were in attendance, the first time in American history that five living chief executives had ever gathered together in one place at one time. It was entirely appropriate that they did so, for all had in one way or the other served out their terms in Nixon's shadow.

FURTHER READING

Ambrose, Stephen, *Nixon: The Education of a Politician, 1913–1962* (New York: Simon and Schuster, 1987).

Ambrose, Stephen, *Nixon: Ruin and Recovery, 1973–1990* (New York: Simon and Schuster, 1991).

Baker, Jean, *Mary Todd Lincoln: A Biography* (New York: W.W. Norton, 1987).

Basler, Roy P., ed., *The Collected Works of Abraham Lincoln*, 9 vols. (New Brunswick, NJ: Rutgers University Press, 1953–1955).

Bergeron, Paul H., *The Presidency of James K. Polk* (Lawrence: University Press of Kansas, 1987).

Brands, H. W., *TR: The Last Romantic* (New York: HarperCollins, 1997).

Brookhiser, Richard, *Founding Father* (New York: Free Press, 1996).

Cramer, Richard Ben, *What it Takes: The Way to the White House* (New York: Vintage Books, 1993).

Dallek, Robert, *Flawed Giant: Lyndon Johnson, 1960–1973* (New York: Oxford University Press, 1998).

Ellis, Joseph J., *Founding Brothers: The Revolutionary Generation* (New York: Vintage, 2001).

Fishel, Wesley L., ed., *Vietnam: Anatomy of a Conflict* (Itasca: F.E. Peacock, 1968).

Flexner, James, *George Washington* (Boston: Little, Brown, 1965).

Goodwin, Doris Kearns, *No Ordinary Time: Franklin and Eleanor Roosevelt: The Homefront in World War Two* (New York: Simon and Schuster, 1994).

Gould, Lewis L., *The Presidency of William McKinley* (Lawrence: University Press of Kansas, 1980).

Linderman, Gerald F., *The Mirror of War: American Society and the Spanish-American War* (Ann Arbor: University of Michigan Press, 1974).

Lyons, Eugene, *Herbert Hoover: A Biography* (New York: Doubleday, 1964).

Madison, James, *The Constitutional Convention: A Narrative History from the Notes of James Madison* (New York: Modern Library, 2005).

McCullough, David, *Truman* (New York: Simon and Schuster, 1992).

McDonald, Forrest, *The American Presidency: An Intellectual History* (Lawrence: University Press of Kansas, 1994).

McKitrick, Eric L., *Andrew Johnson and Reconstruction* (Chicago: University of Chicago Press, 1960).

McPherson, James M., *Ordeal by Fire: The Civil War and Reconstruction* (New York: Alfred A. Knopf, 1982).

Morgan, Ted, *FDR: A Biography* (New York: Simon and Schuster, 1985).

Oates, Stephen B., *Abraham Lincoln: The Man behind the Myths* (New York: HarperCollins, 1984).

Pringle, Henry F., *Theodore Roosevelt* (New York: Smithmark, 1995).

Reeves, Richard, *Nixon: Alone in the White House* (New York: Simon and Schuster, 2001).

Schlesinger, Arthur, Jr., *The Imperial Presidency* (Boston: Houghton Mifflin, 1973).

3

THE ROLE OF THE PRESIDENCY IN AMERICAN POLITICS

"The world is very different now," John F. Kennedy declared in his 1961 Inaugural Address, "for man holds in his mortal hands the power to abolish all forms of human poverty and all forms of human life." Outlining the various challenges that faced Americans at home and abroad, Kennedy invoked a vivid sense of renewal. "Since this country was founded, each generation of Americans has been summoned to give testimony to its national loyalty. The graves of young Americans who answered the call to service surround the globe." He believed that "excessive partiality for one foreign nation of the world, only a few generations have been granted the role of defending freedom in its hour of maximum danger. I do not shrink from this responsibility—I welcome it. I do not believe that any of us would exchange places with any other people or any other generation. The energy, the faith, the devotion which we bring to this endeavor will light our country and all who serve it—and the glow from that fire can truly light the world" (www .presidency.ucsb.edu/ws/index.php ?pid=8032).

THE POWER OF PRESIDENTIAL GENERATIONS

Few presidents have been elected with as keen a sense as Kennedy that a generational changing of the guard was taking place. During the Great Depression and World War II, Americans had watched Franklin Roosevelt grow old and eventually die during the longest tenure in presidential history. He was succeeded by sixty-year-old Harry Truman, who was in turn replaced by sixty-two-year-old Dwight Eisenhower. Altogether that was a lot of gray hair, a long association of presidents with a patriarchal, grandfatherly presence in Americans' lives.

JFK was a welcome breath of fresh air, ushering in a new decade and new times. Roosevelt and Truman were elder statesmen of World War II; Eisenhower had been the supreme allied commander. Kennedy, on the other hand, had been a twentysomething navy patrol boat captain, the first in a long line of rank-and-file World War II veterans who would serve in the White House (George Bush Sr. would be the last). Young, tan, and

The administration of John F. Kennedy, famous for its youth and style, ushered in a period of hope, vigor, and commitment for the United States that would be cruelly cut short by Kennedy's assassination. (John F. Kennedy Library)

handsome, standing on the cusp of one of the most tumultuous decades in American history, Kennedy seemed to embody a fresh age, with new ideals, problems, dreams, and anxieties. His famous call for citizens to "ask not what your country can do for you—ask what you can do for your country" motivated young postwar Americans to engage pressing issues of civil rights, liberty, poverty, and national security. More so than many other presidents, JFK became the bold new face of his era.

Kennedy is an interesting case study in the unique way the presidency blends abstract ideals like duty, honor, and patriotism with stark, black-and-white legal structures like the provisions for the presidency of Article II of the Constitution and with the various virtues, foibles, and aspirations of the flesh-and-blood human beings who have actually occu-

pied the White House. Ideas, the law, and the men themselves have in more or less co-equal parts combined to both preserve the presidency's fundamental structure, now over two centuries old, and oversee the process of change and evolution that has kept the presidency fresh and relevant to changing times and historical circumstances.

In chapter 1 we looked primarily at the Framers and their understanding of what they were doing when they wrote the Constitution's provisions for a national chief executive. In chapter 2 we were introduced to some of the people who served in that high office. But how have all those factors together interacted down through the years to make the presidency a living, developing entity in American life? How has the presidency's structure grown from the barebones scaffolding erected by the Framers in 1787 to the multifaceted and complex edifice that dominates the modern American landscape?

Perhaps the best way to approach these questions would be to think in terms of generations. Of all the presidents, Kennedy was probably the most conspicuously and self-consciously a spokesman for a generational perspective. (He used the word "generation" four times in his Inaugural Address.) But all presidents, to a greater or lesser degree, both reflect and shape the values of the generation to which they belong. In the process, they change—sometimes in subtle ways—the structure of the office itself.

THE REVOLUTIONARY GENERATION

The idea of a "generation" is rooted in the fact that people who are roughly the same age possess broadly shared experiences. Ask any Americans born after 1985, for example, the following question: what is the one big event in your life for which you remember exactly where you were and what you were doing when it occurred? The answer would nearly always be: the attack on the World Trade Center on September 11, 2001. Pose the same question to their parents, however, and the answer might well be the Kennedy assassination in 1963; to their parents it might be the Japanese assault on Pearl Harbor in 1941.

What might have been the answer offered by a Revolutionary war–era American? That generation had a variety of big events from which to choose: the Boston Massacre; the Tea Party; the Stamp Act riots; or perhaps the arrival of a vessel from England bearing news of Parliament's passage of the Sugar Act or closure of Boston's port. Others might have named battles: Lexington and Concord, Bunker Hill, Saratoga, Monmouth, Cowpens, or any of a number of other battles and skirmishes. Still others would likely recall news of British general Cornwallis's surrender at Yorktown in 1781, signaling the end of the conflict.

Those visceral experiences went hand in hand with politics and ideology. The Revolutionary generation stood on the cusp of the Enlightenment, and its leaders read widely: John Locke, David Hume, and Thomas Hobbes were a few of the more common authors. The Revolution itself produced a cohort of indispensable political and intellectual writers: Thomas Paine; Mercy Otis Warren and her brother James; future presidents Thomas Jefferson and John Adams; and a host of lesser-known pamphleteers, newspaper editors, speechmakers, and sermonizers—what modern Americans would call political pundits.

It was in this atmosphere that Americans gathered to create the office of the presidency. We have seen what the Framers brought to the Philadelphia Convention in 1787: a keen sensitivity to the dangers of excess power in an executive; a desire to maintain law and order via that executive while at the same time respecting the balance of authority between an elected president and the people; and a need both to hold presidents accountable and at the same time give them a degree of independence.

This same generation provided the pool for the nation's first six presidents: George Washington, John Adams, Thomas Jefferson, James Madison, James Monroe, and John Quincy Adams. They were often referred to as the Virginia Dynasty, since all but the Adamses hailed from the Old Dominion. The fact of their Virginia roots can be overstated, however, and misses a more important general point: they all came of age during the time that the Revolution and its concerns were vital and immediate. Washington, Adams, Jefferson, and Madison were of course prime movers and shakers of that era: the Revolutionary army's commander in chief, a prime voice of the Boston patriot movement, the author of the Declaration of Independence, and the father of the Constitution. Monroe's ties to the war were not as strong—he fought in the Continental Army but was just twenty-three years old when Cornwallis surrendered at Yorktown—while John Quincy Adams was only age ten as he watched the Battle of Bunker Hill from a rise near the Adams family home. Monroe and the younger Adams were on the very tail end of the Revolutionary generation. But in spirit and intellect they were a part of that time.

The Revolutionary generation of presidents was handed the Constitution while it still had that new law smell, so to speak. Much of what would eventually constitute the familiar trappings of presidential life did not yet exist, and there were endless questions concerning just how the latent powers of the presidency would play themselves out once the Constitution created a living, breathing government. How, for example, would a president exercise his function as commander in chief of the armed forces? How often should a president use the veto, and for what purposes?

"I should consider myself as entering upon an unexplored field," Washington wrote of the presidency in 1788, "enveloped on every side with clouds and darkness." Early in his presidency he wrote a letter to his vice president, John Adams, listing a series of questions about the new office that tugged at his mind. "Whether, after a little time, one day in every week will not be sufficient for receiving visits of Compliment? . . . Whether it would tend to prompt impertinent applications and involve disagreeable consequences to have it known, that the President will, every Morning at 8 Oclock, be at leisure to give Audiences to persons who may have business with him? . . . Whether it would be satisfactory to the Public for the President to make about four great entertainments a year. . . . Whether there would be any impropriety in the President making informal visits—that is to say, in his calling upon his Acquaintainces or public Characters for the purposes of sociability or civility?" (Rhodehamel, 1997, 700, 737).

There were even blank spots concerning relatively minor questions of presidential protocol. Should the holder of the office be addressed as "His Excellency"? "His Highness"? Or perhaps the president should have a slightly milder version of a kingly title: "His Elective Majesty," perhaps, or as one observer suggested, "His Highness the President of the United States and Protector of the

Rights of the Same." The residue of monarchy was also evident when one person mused, "I think the President a kind of Sacred Person." A South Carolinian thought he should be called "Governor of the united People and States of America." Others thought that just "President" would do nicely, while still others thought a mere reference to a "president" lacked gravimen. There are presidents "of Fire Companies and of a Cricket Club," sneered U.S. senator Oliver Ellsworth. In the end, however, republican simplicity won out over such worries, and the new chief executive became "Mr. President" (McDonald, 1994, 157, 213, 224).

These may seem like trivial concerns today; but Washington and others of his generation understood that, there at the dawn of all that is presidential, nothing was trivial. "Many things which appear of little importance in themselves and at the beginning, may have great and durable consequences from their having been established at the commencement of a new general Government," he pointed out (Rhodehamel, 1997, 738).

Whatever the specific answers to these questions might be, the Revolutionary generation at least knew what sort of demeanor it expected from a chief executive. They had grown up around kings, and while most rejected the monarchical model of executive authority per se, they nevertheless wanted their presidents to maintain a good degree of dignity and distance from the more ordinary masses of people. They saw the presidency as an office to be sought in a dignified, statesmanlike

manner. They communicated this desire in a variety of ways: in their half-spoken expectation that only well-educated men of means would ever occupy the White House; in the relatively staid, restrained inaugural ceremonies characteristic of Revolutionary presidents; and in the widespread expectation that only seasoned public servants should even attempt a run at the presidency. All the little questions about ceremony, visits to friends, and the like highlight this generation's keen concern for presidential decorum. "The President in all matters of business and etiquette, can have no object but to demean [lower] himself in his public character, in such a manner as to maintain the dignity of Office, without subjecting himself to the imputation of superciliousness or unnecessary reserve," Washington believed (Rhodehamel, 1997, 738). Few of his contemporaries would have disagreed.

People of the time held a common assumption that the office of secretary of state, and more generally a career in the foreign service, were the best stepping-stones to the presidency. Washington was never an ambassador, but otherwise the revolutionaries were awash in diplomatic experience. John Adams acted as the nation's representative in France, Holland, and England. Jefferson served as Washington's secretary of state and ambassador to France. Madison was Jefferson's secretary of state. Monroe helped negotiate the Louisiana Purchase from France that was orchestrated by Jefferson and Madison. John Quincy Adams was Monroe's secretary of state; by the time he became president, his résumé included diplomatic contacts with the Netherlands, the Germanic states, Russia, England, and Spain.

This well accorded with the Framers' general perspective that the president's role was primarily that of head national diplomat. Nearly all the Revolutionary presidents' more famous utterances while president focused on foreign affairs. Washington's Farewell Address was remembered best for his admonition that the new nation must avoid being sucked into Europe's increasingly troubled affairs. "Nothing is more essential than that permanent, inveterate antipathies against particular nations, and passionate attachments for others, should be excluded," Washington declared, "the nation which indulges towards another a habitual hatred or a habitual fondness is in some degree a slave. It is a slave to its animosity or to its affection, either of which is sufficient to lead it astray from its duty and its interest." Worried about Americans' tendencies to side with either Britain or France in what was rapidly becoming a European-wide conflagration, Washington argued that "excessive partiality for one foreign nation and excessive dislike of another cause those whom they actuate to see danger only on one side, and serve to veil and even second the arts of influence on the other. Real patriots who may resist the intrigues of the favorite are liable to become suspected and odious, while its tools and dupes usurp the applause and confidence of the people, to surrender their interests. The great rule of conduct for us in regard to foreign nations is in extending our commercial relations, to

have with them as little political connection as possible"(www.yale.edu/lawweb/avalon).

Other Revolutionary presidents likewise emphasized foreign affairs. When they turned to specifics in their inaugural speeches, they usually focused on diplomacy. Adams, for example, supported the "system of neutrality and impartiality among the belligerent powers of Europe which has been adopted by this Government and so solemnly sanctioned by both Houses of Congress and applauded by the legislatures of the States and the public opinion." President Monroe worried about the possibility of war with a European nation. "Our distance from Europe and the just, moderate, and pacific policy of our Government may form some security against these dangers," he averred, "but they ought to be anticipated and guarded against" (www.yale.edu/lawweb/avalon).

Context had a great deal to do with this concern. During the era of the Revolutionary presidents, Europe was continually roiled by the wars and rumors of wars sparked by revolution in France and the subsequent Napoleonic conflicts. America still had close economic, political, and cultural ties to its former enemy, Great Britain; and the new nation also had a deep affinity for its chief European benefactor during the Revolution, France. Small wonder, then, that the presidents of the day so often focused on foreign affairs in their speeches.

Not that they gave all that many speeches. The Revolutionary generation could when it wished indulge in fiery oratory—"give me liberty or give me

President James Monroe (standing) presides over a meeting during the writing of the Monroe Doctrine in 1823. The Monroe Doctrine recognized the independence and sovereignty of the new Latin American countries, including Mexico, that had formerly been under Spanish rule. (Bettmann/Corbis)

death!" and the like. But behavior that was acceptable in a legislator, a town councilman, or the leader of a mob was far less so in a chief executive. Too much power accrued in the presidency, too much influence, and too much potential for mischief. Accordingly, the Revolutionaries placed a high value on presidential reticence. Some of this was a matter of temperament. The Revolutionary presidents were, as a rule, men not much taken with oratory as a hobby or a spectator sport. "I hate speeches, messages, addresses, proclamations and

such affected, constrained things," Adams groused to his wife Abigail (McCullough, 2001, 459). When Washington personally visited the Senate to confer about various treaties—as required by the Constitution—and was handled (in his mind) rather brusquely and then made to sit through several hours of speechmaking and debates, he walked out, muttering that he would "be damned if he ever went there again!" (Flexner, 1965, 217).

The Revolutionary generation had no real concept of what others would later term the presidency's "bully pulpit," its potential for shaping national public opinion. This was partly due to the technology of the times—or lack thereof. Early presidents did not possess ready-made media outlets in an age when even printed newspapers were still relatively rare. But the presidents of the Revolutionary generation hesitated to use even the limited means available to them to make their opinions heard. They rarely gave speeches of any kind, other than their Inaugural Addresses and yearly State of the Union messages to Congress. They were not given to writing "private" letters meant for public consumption— Abraham Lincoln would later use this rhetorical tool to powerful effect—and they did not attach to their rare use of the veto power long messages expressing their policymaking opinions—Andrew Jackson would later make effective use of this tool, as well.

In their hearts, the members of the Revolutionary generation hoped that the presidency would be a dignified, elevated, and limited office. Some of the Revolutionaries may well have indulged a private hankering for the good old days of monarchy, but they were also keenly sensitive to the prospect of presidents presuming themselves to be royalty. In an era when clothes and personal appearance were as much a political as a fashion statement, the Revolutionary presidents went out of their way to assume an air of "republican simplicity." Washington carefully chose a suit of simple brown broadcloth for his first inauguration, and right before his inauguration in 1796, John Adams told Abigail to remove

a family coat of arms she had placed on their carriage; it struck the president-elect as pretentious. Americans "shall have a republican President in earnest," he declared (McCullough, 2001, 468).

The Revolutionaries wanted a balance between dignity and democracy, between distance and familiarity, and between intellectual sophistication and what they would have called "republican" simplicity. As representatives of that generation, the first six presidents mirrored the complex concerns of an age that was at once intoxicated with the heady new feeling of creating a New World–style, functioning democracy and at the same time vitally worried about losing the best of the old aristocratic traditions of monarchy and regal splendor with which they had grown to adulthood.

Serving most immediately in the shadow of the Philadelphia Convention, the Revolutionary generation of presidents could be seen as the closest in time and temperament to the Founding Fathers' original vision of what the nation's chief executive was supposed to be and how he was supposed to behave. Those who (quite rightly) venerate the Framers are often tempted to afford equal veneration to the Revolutionary-era presidents, in the process suggesting that the Revolutionaries' vision of the presidency—stately, elevated, and by modern standards severely limited in power and scope—should be seen as the gold standard for all subsequent visions of the office.

But this is a shortsighted and ultimately futile perspective. The presidency of George Washington was not precisely the presidency envisioned by the Framers as they drew up their Constitution only a year and a half before Washington took office. Washington was forced by circumstances, and by the elegant but sometimes excessively circumscribed limitations imposed by the Constitution's simplicity, to adapt, to think anew, and in some cases create new presidential traditions and protocols from scratch. Likewise, the presidencies of Adams, Jefferson, Madison, Monroe, and John Quincy Adams were not quite what the Framers had envisioned. They were, taken as a whole, not presidencies of a particular moment of genius in American history, but rather presidencies that were the product of a generational paradigm and the circumstances of an interesting time in American history, when everything about the United States was new.

THE JACKSONIAN GENERATION

When the Revolution began, Andrew Jackson was only nine years old. He did see some action during the war as a teenage member of a backwoods cavalry unit in the Carolina backcountry. His was not the war of statehouses, political declarations, or heroic nighttime river crossings. Instead, he took a front-row seat to the horrors of the Revolution's guerrilla wars, receiving himself some serious gashes on the head and fingers from a British officer while a prisoner of war, as well as a severe bout with smallpox, contracted in prison, that killed his brother and very nearly killed him as

well. Jackson did everything to extremes. He did not simply like his friends; he was devoted to them, sometimes at considerable personal cost. When his Cabinet was rocked by a scandal involving Margaret Eaton, wife of Jackson's close comrade and the secretary of war, John Henry Eaton, Jackson stood by both Eatons, even when some suggested it might be politically wise to cut them loose. Jackson would have none of it. John Eaton "is more like a son to me than anything else," Jackson exclaimed. "I shall as long as I live estimate his worth and friendship with a grateful heart" (Remini, 1984, 161). He fired the rest of his Cabinet, instead.

On the other hand, he did not merely detest his opponents: he hated them, with a ferocity that bordered on excess. He fought several duels over matters of personal honor, some of which struck observers as "juvenile indiscretions" (Remini, 1977, 123). He railed and stormed against political enemies, real and perceived. Henry Clay was a "designing politician" and a "demagogue"; John C. Calhoun a traitor, "wicked and despicable"; and former president James Monroe "a base infamous hypocrite" (Remini, 1984, 3, 14). He did not just defeat the British at the Battle of New Orleans and the Seminoles in the Florida Everglades; he slaughtered them, with an apparent relish that alarmed some who thought he had willfully presided over the murder of Indian women and children as well as warriors.

This was not the sort of man the Founding Fathers envisioned filling the chair of George Washington. They valued calm and dignity, and while Jackson could actually be quite charming and suave when the situation required— "when it becomes necessary to philosophise and be meek, no man can command his temper better than I," he claimed—Jackson was also capable of ferocious anger, and he carried with him into public life a reputation that he lacked self-control (Remini, 1984, 4). The Founders wanted men whose ambitions were temperate and muted; Jackson's desire for national acclaim and political power ran high and was easily discernable. The Framers founded the presidency's Virginia Dynasty; Jackson was not even sure if he had been born in North or South Carolina.

Some might well have felt that Andrew Jackson in the White House was the Framers' worst nightmare. Or perhaps it would be more fair to say that Jackson, along with other Americans of his age, simply possessed a different set of referent points than his Revolutionary forebears. Memories were growing dim, after all, and what was important to the Framers' generation, what was assumed to be true and what were the governing principles of important political offices like the presidency, might or might not hold sway over subsequent generations. "I do not mean to say, that the scenes of the revolution *are now* or *ever will be* entirely forgotten," a young Abraham Lincoln declared in 1838, "but that like every thing else, they must fade upon the memory of the world, and grow more and more dim by the lapse of time. In history, we hope, they will be read of, and recounted, so long as the bible shall be

Andrew Jackson served two terms as president of the United States, founding a new Democratic Party in the process. He was a strong president who argued with Congress, used the presidential veto power, and left a political legacy known as Jacksonian democracy. (Library of Congress)

read;—but even granting that they will, their influence *cannot be* what it heretofore has been. Even then, they *cannot be* so universally known, nor so vividly felt, as they were by the generation just gone to rest" (Basler, 1953–1955, 1: 115).

The essential constitutional framework put in place by the spirit of 1787 would remain, but all bets were off concerning just how the likes of an Andrew Jackson (or, for that matter, an Abraham Lincoln) would interpret that framework and its applicability to the concerns of the early nineteenth century. Those concerns were legion, for the Jacksonian era was a time of tremendous national growth and change.

Where the presidency was concerned, the most relevant new national trend was a broad increase in voter suffrage. The war had provided most of the key formative experiences for the Revolutionaries; the formative experiences of the Jacksonians were related to market expansion, a tremendous increase in immigration, the growth of cities, and other trends that, taken together, placed greater social, economic, and political power in the hands of more ordinary, middling and working-class white Americans.

The result was a rollicking Jacksonian political culture, its foundation an ever-increasing voter base. The roots of this trend actually extended back into the Revolutionary era, as ordinary Americans demanded (and got) changes in the various state constitutions that lowered voter property requirements and other restrictions, effectively giving them a greater voice in state and local government. Various demographic, social, and political developments during the early decades of the nineteenth century only accelerated the democratization process so that, by the time Jackson entered the White House, virtually any adult white male in America could cast a vote.

Those voters organized with enthusiasm into political parties. Jackson continued the Revolutionary generation's tradition of sounding calls for national unity and governance that rose above party. "It will be my desire so to dis-charge my duties as to foster with our brethren in all parts of the country a spirit of liberal concession and compromise," he declared, "and, by reconciling our fellow-citizens to those partial sacrifices which they must unavoidably make for the preservation of a greater good, to recommend our invaluable Government and Union to the confidence and affections of the American people" (www.yale.edu/lawweb/avalon). To the public, he invariably presented himself as a man for all the people, in all sections and parties. But behind the scenes he was also an adroit and active partisan. He helped direct the actions of Democratic Party planning organizations like the Nashville Central Committee, to which he dispensed advice and information as it coordinated election stratagems. He also cultivated personal relationships with politically prominent newspapermen like Washington, D.C.,'s Duff Green, editor of the influential *United States Telegraph*.

Jackson's successor, Martin Van Buren, was an even more avid manipulator of party machinery. A shrewd, politically savvy New Yorker, Van Buren was nicknamed the Little Magician for his matchless skill at organizing political supporters in ways that would cement their loyalty to him and the new Democratic Party. He knew which government jobs should be awarded to which party allies and when, and he knew when and how to ask for return favors. A master of the backroom deal and the negotiated settlement, the Little Magician had a reputation for seeing all sides of an issue and then making up his mind only when he

As President Andrew Jackson's campaign manager, political confidant, secretary of state, vice president, and finally, handpicked successor, Martin Van Buren played a major role in national politics and the establishment of Jacksonian democracy as a significant political force. (Library of Congress)

was confident that he stood on the winning side. Later generations of Americans might have uncharitably called Van Buren a party hack, and there were people in his time who still clung to the old Revolutionary-era suspicion of parties as unprincipled factions and bemoaned the idea of a man like Martin Van Buren rising first to the level of vice president, and to then the White House itself.

Jackson and Van Buren were also master practitioners of the spoils system, the nineteenth-century nickname for the

practice of awarding plumb government jobs to political allies. ("To the victors belong the spoils," as the saying went.) For a dedicated party man like Van Buren, the spoils system was indispensable. "If you wish to keep up the party," he was told by an ally, "you must induce them to believe that it is in their interest—Some few may adhere to the party from mere conscientious conviction of doing right but interest is a powerful stimulus to make them act energetically and efficiently"—"interest" being a government paycheck (Schlesinger, 1945, 46).

The Framers were no more enamored of a patronage system than they were of parties. The original Constitution made no attempt to address the issue at all, probably because the Framers' generation believed it to be almost a foregone conclusion that presidents would try to find officeholders of merit rather than of a particular faction or party. "I anticipate that one of the most difficult and delicate parts of the duty of my office will be that which relates to nominations for appointments," Washington lamented (Rhodehamel, 1997, 735). Jefferson felt much the same way. "Of the various executive duties, no one excites more anxious concern than that of placing the interests of our fellow citizens in the hands of honest men," he wrote to a group of suppliants in 1801. They had criticized one of Jefferson's appointments, and Jefferson reacted indignantly to the suggestion that politics had (or should) play a role in such decisions. "No duty, at the same time, is so difficult to fill" as such appointments, the president conceded, but in this particular case, he wrote, "it was learnt that his understanding was sound, his integrity pure, his character unstained" (Peterson, 1984, 497). And that, Jefferson felt, should be the only relevant consideration.

The presidents of Jackson's generation continued at least the rhetoric of Revolutionary days, claiming that their various appointments were based on merit, not politics. In many cases this no doubt was true; but in many others, it assuredly was not. The Jacksonian generation had become more or less comfortable with partisan practices and institutions that had made their Revolutionary forebears squirm and would have quickly earned the derogatory label of "faction." Jacksonians did not talk nearly as much about the evils of faction, and they had grown accustomed to the idea that a president was at once both the entire people's representative and the head of his particular party.

Jackson's ascent to the White House in 1828 was a certain high-water mark for this new brand of partisan, populist politics—or low mark, depending upon one's point of view. Old Hickory's managers were adroit practitioners of the new democracy. They were more likely to throw a barbecue than organize a policy debate, more comfortable with a rousing stump speech than a long intellectual address, and understood the aspirations and needs of an ordinary farmer more than a city banker or attorney. During Jackson's first inaugural ceremony, the politics of the new Democratic Party were everywhere evident as thousands of working-class Americans

A nineteenth-century political cartoon brands President Andrew Jackson as a king, trampling on the Constitution, and brandishing his veto power. The Whig Party, composed primarily of opponents of Jackson who viewed him as a tyrannical despot, adopted the name "Whigs" in reference to the political party in England that had opposed King George III in the eighteenth century. (Library of Congress)

crowded into Washington, D.C., in a raucous show of plebeian delight that a "man of the people" would become the nation's leader. The celebration included a near riot at the White House itself as an enthusiastic throng pressed its way through the front doors and wrought havoc. "What a scene did we witness!"

noted one astonished onlooker. *"The Majesty of the People* had disappeared, and a rabble, a mob of boys, negroes, women, children, scrambling, fighting, romping. What a pity, what a pity" (Remini, 1977, 178).

Once he made it into the White House, did Jackson in fact become "King Andrew I"? There were those who might have answered with an emphatic yes. Jackson used the tools available to him with more gusto than any previous chief executive. He vetoed twelve bills during his two terms in office, more than all of the vetoes proffered by the Revolutionary presidents combined.

In his 1832 veto of the National Bank Bill, Jackson showed future presidents how to do more than simply kill congressional legislation. The National Bank had been a touchy subject, symbolic for many Americans of capitalist excess and runaway government power. Jackson felt much the same way—he did not much like banks, as a rule—and in any event he knew a good political opportunity when he saw one. When he killed the bank's charter, he accompanied the deed with a ringing populist message aimed squarely at his Democratic Party constituents. Pointing out that the bank's president and shareholders were not directly accountable to the voters, he asked (rhetorically), "Is there no danger to our liberty and independence in a bank that in its nature has so little to bind it to our country?" There was little doubt about his answer. "It is to be regretted that the rich and powerful too often bend the acts of government to their selfish purposes," he observed, and "when the laws under-

take to . . . make the rich richer and the potent more powerful, the humble members of society, the farmers, mechanics, and laborers who have neither the time nor the means of securing like favors to themselves, have a right to complain of the injustice of their Government. . . . We can at least take a stand against all new grants of monopolies and exclusive privileges, against any prostitution of our Government to the advancement of the few at the expense of the many, and in favor of compromise and gradual reform in our code of laws and system of political economy" (www.yale.edu/lawweb/avalon).

No Revolutionary president would have used a veto in a quite so brazenly political manner. Washington, for example, believed that the veto should be used sparingly, either to fix an administrative oversight or technical defect or to correct Congress when it had so radically veered from the path of wisdom that it endangered the safety and well-being of the whole nation. In fact, Jefferson had to prod Washington into using the veto at some point, fearing that if the nation's foremost Founding Father and first president did not do so, future presidents would not either, and the power would simply fade away from disuse. In not only vetoing the Bank Bill but making an overtly political statement about that legislation, Jackson was signaling a break from the Revolutionary past.

Jackson also exercised a robust view of presidential power by heading off a small dress rehearsal for the Civil War in 1832. That year South Carolina's legislature—a hotbed of anti-Union sentiment even before the Civil War—declared that two tariffs passed by Congress to protect the fledgling American industrial revolution (happening almost entirely in the North) from cheap competition by European manufacturers (supported by those whose goods were purchased throughout the slave South). The South Carolinians not only nullified two federal laws in clear violation of the Constitution's Supremacy Clause; they also declared that any attempt made by federal authorities to collect tariff duties in their state would be met by force and secession from the Union.

As a slaveholding Southerner and leader of a party with a strong southern wing, Jackson might have been expected to empathize at least a bit with the Nullifiers (as they came to be called). But the South Carolina movement was led by John C. Calhoun, a man Jackson thoroughly detested; and besides, Old Hickory's nationalism ran much deeper than any sympathy he may have felt for states' rights. He threatened to send federal troops to occupy Charleston if the Nullifiers took the least step toward secession. In the end, cooler heads on both sides prevailed; Congress agreed to modify its tariff policies a bit to reflect southern concerns, while popular support for radical measures like wrecking the Union rapidly evaporated in South Carolina. President Jackson had left no doubt about where he stood, calling nullification an act of "intended Treason" and informing Vice President Van Buren in no uncertain terms that *The Union shall be preserved"* (Freehling, 1968, 245). He was not creating any radical

new presidential power here; the Constitution specifically gave him the power to put down insurrections. Previous presidents had done so, beginning with Washington's suppression of the so-called Whiskey Rebellion in 1794. But Jackson brought to the Nullification Crisis energy and a certain fierce panache that had been rare in previous chief executives.

Compared to the Founding generation, Jackson was an activist president. But by modern lights, there were definite limits. He did not really invent new presidential prerogatives so much as he breathed fire into those that already existed. Much of his activism was a function of Jackson's personality, ideas, emotions, manners, and preferences, all of which seemed larger than life. But much of it also was a reflection of his times, of a rough-and-tumble new America that could see fit to put an Indian-fighting western populist like Jackson in the White House in the first place.

But populist sloganeering aside, presidents of the Jacksonian generation were still close in time and spirit to their Revolutionary forebears. They continued to use the rhetoric of national unity and asserted the need to rise above party and rule for the common good, even as they settled into the drivers seats of their now indispensable political parties. They may have shoved the boundaries of acceptable presidential behavior outward a bit, but theirs were still remarkably limited ideas concerning what the presidency was and what it should be allowed to do. Different from the spirit of 1787 they may have been, but not so very different.

THE DOUGHFACE GENERATION

The sectional crisis crept up slowly on the White House. Jackson caught a brief glimpse of the future during the nullification controversy. Debates over slave owners' political power relative to the North roiled the presidency of John Tyler (in connection with Texas's eventual entry into the Union), and slavery hovered in the background during President Polk's war with Mexico from 1846 to 1848. But while slavery periodically dominated headlines and clouded presidential brows during the 1830s and 1840s, it had not yet become an ongoing, severe problem in national politics.

By the election of 1852 Andrew Jackson was long dead, having passed away from old age and various infirmities seven years earlier. Almost to his dying breath he was still railing against Clay and Calhoun; asked by someone what he would have done to the Nullifiers if they had tried to take South Carolina out of the Union, the crusty old former president, seventy-eight-years young, thundered, "Hung them, sir, as high as Haman. They should have been a terror to traitors to all time, and posterity would have pronounced it the best act of my life" (Remini, 1984, 517). Calhoun spared the Republic the trouble by dying in bed in 1850; Clay followed him to the grave two years later.

The generation of Jackson, Clay, and Calhoun had seen the problem of slavery looming on the national horizon, but had proven unable to find a resolution. Actually, they had not tried very hard. During

their time slavery was a national itch that only periodically required scratching. Americans' attention was fixed on other concerns, and the nation had not yet arrived at the point where every problem automatically became a presidential problem. When they thought of slavery at all, most Americans saw it as a local matter best handled by white Southerners, and little in the way of sympathy for African Americans' plight entered into the matter.

But by 1848 slavery was increasingly troubling the American national conversation. White Southerners worried over the future: over the growing power of northern cities and factories; over the trickle of runaway slaves headed to those cities, often never to return; and over the possibility that someday enough Yankees might cast enough votes in Congress—or maybe even put a man in the White House—to usher the peculiar institution on its way out of existence. Northerners had their anxieties as well. Perhaps slavery might survive longer than it should, providing a constant drag on the nation's economic development. Perhaps slaveholders might use their undisputed economic power to foist slavery and its dirty work off on Northerners who, while usually feeling little sympathy for black people, nevertheless wanted little to do with catching fugitive slaves and reforging their chains.

In 1848 the recently concluded war with Mexico seemed likely to exacerbate these concerns and perhaps even inflame tensions to the point of outright civil war. The war itself had been a resounding success, with the United States obtaining Texas, California, and all the territory in between. But success was the problem, for now Americans wondered how all that new territory could be equitably divided between free soilers and slaveholders—or whether an equitable approach was even required. Some antislavery Americans sided with Pennsylvania representative David Wilmot, who introduced a proviso requiring all new western territory to be free from slavery. Some proslavery Americans wanted the whole West to be carved up as a vast new slave empire, with perhaps someday Mexico and Central America thrown in to boot. Most people were caught somewhere between these extremes.

The presidency over the next dozen years reflected these divisions. The presidents themselves were often dubbed "doughfaces" by the press. They were Northern men with either outright proslavery sympathies or the wherewithal to keep their mouths shut about the peculiar institution. But more generally, *doughface* seems an apt term for the presidency during the entire decade leading up to the Civil War, reflecting a generation of Americans who wanted badly to avoid having to answer the questions about race and equality that slavery relentlessly shoved in front of them.

Polk had committed himself to serving only one term in office. His successor was Zachary Taylor, Old Rough and Ready, whose wartime exploits and whose lack of any real record on the slavery controversy carried him to victory in 1848. Once in the White House, he brought a hint of Jacksonian spice to the national political table when he snarled

at a delegation of Southerners that he himself would lead the army into a seceding state and hang every secessionist he could find, "with less reluctance than he had hung spies and deserters in Mexico" (Potter, 1976, 91).

As it was, Taylor's untimely and rather curious death in 1850—he became ill after eating cherries and milk at a Washington, D.C., Fourth of July celebration—made the point moot. His vice president and successor, Millard Fillmore, was a bland figure compared to Old Rough and Ready, the conqueror of northern Mexico. Fillmore was a lawyer, U.S. representative, and comptroller of the state of New York. He indulged no fiery rhetoric about hanging traitors and the like; in fact, he seemed to wish fervently that the whole matter would simply go away, and he pursued a low-key approach to leadership while serving out the remainder of Taylor's term. "The general policy of his Administration was wise and liberal," read an 1874 obituary that struggled to find much of anything to say about Fillmore, "and he left the country at peace with all the world and enjoying a high degree of prosperity" (*New York Times*, March 9, 1874). Fillmore's successor, Franklin Pierce, was a typical doughface president, a New Hampshire man who stood out only because of his excessive drinking at Washington parties while serving in Congress—"I have been leading, I need not say, a very agreeable life," he joked. He did not even have that dash of color after he renounced alcohol entirely at the urging of his distraught and temperance-minded wife (Gara, 1991, 52). Pierce was a Yankee with southern friends (including Jefferson Davis, who would serve in Pierce's Cabinet as a very able secretary of war) and a get-along-to-go-along approach to governing that struck some as admirably restrained but others as indicating a lack of presidential moxie. People might well have wondered whether his modesty was all that false when he stated that "no heart but my own can know the personal regret and bitter sorrow over which I have been borne to a position so suitable for others rather than desirable for myself." Where the slavery troubles were concerned, he referred to the Compromise of 1850—a complex piece of legislation that tried to solve the many differences between North and South concerning slavery and the western territories—and rather wistfully declared, "I fervently hope that the question is at rest, and that no sectional or ambitious or fanatical excitement may again threaten the durability of our institutions or obscure the light of our prosperity" (www.yale.edu/lawweb/ avalon).

A group portrait eulogizes the statesmen involved with the Compromise of 1850 and the efforts to preserve the Union. In the front row (from left to right) are the primary figures in the debate: Winfield Scott (in uniform), Lewis Cass, Henry Clay, John C. Calhoun (standing in center), Daniel Webster, and Millard Fillmore (holding a shield). Calhoun and Webster stand with their hands resting on the Constitution with a bust of George Washington between them. (Library of Congress)

Try as he might, Pierce could not simply wish away the signs of growing sectional strife. During his term in the White House, sectional tensions abounded, from growing unrest in Kansas concerning the fate of slavery there and in other western lands, to disagreements between Northerners and Southerners concerning the return of runaway slaves, to arguments in Congress that in one case caused one congressman to assault another with a cane and beat him senseless. Harriet Beecher Stowe's *Uncle Tom's Cabin* (1852) became a runaway best seller in the North during Pierce's time, with its vivid and emotional descriptions of slavery's evil, while in the South, William Grayson delighted whites with his defense of slavery in his poem, *The Hireling and the Slave.* The question was far from at rest, and whatever his intentions—good, bad, or indifferent—Pierce proved ineffective in halting the slide toward disunion.

He wanted a second term, as do most presidents, but the Democrats cast him aside in 1856 and nominated James Buchanan. On the surface, it was not such a bad idea. Buchanan had a distinguished record of public service: a veteran congressman from Pennsylvania (he had served five terms in the House of Representatives), he had an extensive record of diplomatic service in Russia and Great Britain and had served as Polk's secretary of state. On the personal front, he was something of an odd duck, with an air of stuffiness born from his rich background and his seemingly endless career as a mediocre congressman

and diplomat. His own nickname for himself was the Old Public Functionary. He was America's only lifelong bachelor president.

The measure of the man could be taken by observing how, in his Inaugural Address, he made headlines not for an act of leadership, but rather an abdication of responsibility for the sectional crisis in favor of someone else—or rather, nine someone elses, in black robes sitting on the Supreme Court, nine men who were presumably free of the need to play the role of political nonentity, since they did not stand for reelection. Surveying the wrack of sectional strife and how so much of it was piled around the matter of slavery's role in western expansion, Buchanan threw his hands in the air and told America they would all be better off if they let the Supreme Court handle it. "This is, happily, a matter of but little practical importance," he opined. "Besides, it is a judicial question, which legitimately belongs to the Supreme Court of the United States, before whom it is now pending, and will, it is understood, be speedily and finally settled. To their decision, in common with all good citizens, I shall cheerfully submit, whatever this may be" (www.yale.edu/lawweb/avalon).

The pending court case to which Buchanan referred was *Dred Scott v. Sandford* (1857), and the Court's unabashedly proslavery stance on slavery in the territories solved nothing. Even moderate Northerners were stunned by its racist tone, while white Southerners were equally taken aback by Yankee criticism of the highest court in the land.

The mutual recriminations and threats continued unabated, and all the while Buchanan stood by helplessly. Teddy Roosevelt would later appropriately dub him "Buchanan the Little."

The moment of crisis finally arrived in the fall of 1860, when seven southern states withdrew from the Union following the election of a Republican, Abraham Lincoln, to the White House. Before Lincoln took office, Buchanan's supine conception of presidential leadership was laid bare for all to see. He stood idly by while secessionists seized federal property in the South, silenced dissenters, and asserted their right to destroy the American Union. Buchanan responded by both deploring secession as "neither more or less than revolution" and inimical to the Founding Fathers' wishes, while also asserting that as president he did not possess the legal power to "coerce" a state back into the Union (McPherson, 1982, 133).

Taken as a whole, the presidents of the doughface generation were remarkable for their relative lack of activism and unwillingness to expand the office much beyond the bare minimum necessary to govern. Part of this was a product of the constitutional vision that animated many Americans of the day, a vision which held that the federal government—especially the chief executive—must hold itself within the confines of a strictly circumscribed federal sphere that did not intrude upon state and local prerogatives and which exercised little influence over the daily lives of ordinary Americans. Pierce spoke for this point of view as well as any when he told his countrymen that "the dangers of a concentration of all power in the general government of a confederacy so vast as ours are too obvious to be disregarded. You have a right, therefore, to expect your agents in every department to regard strictly the limits imposed upon them by the Constitution of the United States. The great scheme of our constitutional liberty rests upon a proper distribution of power between the State and Federal authorities, and experience has shown that the harmony and happiness of our people must depend upon a just discrimination between the separate rights and responsibilities of the States and your common rights and obligations under the General Government" (http://www.presidency.ucsb.edu/ws/index.php?pid=25816). This was not to say that the doughface presidents were not strong Unionists. "With the Union my best and dearest earthly hopes are entwined," Pierce declared, "Without it what are we individually or collectively?" (www.yale.edu/lawweb/avalon). Even Buchanan, in his limited fashion, was loyal to the nation he led and would have no truck with secessionist extremists. No one in the White House during the 1850s wanted disunion or civil war. But the doughfaces were, on the whole, powerless to prevent it: powerless because of their own temperaments; the party and political realities of their times; and perhaps because, in the words of Republican stalwart William Seward, it really was, at the end of the day, an "irrepressible conflict."

THE "TOUCHED BY FIRE" GENERATION

The more perceptive early presidents had seen storm clouds of disunion gathering on the horizon. Washington felt compelled to remind his countrymen in 1796 that "the unity of government which constitutes you one people is also now dear to you. It is justly so, for it is a main pillar in the edifice of your real independence, the support of your tranquility at home, your peace abroad; of your safety; of your prosperity; of that very liberty which you so highly prize." Even so, he warned, it "is easy to foresee that, from different causes and from different quarters, much pains will be taken, many artifices employed to weaken in your minds the conviction of this truth. . . . It is of infinite moment that you should properly estimate the immense value of your national union to your collective and individual happiness; that you should cherish a cordial, habitual, and immovable attachment to it . . . [while] discountenancing whatever may suggest even a suspicion that it can in any event be abandoned; and indignantly frowning upon the first dawning of every attempt to alienate any portion of our country from the rest, or to enfeeble the sacred ties which now link together the various parts" (Rhodehamel, 1997, 963).

These worries cut across generational lines, for thirty years later Andrew Jackson would warn that "without union our independence and liberty would never have been achieved; without union they never can be maintained." He under-stood how difficult and dangerous the centrifugal forces of disunion might become. "Divided into twenty-four, or even a smaller number, of separate communities, we shall see our internal trade burdened with numberless restraints and exactions; communication between distant points and sections obstructed or cut off; our sons made soldiers to deluge with blood the fields they now till in peace; the mass of our people borne down and impoverished by taxes to support armies and navies, and military leaders at the head of their victorious legions becoming our lawgivers and judges. The loss of liberty, of all good government, of peace, plenty, and happiness, must inevitably follow a dissolution of the Union. In supporting it, therefore, we support all that is dear to the freeman and the philanthropist" (www .yale.edu/lawweb/avalon/presiden/inaug/ jackson2.htm).

But while Jackson and his doughface successors had watched those cracks slowly widen beneath their feet, they remained wedded still to the more passive strains of the Framers' presidency. It may be too much to suggest that the antebellum presidents fiddled while Rome began to burn, but certainly they did little or nothing when the smoke became evident for all to see. Jackson may have threatened to hang secessionists higher than Haman, but neither he nor anyone else in the White House followed through on the threat, either literally or figuratively. Democratic-minded Americans might have taken some small comfort in the fact that the Jacksonian and doughface presidents perfectly mirrored the sentiments of the population at large, in that they did not take the secessionists' threats very seriously until it was far too late.

The Civil War generation of presidents did not have that luxury. Secession and the war that followed would dominate the presidents who led the nation through that war (Lincoln); oversaw the Union's reconstruction (Johnson, Grant, and to a certain extent Hayes); or were, with one exception—Cleveland—veterans of the war (Garfield, Arthur, Harrison, and McKinley) whose military experiences provided a strong background context for their leadership and behavior. The Union's great crisis and its consequences hovered over the White House for years after the guns fell silent. Even as later presidents moved on to address subjects that bore little direct relation to the war—civil service reform, for example—the war was nevertheless always there, always hovering in the background. It was the inescapable event for an American generation that was, in the famous words of Supreme Court justice Oliver Wendell Holmes Jr., "touched by fire."

The Revolutionary generation of presidents confronted the newness of the office, the Jacksonians wrestled with popular democracy's effects, and the doughface presidents spent much of their time hoping the lid would not blow off national sectionalism. Once it did, the Civil War generation of presidents had to confront a key problem: was the office expandable and flexible enough to address the extraordinary circumstances of civil war and the Union's reconstruction,

while still maintaining its essentially democratic character? This was a constitutional issue, as presidents were compelled by circumstances to delve into dark and dusty corners of the Constitution's provisions for the chief executive. It was an institutional issue, with the office itself flexing and expanding in new and unprecedented ways to meet new and unprecedented problems—or not. For it was also a personal issue, as the temperament of the man who happened to be sitting in the office at any particular moment could play a decisive role in determining whether or not powers that were latent in the presidency would be used.

After Abraham Lincoln's election in November 1860, secession-minded Southerners moved quickly to exploit a weakness in the presidential election process: the fact that a president-elect does not technically take the reins of office until his official inauguration ceremony in March, creating a nearly five-month time lag between his election and his actual power to govern. Under normal circumstances the gap is hardly noticeable. But during "secession winter," secessionists in South Carolina, Georgia, Florida, Alabama, Mississippi, Louisiana, and Texas exploited the power vacuum to withdraw their states from the Union, while lame duck James Buchanan did nothing—he was sort of a one-man power vacuum all his own.

From almost the moment he stepped aboard the train that would carry him from his home in Springfield, Illinois, to Washington, D.C., Lincoln found himself confronting problems no president had ever previously faced. Those problems were almost too numerous to list, intrinsic as they were to a modern war and its attendant concerns: not just mobilization of troops, but an entire society, in all of its industrial, political, economic, cultural, and technological facets. Historians still debate whether or not the Civil War was America's first modern war, but there can be no doubt that it posed unprecedented demands and problems.

There were those who sincerely questioned whether the presidency possessed the requisite legal authority to perform the tasks required by the war. There were Americans who doubted the wisdom of the war itself; but if the North insisted upon going to war, few disputed the president's constitutional authority to do the basic things that war required: command the troops, supply them, and so forth. But wars are rarely so simple, and Lincoln faced a variety of difficult questions. Particularly vexing were those related to internal security.

The issue crystallized early in the war over the arrest of a man named John Merryman in Maryland. He was jailed by the army under authority of a proclamation by Lincoln suspending the writ of habeas corpus (basically allowing the army to keep suspects in prison without showing cause) in the state, which had many southern sympathizers. Lincoln's policies also left defendants to the tender mercies of a military court martial, which was far less favorable to defendants than a civilian court of law.

Supreme Court chief justice Roger Taney took great exception to the presi-

dent's policies. A slaveholder and Maryland native, he was no friend of the Lincoln Administration; in addition, he seems to have been genuinely troubled by Lincoln's assumption of the authority to suspend the writ. No previous president had ever done so, on his own hook and without congressional authorization. This was no small matter, for many legal experts (Taney included) believed that the writ could only be suspended by Congress, since the constitutional provision for such an act—"The privilege of the Writ of Habeas Corpus shall not be suspended, unless when in Cases of Rebellion or Invasion the public Safety may require it"—appeared in Article I, which dealt with the legislative branch, rather than Article II's provisions for the presidency.

Taney took it upon himself to rein in the Lincoln Administration, setting definite limits on presidential powers during a civil war and incidentally freeing Merryman. Sitting in his capacity as a federal district court judge (Supreme Court justices pulled double duty in those days), Taney issued a ruling in *Ex parte Merryman* (1861) that tried to do all these things. "The president has exercised a power he does not possess under the constitution," Taney asserted. Outlining the Constitution's provisions for a speedy trial by a jury of the defendant's peers, the right to confront his accusers and have legal representation at trial (none of which was guaranteed in a military tribunal), he declared that "with such provisions in the constitution, expressed in language too clear to be misunderstood by any one, I can see no ground whatever for supposing that the president, in any emergency, or in any state of things, can authorize the suspension of the privileges of the writ of habeas corpus . . . and I can only say that if the authority which the constitution has confided to the judiciary department and judicial officers, may thus, upon any pretext or under any circumstances, be usurped by the military power, at its discretion, the people of the United States are no longer living under a government of laws, but every citizen holds life, liberty and property at the will and pleasure of the army officer in whose military district he may happen to be found." And, he might have added, at the pleasure of the president who commanded that army officer.

This was the most serious assault on presidential authority since the nation's founding, compounded in its power—or mischief—by its occurrence during a time when the nation was fighting for its very survival. The president responded by ignoring Taney and leaving Merryman in jail. Lincoln never conceded Taney's point that the presidency was exceeding its constitutional authority. But he did understand that the Civil War chief executive was going places and doing things never seen or done before by a chief executive. "The dogmas of the quiet past, are inadequate to the stormy present," he told Congress in late 1862. "The occasion is piled high with difficulty, and we must rise with the occasion. As our case is new, so we must think anew, and act anew. We must disenthrall our selves, and then we shall save our country" (Basler, 1953–1955, 5: 537).

Nowhere was this more evident than in the epic, vexed matter of slavery and American race relations. Prior to the war, the presidency had hardly been a leading voice on these issues. Indeed, presidents—and not just the doughfaces—wanted earnestly to avoid these exceedingly touchy subjects if at all possible.

This included Lincoln, too, at least at first. "'I have no purpose, directly or indirectly, to interfere with the institution of slavery in the States where it exists. I believe I have no lawful right to do so, and I have no inclination to do so,'" he declared in his first Inaugural Address, quoting an earlier speech he had made. "Those who nominated and elected me did so with full knowledge that I had made this, and many similar declarations, and had never recanted them" (Basler, 1953–1955, 4: 263). He hoped this would reassure white Southerners enough to abandon the reckless project of secession; but barring that, Lincoln truly believed, in 1861, that the presidency as an institution simply could not do what so many abolitionists wanted (indeed, what he himself would have privately preferred): end the American institution of human bondage by presidential fiat.

Some critics of Lincoln mistook his reluctance to embrace black freedom as latent bigotry, or at best, timidity. The president "can do nothing for *freedom* in a direct manner," grumbled abolitionist William Lloyd Garrison, "but only by circumlocution and delay" (Mayer, 1998, 542). But Garrison and other radical critics misread the president, whose natural

President Abraham Lincoln reads the Emancipation Proclamation to his Cabinet on July 22, 1862.
(Bettmann/Corbis)

inclinations were passive, and who throughout his life was much more given to going around rather than through a problem. He worked his way to a solution to the slavery problem by degrees.

As Lincoln moved toward emancipation, he carried the presidency onto new grounds. In a message to Congress in December 1862, he laid out a detailed plan for federally compensated gradual emancipation, to take place before the year 1900. His proposal took the form of a series of constitutional amendments that would offer federal government bonds to any state that freed its slaves. "Some would perpetuate slavery," he pointed out, "some would abolish it suddenly, and without compensation; some would abolish it gradually, and with compensation; some would remove the freed people from us, and some would retain them with us; and there are yet other minor diversities. Because of these diversities, we waste much strength in struggles among ourselves. By mutual concession we should harmonize, and act together" (Basler, 1953–1955, 5: 531).

Whatever the merits of the plan, its very proposal was extraordinary from the point of view of presidential authority.

No prior president had involved himself quite so directly in the legislative process, and no president had prior to this point proposed constitutional amendments to Congress. As it turned out, neither Congress nor the states took him up on the matter, but the proposal itself was exceptional.

The Emancipation Proclamation was an executive order, itself a rather unusual thing in those days. Executive orders are simply presidential directives issued to agents of the executive department by its boss. There is no specific constitutional provision for such orders, but presidents have argued that they are implied by the provision of Article II, Section 3 that presidents should take care that "the laws be faithfully executed." Until Lincoln's time, executive orders had been issued infrequently—Washington issued only four during his entire tenure in office—and only for relatively inconsequential matters.

Once emancipation was firmly in place, Lincoln never wavered, and in the name of his executive order, he labored quietly behind the scenes to effect policies related to black freedom. This included some quiet but persistent arm-twisting to get border states that were exempted from the Emancipation Proclamation to grant freedom to their slaves. It also included a concerted campaign to bolster passage of the Thirteenth Amendment to finally and forever outlaw slavery, a measure Lincoln knew was vitally necessary, for as an executive order, his proclamation had its limits.

Lincoln also engaged in a quiet campaign to gain the freedmen some small measures of freedom's fruits: protection of their basic legal and civil rights, and perhaps even suffrage, an idea so radical in those times that no American politician, not even the president, dared endorse it with any degree of vigor. But in private he indicated his feelings. Should the Union win the war, he wrote in 1864, "I cannot see, if universal amnesty is granted, how, under the circumstances, I can avoid exacting in return universal suffrage, or, at least, suffrage on the basis of intelligence and military service. How to better the condition of the colored race has long been a study which has attracted my serious and careful attention; hence I think I am clear and decided as to what course I shall pursue in the premises, regarding it a religious duty, as the nation's guardian of these people, who have so heroically vindicated their manhood on the battle-field, where, in assisting to save the life of the Republic, they have demonstrated in blood their right to the ballot, which is but the humane protection of the flag they have so fearlessly defended" (Basler, 1953–1955, 7: 101). Whether Lincoln would have made these private ruminations public after the war by, say, offering to Congress another proposal for constitutional amendments—this time to secure the vote for African Americans—is of course unknown. But by the end of the war he had established precedents for the presidency to become a force for change in American politics and society.

Of course, whether or not a given president would want to exploit this new potential was largely up to the president himself. The office has always been a

Andrew Johnson was one of only two U.S. presidents (the other being Bill Clinton) to be impeached. (Library of Congress)

complex nexus point between the institution and the flesh-and-blood realities of the fallible human beings who actually sat in the chief executive's chair. Lincoln's successor, Andrew Johnson, would provide proof of that. As Lincoln rose to meet the demands of his times, and so expanded the presidency, Johnson shrank from those demands and diminished the office.

The first vice president to succeed an assassinated president, Johnson early on found himself with almost unprecedented political capital at his command. Northerners were energized by their victory over the Confederacy; and coupled with their widespread desire to honor the legacy of Lincoln, the Great Emancipator, this energy might have been channeled into a desire to do something decisive about the South's troubled race relations by extending fundamental

rights to African Americans and by seeing to it that their disgruntled white neighbors allowed them to exercise those rights unmolested. In the immediate aftermath of the Civil War, many white Northerners felt a responsibility toward the freedmen that would become distressingly rare in later years. "It is the duty of the government not only to protect its friends among the white population of the South, but to maintain the rights of the freedmen also," declared one northern newspaper (McKitrick, 1960, 30).

The presidency, grown at least potentially robust during the war, was at the cutting edge of such efforts. Lincoln had seen to this with the Emancipation Proclamation, which tied the White House to black aspirations in a symbolic as well as legal fashion. Lincoln's generation of Americans instinctively thought of the executive branch as the conscience of the nation where the freedmen were concerned. Moreover, the army was the enforcement arm of any Reconstruction aimed at the South, including particularly the policies concerning freedmen and their civil rights—and the president was commander in chief.

Any hope that Andrew Johnson would use the presidency to act vigorously on behalf of the newly freed slaves quickly vanished, however. This was partly due to Johnson's odd political position. He was a lifelong Democrat who had been placed on the Republican national ticket as Lincoln's running mate in 1864 to attract moderates from both parties. The ploy worked in strictly political terms, but it meant that Johnson in effect had no constituency: Democrats no longer trusted him, but he had no Republican base, either. Looking for his own following, he turned to an unlikely source: former Confederates. They in turn had no intention of granting even basic civil rights to their former slaves, and Johnson would accede to their wishes.

Another part of the problem was Johnson's own personality. A tailor from Tennessee who had risen through the political ranks, he relished the role of the solitary achiever who climbed his way to the top alone and unaided. He lacked Lincoln's political skills and negotiating abilities and possessed a deserved reputation as a prickly sort with few close friends. He was also a bigot with little sympathy for African Americans, telling Congress in his 1867 annual message that "wherever [African Americans] have been left to their own devices they have

shown a constant tendency to relapse into barbarism" (Foner, 1988, 180).

Within a year after Lincoln's death, it had become clear that Johnson had no intention of protecting the freedmen. He vetoed the Freedmen's Bureau Act (designed to fund the federal government's chief reconstruction bureau in the South) and the Civil Rights Act of 1866, arguing that both measures represented violations of white Southerners' basic political rights. With reports drifting up from the South concerning widespread incidents of political terrorism and violence perpetrated by new organizations like the Ku Klux Klan, Johnson ordered the army to stay out of the way and allow Southerners to work out their own problems—which meant, in effect, exposing black citizens to the tender mercies of their white neighbors.

Republicans, even those of a relatively moderate variety, were appalled; some seriously wondered if Johnson had been drunk when making his decisions. "Is there no way to arrest the insane course of the President?" asked Senator Thaddeus Stevens (Donald, 1970, 230). Their concerns grew as Johnson began issuing wholesale pardons to former Confederates, thus eliminating any leverage the federal government might have possessed over the very same people who had tried to destroy the Union and who were now engaged in systematically denying civil rights to the freedmen. Johnson felt that his pardons were admirable acts of sectional reconciliation, acts which not incidentally restored full voting rights to men who would now be quite grateful to Andrew Johnson.

Congress responded by refusing to seat Southern representatives elected by the newly pardoned white Southerners—some of whom had the effrontery to show up on the Capitol steps wearing their old Confederate military uniforms—and overriding Johnson's vetoes with the constitutionally prescribed two-thirds majority. Johnson then tried to outflank his congressional opponents by staging in the summer of 1866 an unprecedented public relations campaign, dubbed the "swing around the circle" by the press. Johnson spoke before crowds during a whistle-stop tour between Washington, D.C., and Chicago, defending his Reconstruction policies and castigating those members of his own party who opposed him. No one had ever seen anything quite like it before: a president actively campaigning to win over public opinion. "The Presidents purpose in speaking so much," wrote a New York newspaperman, is that "He thinks he can convince [the people] that he is right and Congress is wrong" (McKitrick, 1960, 429n).

No previous president had done this; and no other president had used the veto power in such a bold—some would say reckless—manner. It could perhaps be argued that Johnson was forging new presidential tools, using pardons, public speaking, and vetoes in unprecedented ways. He even followed Lincoln, in a backhanded way, by involving himself in the process of amending the Constitution, albeit in his case, Johnson threw the weight of his office behind efforts to defeat the Fourteenth Amendment by issuing a message to Congress stating his

belief that Congress could not ratify the amendment—which, among other things, granted basic due process and equal protection rights to all Americans, including (and especially) the freedmen—while excluding eleven former Confederate states from the process.

But in reality, Johnson's wholesale pardoning, his "swing around the circle," his vetoes, and other efforts were driving a wrecking ball through the presidency's prestige and democratic authority. The "swing" was especially embarrassing, as Johnson allowed himself to be baited into unseemly exchanges with hecklers in what were increasingly hostile crowds. In Indianapolis, for example, his speech was greeted with jeers and cries of "Shut up! We don't want to hear from you." Ulysses S. Grant, who reluctantly accompanied the president, was mortified when Johnson stooped to exchanging insults with such people. "I am disgusted with this trip," he reportedly said, "I am disgusted at hearing a man make speeches on his way to his own funeral" (McKitrick, 1960, 428n, 429–430). Needless to say, Johnson's tour did nothing to help his cause, as even Americans who might otherwise have sympathized with his policies were dismayed by such decidedly unpresidential behavior. Referring to "the maudlin speeches by which he has degraded the country as it has never been degraded before" and "reports of pardons sold," one congressman called Johnson "the successor of Jefferson Davis" and "an enormous and malignant usurper, through whom the Republic is imperilled" (Donald, 1970, 279).

The unhappy climax to Johnson's presidency came in 1868 with his impeachment, the first ever for a president. He escaped conviction by only one vote, and soon after left the White House, unable to secure renomination for a second term by either party. "All seems gloom and despair, [but] I have performed my duty to my God, my country, and my family," he defiantly wrote (Castel, 1979, 215). And he did manage to recoup some of his political fortune by campaigning for and eventually winning a seat in the U.S. Senate, entering that body in 1875. He died from a massive stroke just a few weeks into his term, however. Whatever his virtues, it would be difficult to argue with the judgment of historian James Ford Rhodes, who wrote that "of all men in public life, it is difficult to conceive of one so ill-fitted for this delicate work" of Reconstruction (Castel, 1979, 218).

For the Civil War generation, the presidency would never entirely recover from the Johnson fiasco. From Ulysses S. Grant's corruption-riddled two terms through the succession of relatively passive and colorless chief executives who closed out the nineteenth century, the presidency was relegated to a backseat role in policymaking as Congress waxed ascendant. Occasionally, presidents would take a leading role on various issues. Civil service reform became a pet project for Chester Arthur during his stay in the White House; Grover Cleveland tried to clean up pension fraud by refusing to grant pensions to Civil War veterans based on false claims; William McKinley took aim at large business trusts, which he described as "conspira-cies against the public good" (Gould, 1980, 29).

These were not insignificant efforts; and yet more often than not these same presidents found themselves reacting to congressional initiatives on civil service reform, tariffs, railroad monopolies, and the other great political questions of their day. When they momentarily rode the crest of a wave of public and political opinion, it was a wave tossed up by others. Theirs was not the presidency of an Abraham Lincoln, which could risk the wrath of the Supreme Court by suspending the writ of habeas corpus or risk the wrath of racially biased whites by moving boldly forward on issues of freedom and civil rights. Presidential life was subsequently quite a roller-coaster ride for the Civil War generation; it witnessed the office at its most effective and eloquent height during the Lincoln years, as well as the lows of the Johnson years and their aftermath.

THE PROGRESSIVE GENERATION

By 1900 the "touched by fire" generation was moving on. The average Civil War veteran by that time would have been at least middle-aged, and the older men who had actually led both sides during the war were for the most part long gone. Ulysses S. Grant succumbed to throat cancer in 1885, less than a decade after leaving the White House. Former Confederate president Jefferson Davis died in relative obscurity in 1889. William Tecumseh Sherman—who had famously rebuffed attempts to nominate him for the presidency by growling, "if nominated, I will not run; if elected I will not serve"—passed away two years later.

William McKinley was the last Civil War veteran in the White House, an old-fashioned, nineteenth-century man caught on the cusp of a new and very different century. He was "gray and dull," observed one of his biographers, and "remained a catchword for Republican conservatism or an inviting target for scholars who find his Victorian values either cloying or hypocritical" (Gould, 1980, 6). Having been through one war, this mild, guarded president wanted no part of another. The nation, however, thrust one upon him in 1898 following the sinking of the USS *Maine* in Cuba and the near-universal cry for war against Spain. "I pray God that we may be able to keep peace," he lamented. "I have been through one war. I have seen the dead piled up; and I do not want to see another" (Gould, 1980, 78).

But by 1898 the Civil War seemed like a very long time ago, and a new generation of Americans—one that could hardly remember the "dead piled up"— clamored for revenge against the Spanish and, not incidentally, the creation of a new American imperialism on the ashes of the old Spanish Empire. At least one observer was not impressed with McKinley's lack of ardor for war. The president had the "backbone of a chocolate éclair," sneered an assistant secretary of the navy and former police commissioner from New York named Theodore Roosevelt. For his part, McKinley thought Roosevelt was "hotheaded" and "harum scarum" and privately disparaged him as

"that damned cowboy" (Dalton, 2002, 163).

In 1900 the damned cowboy became the chocolate éclair's running mate; and a year later, when an assassin's bullet felled McKinley, Roosevelt was thrust into the presidency. He infuriated some people and inspired many others. Some even thought he was mentally unbalanced. "The President is crazy," fumed one critic, and another referred to one of his speeches as "the ravings of a disordered mind" (Morris, 2001, 508). But love, hate, or fear him, Americans had to admit that Teddy Roosevelt embodied the spirit of a new century and a new age in ways unsurpassed by any previous president.

TR—and he was the first president regularly and affectionately referred to by his initials—was himself quite well aware of his role as chief spokesman for a new century and a new generation of Americans. "We are the heirs of the ages," he told listeners at his inaugural ceremony in 1905, and "our life has called for the vigor and effort without which the manlier and hardier virtues wither away. . . . We have faith that we shall not prove false to the memories of the men of the mighty past. They did their work, they left us the splendid heritage we now enjoy. We in our turn have an assured confidence that we shall be able to leave this heritage unwasted and enlarged to our children and our children's children" (www.yale.edu/lawweb/ avalon/presiden/inaug/troos.htm).

It was Roosevelt who coined the term *bully pulpit* to describe the presidency's powers of persuasion, and he employed that power to great effect. At the dawn of the media age, he was an omnipresent national figure, his trademark persona— barrel chest, pince-nez glasses, and wolfish grin—showcased in cartoons, portraits, and early news films throughout the country. He was a born dramatist who relished big brushstrokes and bold lines, and journalists of the day responded by portraying him as a Robin Hood or a crusader, doing battle with the evil of his day. Roosevelt was an "enchanting Paul Bunyan-ish creature," enthused one contemporary observer (Dalton, 2002, 8).

Previous presidents possessed media images, of course, to a greater or lesser degree; and the best of them knew how to present themselves on the national stage. It is no coincidence that George Washington loved plays or that Abraham Lincoln was a Shakespeare enthusiast. But TR was the first president actively to cultivate a media persona in the more modern sense of the phrase, and this in an age when "media" had come to mean more than newsprint. Roosevelt had at his disposal a highly developed (some would have said sensationalist) early-twentieth-century newspaper industry, the growing power of the camera—in the form of still pictures and films—and voice recordings that could distribute his singular speechmaking capabilities over a much broader range than anything dreamed of by previous chief executives. He saw the possibilities, working directly with writers and journalists to mold his own heroic image in the American mind. He was the first president to do this consistently and well, and his

was the first generation to tolerate and approve of this sort of thing.

Roosevelt's media power was more than just image making; it in turn fed an activist, vigorous presidency. His administration brought high-profile lawsuits against railroads and other huge business monopolies of his day, seeking to establish federal regulatory power over their runaway growth and sometimes predatory practices. A reformer at heart, he was unabashed about what he wanted from Congress on a variety of domestic issues: environmental conservation; labor policies; tariff rates; government regulation of the beef, sugar, and petroleum industries; federal food and drug inspection; and establishment of standards for rail gauges, weights, and measures. He called his collection of domestic policy initiatives the Square Deal program, illustrating his media savvy and understanding of how useful taglines and slogans could be in the new era. Roosevelt even involved himself directly in plans to revamp and beautify downtown Washington, D.C., to the point that one newspaper sarcastically wondered if he planned to change his name to "Butt-insky."

On the foreign policy front, Roosevelt likewise acted with an energy that had not been seen in the White House for decades. He passionately supported America's budding status as an imperial power. "Our place as a nation is and must be with the nations that have left indelibly their impress on the centuries," he declared. "Those that did not expand passed away and left not so much as a memory behind them" (Morris, 2001,

A cartoon depicts a larger-than-life President Theodore Roosevelt standing in a harbor, aggressively digging and throwing dirt in the direction of Bogota, Colombia. The United States aided Panama in its fight for independence from Colombia, which it achieved in 1903. Shortly thereafter a treaty between Panama and the United States enabled the United States to begin construction of the Panama Canal. (Library of Congress)

229). Roosevelt pursued a variety of diplomatic and military agendas to further his expansionist goals. He directed diplomatic and military interventions in Latin America and the Caribbean, called upon Congress to increase funding for the nation's armed forces—particularly the navy—and approve his policies aimed at constructing a canal in Panama.

In what historian Max Boot called "as brazen—and successful—an example of gunboat diplomacy as the world has ever seen," TR bullied and cajoled the Panamanians into awarding the United States a Canal Zone through the center of their nation, under terms extremely favorable to the Roosevelt Administration (2002, 134).

The flavor of TR's foreign policy activism was most evident in his famous Roosevelt Corollary, an amendment to the Monroe Doctrine that he offered during his annual address to Congress in December 1904. One hundred years earlier the Monroe Doctrine had called upon European powers to stay out of Central and South America, which many in the United States considered to be their backyard; Roosevelt now felt compelled to update and reinvigorate that old American policy statement with one of his own. If a nation "keeps order and pays its obligations, then it has no fear of interference from the United States," Roosevelt declared. But "brutal wrongdoing, or an impotence which results in a general loosening of the ties of a civilized society, may finally require intervention by some civilized nation." He left no doubt which civilized nation he had in mind. "In the Western Hemisphere the United States cannot ignore this duty" (Morris, 2001, 326).

The Roosevelt Corollary was a quintessential TR measure: passionate, enthusiastic, brash, and more than a touch bellicose. "Speak softly, but carry a big stick," Roosevelt said during his White House years; but in fact he did not do much of anything softly. His presidency was controversial, it was in many ways unprecedented, and it was a bit of a wild ride at times—but it was never dull.

Neither was Woodrow Wilson's tenure in the White House, despite the fact that his personality was very different from TR's. Wilson was an academic turned politician, a former political science professor and president of Princeton University. Where Teddy Roosevelt's glasses somehow made him look even more exuberant and energetic, Wilson's spare, steel-rimmed frames gave him an austere, almost severe countenance. Where Roosevelt's boyish enthusiasm helped him connect with ordinary people, Wilson was rather aloof, with a bit of a snobbish streak. "The bulk of mankind is rigidly unphilosophical," the college don sniffed. "A truth must become not only plain but also commonplace before it will be seen by the people who go to their work very early in the morning" (Clements, 1992, 5). No one called him WW.

Wilson may not have seemed a terribly endearing man, but he was principled, extremely intelligent, and possessed of exquisite political skills, honed by years of delicately balancing and negotiating between the fractious elements of an academic world while president of Princeton. He also possessed very definite ideas about government and the balance of power between Congress and the presidency; and where Roosevelt's bullish instincts had led him to inject new life into the presidency, Wilson's philosophical mind led him in much the same direction. He argued that, in the wake of the various presidential scandals of the late nineteenth century, Congress had taken on more responsibilities than were necessary or healthy for the nation as a whole. It was a "facile statute-devising machine," he wrote, and as such was unsuited to the debate and development of larger political issues. "The enacting, revising, tinkering, repealing of laws should engross the attention and engage

Woodrow Wilson was a distinguished professor of political science and an innovative president of Princeton University (1902–1910) before he began his remarkable political career as governor of New Jersey (1911–1913) and president of the United States (1913–1921). (Library of Congress)

the entire energy of such a body as Congress," Wilson believed, while well-trained, educated leaders should occupy executive positions like the presidency and use their power to move the broad philosophical direction of the country. "It is only by the action of leading minds that the organic will of a community is stirred to the exercise of either originative purpose or guiding control in affairs" (Clements, 1992, 4).

In shaping that "organic will," Wilson did not neglect domestic policy. TR had his Square Deal, and Wilson, in many ways every bit as astute in managing public opinion, called his domestic programs the New Freedom plan. He continued Roosevelt's policy of keeping a sharp watch on corporate abuses, telling Congress it would be "called upon in every session to intervene in the regulation of business" (Clements, 1992, 35). He supported tariff reductions to prevent creation of special domestic manufacturing interests, and he worked hard to effect what he believed were necessary reforms in the nation's banking and currency policies.

But Wilson's legacy would be in foreign affairs, and especially in his second term, war. He continued TR's policies of robust interventionism in Latin America, sending troops into Haiti and the Dominican Republic when American interests were threatened by unrest in those countries, and authorizing the Punitive Expedition to (unsuccessfully) chase down Mexican bandit Pancho Villa in 1916.

But those efforts paled in comparison to Wilson's eventual involvement in World War I. Unlike Roosevelt, Wilson was a reluctant warrior, and as war spread in Europe in 1914, the president tried carefully to steer clear of the mess, declaring his nation's neutrality and hoping to keep the United States from being sucked into what was fast becoming a charnel house of death and destruction. He wanted America to be in a good position to play the role of arbiter, envisioning a day when the various warring nations would turn to the United States and say, "You were right, and we were wrong. . . . Now, in your self-possession, in your coolness, in your strength, may we not turn to you for counsel and for assistance?" (Clements, 1992, 117). From retirement Roosevelt rather uncharitably groused that Wilson's attempts to stay out of the war offered "a timid and spiritless neutrality," but Wilson's position was popular enough to win him reelection in 1916 with the slogan "he kept us out of war" (Cooper, 1983, 383).

But the president was coming to feel that Americans possessed a moral obligation to intervene in the Europeans' war; and he (like many of his fellow countrymen) grew increasingly incensed at what was perceived to be Germany's high-handed interference with American shipping on the high seas.

Whenever Wilson ran into problems with Congress or party politicians, his instincts led him to appeal directly to the people; and he now used his bully pulpit to explain why Americans should involve themselves in Europe's mess, setting the highest of ideals for the nation as it mobilized. "What we demand in this war, therefore, is nothing peculiar to ourselves," he told Congress in a January 1918 speech, "It is that the world be made fit and safe to live in; and particu-

larly that it be made safe for every peace-loving nation which, like our own, wishes to live its own life, determine its own institutions, be assured of justice and fair dealing by the other peoples of the world as against force and selfish aggression." Not since the days of Lincoln had a president placed the United States and its ideals in such a high global context. "All the peoples of the world are in effect partners in this interest," he intoned, "and for our own part we see very clearly that unless justice be done to others it will not be done to us. The program of the world's peace, therefore, is our program." Wilson's program would come to be known as the Fourteen Points, and they included a variety of strategies designed to promote global peace, including the establishment of a new League of Nations that would, in the president's words, offer "mutual guarantees of political independence and territorial integrity to great and small states alike" (www.firstworldwar.com/source/fourteenpoints.htm).

In the name of these high aspirations, the Wilson Administration oversaw a vast expansion of war-related government activities, many of which had never been tried before. The federal government took over coordination and standardization of key industries like the railroads, established price controls on vital goods and services, and instituted sweeping taxation and bond programs designed to pay for what rapidly became a very expensive undertaking. The government also created powerful new tools to defend the nation's internal security—sometimes too powerful, as federal authorities pursued enemies (real and perceived) with a zealousness that sometimes trampled on Americans' civil rights. The government also got directly involved in the propaganda business. In April 1917 Wilson issued an order establishing the Committee on Public Information, designed to oversee the government's pro-war media efforts and "arouse ardor and enthusiasm" for the war (Clements, 1992, 152).

As a war-making administration, Wilson's regime was unprecedented. In 1918 Congress passed the Overman Act, designed to streamline the ballooning federal war effort by giving Wilson the power to organize new government war agencies with little interference from Congress. For example, Wilson created a War Industries Board and gave it the power to regulate and control the activities of a vast array of business and military industries—all with relatively little input from the legislative branch. The president enthusiastically supported the Overman Act. He had been dismayed by Congress's partisan political wrangling over important wartime legislation, and this law empowered him to act largely as he saw fit in directing the machinery of the executive branch. And that machinery by 1918 had become vast, powerful, and to some Americans ominous. While Wilson was generally careful in using his new powers, a precedent had been set for the ways future presidents could arm the nation for total war.

In Wilson's hands the presidency became a vehicle for the idealistic hopes and dreams of an idealistic generation as he pursued projects that, he was convinced, would not only make the country but the entire world a much safer and better place. But in the end those high expectations ended badly. America and its allies won the war, yes, but Wilson's Fourteen Points shattered on the hard rocks of European cynicism and war-weary Americans' desire to retreat back into isolationism. With congressional opposition to the Treaty of Versailles and the new League of Nations stiffening, Wilson one last time appealed directly to the people, staging a punishing nationwide speaking tour that proved futile—Congress rejected the treaty and kept the United States out of the League—and that broke Wilson's frail health.

Where Roosevelt's enthusiasm had been boisterous and loud, Wilson affected a more intellectual demeanor—but the results were similar. Roosevelt was a man of action who hunted bears, wrestled steers, and fought wars with an unabashed relish; Wilson was a theorist and moralizing reformer who often thought in terms of ideas and abstractions. Historian John Milton Cooper dubbed the two presidents "the Warrior and the Priest." They were very different men; but differences aside, Roosevelt and Wilson both reflected a new century and a new generation that expected their leaders to act with progressive vigor.

Subsequent presidents of the 1920s were a studied contrast to the Warrior and Priest. They were almost de-activist presidents, and consciously so. Roosevelt's successor, William Howard Taft, was an early forerunner to the spirit of the 1920s presidents. Taft was a lawyer and jurist who thought TR's freewheeling ways were constitutionally suspect and sought to scale back Progressive expectations of presidential activism. Following in Woodrow Wilson's footsteps, Warren G. Harding's greatest ambition was simply to get out of the way of a booming postwar economy. He declared that "America's present need is not heroics, but healing; not nostrums, but normalcy; not revolution, but restoration; not agitation, but adjustment; not surgery, but serenity; not the dramatic, but the dispassionate (Trani and Wilson, 1977, 57–58).

Calvin Coolidge was particularly vigorous in his campaign to curb presidential vigor. When he assumed office in 1924, the nation was undergoing a postwar economic boom, and he would do nothing to upset that applecart. "We are not without our problems, but our most important problem is not to secure new advantages but to maintain those which we already possess," he declared. "I find ample warrant for satisfaction and encouragement. . . . Here stands our country, an example of tranquility at home, a patron of tranquility abroad" (www.yale .edu/lawweb/avalon/presiden/inaug/coo lidge.htm). Powered by this profoundly preservationist, conservative vision, Coolidge's days in the White House were a study in principled inactivity and—particularly following Roosevelt's and Wilson's seemingly endless supply of exuberant and intellectual rhetoric— presidential reticence. "A President cannot, with success, constantly appeal to the country," he believed. "After a time he will get no response. The people have

their own affairs to look after" (Coolidge, 1929, 224). Coolidge carried this sensible observation to extremes. A woman at a party once told the president she had bet someone she could get at least three words from him in conversation. "You lose," he replied. (McCoy, 1967, 112)

But it says something about the sea change Roosevelt and Wilson had wrought in the presidency that their immediate successors had to work to lower expectations. And almost despite themselves, Taft, Harding, and Coolidge, each in their own way, contributed to the ongoing growth and development of the twentieth-century White House. Harding was the first president to hire a speechwriter, for example, and Coolidge was an adroit manager of the press when the need arose.

A tipping point had been reached in the way Americans perceived the White House: it was no longer the staid guardian of respectability that it had been for the Founding presidents. Nor was it the halting, fits-and-starts institution of sometime reform and activism that it had been for the Jacksonians. And it had finally recovered from the doughfaces' lassitude and the damage wrought by Johnson and the other Reconstruction chief executives. Twentieth-century Americans either expected big things from the seat occupied by TR and Wilson, or they expected the Hardings and the Coolidges openly to rein in the presidency's latent power. But the power was there; everyone knew this was so.

THE GREATEST GENERATION

If the Progressive generation created the tipping point for creation of the modern presidency, then Roosevelt's cousin Franklin shoved it the rest of the way over. The members of TR's generation found that, by and large, they rather liked having a robust presidency, even if on occasion the times called for that power to lie dormant. But those in FDR's generation discovered that a powerful chief executive was something they desperately needed.

Few generations have been so profoundly tested. Writer and broadcaster Tom Brokaw famously dubbed them the Greatest Generation, the generation of the 1940s, observing that these Americans met "high expectations" of "service, sacrifice, and heroics" during World War II "and then returned home to lead ordinary lives." They were, Brokaw wrote, "the kind of men and women who always have been the foundation of the American way of life" (1998, 16). And it was not just the war. Prior to 1941 the Greatest Generation faced the Great Depression, with its horrible economic and social fallout. That generation needed someone at the helm to explain, repeatedly and eloquently, just where the nation was going and how he intended to get them there. FDR was that man.

Roosevelt had an instinctive grasp for what his generation needed when he assumed office in 1932: not a reticent conservative like Coolidge (or, for that matter, Roosevelt's predecessor, Herbert Hoover); not an abstract professorial lecturer in a Wilsonian mold; and not even TR's patented effervescent exhortations. Mired in economic depression, doubt, and financial disaster, FDR saw that Americans needed a teacher, patient and genial, but firm.

It was a delicate balance, but one that the president was well equipped, by talent and temperament, to strike. He was blessed with fine speaking skills, including a mellifluous voice that lent itself well to radio formats. Like other great presidents, he understood the importance of image making for a president, a knowledge given particular vitality given FDR's need to carefully stage manage every public appearance in ways that hid his polio-induced physical handicaps.

Other circumstances intersected his talents. Cousin Teddy took over the White House at the dawn of the modern media age; FDR's presidency occurred when media technology was more fully blossomed. The press, newsreel footage, and photography were joined by the radios that sat in millions of American households by 1932. Roosevelt's generation was comfortable with media exposure in ways previously unknown, and the president was likewise remarkably comfortable in catering to its media needs. "If a large part of the modern presidency relates to the techniques of public relations and ballyhoo, then Franklin D. Roosevelt deserves recognition as a master of those arts," historian Lewis L. Gould observed (2003, 83).

Americans had also grown accustomed to an activist chief executive on the

President Franklin D. Roosevelt delivers one of his popular fireside chats, a series of evening radio talks to the American public. Roosevelt used these chats to explain New Deal programs during the Great Depression and war policies during World War II. (Library of Congress)

domestic front, with Teddy Roosevelt's trust-busting ways and various other policy initiatives by early-twentieth-century presidents as they tried to influence congressional decision making. But those presidents had merely been dipping their toes in the water compared to FDR, who leapt into the domestic fray with unbridled enthusiasm. His presidency created the "first hundred days" tradition, by which new presidents are measured according to how much they can accomplish during their first one hundred days in office—rather like a presidential wind sprint. Roosevelt did not disappoint, proposing a veritable blizzard of new federal programs during his first hundred days. The contrast with the previous administrations—with Hoover and the studied minimalism of Coolidge and Harding—was striking. Most people approved of the change. "Well, he's taken the ship of state and turned it right around," enthused one of his aides (Morgan, 1985, 375).

This frenzied domestic activism continued throughout his first two terms of office. Following in the footsteps of Teddy's Square Deal and Wilson's New Freedom, Roosevelt called his program the New Deal. The phrase was absolutely appropriate: in scale and type, FDR's programs were revolutionary. A federally subsidized social safety net for older and unemployed Americans, safeguards on banking and investment excesses, worker assistance programs of every shape and size designed to put the millions of Americans displaced by the Great Depression back to work, federal funding for construction projects that brought electricity to rural America, the National Industrial Recovery Act, the Home Owners Loan Corporation, the Farm Security Administration, the Fair Labor Standards Act—Americans had never seen anything quite like it. Some New Deal Programs were successful, others less so, but at least it was clear to everyone that the federal government had no intention of sitting idly by while the Depression wrecked the national economy and social fabric.

What was striking about all of these programs was the commanding presence of the Roosevelt White House in their design and execution. It was "an exceedingly personal enterprise," noted historian Paul Conkin. "Its disparate pro-

grams were unified only by the personality of Franklin D. Roosevelt" (1975, 1). As we've seen, other presidents had made their wishes known to Congress concerning national domestic policy, some more so than others. But none functioned on a par with Roosevelt. His administration created comprehensive and detailed legislative proposals, carefully tracked the progress of bills through the complicated byways of Congress—"I am [informed] on an hourly basis, and the situation changes almost momentarily," he said of one of his bills—and did not hesitate to make his displeasure known when Congress did not act according to his wishes. The same applied to the Supreme Court. The Court had "relegated to the horse and buggy definition of interstate commerce," FDR fumed during a press conference after the justices struck down the National Industrial Recovery Act as unconstitutional (Morgan, 1985, 422–423).

Under the Roosevelt Administration, the executive branch steadily increased in size and complexity, adding new layers of administration and bureaucracy. The trend was not immediately apparent; in fact, during his first six years in office, FDR added no new executive jobs or staff positions, preferring instead to merely flesh out the structure put in place by earlier presidents. Nor was he a grand design type of planner, much preferring a presidency that was fluid and immediately adaptable to changing circumstances. But as the New Deal grew in scope and complexity, so too did FDR's staffing and budget needs—not to mention the larger-than-usual personal retinue required by a man whose physical mobility was limited. By the late 1930s, the executive department had never been so large or complex.

There was no explicit constitutional language authorizing such a domestic blitz, unless one counts Article II's general charge that the president "take Care that the Laws be faithfully executed" or more generally the Preamble's requirement that all federal officials promote the "general Welfare." These were pretty small constitutional hooks upon which to hang FDR's sudden and massive infusion of presidential power. No other president had tried with such unabashed activism to influence the creation of domestic legislation on this scale, and many older, conservative Americans were appalled. On the other hand, there was no specific constitutional prohibition, either, especially when FDR began to speak regularly of governing in a time of emergency and to use that emergency to justify expanding presidential power. "It is to be hoped that the normal balance of executive and legislative authority may be wholly adequate to meet the unprecedented task before us," he declared. "But it may be that an unprecedented demand and need for undelayed action may call for temporary departure from that normal balance of public procedure. . . . But in the event that the Congress shall fail to take one of these two courses, and in the event that the national emergency is still critical, I shall not evade the clear course of duty that will then confront me. I shall ask the Congress for the one remaining instrument to meet the crisis—broad Executive

power to wage a war against the emergency, as great as the power that would be given to me if we were in fact invaded by a foreign foe" (www.yale.edu/lawweb/avalon/presiden/inaug/froos1.htm).

There most certainly was an "emergency" in 1932, with the nation deep in the throes of an unprecedented Depression. But beyond this fact, Roosevelt set a precedent that future presidents would forever be tempted to emulate, which was to justify any expansion of presidential authority by claiming reaction to an "emergency," real or perceived. This could be good or bad, depending upon one's point of view. Roosevelt certainly has his critics in this regard; Republicans of the day made careers out of denouncing Roosevelt's executive excesses. "Delusions of power, dictatorial, [and] intoxicated by authority," were epithets commonly applied to the president by his detractors (Morgan, 1985, 428).

But such arguments aside, it is safe to say that a majority of Americans approved of Roosevelt's grand expansion of presidential authority. The election results speak for themselves. Roosevelt was easily reelected in 1936, and then—shattering the ancient two-term tradition from the days of George Washington—he was elected yet again in 1940. While historians still debate how effective the New Deal was in ending the Depression, there is little doubt that, by 1940, most Americans expected their presidents to lead with verve and energy when the times required. No longer would Americans tolerate a Coolidge-esque deference to congressional authority or any constitutional lectures about separation of powers. They wanted action.

FDR's generation would also eventually place its imprimatur of approval on his equally ambitious foreign policy agenda, though this would not be so evident at first. As the nation seemed to be slowly emerging from the more murky depths of the Depression during the late 1930s, it found itself threatened with new crises abroad, as Europe careened toward war and Japan asserted claims to much of the Pacific Rim. There was very little doubt where the president's loyalties lay: he deeply sympathized with Great Britain and its embattled allies, and he openly worried about Japanese aggression.

The nation, however, was deeply divided. The unhappy aftermath of World War I had left a bad taste in the mouths of many Americans, who shied away from suggestions of any new American intervention in world affairs. Better to stay out of Europe's troubles and let the vast oceans protect America, as they had done for centuries. Some warned of a dark conspiracy to sacrifice American soldiers in the interest not of national safety or democracy, but of protecting rich capitalists. "Perhaps, despite the advice of Washington of no foreign entanglements . . . some miraculous way shall be found to project America into the next maelstrom," thundered isolationist radio broadcaster Charles Coughlin. "And democracy once more, thinking that it has power within its soul, shall rise up to clap and applaud, because the youth of the land is going abroad to make the world safe for what? Safe for dictator-

ship? Safe against communism abroad when we have communism at home? Safe from socialism in France when we have socialism in America? Or safe, safe for the international bankers" (www://historymatters.gmu.edu/d/5111).

FDR had little patience with such thinking. He believed it was delusional to think of America as "a lone island in a world dominated by force," a delusion that might, in his words, lead to the "nightmare of a people lodged in prison . . . and fed through the bars from day to day by the contemptuous, unpitying masters of other continents" (Dallek, 1981, 228). But however he may have felt, Roosevelt had to tread carefully. He pursued tactics less direct but in their way just as activist as those he employed with the New Deal. He called on Congress to initiate arms embargoes to the belligerent powers, he wanted a reduction in protective tariffs to help the industries of embattled nations like England and France, and he pressed for an innovative Lend-Lease program that gave the British a number of American ships and a quantity of military supplies in exchange for the right to use British bases abroad. He did just about everything possible, short of an actual declaration of war, to help Britain and France.

The Japanese made Roosevelt's task simpler with its sudden assault on Pearl Harbor in December 1941, handing the president a symbol that he could employ to great effect in unifying the nation. Hitler also cooperated by very foolishly declaring war on the United States a few days later. Now FDR did not need to tread so carefully; he led a largely unified nation. "Always will we remember the character of the onslaught against us," he declared. "No matter how long it may take us to overcome this premeditated invasion, the American people in their righteous might will win through to absolute victory" (www.law.ou.edu/hist/infamy.html).

During the war itself, the Roosevelt Administration continued to flex the presidency's now bulging muscles. The bureaucracy directed by the executive branch ballooned in size as the presidency led a vast expansion of the nation's economic might. Almost overnight the federal government found itself managing the machinery of a vast wartime economy and a military establishment that dwarfed anything Americans—indeed, the entire world—had ever seen. Price controls, rationing coupons, war bonds, scrap iron drives, propaganda films, the draft, internal security and intelligence activities—all now fell more or less directly under Washington, D.C.,'s aegis.

Leading the nation during such a gargantuan war effort, FDR as commander in chief likewise found himself taking the presidency into new areas of authority and expertise. For example, Roosevelt became the first president to make regular trips abroad. Other presidents had traveled outside the United States while still in office. Cousin Teddy was the first when he visited the Panama Canal project in 1906, and Wilson had made a highly publicized trip to Europe in 1918 to participate in the peace talks that ended World War I. But these visits had been more along the lines of showcase journeys, one-time-only excursions abroad that were notable more for their novelty than anything else. Roosevelt, however, made his visits abroad—particularly conferences with Britain's Winston Churchill and the Soviet Union's Joseph Stalin—integral pieces of his foreign policy mosaic. Here again, FDR found himself going where no previous chief executive had ever quite gone before.

As during the Depression, Roosevelt had his critics, with some wondering whether the presidency was growing too powerful for the good of the country. There was, indeed, a darker side to the White House's wartime authority. FDR authorized internal security measures—such as the internment of thousands of Japanese Americans for no good reason and the use of secret military tribunals to try suspected saboteurs—that set disturbing precedents for the future. Personally honest himself and generally immune to the pursuit of power for power's sake, Roosevelt nevertheless created new avenues of presidential authority that carried the potential for abuse and wandered very far afield from the Revolutionary generation's vision of a limited chief executive.

But again, as during the Depression, the majority of Americans backed FDR and his policies. He won reelection to an unprecedented fourth term in 1940, despite the fact that his return broke the longstanding two-term limit, a tradition begun by George Washington, and also despite the fact that his health was noticeably declining. He would live only three months into his new term, passing

Soviet leader Joseph Stalin (left), U.S. president Franklin D. Roosevelt (center), British prime minister Winston Churchill (right), and various military officers meet on the portico of the Russian Embassy in Tehran, Iran, in 1943. The conference, which was held from November 28 to December 1, 1943, was a meeting of the Big Three to discuss the strategy of the Allies during World War II. (Library of Congress)

---

away suddenly from a cerebral hemorrhage while on vacation at Warm Springs, Georgia. The nation was stunned on a level rarely felt; for this generation, FDR had been *the* president, the only one that mattered. One schoolgirl later recalled that when she heard the news, she felt that "this was going to be the end of the world, because he was the only president I'd ever known" (Goodwin, 1994, 602).

THE WATERGATE GENERATION

For the most part, FDR's generation trusted its presidents, on a visceral level as much as anything else. Roosevelt's fireside chats brought him into many Americans' homes. Truman was "Harry," the sometimes brutally honest midwesterner whom most people tended to trust implicitly. Eisenhower offered a grandfatherly, benign countenance to the presidency, with his golf games and genial smile. Even when these men made mistakes—as in 1960, for example, when Ike had to publicly admit that American aircraft were spying on the Soviet Union following the downing of an American U-2 spy plane by the Soviets—Americans generally were willing to forgive and forget.

Then again, Americans had always tried to give their chief executives the benefit of the doubt; this was the chair filled by the great George Washington, after all. There had been presidential scandals down through the years, of course. Andrew Jackson was peripherally involved in a scandal related to the wife of his secretary of war, Margaret Eaton. Abraham Lincoln fired his first secretary of war, Simon Cameron, at least in part because the latter mixed corruption with general incompetence. Scandals of every stripe plagued the Grant Administration, casting a pall over it through both of its troubled terms. While some of these scandals had weakened the presidency in the short term, they had never caused long-lasting deleterious effects. For most Americans, the man in the White House wore a white hat.

By 1960, however, various circumstances were converging to erode the perpetuation of trust that had protected the presidency for so long. There was first and foremost the ever-expanding power of the office, and this in the nuclear age, when the occupant of the White House literally had his finger on the button that could destroy civilization. And it was not just nuclear weapons, either. For the

first time in history, the cold war generation of Americans chose not to dismantle but rather expand its peacetime armed forces, fearing the ever-present, latent threat of a powerful Soviet military machine. Where previous presidents were required hastily to rebuild the army and navy almost from scratch in times of emergency, the cold war presidents now had millions of soldiers and billions of dollars worth of military equipment at their immediate disposal, all of which could be deployed by the White House before Congress or the American people could (if they felt it necessary) prevent it. Even a career soldier like Eisenhower was alarmed. In one of his last speeches as president, Ike pointed out that "this conjunction of an immense military establishment and a large arms industry is new in the American experience," and he warned that "we must guard against the acquisition of unwarranted influence, whether sought or unsought, by the military-industrial complex. The potential for the disastrous rise of misplaced power exists and will persist" (Richardson, 1979, 186).

In addition to the worries caused by the new military powers at the president's disposal, Americans in the new media age now were able to see, for better or worse, the intimate details of a president's life—warts and all. By the time Kennedy entered the White House in 1960, television had joined radio, films, and still photography as a powerful medium through which the president could establish contact with the American people. For the Progressive generation, the scratchy sound of Teddy Roosevelt's voice on a phonograph had been a novelty. For the Greatest Generation, FDR's fireside chats had been a wonderful new communication device with which presidents could directly interact with everyday Americans. By 1960 all of this was commonplace; with the arrival of television, the new generation of Americans expected face-to-face communication with the president. The media created almost a presumption of such contact; indeed, any president who did not offer at least semi-regular press conferences, weekly radio addresses, and a daily television presence ran the risk of being criticized as isolated and being out of touch.

The White House was a fishbowl like never before, which meant that each and every presidential scar would be visible for all to see. There had always been some skeletons in the White House closet, or at the very least things that presidents preferred to keep from public view. FDR wanted no one to know about his polio-related disabilities, and John F. Kennedy's aides worked overtime to keep people from learning about his own severe health problems—Addison's disease and severe back problems stemming from wartime injuries—as well as his womanizing (which led to still another health concern—venereal disease). Very few people knew of Kennedy's physical or moral failings, however. Members of the White House press corps—who generally liked JFK anyway—buried these stories or dismissed them as unfounded rumors. But the facades became increasingly more difficult to maintain as the number and sophistication of prying eyes

grew and were increasingly trained on the White House.

Kennedy's successor carried a strong aroma of scandal and possible wrongdoing that long predated his career on the national stage. Rumors swirled around Lyndon Johnson concerning the possibility that he had fixed his own election to the Senate, that he possessed questionable relationships with various Texas oil interests, and that he profited illegally from his close ties to the Federal Communications Commission. The ever-growing morass in Vietnam added another layer of distrust to Johnson's already somewhat dubious reputation, with whispers that the president had surreptitiously dragged the country into a questionable Vietnam War by questionable means and that he was unwilling to admit that the entire venture was a mistake. "'Stalemate' is a fighting word in Washington," wrote New York Times reporter Johnnie Apple in 1967. "President Johnson rejects it as a description of the situation in Vietnam. But it is the word used by almost all Americans here [in Vietnam]" (Dallek, 1998, 474–475).

The presidential image in general was starting to show some ragged edges during the 1960s. Still, presidents enjoyed a vast reservoir of goodwill and benefit-of-the-doubt thinking from most Americans, who continued to believe that most of their presidents most of the time were fine men. The old patina of respectability and deferral protected LBJ from much—if not all—finger wagging. He left the White House in 1969 looking tragic rather than sinister, pummeled and finally beaten down by war and its attendant ravages. "WE STILL LOVE YOU, LYNDON," read a college student's sign as he said farewell to Washington, D.C., and traveled back home to Texas (Dallek, 1998, 599). When he died a short time later, it is fair to say that LBJ was a man more admired (and in some ways pitied) than hated, and whatever his failings, he had done the office of president no serious or lasting damage.

For his successor, however, matters would be much different. Richard Nixon would do more to alter fundamentally his generation's perception of the White House than any other president. In him the various circumstances contributing to a profound erosion of public trust in the presidency would finally come together: an exercise of executive authority that struck many as arrogant and deeply disturbing, the blinding glare of the modern media spotlight, and a generation's distrust of its leaders generally.

Like LBJ, Nixon had a reputation as a hard-edged, take-no-prisoners type that stretched back long before he entered the White House; when he became president he brought that tendency with him, along with advisers who quickly became known for their blunt ruthlessness. Chief of Staff Bob Haldeman, for example, became the keeper of the president's schedule, and he severely limited various advisers' "face time" with the president. "Put it in a memo," he told one White House assistant. "The President's time is valuable. This is the system. It is the way the President wants it, and that's the way it's going to be" (Reeves, 2001, 71).

Nixon strove mightily to convey an impression of benign dynamism, of energy and enthusiasm that seemed warm, not sinister. "Add element of lift to each appearance," he advised to himself in a sort of to-do list for the 1970 new year. "Hard work—Imagination—Compassion—Understanding of young—Intellectual expansion. Cool—Strong—Organized—Temperate—Exciting" (Dallek, 1998, 156). Image making of this sort permeated the Nixon White House on all matters, great and small. He once acquired a dog in an attempt to look more family oriented and warm; White House aides had to leave a trail of food leading to Nixon's pocket to coax the animal, who otherwise would not go near the president.

But underneath the showcased puppy dogs and attempts to appear compassionate was the nasty streak of a president who trusted no one, brooded endlessly on the real and perceived machinations of his real and perceived enemies, often watched the film *Patton* (1970) to steel his resolve, and thought of politics as combat. When a confidential letter about a minor domestic matter was leaked to the press, Nixon told Haldeman to execute "the German option." "You first are to find out how many people the letter was sent out to," Nixon ordered, and after compiling a list of these people, "tell them that they have 48 hours for one of them to come up and say he leaked the letter. If they do not [their boss] is to ask for the resignation of all six. This is the battle plan. Execute it" (Dallek, 1998, 195).

The presidency's ruthless tone was evident even before the Watergate scandal erupted; but during that agonizing na-

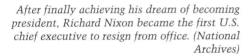

After finally achieving his dream of becoming president, Richard Nixon became the first U.S. chief executive to resign from office. (National Archives)

tional nightmare, his various foibles were laid bare for all to see. This was particularly the case when Nixon was forced to turn over portions of the tapes that recorded his conversations with aides, conversations that revealed him to be a man given to extraordinary hatred, fear, and paranoia as well as a disturbing willingness to use presidential power as a means of curbing government investigations into Watergate's various wrongdoings. On one of the tapes, Haldeman said to Nixon that the FBI should be told, "Stay the hell out of this, this is, ah, business here we don't want you to go any further into it." Haldeman then said to Nixon, "and uh, that would take care of it." Nixon was then heard essentially

agreeing with Haldeman. "All right, fine, I understand it all," he replied to Haldeman's various cover-up machinations (www.nixon.archives.gov/find/tapes/watergate/trial).

As we saw in chapter 2, Watergate was a product of many things, including Nixon's arrogance and myriad insecurities and the willingness of the president and his aides to break the law in the name of both personal ambition and national security. By the time the scandal was over, Nixon was not just tarnished by the fact that he had been forced to leave office under a dire threat of impeachment; he was further tarnished, almost as deeply so, by how the scandal laid bare the flinty, malicious underside of the Nixon presidency. Here was a man who hated, and hated mightily; and the modern presidency had given him enough power that he could translate his hatreds and his inner demons into political reality. He could coldly order thousands of young Americans to their deaths in the jungles of Vietnam and try to bomb the Vietnamese into oblivion in the name of a frighteningly amoral realpolitik; he could create a secret organization within the very walls of the White House—the so-called Plumbers—who with no real checks on their behavior could engage in the most appalling, clandestine, and illegal behavior; and he could give free rein to some of the most destructive impulses of his nature and see some of them translated directly into presidential policymaking. The Greatest Generation could justifiably look with pride on the "imperial presidency" of FDR; the generation that followed could look upon the presidency of Richard Nixon not with pride but trepidation, "imperial" carrying sinister overtones when associated with Nixon and his aides. Small wonder that national trust in the White House plummeted.

The result was a fundamental alteration of the office, but in ways not always easy to detect with the naked eye. The Nixon Administration's behavior did not, for example, create constitutional alterations in the office itself, along the lines of the two-term limit of the Twenty-second Amendment (passed in direct response to FDR's multiple terms). But it did lead to new laws passed by Congress: campaign finance reform, for example, in light of the fact that Wa-

tergate's foundations lay in some egregious abuses of power by the Committee to Re-Elect the President. Watergate also inspired creation of a special prosecutor's office designed to investigate future presidential wrongdoings with an ostensibly independent eye. Also, Nixon's highhanded policies regarding Vietnam contributed to congressional passage of the War Powers Act (1973), which required congressional approval (after the fact) of military actions ordered by the president.

But more important, though less noticeable, were the cultural changes wrought in the White House by Nixon. Americans lost their presidential innocence in the backwash of Watergate. No longer would Americans simply assume that presidents were telling the truth when they spoke, that they exercised power responsibly, or that they were not engineering backroom deals out of the public's sight. Not all of this was Nixon's doing, of course; in fact, one could argue that it was inevitable, albeit a long time coming. But Nixon and his generation together wrought an unforeseen change in circumstances.

CONCLUSION

We still live largely in the Nixon generation of presidents, though Watergate is now over thirty years gone. There is now a darkness about the presidency, a foreboding that is not just the soot left over from the Watergate era. It comes as much from the realization among Americans that the presidency is, for better or worse, the single most powerful political office on earth—indeed, it is the most powerful office in human history. No European monarch has ever commanded the vast economic and military resources available to the presidents. Even at the height of their powers, the Roman emperors could not with a single command create the global conflagration possible in the event of a nuclear war. Even the papacy, when it was the primary vehicle of the Christian faith, could not quite equal a modern president's capacity for shaping public opinion. There is the possibility of much good in this; there is also the potential for much that is bad.

Presidents still echo the Revolutionary generation in their attempts to preserve the semblance of democratic simplicity. Jimmy Carter visibly carried his lunch to work in a brown paper bag and saw to it that journalists recorded the fact. Bill Clinton made it a point to be filmed jogging in ordinary (and frankly rather baggy) gym clothes and eating cheeseburgers at fast-food restaurants. George Bush Jr. was reading stories to grade school children when the terrorist assault on the World Trade Center occurred.

Yet the post-Watergate generation knows that the outwardly still presidential waters run very, very deep. In the 1995 Hollywood film *Nixon,* the president (superbly portrayed by actor Anthony Hopkins) tells a balky supporter that he can if he chooses make the supporter's life very difficult. "Why, Dick," he asks, "are you threatening me?" Hopkins's Nixon smiles thinly, and replies, "Presidents don't threaten. They don't have to."

FURTHER READING

Basler, Roy P., ed., *The Collected Works of Abraham Lincoln,* 9 vols. (New Brunswick, NJ: Rutgers University Press, 1953–1955).

Boot, Max, *The Savage Wars of Peace: Small Wars and the Rise of American Power* (New York: Basic Books, 2002).

Brokaw, Tom, *The Greatest Generation* (New York: Random House, 1998).

Castel, Albert E., *The Presidency of Andrew Johnson* (Lawrence: University Press of Kansas, 1979).

Clements, Kendrick A., *The Presidency of Woodrow Wilson* (Lawrence: University Press of Kansas, 1992).

Conkin, Paul, *The New Deal,* 2nd ed. (Arlington Heights, IL: AHM Pub., 1975).

Coolidge, Calvin, *The Autobiography of Calvin Coolidge* (New York: Cosmopolitan Book Corp., 1929).

Cooper, John M., *The Warrior and the Priest: Woodrow Wilson and Theodore Roosevelt* (Cambridge, MA: Harvard University Press, 1983).

Dallek, Robert, *Franklin D. Roosevelt and American Foreign Policy, 1932–1945* (New York: Oxford University Press, 1981).

Dallek, Robert, *Flawed Giant: Lyndon Johnson, 1960–1973* (New York: Oxford University Press, 1998).

Dalton, Kathleen, *Theodore Roosevelt: A Strenuous Life* (New York: Vintage, 2002).

Donald, David, *Charles Sumner and the Rights of Man* (New York: Alfred A. Knopf, 1970).

Flexner, James, *George Washington* (Boston: Little, Brown, 1965).

Foner, Eric., *Reconstruction: America's Unfinished Revolution, 1863–1877* (New York: Harper and Row, 1988).

Freehling, William W., *Prelude to Civil War: The Nullification Controversy in South Carolina, 1816–1836* (New York: Harper and Row, 1968).

Gara, Larry, *The Presidency of Franklin Pierce* (Lawrence: University Press of Kansas, 1991).

Gelderman, Carol W., *All the President's Words: The Bully Pulpit and the Creation of the Virtual Presidency* (New York: Walker and Co., 1997).

Goodwin, Doris Kearns, *No Ordinary Time: Franklin and Eleanor Roosevelt—The Homefront in World War II* (New York: Simon and Schuster, 1994).

Gould, Lewis, *The Presidency of William McKinley* (Lawrence: University Press of Kansas, 1980).

Gould, Lewis, *The Modern U.S. Presidency* (Lawrence: University Press of Kansas, 2003).

Holt, Michael F., *Political Parties and American Political Development: From the Age of Jackson to the Age of Lincoln* (Baton Rouge: Louisiana State University Press, 1992).

Kennedy, David M., *Over Here: The First World War and American Society* (New York: Oxford University Press, 1980).

Mayer, Henry, *All on Fire: William Lloyd Garrison and the Abolition of Slavery* (New York: St. Martin's, 1998).

McCoy, Donald, *Calvin Coolidge: The Quiet President* (New York: Macmillan, 1967).

McCullough, David, *John Adams* (New York: Simon and Schuster, 2001).

McDonald, Forrest, *The American Presidency: An Intellectual History* (Lawrence: University Press of Kansas, 1994).

McKitrick, Eric L., *Andrew Johnson and Reconstruction* (Chicago: University of Chicago Press, 1960).

McPherson, James M., *Ordeal by Fire: The Civil War and Reconstruction* (New York: Alfred A. Knopf, 1982).

Morgan, Ted, *FDR: A Biography* (New York: Simon and Schuster, 1985).

Morris, Edmund, *Theodore Rex* (New York: Random House, 2001).

Peterson, Merrill, ed., *Thomas Jefferson: Writings* (New York: Library of America, 1984).

Potter, David M., *The Impending Crisis, 1848–1861* (New York: Harper and Row, 1976).

Reeves, Richard, *President Nixon: Alone in the White House* (New York: Simon and Schuster, 2001).

Remini, Robert V., *Andrew Jackson and the Course of American Empire* (New York: Harper and Row, 1977).

Remini, Robert V., *Andrew Jackson and the Course of American Democracy* (New York: Harper and Row, 1984).

Rhodehamel, John, *George Washington: Writings* (New York: Library of America, 1997).

Richardson, Elmo R., *The Presidency of Dwight D. Eisenhower* (Lawrence: University Press of Kansas, 1979).

Schlesinger, Arthur M., *The Age of Jackson* (Boston: Little, Brown, 1945).

Trani, Eugene P., and David L. Wilson, *The Presidency of Warren G. Harding* (Lawrence: University Press of Kansas, 1977).

4

THE POLITICS OF THE PRESIDENCY

"Mr. Lincoln is committed to no one on earth in relation to office—He promised nothing to gain his nomination, and has promised nothing" (Donald, 1995, 250). So said David Davis, Illinois circuit court judge, future Supreme Court justice, and Abraham Lincoln's campaign manager for the 1860 Republican nomination. Rumors were flying that Davis and his fellow Lincoln backers promised jobs and influence to various delegates in return for their support. Word even reached Lincoln, waiting impatiently at his home in Springfield. "Make no contracts that will bind me," he instructed his supporters (Basler, 1953–1955, 4: 50).

Davis was an imposing bear of a man, weighing nearly three hundred pounds and possessed of an ego very nearly as large. He had known Lincoln for nearly twenty-five years, had roomed with him on the Illinois Eighth Circuit as they and other lawyers and judges traveled back roads and hamlets litigating cases of every shape and variety. In the spring of 1860, the judge took it upon himself—along with other Illinois friends of Lincoln—to secure the Republican presidential nomination for Lincoln.

It was a task made easier by the fact that the party—all of six years old in 1860—had seen fit to hold its nominating convention in Chicago, Lincoln's backyard and a town where he had many supporters and friends. Housed in a huge wooden structure nicknamed "the wigwam," the Republicans could smell victory that spring because of their Democratic opponents' split into fractious northern and southern camps over the omnipresent issue of slavery. Republican leaders and their allies were mustering their forces for a Chicago political showdown. New York politico Thurlow Weed—who backed his state's senator, William Seward—was said to have shipped thirteen railroad cars of supporters to the convention.

PRESIDENTS AND THEIR PARTIES

Davis could arguably be called the first campaign manager in American presidential history. In an age when Americans thought outright campaigning by presidential candidates was bad form—the office should seek the man, not the other way around, it was said—Lincoln could not afford to manage the campaign himself. He was tempted. "The taste is in my mouth a little," he told one friend

129

(Gienapp, 2002, 68). To another he confided that "he was almost too much of a candidate to go [to Chicago], and not quite enough to stay at home" (Donald, 1995, 246). But stay at home he did, passing the time as best he could while Davis and others pressed his interests in Chicago.

Davis may have made no "contracts," per se, but he and other Lincoln supporters did do plenty of behind-the-scenes maneuvering in the wigwam. They successfully acted to thwart the cause of Seward, probably the front-runner for the nomination as the convention began, by peeling Seward votes away on the first ballot and then getting a number of delegations to commit to Lincoln as their second choice. They spoke to the delegates from Pennsylvania, who controlled a powerful bloc of votes, trying to convince them that Seward and other better-known Republicans were in fact a little too well-known, having made many enemies as well as friends—so why not go for a relatively obscure but entirely viable choice like Lincoln? They even packed the galleries with pro-Lincoln enthusiasts (not a difficult task, given the wigwam's Illinois location) who cheered wildly whenever Lincoln's name was mentioned, creating the impression that he was backed by a groundswell of popular support within the party.

Lincoln was not present, but he kept close tabs on the proceedings in Chicago, and before the convention he met with Davis and his team to map out their strategy. "I suppose I am not the first choice of a very great many," he astutely observed. But this could be turned to his advantage.

Let Seward and the others founder on their own controversies, Lincoln thought. "Our policy, then, is to give no offence to others—leave them in a position to come to us" (Gienapp, 2002, 69).

It was as masterful a political performance as was ever mounted by a presidential hopeful, for events unfolded pretty much exactly as Lincoln expected. The Chicago convention went through a series of ballots, the first of which favored Seward and other big-name Republicans, but without the margin necessary for victory. As Lincoln's name began creeping up the list, his managers worked to strip delegations away from Seward and the others, arguing that only a man like Lincoln, who had made no powerful enemies, could secure a party victory in November. All the while their stage-managing tactics paid big dividends, with Lincoln supporters raising the roof every time their man was mentioned.

On the convention's third day, Lincoln gained the nomination. When the news arrived via telegraph in Springfield, he was found playing handball in a town alley. Taking the telegraph dispatch, he pointed toward his house and said to the gathering crowd of well-wishers, "I must go home: there is a little short woman there that is more interested in this matter than I am." As he left, a number of men tried to shake his hand. The new Republican nominee joked, "Boys, you had better not come and shake hands with me now that you have an opportunity—for you do not know what influence this nomination may have on me. I am human, you know" (Wilson and Davis, 1998, 492).

He was right, of course; he was both human and a politician. The presidency is by nature a political office. This seems so self-evident as to be almost trite, but it is amazing how often Americans lose sight of this simple fact. Presidents are first and foremost politicians; they are people seeking the highest public office in the land by persuading a majority of the voters to cast their ballots for them. However much Americans of Mr. Lincoln's time—and quite often before and since 1860—wished to pretend otherwise, presidential candidates must by necessity campaign for the office, either overtly or otherwise. It is worse than useless to pretend otherwise. The office has never in fact sought the man.

Yet there is a consistent expectation in American life that presidents should somehow be above the supposedly grubby everyday machinations of the political system. This line of thinking began with the first president, George Washington, and in many ways continues down to the present day. Even modern presidential candidates would do well not to seem too eager for the office; unbridled ambition for the White House still has a rather unseemly air about it.

Appearances notwithstanding, all presidents are, to a greater or lesser extent, party men, deeply enmeshed within the operating systems of their party's machinery. Again, this seems to be self-evident. But just as Americans tend to downplay the role of politics in the presidency, so too do we wish sometimes to believe that our presidents are not partisans, beholden to organized cadres of political backers for their jobs. It all smacks

too much of the stereotypical smoke-filled back room, one-hand-washes-the-other deal making that the nation's political culture grudgingly accepts but still looks upon with suspicion. We like to think that our presidents, at least in their finer moments, can rise above that sort of thing and govern for the good of the entire country.

Presidents themselves are typically well aware of this, and most go out of their way not to appear too overtly partisan in their behavior. In their Inaugural Addresses, for example, presidents very rarely even mention political parties by name; and when they do, they stress the party's lack of importance relative to the national good. "Our two-party system has served us well over the years, but never better than in those times of great challenge when we came together not as Democrats or Republicans, but as Americans united in a common cause," Ronald Reagan declared in 1980 (www.yale.edu/lawweb/avalon). And in 1912 Woodrow Wilson became the first Democratic Party candidate to ascend to the White House in over fifty years, reflecting the party's disastrous popular identification with slavery and secession during and after the Civil War. He could not help but mention the fact. "There has been a change of government," he observed, "The offices of President and Vice-President have been put into the hands of Democrats." But he then immediately distanced himself from any appearance of partisan crowing. "The success of a party means little except when the Nation is using that party for a large and definite purpose," he argued, and "no one can mistake the purpose for which the Nation now seeks to use the Democratic Party. It seeks to use it to interpret a change in its own plans and point of view. . . . We have been refreshed by a new insight into our own life" (www.yale.edu/lawweb/avalon).

It is tempting to dismiss such protestations of nonpartisan unity as a peculiar species of American political hypocrisy. In the name of a rather unrealistic and mythical belief in presidential civic virtue, it could be argued, Americans require their presidents to pretend that they are not what they in fact are: politicians and party stalwarts who run for a highly political office and safeguard whenever possible their party's self-interests.

That said, however, it is also only fair to point out that, although presidents typically act to protect their party's interests, they also sometimes set the needs of their party and their own political self-interests aside when governing. One could argue, for example, that Lincoln's embrace of immediate emancipation as a war aim (and by definition as a Republican Party measure) in the fall of 1862 was politically an extremely risky move. In a nation rife with bigotry and racial prejudice, Republicans had for years carefully delineated their position as supporting only a very gradual disappearance of American slavery, helped along barely (if at all) by government action. Lincoln himself had been elected on just such a platform, one he explicitly restated when he was elected in 1860. And yet less than two years later both he

and his party took the leap in the dark toward emancipation and its consequences. The deed cost Lincoln's party dearly in the off-year elections, and—had events on the battlefield taken a different turn—might have cost him reelection, as well.

Moreover, it would not do to overemphasize a president's party identification when it comes to evaluating his political ideology and ideals. Ideology and party identification have never been entirely consistent in this country, for presidents or any other elected officials. In recent years, Republicans have tended to become overwhelmingly conservative, Democrats liberal. But carry this back just a few years and these intersections become highly problematic. What do we call a Dixiecrat white southern Democrat from the 1960s, for example, who wanted to preserve Jim Crow racism in America? Certainly not a liberal in present-day parlance. American politics is unique in that its party affiliations have often been based upon factors that are entirely separate from ideology.

This has been particularly true where presidents are concerned. Teddy Roosevelt was a trust-busting Progressive reformer; modern Republicans would hardly recognize him. Carry matters still farther back and we find that the Democratic Party, overwhelmingly the party of choice for twenty-first-century African Americans, harbored presidents who were either slaveholders or in one way or another advanced the cause of human bondage; Tennessean James K. Polk, for example, who eventually owned fifty slaves, pursued war with Mexico at least in part to provide his slaveholding Democratic supporters with new land for cotton plantations.

Perhaps the best way to approach the subject of presidential politics would be to think not so much in terms of parties or ideologies, but rather the elections themselves. In chapter 1 we used the Constitution and the Founders' intent as a framework to get at the office and its structure. In chapter 2 we focused on the more well-known presidents by way of understanding the men who have served in the White House. In chapter 3 generations served as a useful vehicle to get at the interaction between these men and the office. Here, we will focus on five presidential elections, using them as platforms, so to speak, to survey the political landscape and better understand the development of American presidential politics.

ELECTION OF 1800

Modern Americans periodically grumble about the contentious and partisan tone of presidential elections. In 2004, for example, political pundits, candidates, and voters complained that the tone set by candidates George Bush Jr. and John Kerry was overly antagonistic. "It has been a fractious, bitter, U.S. election war," observed one of many disturbed onlookers, involving "scare tactics, dirty tricks and vicious personal attacks [that] have been hallmarks of an eight-month, bare-knuckle campaign that has provoked intense emotions in Americans like no other in recent times" (*Toronto Sun*, October 29, 2004).

But presidential elections in this country have always been combative. This was as true at the very beginning of the nation's presidential history as it is now. Indeed, the election of 1800 was one of the more nasty political contests in American history for a variety of reasons, not the least of which was the fact that, for better or worse, it permanently placed political parties at the center of the machinery Americans use to choose their president.

This was certainly not what the Constitution's Framers wanted. The men and women who fought the Revolutionary war almost universally associated "party" with "faction," a group of citizens who put the good of their own selfish interests above that of the common good. Many had been educated to believe that factionalism had destroyed the ancient republics of Greece and Rome, and that political party organizations were a mortal danger to the health of any democracy, feeding the worst angels of human nature. "Parties are the dangerous diseases of civil freedom," argued one Revolutionary. "They are only the first stage of anarchy, cloaked in mild language" (Wood, 1969, 403).

If, say, merchants organized themselves into a party, then that party, if it gained political power, would govern only in the name and interests of merchants, at the expense of farmers, blacksmiths, shipbuilders, or any other nonmerchants. The result, the Revolutionaries believed, would be a government of naked power grabs and low intrigues, at the expense of civic virtue. "It is obvious, that the combination of some hundreds or thousands [of people] for political ends will produce a great aggregate stock or mass of power," wrote political theorist Fisher Ames, and "they will of course, innovate, till the vestiges of private right, and of restraints on public authority, are effaced; until the real people are stripped of all privilege and influence, and become even more abject and spiritless. . . . The success of a faction is ever the victory of a few; and the power of the few can be supported by nothing but force. This catastrophe is fatal" (Hyneman and Lutz, 1983, 2: 1320–1321).

However curious and contradictory it may seem, most Revolutionaries wanted a political system that functioned without politics, where people did not combine themselves into parties or factions and instead understood that the good of the entire American polis should override the good of any one citizen or group. Otherwise, Ames and others of his generation believed, the nation faced a bleak political future, as faction battled faction for control of the nation's resources. "Every faction that may happen to rule will pursue but two objects," Ames wrote, "its vengeance on the fallen party, and the security of its own power against any new one that may rise to contest it" (Hyneman and Lutz, 1983, 2: 1325).

Fear of faction and party had been one reason why a fair number of Revolutionary-era Americans hesitated before creating the presidency in the first place. A powerful chief executive with the backing of a party or faction was a scary thing, smacking of authoritarianism or worse. Critics of the Constitution believed the president would become the chief spokesman for a party of the rich.

"He will be a *minion* of the aristocratics, doing according to their will and pleasure, and confirming every law they may think proper to make, without any regard to their public utility," wrote one Antifederalist. "Every idea of such unlimited powers being lodged in so small number of the *well* born, elevated so far above the rest of their fellow citizens . . . ought to cause the blood of a free citizen to boil with indignation" (Kenyon, 1966, 73).

Some Revolutionaries believed that parties were inevitable, a necessary evil that any complex political community must by nature create. "The object of a free and wise people should be so to balance parties, that from the weakness of all you may be governed by the moderation of the combined judgments of the whole," wrote "A Farmer" in 1788 (Borden, 1965, 27). James Madison made this eminently pragmatic approach to political parties the centerpiece of his famous observations in *Federalist* No. 10. "The causes of faction cannot be removed," he wrote, so "relief is only to be sought in the means of controlling its effects." For Madison this meant enlarging the size of the Republic as much as possible so that factions could counterbalance each other. "Extend the sphere, and you take in a greater variety of parties and interests; you make it less probable that a majority of the whole will have a common motive to invade the rights of other citizens," he wrote, "or if such a common motive exists, it will be more difficult for all who feel it to discover their own strength, and to act in unison with each other" (Rossiter, 1961, 78).

Madison did not specifically mention the presidency in *Federalist* No. 10. And whether they thought parties were a preventable disease of democracy or not, nearly all of the Revolutionaries believed parties should be carefully watched and kept as far away from presidential politics as possible. George Washington, whose word was the gold standard of public discourse for most Americans, fairly ranted against the idea of American political parties, warning his countrymen that "the alternate domination of one faction over another, sharpened by the spirit of revenge, natural to party dissension, which in different ages and countries has perpetrated the most horrid enormities, is itself a frightful despotism." Warming to the subject, he argued that "the common and continual mischiefs of the spirit of party are sufficient to make it the interest and duty of a wise people to discourage and restrain it. It serves always to distract the public councils and enfeeble the public administration. It agitates the community with ill-founded jealousies and false alarms, kindles the animosity of one part against another, foments occasionally riot and insurrection" (www.yale.edu/lawweb/avalon).

Washington could afford to criticize political parties because he became the nation's first president without any party backing. Indeed, he was the closest thing Americans ever had to an apolitical president. He was to all intents and purposes anointed rather than elected to his first term. Even before the ink was dry on the Constitution, everyone knew he would be president. "General Washington it is said will be placed at the head of the new

government," Philadelphian Benjamin Rush wrote to a friend in August 1787 (Schlesinger., 1971, 1: 8). No one would have disagreed.

The only real political question in 1789 concerned who might become Washington's vice president. He was not Washington's running mate, in the modern sense of the word. Under the original provisions of Article II, the second-place candidate in an election was awarded the vice-presidential post. Several prominent Revolutionaries wanted the job: Sam Adams, John Hancock, Henry Knox, and Benjamin Lincoln, to name a few. As they and their supporters jockeyed for position, Americans received a taste of things to come. Should the new vice president hail from Virginia? Given the prominence of Virginia and the South in drafting and supporting the Constitution, and the fact that Washington himself was a Virginian, a Yankee seemed the better choice to provide some regional balance. Support eventually coalesced around John Adams of Massachusetts due to his northern roots, his well-deserved reputation as a brilliant political theorist, and his generally positive attitude toward the new national government (Schlesinger, 1971, 1: 12–13). Adams was decidedly lukewarm to the prospect. "My country in its wisdom contrived for me the most insignificant office that ever the invention of man contrived or his imagination conceived," he groaned to his wife Abigail (McCullough, 2001, 447).

The 1789 election was no election at all, with Washington and Adams attaining their positions more or less by acclamation. But three years later, when

Washington stood for reelection, things had changed. There were signs of a schism developing in the president's Cabinet, with two broad groups coalescing, one around Secretary of State Thomas Jefferson and the other around Secretary of the Treasury Alexander Hamilton.

The two men were profoundly different in personalities, ideals, and ideologies. Jefferson was a Southerner, the author of the Declaration of Independence, and a fierce defender of individual liberty. He never much liked the idea of a strong federal government, had looked with some suspicion on the new Constitution even as he gave it his cautious support—worrying in particular about "the perpetual reeligibility of the President"—and wanted as much as possible to keep government's potential for abuse and tyranny in check. He was also a planter who idealized the independent yeoman farmer as the foundation for American liberty. "I think our governments will remain virtuous for many centuries; as long as they are chiefly agricultural," he wrote to James Madison (Peterson, 1984, 918–919).

Hamilton, on the other hand, was a New York lawyer with strong ties to America's burgeoning business and commercial society. Perhaps the Constitution's most outspoken supporter, he believed a robust national government was necessary to preserve law and order. Moreover, it was good for business. Where Jefferson was a strict constructionist who wanted the government limited only to those powers expressly spelled out in the Constitution, Hamil-

In a distinguished career, Thomas Jefferson served as minister to France, governor of Virginia, secretary of state, vice president, and president of the United States. (National Archives)

ton wanted the document interpreted in such a way as to give the federal government the broadest possible power to deal with the nation's ever-changing economic circumstances. "Every power vested in a government is in its nature sovereign," he wrote, "and includes, by force of the term, a right to employ all the means requisite and fairly applicable to the attainment of the ends of such power, and which are not precluded by restrictions and exceptions specified in the Constitution, or not immoral, or not contrary to the essential ends of political society" (www.yale.edu/lawweb/avalon).

The two men disliked one another. Their personalities were as different as could be: Jefferson, the urbane, polished, dreamy plantation library theorist, Hamilton the rather nervous, impetuous New York lawyer whose mind always turned instinctively to the pragmatic side of issues. Jefferson was a Francophile; Hamilton, an admirer of England. Jefferson came from one of the finest families of the Virginia Tidewater dynasties; Hamilton was illegitimate and had a rather deserved reputation as an unprincipled womanizer. Jefferson saw in Hamilton a threatening tendency toward centralization of power and influence; Hamilton thought the author of the Declaration was an irresponsible dreamer. Each man exaggerated the other's shortcomings; and yet at the same time, both men had a point.

More importantly, they came to represent two competing and antagonistic points of view on a wide range of policy-making issues: monetary and fiscal policies, banking and tax issues, military appropriations, relations with Britain and France, even relatively minor matters of political protocol. Jefferson and Hamilton were the faces of a new American political culture, one that embodied far more than the Cabinet clashes in the Washington Administration. Here was the birthplace of foundational questions of American politics, questions that would dominate the national conversation for decades to follow.

Jefferson's and Hamilton's supporters were not political parties, exactly. The Revolutionaries had lost none of their disdain for parties, even as they laid the groundwork for party organization. But in doing so, they did not think they were behaving as factions, and they certainly

Alexander Hamilton's intelligence and determination helped gain America's independence and forge a vibrant national government. Hamilton created the Federalist Party, which, along with Thomas Jefferson's Republican Party, initiated the two-party political system that still governs American politics. Hamilton was fatally wounded in a duel with political rival Aaron Burr in 1804. (National Archives)

had no intention of legitimizing party organizations as such. A typical Hamilton supporter, for example, did not see himself as a member of a party, but rather as the guardian of the "true" spirit of 1776; those dastardly Jeffersonians were the faction, trying to thwart the proper American civic spirit being displayed by Hamilton and his friends. Conversely, Jefferson's supporters saw themselves as guardians of Revolutionary ideals against the machinations of a Hamiltonian conspiracy, one designed to turn the new American democratic experiment into an oligarchy, or worse. "To recover, therefore, in practice the [despotic] powers which the nation had refused [by rejecting Britain's monarchy] . . . was the steady object of the [Hamiltonian] party," Jefferson later declared. "Ours, on the contrary, was to maintain the will of the majority of the [Constitutional] convention, and of the people" (Peterson, 1984, 1470).

President Washington was caught squarely in the middle of this heated partisan battlefield. Many of the skirmishes were taking place right before his very eyes, in Cabinet meetings where his secretaries of state and Treasury clearly represented two opposing and mutually antagonistic political perspectives. Worse, he was drawn into the fray, as Hamiltonian and Jeffersonian partisans each wanted Washington's endorsement, and were each offended—sometimes to the point of rash intemperance—when such support was not forthcoming. Washington was more often than not sympathetic to Hamilton's point of view, particularly in controversial areas like

creation of a national bank (which Hamilton strongly favored, and Jefferson just as strongly opposed). To his shock and dismay, the president found himself being pilloried in the Jeffersonian press when he took Hamilton's side. Jefferson's more feckless partisans sniped at everything from Washington's lack of a formal education (a sore point with the president) to his generalship during the war. At a New Jersey dinner, one Jeffersonian offered a mocking toast to Washington as the "despot from the South, with Democracy on his lips and tyranny in his heart" (Smith, 1993, 252).

The country was drawing up sides, and Washington was appalled. He was not so naïve as to think America could totally avoid factional disputes, describing party-style politicking as "a fire not to be quenched." But he warned that Americans needed to be vigilant "to prevent [factionalism's] fire from bursting a flame, lest instead of warming it should consume" (Smith, 1993, 282). By 1796 party feelings had indeed burst into a flame of political ardor that Washington found disputatious and unsavory. In many ways he was quite glad to leave the presidency that year; life in the national government had become far too partisan and political for his tastes.

His departure from public life, according to one observer, was "like dropping a hat, for party racers to start, and I expect a great deal of noise, whipping and spurring" (Smith, 1993, 284). Jeffersonians—who now styled themselves Republicans—naturally lined up behind the secretary of state. Alexander Hamilton had made far too many enemies in high places. His supporters—the Federalists—quickly learned another soon-to-be, time-honored truth about presidential politics: namely, that a brilliant presidential candidate sometimes needed to give way to another who was perhaps a bit less so, but also less wreathed in controversy. Fortunately, the Federalists had ready at hand a candidate whose intelligence and learning matched Hamilton but who was a bit less abrasive and much less controversial in his private life: John Adams. Washington's erstwhile vice president became the Federalist candidate for office in 1796 (Schlesinger, 1971, 1: 60–68).

The 1796 election had its share of bitter personal attacks and nasty rhetoric, but it seemed more like a dress rehearsal for the decades of presidential politicking to come. The two sides—it would be a mistake to dignify them with the label "parties"—were half-formed entities, loose coalitions of likeminded men who as yet did not have a terribly clear sense of how to go about fashioning viable political organizations. They squabbled and fought among themselves nearly as much as they did with one another, and the result was an election that seems rather like a half-baked cake, not quite fully formed or mature. Adams won the election, beating out Jefferson largely by portraying himself as the natural heir apparent to the mighty Washington, whose generally pro-Federalist policies Adams endorsed. Adams also offered some hope that he might be able to put the genie of party factionalism back in its bottle. He was a Federalist, yes, but he was a man routinely (some would say notoriously)

John Adams was a prominent member of the Continental Congress and an important diplomat for the colonies during the American Revolution. Adams served as George Washington's vice president and, in 1796, was elected the second president of the United States. His administration was dominated by the growth of the two-party system and the repercussions of the French Revolution. (Library of Congress)

given to a stubborn independence of mind. He and Jefferson were good friends; and at any rate, Adams wholeheartedly shared his generation's deep dislike of political parties, promising to govern with "an equal and impartial regard to the rights, interest, honor, and happiness of all the States in the Union, without preference or regard to a northern or southern, an eastern or western, position, their various political opinions on unessential points or their personal attachments [and] . . . a love of virtuous men of all parties and denominations" (www.yale.edu/lawweb/avalon).

The nation's second president wanted desperately to govern without reference to parties, standing well above the fray of the ugly battles he had witnessed in Washington's Cabinet; but in this he would be profoundly disappointed. During his term in office, the split between Federalists and Republicans grew steadily more pronounced and angry; and, as with Washington, Adams was sucked into the partisan political vortex, whether he wished it or not. Republicans were by and large enthusiastic supporters of the French Revolution—Jefferson waxed eloquent about France constituting "the first chapter . . . of European liberty"—and they grew incensed at the president's attempts to keep America out of the war between France and England and as far as possible from what Adams called the "unnatural irrational and impractical" machinations of the French Revolutionaries (Peterson, 1984, 956–958; Ellis, 2001, 92).

For their part the Federalists, nominally Adams's party colleagues, were chagrined that the president likewise refused to commit the United States to support their favorites, the English. Hamilton in particular had taken to issuing directions to Adams's Cabinet members behind his back, and he privately told other Federalists that he believed Adams was unstable and even mentally unbalanced. Adams gave as good as he got, calling Hamilton "the bastard brat of a Scotch pedlar" (Ellis, 2001, 22). Adams

was very nearly as disgusted as Washington with American politics. "The longer I live and the more I see of public men, the more I wish to be a private one," he wrote. "Modesty is a virtue that can never thrive in public life" (McCullough, 2001, 207).

In retrospect, Adams's neutrality was the wisest course. He kept the United States out of a broiling European-wide conflagration that, had the new nation supported one side at the expense of another, would surely sooner or later have dealt America's interests grievous harm. Adams was smart enough to see this, and he prevented the United States from becoming the tool of either France or England. He was especially worried that the nation might be sucked into the violent excesses of the French Revolution, excesses that Jefferson rather cavalierly dismissed with his famous remark that "the tree of liberty must be refreshed from time to time with the blood of patriots and tyrants" (Peterson, 1984, 911). Adams, on the other hand, was horrified by French bloodletting in the name of democracy, likening the French to "young Schollars from a Colledge or Sailors flushed with recent pay prize money, mounted on wild Horses, lashing and speering, till they kill the Horses and break their own Necks" (Ellis, 2001, 93).

Time would prove that Adams's instincts were largely correct. The French expected American aid and open support of their war with England; when this was not readily forthcoming, French agents meddled in Americans' local politics, embargoed American goods, and seized American ships on the high seas. These actions angered many. On the other hand, many Americans agreed with Jefferson, at least to the extent of believing that the French should be cultivated and their cause actively supported. Everyone knew that the 1800 election would be a climax, a showdown between these diametrically opposed perspectives.

As the election began to heat up, Hamilton stirred the wrath of Adams and his supporters by trying to engineer an unsuccessful behind-the-scenes dumping of the president for Southerner Charles Cotesworth Pinckney. Hamilton then made his feelings about Adams a matter of public record by circulating a letter, titled "Letter from Alexander Hamilton, Concerning the Conduct and Public Character of John Adams, Esq.," in which he argued that the president was "a man of an imagination sublimed and eccentric; propitious neither to the regular display of sound judgment, nor to the perseverance in a systematic plan of conduct . . . [and] to this defect are added the unfortunate foibles of a vanity without bounds, and a jealousy capable of discoloring every subject." For good measure, Hamilton piled on references to Adams's "disgusting egotism," "distempered jealousy," and "ungovernable indiscretion" (Ellis, 2001, 22–23).

Adams was understandably angry at this broadside from a member of his own party. His wrath was also turned against his opponent and theretofore good friend, Thomas Jefferson. Their growing antipathies dated back to their days serving in Washington's Cabinet. When Jefferson had suddenly resigned from the Cabinet in December 1793, Adams privately castigated Jefferson's "want of candor, his obstinate prejudices of both aversion and attachment, his real partiality in spite all his pretensions, [and] his low notions about many things . . . good riddance of bad ware" (McCullough, 2001, 448). By the time Adams entered the presidency, Jefferson's hostility was visible for all to see, and to Adams—who had a tendency to personalize criticism—this hostility went far beyond the mere political differences between two men who wanted the same office.

Tempers ran at a fever pitch for everyone in the weeks leading to the election. By this point America had developed not only two full-fledged political parties but a rollicking and almost totally unrestrained partisan press. Federalist and Republican editors had at the candidates and each other with a venom not previously seen in American public life. A Republican claimed to have heard one Federalist exclaim that Republicans "should be put to death in order to secure the government." A Federalist newspaper warned that Jefferson was bent on establishing a new American monarchy, claiming that it was "whispered that when the Philosopher [Jefferson] gets into the chair, and a suitable force provided at his back, he is to declare himself permanent!" (Sharp, 1995, 252).

Party loyalties cut across—and sometimes conflicted with—state and regional ties as well. South Carolina Federalists had backed Hamilton in his efforts to replace Adams with Pinckney (a native of the Palmetto State), and Adams's Massachusetts supporters worried that their Carolinian brethren's hearts were not really in the cause, whatever their ostensible party loyalties might be. Southern Republicans sometimes expressed misgivings about the loyalties of northern Republicans, and vice versa. Political parties were too new and too inherently suspect for everyone to believe that their unifying effects could outweigh the older and stronger ties to state and region. "Can we, may we rely on the integrity of the southern States?" a nervous New York Republican wrote (Freeman, 2002, 235).

In such an atmosphere of suspicion and distrust, emotions ran high. Each side portrayed itself not as merely one political option but as the only possible moral choice; political opposition itself had not yet attained legitimacy, and the choice before the voters, it was said, was between right and wrong, prosperity and ruin. At stake was nothing less than the legacy of 1776. The election would "clearly evince, whether a Republican form of Government is worth contending for," declared one observer (Freeman, 2002, 229). In this way, Adams and Jefferson were not merely two equally viable candidates contending for high office— one was good and the other evil.

There were even darker hints that extremists on both sides might actually contemplate taking up arms and starting a civil war over the election's outcome. This was not unthinkable in a nation that was only thirteen years old and with memories still fresh of a successful armed uprising against the British crown. "In times like these in which we live, it will not do to be overscrupulous," Hamilton wrote. "It is easy to sacrifice

the substantial interests of society by a strict adherence to ordinary rules" (Freeman, 2002, 229). Others agreed that, should their political enemies gain the upper hand, "ordinary rules" of civility could be jettisoned in favor of victory. In New York, pro-Republican militia units had been formed, and there were rumors that men on both sides were secretly stockpiling muskets to be used in an armed uprising should their side fail to win the election. An abortive slave revolt in Virginia during the summer sparked charges by Federalists that Republicans and their pro-French ideas had fomented the insurrection as a first step toward an American race war. "This dreadful conspiracy originates with some of the French Jacobins," warned one, "aided and abetted by some of our own profligate and abandoned democrats" (Sharp, 1995, 242).

The election returns produced only more confusion. Adams would definitely be a one-term president: he garnered only sixty-five Electoral College votes to Jefferson's seventy-three. Unfortunately, Jefferson's own running mate, Aaron Burr, also received seventy-three votes. Burr possessed strong ties among Republicans in the North, further exacerbating regional tensions within the Republican camp. He also possessed a well-deserved reputation as an unprincipled schemer, one who was perfectly willing to cut the throats of his closest associates to advance his own cause. Three years later he would kill Alexander Hamilton in a duel; not long after that, he would be accused of treason and implicated in a scheme to detach a chunk of western territory from the United States and give it to Great Britain, with himself as governor.

As called for by the Constitution, the entire matter was thrown into the House of Representatives. While the congressmen wrangled, tensions reached a fever pitch. Two mysterious fires, one in the War Department building and another that damaged parts of the Treasury Department's facilities, were seen by some suspicious people as the first signals for what would be an eventual nationwide bloodbath. Republicans believed that the Federalists, who were now most definitely out of the running for the presidency, had set the fires in a desperate attempt to cover up the supposedly widespread corruption of the Adams Administration. "One thing is admitted by the Anglo-Federalists, that the offices of the War and Treasury Departments were burnt down by design," asserted a Republican editor (Sharp, 1995, 251).

Ironically, the Federalists in the end were the deciding factors in the contested election. They disliked Jefferson all right; but the thought of a man like Aaron Burr in the presidency badly scared many of them. After a week of arguing and jockeying, during which tensions in the capital and elsewhere ran at a fever pitch, Federalists from Vermont and Maryland shifted their votes to Jefferson on the thirty-sixth ballot, giving him the victory. For the first time in the nation's history, political power had been transferred, more or less peacefully, from one party to another. Many felt a real crisis had barely been averted. "The country was in as much peril then as in any other era in American history with the

single exception of the Civil War," argues historian James Roger Sharp, "There was no violence, but the threat of violence, like Macbeth's torment by Banquo's ghost, haunted and pre-occupied Americans of that era" (Sharp, 1995, 275).

The election of 1800 revealed a series of fault lines and tensions that would be evident in future presidential contests. There were the ongoing tensions between what was allegedly an apolitical office and the very real political machinations used by the people who wanted that office. There was the need to appear above the partisan fray even as one engaged in the most partisan sort of maneuvering. And there was the ideological split between Federalists and Republicans which, while anchored to specific issues and problems of the time—for example, relations with the French and the creation of a national bank—were also indicative of broader philosophical issues that would dominate American politics for decades: the relative power of national and local governments; the tensions between an agricultural and an industrial economic future; and the extent to which the United States should or should not involve itself in international affairs.

Perhaps most of all, the election of 1800 revealed the tensions and contradictions inherent in a new national political culture that required its participants to be at once both rancorously combative and at the time same willing to forego that rancor in the peaceful transfer of power from one party to another. Americans were obviously quite willing to have at each other with gusto when they chose their presidents, calling each other every nasty name in the book and suspecting each other of the basest motives. Yet when the votes were finally cast, Americans showed that they could then resign themselves to the results with relative grace, shake hands, and retire to lick their wounds, ready to fight again another day. It is a strange contradiction, one that lies at the absolute heart of American presidential politics.

ELECTION OF 1828

The Federalists did not survive the election of 1800. There were a variety of reasons, perhaps the chief of which was their discomfort with the idea of politicking for high office. The party's backbone came from the ranks of the more elitist Revolutionaries, many of whom were at best begrudging advocates of the new American democracy. Even as lowered property restrictions on voting and other factors steadily increased the number of ordinary Americans who could participate in the political process, many Federalists clung to the idea that politics—particularly of the presidential variety—ought to be the realm of gentlemen. It was an attitude that did not bode well for a new century that would witness as one of its chief developments the rise of the ordinary white farmer as the driving force in American politics—a driving force that was not Federalist. "What the Federalists of 1800 could not now face, or even admit, was that the sovereign people had spoken for Jefferson, and not for them," noted historians

Eric McKitrick and Stanley Elkins (1995, 752).

After 1800 there were still Americans who called themselves Federalists. The party continued to have a presence, in greater and lesser degrees, on the local and state level. And there were still many Americans who, when asked, would have espoused Federalist positions on issues like the power of the national government, or the need for a viable national currency, or the merits of Hamilton's economic ideas, or the Adams presidency. But the party could not muster enough organizational strength to field serious national candidates for the White House. Between 1800 and 1828, the only meaningful battle for the presidency occurred in the fight over the Republican Party's nomination. Whoever attained that prize needed only to face the likes of James Ross, Robert Harper, and other Federalist has-beens or never-weres who stood no chance of victory.

Thus have historians sometimes dubbed this period the Era of Good Feelings, that rare, brief moment in American history when there was only one political party competing for the White House. For a generation of antiparty, anti-"faction" Revolutionaries, now growing rather long in the tooth, nothing could have been better news. "I shall hope to . . . obliterate, or rather to unite the names of federalists and republicans," newly elected president Thomas Jefferson wrote in 1801. "The greatest good we can do our country is to heal its party divisions and make them one people" (McKitrick and Elkins, 1995, 754). Party politics and the presidency—here was a phenomenon that required "healing" for Jefferson, and the "good feelings" came from the illusion that, temporarily at least, the American people had become "one people" because their presidents were chosen from one party.

The extent of the good feelings can be exaggerated, however. There was still plenty of political combat between leftover Federalists, their sympathizers, and Republicans on the state and local levels. Moreover, the ideological fissures represented by Republicans and Federalists—local versus federal authority, agrarianism versus industrialization, country versus city—were still very much alive. Indeed, one could argue that these disputes were endemic to the American political system, built into the American political machinery like a computer's operating system. The names of the parties might change, but the arguments would remain.

As we saw in chapter 2, the year 1828 would witness the entrance onto the American political scene of one of the most controversial figures of his day: Andrew Jackson, Tennessee lawyer and slaveholder, victor of the Battle of New Orleans and (for better or worse) various campaigns against Native American tribes. Whatever his virtues and faults, Andrew Jackson was no purveyor of a milquetoast "era of good feelings." He was the sort of man people either loved or loved to hate, with a personality that, in the political arena, inspired extreme reactions.

In his particular political arena, there were additional factors feeding an emotional, partisan political atmosphere.

First and foremost was the ever-expanding suffrage base of voters and the political culture it engendered. Running for office no longer involved well-heeled candidates quietly pumping well-heeled constituents for their votes—the preferred method for the more élitist-minded Federalists. With their closer identification with farmers and agricultural interests and their affiliation with Jefferson's populist "all men are created equal" vision of the American dream, Republicans had always had the upper hand among more ordinary, middling-class voters. With the demise of the Federalists, at least on the national level, Republican Party activists and their allies could now spread their efforts out into the countryside unmolested, trawling for votes in the small towns and farms that made up the grass roots of democratic America.

The voters in those towns and on those farms evinced little interest in exceedingly complex statements of policy-making or civic philosophy by their candidates. A coherent intellectual position on policy issues helped, of course—the voters were not stupid—but often just as important was a candidate or his political supporters' ability to deliver a truly rousing stump speech, one that aroused the heart as well as the head. It did not hurt if the speech was given during a barbecue or picnic. "I do not pretend to be a man of extraordinary talents," declared a typical candidate of the day. "I think I can govern you pretty well. I do not think it will require a very extraordinary smart man to govern you; for to tell you the truth, fellow citizens, I do not think you will be very hard to govern no how" (Sellers, 1991, 165). A young Abraham Lincoln, running for the state legislature in 1832, was even more folksy and succinct. "My name is Abraham Lincoln," he told a group of curious onlookers gathered for a sale along Ritchland Creek in Illinois. "My politics is short and sweet, like the old woman's dance. I am in favor of a national bank, high and protective tariff, and the internal improvement system. If elected I will be thankful. If beaten I can do as I have been doing: work for a living. This is about all. . . . My love to all and your wife in particular" (Wilson and Davis, 1998, 16–17).

Politics on Ritchland Creek and elsewhere in rural America had as much to do with emotions as with reason. The men and women who attended party rallies and debates expected a good show. Politics was their version of a modern-day football game, and party affiliation could cause the same fierce, raucous loyalties that animate a modern Boston Red Sox fan.

Helping them along in their partisan gamesmanship was an increasingly strident American press. Just about anyone with an opinion and a printing press could churn out a sheet or two of foolscap filled with political insults, hubris, praise, and scorn, all jumbled together in ways that made objective news reporting and partisan editorializing difficult to separate. Nearly every town of consequence had at least two newspapers that were arrayed on opposite sides of the political fence and who whaled away at each other with unrestrained partisan zeal. By 1828 the nation sported over 600

newspapers, nearly all of them with an explicit political identification and an axe of one sort or another to grind.

It was an era in which journalists possessed no professional identities to speak of, and so were under no compunction to behave according to agreed-upon standards of professional courtesy and accuracy. Increasing readership and subscription sales were what counted, and editors had a tendency to feed readers' desires for name-calling over substantive debate. Many of these newspapers also tottered on the brink of financial ruin, often barely able to cover their own printing costs; they needed all the help they could get to stay in business and had no reservations about turning to political party men for money.

Combined with the populist political culture and the raucous press was a generation of young American political operatives who were quick studies when it came to party organization and campaigning. They well understood the power of the new populist press, for example, and put dollars and efforts into building what were for that time formidable media networks. They bought local newspapers, installed friendly editors to run them, and solicited articles from talented political writers. "We have at considerable expense established another newspaper in the northern part of New Hampshire," noted Senator Levi Woodbury. "We have organized our fences in every quarter and have begun and shall continue without ceasing to pour into every doubtful region all kinds of useful information" (Remini, 1977, 77). By "useful information" Woodbury meant tidbits of gossip, rumor, and often half-baked facts that could be used by his allies to paste their opponents.

"Organized our fences in every quarter" also had a quasi-military ring. This was appropriate, for party operatives often thought and behaved as if they were arraying their political forces for battle. The early nineteenth century witnessed the rise of America's first real political machines: cadres of party loyalists and supporters who formed elaborate structures of door-to-door activists, committees, precinct captains, and the like. Some borrowed the names of the old wartime organizations from Revolutionary days, calling themselves committees of correspondence or safety. Eventually, Americans of the era would create actual paramilitary outfits with names like the Wide-Awakes that possessed uniforms, rules, and regulations that rivaled the U.S. Army.

These organizations marched in political rallies and parades with battalionlike efficiency, belting out campaign songs and slogans with practiced precision. American party men were learning the value of a well-written song, a value that sometimes met or even exceeded the value of a well-crafted policy statement or party platform. They were discovering the many uses in a democracy of what we would today term media symbolism. The 1828 election would see the introduction of what would eventually become mainstays of presidential politics: campaign buttons, banners, medals, cups, beer mugs, and posters. Candidate images even appeared on cheap papier-mâché snuffboxes.

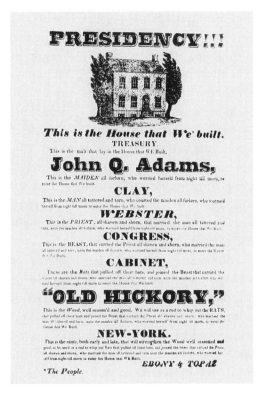

A poster from Andrew Jackson's 1828 presidential campaign. Jackson, the Democratic candidate, beat President John Quincy Adams in what many saw as a realigning election after 1824. (Bettmann/Corbis)

Not everyone was comfortable with the new politics: the rowdy stump speeches, backbiting editors, snuffboxes, and the like. It all seemed to those with longer memories and grayer hairs to be an unseemly way for men to compete for the chair formerly held by George Washington. Divisions over campaign tactics hammered cracks into the Republicans' single-party facade. There were other divisions, as well: between eastern and western party members; Northerners and Southerners; supporters of a strong program of economic development administered by the federal government and those who wanted the government to take a leave-well-enough-alone attitude to the economy. Some Republicans favored a powerful tariff to protect American industrial development; others did not. Some wanted a national bank and a stable national currency; others believed the Constitution gave Washington, D.C., no authority to meddle in such matters.

Four years prior to the election of 1828, these cracks had become visible for all to see. Competition for the party's nomination in 1824—and by extension the presidency itself—became a heated contest between multiple party factions. John Quincy Adams, son of former president John Adams, was the preferred choice for New Englanders and many older Republicans who saw him as a link to the Revolutionary generation. Georgia's William Crawford garnered support among Southerners and states' rights Republicans due to his opposition as a U.S. senator to legislation that would have enlarged the federal government's authority. More appealing to those Republicans who wanted a more powerful federal presence in the nation's economic life was Henry Clay of Kentucky, with his talk of an "American system" of government-funded internal improvements to roads, rivers, and other tools of commerce. And then there was Andrew Jackson, something of a dark horse in 1824 due to his relative lack of political experience but who could muster support among Westerners and expansion-

minded Americans who liked his image as a hero of the Indian wars.

Competition among the four candidates was fierce enough to produce what the nation had not seen in nearly twenty-five years: a presidential election with no clear winner. Jackson's popular appeal among Westerners and his supporters' ability to organize at the grassroots level won him a little over 43 percent of the total vote, while Adams's family pedigree and support among New Englanders gained him a bit over thirty percent. Crawford and Clay split the rest, which meant that no candidate could claim a majority of either the popular vote or the Electoral College. For the first time in a quarter-century, the presidency would be decided in Congress.

As the balloting and jockeying echoed through Congress's chambers during the weeks following the election, rumors grew of a backroom deal negotiated between members of Congress loyal to Adams and those who supported Clay. Adams, it was said, promised Clay a high Cabinet post in return for the Kentuckian's congressional votes. The rumors seemed to have borne fruit when, first, Clay's supporters suddenly switched their votes to Adams—thus putting him in the White House—and, second, when Clay was subsequently appointed secretary of state. Jackson's supporters fumed about a "corrupt bargain" between the new president and his one-time adversary.

Both Adams and Clay denied that any bargain had taken place. Clay in particular claimed that his decision to support Adams rather than Jackson—despite the fact that both he and Jackson were Westerners and, theoretically, bound by sectional loyalties—was motivated by principles rather than self-interest. "The Knaves cannot comprehend how a man can be honest," he fumed. "They cannot conceive that I should have solemnly interrogated my Conscience and asked it to tell me seriously what I ought to do? That it should have enjoined me not to establish the dangerous precedent of elevating in this early stage of the Republic, a Military Chieftain merely because he has won a great victory? . . . I cannot believe that killing 2500 Englishmen at N. Orleans qualifies [Jackson] for the various, difficult, and complicated duties of the Chief Magistracy" (Schlesinger, 1971, 1: 407).

Thus did emotions run high long after the actual election was settled. In the face of this controversy, the Republicans' facade of single-party unity barely persisted. Jackson and his supporters could never forgive the Clay-Adams faction for their machinations (real and perceived), while Clay and many others feared Jackson as a dangerous demagogue-in-the-making. Extremists on both sides literally could not comprehend the perspective of their opponents. "My Dear Sir, is there an intelligent and unbiased man who must not, sooner or later, concur with me?" Clay asked a friend (Schlesinger, 1971, 1: 407). Sentiments like this would make the next presidential election in 1828 a showdown.

Adams was admired by many but beloved by few, with many Americans put off by his often imperious manner and cold intellectualism. He lacked political skills and was not good at cajoling people of different opinions. Adams was "a virtuous man," observed one acquaintance, "whose temper, which is not the best, might be overlooked; he has a great and miscellaneous knowledge, and he is with his pen a powerful debater; but he wants to a deplorable degree that most essential quality, a sound and correct judgment" (Nagel, 1997, 297). It did not help that Adams had to face lingering doubts about the so-called corrupt bargain with Clay and about the fact that he had just barely edged into the White House via a rare and contentious congressional proceeding. That very same Congress would prove throughout his term to be extraordinarily hostile in general, blocking even relatively minor administration efforts, such as sending a delegation to the new pan-American league being formed in Panama and providing federal funding for astronomical laboratories and other institutions of scientific learning. Adams's manner in pursuing such projects was clumsy, leaving him vulnerable to charges that he tried to dictate to Congress. Adams sadly observed that he had been accused of "taken Caesar as my model," and the barbs stung him so badly that he began to lose both weight and sleep, exhibiting signs of what we might today term clinical depression (Nagel, 1997, 304).

Modern political operatives might likewise observe that the president had a crippling image problem. He had an old-fashioned air that did not wear well in the roaring new decades of the nineteenth century. Even though he was only

John Quincy Adams is remembered more for his brilliant achievements as President James Monroe's secretary of state than for his own ineffectual presidency. Although Adams had hoped to make substantial improvements as president, a bitterly divided Congress and his own forbidding personality prevented many positive changes during his tenure. (Library of Congress)

fourteen years old when the American Revolution ended, he seemed to be a leftover from that earlier age. He even had a tendency toward old-fashioned clothes; he was the last president to regularly wear breeches, which were fast going out of style by the 1820s. He had taken the high road to the presidency, the road created by the generation of Revolutionary-era statesmen who preceded him. Traditionally, the secretary of state's job had been seen as the proper stepping-stone to the president's chair; and so Mr. Adams served as President Monroe's secretary of state. The Founders perceived the presidency as primarily a foreign policy job; and so Mr. Adams served as America's minister to the Netherlands, Russia, and Germany, preceded by an apprenticeship under his father when the latter served as an American ambassador in Europe. John Quincy was no mere placeholder in these

positions, either. He was an effective, astute diplomat. He had been long groomed for the White House by a father whose pride knew no bounds when his son became president in 1824 and who was acutely aware that John Quincy's presidency must necessarily reflect and be reflected by his own turn as the nation's chief executive. John Adams "was considerably affected by the fulfillment of his highest wishes," noted one family member in 1824, like "that old man who was pronounced by Solon to be the highest of mortals when he expired on hearing of his son's success at the Olympic games" (McCullough, 2001, 639).

This was all well and good; but in the embryonic media age of the early nineteenth century, it lacked a certain panache. Jackson, on the other hand, was colorful and controversial. In modern journalistic parlance, he made for good copy. And Jackson's supporters were fast learners in the game of populist politics. As the campaign season began to heat up, they trotted out the stories of Jackson's heroic deeds at the Battle of New Orleans, his Indian campaigns, and his frontier moxie. They also set their sights on the president, "going negative" (in modern parlance) and taking full advantage of Adams's various character foibles and image problems.

The partisan sniping in the press reached a crescendo of charge and countercharge during the summer and fall of 1828. Adams was pilloried for his old-school identification with the Revolutionary era, his "dandy dress of 'nankeen' pantaloons and silk stockings," and his bookish inclinations, which made him, according to his critics, a bona fide member of the "New England aristocracy" (Hargreaves, 1985, 287). The more creative among Jackson's supporters claimed that Adams was once a pimp who ran a house of ill-repute while living in Paris, and that his campaign manager, Henry Clay, was "a shyster, pettifogging in a bastard suit before a country squire" (Bowers, 1922, 32).

Adams's supporters gave as good as they got. "General Jackson's mother was a COMMON PROSTITUTE, brought into this country by the British soldiers!" screamed one opposition newspaper. Others called Jackson a drunkard, a gambler, a murderer, a duelist, and a home wrecker. That last charge related to Jackson's marriage, about which it was said he had first lived with and then wed his wife Rachel while she was still married to another man. There was a morsel of

A lithograph depicts General Andrew Jackson leading U.S. forces to an overwhelming victory over the British at the Battle of New Orleans on January 8, 1815. (Library of Congress)

truth to the claim; after she married Andrew Jackson, some confusion had ensued over the actual status of Rachel's divorce from her first husband, Lewis Robards; when this was discovered, she quickly filed the proper paperwork and got her divorce. No harm, no foul—or so she thought. But hostile anti-Jackson newspapermen spun all sorts of wild rumors about the affair: that Rachel had lived in sin with Andrew as his ostensible housekeeper; that Jackson had bought the first husband's silence while he and Rachel knowingly committed adultery and bigamy for several years; and that a 1790 jury found Rachel guilty of desertion and that she "hath, and doth still, live[s] in adultery with another man" (Remini, 1977, 118–119, 134).

Normally, Jackson would have shot someone over such an accusation, or at least delivered a good tongue-lashing. But many of the old restrictions on presidential behavior remained firmly in place, among them the Revolutionaries' custom that presidents ought not appear too eager for the office and should therefore remain silent. Jackson was smart enough not to deliver any fiery public speeches that would have merely given credence to the already common charge among his enemies that he was a potential dictator in the making. So when the stories about his marriage broke, he fumed only in private, calling Henry Clay "the bases[t], meanest scoundrel, that ever disgraced the image of his god" and asserting that "nothing [is] too mean and low for him to condescend to, *secretly* to carry his cowardly, and base purpose of slander into effect; even the aged and virtuous female, is not free from his secret combination of base slander" (Remini, 1977, 120). For her part, Rachel was so mortified that her already precarious health broke down completely, and she died shortly before her husband took office. Whether this was directly related to the rumors about her divorce is impossible to say; but Jackson forever after blamed Clay and others in the opposition for his wife's death.

The campaign's tone grew ever nastier in the weeks leading up to the election. "A vote for Jackson meant a vote for a man who thinks that if he takes a fancy to his neighbor's pretty wife, he 'has nothing to do but take a pistol in one hand and a horsewhip in another and . . . possess her,'" said one critic (Marszalek, 1997, 16). Jackson's supporters were no more charitable. "When it comes to an act upon any policy or principle not connected with a hatred of Jackson," snarled a Jackson editor, the pro-Adams, pro-Clay party "must fall to pieces. . . . It contains all the elements of dissolution, and is destined to share the fate of other monstrous alliances" (Bowers, 1922, 348).

In addition to this sort of extreme negative campaigning, the two sides made full use of populism's new campaign tools. Jackson's people were particularly enthusiastic in their democratic campaigning, staging parades, rallies, barbecues, dinners, and stump speeches all over the countryside. They made special use of Jackson's nickname, Old Hickory, by encouraging the planting of hickory trees as an election activity and organizing themselves into quasi-formal clubs called the Hurra Boys, who distributed hickory sticks, brooms, canes, and other Jackson memorabilia. The general's handlers also used campaign songs to great effect. One in particular, "The Hunters of Kentucky," extolled Jackson's virtues at the Battle of New Orleans:

But Jackson, he was wide awake,
And was not scared at trifles,
For well he knew Kentucky's boys,
With their death-dealing rifles,
He led them down to cypress swamp,
The ground was low and mucky,
There stood John Bull in martial pomp,
And here stood old Kentucky.

(Remini, 1977, 134)

At the end of the day, Jackson's supporters proved more adept at such matters than Adams's more traditional-minded friends. The general beat the Founding Father's son handily, mustering 56 percent of the popular vote and 178 Electoral College votes, while Adams garnered 44 percent and 83 College votes. Adams dominated on his home turf—upper New England—but Jackson was stronger everywhere else, including the growing West and the slaveholding South.

No one could disguise the fact that this was a resounding defeat for Adams. "The sun of my political life sets in the deepest gloom," he remarked, and vowed to be only stiffly cordial to the president-elect, whom, he claimed, had "slandered me" (Nagel, 1997, 321). For his part, Jackson did not feel much like celebrating, for his beloved wife Rachel took ill and passed away within days after he received news of his victory. She was "a being so gentle and so virtuous, slander might wound but could not dishonor [her]," Jackson believed, referring even at this dark moment to the accusations of bigamy leveled by Adams's supporters (Remini, 1977, 156).

Any doubts that a crossroads had been reached in American presidential politics were erased when Jackson held his inaugural ceremony. Previous ceremonies had been austere, statesmanlike affairs; Jackson's inauguration took on the air of a raucous party. "It was a proud day for the people," observed a journalist, for "General Jackson is *their own* president" (Schlesinger Jr., 1945, 6). Thousands witnessed Jackson's oath and cheered lustily

as the new president kissed the Bible and then shook hands with Supreme Court chief justice John Marshall. The crowd then surged forward in a frenzy, snapping the chain separating it from the Capitol's Portico and surging around Jackson to offer backslaps and handshakes galore. Overwhelmed and in some danger of being trampled, the president was forced to retreat back inside the Capitol while city marshals tried to restore order outside (Remini, 1977, 177).

The festive atmosphere grew rather ugly at the White House itself, where a small reception had been scheduled. The crowd descended upon the building, forcing its way inside and again putting Jackson in peril; he was pressed against a back wall near the White House's south entrance and had to be escorted outside by a ring of protectors who feared he would be suffocated. The crowd then took over the place, tearing down curtains and breaking up pieces of furniture for souvenirs and calling for refreshments in such a menacing way that the terrified White House staff set up bowls of spiked punch and bucketfuls of harder liquor on the front lawn in a desperate attempt to appease the crowd. "What a scene did we witness!" exclaimed one onlooker, "*The Majesty of the People* had disappeared, and a rabble, a mob, of boys, negroes, women, children, scrambling, fighting, romping. What a pity, what a pity" (Remini, 1977, 177–178).

Jackson's ascendancy marked far more than just a new lack of political decorum. He was almost inevitably a divisive figure, and his victory left enough controversy and bitter feelings to permanently split Jefferson's old Republican coalition. Anti-Jackson Republicans united with remnants of the old Federalists to form a new party, at first dubbed merely the Opposition—a fact that in itself speaks volumes about how much Andrew Jackson defined even his opponents—and then the National Republicans, they later christened themselves the Whigs after an old English party dedicated to opposing tyrannical policies emanating from the monarchy. Again, the name says it all concerning its followers' perceptions of Jackson and their fears of his possible abuse of power.

Jackson's people at first called themselves the Democratic Republicans, but later shortened this to simply the Democrats. Where Whigs had a tendency to look with suspicion on the "majesty of the people," Democrats reveled in their populist image. It did not seem to much matter that, by and large, Democratic candidates would be drawn from the upper crust of society—Jackson himself was a well-heeled Tennessee slave owner and lawyer, after all. What mattered was Democratic mastery of the language and the symbols of populist politics. They would use these skills to dominate the White House for the next thirty years.

A new two-party rivalry was born. The "good feelings," such as they were, came abruptly to an end. The year 1828 set a certain tone for presidential elections in the antebellum era. Whether that tone was good or bad depended upon one's point of view. The more populist-minded Americans loved the idea that politicians no longer could limit themselves to gen-

teel persuasion in drawing rooms and other environs of the rich. They could no longer count on their money and class status to elevate them to high office; now, any man who wanted to be president of the United States would be forced to pay attention to the needs and wants of more ordinary Americans.

Others, however, believed the new democracy introduced a coarseness into the nation's political discourse. Andrew Jackson had been elected in 1828 with a variety of rather tawdry issues swirling around him—accusations of bigotry and the like. Some wondered if the office of George Washington and Thomas Jefferson should be reduced to the level of stump speeches, barbecues, and mudslinging. Such criticisms may have had merit, but in the end that really did not matter very much. The engine of populist democracy was humming by 1828, driven by ever-lowering suffrage requirements, the burgeoning population of white males, and a growing American press corps that could supply virtually anyone with cheap newspaper copy whose truth and accuracy was guaranteed by no one.

Americans were discovering the value of symbolism in their political conversations: the fact that, in a democracy, a single well-placed symbol—a hickory stick, for example—a catchy song, or a well-timed stump speech could turn an entire election. And Americans were discovering that presidential politics, for better or worse, could be driven by symbolism and media commentary as much as substantive debate or arguments about policy.

ELECTION OF 1864

Few presidents have ascended to office in the wake of more vindictiveness or even outright character assassination than Abraham Lincoln. Once David Davis helped get him his nomination, Lincoln became the target of vilification that met and sometimes even exceeded the charges of pimping and bigamy leveled at Adams and Jackson thirty years earlier. He was assailed as a Black Republican, a "horrid looking wretch," and a "bloodthirsty tyrant" who was "slouchy, ungraceful, round shouldered . . . and ugly in every way." One Southerner declared that a Lincoln victory in 1860 would usher in "robberies, rapes, and murders of the poorer whites by the emancipated blacks [who] would then disfigure the whole fair face of this prosperous, smiling, and happy Southern land" (Oates, 1977, 181, 187–188).

Most Southerners had never even heard of Lincoln before 1860. They did know what he represented, however. Lincoln was the candidate of the new Republican Party, barely six years old in 1860. It had been constructed partly on the ruins of the Whigs, the loose anti-Jackson coalition that had never quite managed to mount a sustained challenge to the Democrats' presidential dominance during the 1840s and 1850s. During that time the Whigs managed to elect only two presidents, William Henry Harrison and Zachary Taylor, elderly military figures who shared two important characteristics: they were both exceedingly vague in their core political convic-

tions—which worked to the Whigs' advantage—and they both managed to die very early in office—which most assuredly did not. The Whigs also had a tendency to quarrel among themselves, squaring off over state and regional differences; disagreements about slavery (of course); and the efficacy of immigration, which helped create pro- and anti-immigration wings within the party. By the early 1850s, these various cracks had widened to the point that the entire party edifice crumbled away. "The Whig party *as such* is dead and buried," remarked one party stalwart in 1852 (Holt, 1999, 1976).

American politics abhors a vacuum, however, and almost immediately on the heels of the Whig Party's demise, a new and stronger alternative rose to take its place. The catalyst was Congress's passage of the Kansas-Nebraska Act of 1854, which opened the West to slavery by popular vote. For antislavery Americans like Lincoln, this was a betrayal of the Founding Fathers' principal wish that slavery be contained in the Old South like a dangerous virus and slowly allowed to die. Moreover, voting slavery up or down was a form of racism that Lincoln and many others could not abide. "If we admit that a negro is not a man, then it is right for the Government to own him and trade in the race, and it is right to allow the South to take their peculiar institution with them and plant it upon the virgin soil of Kansas and Nebraska," Lincoln argued. "But if the negro, upon soil where slavery is not legalized by law and sanctioned by custom, *is* a man, then there is not even the shadow of popular sovereignty in allowing the first settlers upon such soil to decide whether it shall be right in all future time to hold men in bondage there" (Basler, 1953–1955, 2: 239).

Kansas-Nebraska was eminently a Democratic measure, sponsored by the nation's leading congressional Democrat, Stephen Douglas; the act's critics could not very well oppose it within that party's ranks. Looking for a new home, antislavery Democrats like Salmon Chase of Ohio joined with antislavery members of the now-defunct Whig Party like Abraham Lincoln; entrepreneurial-minded free labor enthusiasts like New York's former Whig boss Thurlow Weed (who often cared more about creating new business opportunities for American capital than the slavery issue); and other homeless former Whigs who for one reason or another could not stomach an alliance with the party of Andrew Jackson. The resulting loose collection of men with vaguely similar principles (but nearly as many divisions and disagreements) dubbed itself the Republican Party. "Upon those men who are, in sentiment, opposed to the spread, and nationalization of slavery, rests the task of preventing it. The Republican organization is the embodiment of that sentiment," Lincoln wrote in 1857, and the new party "is, to-day, the best hope of the nation, and of the world" (Basler, 1953–1955, 2: 391).

Since the new party had as one of its stated aims the containment and eventual elimination of slavery, Republicans of any kind scared Southerners to death.

"Let the consequences be what they may, whether the Potomac [River] is crimsoned in human gore, and Pennsylvania Avenue is paved ten fathoms deep with mangled bodies," raged one Southerner, "the South, will never submit to such humiliation and degradation as the inauguration of Abraham Lincoln" (McPherson, 1982, 122). In some quarters of the Republican Party, the antipathy was entirely mutual. "We are not one people," claimed Republican newspaperman Horace Greeley. "We are a people for Freedom and a people for Slavery. Between the two, conflict is inevitable" (Foner, 1988, 310).

In 1860 Lincoln's name did not even appear on many Southern ballots. That was the problem. By putting him in the White House, Northerners proved they could elect a president with no Southern input at all. Yankee population growth, money, and economic might would someday overwhelm the South and its plantation-based way of life, and there was not much Southerners could do about it. Abraham Lincoln was symbolic of this fact; it did not even much matter what he actually said or did.

Not that he actually said or did very much during the 1860 election; Lincoln let the party stalwarts do that, which was expected. By 1860 American presidential politics possessed certain elements that had been in place since the days of Andrew Jackson. Political parties now reigned supreme, and while politicians might still sometimes give lip service to the old idea of choosing a president who stood above party factionalism, in reality Americans had grown comfortable with the notion that parties ruled the process of selection and election. Party operatives had perfected what historian David Potter in *The Impending Crisis* (1976) dubbed the "hurrah" style of campaigning, with loud rallies, free-flowing alcohol, and raucous rhetoric. In 1860 "hurrah" campaigning reached a zenith as Republicans organized quasi-military marching clubs called the Wide Awakes. Northern Democrats countered with the Little Dougs, named after their candidate Stephen Douglas, while southern Democrats marched as National Democratic Volunteers. Presidential candidates were still expected to remain silent, but their supporters did plenty of talking, abetted by a popular press that whipped up support for some candidates and fanned the flames of hatred for others.

Four years later, hatred for Lincoln had not abated in Democratic circles. The hardcore southern wing of the party was gone, of course, but there were plenty of conservative and moderate northern Democrats nursing grudges. There were even a fair number of Copperheads within the party ranks; that is, men whose antipathy toward the Lincoln Administration and antiwar sentiments generally were so pronounced that their very loyalty to the Union might be called into question. Arguing that Lincoln had become the dupe of Yankee "Negrophiles" and "Abolition Puritans" like William Lloyd Garrison and Frederick Douglass, some extremists in the West even spoke openly of seceding and striking a separate peace with the Confederacy.

Lincoln faced a touchy political and legal dilemma in the spring of 1863 when one such Copperhead, Ohio Democrat Clement Vallandigham, delivered such an incendiary speech against the administration and its policies—particularly the draft, which Vallandigham urged his listeners to resist by whatever means necessary—that Ohio's military commander, General Ambrose Burnside, had him arrested and tried by a military tribunal, which sentenced him to prison. Lincoln had not really wanted Vallandigham arrested, but handed a fait accompli by one of his own generals, the president could not very well back down. He did drop Vallandigham's jail sentence, banishing him to the Confederacy instead. Democrats made much of the incident, accusing Lincoln of tyranny and unconstitutional usurpation of authority. Lincoln's response was pragmatic. "Must I shoot a simple-minded soldier boy who deserts, while I must not touch a hair of a wiley [sic] agitator who induces him to desert?" Lincoln wrote to one of his critics, "This is none the less injurious when effected by getting a father, or brother, or friend, into a public meeting, and there working upon his feeling, till he is persuaded to write the soldier boy, that he is fighting in a bad cause, for a wicked administration of a contemptable [sic] government, too weak to arrest and punish him if he shall desert. I think that in such a case, to silence the agitator, and save the boy, is not only constitutional, but, withal, a great mercy" (Basler, 1953–1955, 6: 266–267).

The Vallandigham controversy offers an apt illustration of the political problems facing a wartime president like Abraham Lincoln. Criticism of the nation's chief executive, in any democracy, was to be expected—even encouraged. But how far exactly might such criticism go during a war, when the stakes were so high? In peacetime, an offhand or injudicious remark by a politician or journalist might be offensive, distasteful, or untrue, and in the process might cost someone their reputation. In a war, however, such behavior could cost lives. But then again, just how far might a president go in suppressing such behavior in the name of national security? Might he not go so far as to endanger the founding principles of the nation itself?

With 1864 approaching, Americans would have an opportunity to pass judgment on Lincoln's policies concerning Copperheads as well as other matters related to the war. Topping the list was emancipation, an administration policy that evoked the most savage sort of opposition from Democrats. "I reject it now; I utterly spit at and despise it," seethed one (Klingaman, 2001, 108). The Democratic Party platform during the 1862 congressional elections accused emancipation-minded Republicans of pursuing "butchery of women and children," "lust and rapine," and "arson and murder" (Klingaman, 2001, 199).

There were plenty of other wartime issues the Democrats could target. One was the Vallandigham affair, of course, which party spokesmen exploited to full effect, circulating the embattled Ohioan's own proclamation from jail that "I am a Democrat—for constitu-

tion, for law, for the Union, for liberty—that is my only crime" (Paludan, 1988, 242). Democrats ripped other administration excesses in the area of civil liberties (real or imagined), arguing that Lincoln had become a tyrant with his arrests and occasional suspensions of the writ of habeas corpus. The general military conduct of the war also provided plenty of grist for the opposition party's mill, as did various economic policies backed by the president to finance the war. Among them was the Legal Tender Act, which created a uniform national currency for the first time in American history. People had balked at attempts to do this in earlier times, and there were still some who thought the government was overreaching in transforming the economy in such ways. Being the president and the leader of the party promoting these policies, Lincoln came in for more than his share of abuse.

Republicans were nervous, particularly when the state and congressional elections in late 1862 cost the party dearly. Democrats gained seats in several state legislatures and won control of the congressional delegations from Ohio, Indiana, New York, Pennsylvania, and even Lincoln's home state of Illinois. Emancipation had become party policy at this point, and the Democrats made Lincoln's party pay dearly for the fact among voters hostile to African Americans and their problems. Military reverses contributed to the problem, as well as a general war weariness that made the administration a target for more than its fair share of abuse. The president summed the problem up rather nicely. "Three main causes told the whole story," he wrote, "1. The democrats were left in a majority by our friends going to the war. 2. The democrats observed this & determined to reinstate themselves in power, and 3. Our newspaper's, by vilifying and disparaging the administration, furnished them all the weapons to do it with. Certainly, the ill-success of the war had much to do with this" (Basler, 1953–1955, 5: 494).

Some Republicans wanted to dump Lincoln, believing he had become a liability. From the more conservative spectrum came party members who felt that his attachment to emancipation fatally compromised his ability to connect with moderate and conservative white Americans, many of whom had no use for the freedmen or their problems. He is "an awful, woeful ass," moaned a conservative Republican journalist (Donald, 1995, 424). But a more serious threat to Lincoln came from Radicals at the other end of the party spectrum, who felt Lincoln had been far too slow and conservative in his embrace of emancipation and freedmen's rights. "Mr. President, you are murdering your country by inches in consequence of the inactivity of the military and the want of a distinct policy towards slavery," U.S. senator Benjamin Wade had scolded him early in the war (Donald, 1995, 332). Even after Lincoln came around to their way of thinking and freed the slaves, many Radicals felt far from satisfied, worrying over Lincoln's apparently conciliatory attitude toward white Southerners and his refusal to openly embrace measures like universal suffrage for the freedmen or wholesale confiscation of the rebels' property.

A few Radicals were disgruntled enough to begin casting about for alternatives. Some tried to draft the party's first presidential nominee from 1856, John C. Fremont, for a second run at the White House. Fremont held a certain fascination for abolitionists, because as the ranking Union general in Missouri in 1862, he had issued an emancipation decree for Missouri's slaves (which Lincoln later revoked, fearing the political repercussions). But Fremont was also a rather erratic sort, pompous and possessing a spotty military record; his candidacy to supplant Lincoln never advanced very far. More serious were the machinations of Lincoln's secretary of the Treasury, Salmon Chase. A rather humorless, ambitious, and difficult man, Chase had always held an ambivalent opinion of the president, believing that whatever Lincoln accomplished, Chase himself could surely have done better. He too was a favorite in Radical circles, with impeccable credentials dating back to his days as an antislavery lawyer trying cases in Ohio. Chase badly wanted the nomination and worked to encourage behind-the-scenes attempts to undermine Lincoln in party circles, for example, by approving an anonymous pamphlet that attacked the president for his "vascillation [sic]" and "the feebleness of his will." The president knew very well what Chase was doing. "I am entirely indifferent as to success or failure in these schemes, so long as he does his duty,"

Lincoln calmly responded (Donald, 1995, 479–481).

In the end, it did not much matter, because even his loudest Republican critics understood what an unmitigated disaster it would be if they dumped their own president in the middle of a war. And Lincoln himself knew how to navigate these treacherous political waters. A natural-born compromiser and a very shrewd politician, Lincoln aimed for the middle ground, somewhere between the radical and conservative wings of his party, and indeed of the nation as a whole. He dumped Vice President Hannibal Hamlin—a former governor, representative, and senator from Maine with a strong antislavery pedigree—in favor of Tennessee Unionist Andrew Johnson, who Lincoln and his supporters hoped would peel away moderate Democratic votes, especially in the border states. Lincoln even approved a temporary name change for his party, from Republican to National Union Party, again the better to attract moderates and conservatives who had come to associate the Republican label with radicalism. In the meantime, he struck a practical note concerning his reelection: "I have not permitted myself, gentlemen, to conclude that I am the best man in the country," he told a delegation from the National Union League in June 1864, "but I am reminded, in this connection, of a story of an old Dutch farmer, who remarked to a companion once that 'it was not best to swap horses when crossing streams'" (Basler, 1953–1955, 7: 385).

A campaign banner for President Abraham Lincoln (left) and his new running mate, Andrew Johnson, in the 1864 presidential election. Lincoln won reelection but was assassinated the following year. (Library of Congress)

The Democrats aimed for a certain middle ground themselves—and their problems aptly illustrate the political difficulties faced by the party that is out of power during a war. On the one hand, they needed to respect those members in its ranks who had honest disagreements with the administration about its policies. On the other hand, the party could not afford to be identified too closely with the Copperheads, lest it become tainted as the home of treason. It was bad enough that most of the major leaders of the Confederacy had been Democrats before the war (Republicans would take every opportunity to remind voters of this fact); if the party became too outspoken in its opposition, the thousands of fathers, brothers, and sons of the men serving in the Union army—not to mention the soldiers themselves—might well conclude that a vote for a Democrat was a vote against the men in the combat zone.

Former general George McClellan seemed to be the perfect solution to the Democrats' problems. His military status would insulate him from charges of copperheadism, gain votes among the army's rank and file (where Little Mac enjoyed huge popularity), and lend an air of legitimacy to his candidacy. He was no friend of the Lincoln Administration—he once referred to the president as "the original gorilla"—and he certainly had no sympathy for emancipation or other administration measures like suspending the writ of habeas corpus (thereby jailing suspected Copperheads without a trial). "It is too infamous," McClellan wrote; Lincoln was "inaugurating servile war, emancipating the slaves, and at one stroke of the pen changing our free institutions into a despotism—for such I regard as the natural effect of the last Proclamation suspending the Habeas Corpus throughout the land" (Sears, 1988, 324).

When they nominated McClellan, the Democrats handed him a problematic platform that seemed to at once call for an end to hostilities and a vigorous prosecution of the war. The opening paragraph pledged that Democrats "will adhere with unswerving fidelity to the Union under the Constitution as the only solid foundation of our strength, security, and happiness as a people." On the other hand, the next plank in the platform (authored by Clement Vallandigham himself) blasted the Lincoln Administration's efforts to restore that very same Union. "After four years of failure to restore the Union by the experiment of war, during which . . . public liberty and private right alike trodden down, and the material prosperity of the country essentially impaired," the convention declared, "justice, humanity, liberty, and the public welfare demand that immediate efforts be made for a cessation of hostilities, with a view of an ultimate convention of the States, or other peaceable means, to the end that, at the earliest practicable moment, peace may be restored on the basis of the Federal Union of the States" (www.sewanee.edu/ faculty/Willis/Civil_War/ documents/democratic.html). "On the basis of the Federal Union" moved the party away from sounding like an all-out Copperhead organization, but the call for a truce and negotiation—with white Southerners who had never shown much inclination toward either, unless on the basis of Confederate independence—suggested otherwise. To further the confusion, the convention saddled McClellan with an extreme peace candidate and Vallandigham ally as a running mate, George H. Pendleton of Ohio.

A Democratic Party campaign banner for the presidential election of 1864 includes portraits of presidential contender George B. McClellan (left) and his running mate, George H. Pendleton. (Library of Congress)

At their convention in Baltimore, the Republicans hammered together a platform that was more internally consistent than their opponents'. It issued an unequivocal call for victory against the Confederacy, supported emancipation and the arming of black troops (neither of which were even mentioned in the Democrats' platform), and endorsed the administration's internal security and economic measures. It left no middle ground on the matter of the war's justice or its prosecution. "It is the highest duty of every American citizen to maintain against all their enemies the integrity of the Union and the paramount authority of the Constitution and laws of the United States," the platform declared, and stated that "we pledge ourselves, as Union men . . . to do everything in our power to aid the Government in quelling by force of arms the Rebellion now raging against its authority, and in bringing to the punishment due to their crimes the Rebels and traitors arrayed against it" (www.sewanee.edu/faculty/Willis/Civil_War/documents/republican.html).

Democrats moved quickly to exploit all the baggage attached to administration policies, attacking Lincoln's record on civil liberties, his economic policies, and whatever other problems could be laid at the president's doorstep. Vallandigham accused Lincoln of using federal patronage powers to build himself up like a king, declaring that Lincoln "is the God whose priests are a hundred and fifty thousand [federal workers] and whose worshipers are a whole army of jobbers and contractors" (Baker, 1983, 156).

But the real hot-button issue was emancipation, and here Democrats focused most of their efforts, playing the race card with stunning ferocity. They claimed that the first of Lincoln's Ten Commandments held that "Thou shalt have no other God but the negro" (Donald, 1995, 537). Lincoln "is brutal in all his habits," railed one newspaper editorial. "Filthy black niggers, greasy, sweating, and disgusting, now jostle white people and even ladies everywhere, even at the President's levees." Others referred to Lincoln as "Abraham Africanus the First" and spread rumors that African American blood ran in his veins (McPherson, 1982, 790). Nor were the racial slurs limited to Lincoln; a widely circulated cartoon portrayed a "negro ball" involving white Republican men and lascivious black women (Vorenberg, 2001, 161). The particular theme of race mixing, or miscegenation, touched a very sensitive spot in many whites' minds, and Democrats pushed it for all it was worth.

The 1864 election was the most racially charged in American history. Republicans labored hard to link Democrats with treason and support for the enemy. Some suggested that McClellan was so deeply dissatisfied with administration policies that his very loyalty was questionable. Just as the Democrats tried to blur the lines between radical antislavery Republicans and the party's more moderate wing, so too did Republicans suggest that there essentially was no difference between a Copperhead and a Democrat. Rumors abounded of dark plots, abetted by Democrats, to poison northern water supplies, free Confederate prisoners from northern jails, and assassinate the president. "I have facts in my possession which I wish to reveal to you alone, in relation to a conspiracy against you and this glorious Union," ran a breathless letter from New York newspaperman Horace Greeley. "When I reveal it to you, some of the most prominent men of the Democracy of this city will be brought out as Traitors and Conspirators" (Holzer, 2006, 345). "REBELLION IN THE NORTH!! EXTRAORDINARY DISCLOSURE! Val[landigham]'s Plan to

Overthrow the Government!" read one overwrought Republican headline (McPherson, 1982, 448). And if the Democrats harped on fears of African Americans, Republicans countered with a strained anti-Semitic argument that Democratic operatives were in league with Jewish business at home and abroad to undermine the Republicans' wartime financial plans. One man even went so far as to suggest that McClellan had been nominated by "a cabal of Jews at Chicago" (Neely, 1991, 155).

All the talk of freedmen and race aside, the election would turn on military matters, in particular two factors: what would happen on the battlefield and what would happen in the heads of soldiers in the field. The president naturally had his share of detractors in the ranks, and he sometimes took heat for his lack of military decorum and sloppy appearance during troop reviews. "There is no need of your being so infernally awkward," groused a friend who had heard such complaints. "For God's sake, consult somebody, some military man, as to what you ought to do on these occasions" (Davis, 1999, 42). But more often the men in blue admired and rather liked the president's homeliness and unmilitarylike appearance. Many had come to see him as a sort of father figure, referring to him affectionately as Old Abe and Father Abram. "What a depth of devotion, sympathy, and reassurance were conveyed through his smile," wrote a soldier, and "how our hearts went out to him" (Davis, 1999, 69). Lincoln did what he could to see to it that soldiers were given every opportunity to express their admiration, granting furloughs to those soldiers who hailed from a state other than the nineteen that allowed them to vote in the field. A full 78 percent would cast their ballots for him (Paludan, 1988, 289).

Still, the contest was touch and go for a while. Horrendous battlefield deaths throughout the first half of 1864 at places like Spotsylvania and Cold Harbor deepened northern gloom. During the summer Lincoln himself grew despondent, particularly when some of his own advisers told him that war weariness and Democratic craftiness would indeed deny him a second term. "I told Mr. Lincoln that his re-election was an impossibility," Republican Party boss Thurlow Weed recalled. "At any rate, nobody here [New York] doubts it; nor do I see any body from other States who authorizes [sic] the slightest hope of success." In August, Lincoln wrote out a note that read, "This morning, as for some days past, it seems exceedingly probable that this Administration will not be re-elected. Then it will be my duty to so co-operate with the President elect, as to save the Union between the election and the inauguration; as he will have secured his election on such ground that he can not possibly save it afterwards." (Basler, 1953–1955, 7: 514–515). Lincoln asked all of his Cabinet members to sign the note without reading it, then carefully tucked it away, thinking he might have to use it for a lost election.

Lincoln and his supporters need not have been quite so concerned for, in the end, he beat McClellan rather handily. The president garnered 55 percent of the popular vote and dominated the Electoral College, racking up 212 electoral votes to McClellan's 12. The Republicans carried every state but New Jersey, Delaware, and Kentucky. To a supporter McClellan groused that it was "a struggle of honor[,] patriotism and truth against deceit[,] selfishness and fanaticism, and I think we have played well our parts" (Sears, 1988, 386). Lincoln was more generous, as was his wont. "While deeply grateful for this mark of [the voters'] confidence in me," he declared, "if I know my heart, my gratitude is free from any taint of personal triumph. I do not impugn the motives of any one opposed to me. It is no pleasure to me to triumph over any one; but I give thanks to the Almighty for this evidence of the people's resolution to stand by free government and the rights of humanity" (Basler, 1953–1955, 8: 96).

In many ways the presidential election of 1864 set the agenda for presidential elections over the next several decades. It marked the beginning of Republican dominance in the White House, a control perpetuated by the party's habit of nominating and electing former Union officers and by its continual invocation of wartime memories and American patriotism. Some would call this strategy "waving the bloody shirt," after the habit among some GOP activists of literally displaying bloodstained uniforms left over from the war at campaign rallies—a non-too-subtle reminder that they were the party of victory and the preservation of the Union. "We charge the Democratic party with being the same in character and spirit as when it sympathized with treason," the Republican party platform of 1876 declared, "with reasserting and applauding in the national capitol the sentiments of unrepentant rebellion; with sending Union soldiers to the rear, and promoting Confederate soldiers to the front, . . . [and] we warn the country against trusting a party thus alike unworthy, recreant, and incapable" (www.presidency.ucsb.edu).

For their part, Democrats would very often live in the Civil War past as well, becoming the party of choice for unreconstructed white supremacists in the South and staunch supporters of Jim Crow America. The party had always possessed a strong proslavery southern wing, which after the war would morph into a Jim Crow segregationist wing exerting a strong gravitational pull on Democratic politics well into the twentieth century.

But perhaps what is most remarkable about the 1864 election is merely the fact that it occurred at all. Few nations could afford, in the midst of a ruinous civil war, to pause and allow its citizens to pass judgment on their political and military leaders in such a fashion. President Lincoln himself said it best when addressing a group of well-wishers a few days after his victory. "The election, along with its incidental, and undesirable strife, has done good," Lincoln argued. "It has demonstrated that a people's government can sustain a national election, in the midst of a great civil war. . . . It shows also how *sound*, and how *strong* we still are. . . . Gold is good in its place; but living, brave, patriotic men, are better than gold" (Basler, 1953–1955, 8: 101).

ELECTION OF 1932

The Civil War seemed like a very long time ago to Americans in 1932. Nineteen years before, President Woodrow Wilson—the first Democrat elected to the White House since Grover Cleveland in 1892—had presided over the fiftieth anniversary reunion of the Battle of Gettysburg. A Southerner who had witnessed the defeated veterans of Lee's army returning while a boy, Wilson pronounced his benediction on the cause, North and South, and suggested that memories had finally faded enough to effect a full-blown sectional reconciliation. "How wholesome and healing the peace has been!" Wilson declared. "We have found one another again as brothers and comrades" (Blight, 2001, 11).

Reconciliation there may have been, but one political fact had not changed; the White House had been a Republican bastion ever since Lincoln's death. Cleveland and Wilson briefly broke the string of Republican chief executives, but otherwise the GOP dominated presidential politics. In the process the party became the province of what one observer called "political condottieri"—professional political operators like Simon Cameron of Pennsylvania, Roscoe Conkling and "Boss" Tweed of New York, and other power brokers who wheeled and dealed in votes, often in a corrupt and unprincipled manner.

Certain political assumptions had accompanied the Republicans' presidential supremacy. The party always possessed a strong free labor, economic development wing whose views eventually hardened into an orthodoxy that required its presidential candidates to possess strong big-business credentials. There were occasional blips on the screen—Teddy Roosevelt's trust-busting ways in the early 1900s that were aimed at corporate misdeeds and which made big headlines—but for the most part, "Republican" was synonymous in Americans' minds with the twentieth-century's explosive capitalist and industrial growth, and party stalwarts wanted government largely to get out of business's way. Regulation of the market was fine, so long as it did not come to resemble government ownership of key economic sectors. As Herbert Hoover put it, there was a "determination of the American people that regulation of private enterprise and not Government ownership or operation is the course rightly to be pursued in our relation to business" (www.yale.edu/lawweb/avalon).

Voters equally identified the party with limited presidential power. This was partly a function of the general decline in presidential influence vis-à-vis Congress during the late nineteenth century, when the impeachment of Andrew Johnson and the various scandals surrounding the administrations of Ulysses S. Grant tipped the balance of power in favor of Congress. But it was also part and parcel of a Republican laissez-faire political economy. Again, Teddy Roosevelt provided something of an exception, with his robust embrace of the "strenuous life" and the Progressive approach to various government reforms. But there were definite limits to how far even TR would go in the name of reining

in business's excess. He took pains not to appear a fellow traveler of the great bugaboo of the age, socialism, with its goal of bringing all segments of American life under government's heel. "Roosevelt saw his job as leading the nation toward reform through gradual, constitutional means—with an occasional jump start of an executive order," wrote biographer Kathleen Dalton (Dalton, 2002, 325).

At the same time, the GOP's traditional identification with the rights and concerns of African Americans eroded. Since its birth the party had possessed both a civil liberties and a big business wing, and by 1880 the latter enjoyed a definite ascendancy, as Americans saw fit to abandon Reconstruction and leave African Americans in the South to the tender mercies of their former Confederate neighbors. Republicans found more political capital in touting their business credentials than pursuing increasingly unpopular programs for the freedmen and increasingly paid only lip service to easing the plight of blacks groaning under the weight of post-slavery poverty and injustice. The GOP was still the party of choice for most African Americans, but it was clear by the turn of the twentieth century that the party's ruling powers had lost interest in them, to the point that some disgruntled blacks tried (unsuccessfully) to establish an independent organization, the Afro-American National League, to protect black interests.

The Democrats, meanwhile, were hamstrung in their efforts to regain control of the White House by a variety of factors. The residue of Confederate defeat hung about the party for the rest of the nineteenth century, helped along by their Republican opponents' habit of nominating former Union officers and relentlessly "waving the bloody shirt" to remind voters just who had prevailed during the century's preeminent conflict. Republican cartoonist Thomas Nast used a donkey to portray Democrats' antiwar stubbornness (the original donkey was labeled a "copperhead" and a "jackass"), and while the party would eventually come to embrace the donkey as its mascot, it was originally meant to illustrate, among other things, a party that had become badly out of touch with the nation.

Democrats did have a Progressive wing, and its influence was steadily increasing. The gap between rich and poor grew wider during the Gilded Age, and since the GOP was quite rightly associated with big business, shrewd Democratic operatives could exploit this fact by suggesting that their party was in fact the proper place to protect the interests of working Americans. But Democrats had no unified plan concerning how they might do this. Gold Democrats, for example, wanted a currency based on the gold standard, while Silver Democrats argued for a currency rooted in the nation's large stockpiles of silver bullion. Other Democrats quarreled over tariff policies, the party's proper response to the nation's burgeoning labor movement, and other issues that seemed to divide more often than unite. Beyond that, the party simply seemed to be forever catching its breath, trying forever to play catch-up to a Republican Party that had pretty much

controlled the nation's political agenda since 1865. One disgruntled observer sourly noted that the Democrats "camped every four years exactly where the Republican Party camped four years before" (Rutland, 1979, 129).

The party could make a serious run at the White House. In 1880, for example, Winfield Scott Hancock mustered a little over 48 percent of the popular vote against the Republicans' James A. Garfield, and Grover Cleveland prevailed twice in nonconsecutive elections (the only president to do so). In fact, many of the presidential elections between 1864 and 1900 were quite close, reflecting a more divided and ambivalent electorate than the Republicans' dominance of the White House during the period would suggest. But in the North especially, the Democrats' legacy and mandate remained unclear. The Republicans spent decades positioning themselves as the party of wartime victory (the Civil War, the Spanish-American conflict), patriotism, and economic might. Democrats could claim a wartime victory during World War I under Wilson's watch (though that particular victory created a good amount of disillusionment and alienation) and some important Progressive reforms in Congress. But the party lacked an easily identifiable, appealing identity, and it had a disturbing tendency to shoot itself in the foot—as in 1896, when it nominated the brilliant but erratic William Jennings Bryan to run against the GOP's William McKinley. According to one acerbic observer, "Lunacy having dictated [the Democratic Party platform], it was perhaps natural that should evolve . . . there is peril in making [a party] ridiculous. The nomination of the 'boy orator' for the White House at this stage of the nation's affairs . . . comes perilously near taking this fatal step" (Rutland, 1979, 151). Bryan lost to McKinley in a landslide.

When Herbert Hoover was elevated to the White House in 1928, he seemed to be yet another typical Republican success story. Born into modest circumstances in a pious Quaker family, Hoover earned a degree in engineering from Stanford University and made his fortune in the mining industry. Thrifty, hardworking, and devout, he seemed to be the embodiment of the American character—or at least the Republican version thereof. "A society's inspiration is individual initiative. Its stimulus is competition," he believed. "It is the essence of [American] democracy that progress of the mass must arise from progress of the individual" (Burner, 1979, 139). Those individuals, he believed, should be left as free from government interference as possible, to maximize their drive and entrepreneurship. Volunteerism and private charity were the answer in times of crisis, not government intervention. "Neighborly obligation" could solve the world's ills.

In back of Hoover stood over a decade's worth of economic prosperity; the Roaring Twenties had seen the nation's burgeoning industrial economy grow at an unprecedented rate, bringing good times for large numbers of Americans. Neither the new president nor anyone else saw much reason to think this would change anytime soon. In his Inaugural Address,

Brilliantly successful as an engineer and humanitarian, Herbert Hoover failed as a president to lead the United States effectively during the Great Depression. (Library of Congress)

Hoover sounded an optimistic note. "If we survey the situation of our Nation both at home and abroad, we find many satisfactions," he declared. "We have emerged from the losses of the Great War and the reconstruction following it with increased virility and strength. . . . We have reached a higher degree of comfort and security than ever existed before in the history of the world. Through liberation from widespread poverty, we have reached a higher degree of individual freedom than ever before. The devotion to and concern for our institutions are deep and sincere. We are steadily building a new race—a new civilization great in its own attainments" (www.yale.edu/lawweb/avalon).

But the times were changing, pulling the rug of prosperity right out from under Hoover's feet. He was no fool, and he was a good businessman; he saw trouble coming as far back as 1928, when he warned Federal Reserve officials that the nation's runaway fascination with the stock market, predicated often on dollar values that did not really exist, was irrational and dangerous. "The only trouble with capitalism is capitalists," he grumbled. "They're too damned greedy" (Burner, 1979, 246–247). Black Friday and the Crash of 1929 would prove the president prescient.

But as we saw in chapter 2, Hoover was inadequate to the task of addressing the Depression's wrenching social and economic problems. He was not up to the politics of the day, either. As a coalition builder he left much to be desired, managing often to irritate Democrats and his own party members alike; nor was he much given to the arm-twisting that would have been necessary to bring businessmen and corporate leaders into line with government attempts to curb the Depression. He never really had good relations with the media, either, preferring to insulate himself from their questions whenever possible and becoming increasingly sensitive as editorialists brought his administration under fire. "I have not in my experience in Washington seen anything so rotten in an attitude of the press towards the President of the United States," he groused (Burner, 1979, 254).

More generally, the Republicans' prevailing political ideology of laissez-faire governing and trust in businessmen seemed hopelessly obsolete to many who now stood in soup lines and begged on street corners in the shadows of the edifices erected by the captains of industry. It was hard to convince desperate Americans that merely trusting capitalism's invisible hand would be enough to staunch the economic bleeding felt in all corners of American life. The GOP had placed most of its eggs in one basket: industrialization and big business. If Americans were to blame big business and industry for the Crash of 1929, the Republican Party could find itself caught in the backlash.

A variety of other forces were combining to give Democrats real hope. The off-year congressional elections of 1930 saw the GOP lose eight seats in the Senate, giving the party a razor-thin majority of forty-eight seats to the Democrats' forty-seven (and one member of the independent Farmer-Labor party). Of those forty-eight, Hoover bemoaned the fact that several voted with what he thought of as the "left wing." While the Democrats still sported a conservative southern element that wanted little to do with government activism, there were signs of a growing working-class, urban, and minority bloc of voters who might be persuaded to support a Democratic challenger to the Republicans' White House hegemony.

The pieces were in place for a major sea change in American politics. What the Democratic Party now needed was a person who understood the changes in the party's makeup and possessed the requisite political skills and media savvy to forge them into a functioning coalition.

Few would have predicted that Franklin Delano Roosevelt could lead such a coalition. Born into wealth and privilege, he never stood in a soup line, worked in a factory, or knew the pain of discrimination. Well-mannered, cultured, and charming, Roosevelt seemed much more suited for a summer in the Hamptons or a New York soiree than for a place in the front lines battling poverty. "He was rather a snob," recalled one of his college friends, and "as far as I know, he was not then interested in the working man. . . . He did not have the 'common touch' . . . [and] seemed ill at ease with people outside of his group. When as a young man he found himself in a rundown district of Boston, the very idea that such conditions even existed was a revelation. 'My God, I didn't know anyone lived like that'," he exclaimed (Ward, 1985, 240, 319).

Beneath the surface, however, was a man with exquisite political skills that were peculiarly appropriate for his day and age. In a time when politicians increasingly found themselves under the glaring spotlights created by the new media of film and radio, Roosevelt was a consummate actor who knew how to project an image. He fairly exuded charm and enthusiasm. "You know I am seldom carried away," one Democratic Party boss told a reporter in 1924 after hearing a Roosevelt speech, but "he has the most magnetic personality of any individual I have ever met" (Morgan, 1985, 271).

Roosevelt also possessed a keen eye for just the sort of image Americans wanted at any given time. Mired in the throes of the Depression, he understood that Americans desperately needed leaders who at least acted as if they knew what they were doing, and he obliged with constant images of his happy, smiling face and a barrage of speeches and radio "chats" with his soothing, mellifluous voice. There were those who felt he was not all that bright—"a kind of amiable boy scout," scoffed one critic—but this was more than offset by his ability to project understanding, sympathy, and charm (Kennedy, 1999, 101).

He offered an interesting contrast to Hoover, who was the embodiment of a complacent Republican establishment that had grown too accustomed to power and had possessed the keys to the White House for too long. President Hoover was not without his merits, and it was far from certain that a Democratic administration could do any better. Still, Americans in 1932 could be forgiven if they thought that a change, any change at all, was preferable to their current miserable situation.

The Republicans renominated Hoover, but without much enthusiasm. By this point, sour-minded Americans had tagged nearly every bad thing or experience related to the Depression with his last name: "Hoovervilles" were cardboard shanties, a "Hoover flag" was an empty pocket turned inside out, even a controversial tariff measure that some felt had contributed to the panic (and which the president had only grudgingly signed into law) became the "Hoover tariff." Republicans knew they had been saddled with a dead horse. "He is more unpopular than Judas Iscariot," one party operative observed (Mayer, 1967, 421). There was some talk of dumping Hoover in favor of former president Calvin Coolidge or some minor figure in the party; but in the end, Hoover's status as the incumbent and his political connections within the party were enough to hand him the nomination rather easily, all things considered.

Roosevelt had to work harder to get his nomination. There was blood in the water; everyone knew the Republicans were vulnerable and that the presidency was probably there for the taking. Roosevelt's chief competitor was John Nance Garner, a well-connected Texan, Speaker of the House of Representatives, and hero of the party's southern wing, who was if anything more conservative than many Republicans—"the great trouble today is that we have too many laws," he once declared (Kennedy, 1999, 61).

The party platform offered a long laundry list of reforms aimed at fixing everything broken by the Depression and laying the blame squarely on the shoulders of their opponents. Republicans "have ruined our foreign trade; destroyed the values of our commodities and products, crippled our banking system, robbed millions of our people of their life savings, and thrown millions more out of work," the platform argued, and in the process "produced wide-spread poverty and brought the government to a state of financial distress unprecedented in time of peace" (www.presidency.ucsb.edu). Reflecting a growing Democratic Party skill

at marketing itself in the new media age of politics, the party reduced its ideas to a simple phrase: the "three Rs: relief, recovery, and reform." And Roosevelt went still further, helping to create the brilliant phrase "the New Deal" to describe the party's program. And in another demonstration of media savvy, FDR flew directly to Chicago to deliver his acceptance speech for the party's nomination, a move doubly innovative, given the long-standing tradition that presidential candidates should remain outdoors while their nominating conventions met and that commercial airflight itself was still very new.

By contrast, the Hoover campaign looked and felt beaten almost from day one. Its platform was an extremely long, nearly unreadable list of the problems caused by the Depression, capped with a ringing declaration that "the Republican Party faces the future unafraid! With courage and confidence in ultimate success, we will strive against the forces that strike at our social and economic ideals, our political institutions" (www.presidency.ucsb.edu). But the statement smacked of a false bravado.

The campaign itself was, practically speaking, without surprise or much drama. While FDR saw to it that his image of energy and charm pervaded the nation's newspapers and airwaves, Hoover withdrew from the public eye, making few statements to the press and preferring to pass out written policy statements to baffled reporters. "Did it ever occur to you that we went through the campaign . . . without one kindly story circulated about Hoover or any of

Franklin D. Roosevelt campaigns for president with daughter Anna (center) and wife Eleanor (right) on October 24, 1932. Roosevelt would go on to defeat the incumbent president Herbert Hoover and remain in office until his death in 1945. (Franklin D. Roosevelt Library)

---

his friends?" moaned one Republican to a friend (Fausold, 1985, 205).

The results were predictable. Roosevelt won in a landslide, carrying every state but Pennsylvania, Delaware, Rhode Island, Maine, Vermont, and New Hampshire. Nearly 23 million Americans voted for FDR and his New Deal, as opposed to a bit under 16 million for Hoover. The Electoral College tally was even more lopsided: 472 for Roosevelt,

59 for Hoover. "As we expected, we were defeated in the election," was Hoover's terse response (Fausold, 1985, 213).

While the election itself was one of the less exciting contests in American presidential history, its results were profound. FDR brought to the White House a whole new attitude, startling in its contrast to previous decades of Republican laissez-faire leadership. Now presidents would be judged not by their capacity for self-restraint in the exercise of executive authority—a largely forgotten strain of thought about the presidency that had originated with Washington and his generation's concerns about the presidency's quasi-monarchical potential—but rather by their activity, energy level, and enthusiasm. Roosevelt set the precedent of presidents being held accountable for how much new policy they could create within the first one hundred days of their terms, how well they handled press conferences and the glaring media spotlight, and how much élan and poise they could muster while dwelling in the media fishbowl of the White House. After FDR it would be unthinkable for a president to take pride in his reticence (as Calvin Coolidge had done) or to express an overt disdain for professional journalism and the media (as Hoover had often seemed to do). Roosevelt ensured that future presidents would have at least to look busy; the political consequences of doing otherwise could be enormous.

There would be those who saw in Roosevelt's activism a subversion of the bedrock principle that presidents should exercise careful restraint in pulling the levers of federal executive power. In the years that followed his election, Republican opponents hammered on the theme that FDR's New Deal activism (and later, his robust foreign policy) would spell disaster for the country by touching off a reckless spate of government spending that might eventually land the nation in bankruptcy. Herbert Hoover himself tried briefly to resuscitate his reputation with a possible run at the White House in 1936 by sounding these themes and

pressing his fellow Republicans to reject FDR's activism and "raise the standard in defense of fundamental American principle" (Wolfskill, 1969, 237).

Hoover did not get very far; more generally, for the next two decades Republicans would be frustrated in their attempts to regain the White House. Roosevelt eventually served for thirteen years, ignoring the old two-term limit tradition established by George Washington and becoming by far the longest sitting president in American history. Following his death in 1945, Harry Truman took over. Truman gave the GOP hope. He seemed vulnerable, an obscure Missouri senator who had a plainspoken quality that sometimes shaded off into an embarrassing frankness and who lacked FDR's consummate political skills. But Truman stunned everyone by beating colorless Republican stalwart Tom Dewey in 1948, denying the GOP a return to presidential power. Former general Dwight Eisenhower's two-term stint as president from 1952 to 1960 provided only a brief Republican interlude before Democrats John F. Kennedy and Lyndon Johnson again gave Democrats control of the White House for most of the 1960s. Overall, in the middle of the twentieth century the White House became a Democratic bastion.

Part of the problem for Republicans was FDR's enormous personal popularity, and another part of it was the times. First the Great Depression and then World War II convinced most Americans that changing horses in midstream would be unwise—and so they stuck with Roosevelt. After his death, the cold war with Russia also seemed to be a poor time to make a massive change in national leadership—and so they stuck with Truman, a Democrat and Roosevelt's immediate successor. By 1960, the Roosevelt coalition was a powerful enough force that its core strength of blue-collar workers, city dwellers, and civil rights supporters were effectively able to wrest control of the party from the hoary old white Southern Dixiecrat wing and deliver the presidency to Kennedy and Johnson, both men with strong antipoverty and civil rights records.

Past a certain point, there was not much Republicans could do about the political dynamics of these developments. But the GOP created its own political difficulties as well. By the time Roosevelt entered office, the Republican Party was showing unmistakable signs of having been in power for too long: complacency; stale ideas; and concentration of party control in the hands of a few insiders, some of whom were unscrupulous and even corrupt. Waving the bloody shirt had long since faded into obscurity, and the morally ambivalent ground that big business came increasingly to occupy made the GOP's pro-capitalist politics an iffy proposition, at best. Americans would no longer reflexively support a candidate who was overtly allied with the captains of industry; nor would they be inclined to give the benefit of the doubt to a party whose more memorable presidents since the days of Teddy Roosevelt were men who fervently believed that he who governed least, governed best.

In contrast, the Democratic Party seemed to be riding the crest of progress. With an energized new base, the party pursued bold (and sometimes controversial) new programs in domestic spending and robust government activism under Roosevelt, Truman, Kennedy, and Johnson. Those four together painted a picture of federal government domestic activism to combat racism, discrimination, poverty, and unemployment and of robust foreign policy activism directed first at the Axis powers of World War II and then at the postwar Communist regimes in Russia and China. "I do not believe that the Great Society is the ordered, changeless, and sterile battalion of the ants," Johnson declared in 1965. "It is the excitement of becoming—always becoming, trying, probing, falling, resting, and trying again—but always trying and always gaining" (www.yale.edu/lawweb/avalon). "Always trying, always gaining"—a long way, indeed, from the days of Calvin Coolidge and Herbert Hoover.

ELECTION OF 1980

In 1973 Arthur Schlesinger Jr. penned *The Imperial Presidency*, one of the most important and influential books ever written about the office. In it he argued that the American president had become far too powerful for the office and the nation's own good. Tracing the history of the presidency's development from the Founding era through the twentieth century, Schlesinger argued that "presidential primacy, so indispensable to the political order, has turned into presidential supremacy." He worried in particular about separation of powers issues between the executive and legislative branches, writing critically about "the shift in the *constitutional* balance . . . that is, the appropriation by the Presidency, and particularly by the contemporary Presidency, of powers reserved by the Constitution and by long historical practice to Congress" (Schlesinger, 1973, viii).

Schlesinger was at once both peculiarly qualified and a peculiar choice to write such a volume: qualified, in that he was a historian with impeccable credentials and a razor-sharp analytical mind, peculiar in that he had served as an adviser in the Kennedy Administration, whose Camelot public image and generally optimistic outlook would seem to have been the very antithesis of the dark warnings Schlesinger sounded about the growth of presidential power. The enormously popular JFK did receive some kudos from Schlesinger, who argued that Kennedy had acted to curb the profligate use of "executive privilege" pioneered under his predecessor, Dwight Eisenhower, as a tool by which presidents could almost unilaterally exercise authority without congressional input or oversight. But even Kennedy, Schlesinger argued, had contributed to the drift toward ever greater executive power. "In foreign affairs Congress and the executive [under Kennedy] alike, as if under hypnosis, unquestionably accepted the thesis of executive supremacy," Schlesinger argued (Schlesinger, 1973, 172).

Whether Americans actually cared or not was another matter. Presidents seemed almost instinctively to understand that, since FDR's election in 1932, the public wanted and expected big, bold actions from their presidents. Harry Truman tore a page from Roosevelt's book and labeled his own ambitious domestic program the Fair Deal, pressing Congress for new social spending initiatives in education, unemployment insurance, health care, tax reform, and labor relations. "We must go on," he told Congress. "We must widen our horizon further." To that end, Truman sought to maintain many of the World War II–era measures of expansive federal power into peacetime, using powerful new tools like federal price controls and labor-management regulations to further direct the American economy from on high, this time in the name of social justice. "We must consider the redevelopment of large areas of the blighted and slum sections of our cities so that in the truly American way they may be remade to accommodate . . . every income group," he declared (McCullough, 1992, 468).

Lyndon Johnson pressed still further, trying to use the enormous political goodwill and national unity he inherited as Kennedy's successor to end poverty in America altogether through government action. Calling his program the Great Society, LBJ pressed for sweeping new government programs in just about every walk of life, from poverty relief to higher education. The economic boom times of the 1960s meant that the government had money to spend, and LBJ pressed for action. "The challenge of the next half century is whether we have the wisdom to use that wealth to enrich and elevate our national life," he declared (Goodwin, 1976, 211). Funded by Congress but conceived by the president, the Great Society was almost certain to create ever-greater opportunities for presidential expansion and power. Publicly, Johnson placed these developments on the high moral plane of moral duty; privately, this intensely ambitious man strove to make a name for himself by passing more domestic legislation than did FDR during the New Deal's heyday. "I'm no budget slasher," he proudly told his supporters. "I am a Roosevelt New Dealer. As a matter of fact, John F. Kennedy was a little too conservative to suit my tastes" (Dallek, 1998, 61).

Even Eisenhower—something of a grandfatherly figure and an apparent throwback to the days of Coolidge and Hoover with his image of relaxed presidential golf games and genial smiles—oversaw the steady growth of executive power during his watch. Where Johnson's specialty would be growing the president's authority in domestic matters, Ike saw to it that White House influence grew in foreign affairs, particular regarding the gathering of intelligence and its implementation. He used the Central Intelligence Agency to engineer coups in the Middle East, Central America, and Southeast Asia, all largely without congressional influence or oversight. "In no way perhaps did [Eisenhower] more effectively deprive the Congress of a voice in foreign policy than by confiding so much power to an agency so securely out of congressional reach," Schlesinger argued. "Though the CIA

was persistently, ingeniously and sometimes irresponsibly engaged in undertakings that confronted the nation with the possibility of war, Congress had no effective means of control or of oversight" (Schlesinger, 1973, 167). And what Eisenhower initiated, his vice president and the future president Richard Nixon would develop into almost an art form, using various clandestine operations in Vietnam and elsewhere to further his policy objectives with even less monitoring or restraint from other agencies than was the case with his predecessors. Disdaining the CIA as made up of "Ivy League liberals" and the State Department as the dead hand of bureaucracy, Nixon pressed for personal, solitary control of the nation's foreign affairs, away from the prying eyes of the American people, Congress, and sometimes even his own advisers. "It was significant that the contemporary statesman Nixon most admired was Charles de Gaulle of France," observed historian William Bundy. "Secrecy, aloofness, an aura of mystery, limiting personal statements and achieving maximum surprise and effect with those he did make, frequent dissimulation of his true purposes to keep criticism at bay—all these were leaves from de Gaulle's book that Nixon was prepared by instinct and calculation to borrow" (Bundy, 1998, 55).

Prior to 1980 it would have been difficult to put a consistent political or ideological label on any of these various manifestations of the imperial presidency. Democrats tended to create activist presidents because the party's prevailing liberal orthodoxy suggested the importance of government activism to right the wrongs of a capitalist system that sometimes ran amok. Democrats could therefore often be heard to argue for the virtues of a strong man at the presidential helm to press the various domestic initiatives embodied in the New Deal, the Fair Deal, and the Great Society. The Republicans' history of laissez-faire economic policies and generally conservative tendencies would have suggested the appeal of a more limited approach to federal power in general and presidential power in particular. Yet when push came to shove, Eisenhower did not hesitate to expand executive authority in foreign policy and intelligence operations, and Richard Milhous Nixon was hardly a model of presidential restraint. Whether any given liberal or conservative, Democratic or Republican presidential candidate pressed for more or less power depended a great deal upon the times and the circumstances. And at the end of the day, neither party was willing to place a significant brake on runaway presidential power.

Moreover, it would be a mistake to presume too close an alignment of party and ideology in American politics. "Democrat" has not always been synonymous with "liberal." By the same token, Republicans have not always been ideological conservatives. That said, however, there have been periods in American history when party politics did align itself more or less predictably in ideological terms. This process reached a critical mass for Republicans in 1964 with the nomination of Arizona's Barry Goldwater to face Lyndon Johnson.

Many observers were astonished that the GOP would nominate a man like Goldwater: he was irascible, brilliant, and uncompromising, a fire-breathing Arizona senator who spoke his mind no matter what the cost or consequences. In newspaper columns and a 1960 book, *The Conscience of a Conservative,* Goldwater espoused a brand of right-wing politics that emphasized a strong, anti-Communist national defense; limited federal power; a drastic reduction in the size of the New Deal welfare state; and a return to old-time religious values and virtues as a way of restoring what he believed was the nation's tattered moral fabric. "Now, my fellow Americans, the tide has been running against freedom," he thundered in his acceptance speech during the 1964 convention. "Our people have followed false prophets. We must, and we shall, return to proven ways—not because they are old, but because they are true." To those who labeled him an extremist, Goldwater replied that "extremism in the defense of liberty is no vice. And let me remind you also that moderation in the pursuit of justice is no virtue" (www.washingtonpost.com/wp-srv/politics/daily/may98/goldwaterspeech.htm).

Goldwater's worst tendencies played right into the Democrats' hands—and they played their cards masterfully. They relentlessly portrayed the Arizona senator as a conservative extremist whose views might someday cost the nation dearly. Their masterstroke was a controversial television ad depicting a little girl holding a flower in a field, followed by an immense atomic bomb explosion. A somber voice (with a Texas twang that sounded quite a bit like LBJ) then intoned, "These are the stakes—to make a world in which all of God's children can live, or to go into the dark. We must love each other, or we must die. Vote for President Johnson on November 3. The stakes are too high for you to stay home" (Dallek, 1998, 175). The implication was clear: Goldwater was a madman who might just push the nuclear button if given an opportunity. The ad was controversial and not entirely fair; it was also extremely effective, particularly given Goldwater's own comments: "Let's lob [a nuclear weapon] into the men's room of the Kremlin," he once exclaimed (Dallek, 1998, 131). Conservative true believers were delighted, moderates were shocked, and the Democrats were victorious. Johnson crushed Goldwater in the election.

As a man campaigning for president, Goldwater was a disaster; but as a bellwether of change for the Republican Party, he was a prophet. His fire-and-brimstone conservatism may have alienated many middle-of-the-road Americans, but it galvanized a potent Republican base of suburban white voters, evangelical Christians, and anti-Communist hardliners, what Richard Nixon later termed the "silent majority." This silent majority was hazy, amorphous, and difficult to define precisely. "[Nixon] has given a voice to a majority that did not know it was a majority," one reporter later observed (Reeves, 2001, 104). But they were out there, and they wanted curbs to federal power—including the imperial presi-

dency—because they were suspicious of the changes wrought by the 1960s in areas of civil rights and particularly affirmative action programs. They were heartsick over America's losses during the Vietnam War and wanted to restore the nation's tarnished image abroad. Perhaps most of all, they wanted out of what many perceived as a persistent national melancholy, fueled by the scandals of Watergate, bad economic news, an ongoing fuel and energy shortage, and the seemingly endless frictions caused by American racial strife.

Whatever his virtues, the nation's next president, Jimmy Carter, was not the man to quiet these worries. Watching Ford struggle with the legacy of his former boss just hammered home the obvious to Democratic political strategists: they needed to run someone for president who was as far removed from the sad world of Richard Nixon as possible. Jimmy Carter fit the bill. A peanut farmer from Georgia and a devout Baptist, he wore his sincerity, his faith, and his principles on his sleeve for all to see. He was an orthodox, rock-solid liberal Democrat in the New Deal mode with a strong record of public support for civil rights, antipoverty programs, and government intervention to restrain the excesses of American capitalism.

He was the first president elected after Richard Nixon, replacing Nixon's vice president, Gerald Ford. Ford had unfortunately (and unfairly) inherited much of the stench left from Nixon's various wrongdoings. He pardoned Nixon of any crimes he might have committed in connection with Watergate, unleashing a torrent of abuse and charges of cronyism; he was also unlucky enough to preside over the humiliating final days of America's involvement in Vietnam, when the nation's first losing war effort could be seen on national television. This was hardly Ford's fault, but he was nevertheless targeted for criticism largely on the basis of his simply being in the White House at the time.

Carter beat Ford in a close 1976 election and then proceeded to behave as little like Nixon as possible. Where Nixon had been obsessively secretive, Carter was frankly, brutally honest—sometimes too much so. In the midst of a fuel shortage during the summer of 1979, when long lines were forming at the nation's gas stations and the federal government seemed incapable of fixing the problem, the president made matters worse by offering observations in a nationally televised speech that seemed to suggest the American people themselves were to blame on some inchoate, psychological level. "I want to talk to you right now about a fundamental threat to American democracy," he declared. "The threat is nearly invisible in ordinary ways. It is a crisis of confidence. It is a crisis that strikes at the very heart and soul and spirit of our national will. We can see this crisis in the growing doubt about the meaning of our own lives and in the loss of a unity of purpose for our nation." Carter listed a variety of national ills and anxieties—"What you see too often in Washington and elsewhere around the country is a system of government that seems incapable of action"—and then offered a scolding, preachy tone that was grating to quite a few of his listeners. "In a nation that was proud of hard work, strong families, close-knit communities, and our faith in God, too many of us now tend to worship self-indulgence and consumption," he declared. "Human identity is no longer defined by what one does, but by what one owns" (www.pbs.org/wgbh/amex/carter/filmmore/ps_crisis.html).

This was startling stuff, coming as it did from the man who occupied FDR's old chair. Roosevelt had built the modern Democratic Party and practically reinvented the presidency by projecting confidence, enthusiasm, and boundless energy. He knew better than to expose any doubts he may have had about the American people, and he certainly would never have openly speculated on the state of America's soul. Carter was sincere enough. "I'll never tell a lie," he often said. To which one campaign aide jokingly replied, "We're gonna lose the liar vote!" (Boller, 1984, 549).

Carter also seemed genuinely to want a reversal of the imperial presidency. He made a point of being seen by reporters and cameras as he helped carry his family's furniture into the White House, and carried his lunch to work in a brown paper bag. On a more substantive front, he did away with the chief of staff as an excessively autocratic office, preferring instead to give various department heads direct access to him personally.

This was all well and good, but sometimes the Brown Bag president seemed overwhelmed by what was still the imperial presidency. During the 1979 Iranian hostage crisis, when Islamic extremists seized the American embassy in Tehran and took sixty-six Americans captive, the president appeared out of his depth. To be fair, his options were limited. But he unwisely announced that resolution of the hostage crisis would thenceforth be the centerpiece of his presidency, thus drawing still more attention to a problem that called for a more nuanced, low-key approach. He also managed to project an image of unacceptable presidential weakness when he authorized an attempt to rescue the hostages via a helicopter and commando raid on Tehran. The raid went horribly wrong, with equipment malfunctions, faulty intelligence, and in the end, utter failure. As commander in chief, Carter bore the brunt of the blame, and this with the election of 1980 looming. Public approval of his management of the Iranian crisis dipped below 30 percent.

Republicans sensed their own opportunity in 1980; just as Democrats had gone looking for the anti-Nixon in the wake of Watergate and Vietnam, Republicans wanted an anti-Carter, someone who could speak to American fears and insecurities in the era of inflation, energy crises, and the hostage crisis. California's governor Ronald Reagan fit that bill. Reagan was a former actor who had a keen grasp of how and when to project a certain image to his audience; and he knew, that, in the wake of Nixon's misdeeds and Carter's impotence, what Americans really wanted was a leader who seemed confident, determined, and above all optimistic. Whatever their virtues, neither Nixon, Ford, nor Carter could fairly be accused of projecting a

consistently sunny disposition. Americans needed presidential optimism, and they needed a president who knew how to at least seem confident in an era of economic problems, wrenching scandals, and lost wars.

But Ronald Reagan was more than just a smart tactical choice. He continued the process, begun by Goldwater, of decisively placing the Republican Party within the conservative camp. A former Roosevelt Democrat, Reagan broke ranks with New Deal politics when he decided that FDR's policies had made the federal government much too large and omnipresent. Reagan became a staunch conservative, advocating the New Federalism approach of shifting power back to the states, decreasing the influence of Washington, D.C., over various sectors of American life, and returning the nation to the decentralized, pro-business, laissez-faire economic policies of the Republican yesteryear. At the same time, he wanted to expand the federal government in one area of involvement that was near and dear to conservatives' hearts: national defense. Even as he advocated tax cuts and slashed federal budgets, he wanted to increase spending on the military budget, the better to play a strong hand in diplomacy against the Soviet Union—what he would later call the "evil empire."

Reagan also continued a Republican Party political strategy, foreshadowed by Goldwater but given its real impetus by Richard Nixon, of appealing to white conservatives in the South. A bastion of Democratic Party power since the days of Andrew Jackson, the white South had

Republican presidential candidate Ronald Reagan flashes a big grin at a campaign stop in Columbia, South Carolina, on October 10, 1980. (Ronald Reagan Library)

begun showing signs of a shift to the GOP during the 1960s, a tendency Richard Nixon encouraged in 1968. Democrats then and since denounced this so-called "southern strategy" as unabashed race-baiting and an appeal to the former Confederate South's worst instincts. Republicans hotly denied this, and do so to this day. Still, Reagan delivered the first speech of his 1980 campaign in Philadelphia, Mississippi, a small town that made national headlines in 1964, when three civil rights workers were murdered there by local white supremacists. To make matters worse, he made no mention at all of the three dead activists in his speech. While it is a reach to suggest that Reagan and his supporters were bigots, one could fairly suggest that, at the very least, they were careless where the racial context of their southern strategy was concerned—so much so that black voters, who had been leaving the GOP's ranks since the New Deal, now deserted the party of Lincoln wholesale. A few prominent exceptions aside, they have not returned.

But whatever the cost and whatever their motives, Reagan supporters succeeded in building a powerful political foundation for their party, shades of FDR's historic coalition building in the early 1930s; and in 1980 it was a blueprint for victory. The party nominated Reagan and called for a return to fiscal responsibility. "We will stand united as a party behind a bold program of tax rate reductions, spending restraints, and regulatory reforms that will inject new life into the economic bloodstream of this country," the party platform read. The GOP also heavily emphasized a strong national defense, declaring that its ranks were "united in a belief that America's international humiliation and decline can be reversed only by strong presidential leadership and a consistent, far-sighted foreign policy, supported by a major upgrading of our military forces, a strengthening of our commitments to our allies, and a resolve that our national interests be vigorously protected." "Ultimately," the party argued, "those who practice strength and firmness truly guard the peace" (www.presidency .ucsb.edu).

The platform also offered a seething indictment of the Democrats and their president. Specifically reminding Americans of the nation's economic ills and above all the Iranian hostage crisis— "never before in modern history has the United States endured as many humiliations, insults, and defeats as it has during the past four years"—Republicans severely chastised their opponents for weakness and a rudderless direction from the White House. "Divided, leaderless, unseeing, uncomprehending, they plod on with listless offerings of pale imitations of the same policies they have pursued so long, knowing full well their

futility," the platform read, and "the Carter Administration is the unhappy and inevitable consequence of decades of increasingly outmoded Democratic domination of our national life" (www.presidency.ucsb.edu).

With the Iranian hostage crisis still simmering, Carter faced a tide of discontent in his own party. His biggest challenger was John F. Kennedy's young brother Teddy, senator from Massachusetts and bearer of the Kennedy family's still-powerful political mantle. Carter's "political liabilities seemed so clear to so many leaders of his own party that Democratic VIP's from all over the country were literally lining up behind one another . . . outside [Kennedy's] office," noted one reporter (Ranney, 1981, 43). But an old scandal involving the death of a young woman in Kennedy's company in 1969 resurfaced in the press and doomed his run at the White House. Meanwhile, no other serious candidate surfaced to challenge Carter in his quest for a second term, and he won renomination despite many Democrats' misgivings.

The president put the best possible face on matters. In his acceptance speech, Carter repeatedly invoked memories of the Democrats' tried-and-true champions. "We are the party of a great President who knew how to get reelected—Franklin Delano Roosevelt," he declared, "and we are the party of a courageous fighter who knew how to give 'em hell—Harry Truman." Carter also used his strongest political weapons: his fundamental honesty and sense of compassion. "I'm wiser tonight than I was 4 years ago," he rather ruefully ob-

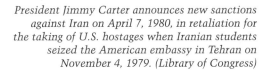

President Jimmy Carter announces new sanctions against Iran on April 7, 1980, in retaliation for the taking of U.S. hostages when Iranian students seized the American embassy in Tehran on November 4, 1979. (Library of Congress)

served, and he told Americans that he had "crisscrossed this country and I listened to thousands and thousands of people—housewives and farmers, teachers and small business leaders, workers and students, the elderly and the poor, people of every race and every background and every walk of life. It was a powerful experience—a total immersion in the human reality of America" (www.presidency.ucsb.edu/shownomination.php?convid=6). The president suggested that his various experiences with the nation's domestic and foreign affairs gave him a hard but valuable education in the vicissitudes and problems of modern American life—certainly more valuable than his opponent's experience as an actor and governor of California.Carter also waged

a vigorous negative campaign against Reagan, portraying the Republican nominee as an intellectual lightweight with no serious appreciation of the nation's vast problems. "Why throw this bum out who has some experience for a bum who has no experience?" quipped a Carter aide in private (Ranney, 1981, 147). The remark illustrated an unfortunate habit among Carter supporters of simply not taking the Reagan candidacy seriously. "The American people are not going to elect a seventy-year-old, right-wing, ex-movie actor to be president," Carter adviser Hamilton Jordan confidently predicted (Ranney, 1981, 212).

While Carter sounded a sadder-but-wiser note and his people set about trying to undermine Reagan's reputation, the former movie actor campaigned by doing what he did best. He brushed aside talk of his shallow intellect and thin list of accomplishments, declared that it was "morning in America again," and displayed a breezy sense of optimism that was in some ways more akin to FDR's legacy than Carter's own efforts. Reagan hammered on the themes his party had laid out in its platform: tax cuts, defense spending, and a tough foreign policy. Reagan also tapped into a broad American disillusionment with the federal government and Washington, D.C.'s "inside the beltway" operatives and politicians, for whom many Americans felt a vague but powerful disdain. "I used to fantasize what it would be like if everyone in government would quietly slip away and close the doors and disappear," Reagan declared, "see how long it would take the people of this country to miss them. I think that life would go on, and the people would keep right on doing the things they are, and we would get along a lot better than we think" (Boller, 1984, 358).

He was also aided by a fortuitous turn of events in Iran. After nearly a year of tense, behind-the-scenes negotiations with the Iranians, President Carter was confident he could achieve their freedom just in time to give him a big boost at the polls. But the negotiations dragged on, dashing Carter's hopes that he might be able to free the hostages before voters went to the polls. There were dark rumors of a separate deal, a so-called October surprise, between secret negotiators for the Reagan campaign and the Iranians, the gist of which was that Reagan had engineered a delay in their release

until after the election. Those allegations were never proven, but whatever the case may be, there is little doubt that the hostage drama did its part in sinking an already lackluster Democratic campaign.

In the end, even those Americans who did not particularly care much for Reagan often found themselves thinking, in the words of one observer, that "Carter is such a disaster he has to go" (Ranney, 1981, 173). Reagan soundly defeated Carter, carrying all but seven states and racking up an impressive 489 electoral college votes to Carter's forty-nine. Reagan was helped by the surprisingly strong candidacy of independent John Anderson, who tapped into many Americans' growing disdain for political parties and siphoned some votes that might have otherwise gone to Carter. But in the end, no one could have saved the Brown Bag president, who left office still smarting under the cloud of the hostage crisis. (The hostages would be freed the very day Reagan took office, another point that infuriated Democrats.)

In the end, Carter could never quite believe that the former movie actor, a man who the president and many of his supporters believed was hopelessly out of his depth, had prevailed. Just before Reagan's inauguration, the president-elect had a lengthy phone conversation with the outgoing president about the hostage situation. "What did [Reagan] say, Mr. President?" Hamilton Jordan asked Carter when he hung up. "Well, I briefed him on what was happening to the hostages. He mostly listened. But when I finished, he said, 'What hostages?'" (Ranney, 1981, 367–368).

FURTHER READING

Baker, Jean H., *Affairs of Party: The Political Culture of Northern Democrats in the Mid-Nineteenth Century* (Ithaca, NY: Cornell University Press, 1983).

Basler, Roy P., *The Collected Works of Abraham Lincoln*, 9 vols. (New Brunswick, NJ: Rutgers University Press, 1953–1955).

Blight, David W., *Race and Reunion: The Civil War in American Memory* (New York: Belknap Press, 2001).

Boller, Paul, *Presidential Campaigns* (New York: Oxford University Press, 1984).

Borden, Morton, *The Antifederalists* (East Lansing: Michigan State University Press, 1965).

Bowers, Claude G., *The Party Battles of the Jackson Period* (Boston: Houghton-Mifflin, 1922).

Bundy, William P., *A Tangled Web: The Making of Foreign Policy in the Nixon Presidency* (New York: Hill and Wang, 1998).

Burner, David, *Herbert Hoover: A Public Life* (New York: Alfred A. Knopf, 1979).

Cannon, Lou, *President Reagan: The Role of a Lifetime* (New York: Simon and Schuster, 1991).

Dallek, Robert, *Flawed Giant: Lyndon Johnson and His Times, 1961–1973* (New York: Oxford University Press, 1998).

Dalton, Kathleen, *Theodore Roosevelt: The Strenuous Life* (New York: Vintage Books, 2002).

Davis, William C., *Lincoln's Men: How President Lincoln became Father to an Army and a Nation* (New York: Free Press, 1999).

Donald, David, *Lincoln* (New York: Simon and Schuster, 1995).

Dusinberre, William, *Slavemaster President: The Double Career of James Polk* (New York: Oxford University Press, 2003).

Ellis, Joseph J., *Founding Brothers: The Revolutionary Generation* (New York: Vintage Books, 2001).

Fausold, Martin L., *The Presidency of Herbert C. Hoover* (Lawrence: University Press of Kansas, 1985).

Fausold, Martin L., *Passionate Sage: The Character and Legacy of John Adams* (New York: W.W. Norton, 1993).

Foner, Eric, *Reconstruction: America's Unfinished Revolution, 1863–1877* (New York: Harper and Row, 1988).

Freeman, Joanne B., *Affairs of Honor: National Politics in the New Republic* (New Haven, CT: Yale University Press, 2002).

Gienapp, William, E., *Abraham Lincoln and Civil War America* (New York: Oxford University Press, 2002).

Goodwin, Doris Kearns, *Lyndon Johnson and the American Dream* (New York: Harper and Row, 1976).

Hargreaves, Mary W. M., *The Presidency of John Quincy Adams* (Lawrence: University Press of Kansas, 1985).

Holt, Michael F., *The Rise and Fall of the American Whig Party: Jacksonian Politics and the Onset of Civil War* (New York: Oxford University Press, 1999).

Holzer, Harold, *Dear Mr. Lincoln: Letters to the President* (Carbondale: Southern Illinois University Press, 2006).

Hyneman, Charles S., and Donald S. Lutz, eds., *American Political Writing during the Founding Era, 1760–1805*, 2 vols. (Indianapolis, IN: Liberty Press, 1983).

Kennedy, David M., *Freedom from Fear: The American People in Depression and War, 1929–1945* (New York: Oxford University Press, 1999).

Kenyon, Cecelia, *The Antifederalists* (Indianapolis, IN: Bobbs-Merrill, 1966).

Klingaman, William K., *Abraham Lincoln and the Road to Emancipation* (New York: Viking, 2001).

Marszalek, John F., *The Petticoat Affair: Manners, Mutiny, and Sex in Andrew Jackson's America* (Baton Rouge: Louisiana State University, 1997).

Mayer, George H., *The Republican Party, 1854–1964* (New York: Oxford University Press, 1967).

McCullough, David, *Truman* (New York: Simon and Schuster, 1992).

McCullough, David, *John Adams* (New York: Simon and Schuster, 2001).

McKitrick, Eric, and Stanley Elkins, *The Age of Federalism: The Early American Republic, 1788–1800* (New York: Oxford University Press, 1995).

McPherson, James M., *Ordeal by Fire: The Civil War and Reconstruction* (New York: Alfred A. Knopf, 1982).

Morgan, Ted, *FDR: A Biography* (New York: Simon and Schuster, 1985).

Nagel, Paul C., *John Quincy Adams: A Public Life, a Private Life* (New York: Alfred A. Knopf, 1997).

Neely, Mark, *The Fate of Liberty: Abraham Lincoln and Civil Liberties* (New York: Oxford University Press, 1991).

Oates, Stephen B., *With Malice toward None: The Life of Abraham Lincoln* (New York: Harper and Row, 1977).

Paludan, Philip S., *A People's Contest: The Union and the Civil War, 1861–1865* (New York: Harper and Row, 1988).

Peterson, Merrill D., ed., *Thomas Jefferson: Writings* (New York: Library of America, 1984).

Potter, David M., *The Impending Crisis, 1848–1861* (New York: Harper and Row, 1976).

Ranney, Austin, *The American Elections of 1980* (Washington, DC: American Enterprise Institute, 1981).

Reeves, Richard, *President Nixon: Alone in the White House* (New York: Simon and Schuster, 2001).

Remini, Robert, *Andrew Jackson and the Course of American Empire* (New York: Harper and Row, 1977).

Rossiter, Clinton, ed., *The Federalist Papers* (New York: Signet, 1961).

Rutland, Robert A., *The Democrats, from Jefferson to Carter* (Baton Rouge: Louisiana State University Press, 1979).

Schlesinger, Arthur, Jr., *The Age of Jackson* (Boston: Little, Brown, 1945).

Schlesinger, Arthur, Jr., ed., *History of American Presidential Elections, 1789–1968*, 4 vols. (New York: Chelsea House, 1971).

Schlesinger, Arthur, Jr., *The Imperial Presidency* (Boston: Houghton-Mifflin, 1973).

Sears, Stephen W., *George B. McClellan: The Young Napoleon* (New York: Ticknor and Fields, 1988).

Sellers, Charles G., *The Market Revolution, 1815–1846* (New York: Oxford University Press, 1991).

Sharp, James, *American Politics in the Early Republic: The New Nation in Crisis* (New Haven, CT: Yale University Press, 1995).

Smith, Richard, *Patriarch: George Washington and the New American Nation* (Boston: Houghton-Mifflin, 1993).

Vorenberg, Michael, *Final Freedom: The Civil War, the Abolition of Slavery, and the Thirteenth Amendment* (Cambridge, MA: Harvard University Press, 2001).

Ward, Geoffrey C., *Before the Trumpet: Young Franklin Roosevelt, 1882–1905* (New York: Harper and Row, 1985).

Wilson, Douglas L., and Rodney O. Davis, eds., *Herndon's Informants: Letters, Interviews, and Statements about Abraham Lincoln* (Urbana: University of Illinois Press, 1998).

Wolfskill, George, *All but the People: Franklin D. Roosevelt and His Critics, 1933–1939* (New York: Macmillan, 1969).

Wood, Gordon S., *The Creation of the American Republic, 1776–1787* (Chapel Hill: University of North Carolina Press, 1969).

5

THE WHITE HOUSE'S RELATIONS WITH OTHER BRANCHES

"The Vice Presidency ain't worth a pitcher of warm spit," John Nance Garner famously observed (Dailey, 1996, 146). "Cactus Jack" knew what he was talking about, having served as Franklin Roosevelt's second-in-command for seven years. On the surface, he appeared to be a good choice as FDR's running mate: a politically savvy, well-connected Texan who was reelected to his seat in the House of Representatives an astounding fifteen times and served two terms as House Speaker. Given Roosevelt's New Deal ambitions, it certainly did not hurt to have a man with Garner's congressional connections and experience readily at hand.

Except that Roosevelt rarely consulted Cactus Jack on much of anything. When he did, the two men spent much of their time arguing, with Garner's advice nearly always overruled. He opposed FDR's aggressive pro-British foreign policies, including the Lend-Lease program that the president used to send Britain vital war matériel. Garner was no admirer of the president's domestic policies, either. FDR suspected him of secretly undermining New Deal initiatives in Congress and cut Garner out of important policymaking decisions. "The Vice-President is not here so we can talk freely," Roosevelt caustically told his Cabinet on one occasion (Morgan, 1985, 318). Disgusted with Roosevelt's pursuit of a third term—at least in part because Garner wanted the 1940 nomination for himself—the thoroughly disillusioned vice president retired to his Texas ranch.

SEPARATING THE POWERS

Most vice presidents eventually develop Garner's "warm spit" perspective on their job. The nation's first vice president, John Adams, wrote dejectedly to his wife Abigail in 1793 that "my country in its wisdom contrived for me the most insignificant office that was the invention of man." Blessed with a brilliant intellect and energetic character, Adams was chagrined to discover that, as vice president, "I can do neither good or evil, [and] I must be borne away by others and meet the common fate" (Smith, 1962, 2: 844).

For some this was not an altogether difficult experience, because their expectations were so low. How much influence could Indiana lawyer Charles Fairbanks really have hoped to wield, for example, as the vice president for a dynamic, activist chief executive like Teddy Roosevelt? Fairbanks was added to TR's ticket by Republican power brokers at the last minute and against Roosevelt's wishes—he preferred the more energetic Robert Hitt, representative from Illinois—and the president responded by excluding Fairbanks from serious policy debates or decisions.

But for others, the experience was all the more galling because their expectations were initially so high. Plucked from other positions of importance—sometimes reluctantly—some vice presidents have been dismayed to learn how little influence they actually exert.

Lyndon Johnson is an example. He was arguably the most talented legislator of the twentieth century, an expert in the arcane ways of Congress and an effective backroom negotiator. He strode through the halls of Congress and the Democratic Party like a colossus, wielding power and influence on a level matched by few. "Lyndon Johnson just towered over me and intimidated me terribly," remembered one colleague. "He's the one person who had my number all his life" (Dallek, 1998, 5).

There were some who believed he was reaching beneath himself in accepting the position as Kennedy's running mate. Certainly Johnson felt no admiration for the much-younger Kennedy, whom he privately dismissed as "the boy." "He's just a flash in the pan," Johnson complained to fellow congressman Tip O'Neill, "and he's got no record of substance to run on" (Dallek, 1991, 565). But LBJ also knew that the vice presidency

would increase his national stature and would be good for the southern wing of the Democratic Party. Moreover, Johnson was no obscure backbench politician: he was Lyndon Baines Johnson, master of the United States Senate. "Johnson seemed to be thinking about what he could make of the vice presidency," biographer Robert Dallek argues, and asking, "could he make it into something more than it traditionally had been?" (Dallek, 1991, 576). Johnson believed he could form an unprecedented bridge between the presidency and Congress, using his position as second-in-command with the former and his influence in the latter to decisively affect Washington politics. He might even become something of a power behind the throne, given the lack of experience evident in "the boy."

In this he would be cruelly disappointed. The lesson was brought home to him quite early, just a few days before he took office. Johnson attended a caucus of Democratic senators, bent on assuming his old leadership role. Instead, he was none-too-politely told to butt out. As he left the room shaking with anger, LBJ stormed, "I now know the difference between a caucus and a cactus. In a cactus, all the pricks are on the outside" (Dallek, 1991, 8).

At least Johnson's miseries were relatively short-lived. He had the fortune, rising from great misfortune, directly to succeed his boss in office when Kennedy was assassinated in 1963. Most vice presidents have not been so blessed. Only fourteen have eventually served as president.

Indeed, despite his status as the president-in-waiting, more of a given vice president's power—such as it is—comes from his role as president of the Senate, as provided by Article I, Section 3 of the Constitution. The office does not give him license to become too directly involved in the Senate's proceedings, however: he only has a vote in case of a tie. A total of 233 such votes have been cast during the nation's history, over half before 1850. The vice presidency is the only office mentioned in the Constitution with such a direct crossover authority between the executive and legislative branches. There are a variety of contact points between the presidency, Congress, and the Supreme Court, to be sure; but the vice president is the only federal officeholder who possesses two jobs in two branches.

This highlights the fact that the Framers took separation of powers very seriously. In fact, some objected to giving the vice president any role in the legislative branch at all. During the Philadelphia Convention, Elbridge Gerry declared that, if they allowed the vice president to act as the Senate's president as well, "we might as well put the President himself at the head of the Legislature. The close intimacy that must subsist between the President and vice-president makes it absolutely improper." Gerry was worried enough to propose that the vice presidency be done away with altogether. George Mason agreed with Gerry's sentiments, declaring that "the office of vice-President [was] an encroachment on the rights of the Senate; and that it mixed too much

the Legislative and Executive, which as well as the Judiciary department, ought to be kept as separate as possible" (Madison, 2005, 596). Limiting the vice president to action only in case of tie votes was a way for the Framers to alleviate such fears.

But in reality, there are many intersection points between the executive and the other two branches. Party membership is of course a constant source of mutual contact between presidents, members of Congress, and judges, not to mention officeholders, staffers, and other federal government employees. Presidents are expected to act at least in part with the interests of their fellow Republicans and Democrats in mind when they shape policy. Indeed, it is not uncommon to refer to a given president as the "head of the party"—understandable, since he is often the most highly visible representative of his party.

Political considerations aside, there are likewise numerous formal contact points between the executive and the other two branches embedded within the language of the Constitution. Presidents appoint Supreme Court justices, for example, with the Senate's advice and consent. Article II, Section 3 requires that he "shall from time to time give to the Congress Information of the State of the Union, and recommend to their Consideration such Measures as he shall judge necessary and expedient." Congress can impeach presidents and vice presidents, the Senate advises the president on treaties, members of Congress determine the day and time for choosing presidential electors—the list is long.

But this covers only the dry, structural aspect of government. Presidents, members of Congress, judges, and their various entourages are also flesh-and-blood human beings. They run into each other on the streets of Washington, D.C., know each other's families and friends, sometimes dine together, speak at the same public functions, and very often come from similar socioeconomic backgrounds, circumstances, and professions. Twenty-five of forty-three presidents have been lawyers, for example, as have nearly all Supreme Court justices and who knows how many members of Congress.

These shared personal experiences and day-to-day contacts have more influence than we might think. In 1856 Supreme Court chief justice Roger B. Taney apparently informed president-elect and fellow Democrat James Buchanan that a court case was in the offing that could provide a legal solution to the thorny problem of what to do about slavery in America's western territories. Buchanan subsequently made a brief reference to this in his Inaugural Address, telling listeners that the problem of slavery in the territories "is a judicial question, which legitimately belongs to the Supreme Court of the United States, before whom it is now pending, and will, it is understood, be speedily and finally settled. To their decision, in common with all good citizens, I shall cheerfully submit, whatever this may be" (www.yale.edu/lawweb/avalon/presiden/inaug/buchanan.htm). In this particular case, contact between the executive and judicial branches was less than beneficial, for

when the Court decision in question turned out to be the extremely pro-southern *Dred Scott v. Sandford*, more than a few Americans believed a cozy conspiracy had been hatched between Taney and Buchanan to preserve the prerogatives of their party's white, southern wing. Republican senator William Seward, for example, saw a "judicial usurpation [that] is more odious and intolerable than any other among the manifold practices of tyranny" (Fehrenbacher, 1978, 473).

Separation of powers is therefore actually a bit of a misnomer. The Framers did not want the branches totally separated; quite the contrary. They wanted a close enough mix so that everyone could keep an eye on one another, rather like see-through walls that would keep the president, Congress, and the Supreme Court from developing close enough ties to become dangerous, but permeable enough so that the branches could do the nation's business and keep each other from misbehaving. A careful balance, therefore, had to be struck by the Framers: contact between the branches, yes, but not too much. "The accumulation of all powers, legislative, executive, and judiciary, in the same hands . . . may justly be pronounced the very definition of tyranny," James Madison observed (Rossiter, 1961, 269). Yet he and the other Framers believed they had avoided both that form of tyranny and an excessively wide gulf between the government's officers that might render the government inoperable. "The political apothegm [of separation of powers] does not require that the legislative, executive, and judiciary departments should be wholly unconnected with each other," Madison further explained (Rossiter, 1961, 276).

What is the best way to understand how the Constitution's permeable walls have operated upon the presidency during its history? Throughout this volume, we have been using various approaches to the vast field of presidential history to highlight certain issues and events: the Framers and their constitutional structuring of the office; certain "big-name" presidents and their presidential personalities; generational influences on the office's growth and development; and key elections illuminating the political dimension of the presidency.

Perhaps the various forms of interaction between the presidency, Congress, and the Supreme Court might best be observed by examining the nation's major wars. Obviously, there are other ways to do this, but wars have a tendency to throw such matters into sharp relief. Congress and the president share war-making powers and must find ways of cooperating to prosecute successfully a major war effort; sometimes these ways are unprecedented in nature and scope. The Supreme Court likewise finds itself compelled carefully to monitor presidential behavior, and occasionally it reins in the chief executive when he oversteps his constitutional boundaries.

We will address these matters by focusing on issues related to war making that arose during the presidencies of four men: Thomas Jefferson, James Polk,

Abraham Lincoln, and Franklin Roosevelt. In each case, the business of war compelled these presidents to interact with Congress and the Supreme Court in ways more frequent and often more controversial than has been the case during peacetime. And while overgeneralization is always best avoided, it is safe to say that, on the whole, these interactions illustrate a more or less consistent trend in American history: the steady gravitation of power away from Congress and the Supreme Court and toward the men occupying the White House. This has been equally true in war and peace.

THOMAS JEFFERSON, COMMANDER IN CHIEF

In the early years of their new nation, American merchants and commercial capitalists pressed aggressively outward into various trading partnerships abroad as vessels from Boston, New York, and other hubs of the market revolution delivered and procured goods from all over the globe. What was left of the old pre–Revolutionary war bonds of mercantilism—whereby American colonists had been required by law to trade only with Great Britain—were now gone, and Yankee traders could push their way into all sorts of new and potentially lucrative markets with no British interference.

On the other hand, they would no longer enjoy the protection of His Majesty's Royal Navy. British cannon had kept the more aggressive and rapacious foreigners from preying too mercilessly on American commerce, but now it was more or less open season on Americans abroad. Americans' penury and suspicion of professional military men meant that the fledgling nation had almost no navy to speak of by which it could guard its own commercial interests. Congress technically funded the construction of six frigates in 1794, a pathetic number compared to the hundreds of vessels the mighty British and French navies could bring to bear on the high seas; and even of the six, just three had been constructed by 1800.

This suited the states' rights–oriented philosophy of President Thomas Jefferson well. The author of the Declaration of Independence had always felt that Americans required little government help in pursuing happiness. When he assumed office in 1801, he quickly set about reducing the already minuscule executive branch to truly skeletal levels. Under his watch, budget requests from the executive department were limited to only the basic necessities, department employees were cut to the bare minimum necessary to function, and he himself had only one private secretary (the redoubtable Meriwether Lewis of Lewis and Clark fame). He took pride in forcing the presidency to make do with less.

Jefferson was, after all, monarchy's most visible and vocal critic in America. Most of the Declaration of Independence was a scathing indictment of one man, George III, and what Jefferson saw as his tyrannical rule from the throne. The new American presidency was a form of one-man rule, as well, and the office had

made him nervous since he first perused copies of the finished Constitution in 1787. (He had not been present at the Philadelphia Convention.) I "found articles which I thought were objectionable," he later wrote; among other matters, "the re-eligibility of the President for life, I quite disapproved" (Petersen, 1984, 72). Writing to his good friend John Adams, Jefferson was even more blunt. The "President seems a bad edition of the Polish king," he lamented, "once in office, and possessing the military force of the union, without either the aid or check of a council, he would not easily be dethroned, even if the people could be induced to withdraw their votes from him" (Peterson, 1984, 913).

Given such concerns about the president's latent powers as commander in chief, it is perhaps not surprising that military appropriations were threadbare during the Jefferson Administration. The president did sign the bill authorizing the creation of the United States Military Academy at West Point, believing that it was more valuable as an institution of higher learning for engineering and science than war, and that its admissions policies—open to anyone who could secure the recommendation of a member of Congress—would tend to have a democratizing effect on what might otherwise become an aristocratic American officer corps (Malone, 1948, 5: 510). But he had little patience for measures expanding the size of the nation's tiny regular army, nor was he a very enthusiastic booster of the navy. "It is necessary we should possess some [naval] power," he ruefully observed, but "to aim at such a navy as the greater nations of Europe possess, would be a foolish and wicked waste of the energies of our countrymen." For Jefferson, vast naval expenditures were precisely the problem with Europe's bloated monarchies. To build a grand American navy, he argued, "would be to pull on our own heads that load of military expence, which makes the European laborer go supperless to bed, and moistens his bread with the sweat of his brows. . . . A small naval force then is sufficient for us, and a small one is necessary" (Petersen, 1984, 301).

Foreign adversaries were not impressed by Jefferson's ideology. This was particularly so among the chieftains along Africa's Mediterranean coast, the Muslim lords of Barbary, Tunis, Algiers, and Tripoli, who for decades had preyed upon European shipping near their coastal waters, stealing the vessels' contents and sometimes holding their crews for ransom. European rulers had learned to play a carrot-and-stick game of diplomacy with these pirates and their rulers, paying them off when the expense was not too high and occasionally assaulting their ports and cities when it seemed necessary.

Prior to the Revolution, Americans had largely been insulated from this game; but after independence the gloves came off, and during the first years of the new nation's existence, pirates began to seize American ships and crews. In 1793, for example, the American vessel *Polly* was captured by the Algerians and its crew put to work at hard labor breaking rocks, while their captors jeered at and abused them. "Now I have got you, you Christian dogs," exclaimed one, "you shall eat stones" (Boot, 2002, 9).

The capture of the *Polly* and other vessels became the subject of intense debate in Congress as the nation's representatives wrestled with the problem of how best to respond. Some wanted war, while others thought the old European model of bribery and tolerance worked best. Years before, Congress had actually authorized payment of up to $80,000 to negotiate some sort of mutually agreeable arrangement between America and the Barbary states. Then ambassador to France, Jefferson had been stunned to learn, however, that Tripoli alone would have quickly drained that fund with its demands, which included not only an annual lump sum of 30,000 guineas for the Tripoli government, but also a hefty private bribe for Tripoli's ambassador (McCullough, 2001, 354). It was an abject lesson in the realities of Mediterranean diplomacy and power politics that Jefferson would remember when he entered the White House.

But was this fundamentally his problem, or was it a matter for Congress to address? No one knew exactly where the precise lines of authority lay between the president and Congress in matters of foreign affairs and war. In Washington's Cabinet, for example, both Thomas Jefferson (secretary of state) and Alexander Hamilton (secretary of the Treasury) agreed that America should declare its neutrality when war broke out between Britain and France in the early 1790s, but they disagreed on whether Congress or the president possessed the proper authority to do so.

Despite his philosophy of limited presidential power, Jefferson was actually a fairly activist president—at least within the context of his times—when it came to relations with the legislative branch. Washington and Adams were extremely scrupulous in their dealings with Congress, with the first president in particular taking great care not to encroach upon the boundaries of congressional authority. He took no action to steer measures he liked through the legislative process, and he issued a grand total of two vetoes during his entire eight years in office, both addressing minor procedural matters. "The election of the different branches of Congress by freemen, either directly or indirectly, is the pivot on which turns the first wheel of government, a wheel which communicates motion to all the rest," he argued; and "all the rest" included the presidency, which should seldom, in Washington's mind, serve as the primary mover and shaker of federal action (Flexner, 1974, 168).

Washington's successor, John Adams, had similar sentiments. Adams had once been accused—unfairly—of harboring secret monarchist tendencies, so he was perhaps more sensitive than most to accusations of executive excess. He possessed more legislative experience than Washington, having served first in the Continental Congress and then as the Senate's president in his capacity as vice president. He kept an eye on Congress's doings generally, sent it messages of various kinds requesting action (mostly on foreign policy issues related to the ongoing problems in Europe), and became the first president to call Congress into special session (a power expressly granted to him by the Constitution), asking members to discuss delicate negotiations with France, whose behavior had placed it on the brink of war with the United States. He certainly had his share of bile directed toward him by opposition representatives and senators eager to embarrass both the president and his fledgling political party, the Federalists—and Adams being Adams, he sometimes heartily returned the favor. But the president largely steered clear of Congress's everyday deliberations, and he did not veto any bills at all during his four years in office.

Following in the footsteps of his two predecessors, Thomas Jefferson said all the right things, referring deferentially to Congress's sovereign authority and calling it the nation's "grand council" (McDonald, 1994, 259). Like Adams, he vetoed no bills. But he allowed his secretary of the Treasury, Albert Gallatin, to participate openly in the drafting of legislation related to the nation's financial structure, something neither Washington nor Adams would have done, and he enlisted the help of sympathetic senators and representatives to steer bills through Congress. Jefferson also used the mechanisms available to him as leader of the Republican Party (the only viable national political party in America at that time) to influence Congressional procedures. This is not to say that Jefferson tried to dominate the legislative branch, like some later chief executives; but he was not interested in maintaining Washington's thick wall of separation, either. "It would be nearer the truth to say that Jefferson embodied himself with Congress," observed historian Dumas Malone, "than that he sought to establish executive supremacy. . . . What he sought and gained was not subservience but a high degree of cooperation" (Malone, 1948, 1: 111).

Moreover, when it came to war, Jefferson was the first in a long line of presidents—down to the present day—who felt that the man occupying the presidential chair ought to take a leading role vis-à-vis Congress. "In times of peace the people look most to their representatives, but in war, to the executive solely," he wrote (Peterson, 1984, 1218). And where the Barbary problem was concerned, Jefferson frankly admitted that, in his opinion, "it would be best to effect a peace thro' the medium of war." He listed his reasons to John Adams: "1. Justice is in favor of this opinion. 2. Honor favors it. 3. It will procure us respect in Europe, and respect is a safeguard to interest" (Peterson, 1984, 855).

When the Mediterranean pirate issue reared its head during his administration, Jefferson was therefore inclined to act with dispatch and take the lead, with Congress following, and not the other way around. A renewed series of seizures by Tripolitan raiders in 1801 motivated Jefferson to dispatch a naval squadron to that nation's waters, spurred by the pasha of Tripoli's demand for more tribute money from the United States—a demand, according to Jefferson, that was "unfounded either in right or compact"—and eventually the pasha's declaration of outright war against the United States. Venturing into Tripoli's waters, the American schooner *Enterprise* engaged and heavily damaged a Tripolitan cruiser, killing or wounding sixty of the cruiser's eighty crewmen without the loss of a single American life. The little affair demonstrated, in Jefferson's grandiloquent language, that "it is not a want of virtue which makes us seek their peace, but a conscientious desire to direct the energies of our nation to the multiplication of the human race, and not its destruction" (Peterson, 1984, 502).

For a man who made much of his principled reluctance to build an American military establishment, Jefferson seemed quite pleased with the results of this demonstration of naval might. He dispatched three more squadrons to Tripoli in 1802 and 1803. They blockaded the Tripoli coast, fired on the city of Tripoli itself, and in 1805 mounted an amphibious assault that compelled the pasha to sign a peace treaty with the United States (and inspired the famous lines in the Marine Corps hymn, "From the Halls of Montezuma/To the shores of Tripoli").

His efforts were actually not always so triumphant. In the summer of 1803 the president's Tripolitan naval squadron made a fairly impressive showing, at least for the American navy of the era: the 44-gun heavy frigate *Constitution*

The U.S. Navy bombards Tripoli in August 1804 in an action against a ruler who supported the Tripolitan (Barbary) pirates. In 1801, the pasha of Tripoli demanded a higher tribute payment from the United States for protection of its ships from the pirates; President Thomas Jefferson's refusal to pay led to the Tripolitan War. (Hulton Archive/Getty Images)

(Old Ironsides, the pride of the fleet) and several other well-armed vessels, including the 36-gun *Philadelphia*. Taking up a blockading position off Tripoli in late October, the *Philadelphia* managed to run herself aground on a nearby reef and was captured by the Tripolitans. Her crew was paraded through the streets of the cities stripped to their underwear and then forced to labor as slaves, while their ship was repaired and pressed into the pasha's service. American military men bristled at the consequences of this embarrassing display of weakness. "If it had not been for the capture of the *Philadelphia*," groused one naval officer,

"I have no doubt, but we should have had peace with Tripoli this Spring" (Boot, 2002, 18–19). The president was not very proud of this ignominious little affair, either, and he glossed over it in his 1804 State of the Union Address, blandly remarking that "the activity and success of the small force employed in the Mediterranean in the early part of the present year . . . will, I trust, by the sufferings of war, reduce the barbarians of Tripoli to the desire of peace on proper terms" (www.presidency.ucsb.edu/ws/index.php?pid=29446).

On the whole, this first presidential exercise in waging small war could be judged a guarded success. Jefferson chose to pursue a course that lay somewhere between full-blown war and appeasement of the Mediterranean pirates, a course driven partly by his own personal distaste for wars and things military and partly by the circumstances of his times. Americans of the early nineteenth century wanted their government small and limited and looked with suspicion upon anyone who might want to beef up the peacetime army and navy as extravagant at best, and potentially despotic at worst. Jefferson was neither, and in his annual dispatch of navy squadrons to the Mediterranean coast, he eventually achieved his end—peace with the Tripolitan pirates and their allies—without large expense or loss of life. To his way of thinking, Jefferson's strategy was both effective and cheap. "The small vessels authorized by Congress with a view to the Mediterranean service, have been sent into that sea, and will be able more effectively to confine the Tripoline cruisers within their harbors," the president asserted, "and supersede the necessity of convoy expenses to our commerce in that quarter" (Peterson, 1984, 513).

More to the point, relations between Jefferson and Congress during the Tripolitan affair were encouraging. As Jefferson himself pointed out, Congress generally concurred with his actions and behaved accordingly. In addition to funding the squadrons, Congress in February 1802 passed a law authorizing Jefferson to employ force in defending American interests overseas. For his part, the president was careful not to advance beyond what he considered to be the purely de-

fensive measure of deploying small squadrons; anything more, in his opinion, would require a declaration of war from Congress, a potentially divisive and expensive move that neither he nor most members of Congress really wanted. A few of the more die-hard Federalists protested that this smacked of executive weakness; Alexander Hamilton, for example, wanted more vigorous presidential action in the Mediterranean and wondered, "What will the world think of the fold which has such a shepherd" (Malone, 1948, 3: 98). But Jefferson's carefully prescribed strategy preserved the political peace with Congress as well as the president's spare military budget.

Jefferson's activities and Congress's response to the Barbary pirates offer an example of the way early Americans understood cooperation between the two branches and the way each should behave. Not very far removed from the days when European monarchs impinged upon parliamentary prerogatives, Americans of Jefferson's age wanted clear boundaries beyond which neither branch would go.

But what of the new government's third branch? What might the Supreme Court have to say concerning presidential war making in particular, and the presidency's powers in general?

It was not immediately apparent that the nation's highest court had any business offering its opinion on presidential matters at all. The language of the Constitution created no explicitly stated role for the Court in either expanding or restraining presidential power. The only contact point between the Court and the executive branch was the president's power to appoint the Court's members—with the Senate's advice and consent. Indeed, there were many more numerous and consequential contact points between the Court and Congress than the president, with the nation's legislature empowered to establish the size and shape of the federal judiciary beneath the Supreme Court, determine the precise parameters of the federal system's appellate powers, and decide what exactly constituted the best punishment for treasonous behavior.

In all of these matters, the president possessed no constitutionally defined role at all; and while the Framers never quite said so directly, one suspects they wanted it that way, and for sound political reasons. In an era that was characterized by many Americans' rising antipathy toward powerful men like kings, it made sense to keep a fairly thick wall of separation between the most powerful elected individual in the new national government—the president—and those who might easily be perceived as the most powerful nonelected individuals in the new national government—the Supreme Court. The Constitution's supporters went to a great deal of trouble to reassure their nervous countrymen that the new federal tribunal would be, in the words of Alexander Hamilton, "the weakest of the three departments of power." Conceding the point that a judiciary unduly influenced by either the president or Congress would be dangerous and liable to corruption, Hamilton continued by arguing that "this independence of the judges is equally requi-

site to guard the Constitution and the rights of individuals from the effects of those ill humors, which the arts of designing men, or the influence of particular conjunctures, sometimes disseminate among the people themselves, and which . . . occasion dangerous innovations in the government, and serious oppressions of the minor party in the community" (Rossiter, 1961, 117–121).

It was John Marshall, the Supreme Court's third chief justice (and the first chief justice to treat the job with much gravity) who established the Court's modern role as arbiter of the Constitution's meaning. But when John Marshall created the Court's power of judicial review in *Marbury v. Madison* (1803), the decision had more direct bearing on Congress than the president. Despite the fact that the case named Jefferson's secretary of state, James Madison, as the defendant, it really turned on the validity of a congressional act that empowered Madison to appoint federal judges. Marshall's assertion that the Court could rule on the constitutionality of that act and other acts of Congress was broad enough that by implication it covered the executive branch as well and was generally understood as such. But in fact *Marbury* barely mentioned the presidency and offered no future guidelines concerning what boundaries—if any—the Court might someday place on the nation's highest executive officer.

But then the early American presidency gave the Supreme Court few opportunities to offer such guidelines. Put simply, the presidents who served during the nation's first decades did not do very much. The executive department was minuscule, the presidents themselves were careful not to create even the appearance of overreach or impropriety, and Americans in general possessed low expectations of their new federal government.

War was the exception, however. The Constitution empowered the president, as the commander in chief, to reach directly into Americans' lives—though in what ways and how far was not entirely clear, at least not in the early days of the Republic. The language in Article II was sparse, declaring merely that "the President shall be commander in chief of the Army and Navy of the United States, and of the militia of the several states, when called into the actual service of the United States."

The notes from the Philadelphia Convention were not much help. The delegates were apprehensive about delivering presidents too much war-making authority (as they were worried about nearly all questions of executive power), seeing war and its concomitant bestowal of literally the power of life and death on government authorities as perhaps the most direct means by which an individual American citizen's rights might be curtailed. Small wonder, then, that the Founders—worried as they constantly were about the abridgment of personal liberties—expressed an earnest desire to deny excessive military power to the new executive branch.

The Constitution's defenders tried to further allay fears of an omnipotent American military chieftain by pointing out that the president would be much less independent in his war-making authority than Britain's monarch. "In this respect his authority would be nominally the same with that of the king of Great Britain," Hamilton wrote in *Federalist No. 69*, "but in substance much inferior to it. It would amount to nothing more than the supreme command and direction of the military and naval forces, as first General and admiral of the Confederacy; while that of the British king extends to the Declaring of war and to the raising and regulating of fleets and armies, all which, by the Constitution under consideration, would appertain to the legislature" (http://www.yale.edu/lawweb/avalon/federal/fed69.htm).

But beyond this simple fact of separation between executive and legislative powers, many questions remained concerning the precise boundaries of presidential war-making power. One could argue that the Supreme Court was the logical arbiter of such matters, but the early Court had little to say concerning either war or the presidency in general.

This would change in 1799. Ironically enough, in that year the United States was not, technically speaking, at war. In fact, that was the point.

Ever since the outbreak of the French Revolution ten years previously, Americans had walked a thin line between support for the revolutionaries—many of whom waved copies of the Declaration of Independence as they dismantled the French monarchy—and revulsion at their excesses. The French seemed at once exhilaratingly democratic and shockingly brutal—often both at once. American ambivalence quickened when

France was drawn into conflict with her ancient enemy, Great Britain. Some Americans still felt close enough to Britain culturally and economically that they were reluctant to make war on their old mother country. Others argued that America was obligated to support France, the nation that had provided critical support for the patriot cause during the difficult days of the American Revolution and that was now in the throes of a revolution fed by and similar to that which had moved the heroes of 1776. "We wish to omit no opportunity of convincing [the French] how cordially we desire the closest union with them," Thomas Jefferson wrote in 1793. "Mutual good offices, mutual affection and similar principles of government seem to have destined the two people for the most intimate communion, and even for a complete exchange of citizenship among the individuals composing them" (Peterson, 1984, 1003).

When Jefferson became president seven years later, however, he confronted a much different situation. French enthusiasm for American democracy and the stylings of American Revolutionaries had since turned into a barely controlled fury at the United States for maintaining neutrality between the warring European powers. When the French Directory issued a decree in 1796 declaring that France now intended to "treat neutral vessels, either as to confiscation, as to searches, or capture, in the same manner as they shall suffer the English to treat them," French naval commanders took this as a license to seize American ship-

ping on the high seas, steal their cargoes, and impress American sailors into service" (McKitrick and Elkins, 1995, 538–539).

Faced with the fact that the U.S. Navy existed largely in name only, Congress in 1798 passed legislation designed to encourage merchant vessels to protect themselves. It awarded a portion of the cargo from any American vessel taken by the French and then retaken by an American vessel, as compensation and an incentive for merchants to arm their ships and protect one another. Accordingly, in 1799 the American merchant vessel *Ganges* recaptured from the French a merchant vessel called the *Eliza*. Under the provisions of the law the *Ganges* owner, Captain Tingy, claimed one-half of the *Eliza*'s cargo as prize. Citing a technicality in the law, the *Eliza*'s owner, John Bas, argued that Tingy was entitled to only one-eighth of the cargo. The entire matter wound up before the Supreme Court.

On the surface, *Bas v. Tingy* (1800) had relatively little to do with presidential war-making powers, or any other presidential authority. Much of the opinion was taken up with the justices trying to find a distinction between a "declared" war by Congress and the quasi-war being waged by the merchant vessels. Bas argued that Tingy was not due one-half of his cargo because, no war having actually been declared by Congress, there was no state of "war" as required by the statute. Tingy's lawyers in turn argued that a de facto war did in fact exist between America and France. Much of their wrangling

The USS Constellation *battles the French frigate* l'Insurgente *in the waters of the West Indies, during the French-American Quasi-War on February 9, 1799. (Naval Historical Foundation)*

involved congressional intent, with the president barely mentioned at all.

But lying beneath these issues was the matter of presidential war making and, by extension, his general authority as the nation's chief executive. And still further beneath these matters was the fundamental issue of presidential flexibility, a matter that had bedeviled American constitutionalism since the office was first created in 1787. The crux of *Bas v. Tingy* was simply this: could some government

entity (that is, the president) other than Congress create a state of war without overt congressional permission?

The Court awarded Tingy his one-half cargo compensation, and in doing so affirmed, implicitly at least, that there were broad areas in American war making that the presidency could pursue without overt congressional permission. Identifying a formally declared war by Congress a "perfect war," Justice Bushrod Washington wrote that "hostilities may subsist between two nations more confined in its nature and extent; being limited as to persons, places, and things; and this is more properly termed imperfect war. . . . It is public war, because it is an external contention by force, between some of the members of the two nations, authorized by the legitimate powers." Washington did not suggest that the president, by himself, might be such a "legitimate power," and future justices chose not to pursue his somewhat vague distinction between "perfect" and "imperfect" wars. But he and his brethren in *Bas v. Tingy* had left a crack in the door through which a future chief executive could, if he so chose, wage an armed conflict on at least a limited scale without necessarily requiring a formal congressional declaration. While it would not be immediately apparent, Washington had just laid the groundwork for nearly two centuries of presidential war making with little or no prior congressional approval.

A quarter-century later, the Supreme Court was again confronted with questions surrounding presidential war making, this time directly involving presidential action. At issue was an order issued by President Madison during the War of 1812 that pressed the state militia of New York into national service. When it became apparent that this might mean ordering the men to serve outside the state, a militiaman named Jacob Mott objected, filing a lawsuit against the federal government that argued against the president's power to seize control of New York's militia.

Martin v. Mott (1827) presented the question of presidential war-making au-

thority in a more direct manner than *Bas v. Tingy*. Justice Joseph Story, writing for the Court, recognized this was "a very high and delicate" matter. "A free people are naturally jealous of the exercise of military power," he pointed out, and it was a power only to be exercised in "cases of invasion, or of imminent danger of invasion." The question, then, was whether Congress or the president was the better judge concerning whether or not such a situation had arisen.

Story and the Court came down firmly on the president's side. "We are all of the opinion, that the authority to decide whether the exigency has arisen, belongs exclusively to the President, and that his decision is conclusive upon all other persons." This included Jacob Mott, who lost his case, but the matter went much further than one disgruntled militiaman. The Supreme Court had now widened *Bas v. Tingy's* crack into a rather wide breach, arguing that war presented special circumstances, whereby there might simply not be enough time to consult with other authorities—militia officers, state legislators, or even, by implication, U.S. congressmen—before ordering American troops into combat. "In many instances, the evidence upon which the President might decide that there is imminent danger of invasion, might be of a nature not constituting strict technical proof," Story pointed out, "or the disclosure of the evidence might reveal important secrets of state, which the public interest, and even safety, might imperiously demand to be kept in concealment" (*Martin v. Mott,* 25 U.S. 19).

CONGRESS AND "MR. POLK'S WAR"

Over three decades would pass before Congress and the presidency had occasion to interact again on wartime matters. While the nation did fight occasional small-scale skirmishes and minor wars with various Native American tribes between 1815 (the end of hostilities with Great Britain) and 1846 (the beginning of the Mexican War), it engaged in no major military conflicts that might call into question the presidency's war-making capacity.

In the meantime, Jacksonian-era presidents forged a relationship with Congress that was in many ways more direct and more advanced than that employed by early chief executives. The key was the political party, a phenomenon unlooked for and largely despised by the Framers but embraced by their descendants as a necessary fact of modern American political life.

Presidents now had more sophisticated party tools at their disposal than previously. They could connect with big boss–style party leaders like New York's Thurlow Weed and Pennsylvania's Simon Cameron, men who in turn could command organized cadres of the party faithful down to the level of the town and neighborhood and could deliver support and votes from their party "machinery" as needed. Granted, the level of organization was not nearly as sophisticated as it would someday become. Later in the century party bosses would weld together sophisticated structures of local, state, and national party loyalists that sometimes rivaled military outfits; the Wide-Awakes of the early Republican Party, for example, adopted paramilitary uniforms and ranks and marched in martial formation. Eventually, many people would come to see something undemocratic in the spectacle and call for reform. But compared to what had come before them, Jacksonian-era party activists created surprisingly effective and disciplined organizations.

These organizations reached their apogee during presidential elections. The coming-out party, of sorts, for the modern party-led political rally system of electing presidents was the presidential election of 1840, pitting military hero William Henry Harrison of the Whigs against the Democrats' Martin Van Buren. Harrison possessed more military than political experience—he was the hero of the Battle of Tippecanoe (1811) against Tecumseh's Indian Confederation—and not much in the way of a discernible political philosophy. His supporters compensated by highlighting Harrison's military career with the catchy slogan "Tippecanoe and Tyler, Too!" the last part in reference to his running mate, John Tyler. They also had a field day marketing Harrison as a man of the people, playing upon what were supposed to be disparaging remarks about Harrison leveled by an opposition newspaper. "Give him a barrel of hard cider and settle a pension of two thousand a year on him," sneered the paper's editor, "and my word for it, he will sit . . . by the side of a 'sea coal' fire, and study moral philosophy" (http://www.whitehouse.gov/history/presidents/wh9.html).

Whigs turned the sneer into a propaganda coup, depicting their man as a populist folk hero, replete with banners flying images of log cabins and cider jugs. "No ruffled shirt, no silken hose/No airs does Tip display" went a campaign poem; instead "he goes in homespun 'hodding gray.'" Songwriting became a particularly popular pursuit, as Harrison's supporters concocted dozens of little rhymes and ditties, eventually collected in a little book titled *The Log Cabin Sing-book*. Whigs also constructed model log cabins in town squares all over the country; a "log-cabin raising" sponsored by the local Tippecanoe Club became quite the social event. (Gunderson, 1957, 123–124). Thus was the modern party media campaign born, a campaign that could be used not only to garner votes but to knit together party loyalists at all levels.

These party loyalists could be further linked to a president's agenda after he attained office through the use of patronage power. Jacksonian-era presidents distributed valuable political jobs among their supporters, ensuring their loyalty and giving the executive branch a presence in the far corners of the federal government. "To the victor belongs the spoils," exulted New York politician William Marcy, defending his man Andrew Jackson's habit of rewarding party supporters with government jobs. Revolutionary-era Americans would have seen this "spoils system" as shameless factionalism and insisted it had no place in presidential politics, but Jacksonians were much more comfortable with such practices.

A key figure in the development of party machinery and its connection to the White House was the man Harrison defeated in 1840. Martin Van Buren had been known as the Little Magician (he was a spare 5 feet 6 inches) in his home state of New York for his clever manipulations of party politics and loyalties to get ahead in the state's Democratic Party and consolidate his power. He came to the White House in 1836 as Andrew Jackson's vice president and handpicked successor, having deftly outmaneuvered South Carolina's favorite son, John C. Calhoun, for the role of Jackson's heir apparent by playing upon Jackson's displeasure with Calhoun on a variety of matters.

Words like "crafty" and "devious" were often applied to Van Buren. While this was in many respects unfair, it was true that the Little Magician had a taste for informal political conversations (what a later generation might have referred to as doing business on the golf course), backroom maneuvering, and political deal making. He was innately cautious and not given to brash political moves, preferring first to determine which direction the political winds were blowing and then to adjust his sails accordingly. "Even his best friends were apprehensive that he was over cautious," observed an acquaintance (Curtis, 1970, 18).

Bold or not, President Van Buren was keener than most of his predecessors in his desire to keep an eye on the workings of Congress, and party connections helped him to do so. He wanted a disciplined Democratic Party, with members of Congress loyal to the party—and to him—in pursuit of a mature political agenda. To that end he maintained contacts on Capitol Hill, and he tried (with at best mixed success) to mediate disputes between warring factions within the party's membership. To modern eyes, this was meager fare. "He did not propose to unite the faithful behind a vast legislative program," observed one historian. "Such an idea was alien to his day" (Curtis, 1970, 63). What he did want was a cooperative, relatively harmonious Congress, run by the leadership of his own Democratic Party in an orderly fashion.

The Framers' generation of presidents had been very ambivalent about the idea of political parties and reluctant to involve themselves much at all in congressional affairs. Van Buren, in contrast, specifically wanted a policy of "resuscitating old party feelings" (Wilson, 1984, 37). He believed that party combat in Congress and in the polis generally was a natural and good phenomenon, indicative of a healthy, robust republic. Unlike many others of his day, Van Buren was not much enamored of the so-called Era of Good Feelings, that period between 1800 and 1828 when American politics was dominated by one party, the Jeffersonian Republicans. To the Little Magician, it was unrealistic to expect one party, however well-intentioned, to represent the interests of every American. Factionalism, to him, was a good thing. "Every community that enjoys the least semblance of freedom is kept in contention by the antagonist principle," he wrote to Andrew Jackson, and that prin-

ciple was given organized expression in the party system (Wilson, 1984, 36).

Certainly by 1846 the Era of Good Feelings had long since ended, and the nation found itself once again—and thereafter—possessed of a robust, raucous two-party rivalry. Jefferson's Republicans had split in 1828 over Jackson's controversial presidency, with Jackson's supporters assuming the moniker Democrats while his many opponents united under the Whig banner. The Whigs were more inclined to favor a stronger government presence in American economic life (though they wanted careful limits placed on executive power) and were the natural home of moral reformers of various stripes. Generally speaking, Democrats represented the interests of farmers and southern planters; had a strong states' rights streak in their approach to government authority; and were ardent expansionists, calling upon the nation to realize its Manifest Destiny of extension to the Pacific Ocean.

When James K. Polk became president in 1845, there were those who felt he diminished the office. John Quincy Adams sneered that he was "just qualified for an eminent County Court lawyer" (Stephanson, 1995, 34). But he was a dedicated Jacksonian Democrat and an even more committed expansionist. "The jurisdiction of the United States, which at the formation of the Federal Constitution was bounded by the St. Mary's on the Atlantic, has passed the capes of Florida and been peacefully extended to the Del Norte," he exulted, and like many of his fellow countrymen, the president saw this expansion as the natural

James K. Polk served as president of the United States from 1845 to 1849. During his administration, more than one million square miles of new territory were added to the nation. This expansion revived the slavery controversy, polarizing the country. (Library of Congress)

extension of American ideals of democracy and self government. "In contemplating the grandeur of this event it is not to be forgotten that the result was achieved in despite of the diplomatic interference of European monarchies," he declared. "European Governments may learn how vain diplomatic arts and intrigues must ever prove upon this continent against that system of self-government which seems natural to our soil, and which will ever resist foreign interference" (www.presidency.ucsb.edu/ws/index.php?pid=29486).

Polk was a rare bird in that he was at once both ambitious and publicly committed to serving only one term in office—the only president to ever limit himself in this fashion. This commitment was a function of his states' rights philosophy, a point of view that looked

askance at any serious expansion of federal power. As a good Jacksonian Democrat and states' rights Southerner, he was obsessed with the problem of limiting federal influence and his office's own power. In his Inaugural Address, Polk spoke at length on the matter, telling his audience that "it will be my desire to guard against that most fruitful source of danger to the harmonious action of our system which consists in substituting the mere discretion and caprice of the Executive or of majorities in the legislative department of the Government for powers which have been withheld from the Federal Government by the Constitution." Where Congress was concerned, he took pains to point out that he would act as an adviser only, and that his advice would always lean toward limitation rather than expansion of government power. "Ours was intended to be a plain and frugal government," he argued, "and I shall regard it to be my duty to recommend to Congress and, as far as the Executive is concerned, to enforce by all the means within my power the strictest economy in the expenditure of the public money which may be compatible with the public interests" (www.yale.edu/lawweb/ avalon/presiden/inaug/polk.htm).

This laissez-faire approach to federal power existed somewhat uneasily alongside his robust expansionism; one might think that a president committed to growing the territory of the United States would surely also be interested in expanding his own reach, as well, if for no other reason than to assist Manifest Destiny by executive fiat. Certainly such groundwork had been laid by Thomas Jefferson (whom Polk greatly admired) when Jefferson had purchased Louisiana from France forty years earlier. Like Polk, Jefferson had also been committed to states' rights; and, like Polk, Jefferson would lay such constitutional scruples to one side when they conflicted with opportunities to grow the nation's borders.

President Polk faced two such opportunities, but both were fraught with peril as well as promise. As a candidate, Polk had two dominant goals: solve the "Oregon" problem and the "Texas" problem on terms beneficial to his fellow American expansionists. Where the former was concerned, the Americans and the British had long maintained mutually antagonistic claims to Oregon and had created a rather uneasy joint occupa-

tion mechanism by which the two nations were both allowed access to the territory. Such an arrangement could not last forever, and both sides knew it. For his part, Polk pressed the American claim to Oregon from the moment he took office. "Our title to the whole of the Territory of Oregon is clear and unquestionable," read the Democrats' 1844 platform. "No portion of the same ought to be ceded to England or any other power. . . . The reoccupation of Oregon and the re-annexation of Texas at the earliest practicable period are great American measures" (www.presidency.ucsb.edu/showplatforms.php?platindex =D1844). Polk solved the Oregon problem with diplomacy, negotiating an eventual evacuation of British subjects south of the forty-ninth parallel and giving British Canada the territory north of that line.

Texas, however, was a far more complicated and thorny problem, involving sectional tensions between North and South and a smoldering border dispute with Mexico concerning whether the Rio Grande River or the Nueces River constituted Texas's southernmost border. These had first become serious national issues during the preceding administration of John Tyler.

Tyler became more than the mere afterthought of "Tippecanoe and Tyler, Too!" when President Harrison died suddenly from pneumonia in April 1841. "His Accidency"—as he was contemptuously labeled by critics—was, like Polk, an expansionist who wanted Texas added to the United States. Texans had won their independence from Mexico five years previously and desired admission into the Union. If Texas had been a territory, Congress would have been directly and intimately involved with its passage into statehood, with all of the eddies and currents of congressional politics complicating the matter. But Texas was an independent nation, and this gave President Tyler the opportunity he needed to negotiate a treaty under his Article II power. Congress still had to ratify the administration's treaty, of course. But expansionism enjoyed widespread support on Capitol Hill, and Texas was eventually annexed to the United States. "The Lone Star of Texas . . . has passed on and become fixed forever in that glorious constellation which all freemen and lovers of freedom in the world must reverence and adore—the American Union," enthused one Texan (Merk, 1978, 309).

Thanks to Tyler, Texas's border problem with Mexico was now America's problem, and it threatened to exacerbate smoldering sectional tensions over slavery. Texas was settled largely by men and women from Tennessee, Kentucky, and other slave-owning areas. They brought their slaves with them, meaning that Texas would inevitably become a slave state itself when it was finally admitted into the Union. A slave-owning state—or two, or perhaps three or four. White Southerners exulted that Texas could be broken up into pieces, each piece with its own representatives and senators, who could in turn protect southern interests on Capitol Hill for decades to come. Northerners were understandably dismayed at the prospect. "The annexation

of Texas looks like one of those events which retard or retrograde the civilization of ages," groused Ralph Waldo Emerson, an opponent of slavery (Bauer, 1974, 10).

Polk possessed a decidedly pro-southern point of view on the matter. He was himself a slaveholder, and he owed his election to southern voters. Expansion was also a prominent Democratic Party goal. John O'Sullivan—the man who coined the term *Manifest Destiny*—was, after all, a die-hard Democrat, and wrote those words for a party newspaper organ, the *Democratic Review*. The Democrats' new president was therefore determined to settle the Texas-Mexico border dispute in Texas's favor as a matter of personal preference and regional and party loyalty all at once. He sent a series of delegations to Mexico City to negotiate settlement of the Texas matter and instructed his diplomats to press for the Rio Grande River as the new state's southern border.

But Mexico would not budge, and as the arguments between the sides dragged on, both engaged in an increasing amount of saber rattling. Polk stationed American soldiers under Zachary Taylor near the disputed zone, and Mexico responded with a sizeable force of its own, staring down the Americans from across the Rio Grande. With soldiers in such close proximity, perhaps it was just a matter of time between the two sides clashed. On April 25, 1846, Mexican troops crossed the Rio Grande and attacked a small party of American dragoons at Port Isabel, killing eleven and capturing over eighty more, including the detachment's commander. Taylor immediately informed the president of the clash and informed a colleague that "hostilities may now be considered as commenced" (Bauer, 1974, 48).

Perhaps. But there was as yet no declaration of war to that effect from a badly divided Congress. President Polk, who had by now concluded that a war was inevitable, seized upon the Port Isabel skirmish to ramrod a declaration of war through Congress. He found out about the incident on May 9, a Saturday when most congressmen were enjoying a weekend respite from their tasks. Bright and early Monday morning, they were greeted with a rather breathless message from the president that "Mexico has passed the boundary of the United States, has invaded our territory and shed American blood upon the American soil. She has proclaimed that hostilities have commenced, and that the two nations are now at war" (www.pbs.org/weta/thewest/resources/archives/two/mexdec.htm). With some members of Congress believing that "passed the boundary of the United States" meant a wholesale Mexican invasion of Texas soil—rather than merely a skirmish in the disputed area just north of the Rio Grande, the status of which was certainly open to question—Congress on May 13 quickly gave Polk his declaration of war, overriding the opposition of antislavery congressmen.

But when rumors quickly emerged that Mexico's "invasion" was not much of an invasion at all, many congressmen grew incensed, to the point where some supported a vote of censure against the president. Censure was a legislative device with roots in the early British Parliament and was designed for use by legislators to express disapproval of the behavior displayed by one of their own. Just two years prior to the start of the Mexican War, for example, Benjamin Tappan of Ohio was censured by the Senate for leaking to the press a copy of a message that President John Tyler had confidentially sent to the Senate concerning Texas's annexation. Censure was considered to be a part of the Constitution's provision that "Each House may determine the Rules of its proceedings, [and] punish its members for disorderly behavior." But it carried no weight beyond the social stigma and political consequences it might engender. And as far as the presidency was concerned, censure had no constitutional foundation at all (www.senate.gov/artandhistory/history/common/briefing/Expulsion_Censure.htm).

Nevertheless, it had been done—once. In 1830 Congress formally censured Andrew Jackson when Old Hickory took the federal government's money out of the National Bank and deposited it in various state (or "pet") banks, thus wrecking the National Bank and deeply angering Bank supporters. The censure resolution claimed that Jackson had "assumed upon himself authority and power not conferred by the Constitution and laws, but in derogation of both" (Remini, 1984, 151). Jackson privately denounced the censure as a "false clamour" motivated by "spite and envy." Publicly, he sent an angry message to the Senate, defending his banking policies and informing Congress that it possessed no legal authority "to take up, consider and decide upon the official acts of the Executive" (Remini, 1984, 152–153). The president went on to assert the then-novel proposition that the chief executive was responsible to the people, not Congress. In doing so, Jackson biographer Robert Remini argued, Jackson "liberated the chief executive from the position of prime minister responsible only to Congress" (Remini, 1984, 159).

This was on the level of political and constitutional theory. On the practical level, the censure resolution lit Andrew Jackson's already notoriously short fuse and ignited a fierce war of words in the press and on the floor of Congress—but it otherwise accomplished very little in the way of concrete policymaking. At the end of the day, Jackson prevailed over the National Bank and eventually won reelection to a second term. The censure certainly did not destroy his career, as his enemies predicted it might. It was "the last stroke upon the last nail driven into the coffin of Jacksonianism," Henry Clay exulted (Petersen, 1984, 244). He could not have been more mistaken.

Nevertheless, eighteen years later, angry Whigs and their Democratic supporters dusted off the censure as a means of expressing their disapproval of Mr. Polk. The measure was sponsored by George Ashmun of Massachusetts, an outspoken opponent of the administration and the war. Ashmun attached the censure as a rider on a resolution offering Congress's vote of thanks to General Zachary Taylor for his victory at the Battle of Buena Vista. Feelings were riding high enough in the House that the censure amendment actually passed, very narrowly, by a vote of 82 to 81. It failed in the Senate, however, and so to this day, Andrew Jackson remains the only president ever to have received a censure from Congress.

One of those eighty-two representatives voting in the affirmative was a relatively unknown representative from Illinois, Abraham Lincoln. Like many Whigs, Lincoln disliked the war and the circumstances surrounding it. He voiced his displeasure on the matter in no uncertain terms during a blistering speech on the floor of the House. "The President, in his first war message of May 1846, declares that the soil was *ours* on which hostilities were commenced by Mexico," Lincoln pointed out. But according to the Illinois congressman, this was not so. And in practicing this bit of chicanery upon the nation's legislators, Lincoln argued, Polk had embarrassed the nation and himself. "My way of living leads me to be about the courts of justice," Lincoln declared, "and there, I have sometimes seen a good lawyer, struggling for his client's neck, in a desperate case, employing every artifice to work round, befog, and cover up, with many words, some point arising in the case, which he *dared* not admit, and yet *could* not deny. Party bias may help to make it appear so; but with all the allowance I can make for such bias, it still does appear to me, that just such, and from just such necessity, is the President's struggle in this case" (Basler, 1953–1955, 1: 438).

Lithograph depicting the Battle of Buena Vista, fought between Mexican general Antonio López de Santa Anna's Army of the North and U.S. general Zachary Taylor's Army of Occupation on February 23, 1847. The final battle in northern Mexico and a demoralizing loss for the Mexican army, it was a significant turning point in the Mexican War. (Library of Congress)

Lincoln thought this rebuke would earn him the approbation of his friends and fellow Whigs back home in Illinois—and, just possibly, a second congressional term. Instead, he found himself raked over the coals by an Illinois Democratic press that accused him of disloyalty. A Morgan County Democratic Party rally denounced Lincoln's "base, cowardly, and treasonable assault on President Polk" (Donald, 1995, 125). Even Lincoln's friends warned him that he had pushed matters too far, both with the speech and his vote in favor of the Ashmun amendment.

Nonplussed, Lincoln defended himself in a letter to his law partner, Billy Herndon, that explained his reasons. "That [censure] vote affirms that the war was unnecessarily and unconstitutionally commenced by the President; and I will stake my life, that if you had been in my place, you would have voted just as I did," he informed Herndon. Apparently, Herndon had suggested Lincoln might have been better served by simply abstaining from the Ashmun vote altogether. Lincoln did not much care for this option, either. "Would you have gone out of the House—skulked the vote? I expect not. If you had skulked one vote, you would have had to skulk many more, before the end of the session." He also took exception to the charge made by some Democrats that his opposition to Mr. Polk's war had led him to deprive American soldiers of much-needed money and supplies by voting against military appropriations bills. "This vote, has nothing to do, in determining my votes on the questions of supplies," Lincoln retorted. "I have always intended, and still intend, to vote supplies; perhaps not in the precise form recommended by the President, but in a better form for all purposes. . . . It is in this particular you seem to be mistaken. The [pro-war Democrats] are untiring in their effort to make the impression that all who vote supplies, or take part in the war, do, of necessity, approve the Presidents conduct in the beginning of it; but the whigs have, from the beginning, made and kept the distinction between the two" (Basler, 1953–1955, 1: 448).

There in a nutshell was the dilemma faced by members of Congress who oppose a president trying to go to war. On a constitutional level, Congress is a co-equal partner in the business of war making; the president is the commander in chief, while Congress raises and funds the armed forces and makes the rules governing their behavior. But on the level of practical politics, the president holds all the cards. He is the titular head of a party organization that he can use, if he is skillful, to bring to heel representatives and senators within the ranks. In a media-driven democracy, presidents also have the advantage of being singular dynamic figures who can focus national attention with greater alacrity than the often-faceless legislators who cannot collectively or alone command the same level of media attention.

Most of all, as commander in chief, the president can call upon Americans' immense reservoirs of patriotism and goodwill during war. When shots are fired at American troops, the nation's citizenry tends to rally around the flag and support its president as a matter of national pride. Indeed, to many Americans, supporting the president and supporting the soldiers in the field are very nearly one and the same thing. Few members of Congress possess the standing and power to confront this dynamic.

ABRAHAM LINCOLN, THE JOINT COMMITTEE, AND THE LIMITS OF NECESSITY

Abraham Lincoln may have later looked back wistfully—or even with a touch of chagrin—on his congressional days of opposition to Polk's war with Mexico. Fifteen years later, he would find himself dealing with his own set of vocal congressional critics; and they were far more organized and effective than Lincoln's own rather lonely crusade against Polk could ever have been.

At issue during the Civil War was not a declaration of war as such. Congress never actually declared war on the Confederacy, for to do so would have presented a legal quandary. The Lincoln Administration always held that, as a matter of law, the Confederate States of

America did not exist; "Confederates" were really only Americans in rebellion against their legitimate government in Washington, D.C. A declaration of war against the Confederacy would have been tantamount to the United States declaring war against itself—a palpable absurdity, at least from the North's point of view. Northerners were therefore spared the spectacle of Congress and the president tussling over which branch possessed the constitutional right to declare a war.

The constitutional questions presented by the war were actually far more subtle and complex. All agreed that some sort of war existed between the North and the South, however one wished to characterize or call it. Disagreements arose between the White House, Congress, and the Supreme Court concerning the myriad of details surrounding that war's conduct. The war presented a whole host of new and thorny problems, many of which had never been encountered before, for the simple reason that America had never fought this sort of war before. Scholars of the Civil War disagree whether it was the first "modern" war in American (indeed, world) history. But modern or not, it was certainly quite unprecedented in scope and complexity, placing more Americans in harm's way than had any previous war.

When the war began in 1861, the federal administrative machinery had hardly evolved at all to meet the new crisis. Not much had changed in the government's frugal, some might say threadbare, makeup since the days of Andrew Jackson. A person needed only to walk the streets of pre-war Washington, D.C., to see firsthand evidence of this. Prior to 1860, the nation's capital was a sleepy hamlet of only a few thousand souls, many of whom abandoned the place when hot summer weather arrived. "It was a Southern town," noted one observer, "without the picturesqueness, but with the indolence, the disorder and the want of sanitation" (Leech, 1941, 11).

There were comparatively few government buildings for the simple reason that there were few government employees. Even the Capitol dome symbolized the national government's embryonic state. In 1850 Congress had allocated $500 for renovations to its building, with the replacement of the old wooden and copper dome with marble being an integral part of its plan. But construction proceeded so slowly that ten years later the dome was still only half finished. President-elect Lincoln took the oath of office among construction paraphernalia and half-finished marble blocks.

Where formal relations between the presidency and Congress were concerned, lack of development was likewise evident. Many of the old taboos against direct contact were still in place. Presidents still did not deliver their State of the Union Addresses in person. Vetoes were a relative rarity; out of the 2,550 vetoes issued by presidents, only fifty-two occurred before 1860. Even contact that today seems trivial could upset members of Congress anxious to guard their turf against presidential encroachment, perceived and real. In 1863, for example, Lincoln sent along with his signature on a military appropriations bill a statement of his views concerning the nation's monetary policy. "It must be confessed that the message partook somewhat of the character of a lecture," noted one newspaper reporter, "but the turmoil, buzzing and fretting of Congress was unnecessary and undignified. . . . Representatives grumbled and swore, and Senators were indignant, and being so lectured, would not even print the message" (Burlingame and Ettlinger, 1997, 19).

Such incursions into congressional dignity were rare, perhaps in part because the White House was ill-equipped to monitor the nation's legislators on anything like a regular basis. The president's connections with Congress were informal and ramshackle. He had no formal liaison with Congress, no real administrative network to speak of, and did not offer a formal legislative agenda beyond whatever recommendations might appear in his State of the Union Address. In the wake of the Panic of 1857 Lincoln's predecessor, James Buchanan, gently suggested that "under these circumstances a loan may be required before the close of your present session; but this, although deeply to be regretted, would prove to be only a slight misfortune when compared with the suffering and distress prevailing among the people." Even so, Buchanan hastily added, Congress "may be without the power to extend relief" (www.presidency.ucsb.edu/ws/index.php?pid=29498).

The president did not have the means to monitor systematically how Congress would act upon such recommendations.

President Abraham Lincoln poses for a formal portrait with his two personal secretaries, John Nicolay (left) and John Hay on November 8, 1863. (Library of Congress)

Indeed, he could not really monitor much of anything. The executive branch's staff was skeletal. Even at the height of the Civil War, Lincoln employed a grand total of two private secretaries, John Nicolay and John Hay. The two young men oversaw the day-to-day scheduling of Lincoln's appointments, helped answer the great volumes of mail that crossed the president's desk, and acted as door wardens to the president's office—not a difficult task, since Lincoln chose to see nearly anybody who wandered by. "Nobody ever wanted to see the president who did not," irritably remarked Secretary of State William Seward. "There was never a man so accessible to all sorts of proper and improper persons" (Burlingame and Ettlinger, 1997, 221).

Connections of party politics and loyalties created links between the executive and legislative branches; the spoils system remained alive and well throughout the antebellum era, and presidents were routinely greeted with requests from this or that congressman to grant jobs and other emoluments to favored constituents. When Lincoln took office in 1860, he represented a new party, the Republicans, a loose-knit coalition of antislavery activists, free soilers, and business-minded people keen to use government power to develop the nation's economy. If anything, the members of this new organization were even more hungry than usual for the rewards of political office. President-elect Lincoln was buried under the requests and demands of office seekers trying to cash in on Republicans' newfound authority.

Republicans also had the usual backroom and quasi-formal "business on the golf course" access to the Lincoln White House. One interesting connection in this regard was the friendship that blossomed between Republican senator Charles Sumner and First Lady Mary Lincoln. Sumner was an antislavery Bostonian and Radical Republican who had gained national attention in 1854 when his intemperate remarks about a South Carolina colleague led to his being beaten with a cane by the Carolinian's

outraged cousin. At first glance he seemed an unlikely friend to Mary, daughter of a Kentucky slaveholder. But Mary was captivated by Sumner's charm and gift for social conversation, and he soon became a frequent White House dinner guest. "He appreciated my noble husband," Mary later observed, "and I learned to converse with him, with more freedom and *confidence* than any of my other friends" (Donald, 1995, 476).

Sumner did more than just keep the First Lady entertained. He pressed his antislavery views on Mary, who in turn tried to steer her husband toward emancipation as a war goal. Mary also came to Sumner for various political and personal favors, introducing him for example to "two colored persons who came to us very highly recommended from some of our loyal families in Philadelphia" and asking the senator to meet with them about some unknown issue (Baker, 1987, 233). The president understood how these connections worked as well. He carefully cultivated Sumner's friendship and esteem as a way of influencing the Republicans' Radical contingent in Congress.

This sort of informal coalition of dinner companions, party loyalists, and the like had worked well enough before the war to ensure that the federal government's business functioned more or less smoothly. The government did so little that Americans could get by and still nurse their Revolutionary-era ideals about presidents who possessed so few formal channels to Congress that there was no risk of any dangerous tyrannies or untoward influence between the two branches.

But to paraphrase Lincoln, the quiet dogmas of the past were inadequate for the stormy Civil War present. The war effort was too complex for the mom-and-pop operation that was the antebellum federal government. Almost overnight Washington, D.C., was overrun by a new wave of clerks, bureaucrats, workers, and officials of all shapes and sizes brought in to administer the biggest war effort to that point in the nation's history.

With all the new people in uniform came a whole host of new problems. Before the war, the U.S. Army numbered around 10,000 men; by the end of the war's first year, there were more than five times that number defending Washington, D.C., and a great many more scattered in armies around the country. Americans had never tried to arm, feed, discipline, or lead that many soldiers at once; the task took their collective breaths away. "A French army of half the size of ours could be supplied with what we waste," one general believed (McPherson, 1982, 198).

Some in Congress wondered if the new president was equal to the task of managing the Union's new military leviathan. After all, prior to 1860 Lincoln had never been in charge of anything larger than his own law office, and more than one member of Congress noted that the man was a terrible administrator, disorganized and given to distraction by details and individual supplicants looking for favors or jobs or merely trying to dispense helpful advice. "The difficulty with Mr. Lincoln is that he has no conception of his situation," Sumner believed, and worse, he had "no system in his composition" (Donald, 1995, 285).

Secretary of War Simon Cameron likewise did little to inspire confidence. Lincoln felt compelled to reward the Pennsylvania politico with a Cabinet post, despite Cameron's reputation for corruption and his general inexperience at military matters. "Everything goes in confused disorder," Secretary of the Treasury Salmon Chase observed of the War Department. "Gen. [Winfield] Scott [the army's commander] gives an order, Mr. Cameron gives another. Half of both are executed neutralizing each other" (Burlingame and Ettlinger, 1997, 6) The Cameron-led War Department quickly became a dismaying tangle of inefficiency and corruption. Senator Orville Browning rightly informed Lincoln that Cameron had "lost, or rather failed to secure the confidence of the country" (Donald, 1995, 325). A growing chorus of congressmen called for Cameron's resignation.

Most of all, perhaps, the nation's legislators worried about the Union's young commanding general, George B. McClellan, who replaced Scott late in 1861. "Little Mac" came to the army with an impressive résumé—topflight graduate of West Point, protégé of Winfield Scott, successful businessman—and he had scored a series of small victories in western Virginia during the war's early months. He was hailed as a national savior, but he also had his share of faults: an overweening ego, a propensity for delay (Lincoln sardonically observed that his general had the "slows"), and a taste for politics that placed him decidedly on the conservative, Democratic end of the spectrum. That party, wounded and dispirited by the disaffection of most of its southern wing into the Confederacy, was already contemplating a McClellan candidacy against Lincoln in 1864, and Little Mac did nothing to discourage such talk. One hostile Republican newspaper even wondered whether McClellan's reluctance to attack the enemy masked some hidden political agenda. Perhaps the general hesitated out of worry "that he would be likely to kill several thousand good voters, whom he might need in 1864 when he runs for President as the candidate of the reunited and reinvigorated Sham Democracy" (Sears, 1988, 154).

Republicans in Congress felt growing angst about the Lincoln Administration's conduct of the war and the behavior of the army's commanding general. A nasty little combat disaster in the fall of 1861 was the catalyst for translating that angst into action. On October 21, a detachment of Union soldiers was overwhelmed by a force of Confederates at a place called Ball's Bluff in Virginia. The Union suffered nearly 1,000 casualties, including 500 prisoners. Among the dead was Edward Baker, a popular Oregon senator and close friend of Abraham Lincoln. "This has been a heavy day," John Hay noted in his diary when the president received the news (Burlingame and Ettlinger, 1997, 27).

In the overall scheme of things, Ball's Bluff was not much—small potatoes, compared with the titanic battles to come. But it rubbed many Americans the wrong way. Union forces had been trapped with their backs to a river and no reinforcements close at hand. It also seemed apparent that the Union commander on the scene, General Charles Stone, had been taken unawares by a surprisingly strong rebel force. And where, many asked, was the Little Napoleon when this fiasco unfolded?

Ball's Bluff seemed to be a straw that might break the camel's back of the Union cause, a back that was swaying under a dismaying series of reverses during that terrible first year of the war. Moreover, it would be difficult to imagine an incident that more thoroughly connected the White House and Capitol Hill: a dead senator who was at once well liked and respected by many of his brethren in the Congress and who was also Lincoln's friend. (Even the Supreme Court had a presence here, in a way; future Justice Oliver Wendell Holmes Jr., a lad of twenty at the time, was seriously wounded in the battle). Responding to the public furor over the Ball's Bluff debacle, Republican members of Congress took the unusual step of forming their own war review board, the Joint Committee on the Conduct of the War. The nation had never seen anything quite like it before. Congress had earlier conducted occasional brief forays into the conduct (rather than the funding) of war making, most notably in 1792, when it investigated the army's mishandling of attempts to drive Indian tribes from the Northwest Territory. But it had never tried to insert itself quite so persistently and permanently into the business of making war, and no congressmen had ever impinged so directly on presidential prerogatives. The Constitution's language indicating that the president was commander in chief of the armed forces seemed to indicate a high degree of independence in his direction of the army's and navy's day-to-day operations. Congress possessed no overt constitutional authority to intervene, though one could argue that its Article I mandate to fund the military and make rules for its conduct provided some constitutional platform for the Joint Committee's formation.

Constitutional or not, some observers were unsure if the committee was a very good idea. There were the usual worries about mixing the branches too closely together, albeit in this case the issue seemed to be more of congressional tyranny over the president rather than the other way around. There was also the ever-present dimension of party politics. The committee was widely viewed as a tool of the Republicans' Radical wing, whose members were uncertain about the loyalties of West Point–trained generals—many of whom were Democrats and had former friends in the Confederate army's ranks—and wanted to bring the army into line with what would soon become the nation's emancipation policies. One Radical senator and future committee member, Zachariah Chandler of Michigan, claimed that army generals had "actually express[ed] their sympathy with the enemy" and spoke of the con-

flict as a "damned black Republican war" (Tap, 1998, 25). Everyone knew that one impetus behind the committee's formation was rooting out such sentiments and chastising those who expressed them—a decidedly political agenda that could turn the committee into a poisonous brew of political conflict mixed with internecine struggle between the executive and legislative branches.

Lincoln was not much taken with the idea of a congressional oversight committee, either. He did not have a problem with the committee members' politics—after all, his own Emancipation Proclamation in effect created the "black Republican" dimension of the war—and he worked hard to cultivate the goodwill of Sumner and other influential Radicals. But like nearly every man who has ever sat in the president's chair, he was wary of legislative encroachment upon his powers, particularly a power like wartime commander in chief, which presidents with some justification see as their special bailiwick. Lincoln was no exception. He "viewed the creation of the Committee on the Conduct of the War with some anxiety," Lincoln biographer David Donald observed, "fearing that it might turn into an engine of agitation against the administration" (Donald, 1995, 327). This was no idle fear, given that the committee's chair was the Radical Benjamin F. Wade, an outspoken and often severe critic of the Lincoln Administration's perceived slowness and conservatism on matters related to slavery and emancipation.

But the president was too good a politician to make an open fight of the matter.

He needed to preserve the fragile coalition that was the Republican Party, carefully balancing its conservative wing—business-oriented and suspicious of any drastic plans for prosecuting the war with excessive vengeance or for fundamentally remaking southern society—and its Radical wing, with its insistence on a vigorous war effort and far-reaching changes in the South. The Joint Committee was dominated by Radicals, and Lincoln needed them; so he largely kept quiet as the committee members did their jobs.

The committee focused much of its ire on George McClellan and his sympathizers in the army's ranks. There was a lot of room for criticism. The Little Napoleon had been all too open about his presidential ambitions, his Democratic Party sympathies, and his towering distaste for anything resembling emancipation. "I confess to a prejudice in favor of my own race, and can't learn to like the odor of either Billy goats or niggers," he once declared (Sears, 1988, 116). Such attitudes exposed him to the hostility of committed antislavery men like Benjamin Wade, but might have been overlooked had Little Mac achieved battlefield success. He did not. After constant prodding by an impatient press, Republican congressmen, and the president, McClellan launched what would eventually be the disastrous and unsuccessful campaign to take Richmond by way of an area of Virginia known as the Peninsula. Along the way, McClellan proved himself to be obstinate, overly cautious, and given to delusions about the size and strength of the enemy. He routinely exaggerated its numbers past the point of reason and then used those exaggerations to avoid decisive action. McClellan "had the capacity to make arrangements properly for a great conflict," Lincoln shrewdly observed, but "he became nervous and oppressed with the responsibility and refused to meet the crisis" (Sears, 1988, 169).

There were those in Congress and on the committee who were far less benign in their assessments of McClellan. Wade openly accused McClellan of cowardice, and others on the committee thought the problem extended to out-and-out disloyalty. Chandler believed not only that McClellan's loyalties were suspect, but that he had stocked the ranks of the Army of the Potomac with likeminded southern sympathizers. This was not entirely fair; no hard evidence exists to suggest that General McClellan or his army friends secretly sympathized with the Confederacy. But they were uneasy with Republican policies like property confiscation and emancipation, and the committee devoted much of its time and energy to the task of rooting out Confederate sympathizers, real and imagined, within the army's ranks. In the process, its tone and rhetoric grew increasingly partisan and sharp. Denouncing the "poorly disguised rebel sympathy of sniveling hypocrites," for example, committee member George Julian vowed that "the defenders of slavery and its despicable apologists will be nailed to the world's pillory" (Tap, 1998, 118). Julian and his Radical colleagues wanted to use the committee as a platform to do so.

That said, however, the committee performed tasks other than acting as a political watchdog, some of them worthwhile and largely above the fray of partisan combat. It investigated fraudulent army contracts and looked into (well-founded) accusations of Union army atrocities at Sand Creek, Colorado Territory, and Confederate army atrocities at Fort Pillow, Tennessee. It also investigated reports of Union prisoner abuse by Confederate authorities, describing the conditions in which Union POWs languished as of a sort "that no language can adequately describe" (Tap, 1998, 203). And the committee offered its advice on various Reconstruction schemes, predictably assailing the Lincoln Administration's rather lenient approach as too tepid and supporting efforts at property confiscation and other Radical measures deemed necessary to bring white Southerners to heel and protect freedmen's rights.

The committee cast quite a wide net—but to what end? From the very beginning, no one was quite sure what the committee was supposed to do. It did not draft legislation or create tangible policy recommendations. It possessed no constitutional authority to issue orders to army officers or make any other administrative changes that it might deem worthwhile. When it released its official report on the Army of the Potomac's operations in April 1863, it offered a blistering indictment of McClellan and his strategies, declaring that, had McClellan's operations "corresponded with the success of our arms in other parts of the country, there is reason to believe that the termination of the campaign of 1862 would have seen the rebellion well-nigh,

if not entirely overthrown" (Tap, 1998, 162). But beyond offering grist for the mills of pro- and antiadministration newspapers, this meant little, for the committee lacked the president's power as commander in chief to turn words into deeds. Lincoln did nothing to protect McClellan and other Democratic generals from the committee, but he was not much disposed to heed its advice, either (Paludan, 1994, 104–105). Whatever the committee members' aspirations, Lincoln continued to conduct the war's day-to-day operations.

In the end, this first extensive congressional foray into presidential war making produced mixed results. The committee made perhaps some positive contributions to the war effort by highlighting various abuses and atrocities committed on both sides and keeping the ever-important matter of African American civil rights firmly in the limelight. It also kept some generals on their respective toes by standing as an ever-present threat for reviewing their behavior and making their shortcomings public.

Nor is it entirely fair to simply dismiss the committee as a tool of the Radical Republicans that politicized the war and its conduct. The war was "political" from the day it began; all wars are political. And however much McClellan and his Democratic fellow travelers in the Army of the Potomac wished to decry the committee's political agenda in criticizing their behavior, they were hardly innocent of such matters themselves. McClellan's dalliance with the Democratic Party's power brokers in Congress began from very nearly the day he assumed com-

President Abraham Lincoln visits General George B. McClellan and his staff at Antietam, Maryland, on October 3, 1862, a few weeks after the Battle of Antietam, the bloodiest battle of the Civil War. Lincoln tried to persuade McClellan to pursue Robert E. Lee's retreating army. McClellan's failure to do so led Lincoln to dismiss him as commander of the Army of the Potomac. (Library of Congress)

mand (as can be said of many of the men he appointed to positions beneath him in the army's power structure). He willingly assumed the mantle of mouthpiece for the North's conservatives and thus could hardly complain if Congress's Radicals found an outlet for their own agenda—an agenda that included, to their credit, defending the rights of several million African Americans.

Still, the Joint Committee on the Conduct of the War must serve as a rather sobering lesson concerning the limits of congressional involvement in presidential war making—or presidential power in general. Aside from a few relatively limited tasks—reviewing the president's Supreme Court appointees, for example—the Framers purposely avoided creating well-defined lines of demarcation between the president and the other two branches. They had good reasons for doing so. But in times of war and other moments of national crisis, this has meant that the executive and legislative branches create what can best be described as hastily constructed bridges between their respective territories, and sometimes those bridges are shaky.

ROOSEVELT'S WARS

By 1941 the Joint Committee on the Conduct of the War and the Civil War were distant memories. Congress and the presidency had occasion to interact on warmaking issues in a significant way only twice between the Civil War and World War I. In 1898 Congress responded to angry public sentiment over the supposed Spanish bombing of the battleship *Maine* by declaring war on Spain. As we saw in chapter 2, the nation's legislators actually had to dragoon an unenthusiastic President McKinley into war, rather than *vice versa.* Publicly, McKinley put the best face he could on a war he believed was a bad idea. Privately, he and his advisers fumed at the rhetoric emanating from members of Congress who asserted that the nation wanted a showdown with Spain. "The ranters in Congress, the blatherskites who do the talking upon the street-corners and at the public meetings, and the scavengers of the sensational press misrepresent public opinion . . . when they assert that this country is for war," complained McKinley's secretary George Cortelyou (Trask, 1981, 56). Yet in the end, the war turned out well enough and was over quickly enough that such disagreements between the president and his more aggressive colleagues on Capitol Hill had little real effect on how the war was fought and won.

Almost two decades later, Woodrow Wilson's mixture of idealism and dismay at Germany's unrestricted submarine warfare on American shipping led him to request a declaration of war against the kaiser, a request Congress readily granted. Wilson proved to be a remarkably effective manager of executive-legislative relationships during his tenure in the White House. Drawing on his expertise as a political science professor, Wilson managed his relationships with key members of Congress using a hands-on approach that enabled him in many cases to influence deliberations on measures he deemed desirable. This was particularly the case when America went to war; in 1917 alone he visited Capitol Hill five times to explain the nation's progress toward hostilities with Germany. "It was necessary for me by very slow stages indeed . . . to lead the country on to a single way of thinking," he believed, and much of this leadership he exercised by way of influence in Congress (Kennedy, 1980, 10–11).

When all was said and done, however, executive-legislative relationships did not change much between the Civil War era and the 1930s. Yes, presidents like Wilson could develop techniques to get their programs through Congress, and in doing so wielded a more active and effective influence on the lawmaking process than their predecessors. But this was still an ad hoc change, dependent on the skills and desires of a given president; no formal machinery was put in place to routinize such behavior. Nor was Congress necessarily compelled to listen to any president, whatever the circumstances.

President Woodrow Wilson addresses a large crowd in Tacoma, Washington, on September 18, 1919, as he tours the country promoting U.S. membership in the League of Nations. Wilson was instrumental in the creation of the organization. (Library of Congress)

For all of his success, Woodrow Wilson suffered a spectacular failure in his relations with Congress when in 1919 the Senate failed to ratify the Treaty of Versailles (which the president had personally helped to negotiate in Paris) and refused to allow the United States to join Wilson's beloved League of Nations. The president pulled out all the stops, holding private meetings with individual senators and directly consulting with the Senate Foreign Relations Committee. When these tactics failed to produce a pro-treaty majority, matters turned rather ugly. Wilson embarked on an unusual private speaking tour of the nation's heartland and applied a rhetorical tongue-lashing to his congressional detractors that set a certain low-water mark for executive-legislative cooperation. "Opposition [in the Senate] is the specialty of those who are Bolshevistically inclined," he fumed, pushing the popular hot button of anti-Bolshevik and anti-Communist fears (Clements, 1992, 195). The opposition gave as good as it got, calling the treaty an "inhuman monster" and claiming that the treaty's creation of a League of Nations amounted to a humiliating surrender of national sovereignty. The entire affair placed no one in a flattering light.

What about the nation's third branch, the Supreme Court? During the Civil War, the Court had either stayed out of war-related policies or deferred to the president's judgment. In the *Prize Cases* decision of 1863, the Court gave the president broad discretion in how he defined Confederate combatants, either as enemy aliens or rebellious American citizens, depending upon whatever circumstances required. The following year the Court also allowed Lincoln to try by military court-martial and then banish an Ohio politician, Clement Vallandigham, to the Confederacy as punishment for a speech he gave criticizing the draft. In neither case did the Court deliver a ringing affirmation of executive authority. In fact, both decisions were relatively narrow; *Ex parte Vallandigham* (1864) was decided on matters of appellate jurisdiction. But the gist of the Court's position was clear: in matters of war, the president generally knew best. "Whether the President in fulfilling his duties, as Commander in chief, in suppressing an insurrection, has met with such armed hostile resistance, and a civil war of such alarming proportions as will compel him to award them the character of belligerents, is a question to be decided by him," noted

the Court in *Prize Cases*, "and this Court must be governed by the decisions and acts of the political department of the Government to which this power was entrusted." (*Prize Cases*, 67 U.S. 635).

After the war was over, the Court saw fit to qualify the position it had taken in the Vallandigham affair, reflecting perhaps the subsidence of the war's heated feelings. What had seemed acceptable during the war now seemed beyond the pale, as the Court ruled in *Ex parte Milligan* (1866) that the president could not try an American citizen in a military court while the civilian judicial system was still operational. More generally, the Court tried to clarify the President's wartime powers vis-à-vis Congress. "[The] Constitution has delegated to Congress the power of originating war by declaration," the Court conceded. "[But] after war is originated . . . the whole power of conducting it . . . is given to the President." But does this mean, the Court asked, that the "President, in time of war, upon his own mere will and judgment, [has] the power to bring before his military officers any person in the land, and subject him to trial and punishment, even to death?" The Court thought not. "Upon the text of the original Constitution, as it stood when it was ratified, there is no color for the assumption that President, without act of Congress, could create military commissions for the trial of persons not military, for any cause or under any circumstances whatever." (*Ex parte Milligan*, 71 U.S. 2).

As limitations go, this was mild fare, hemming in only one part of presidential war-making authority while explicitly authorizing him elsewhere to wage war with few restraints from Congress. The Supreme Court showed a tendency it has displayed throughout its history in allowing presidents wide leeway as commanders in chief. Of the three branches, the Supreme Court has the least to do with military matters. All things considered, in fact, the nation's highest court has had relatively little to say about executive power in general, except to affirm its generally robust nature.

Meantime, in the wake of the Johnson impeachment after the Civil War, Congress became the dominant branch of the federal government, and in so doing grew in power and sophistication. With the vastly increased pace of industrial and urban growth during the later part of the nineteenth century came a whole host of new problems, ranging from workplace conditions to food safety. Congress responded by creating nascent regulatory commissions, an innovation that involved federal officials in areas of American life theretofore untouched by Washington, D.C.

During this time, presidents still did not develop much in the way of extensive administrative connections with Congress, relying on the earlier network of informal connections and party loyalties to wield influence on the legislative branch. Presidents routinely called for civil service reform throughout the Gilded Age, for example, responding to public concerns that government jobs should be distributed on the basis of merit rather than the old political spoils

system. "Honorable party service will certainly not be esteemed by me a disqualification for public office, but it will in no case be allowed to serve as a shield of official negligence, incompetency, or delinquency," Benjamin Harrison declared in 1881. "It is entirely creditable to seek public office by proper methods and with proper motives, and all applicants will be treated with consideration. . . . We shall not, however, I am sure, be able to put our civil service upon a nonpartisan basis until we have secured an incumbency that fair-minded men of the opposition will approve for impartiality and integrity" (www.presidency.ucsb.edu/ws/index.php?pid=25825).

But a call for reform in a speech was an uncertain instrument whose effectiveness depended on a variety of factors the president could not control. Congressmen could—and did—simply choose to ignore a president's ideas, particularly if that president was weak or lacked strong public support. There was a question of origin here that muddied the whole matter of presidential influence. If Congress chose to act on a suggestion by the president, was it doing so because of the president's power and effective influence or because both president and Congress were simply responding to a strong public demand for measures like civil service reform? Was the president leading or following?

There was a deferential tone to presidential directives—suggestions, really—about congressional methods and measures. Most presidents, most of the time, couch their demands in a deferential manner, but memories of Andrew Johnson hovered over the White House like a dark cloud throughout the last decades of the nineteenth century. While that affair could arguably have been seen as constituting an embarrassment to Congress as well as the presidency, in effect it gave presidents pause concerning just how much they could demand from the nation's legislators. Chester Arthur vetoed a massive appropriations bill in 1882, for example, and explained his actions with a remonstrance that likely had little effect at all on those listening to his State of the Union Address. "This leads me to offer a suggestion which I trust will commend itself to the wisdom of Congress," he gently suggested. "Is it not advisable that grants of considerable sums of money for diverse and independent schemes of internal improvement should be made the subjects of separate and distinct legislative enactments? It will scarcely be gainsaid, even by those who favor the most liberal expenditures for such purposes as are sought to be accomplished by what is commonly called the river and harbor bill, that the practice of grouping in such a bill appropriations for a great diversity of objects, widely separated either in their nature or in the locality with which they are concerned, or in both, is one which is much to be deprecated unless it is irremediable. It inevitably tends to secure the success of the bill as a whole, though many of the items, if separately considered, could scarcely fail of rejection. By the adoption of the course I have recommended every member of Congress, whenever opportunity should arise for giving his influence

and vote for meritorious appropriations, would be enabled so to do without being called upon to sanction others undeserving his approval" (www.presidency.ucsb.edu/ws/index.php?pid=29523).

This could have been seen as either a suggestion that Congress revamp its appropriations practices (it did not) or that the president be granted a line-item veto (he was not). In any event, it was, in fact, merely a suggestion, made by a president with weak means to work his will on Capitol Hill. In this Arthur was not alone. His fellow Gilded Age chief executives chose their battles carefully, avoided alienating Congress whenever possible, and generally gave future generations of schoolchildren good reasons for not remembering their names.

As in so many other areas, Teddy Roosevelt proved to be a pioneer in changing the passive face of executive relations with Congress. TR brought a whole raft of Progressive ideas to the presidency, backed by his inimitable energy, enthusiasm, and (at times) overweening belligerence. Teddy wanted to break up large private-sector monopolies that he and many others believed were damaging the free enterprise system; he wanted to conserve soil, forest, and water resources; he wanted to revamp an aging army and navy; and the list went on and on. Such efforts earned Roosevelt plaudits from Progressives, who saw his activist presidency as key to wise decision making in the new era. More conservative Americans, however, saw danger afoot in an activist chief executive who, they feared, might run roughshod over the people's representatives. More generally, Roosevelt simply found it difficult to impose his outsized will upon the disparate souls—each with an ego and agenda—that inhabited the halls of Congress. He had to by turns schmooze, cajole, and threaten the senators and representatives to get his way, an experience he found frustrating and exhausting. It was "one long experiment of checking one's own impulses with an iron hand," he ruefully observed, "and learning to subordinate one's own desires to what some hundreds of associates can be forced or cajoled or led into desiring" (Dalton, 2002, 230).

At times, TR felt compelled simply to ignore Congress altogether, and in so doing he trod upon some dangerous constitutional grounds. This was most evident in his pursuit of policies leading to the construction of an American-operated canal across the Isthmus of Panama. Long an advocate of a robust two-ocean American navy, the president believed a waterway across Panama was vital to the nation's security. "No single great material work which remains to be undertaken on this continent is of such consequence to the American people as the building of a canal across the Isthmus connecting North and South America," he told Congress in his first State of the Union Address. "It is emphatically a work which it is for the interest of the entire country to begin and complete as soon as possible; it is one of those great works which only a great nation can undertake with prospects of success, and which when done are not only permanent assets in the nation's material interests, but standing monuments to its con-

structive ability" (www.presidency.ucsb.edu/ws/index.php?pid=29542).

To Roosevelt, the Panama Canal project was essentially a military project, and its pursuit fell within his powers as commander in chief and as the nation's chief diplomatic officer. But the project was not without controversy, both at home and abroad. Quite a few Americans were disturbed by TR's ham-handed approach to the affair, as he first tried to negotiate with the Colombian government to buy the canal's right-of-way (Colombia controlled Panama at the time) and then—when the Colombians dragged their feet—helped engineer a Panamanian revolution that installed leaders more amenable to TR's wishes. Opposition members of Congress leveled angry charges of imperialistic arrogance. Roosevelt contemptuously dismissed his congressional critics. "I took the canal zone and let Congress debate," he bragged, "and while the debate goes on the canal does also" (Harbaugh, 1975, 204).

But critics of an activist presidency had not seen anything yet. Teddy's cousin Franklin would truly revolutionize presidential relations with Congress and the Supreme Court, setting in motion forces that eventually eclipsed the other two branches—at least in the eyes of the general public—and created a dominating role for the presidency that continues until this day.

The Depression and FDR's response to that harrowing national crisis was a major catalyst for these developments. As we saw in chapter 2, Roosevelt used a variety of techniques—his communication skills, his media savvy, his deft manipulation of political party machinery—to ride shotgun on various New Deal legislative programs through Congress. He had his share of allies on Capitol Hill, of course, as what is now known as the Roosevelt coalition created a major new Democratic Party alliance between blue-collar Americans, urban dwellers, civil rights activists, and labor union organizers. New Deal supporters in the Senate and the House gave FDR a powerful cadre of allies as he tried to enact work relief programs, banking and stock market reforms, Social Security and public works programs, and a whole host of other measures.

Previous presidents had adopted a deferential tone toward Congress in large part because the nation's legislative branch could claim to be the collective voice of the American masses. FDR turned this reasoning on its head, bluntly telling Congress that it was he who spoke for the voice of the people in calling for drastic economic and political reform. "I come before you . . . not to make requests for special or detailed items of legislation," he told Congress in his 1934 State of the Union Address. "I come, rather, to counsel with you, who, like myself, have been selected to carry out a mandate of the whole people, in order that without partisanship you and I may cooperate to continue the restoration of our national well being and, equally important, to build on the ruins of the past a new structure designed better to meet the present problems of modern civilization." The president called for Congress to rise above partisan political bickering in addressing the suffering caused by the Depression. "Without regard to party, the overwhelming majority of our people seek a greater opportunity for humanity to prosper and find happiness," he informed Congress in 1934. "They recognize that human welfare has not increased and does not increase through mere materialism and luxury, but that it does progress through integrity, unselfishness, responsibility and justice" (http://www.presidency.ucsb.edu/ws/index.php?pid=14683).

The president, however, was being disingenuous when he claimed he wanted to merely "counsel" Congress. He was not the sort of man who would settle for mere suggestions in his State of the Union Addresses or for passively counting on the exertions of others, even his own party allies. With the Depression dragging on year after year, and the recovery spotty and uneven at best, Roosevelt took steps to work his will in Congress on a scale and with a verve never before seen in the American presidency. He called Congress into special session in early 1933 with the expressed purpose of enacting new measures to alleviate the Depression, and during that session he sent no less than fifteen special messages to Congress calling for various legislative reforms. Later dubbed Roosevelt's One Hundred Days, the special session produced a blizzard of new laws desired by FDR and his allies. "Here at last was a leader who could lead, and a Congress that could be made to follow," observed historian David Kennedy (Kennedy, 1999, 139).

The president's activism vis-à-vis Congress continued for far longer than one hundred days. Every year during the 1930s his State of the Union Addresses offered long laundry lists of programs he desired and evils he wished to vanquish. He kept close tabs on how New Deal legislation was faring as it worked its way through the halls of Congress. He appointed an old ally from his days as governor of New York, Harry Hopkins, to act as an administrator of all the sprawling new federal relief programs. "Boys—this is our hour," Hopkins enthused to his staff. "We've got to get everything we want—a works program, social security, wages and hours, everything—now or never" (Kennedy, 1999, 217).

In pursuing these goals, Roosevelt's administration made no apologies for its intrusion into the affairs of Congress. Ever since the days of George Washington, presidents had been reluctant to breach the wall of separation of powers between executive and legislative functions. FDR wanted to keep that wall intact, but he also wanted the wall to be as permeable as possible. "Out of these friendly contacts [between the president and Congress] we are, fortunately, building a strong and permanent tie between the legislative and executive branches of the Government," he declared. "The letter of the Constitution wisely declared a separation, but the impulse of common purpose declares a union. In this spirit we join once more in serving the American people" (www.presidency.ucsb.edu/ ws/index.php?pid=14683).

For FDR, combating the Great Depression was just that—combat, a waging of war against an implacable economic foe. A shrewd observer of public opinion,

Roosevelt understood that Americans would rally around an activist president in a time of war—indeed, they expected energy on the part of the nation's commander in chief. The Great Depression was not a war, and the New Deal was not combat, per se—and yet FDR often used martial metaphors whenever he described his administration's programs. "Our greatest primary task is to put people to work . . . [which] can be accomplished in part by direct recruiting by the Government itself, treating the task as we would treat the emergency of a war," he declared in his first inaugural address (www.presidency.ucsb.edu/ws/index.php ?pid=14473).

Congressional critics of Roosevelt were disturbed by this robust flexing of presidential muscle, however it may have been justified, and they said so often and loudly. But FDR's most potent critics sat on the nation's highest court. Occasional spates of reformism aside (the Warren Court of the 1950s and 1960s, for example), the Supreme Court has throughout most of its history been an essentially conservative institution, acting far more often to preserve than to change existing American institutions. By the 1930s the Court had an established track record of laissez-faire economics and a tendency to look askance at any government regulation of capitalism that might conceivably interfere with what it saw as the free exchange of goods and services.

If Roosevelt thought the justices would buy his New-Deal-as-war-making political metaphor, he was mistaken. The Court served notice that it would not simply award the presidency the wide latitude previously allowed to it in other national emergencies like the Civil War. A 1936 decision, *Schechter v. United States*, struck down key provisions of the National Industrial Recovery Act of 1933 as an unconstitutional intrusion of executive power into local economic decision making. The ruling was delivered in such a way that it threatened to bring down many of FDR's New Deal aspirations. Indeed, administration insiders and the press called the day on which the *Schechter* decision was delivered Black Monday. Justice Brandeis even went so far as to send a private note to Roosevelt's aides (an extremely unusual occurrence, harkening back to the days of Buchanan, Taney, and *Dred Scott*), warning Roosevelt that he had been "living in a fool's paradise" with his extraordinarily activist decision making. "This is the end of this business of centralization," he lectured. "We're not going to let this government centralize everything. It has come to an end" (Davis, 1993, 517).

Angry and stunned, Roosevelt experienced a rare moment in which his political talents deserted him and he badly overreached. Convinced that the American people were no more enamored of Court obstructionism than himself—and would therefore support nearly anything the president might do to cut the Supreme Court down to size—FDR proposed in a message to Congress a plan that would have allowed him to add a new justice to the Supreme Court anytime a sitting justice over the age of seventy refused to retire. Roosevelt hoped

A political cartoon satirizes the court-packing plan proposed by President Franklin D. Roosevelt in 1937. Roosevelt's plan represented an attempt to control Supreme Court decisions related to his New Deal legislation. (Bettmann/Corbis)

that this would either encourage elderly justices to step down (reflecting his belief that the people who opposed the New Deal were fossilized reactionaries) or allow him to add judges who were pro–New Deal and would eventually drown out the more conservative voices already on the Court. Dubbed FDR's "court- packing plan," it was a measure designed to bring the nation's highest tribunal to the president's heel.

While many Americans may have been dismayed at the Court's lack of support for the New Deal, many more were shocked at this instance of presidential aggression toward the judicial branch. Granted, there was nothing unconstitutional about it, on its face. The Constitution does not specify the precise number of justices allowed to sit on the Court, and Congress has the authority to organize federal judicial appointments as it sees fit. But as a matter of political culture, Americans revere separation of powers as a time-honored American principle, and they quickly saw what Roosevelt was trying to do. Howls of protest greeted the court plan as it tried to make its way through Congress. "He knew that hell would break loose," rightly observed the House Speaker (Morgan, 1985, 471). Much of the uproar related not only to the Court, but also to what many saw as FDR's high-handed methods in trying to ram the scheme through Congress, wounding sensibilities in the legislative branch as well. "I don't like your method," snapped one Democratic Party ally. "I suppose you are in a hurry and this is *your* Congress" (Morgan, 1985, 471). In the end, the plan died in Congress, never to be revived.

If the Great Depression was a "war" in the symbolic sense to Roosevelt, December 7, 1941, quickly landed Roosevelt in the real thing. The methods Roosevelt introduced in his relations with Congress during the New Deal in many ways would be accentuated and expanded after Pearl Harbor. Now an entire nation was under arms on a scale unprecedented. It would be "hard work—grueling work—day and night, every hour and every minute," Roosevelt warned during a fireside chat two days after the Japanese attack, but "we are going to win the war

and we are going to win the peace that follows . . . [and] we know that the vast majority of the members of the human race are on our side. . . . For in representing our cause, we represent theirs as well" (Davis, 2000, 350).

To pursue such lofty goals as defending freedom and spreading an American brand of liberty, the United States engaged in truly Herculean efforts. The raw numbers alone are astonishing. Sixteen million men and women were drafted into the American armed forces during the war, an unprecedented number for a nation accustomed to small armies and citizen soldiers. Those new servicemen and women were liberally supplied with millions of socks, shoes, guns, bullets, gas masks, helmets, and so on, the nearly endless paraphernalia of modern warfare. Auto manufacturers converted from the construction of sedans to Sherman tanks and jeeps; makers of aircraft shifted from passenger planes to B-17 bombers, many of which were constructed by a host of Rosie the Riveters, women pressed into new roles by a nation desperate for labor. The level of production was prodigious. One shipyard built an entire Liberty Ship in just a bit over four days.

With this grand war making came a tremendous explosion in the size and complexity of the federal government. Almost overnight an army of new federal employees appeared in Washington, D.C., and around the country. Two floors were hastily added to the planned three stories for the new Department of Defense building, dubbed "the Pentagon" because of its pentagonal shape. The Pentagon opened in the middle of the war and would eventually house over 35,000 employees. From the sprawling new Pentagon and elsewhere came a veritable flood of orders, contracts, and demands. During the first six months of 1942 alone, the military handed out over $100 billion in contracts.

Attempting to cope with the complications created by this massive new mobilization program, FDR—with characteristic vigor—formed a host of new agencies and bureaucracies. These included not just the War Planning Board (WPB) and the Office of War Mobilization (OWM), but also the War Manpower Commission (WMC), the National War Labor Board (NWLB), the Board of Economic Welfare (BEW), and scores of smaller agencies that flowered outward in the government's now seemingly endless organizational flowcharts. Much of this was merely an extension of the president's New Deal days, a massive expansion of what was already an activist executive branch into new corners of American life. The war simply gave Americans a more vivid, focused purpose than ending poverty or combating the effects of banking and financial crisis.

Congress was not always a pliant instrument of the president's agenda. The Democratic Party in fact suffered serious losses during the 1942 off-year elections, and there were quite a few anti–New Dealers on Capitol Hill. But despite this—or perhaps because of it—FDR continued his hands-on approach to congressional activities. He was not at all shy about making his wishes known concerning military appropriations, economic planning, manpower recruitment,

and a whole host of other war-related issues. In his first State of the Union Address after Pearl Harbor, he gave the people's representatives a huge laundry list of goals: tens of thousands of new planes and tanks, hundreds of thousands of new guns, millions of tons of new ships. "Let no man say it cannot be done," he urged (Goodwin, 1994, 313). As the war progressed, the president became so immersed in the details of running a far-flung military operation that he had to devote less attention to Congress's daily affairs. Even so, his was an unmistakable and largely unprecedented presence in the deliberations of a legislative body that had theretofore often been walled off from executive interference.

For its part, the Supreme Court seemed to have taken notice of the president's general popularity and political skill. Yes, the court-packing plan was a debacle, arguably the biggest political disaster of FDR's long tenure in office. But after 1937 the Court proved more amenable to the expansionist reading of federal power championed by FDR and his Democratic Party followers as it upheld a variety of state and federal economic regulations that it had earlier decided were unconstitutional. And during World War II the Court likewise proved generally amenable to the Roosevelt Administration's policies, including such controversial measures as the forced internment of Japanese Americans.

Some have argued that the Court engaged in what was facetiously termed the "switch in time to save nine." That is, the nine men in black who sat on the nation's highest tribunal made an essentially political decision to avoid another court-packing plan—one that might actually succeed—by acquiescing to Roosevelt. Others suggest that the Court as well as the nation was already well on its way, even before the court-packing plan, to a reconceptualization of government's role in the nation's economy and that the justices' decisions reflected this fact. Whatever the case may be, after the court-packing plan, Roosevelt found the Court to be a friendlier place for his policies and a more or less willing ally in the expansion of executive authority. This was particularly true after 1939, when a series of deaths and resignations among the older justices gave FDR the opportunity to appoint replacements who sympathized with him and his policies. By the time of Roosevelt's death in 1945, the Supreme Court was well on its way to the era of judicial activism that would eventually witness its pivotal role in the civil rights revolution of the 1960s.

SHADOWS OF FDR

For better or worse, Roosevelt revolutionized the relationship between the presidency, Congress, and the Supreme Court—revolutionized it by diminishing the independence and power of the other federal branches. By the end of World War II, the presidency was firmly established as the dominant political office in America and the world's most powerful job. It has remained so ever since.

To his admirers, Roosevelt was a gifted revolutionary. He modernized the presidency, finally transforming it from its laissez-faire origins into a vital part of American democracy. A great many Americans then and since have sympathized with Roosevelt's values—rescuing the victims of the Great Depression, defeating the twin evils of Nazism and Japanese imperialism—and have argued with fervor that he was an American hero. And if in the process of this crusade Congress and the Supreme Court lost power and stature, what of it? For all of its virtues, Congress had long been dominated by some of the more reactionary elements in American society: isolationists; white segregationists; staunchly conservative businesspeople who opposed nearly any government interference with their profit margin; and so forth. Roosevelt at least tried to address problems of poverty, bigotry, and general backwardness that plagued American life, and if the result was an enormously ballooned executive branch that would dwarf Congress in public perception and authority, then that was a relatively small price to pay. Or so the argument goes.

On the other hand, there were thoughtful observers who worried that the sea change in favor of executive authority at the expense of Congress was an ominous development, a turning of the ratchet irreversibly in the direction of Big Brother–type centralized power at the expense of individual autonomy and local authority. It is probably no coincidence that the amplification of presidential power under FDR coincided with the erosion of public interest in state and local politics, declining voter participation in off-year (that is, nonpresidential) elections, and a general apathy toward participation in grassroots campaigning and policymaking.

All eyes would now be focused on the media fishbowl that was the White House. Congress and the Supreme Court increasingly became secondary attractions in the public mind, a fact that strikes some observers as an unhealthy development in American democracy. Whatever its virtues as a response to modern problems like depression and war, this was clearly not what the designers of the office envisioned in 1787.

Roosevelt's multiple terms likewise caused consternation in the minds of some. He remains the only president in American history to serve more than two terms in office. After his death, Republicans pushed through a new amendment to the Constitution that forbade such a thing outright. Ratified in 1951, the Twenty-second Amendment held that "no person shall be elected to the office of the President more than twice, and no person who has held the office of President, or acted as President, for more than two years of a term to which some other person was elected President shall be elected to the office of the President more than once." While few seriously believed that FDR himself wanted to become a despot, many Americans feared that in the future a man with his talents—media presence, political gifts, and a strong party base— and fewer scruples might turn the now all-powerful office of the presidency into something disturbing and dangerous that the other two branches might not be able to control.

If this were to ever happen, one suspects that it would occur under the aegis of a war. As we have seen, wars provide American presidents with authority that is largely unrivaled by Congress or the Supreme Court. Since FDR's time, other presidents have used wars as a means to further enhance White House authority. Lyndon Johnson would dramatically increase America's involvement in Vietnam during the mid-1960s with relatively little oversight by Congress—and with tragic results. In the 1970s and 1980s American presidents would literally have the power of global destruction at their fingertips as commanders in chief of a fearful nuclear arsenal. And at the turn of the twenty-first century, President George Bush Jr. would use the terrorist assault on the World Trade Center and the Pentagon in 2001 to begin conventional wars in Afghanistan and Iraq and wage a low-grade "war on terror" that many Americans felt impinged upon individual liberties and played fast and loose with international law.

In all of these developments, Congress and the Supreme Court have been relegated to the role of relative bystanders. Few members of Congress in the post-FDR era can muster the political capital necessary to oppose openly a sitting president who wants to wage war, and the Supreme Court continues to defer to the judgment of the commander in chief in the White House regarding wars and their consequences. And as wars go, so goes the general trend of modern American politics. We do indeed have an imperial presidency, for better or worse.

FURTHER READING

Baker, Jean H., *Mary Todd Lincoln: A Biography* (New York: W.W. Norton, 1987).

Basler, Roy P., ed., *The Collected Works of Abraham Lincoln*, 9 vols. (New Brunswick, NJ: Rutgers University Press, 1953–1955).

Bauer, K. Jack, *The Mexican War, 1846–1848* (New York: Macmillan, 1974).

Boot, Max, *The Savage Wars of Peace: Small Wars and the Rise of American Power* (New York: Basic Books, 2002).

Burlingame, Michael, and John R. T. Ettlinger, eds., *Inside Lincoln's White House: The Complete Civil War Diary of John Hay* (Carbondale: Southern Illinois University Press, 1997).

Burlingame, Michael, and John R. T. Ettlinger, eds., *Lincoln Observed: Civil War Dispatches of Noah Brooks* (Baltimore, MD: Johns Hopkins University Press, 1997).

Clements, Kendrick A., *The Presidency of Woodrow Wilson* (Lawrence: University Press of Kansas, 1992).

Curtis, James C., *The Fox at Bay: Martin Van Buren and the Presidency, 1837–1841* (Lexington: University Press of Kentucky, 1970).

Dailey, G. Wayne, *Next Door to Power* (n.p.: G. Wayne Dailey, 1996).

Dallek, Robert, *Lone Star Rising: Lyndon Johnson and His Times, 1908–1960* (New York: Oxford University Press, 1991).

Dallek, Robert, *Flawed Giant: Lyndon Johnson and His Times, 1961–1973* (New York: Oxford University Press, 1998).

Dalton, Kathleen, *Theodore Roosevelt: A Strenuous Life* (New York: Alfred A. Knopf, 2002).

Davis, Kenneth W., *FDR, into the Storm, 1937–1940: A History* (New York: Random House, 1993).

Davis, Kenneth W., *FDR, the War President, 1940–1943: A History* (New York: Random House, 2000).

Donald, David, *Lincoln* (New York: Simon and Schuster, 1995).

Fehrenbacher, Don E., *The Dred Scott Case, Its Significance in Law and Politics* (New York: Oxford University Press, 1978).

Flexner, James, *Washington: The Indispensable Man* (Boston: Little, Brown, 1974).

Goodwin, Doris Kearns, *No Ordinary Time: Franklin and Eleanor Roosevelt: The Homefront in World War II* (New York: Simon and Schuster, 1994).

Gunderson, Robert G., *The Log-Cabin Campaign* (Lexington: University of Kentucky Press, 1957).

Harbaugh, William Henry, *The Life and Times of Theodore Roosevelt* (New York: Oxford University Press, 1975).

Kennedy, David M., *Over Here: The First World War and American Society* (New York: Oxford University Press, 1980).

Kennedy, David M., *Freedom from Fear: the American People in Depression and War, 1929–1945* (New York: Oxford University Press, 1999).

Leech, Margaret, *Reveille in Washington, 1860–1865* (New York: Harper and Bros., 1941).

Madison, James, *The Constitutional Convention: A Narrative History from the Notes of James Madison* (New York: Modern Library, 2005).

Malone, Dumas, *Jefferson and His Time*, 6 vols. (Boston: Little, Brown, 1948).

McCullough, David, *John Adams* (New York: Simon and Schuster, 2001).

McDonald, Forrest, *The American Presidency: An Intellectual History* (Lawrence: University Press of Kansas, 1994).

McKitrick, Eric, and Stanley Elkins, *The Age of Federalism: The Early American Republic, 1788–1800* (New York: Oxford University Press, 1995).

McPherson, James M., *Ordeal by Fire: The Civil War and Reconstruction* (New York: Alfred A. Knopf, 1982).

Merk, Frederick, *History of the Westward Movement* (New York: Alfred A. Knopf, 1978).

Millett, Allan R., *For the Common Defense: A Military History of the United States of America* (New York: Free Press, 1984).

Morgan, Ted, *FDR: A Biography* (New York: Simon and Schuster, 1985).

Paludan, Philip S., *The Presidency of Abraham Lincoln* (Lawrence: University Press of Kansas, 1994).

Peterson, Merrill D., ed., *Thomas Jefferson: Writings* (New York: Library of America, 1984).

Remini, Robert V., *Andrew Jackson and the Course of American Empire, 1833–1845* (New York: Harper and Row, 1984).

Rossiter, Clinton, ed., *The Federalist Papers* (New York: Signet, 1961).

Sears, Stephen W., *George B. McClellan: The Young Napoleon* (New York: Ticknor and Fields, 1988).

Smith, Page, *John Adams*, 2 vols. (Garden City, NY: Doubleday, 1962).

Stephanson, Anders, *Manifest Destiny: American Expansionism and the Empire of Right* (New York: Hill and Wang, 1995).

Tap, Bruce, *Over Lincoln's Shoulder: The Committee on the Conduct of the War* (Lawrence: University Press of Kansas, 1998).

Trask, David F., *The War with Spain in 1898* (New York: Macmillan, 1981).

Wilson, Major L., *The Presidency of Martin Van Buren* (Lawrence: University Press of Kansas, 1984).

GLOSSARY OF CONCEPTS AND PEOPLE

Adams, John: The second president of the United States, 1797–1801. Federalist. Also America's first vice president under George Washington. Lost a bitter and closely fought election for a second term to Thomas Jefferson. Widely considered to be among the most brilliant minds of the Founders' generation.

Adams, John Quincy: The sixth president of the United States, 1825–1829. Jeffersonian Republican. Son of second president John Adams. Lost a bitter election to Andrew Jackson in 1828 and afterward pursued a prominent career as a U.S. representative and antislavery advocate.

Agnew, Spiro T.: Vice president (1969–1973) during Richard Nixon's administration (1969–1974). Forced to resign from the vice presidency in 1973 following charges of tax fraud; he is the only vice president to have ever resigned from office.

Arthur, Chester Alan: The twenty-first president of the United States, 1881–1885. Republican. Served as James Garfield's vice president and ascended to the presidency when Garfield was assassinated in 1881.

Barkley, Alben W.: Vice president during Harry S. Truman's second term (1949–1953). Kentucky lawyer and former Senate majority leader.

Breckinridge, John C.: Vice president during the administration of James Buchanan (1857–1861) and candidate for the Democratic Party's southern wing during the 1860 presidential election. Later a Confederate general and the last secretary of war of the Confederacy.

Buchanan, James: The fifteenth president of the United States, 1857–1861. Democrat. Was president during the secession crisis, doing little as the nation careened toward a civil war. The nation's only bachelor president.

bully pulpit: Nickname given to the modern presidency's power to sway public opinion via his media presence. First applied to Theodore Roosevelt's oratorical skills.

Burr, Aaron: Vice president during Thomas Jefferson's first term (1801–1805). Controversial figure who shot and killed Alexander Hamilton in a duel and was later accused of trying to start his own republic on the western frontier.

Bush, George Herbert Walker (George Bush Sr.): The forty-first president of the United States, 1989–1993. Republican. Vice president under Ronald Reagan (1981–1989) and former director of the CIA. Led the nation during the Persian Gulf War.

Bush, George Walker (George Bush Jr.): The forty-third president of the United States, 2001–present (as of 2007). Republican. Elected following crisis during election of 2000, when the vote count was disputed in the state of Florida. Led the nation during the September 11, 2001, terrorist attack on the World Trade Center in New York and during the war with Iraq.

Cabinet: The heads of the various branches of the executive department (war, Treasury, state, interior, etc.) who routinely meet to advise and consult with the president. The numbers and influence of Cabinet members have varied over time. There is no formal provision for a cabinet in the Constitution, but President George Washington quickly established one as a way to administer the new executive branch, and it has since become a time-honored presidential institution.

Calhoun, John C.: Vice president during the presidency of John Quincy Adams (1825–1829) and the first term of Andrew Jackson's presidency (1829–1833). South Carolina planter and architect of early constitutional theories allowing state nullification of federal laws and secession.

Camp David: Retreat constructed in the Maryland mountains in 1942 as a place for the president to vacation and occasionally conduct summits and conferences. FDR originally named it Shangri-la, but President Dwight Eisenhower renamed it Camp David in 1953 in honor of his grandson.

Carter, James Earl, Jr.: The thirty-ninth president of the United States, 1977–1981. Democrat. Led the nation during a major economic recession and the Iranian hostage crisis, and helped broker a historic peace arrangement between Israel and Egypt known as the Camp David Accords in 1978.

Cheney, Richard B.: Served as vice president during the George Bush Jr. Administration (2001–present [as of 2007]). Seen by many as one of the most influential vice presidents in American history; has acted as the president's chief adviser regarding the administration's most controversial policies, included the war in Iraq.

chief executive: Another name for the president, reflecting his status as head of the nation's executive branch.

Cleveland, Grover: The twenty-second and twenty-fourth president of the United States, 1885–1889 and 1893–1897. Democrat. The only president to serve two nonconsecutive terms.

Clinton, George: Vice president during Thomas Jefferson's second term (1805–1809) and James Madison's first term (1809–1813). Former governor of New York and Revolutionary war hero.

Clinton, William Jefferson: The forty-second president of the United States, 1993–2001. Democrat. Second president to be impeached, following the Monica Lewinsky scandal.

Colfax, Schuyler: Vice president during the first term of Ulysses S. Grant (1869–1873). Indiana newspaperman, representative, and Speaker of the House.

commander in chief: The president's official title as head of the nation's armed forces.

Coolidge, Calvin: The thirtieth president of the United States, 1923–1929. Republican. Vice president to Warren G. Harding, ascended to the presidency following Harding's death in 1923. Famous for his reticence.

Curtis, Charles: Vice president during Herbert Hoover's presidency (1929–1933). Kansas attorney with strong ancestral ties to the Kaw Indian tribe.

Dallas, George M.: Vice president during the presidency of James K. Polk (1845–1849). Pennsylvania lawyer and ambassador to Russia and Great Britain.

Dawes, Charles D.: Vice president during Calvin Coolidge's administration (1925–1929). Ohio lawyer and civil engineer who was heavily involved in railroad and banking issues.

Eisenhower, Dwight David: The thirty-fourth president of the United States, 1953–1961. Republican. Famous World War II general, president at the height of the cold war with the Soviet Union.

Electoral College: Electors chosen by the voters in each state in a manner decided by the state's legislators. The electors in each state together cast votes for the presidency. Each state receives a certain number of votes, according to its population. Technically, an election result may be overturned by the Electoral College; to date this has never happened.

executive order: An order issued by the president putting into effect some policy or procedure desired by him that falls under the purview of the executive branch. An executive order can be rescinded at any time by a later president.

Fairbanks, Charles W.: Vice president during Theodore Roosevelt's second term (1905–1909). An Indiana attorney, he aggressively defended the gold standard during the heated monetary debates of the late nineteenth century.

Fillmore, Millard: The thirteenth president of the United States, 1850–1853. Whig. Zachary Taylor's vice president, ascended to the presidency upon Taylor's death. The last Whig president.

fireside chats: Franklin D. Roosevelt's series of broadcasts during the Great Depression, designed to alleviate Americans' fears about the economic crisis and project his will and persona through the new medium of radio.

Ford, Gerald Rudolph: The thirty-eighth president of the United States, 1974–1977. Republican. Richard Nixon's vice president, ascended to the presidency when Nixon resigned following the Watergate scandal. Later pardoned Nixon, an act that was highly controversial.

Fourteen Points: Woodrow Wilson's plan to bring peace and prosperity to post–World War I Europe. Its centerpiece was the creation of a new League of Nations, designed to settle international disputes without bloodshed.

Garfield, James Abram: The twentieth president of the United States, 1881. Republican. Spent only a brief time in office before his assassination by a disgruntled job seeker.

Garner, John N.: Vice president during Franklin D. Roosevelt's first two terms (1933–1941). Talented representative and Texas powerhouse, Cactus Jack opposed many of FDR's New Deal policies.

Gerry, Elbridge: Vice president during James Madison's second term (1813–1817). One of the signers of the Declaration of Independence and a Framer of the U.S. Constitution.

Gore, Albert A.: Vice president during the Bill Clinton administration (1993–2001). Son of legendary Tennessee senator Al Gore Sr., ran unsuccessfully against George Bush Jr. in the controversial election of 2000.

Grant, Ulysses Simpson: The eighteenth president of the United States, 1869–1877. Republican. Famous Union Civil War general. His administration was characterized by numerous Cabinet scandals.

Great Society: Name given to Lyndon Johnson's ambitious program of domestic initiatives designed to alleviate various social and economic ills in 1960s America and eventually end poverty altogether.

Hamlin, Hannibal: Vice president during the first term of Abraham Lincoln's presidency (1861–1865). Former senator from and governor of Maine.

Harding, Warren Gamaliel: The twenty-ninth president of the United States, 1921–1923. Republican. Was the third president to die a natural death in office (FDR was the last).

Harrison, Benjamin: The twenty-third president of the United States, 1889–1893. Republican. Known as "Kid Gloves" Harrison because of his wealth.

Harrison, William Henry: The ninth president of the United States, 1841. Whig. First Whig president, died of pneumonia shortly after taking office. Was the first president to die in office.

Hayes, Rutherford Birchard: The nineteenth president of the United States, 1877–1881. Republican. Elected to the presidency as part of a compromise to end Reconstruction in the South.

Hendricks, Thomas A.: Vice president who served during Grover Cleveland's first term of office (1885). An Indiana attorney, he died from a stroke while in office.

Hobart, Garrett A.: Vice president during William McKinley's first administration (1897–1899). Died suddenly in office in 1899. There being no constitutional provision for vice presidential succession at the time, the office remained vacant until 1901, when Theodore Roosevelt gained the office as McKinley's running mate during the 1900 election.

Hoover, Herbert Clark: The thirty-first president of the United States, 1929–1933. Republican. Presidency marred by the onset of the Great Depression in 1929, for which he received much of the blame.

Humphrey, Hubert H.: Vice president during Lyndon Johnson's second term (1965–1969). He supported the Vietnam War, which may well have cost him the presidential election against Nixon in 1968.

impeachment: Power granted to Congress to remove a president who has committed "high crimes and misdemeanors." When articles of impeachment are passed by the House of Representatives, the Senate constitutes a trial, over which the Supreme Court's chief justice presides, whereby the senators decide if removal from office is warranted. To date, no president has ever been removed from office by impeachment. Two presidents, Andrew Johnson and William Jefferson Clinton, have been impeached without conviction or removal. A third, Richard Milhous Nixon, resigned under the imminent threat of impeachment.

Inaugural Address: Speech given by a president following his swearing-in ceremony.

Jackson, Andrew: The seventh president of the United States, 1829–1837. Democrat. Old Hickory, founder of the Democratic Party with his election in 1828. Involved in several high profile controversies: battles over the creation of a National Bank; the disposition of the Cherokee Indians; a scandal involving the wife of a prominent Cabinet member; and an attempt by South Carolina to nullify a federal tariff law.

Jefferson, Thomas: The third president of the United States, 1801–1809. Jeffersonian Republican. Author of the Declaration of Independence and widely seen as the greatest mind of the Founding generation. Highlights of his presidency were the purchase of the Louisiana Territory from France and then the ordering of the famous Lewis and Clark Expedition to explore the territory's borders.

Johnson, Andrew: The seventeenth president of the United States, 1865–1868. Republican. Abraham Lincoln's second vice president, ascended to the presidency when Lincoln was assassinated. Disagreements with Congress on Reconstruction led to his impeachment and near conviction in 1868.

Johnson, Lyndon Baines: The thirty-sixth president of the United States, 1963–1969. Democrat. John F. Kennedy's vice president, ascended to the presidency following

JFK's assassination. Renowned for his War on Poverty programs to combat poverty and for embroiling the nation deeply in the Vietnam War.

Johnson, Richard M.: Vice president during the presidency of Martin Van Buren (1837–1841). Hero of the War of 1812.

Joint Chiefs of Staff: Presidential advisory board established in 1949 as a way to coordinate the efforts of the four armed forces (army, navy, air force, marines) and provide the president with general strategic and war-making advice and information.

Kennedy, John Fitzgerald: The thirty-fifth president of the United States, 1961–1963. Democrat. Youngest man to be elected to the presidency; assassinated in 1963. Famous for boyish good looks, Camelot atmosphere in the White House. Led nation during showdown with Soviet Union over the placement of Soviet nuclear missiles in Cuba.

King, William Rufas DeVane: Vice president during the presidency of Franklin Pierce (1853). Died shortly after taking the oath of office, served the shortest term of any American vice president.

Lincoln, Abraham: The sixteenth president of the United States, 1861–1865. Republican. Widely thought to be the greatest president in American history. Led the North to victory during the Civil War and signed the Emancipation Proclamation, ending American slavery. Assassinated during second term by actor John Wilkes Booth.

line-item veto: A proposed power to be given the president, whereby the president can selectively veto some parts of a bill while approving others. This power has often been debated but never actually granted to the president.

Madison, James: The fourth president of the United States, 1809–1817. Jeffersonian Republican. Revered as Father of the Constitution. Presidency marked by renewed war with Great Britain in 1812.

Marshall, Thomas R.: Vice president during Woodrow Wilson's presidency (1913–1921). Indiana attorney more highly regarded for his amiable personality than any political or administrative skills.

McKinley, William: The twenty-fifth president of the United States, 1897–1901. Republican. Led the nation during the Spanish-American War. Assassinated during second term by anarchist Leon Czolgosz.

Mondale, Walter F.: Vice president during the Jimmy Carter administration (1977–1981). Minnesota lawyer and educator, ran unsuccessfully for the presidency against Ronald Reagan in 1984.

Monroe, James: The fifth president of the United States, 1817–1825. Jeffersonian Republican. Presidency marked by enunciation of the Monroe Doctrine, demanding that Europeans stay out of the affairs of nations in the Western Hemisphere.

Morning in America: Slogan employed by Ronald Reagan during his 1980 presidential campaign, designed to convince Americans that the "national malaise" proclaimed by his predecessor, Jimmy Carter, was over.

Morton, Levi P.: Vice president during Benjamin Harrison's administration (1889–1893). A Vermont financier and governor of New York.

National Security Adviser: Executive branch member who advises the president on various national security matters. The office was created by Dwight Eisenhower in 1953. It is a position appointed by the president alone.

New Deal: Franklin Roosevelt's revolutionary package of domestic reform measures, designed to bring the nation out the Great Depression of the 1930s.

Nixon, Richard Milhous: The thirty-seventh president of the United States, 1969–1974. Republican. His presidency's high marks were putting an end to American involvement in Vietnam, détente with Russia, and establishing diplomatic relations with Communist China. Low marks were the Watergate scandal and his subsequent resignation from the presidency in 1974. He is the only president to have resigned from office.

pardoning power: The Constitution grants presidents the power to pardon any American convicted of any crime. This power cannot be overridden by another branch of government.

patronage: The power of a president to distribute federal offices to loyal supporters, often for political reasons.

Pierce, Franklin: The fourteenth president of the United States, 1853–1857. Democrat. As president faced rising sectional tensions between North and South, especially in Bleeding Kansas.

pocket veto: A veto action by a president in which he does not actually veto a bill, but rather simply refuses to sign it within the ten-day period allotted by the Constitution. If he does this and the congressional session that produced the bill expires, the bill also expires. Pocket vetoes have been used primarily for political effect by presidents who do not wish to sign a given bill but also do not wish to give offense to a bill's congressional supporters by the physical act of writing out a veto. In 1929 James Madison became the first president to use a pocket veto.

Polk, James Knox: The eleventh president of the United States, 1845–1849. Democrat. Ardent expansionist who fought a successful war with Mexico that added the western third of the continent to the United States. Settled disputes over Oregon Territory with Great Britain.

Quayle, J. Danforth: Vice president during the George Bush Sr. administration (1989–1993). Indiana lawyer, U.S. representative and senator, seen by many as a spokesman for the Republican Party's more conservative constituency.

Reagan, Ronald: The fortieth president of the United States, 1981–1989. Republican. Called the Great Communicator for his speech-making skills. Proclaimed that it was "Morning in America" again and oversaw a massive arms buildup vis-à-vis the Soviet Union that many regard as instrumental in the latter nation's disintegration during the late 1980s.

Rockefeller, Nelson A.: Vice president during the Gerald Ford administration (1974–1977). Wealthy lawyer from Maine, former governor of New York, seen by many as a spokesman for the Republican Party's moderate wing.

Roosevelt, Franklin Delano: The thirty-second president of the United States, 1933–1945. Democrat. Led the nation during the Great Depression and World War II. The only president to serve more than two terms in office. Died in Warm Springs, Georgia. Last president to die in office.

Roosevelt, Theodore: The twenty-sixth president of the United States, 1901–1909. Republican. Vice president under William McKinley, ascended to the presidency upon McKinley's assassination. The youngest man ever to become president. Famous for his advocacy of the "strenuous life" and his use of the presidency's "bully pulpit" to sway popular opinion.

Secret Service: The president's bodyguard, formed in 1865. Part of the Treasury Department.

Sherman, James S.: Vice president during William Howard Taft's administration (1909–1912). New York lawyer who served in the U.S. House of Representatives prior to his vice presidency. Died before his term expired.

State of the Union Address: Constitutionally mandated annual report to Congress from the president concerning the state of the nation. Usually includes suggestions concerning future policymaking initiatives.

Stevenson, Adlai B.: Vice president during Grover Cleveland's second term (1893–1897). Illinois lawyer and state district attorney who would later run unsuccessfully as William Jennings Bryan's running mate.

Taft, William Howard: The twenty-seventh president of the United States, 1909–1913. Republican. After the presidency would serve on the Supreme Court, the only president to have ever done so.

Taylor, Zachary: The twelfth president of the United States, 1849–1850. Whig. Died soon after assuming office from stomach complications following a Fourth of July picnic.

Tippecanoe and Tyler, Too: Famous slogan from the 1840 presidential election, "Tippecanoe" referring to the Whig presidential candidate William Henry Harrison's victory at the Battle of Tippecanoe, and "Tyler" referring to his running mate, John Tyler.

Tompkins, Daniel D.: Vice president during the presidency of James Monroe (1817–1825). Former governor of New York and state supreme court justice.

Truman, Harry S.: The thirty-third president of the United States, 1945–1953. Democrat. Vice president under Franklin Roosevelt, ascended to the presidency when FDR died in office. Led the nation during the Korean War.

Tyler, John: The tenth president of the United States, 1841–1845. Whig. Vice president under William Henry Harrison, ascended to the presidency after Harrison's death in office. Primary accomplishment was his controversial annexation of Texas.

Van Buren, Martin: The eighth president of the United States, 1837–1841. Democrat. Consummate party politician, seen by many as a master of political intrigue.

veto: The act of a president in striking down a bill that has passed both houses of Congress. According to the Constitution, a veto may be overridden by a two-thirds majority vote in both House and Senate. Historically, fewer than 10 percent of presidential vetoes have been overridden.

Wallace, Henry: Vice president during Franklin Roosevelt's third term (1941–1945). His reputation for supporting labor radicalism and other leftist causes led FDR to dump him in favor of Harry Truman as a running mate for the 1944 election.

Washington, George: The first president of the United States, 1789–1797. Federalist. Father of the Country and victorious American general during the Revolutionary war. Established many of the institutions and traditions of the office of the president.

Watergate: Name commonly given to the scandal that engulfed the Nixon Administration in 1972 and led to the president's resignation in 1974. Watergate is the name of a large apartment and office building in Washington, D.C. In June 1972 several men were caught breaking into the Democratic Party's national headquarters there, triggering the scandal.

Wheeler, William: Vice president during the presidency of Rutherford B. Hayes (1877–1881). Reputation for honesty during a scandal-plagued era in American politics made him an acceptable, if colorless, running mate for Hayes.

White House: The president's official residence in Washington, D.C. The cornerstone of the building was laid in 1792; President John Adams and his family were the first occupants. Earned the name "White House" when white paint was used to cover the burn stains from the British army's torching of the building during the War of 1812.

Wilson, Henry: Vice president during Ulysses S. Grant's second term (1872–1875). Serious health problems kept him from performing many of the duties of vice president during his tenure in office. Died before his term expired.

Wilson, Woodrow: The twenty-eighth president of the United States, 1913–1921. Democrat. College professor and president, idealist who led the nation during World War I. Fought unsuccessfully to persuade America to enter the League of Nations.

INAUGURAL ADDRESSES

(Edited Highlights)

Inaugural Addresses are arguably the most important and revealing speeches delivered by American presidents. Indeed, during the nation's early years, when speech making by presidents was thought to be somewhat gauche, Inaugural Addresses were often nearly the only examples available of a given president's ideas and ideals.

The following three sections offer edited excerpts from the presidents' Inaugural Addresses, from the first such speech delivered by George Washington in 1789 through George Bush Jr.'s 2005 address. In choosing what to include, I have focused particularly on (1) statements that have subsequently achieved particular fame (Lincoln's "with malice toward none" passage in 1864, for example); (2) statements that reflect a given president's attitude toward the office or his general state of mind; and (3) offer broad statements of a president's values and principles and those of his times. I have excluded passages that seemed overly obscure or to be of little general interest to students or historians (Washington's very terse second Inaugural Address, for example). Unless otherwise indicated, text is taken from the Avalon Project's Web site at Yale University (http://www.yale.edu/lawweb/avalon/presiden/inaug/inaug.htm).

INAUGURAL ADDRESSES
1789–1865

GEORGE WASHINGTON

April 30, 1789

In this Inaugural Address, Washington expresses his trepidation at the immense responsibilities facing him as the nation's first chief executive. Note also his desire that Americans rise above factionalism and act in the spirit of the greater national good.

Among the vicissitudes incident to life no event could have filled me with greater anxieties than that of which the notification was transmitted by your order, and received on the 14th day of the present month. On the one hand, I was summoned by my Country, whose voice I can never hear but with veneration and love, from a retreat which I had chosen with the fondest predilection, and, in my flattering hopes, with an immutable decision, as the asylum of my declining years—a retreat which was rendered every day more necessary as well as more dear to me by the addition of habit to inclination, and of frequent interruptions in my health to the gradual waste committed on it by time. On the other hand, the magnitude and difficulty of the trust to which the voice of my country called me, being sufficient to awaken in the wisest and most experienced of her citizens a distrustful scrutiny into his qualifications, could not but overwhelm with despondence one who (inheriting inferior endowments from nature and unpracticed in the duties of civil administration) ought to be peculiarly conscious of his own deficiencies. In this conflict of emotions all I dare aver is that it has been my faithful study to collect my duty from a just appreciation of every circumstance by which it might be affected. All I dare hope is that if, in executing this task, I have been too much swayed by a grateful remembrance of former instances, or by an affectionate sensibility to this transcendent proof of the confidence of my fellow-citizens, and have thence too little consulted my incapacity as well as disinclination for the weighty and untried cares before me, my error will be palliated by the motives which mislead me, and its consequences be judged by my country with some share of the partiality in which they originated.

Such being the impressions under which I have, in obedience to the public summons, repaired to the present station, it would be peculiarly improper to omit in this first official act my fervent supplications to that Almighty Being who rules over the universe, who presides in the councils of nations, and whose providential aids can supply every human defect, that His benediction may consecrate to the liberties and happiness of the people of the United States a Government instituted by themselves for these essential purposes, and may enable every instrument employed in its administration to execute with success the functions allotted to his charge. In tendering this homage to the Great Author of every public and private good, I assure myself that it expresses your sentiments not less than my own, nor those of my fellow-citizens at large less than either. No people can be bound to acknowledge and adore the Invisible Hand which conducts the affairs of men more than those of the United States. Every step by which they have advanced to the character of an independent nation seems to have been distinguished by some token of providential agency; and in the important revolution just accomplished in the system of their united government the tranquil deliberations and voluntary consent of so many distinct communities from which the event has resulted can not be compared with the means by which most governments have been established without some return of pious gratitude, along with an humble anticipation of the future blessings which the past seem to presage. These reflections, arising out of the present crisis, have forced themselves too strongly on my mind to be suppressed. You will join with me, I trust, in thinking that there are none under the influence of which the proceedings of a new and free government can more auspiciously commence.

By the article establishing the executive department it is made the duty of the President "to recommend to your consideration such measures as he shall judge necessary and expedient." The circumstances under which I now meet you will acquit me from entering into that subject further than to refer to the great constitutional charter under which you are assembled, and which, in defining your powers, designates the objects to which your attention is to be given. . . . I behold the surest pledges that as on one side no local prejudices or attachments, no separate views nor party animosities, will misdirect the comprehensive and equal eye which ought to watch over this great assemblage of communities and interests, so, on another, that the foundation of our national policy will be laid in the pure and immutable principles of private morality, and the pre-eminence of free government be exemplified by all the attributes which can win the affections of its citizens and command the respect of the world. I dwell on this prospect with every satisfaction which an ardent love for my country can inspire, since there is no truth more thoroughly established than that there exists in the economy and course of nature an indissoluble union between virtue and happiness; between duty and advantage; between the genuine maxims of an honest and magnanimous policy and the solid rewards of public prosperity and felicity; since we ought to be no less persuaded that the propitious smiles of Heaven can never be expected on a nation that disregards the eternal rules of order and right which Heaven itself has ordained; and since the preservation of the sacred fire of liberty and the destiny of the republican model of government are justly considered, perhaps, as deeply, as finally, staked on the experiment entrusted to the hands of the American people. . . .

I assure myself that whilst you carefully avoid every alteration which might endanger the benefits of an united and effective government, or which ought to await the future lessons of experience, a reverence for the characteristic rights of freemen and a regard for the public harmony will sufficiently influence your deliberations on the question how far the former can be impregnably fortified or the latter be safely and advantageously promoted. . . .

Having thus imparted to you my sentiments as they have been awakened by the occasion which brings us together, I shall take my present leave; but not without resorting once more to the benign Parent of the Human Race in humble supplication that, since He has been pleased to favor the American people with opportunities for deliberating in perfect tranquillity, and dispositions for deciding with unparalleled unanimity on a form of government for the security of their union and the advancement of their happiness, so His divine blessing may be equally conspicuous in the enlarged views, the temperate consultations, and the wise measures on which the success of this Government must depend.

JOHN ADAMS

March 4, 1797

Adams was an avid reader of history, and it shows in his speech, during which he offered a review of the Revolution and effusive praise for George Washington. Washington's long shadow over the Adams presidency is quite evident here, as was Adams's desire—common to his generation—to avoid factional disputes.

When it was first perceived, in early times, that no middle course for America remained between unlimited submission to a foreign legislature and a total independence of its claims, men of reflection were less apprehensive of danger from the formidable power of fleets and armies they must determine to resist than from those contests and dissensions which would certainly arise concerning the forms of government to be instituted over the whole and over the parts of this extensive country . . ..

The zeal and ardor of the people during the Revolutionary war, supplying the place of government, commanded a degree of order sufficient at least for the temporary preservation of society. . . . [But] universal languor, jealousies and rivalries of States, decline of navigation and commerce, discouragement of necessary manufactures, universal fall in the value of lands and their produce, contempt of public and private faith, loss of consideration and credit with foreign nations, and at length in discontents, animosities, combinations, partial conventions, and insurrection, threaten[ed] some great national calamity.

In this dangerous crisis the people of America were not abandoned by their usual good sense, presence of mind, resolution, or integrity. Measures were pursued to concert a plan to form a more perfect union, establish justice, insure domestic tranquillity, provide for the common defense, promote the general welfare, and secure the blessings of liberty. The public disquisitions, discussions, and deliberations issued in the present happy Constitution of Government.

Employed in the service of my country abroad during the whole course of these transactions, I first saw the Constitution of the United States in a foreign country. Irritated by no literary altercation, animated by no public debate, heated by no party animosity, I read it with great satisfaction, as the result of good heads prompted by good hearts, as an experiment better adapted to the genius, character, situation, and relations of this nation and country than any which had ever been proposed or suggested. In its general principles and great outlines it was conformable to such a system of government as I had ever most esteemed, and in some States, my own native State in particular, had contributed to establish. Claiming a right of suffrage, in common with my fellow-citizens, in the adoption or rejection of a constitution which was to rule me and my posterity, as well as them and theirs, I did not hesitate to express my approbation of it on all occasions, in public and in private. It was not then, nor has been since, any objection to it in my mind that the Executive and Senate were not more permanent. Nor have I ever entertained a thought of promoting any alteration in it but such as the people themselves, in the course of their experience, should see and feel to be necessary or expedient, and by their representatives in Congress and the State legislatures, according to the Constitution itself, adopt and ordain. . . .

I have repeatedly laid myself under the most serious obligations to support the Constitution. The operation of it has equaled the most sanguine expectations of its friends, and from an habitual attention to it, satisfaction in its administration, and delight in its effects upon the peace, order, prosperity, and happiness of the nation I have acquired an habitual attachment to it and veneration for it.

What other form of government, indeed, can so well deserve our esteem and love? . . .

In the midst of these pleasing ideas we should be unfaithful to ourselves if we should ever lose sight of the danger to our liberties if anything partial or extraneous should infect the purity of our free, fair, virtuous, and independent elections. If an election is to be determined by a majority of a single vote, and that can be procured by a party through artifice or corruption, the Government may be the choice of a party for its own ends, not of the nation for the national good. If that solitary suffrage can be obtained by foreign nations by flattery or menaces, by fraud or violence, by terror, intrigue, or venality, the Government may not be the choice of the American people, but of foreign nations. It may be foreign nations who govern us, and not we, the people, who govern ourselves; and candid men will acknowledge that in such cases choice would have little advantage to boast of over lot or chance.

Such is the amiable and interesting system of government (and such are some of the abuses to which it may be exposed) which the people of America have exhibited to the admiration and anxiety of the wise and virtuous of all nations for eight years under the administration of a citizen [Adams's immediate predecessor, George Washington] who, by a long course of great actions, regulated by prudence, justice, temperance, and fortitude, conducting a people inspired with the same virtues and animated with the same ardent patriotism and love of liberty to independence and peace, to increasing wealth and unexampled prosperity, has merited the gratitude of his fellow-citizens, commanded the highest praises of foreign nations, and secured immortal glory with posterity.

In that retirement which is his voluntary choice may he long live to enjoy the delicious recollection of his services, the gratitude of mankind, the happy fruits of them to himself and the world, which are daily increasing, and that splendid prospect of the future fortunes of this country which is opening from year to year. His name may be still a rampart, and the knowledge that he lives a bulwark, against all open or secret enemies of his country's peace. This example has been recommended to the imitation of his successors by both Houses of Congress and by the voice of the legislatures and the people throughout the nation.

On this subject it might become me better to be silent or to speak with diffidence; but as something may be expected, the occasion, I hope, will be admitted as an apology if I venture to say that if a preference, upon principle, of a free republican government, formed upon long and serious reflection, after a diligent and impartial inquiry after truth; if an attachment to the Constitution of the United States, and a conscientious determination to support it until it shall be altered by the judgments and wishes of the people, expressed in the mode prescribed in it; if a respectful attention to the constitutions of the individual States and a constant caution and delicacy toward the State governments; if an equal and impartial regard to the rights, interest, honor, and happiness of all the States in the Union, without preference or regard to a northern or southern, an eastern or western, position, their various political opinions on unessential points or their personal attachments; if a love of virtuous men of all parties and denominations; if a love of science and letters and a wish to patronize every rational effort to encourage schools, colleges, universities, academies, and every institution for propagating knowledge, virtue, and religion among all classes of the people, not only for their benign influence on the happiness of life in all its stages and classes, and of society in all its forms, but as the only means of preserving our Constitution from its natural enemies, the spirit of sophistry, the spirit of party, the spirit of intrigue, the profligacy of corruption, and the pestilence of foreign influence, which is the angel of destruction to elective governments; if a love of equal laws, of justice, and humanity in the interior administration; if an inclination to improve agriculture, commerce, and manufacturers for necessity, convenience, and defense; if a spirit of equity and humanity toward the aboriginal nations of America, and a disposition to meliorate their condition by inclining them to be more friendly to us, and our citizens to be more friendly to them; if an inflexible determination to maintain peace and inviolable faith with all nations, and that system of neutrality and impartiality among the belligerent powers of Europe which has been adopted by this Government and so solemnly sanctioned by both

Houses of Congress and applauded by the legislatures of the States and the public opinion, until it shall be otherwise ordained by Congress; if a personal esteem for the French nation, formed in a residence of seven years chiefly among them, and a sincere desire to preserve the friendship which has been so much for the honor and interest of both nations; if, while the conscious honor and integrity of the people of America and the internal sentiment of their own power and energies must be preserved, an earnest endeavor to investigate every just cause and remove every colorable pretense of complaint; if an intention to pursue by amicable negotiation a reparation for the injuries that have been committed on the commerce of our fellow-citizens by whatever nation, and if success can not be obtained, to lay the facts before the Legislature, that they may consider what further measures the honor and interest of the Government and its constituents demand; if a resolution to do justice as far as may depend upon me, at all times and to all nations, and maintain peace, friendship, and benevolence with all the world; if an unshaken confidence in the honor, spirit, and resources of the American people, on which I have so often hazarded my all and never been deceived; if elevated ideas of the high destinies of this country and of my own duties toward it, founded on a knowledge of the moral principles and intellectual improvements of the people deeply engraven on my mind in early life, and not obscured but exalted by experience and age; and, with humble reverence, I feel it to be my duty to add, if a veneration for the religion of a people who profess and call themselves Christians, and a fixed resolution to consider a decent respect for Christianity among the best recommendations for the public service, can enable me in any degree to comply with your wishes, it shall be my strenuous endeavor that this sagacious injunction of the two Houses shall not be without effect . . ..

And may that Being who is supreme over all, the Patron of Order, the Fountain of Justice, and the Protector in all ages of the world of virtuous liberty, continue His blessing upon this nation and its Government and give it all possible success and duration consistent with the ends of His providence.

THOMAS JEFFERSON

First Address: March 4, 1801

Jefferson took office following one of the most contentious elections in American history. He therefore felt compelled to sound a note of reconciliation and bipartisanship, sounding again the Revolutionary generation's call to rise above partisan strife. He also took Washington's cue and expressed a sense of humility in the face of the presidency's heavy responsibilities. Note also his references to government restraint; fearing what he felt were his opponents' tendencies to seek too much power for the federal government, Jefferson espoused a philosophy of limited, restrained government authority.

Called upon to undertake the duties of the first executive office of our country, I avail myself of the presence of that portion of my fellow-citizens which is here assembled to express my grateful thanks for the favor with which they have been pleased to look toward me, to declare a sincere consciousness that the task is above my talents, and that I approach it with those anxious and awful presentiments which the greatness of the charge and the weakness of my powers so justly inspire. A rising nation, spread over a wide and fruitful land, traversing all the seas with the rich productions of their industry, engaged in commerce with nations who feel power and forget right, advancing rapidly to destinies beyond the reach of mortal eye—when I contemplate these transcendent objects, and see the honor, the happiness, and the hopes of this beloved country committed to the issue and the auspices of this day, I shrink from the contemplation, and humble myself before the magnitude of the undertaking. Utterly, indeed, should I despair did not the presence of many whom I here see remind me that in the other high authorities provided by our Constitution I shall find resources of wisdom, of virtue, and of zeal on which to rely under all difficulties. To you, then, gentlemen, who are charged with the sovereign functions of legislation, and to those associated with you, I look with encouragement for that guidance and support which may enable us to steer with safety the vessel in which we are all embarked amidst the conflicting elements of a troubled world.

During the contest of opinion through which we have passed [the hotly contested election of 1800, which was eventually decided in the House of Representatives] the animation of discussions and of exertions has sometimes worn an aspect which might impose on strangers unused to think freely and to speak and to write what they think; but this being now decided by the voice of the nation, announced according to the rules of the Constitution, all will, of course, arrange themselves under the will of the law, and unite in common efforts for the common good. All, too, will bear in mind this sacred principle, that though the will of the majority is in all cases to prevail, that will to be rightful must be reasonable; that the minority possess their equal rights, which equal law must protect, and to violate would be oppression. Let us, then, fellow-citizens, unite with one heart and one mind. Let us restore to social intercourse that harmony and affection without which liberty and even life itself are but dreary things. And let us reflect that, having banished from our land that religious intolerance under which mankind so long bled and suffered, we have yet gained little if we countenance a political intolerance as despotic, as wicked, and capable of as bitter and bloody persecutions. During the throes and convulsions of the ancient world, during the agonizing spasms of infuriated man, seeking through blood and slaughter his long-lost liberty, it was not wonderful that the agitation of the billows should reach even this distant and peaceful shore; that this should be more felt and feared by some and less by others, and should divide opinions as to measures of safety. But every difference of opinion is not a difference of principle. We have called by different names brethren of the same principle. We are all Republicans, we are all Federalists. If there be any among us who would wish to dissolve this Union or to change its republican form, let them stand undisturbed as monuments of the safety with which error of opinion may be tolerated where reason is left free to combat it. I know, indeed, that some honest men fear that a republican government can not be strong, that this Government is not strong enough; but would the honest patriot, in the full tide of successful experiment, abandon a government which has so far kept us free and firm on the theoretic and visionary fear that this Government, the world's best hope, may by possibility want energy to preserve itself? I trust not. I believe this, on the contrary, the strongest Government on earth. I believe it the only one where every man, at the call of the law, would fly to the standard of the law, and would meet invasions of the public order as his own personal concern. Sometimes it is said that man can not be trusted with the government of himself. Can he, then, be trusted with the government of others? Or have we found angels in the forms of kings to govern him? Let history answer this question.

Let us, then, with courage and confidence pursue our own Federal and Republican principles, our attachment to union and representative government. Kindly separated by nature and a wide ocean from the exterminating havoc of one quarter of the globe; too high-minded to endure the degradations of the others; possessing a chosen country, with room enough for our descendants to the thousandth and thousandth generation; entertaining a due sense of our equal right to the use of our own faculties, to the acquisitions of our own industry, to honor and confidence from our fellow-citizens, resulting not from birth, but from our actions and their sense of them; enlightened by a benign religion, professed, indeed, and practiced in various forms, yet all of them inculcating honesty, truth, temperance, gratitude, and the love of man; acknowledging and adoring an overruling Providence, which by all its dispensations proves that it delights in the happiness of man here and his greater happiness hereafter—with all these blessings, what more is necessary to make us a happy and a prosperous people? Still one thing more, fellow-citizens—a wise and frugal Government, which shall restrain men from injuring one another, shall leave them otherwise free to regulate their own pursuits of industry and improvement, and shall not take from the mouth of labor the bread it has earned. This is the sum of good government, and this is necessary to close the circle of our felicities.

About to enter, fellow-citizens, on the exercise of duties which comprehend everything dear and valuable to you, it is proper you should understand what I deem the essential principles of our Government, and consequently those which ought to shape its Administration. I will compress them within the narrowest compass they will bear, stating the general principle, but not all its limitations. Equal and exact justice to all men, of whatever state or persuasion, religious or political; peace, commerce, and honest friendship with all nations, entangling alliances with none; the support of the State governments in all their rights, as the most competent administrations for our domestic concerns and the surest bulwarks against antirepublican tendencies; the preservation of the General Government in its whole constitutional vigor, as the sheet anchor of our peace at home and safety abroad; a jealous care of the right of election by the people—a mild and safe corrective of abuses which are lopped by the sword of revolution where peaceable remedies are unprovided; absolute acquiescence in the decisions of the majority, the vital principle of republics, from which is no appeal but to force, the vital principle and immediate parent of despotism; a well-disciplined militia, our best reliance in peace and for the first moments of war till regulars may relieve them; the supremacy of the civil over the military authority; economy in the public expense, that labor may be lightly burthened; the honest payment of our debts and sacred preservation of the public faith; encouragement of agriculture, and of commerce as its handmaid; the diffusion of information and arraignment of all abuses at the bar of the public reason; freedom of religion; freedom of the press, and freedom of person under the protection of the habeas corpus, and trial by juries impartially selected. These principles form the bright constellation which has gone before us and guided our steps through an age of revolution and reformation. The wisdom of our sages and blood of our heroes have been devoted to their attainment. They should be the creed of our political faith, the text of civic instruction, the touchstone by which to try the services of those we trust; and should we wander from them in moments of error or of alarm, let us hasten to retrace our steps and to regain the road which alone leads to peace, liberty, and safety.

I repair, then, fellow-citizens, to the post you have assigned me. With experience enough in subordinate offices to have seen the difficulties of this the greatest of all, I have learnt to expect that it will rarely fall to the lot of imperfect man to retire from this station with the reputation and the favor which bring him into it. Without pretensions to that high confidence you reposed in our first and greatest revolutionary character, whose preeminent services had entitled him to the first place in his country's love and destined for him the fairest page in the volume of faithful history, I ask so much confidence only as may give firmness and effect to the legal administration of your affairs. I shall often go wrong through defect of judgment. When right, I shall often be thought wrong by those whose positions will not command a view of the whole ground. I ask your indulgence for my own errors, which will never be intentional, and your support against the errors of others, who may condemn what they would not if seen in all its parts. The approbation implied by your suffrage is a great consolation to me for the past, and my future solicitude will be to retain the good opinion of those who have bestowed it in advance, to conciliate that of others by doing them all the good in my power, and to be instrumental to the happiness and freedom of all.

Relying, then, on the patronage of your good will, I advance with obedience to the work, ready to retire from it whenever you become sensible how much better choice it is in your power to make. And may that Infinite Power which rules the destinies of the universe lead our councils to what is best, and give them a favorable issue for your peace and prosperity.

Second Address: March 4, 1805

In his second address, Jefferson offered a justification for his administration's policies on a litany of controversial subjects, but in particular the Louisiana Purchase and government policies toward the Indians. His statements about Indians reveal the combination of altruism, arrogance, and prejudice that governed many Americans' attitudes toward Indians and their fate. Jefferson also offered his criticisms of fast-growing and raucous American newspapers.

Proceeding, fellow citizens, to that qualification which the constitution requires, before my entrance on the charge again conferred upon me, it is my duty to express the deep sense I entertain of this new proof of confidence from my fellow citizens at large, and the zeal with which it inspires me, so to conduct myself as may best satisfy their just expectations.

On taking this station on a former occasion, I declared the principles on which I believed it my duty to administer the affairs of our commonwealth. My conscience tells me that I have, on every occasion, acted up to that declaration, according to its obvious import, and to the understanding of every candid mind.

In the transaction of your foreign affairs, we have endeavored to cultivate the friendship of all nations, and especially of those with which we have the most important relations. We have done them justice on all occasions, favored where favor was lawful, and cherished mutual interests and intercourse on fair and equal terms. We are firmly convinced, and we act on that conviction, that with nations, as with individuals, our interests soundly calculated, will ever be found inseparable from our moral duties; and history bears witness to the fact, that a just nation is taken on its word, when recourse is had to armaments and wars to bridle others. . . .

I know that the acquisition of Louisiana [a reference to Jefferson's 1803 purchase of Louisiana from France for fifteen million dollars, adding to the nation almost 530 million acres of new land] has been disapproved by some, from a candid apprehension that the enlargement of our territory would endanger its union. But who can limit the extent to which the federative principle may operate effectively? The larger our association, the less will it be shaken by local passions; and in any view, is it not better that the opposite bank of the Mississippi should be settled by our own brethren and children, than by strangers of another family? With which shall we be most likely to live in harmony and friendly intercourse? . . .

The aboriginal inhabitants of these countries I have regarded with the commiseration their history inspires. Endowed with the faculties and the rights of men, breathing an ardent love of liberty and independence, and occupying a country which left them no desire but to be undisturbed, the stream of overflowing population from other regions directed itself on these shores; without power to divert, or habits to contend against, they have been overwhelmed by the current, or driven before it; now reduced within limits too narrow for the hunter's state, humanity enjoins us to teach them agriculture and the domestic arts; to encourage them to that industry which alone can enable them to maintain their place in existence, and to prepare them in time for that state of society, which to bodily comforts adds the improvement of the mind and morals. We have therefore liberally furnished them with the implements of husbandry and household use; we have placed among them instructors in the arts of first necessity; and they are covered with the aegis of the law against aggressors from among ourselves.

But the endeavors to enlighten them on the fate which awaits their present course of life, to induce them to exercise their reason, follow its dictates, and change their pursuits with the change of circumstances, have powerful obstacles to encounter; they are combated by the habits of their bodies, prejudice of their minds, ignorance, pride, and the influence of interested and crafty individuals among them, who feel themselves something in the present order of things, and fear to become nothing in any other. These persons inculcate a sanctimonious reverence for the customs of their ancestors; that whatsoever they did, must be done through all time; that reason is a false guide, and to advance under its counsel, in their physical, moral, or political condition, is perilous innovation; that their duty is to remain as their Creator made them, ignorance being safety, and knowledge full of danger; in short, my friends, among them is seen the action and counteraction of good sense and bigotry; they, too, have their anti-philosophers, who find an interest in keeping things in their present state, who dread reformation, and exert all their faculties to maintain the ascendency of habit over the duty of improving our reason, and obeying its mandates.

In giving these outlines, I do not mean, fellow citizens, to arrogate to myself the merit of the measures; that is due, in the first place, to the reflecting character of our citizens at large, who, by the weight of public opinion, influence and strengthen the public measures; it is due to the sound discretion with which they select from among themselves those to whom they confide the legislative duties; it is due to the zeal and wisdom of the characters thus selected, who lay the foundations of public happiness in wholesome laws, the execution of which alone remains for others; and it is due to the able and faithful auxiliaries, whose patriotism has associated with me in the executive functions.

During this course of administration, and in order to disturb it, the artillery of the press has been levelled against us, charged with whatsoever its licentiousness could devise or dare. These abuses of an institution so important to freedom and science, are deeply to be regretted, inasmuch as they tend to lessen its usefulness, and to sap its safety; they might, indeed, have been corrected by the wholesome punishments reserved and provided by the laws of the several States against falsehood and defamation; but public duties more urgent press on the time of public servants, and the offenders have therefore been left to find their punishment in the public indignation.

Nor was it uninteresting to the world, that an experiment should be fairly and fully made, whether freedom of discussion, unaided by power, is not sufficient for the propagation and protection of truth—whether a government, conducting itself in the true spirit of its constitution, with zeal and purity, and doing no act which it would be unwilling the whole world should witness, can be written down by falsehood and defamation. The experiment has been tried; you have witnessed the scene; our fellow citizens have looked on, cool and collected; they saw the latent source from which these outrages proceeded; they gathered around their public functionaries, and when the constitution called them to the decision by suffrage, they pronounced their verdict, honorable to those who had served them, and consolatory to the friend of man, who believes he may be intrusted with his own affairs.

No inference is here intended, that the laws, provided by the State against false and defamatory publications, should not be enforced; he who has time, renders a service to public morals and public tranquillity, in reforming these abuses by the salutary coercions of the law; but the experiment is noted, to prove that, since truth and reason have maintained their ground against false opinions in league with false facts, the press, confined to truth, needs no other legal restraint; the public judgment will correct false reasonings and opinions, on a full hearing of all parties; and no other definite line can be drawn between the inestimable liberty of the press and its demoralizing licentiousness. If there be still improprieties which this rule would not restrain, its supplement must be sought in the censorship of public opinion.

Contemplating the union of sentiment now manifested so generally, as auguring harmony and happiness to our future course, I offer to our country sincere congratulations. With those, too, not yet rallied to the same point, the disposition to do so is gaining strength; facts are piercing through the veil drawn over them; and our doubting brethren will at length see, that the mass of their fellow citizens, with whom they cannot yet resolve to act, as to principles and measures, think as they think, and desire what they desire; that our wish, as well as theirs, is, that the public efforts may be directed honestly to the public good, that peace be cultivated, civil and religious liberty unassailed, law and order preserved; equality of rights maintained, and that state of property, equal or unequal, which results to every man from his own industry, or that of his fathers. When satisfied of these views, it is not in human nature that they should not approve and support them; in the meantime, let us cherish them with patient affection; let us do them justice, and more than justice, in all competitions of interest; and we need not doubt that truth, reason, and their own interests, will at length prevail, will gather them into the fold of their country, and will complete their entire union of opinion, which gives to a nation the blessing of harmony, and the benefit of all its strength.

I shall now enter on the duties to which my fellow citizens have again called me, and shall proceed in the spirit of those principles which they have approved. I fear not that any motives of interest may lead me astray; I am sensible of no passion which could seduce me knowingly from the path of justice; but the weakness of human nature, and the limits of my own understanding, will produce errors of judgment sometimes injurious to your interests. I shall need, therefore, all the indulgence I have heretofore experienced—the want of it will certainly not lessen with increasing years. I shall need, too, the favor of that Being in whose hands we are, who led our forefathers, as Israel of old, from their native land, and planted them in a country flowing with all the necessaries and comforts of life; who has covered our infancy with his providence, and our riper years with his wisdom and power; and to whose goodness I ask you to join with me in supplications, that he will so enlighten the minds of your servants, guide their councils, and prosper their measures, that whatsoever they do, shall result in your good, and shall secure to you the peace, friendship, and approbation of all nations.

James Madison

First Address: March 4, 1809

The shadow of Europe's ongoing wars and conflicts are evident in Madison's first Inaugural Address, as he took a cue from his predecessors and announced his nation's ongoing attempts to maintain a precarious neutrality. At the same time, however, he also took note of the nation's booming prosperity, as he ascended to the White House during the first stirrings of the Market Revolution. Also, the fourth paragraph below— possibly the longest sentence in the history of presidential speech making—offers a sort of microcosm of the nation's general political values at the turn of the century.

Unwilling to depart from examples of the most revered authority, I avail myself of the occasion now presented to express the profound impression made on me by the call of my country to the station to the duties of which I am about to pledge myself by the most solemn of sanctions. . . .

The present situation of the world is indeed without a parallel and that of our own country full of difficulties. The pressure of these, too, is the more severely felt because they have fallen upon us at a moment when the national prosperity being at a height not before attained, the contrast resulting from the change has been rendered the more striking. Under the benign influence of our republican institutions, and the maintenance of peace with all nations whilst so many of them were engaged in bloody and wasteful wars, the fruits of a just policy were enjoyed in an unrivaled growth of our faculties and resources. Proofs of this were seen in the improvements of agriculture, in the successful enterprises of commerce, in the progress of manufacturers and useful arts, in the increase of the public revenue and the use made of it in reducing the public debt, and in the valuable works and establishments everywhere multiplying over the face of our land. . . .

Indulging no passions which trespass on the rights or the repose of other nations, it has been the true glory of the United States to cultivate peace by observing justice, and to entitle themselves to the respect of the nations at war by fulfilling their neutral obligations with the most scrupulous impartiality. If there be candor in the world, the truth of these assertions will not be questioned; posterity at least will do justice to them. . . .

To cherish peace and friendly intercourse with all nations having correspondent dispositions; to maintain sincere neutrality toward belligerent nations; to prefer in all cases amicable discussion and reasonable accommodation of differences to a decision of them by an appeal to arms; to exclude foreign intrigues and foreign partialities, so degrading to all countries and so baneful to free ones; to foster a spirit of independence too just to invade the rights of others, too proud to surrender our own, too liberal to indulge unworthy prejudices ourselves and too elevated not to look down upon them in others; to hold the union of the States as the basis of their peace and happiness; to support the Constitution, which is the cement of the Union, as well in its limitations as in its authorities; to respect the rights and authorities reserved to the States and to the people as equally incorporated with and essential to the success of the general system; to avoid the slightest interference with the right of conscience or the functions of religion, so wisely exempted from civil jurisdiction; to preserve in their full energy the other salutary provisions in behalf of private and personal rights, and of the freedom of the press; to observe economy in public expenditures; to liberate the public resources by an honorable discharge of the public debts; to keep within the requisite limits a standing military force, always remembering that an armed and trained militia is the firmest bulwark of republics—that without standing armies their liberty can never be in danger, nor with large ones safe; to promote by authorized means improvements friendly to agriculture, to manufactures, and to external as well as internal commerce; to favor in like manner the advancement of science and the diffusion of information as the best aliment to true liberty; to carry on the benevolent plans which have been so meritoriously applied to the conversion of our aboriginal neighbors from the degradation and wretchedness of savage life to a participation of the improvements of which the human mind and manners are susceptible in a civilized state—as far as sentiments and intentions such as these can aid the fulfillment of my duty, they will be a resource which can not fail me . . ..

But the source to which I look or the aids which alone can supply my deficiencies is in the well-tried intelligence and virtue of my fellow-citizens, and in the counsels of those representing them in the other departments associated in the care of the national interests. In these my confidence will under every difficulty be best placed, next to that which we have all been encouraged to feel in the guardianship and guidance of that Almighty Being whose power regulates the destiny of nations, whose blessings have been so conspicuously dispensed to this rising Republic, and to whom we are bound to address our devout gratitude for the past, as well as our fervent supplications and best hopes for the future.

Second Address: March 4, 1813

The shadow of war with England hung over Madison's second address, and he devoted most of his attention to explaining the causes and justifications of the war. He also used the opportunity to castigate the British conduct of the war in very harsh terms.

Seventeen months after he gave this speech, the British would lay waste to the city in which Madison gave his speech, torching the presidential mansion so badly that it had to be repainted a bright white to cover the soot stains (hence the White House).

About to add the solemnity of an oath to the obligations imposed by a second call to the station in which my country heretofore placed me, I find in the presence of this respectable assembly an opportunity of publicly repeating my profound sense of so distinguished a confidence and of the responsibility united with it. The impressions on me are strengthened by such an evidence that my faithful endeavors to discharge my arduous duties have been favorably estimated, and by a consideration of the momentous period at which the trust has been renewed. From the weight and magnitude now belonging to it I should be compelled to shrink if I had less reliance on the support of an enlightened and generous people, and felt less deeply a conviction that the war with a powerful nation, which forms so prominent a feature in our situation, is stamped with that justice which invites the smiles of Heaven on the means of conducting it to a successful termination.

May we not cherish this sentiment without presumption when we reflect on the characters by which this war is distinguished?

It was not declared on the part of the United States until it had been long made on them, in reality though not in name; until arguments and postulations had been exhausted; until a positive declaration had been received that the wrongs provoking it would not be discontinued; nor until this last appeal could no longer be delayed without breaking down the spirit of the nation, destroying all confidence in itself and in its political institutions, and either perpetuating a state of disgraceful suffering or regaining by more costly sacrifices and more severe struggles our lost rank and respect among independent powers.

On the issue of the war are staked our national sovereignty on the high seas and the security of an important class of citizens whose occupations give the proper value to those of every other class. Not to contend for such a stake is to surrender our equality with other powers on the element common to all and to violate the sacred title which every member of the society has to its protection. I need not call into view the unlawfulness of the practice by which our mariners are forced at the will of every cruising officer from their own vessels into foreign ones, nor paint the outrages inseparable from it. The proofs are in the records of each successive Administration of our Government, and the cruel sufferings of that portion of the American people have found their way to every bosom not dead to the sympathies of human nature.

As the war was just in its origin and necessary and noble in its objects, we can reflect with a proud satisfaction that in carrying it on no principle of justice or honor, no usage of civilized nations, no precept of courtesy or humanity, have been infringed. The war has been waged on our part with scrupulous regard to all these obligations, and in a spirit of liberality which was never surpassed.

How little has been the effect of this example on the conduct of the enemy!

They have retained as prisoners of war citizens of the United States not liable to be so considered under the usages of war.

They have refused to consider as prisoners of war, and threatened to punish as traitors and deserters, persons emigrating without restraint to the United States, incorporated by naturalization into our political family, and fighting under the authority of their adopted country in open and honorable war for the maintenance of its rights and safety. Such is the avowed purpose of a Government which is in the practice of naturalizing by thousands citizens of other countries, and not only of permitting but compelling them to fight its battles against their native country.

They have not, it is true, taken into their own hands the hatchet and the knife, devoted to indiscriminate massacre, but they have let loose the savages armed with these cruel instruments; have allured them into their service, and carried them to battle by their sides, eager to glut their savage thirst with the blood of the vanquished and to finish the work of torture and death on maimed and defenseless captives. And, what was never before seen, British commanders have extorted victory over the unconquerable valor of our troops by presenting to the sympathy of their chief captives awaiting massacre from their savage associates. And now we find them, in further contempt of the modes of honorable warfare, supplying the place of a conquering force by attempts to disorganize our political society, to dismember our confederated Republic. Happily, like others, these will recoil on the authors; but they mark the degenerate counsels from which they emanate, and if they did not belong to a sense of unexampled inconsistencies might excite the greater wonder as proceeding from a Government which founded the very war in which it has been so long engaged on a charge against the disorganizing and insurrectional policy of its adversary.

To render the justice of the war on our part the more conspicuous, the reluctance to commence it was followed by the earliest and strongest manifestations of a disposition to arrest its progress. The sword was scarcely out of the scabbard before the enemy was apprised of the reasonable terms on which it would be resheathed. Still more precise advances were repeated, and have been received in a spirit forbidding every reliance not placed on the military resources of the nation.

These resources are amply sufficient to bring the war to an honorable issue. Our nation is in number more than half that of the British Isles. It is composed of a brave, a free, a virtuous, and an intelligent people. Our country abounds in the necessaries, the arts, and the comforts of life. A general prosperity is visible in the public countenance. The means employed by the British cabinet to undermine it have recoiled on themselves; have given to our national faculties a more rapid development, and, draining or diverting the precious metals from British circulation and British vaults, have poured them into those of the United States. It is a propitious consideration that an unavoidable war should have found this seasonable facility for the contributions required to support it. When the public voice called for war, all knew, and still know, that without them it could not be carried on through the period which it might last, and the patriotism, the good sense, and the manly spirit of our fellow-citizens are pledges for the cheerfulness with which they will bear each his share of the common burden. To render the war short and its success sure, animated and systematic exertions alone are necessary, and the success of our arms now may long preserve our country from the necessity of another resort to them. Already have the gallant exploits of our naval heroes proved to the world our inherent capacity to maintain our rights on one element. If the reputation of our arms has been thrown under clouds on the other, presaging flashes of heroic enterprise assure us that nothing is wanting to correspondent triumphs there also but the discipline and habits which are in daily progress.

JAMES MONROE

First Address: March 4, 1817

President Monroe's first address was more upbeat than the second one of his immediate predecessor. America had managed to survive the War of 1812, Europe's various conflicts were starting to subside, and the new president was able to turn his attention to the nation's burgeoning economy and general prosperity. Monroe found much to his liking.

I should be destitute of feeling if I was not deeply affected by the strong proof which my fellow-citizens have given me of their confidence in calling me to the high office whose functions I am about to assume. . . .

   In commencing the duties of the chief executive office it has been the practice of the distinguished men who have gone before me to explain the principles which would govern them in their respective Administrations. In following their venerated example my attention is naturally drawn to the great causes which have contributed in a principal degree to produce the present happy condition of the United States. They will best explain the nature of our duties and shed much light on the policy which ought to be pursued in future. . . .

   To whatever object we turn our attention, whether it relates to our foreign or domestic concerns, we find abundant cause to felicitate ourselves in the excellence of our institutions. During a period fraught with difficulties and marked by very extraordinary events the United States have flourished beyond example. Their citizens individually have been happy and the nation prosperous. . . .

   And if we look to the condition of individuals what a proud spectacle does it exhibit! On whom has oppression fallen in any quarter of our Union? Who has been deprived of any right of person or property? Who restrained from offering his vows in the mode which he prefers to the Divine Author of his being? It is well known that all these blessings have been enjoyed in their fullest extent; and I add with peculiar satisfaction that there has been no example of a capital punishment being inflicted on anyone for the crime of high treason. . . .

Such, then, is the happy Government under which we live—a Government adequate to every purpose for which the social compact is formed; a Government elective in all its branches, under which every citizen may by his merit obtain the highest trust recognized by the Constitution; which contains within it no cause of discord, none to put at variance one portion of the community with another; a Government which protects every citizen in the full enjoyment of his rights, and is able to protect the nation against injustice from foreign powers. . . .

Fortunate as we are in our political institutions, we have not been less so in other circumstances on which our prosperity and happiness essentially depend. Situated within the temperate zone, and extending through many degrees of latitude along the Atlantic, the United States enjoy all the varieties of climate, and every production incident to that portion of the globe. Penetrating internally to the Great Lakes and beyond the sources of the great rivers which communicate through our whole interior, no country was ever happier with respect to its domain. Blessed, too, with a fertile soil, our produce has always been very abundant, leaving, even in years the least favorable, a surplus for the wants of our fellow-men in other countries. . . . Our manufactures find a generous encouragement by the policy which patronizes domestic industry, and the surplus of our produce a steady and profitable market by local wants in less-favored parts at home.

Such, then, being the highly favored condition of our country, it is the interest of every citizen to maintain it. What are the dangers which menace us? If any exist they ought to be ascertained and guarded against. . . .

It is only when the people become ignorant and corrupt, when they degenerate into a populace, that they are incapable of exercising the sovereignty. Usurpation is then an easy attainment, and an usurper soon found. The people themselves become the willing instruments of their own debasement and ruin. Let us, then, look to the great cause, and endeavor to preserve it in full force. Let us by all wise and constitutional measures promote intelligence among the people as the best means of preserving our liberties.

Dangers from abroad are not less deserving of attention. Experiencing the fortune of other nations, the United States may be again involved in war, and it may in that event be the object of the adverse party to overset our Government, to break our Union, and demolish us as a nation. Our distance from Europe and the just, moderate, and pacific policy of our Government may form some security against these dangers, but they ought to be anticipated and guarded against. Many of our citizens are engaged in commerce and navigation, and all of them are in a certain degree dependent on their prosperous state. Many are engaged in the fisheries. These interests are exposed to invasion in the wars between other powers, and we should disregard the faithful admonition of experience if we did not expect it. We must support our rights or lose our character, and with it, perhaps, our liberties. A people who fail to do it can scarcely be said to hold a place among independent nations. National honor is national property of the highest value. The sentiment in the mind of every citizen is national strength. It ought therefore to be cherished.

To secure us against these dangers our coast and inland frontiers should be fortified, our Army and Navy, regulated upon just principles as to the force of each, be kept in perfect order, and our militia be placed on the best practicable footing. . . .

Other interests of high importance will claim attention, among which the improvement of our country by roads and canals, proceeding always with a constitutional sanction, holds a distinguished place. . . .

Our manufacturers will likewise require the systematic and fostering care of the Government. Possessing as we do all the raw materials, the fruit of our own soil and industry, we ought not to depend in the degree we have done on supplies from other countries. While we are thus dependent the sudden event of war, unsought and unexpected, can not fail to plunge us into the most serious difficulties. It is important, too, that the capital which nourishes our manufacturers should be domestic, as its influence in that case instead of exhausting, as it may do in foreign hands, would be felt advantageously on agriculture and every other branch of industry. Equally important is it to provide at home a market for our raw materials, as by extending the competition it will enhance the price and protect the cultivator against the casualties incident to foreign markets.

With the Indian tribes it is our duty to cultivate friendly relations and to act with kindness and liberality in all our transactions. Equally proper is it to persevere in our efforts to extend to them the advantages of civilization.

The great amount of our revenue and the flourishing state of the Treasury are a full proof of the competency of the national resources for any emergency, as they are of the willingness of our fellow-citizens to bear the burdens which the public necessities require. . . .

Equally gratifying is it to witness the increased harmony of opinion which pervades our Union. Discord does not belong to our system. Union is recommended as well by the free and benign principles of our Government, extending its blessings to every individual, as by the other eminent advantages attending it. The American people have encountered together great dangers and sustained severe trials with success. They constitute one great family with a common interest. . . .

Never did a government commence under auspices so favorable, nor ever was success so complete. If we look to the history of other nations, ancient or modern, we find no example of a growth so rapid, so gigantic, of a people so prosperous and happy. In contemplating what we have still to perform, the heart of every citizen must expand with joy when he reflects how near our Government has approached to perfection; that in respect to it we have no essential improvement to make; that the great object is to preserve it in the essential principles and features which characterize it, and that is to be done by preserving the virtue and enlightening the minds of the people; and as a security against foreign dangers to adopt such arrangements as are indispensable to the support of our independence, our rights and liberties. If we persevere in the career in which we have advanced so far and in the path already traced, we can not fail, under the favor of a gracious Providence, to attain the high destiny which seems to await us. . . .

Second Address: March 5, 1821

Monroe's second address reviewed the end of the War of 1812 and offered general observations about the nation's ongoing prosperity. Of special interest here are Monroe's statements about government policies toward Native Americans.

I shall not attempt to describe the grateful emotions which the new and very distinguished proof of the confidence of my fellow-citizens, evinced by my reelection to this high trust, has excited in my bosom . . ..

As soon as the war [of 1812] had terminated, the nation, admonished by its events, resolved to place itself in a situation which should be better calculated to prevent the recurrence of a like evil, and, in case it should recur, to mitigate its calamities. With this view, after reducing our land force to the basis of a peace establishment, which has been further modified since, provision was made for the construction of fortifications at proper points through the whole extent of our coast and such an augmentation of our naval force as should be well adapted to both purposes. . . .

It need scarcely be remarked that these measures have not been resorted to in a spirit of hostility to other powers. Such a disposition does not exist toward any power. Peace and good will have been, and will hereafter be, cultivated with all, and by the most faithful regard to justice. They have been dictated by a love of peace, of economy, and an earnest desire to save the lives of our fellow-citizens from that destruction and our country from that devastation which are inseparable from war when it finds us unprepared for it. It is believed, and experience has shown, that such a preparation is the best expedient that can be resorted to prevent war. . . .

At the period adverted to the powers of Europe, after having been engaged in long and destructive wars with each other, had concluded a peace, which happily still exists. . . .

Our attitude has therefore been that of neutrality between them, which has been maintained by the Government with the strictest impartiality. No aid has been afforded to either, nor has any privilege been enjoyed by the one which has not been equally open to the other party, and every exertion has been made in its power to enforce the execution of the laws prohibiting illegal equipments with equal rigor against both . . ..

Respecting the attitude which it may be proper for the United States to maintain hereafter between the parties, I have no hesitation in stating it as my opinion that the neutrality heretofore observed should still be adhered to. . . .

The situation of the United States in regard to their resources, the extent of their revenue, and the facility with which it is raised affords a most gratifying spectacle. . . .

The care of the Indian tribes within our limits has long been an essential part of our system, but, unfortunately, it has not been executed in a manner to accomplish all the objects intended by it. We have treated them as independent nations, without their having any substantial pretensions to that rank. The distinction has flattered their pride, retarded their improvement, and in many instances paved the way to their destruction. The progress of our settlements westward, supported as they are by a dense population, has constantly driven them back, with almost the total sacrifice of the lands which they have been compelled to abandon. They have claims on the magnanimity and, I may add, on the justice of this nation which we must all feel. We should become their real benefactors; we should perform the office of their Great Father, the endearing title which they emphatically give to the Chief Magistrate of our Union. Their sovereignty over vast territories should cease, in lieu of which the right of soil should be secured to each individual and his posterity in competent portions; and for the territory thus ceded by each tribe some reasonable equivalent should be granted, to be vested in permanent funds for the support of civil government over them and for the education of their children, for their instruction in the arts of husbandry, and to provide sustenance for them until they could provide it for themselves. My earnest hope is that Congress will digest some plan, founded on these principles, with such improvements as their wisdom may suggest, and carry it into effect as soon as it may be practicable.

Europe is again unsettled and the prospect of war increasing. Should the flame light up in any quarter, how far it may extend it is impossible to foresee. It is our peculiar felicity to be altogether unconnected with the causes which produce this menacing aspect elsewhere. With every power we are in perfect amity, and it is our interest to remain so if it be practicable on just conditions. . . .

In our whole system, national and State, we have shunned all the defects which unceasingly preyed on the vitals and destroyed the ancient Republics. In them there were distinct orders, a nobility and a people, or the people governed in one assembly. Thus, in the one instance there was a perpetual conflict between the orders in society for the ascendency, in which the victory of either terminated in the overthrow of the government and the ruin of the state; in the other, in which the people governed in a body, and whose dominions seldom exceeded the dimensions of a county in one of our States, a tumultuous and disorderly movement permitted only a transitory existence. In this great nation there is but one order, that of the people, whose power, by a peculiarly happy improvement of the representative principle, is transferred from them, without impairing in the slightest degree their sovereignty, to bodies of their own creation, and to persons elected by themselves, in the full extent necessary for all the purposes of free, enlightened and efficient government. The whole system is elective, the complete sovereignty being in the people, and every officer in every department deriving his authority from and being responsible to them for his conduct. . . .

Our physical attainments have not been less eminent. Twenty-five years ago the river Mississippi was shut up and our Western brethren had no outlet for their commerce. What has been the progress since that time? The river has not only become the property of the United States from its source to the ocean, with all its tributary streams (with the exception of the upper part of the Red River only), but Louisiana, with a fair and liberal boundary on the western side and the Floridas on the eastern, have been ceded to us . . . .. Our population has augmented in an astonishing degree and extended in every direction. We now, fellow-citizens, comprise within our limits the dimensions and faculties of a great power under a Government possessing all the energies of any government ever known to the Old World, with an utter incapacity to oppress the people.

Entering with these views the office which I have just solemnly sworn to execute with fidelity and to the utmost of my ability, I derive great satisfaction from a knowledge that I shall be assisted in the several Departments by the very enlightened and upright citizens from whom I have received so much aid in the preceding term. With full confidence in the continuance of that candor and generous indulgence from my fellow-citizens at large which I have heretofore experienced, and with a firm reliance on the protection of Almighty God, I shall forthwith commence the duties of the high trust to which you have called me.

JOHN QUINCY ADAMS

March 4, 1825

Adams's broad intellectual bent is evident here as he offers one of the more lyrical presidential passages concerning the nation's expansion during the era of Manifest Destiny. His Revolutionary-era dislike of party factionalism is likewise evident.

In compliance with an usage coeval with the existence of our Federal Constitution, and sanctioned by the example of my predecessors in the career upon which I am about to enter, I appear, my fellow-citizens, in your presence and in that of Heaven to bind myself by the solemnities of religious obligation to the faithful performance of the duties allotted to me in the station to which I have been called. . . .

The year of jubilee since the first formation of our Union has just elapsed that of the declaration of our independence is at hand. The consummation of both was effected by this Constitution. . . .

Since that period a population of four millions has multiplied to twelve. A territory bounded by the Mississippi has been extended from sea to sea. New States have been admitted to the Union in numbers nearly equal to those of the first Confederation. Treaties of peace, amity, and commerce have been concluded with the principal dominions of the earth. The people of other nations, inhabitants of regions acquired not by conquest, but by compact, have been united with us in the participation of our rights and duties, of our burdens and blessings. The forest has fallen by the ax of our woodsmen; the soil has been made to teem by the tillage of our farmers; our commerce has whitened every ocean. The dominion of man over physical nature has been extended by the invention of our artists. Liberty and law have marched hand in hand. All the purposes of human association have been accomplished as effectively as under any other government on the globe, and at a cost little exceeding in a whole generation the expenditure of other nations in a single year.

Such is the unexaggerated picture of our condition under a Constitution founded upon the republican principle of equal rights. To admit that this picture has its shades is but to say that it is still the condition of men upon earth. From evil—physical, moral, and political—it is not our claim to be exempt. We have suffered sometimes by the visitation of Heaven through disease; often by the wrongs and injustice of other nations, even to the extremities of war; and, lastly, by dissensions among ourselves—dissensions perhaps inseparable from the enjoyment of freedom, but which have more than once appeared to threaten the dissolution of the Union, and with it the overthrow of all the enjoyments of our present lot and all our earthly hopes of the future. The causes of these dissensions have been various, founded upon differences of speculation in the theory of republican government; upon conflicting views of policy in our relations with foreign nations; upon jealousies of partial and sectional interests, aggravated by prejudices and prepossessions which strangers to each other are ever apt to entertain.

It is a source of gratification and of encouragement to me to observe that the great result of this experiment upon the theory of human rights has at the close of that generation by which it was formed been crowned with success equal to the most sanguine expectations of its founders. Union, justice, tranquillity, the common defense, the general welfare, and the blessings of liberty—all have been promoted by the Government under which we have lived. Standing at this point of time, looking back to that generation which has gone by and forward to that which is advancing, we may at once indulge in grateful exultation and in cheering hope. From the experience of the past we derive instructive lessons for the future. Of the two great political parties which have divided the opinions and feelings of our country, the candid and the just will now admit that both have contributed splendid talents, spotless integrity, ardent patriotism, and disinterested sacrifices to the formation and administration of this Government, and that both have required a liberal indulgence for a portion of human infirmity and error. The revolutionary wars of Europe, commencing precisely at the moment when the Government of the United States first went into operation under this Constitution, excited a collision of sentiments and of sympathies which kindled all the passions and imbittered the conflict of parties till the nation was involved in war and the Union was shaken to its center. This time of trial embraced a period of five and twenty years, during which the policy of the Union in its relations with Europe constituted the principal basis of our political divisions and the most arduous part of the action of our Federal Government. With the catastrophe in which the wars of the French Revolution terminated, and our own subsequent peace with Great Britain, this baneful weed of party strife was uprooted. From that time no difference of principle, connected either with the theory of government or with our intercourse with foreign nations, has existed or been called forth in force sufficient to sustain a continued combination of parties or to give more than wholesome animation to public sentiment or legislative debate. Our political creed is, without a dissenting voice that can be heard, that the will of the people is the source and the happiness of the people the end of all legitimate government upon earth; that the best security for the beneficence and the best guaranty against the abuse of power consists in the freedom, the purity, and the frequency of popular elections; that the General Government of the Union and the separate governments of the States are all sovereignties of limited powers, fellow-servants of the same masters, uncontrolled within their respective spheres, uncontrollable by encroachments upon each other; that the firmest security of peace is the preparation during peace of the defenses of war; that a rigorous economy and accountability of public expenditures should guard against the aggravation and alleviate when possible the burden of taxation; that the military should be kept in strict subordination to the civil power; that the freedom of the press and of religious opinion should be inviolate; that the policy of our country is peace and the ark of our salvation union are articles of faith upon which we are all now agreed. If there have been those who doubted whether a confederated representative democracy were a government competent to the wise and orderly management of the common concerns of a mighty nation, those doubts have been dispelled; if there have been projects of partial confederacies to be erected upon the ruins of the Union, they have been scattered to the winds; if there have been dangerous attachments to one foreign nation and antipathies against another, they have been extinguished. Ten years of peace, at home and abroad, have assuaged the animosities of political contention and blended into harmony the most discordant elements of public opinion. There still remains one effort of magnanimity, one sacrifice of prejudice and passion, to be made by the individuals throughout the nation who have heretofore followed the standards of political party. It is that of discarding every remnant of rancor against each other, of embracing as countrymen and friends, and of yielding to talents and virtue alone that confidence which in times of contention for principle was bestowed only upon those who bore the badge of party communion.

The collisions of party spirit which originate in speculative opinions or in different views of administrative policy are in their nature transitory. Those which are founded on geographical divisions, adverse interests of soil, climate, and modes of domestic life are more permanent, and therefore, perhaps, more dangerous. It is this which gives inestimable value to the character of our Government, at once federal and national. It holds out to us a perpetual admonition to preserve alike and with equal anxiety the rights of each individual State in its own government and the rights of the whole nation in that of the Union. Whatsoever is of domestic concernment, unconnected with the other members of the Union or with foreign lands, belongs exclusively to the administration of the State governments. Whatsoever directly involves the rights and interests of the federative fraternity or of foreign powers is of the resort of this General Government. The duties of both are obvious in the general principle, though sometimes perplexed with difficulties in the detail. To respect the rights of the State governments is the inviolable duty of that of the Union; the government of every State will feel its own obligation to respect and preserve the rights of the whole. The prejudices everywhere too commonly entertained against distant strangers are worn away, and the jealousies of jarring interests are allayed by the composition and functions of the great national councils annually assembled from all quarters of the Union at this place. Here the distinguished men from every section of our country, while meeting to deliberate upon the great interests of those by whom they are deputed, learn to estimate the talents and do justice to the virtues of each other. The harmony of the nation is promoted and the whole Union is knit together by the sentiments of mutual respect, the habits of social intercourse, and the ties of personal friendship formed between the representatives of its several parts in the performance of their service at this metropolis. . . .

In this brief outline of the promise and performance of my immediate predecessor the line of duty for his successor is clearly delineated. To pursue to their consummation those purposes of improvement in our common condition instituted or recommended by him will embrace the whole sphere of my obligations. To the topic of internal improvement, emphatically urged by him at his inauguration, I recur with peculiar satisfaction. It is that from which I am convinced that the unborn millions of our posterity who are in future ages to people this continent will derive their most fervent gratitude to the founders of the Union; that in which the beneficent action of its Government will be most deeply felt and acknowledged. The magnificence and splendor of their public works are among the imperishable glories of the ancient republics. The roads and aqueducts of Rome have been the admiration of all after ages, and have survived thousands of years after all her conquests have been swallowed up in despotism or become the spoil of barbarians. Some diversity of opinion has prevailed with regard to the powers of Congress for legislation upon objects of this nature. The most respectful deference is due to doubts originating in pure patriotism and sustained by venerated authority. But nearly twenty years have passed since the construction of the first national road was commenced. The authority for its construction was then unquestioned. To how many thousands of our countrymen has it proved a benefit? To what single individual has it ever proved an injury? Repeated, liberal, and candid discussions in the Legislature have conciliated the sentiments and approximated the opinions of enlightened minds upon the question of constitutional power. I can not but hope that by the same process of friendly, patient, and persevering deliberation all constitutional objections will ultimately be removed. The extent and limitation of the powers of the General Government in relation to this transcendently important interest will be settled and acknowledged to the common satisfaction of all, and every speculative scruple will be solved by a practical public blessing. . . .

ANDREW JACKSON

First Address: March 4, 1829

Jackson's inauguration was raucous and even a little scary, with lusty cheers given by the common Americans who attended the ceremony and a near riot at the White House reception. By contrast, Jackson's speech was elegant, brief, and rather low-key.

About to undertake the arduous duties that I have been appointed to perform by the choice of a free people, I avail myself of this customary and solemn occasion to express the gratitude which their confidence inspires and to acknowledge the accountability which my situation enjoins. While the magnitude of their interests convinces me that no thanks can be adequate to the honor they have conferred, it admonishes me that the best return I can make is the zealous dedication of my humble abilities to their service and their good.

As the instrument of the Federal Constitution it will devolve on me for a stated period to execute the laws of the United States, to superintend their foreign and their confederate relations, to manage their revenue, to command their forces, and, by communications to the Legislature, to watch over and to promote their interests generally. And the principles of action by which I shall endeavor to accomplish this circle of duties it is now proper for me briefly to explain.

In administering the laws of Congress I shall keep steadily in view the limitations as well as the extent of the Executive power trusting thereby to discharge the functions of my office without transcending its authority. With foreign nations it will be my study to preserve peace and to cultivate friendship on fair and honorable terms, and in the adjustment of any differences that may exist or arise to exhibit the forbearance becoming a powerful nation rather than the sensibility belonging to a gallant people.

In such measures as I may be called on to pursue in regard to the rights of the separate States I hope to be animated by a proper respect for those sovereign members of our Union, taking care not to confound the powers they have reserved to themselves with those they have granted to the Confederacy.

The management of the public revenue—that searching operation in all governments—is among the most delicate and important trusts in ours, and it will, of course, demand no inconsiderable share of my official solicitude. Under every aspect in which it can be considered it would appear that advantage must result from the observance of a strict and faithful economy. This I shall aim at the more anxiously both because it will facilitate the extinguishment of the national debt, the unnecessary duration of which is incompatible with real independence, and because it will counteract that tendency to public and private profligacy which a profuse expenditure of money by the Government is but too apt to engender. Powerful auxiliaries to the attainment of this desirable end are to be found in the regulations provided by the wisdom of Congress for the specific appropriation of public money and the prompt accountability of public officers.

With regard to a proper selection of the subjects of impost with a view to revenue, it would seem to me that the spirit of equity, caution and compromise in which the Constitution was formed requires that the great interests of agriculture, commerce, and manufactures should be equally favored, and that perhaps the only exception to this rule should consist in the peculiar encouragement of any products of either of them that may be found essential to our national independence.

Internal improvement and the diffusion of knowledge, so far as they can be promoted by the constitutional acts of the Federal Government, are of high importance.

Considering standing armies as dangerous to free governments in time of peace, I shall not seek to enlarge our present establishment, nor disregard that salutary lesson of political experience which teaches that the military should be held subordinate to the civil power. The gradual increase of our Navy, whose flag has displayed in distant climes our skill in navigation and our fame in arms; the preservation of our forts, arsenals, and dockyards, and the introduction of progressive improvements in the discipline and science of both branches of our military service are so plainly prescribed by prudence that I should be excused for omitting their mention sooner than for enlarging on their importance. But the bulwark of our defense is the national militia, which in the present state of our intelligence and population must render us invincible. As long as our Government is administered for the good of the people, and is regulated by their will; as long as it secures to us the rights of person and of property, liberty of conscience and of the press, it will be worth defending; and so long as it is worth defending a patriotic militia will cover it with an impenetrable aegis. Partial injuries and occasional mortifications we may be subjected to, but a million of armed freemen, possessed of the means of war, can never be conquered by a foreign foe. To any just system, therefore, calculated to strengthen this natural safeguard of the country I shall cheerfully lend all the aid in my power.

It will be my sincere and constant desire to observe toward the Indian tribes within our limits a just and liberal policy, and to give that humane and considerate attention to their rights and their wants which is consistent with the habits of our Government and the feelings of our people.

The recent demonstration of public sentiment inscribes on the list of Executive duties, in characters too legible to be overlooked, the task of reform, which will require particularly the correction of those abuses that have brought the patronage of the Federal Government into conflict with the freedom of elections, and the counteraction of those causes which have disturbed the rightful course of appointment and have placed or continued power in unfaithful or incompetent hands.

In the performance of a task thus generally delineated I shall endeavor to select men whose diligence and talents will insure in their respective stations able and faithful cooperation, depending for the advancement of the public service more on the integrity and zeal of the public officers than on their numbers.

A diffidence, perhaps too just, in my own qualifications will teach me to look with reverence to the examples of public virtue left by my illustrious predecessors, and with veneration to the lights that flow from the mind that founded and the mind that reformed our system. The same diffidence induces me to hope for instruction and aid from the coordinate branches of the Government, and for the indulgence and support of my fellow-citizens generally. And a firm reliance on the goodness of that Power whose providence mercifully protected our national infancy, and has since upheld our liberties in various vicissitudes, encourages me to offer up my ardent supplications that He will continue to make our beloved country the object of His divine care and gracious benediction.

Second Address: March 4, 1833

A key theme in Jackson's second address was the ongoing debate over the relative powers of the state and federal governments. Here Jackson faithfully articulates the prevailing philosophy of his administration: respect for each within its own constitutionally prescribed sphere.

The will of the American people, expressed through their unsolicited suffrages, calls me before you to pass through the solemnities preparatory to taking upon myself the duties of President of the United States for another term. . . .

So many events have occurred within the last four years which have necessarily called forth—sometimes under circumstances the most delicate and painful—my views of the principles and policy which ought to be pursued by the General Government that I need on this occasion but allude to a few leading considerations connected with some of them.

The foreign policy adopted by our Government soon after the formation of our present Constitution, and very generally pursued by successive Administrations, has been crowned with almost complete success, and has elevated our character among the nations of the earth. To do justice to all and to submit to wrong from none has been during my Administration its governing maxim, and so happy have been its results that we are not only at peace with all the world, but have few causes of controversy, and those of minor importance, remaining unadjusted.

In the domestic policy of this Government there are two objects which especially deserve the attention of the people and their representatives, and which have been and will continue to be the subjects of my increasing solicitude. They are the preservation of the rights of the several States and the integrity of the Union.

These great objects are necessarily connected, and can only be attained by an enlightened exercise of the powers of each within its appropriate sphere in conformity with the public will constitutionally expressed. To this end it becomes the duty of all to yield a ready and patriotic submission to the laws constitutionally enacted and thereby promote and strengthen a proper confidence in those institutions of the several States and of the United States which the people themselves have ordained for their own government.

My experience in public concerns and the observation of a life somewhat advanced confirm the opinions long since imbibed by me, that the destruction of our State governments or the annihilation of their control over the local concerns of the people would lead directly to revolution and anarchy, and finally to despotism and military domination. In proportion, therefore, as the General Government encroaches upon the rights of the States, in the same proportion does it impair its own power and detract from its ability to fulfill the purposes of its creation. Solemnly impressed with these considerations, my countrymen will ever find me ready to exercise my constitutional powers in arresting measures which may directly or indirectly encroach upon the rights of the States or tend to consolidate all political power in the General Government. But of equal and, indeed of incalculable, importance is the union of these States, and the sacred duty of all to contribute to its preservation by a liberal support of the General Government in the exercise of its just powers. You have been wisely admonished to "accustom yourselves to think and speak of the Union as of the palladium of your political safety and prosperity, watching for its preservation with Jealous anxiety, discountenancing whatever may suggest even a suspicion that it can in any event be abandoned, and indignantly frowning upon the first dawning of any attempt to alienate any portion of our country from the rest or to enfeeble the sacred ties which now link together the various parts." Without union our independence and liberty would never have been achieved; without union they never can be maintained. Divided into twenty-four, or even a smaller number, of separate communities, we shall see our internal trade burdened with numberless restraints and exactions; communication between distant points and sections obstructed or cut off; our sons made soldiers to deluge with blood the fields they now till in peace; the mass of our people borne down and impoverished by taxes to support armies and navies, and military leaders at the head of their victorious legions becoming our lawgivers and judges. The loss of liberty, of all good government, of peace, plenty, and happiness, must inevitably follow a dissolution of the Union. In supporting it, therefore, we support all that is dear to the freeman and the philanthropist.

The time at which I stand before you is full of interest. The eyes of all nations are fixed on our Republic. The event of the existing crisis will be decisive in the opinion of mankind of the practicability of our federal system of government. Great is the stake placed in our hands; great is the responsibility which must rest upon the people of the United States. Let us realize the importance of the attitude in which we stand before the world. Let us exercise forbearance and firmness. Let us extricate our country from the dangers which surround it and learn wisdom from the lessons they inculcate.

Deeply impressed with the truth of these observations, and under the obligation of that solemn oath which I am about to take, I shall continue to exert all my faculties to maintain the just powers of the Constitution and to transmit unimpaired to posterity the blessings of our Federal Union. At the same time, it will be my aim to inculcate by my official acts the necessity of exercising by the General Government those powers only that are clearly delegated; to encourage simplicity and economy in the expenditures of the Government; to raise no more money from the people than may be requisite for these objects, and in a manner that will best promote the interests of all classes of the community and of all portions of the Union. Constantly bearing in mind that in entering into society "individuals must give up a share of liberty to preserve the rest," it will be my desire so to discharge my duties as to foster with our brethren in all parts of the country a spirit of liberal concession and compromise, and, by reconciling our fellow-citizens to those partial sacrifices which they must unavoidably make for the preservation of a greater good, to recommend our invaluable Government and Union to the confidence and affections of the American people.

Finally, it is my most fervent prayer to that Almighty Being before whom I now stand, and who has kept us in His hands from the infancy of our Republic to the present day, that He will so overrule all my intentions and actions and inspire the hearts of my fellow-citizens that we may be preserved from dangers of all kinds and continue forever a united and happy people.

MARTIN VAN BUREN

March 4, 1837

Martin Van Buren was a consummate politician, the Little Magician who shrewdly manipulated party politics to gain power and affect public policy. Ascending to the presidency as Jackson's ally and successor, Van Buren would in a very long and convoluted address paint a rosy picture of the nation's prosperity; a few months later, however, the Panic of 1837 made hash of Van Buren's optimism and contributed to his status as a one-term president. Van Buren was also the first president to address directly the growing unrest over the subject of slavery; and here too he expressed what would turn out to be an overly optimistic assessment.

The practice of all my predecessors imposes on me an obligation I cheerfully fulfill—to accompany the first and solemn act of my public trust with an avowal of the principles that will guide me in performing it and an expression of my feelings on assuming a charge so responsible and vast. . . .

Though not altogether exempt from embarrassments that disturb our tranquility [sic] at home and threaten it abroad, yet in all the attributes of a great, happy, and flourishing people we stand without a parallel in the world. Abroad we enjoy the respect and, with scarcely an exception, the friendship of every nation; at home, while our Government quietly but efficiently performs the sole legitimate end of political institutions—in doing the greatest good to the greatest number—we present an aggregate of human prosperity surely not elsewhere to be found.

How imperious, then, is the obligation imposed upon every citizen, in his own sphere of action, whether limited or extended, to exert himself in perpetuating a condition of things so singularly happy! . . .

Half a century, teeming with extraordinary events, and elsewhere producing astonishing results, has passed along, but on our institutions it has left no injurious mark. From a small community we have risen to a people powerful in numbers and in strength; but with our increase has gone hand in hand the progress of just principles. The privileges, civil and religious, of the humblest individual are still sacredly protected at home, and while the valor and fortitude of our people have removed far from us the slightest apprehension of foreign power, they have not yet induced us in a single instance to forget what is right. Our commerce has been extended to the remotest nations; the value and even nature of our productions have been greatly changed; a wide difference has arisen in the relative wealth and resources of every portion of our country; yet the spirit of mutual regard and of faithful adherence to existing compacts has continued to prevail in our councils and never long been absent from our conduct. We have learned by experience a fruitful lesson—that an implicit and undeviating adherence to the principles on which we set out can carry us prosperously onward through all the conflicts of circumstances and vicissitudes inseparable from the lapse of years.

The success that has thus attended our great experiment is in itself a sufficient cause for gratitude, on account of the happiness it has actually conferred and the example it has unanswerably given. But to me, my fellow-citizens, looking forward to the far-distant future with ardent prayers and confiding hopes, this retrospect presents a ground for still deeper delight. It impresses on my mind a firm belief that the perpetuity of our institutions depends upon ourselves; that if we maintain the principles on which they were established they are destined to confer their benefits on countless generations yet to come, and that America will present to every friend of mankind the cheering proof that a popular government, wisely formed, is wanting in no element of endurance or strength. Fifty years ago its rapid failure was boldly predicted. Latent and uncontrollable causes of dissolution were supposed to exist even by the wise and good, and not only did unfriendly or speculative theorists anticipate for us the fate of past republics, but the fears of many an honest patriot overbalanced his sanguine hopes. Look back on these forebodings, not hastily but reluctantly made, and see how in every instance they have completely failed. . . .

Certain danger was foretold from the extension of our territory, the multiplication of States, and the increase of population. Our system was supposed to be adapted only to boundaries comparatively narrow. These have been widened beyond conjecture; the members of our Confederacy are already doubled, and the numbers of our people are incredibly augmented. The alleged causes of danger have long surpassed anticipation, but none of the consequences have followed. The power and influence of the Republic have arisen to a height obvious to all mankind; respect for its authority was not more apparent at its ancient than it is at its present limits; new and inexhaustible sources of general prosperity have been opened; the effects of distance have been averted by the inventive genius of our people, developed and fostered by the spirit of our institutions; and the enlarged variety and amount of interests, productions, and pursuits have strengthened the chain of mutual dependence and formed a circle of mutual benefits too apparent ever to be overlooked.

In justly balancing the powers of the Federal and State authorities difficulties nearly insurmountable arose at the outset and subsequent collisions were deemed inevitable. Amid these it was scarcely believed possible that a scheme of government so complex in construction could remain uninjured. From time to time embarrassments have certainly occurred; but how just is the confidence of future safety imparted by the knowledge that each in succession has been happily removed! Overlooking partial and temporary evils as inseparable from the practical operation of all human institutions, and looking only to the general result, every patriot has reason to be satisfied. . . .

The last, perhaps the greatest, of the prominent sources of discord and disaster supposed to lurk in our political condition was the institution of domestic slavery. Our forefathers were deeply impressed with the delicacy of this subject, and they treated it with a forbearance so evidently wise that in spite of every sinister foreboding it never until the present period disturbed the tranquillity of our common country. Such a result is sufficient evidence of the justice and the patriotism of their course; it is evidence not to be mistaken that an adherence to it can prevent all embarrassment from this as well as from every other anticipated cause of difficulty or danger. . . . Perceiving before my election the deep interest this subject was beginning to excite, I believed it a solemn duty fully to make known my sentiments in regard to it. . . . I then declared that if the desire of those of my countrymen who were favorable to my election was gratified "I must go into the Presidential chair the inflexible and uncompromising opponent of every attempt on the part of Congress to abolish slavery in the District of Columbia against the wishes of the slaveholding States, and also with a determination equally decided to resist the slightest interference with it in the States where it exists." . . . It now only remains to add that no bill conflicting with these views can ever receive my constitutional sanction. These opinions have been adopted in the firm belief that they are in accordance with the spirit that actuated the venerated fathers of the Republic, and that succeeding experience has proved them to be humane, patriotic, expedient, honorable, and just. If the agitation of this subject was intended to reach the stability of our institutions, enough has occurred to show that it has signally failed, and that in this as in every other instance the apprehensions of the timid and the hopes of the wicked for the destruction of our Government are again destined to be disappointed. . . .

What can be more gratifying than such a retrospect as this? We look back on obstacles avoided and dangers overcome, on expectations more than realized and prosperity perfectly secured. To the hopes of the hostile, the fears of the timid, and the doubts of the anxious actual experience has given the conclusive reply. We have seen time gradually dispel every unfavorable foreboding and our Constitution surmount every adverse circumstance dreaded at the outset as beyond control. . . .

WILLIAM HENRY HARRISON

March 4, 1841

In a long speech that wound its way back to classic antiquity, Harrison hit upon most of the major themes that dominated politics of the Jacksonian Era: assurances of limited presidential power (Harrison had previously and here again pledged himself to a single term in office); separation of executive and legislative operations; and a strict and limited interpretation of the Constitution. Harrison also sounded warnings about the growing agitation over slavery and reiterated his predecessors' promises to deal in a kindly, paternalistic manner with the Indians—promises that were at best imperfectly realized.

Called from a retirement which I had supposed was to continue for the residue of my life to fill the chief executive office of this great and free nation, I appear before you, fellow-citizens, to take the oaths which the Constitution prescribes as a necessary qualification for the performance of its duties. . . .

There are certain rights possessed by each individual American citizen which in his compact with the others he has never surrendered. Some of them, indeed, he is unable to surrender, being, in the language of our system, unalienable. . . . These precious privileges, and those scarcely less important of giving expression to his thoughts and opinions . . . [derive] from no charter granted by his fellow-man. He claims them because he is himself a man, fashioned by the same Almighty hand as the rest of his species and entitled to a full share of the blessings with which He has endowed them. Notwithstanding the limited sovereignty possessed by the people of the United States and the restricted grant of power to the Government which they have adopted, enough has been given to accomplish all the objects for which it was created. It has been found powerful in war, and hitherto justice has been administered, and intimate union effected [sic], domestic tranquility [sic] preserved, and personal liberty secured to the citizen. As was to be expected, however, from the defect of language and the necessarily sententious manner in which the Constitution is written, disputes have arisen as to the amount of power which it has actually granted or was intended to grant. . . .

The great danger to our institutions does not appear to me to be in a usurpation by the Government of power not granted by the people, but by the accumulation in one of the departments of that which was assigned to others. Limited as are the powers which have been granted, still enough have been granted to constitute a despotism if concentrated in one of the departments. This danger is greatly heightened, as it has been always observable that men are less jealous of encroachments of one department upon another than upon their own reserved rights. When the Constitution of the United States first came from the hands of the Convention which formed it, many of the sternest republicans of the day were alarmed at the extent of the power which had been granted to the Federal Government, and more particularly of that portion which had been assigned to the executive branch. There were in it features which appeared not to be in harmony with their ideas of a simple representative democracy or republic, and knowing the tendency of power to increase itself, particularly when exercised by a single individual, predictions were made that at no very remote period the Government would terminate in virtual monarchy. It would not become me to say that the fears of these patriots have been already realized; but as I sincerely believe that the tendency of measures and of men's opinions for some years past has been in that direction, it is, I conceive, strictly proper that I should take this occasion to repeat the assurances I have heretofore given of my determination to arrest the progress of that tendency if it really exists and restore the Government to its pristine health and vigor, as far as this can be effected by any legitimate exercise of the power placed in my hands.

I proceed to state in as summary a manner as I can my opinion of the sources of the evils which have been so extensively complained of and the correctives which may be applied. Some of the former are unquestionably to be found in the defects of the Constitution; others, in my judgment, are attributable to a misconstruction of some of its provisions. Of the former is the eligibility of the same individual to a second term of the Presidency. . . . Republics can commit no greater error than to adopt or continue any feature in their systems of government which may be calculated to create or increase the lover of power in the bosoms of those to whom necessity obliges them to commit the management of their affairs; and surely nothing is more likely to produce such a state of mind than the long continuance of an office of high trust. . . . I give my aid to it by renewing the pledge heretofore given that under no circumstances will I consent to serve a second term. . . .

To assist or control Congress . . . in its ordinary legislation could not, I conceive, have been the motive for conferring the veto power on the President. . . .

I consider the veto power, therefore given by the Constitution to the Executive of the United States solely as a conservative power, to be used only first, to protect the Constitution from violation; secondly, the people from the effects of hasty legislation where their will has been probably disregarded or not well understood, and, thirdly, to prevent the effects of combinations violative of the rights of minorities. . . .

The General Government has seized upon none of the reserved rights of the States. As far as any open warfare may have gone, the State authorities have amply maintained their rights. . . . But there is still an undercurrent at work by which, if not seasonably checked, the worst apprehensions of our antifederal patriots will be realized, and not only will the State authorities be overshadowed by the great increase of power in the executive department of the General Government, but the character of that Government, if not its designation, be essentially and radically changed. This state of things has been in part effected by causes inherent in the Constitution and in part by the never-failing tendency of political power to increase itself. By making the President the sole distributer [sic] of all the patronage of the Government the framers of the Constitution do not appear to have anticipated at how short a period it would become a formidable instrument to control the free operations of the State governments. . . . But it is not by the extent of its patronage alone that the executive department has become dangerous, but by the use which it appears may be made of the appointing power to bring under its control the whole revenues of the country. . . . It was certainly a great error in the framers of the Constitution not to have made the officer at the head of the Treasury Department entirely independent of the Executive. He should at least have been removable only upon the demand of the popular branch of the Legislature. I have determined never to remove a Secretary of the Treasury without communicating all the circumstances attending such removal to both Houses of Congress. . . .

There is no part of the means placed in the hands of the Executive which might be used with greater effect for unhallowed purposes than the control of the public press. The maxim which our ancestors derived from the mother country that "the freedom of the press is the great bulwark of civil and religious liberty" is one of the most precious legacies which they have left us. We have learned, too, from our own as well as the experience of other countries, that golden shackles, by whomsoever or by whatever pretense imposed, are as fatal to it as the iron bonds of despotism. The presses in the necessary employment of the Government should never be used "to clear the guilty or to varnish crime." A decent and manly examination of the acts of the Government should be not only tolerated, but encouraged.

Upon another occasion I have given my opinion at some length upon the impropriety of Executive interference in the legislation of Congress—that the article in the Constitution making it the duty of the President to communicate information and authorizing him to recommend measures was not intended to make him the source in legislation, and, in particular, that he should never be looked to for schemes of finance. . . . The delicate duty of devising schemes of revenue should be left where the Constitution has placed it—with the immediate representatives of the people. For similar reasons the mode of keeping the public treasure should be prescribed by them, and the further removed it may be from the control of the Executive the more wholesome the arrangement and the more in accordance with republican principle. . . .

I have spoken of the necessity of keeping the respective departments of the Government, as well as all the other authorities of our country, within their appropriate orbits. This is a matter of difficulty in some cases, as the powers which they respectively claim are often not defined by any distinct lines. Mischievous, however, in their tendencies as collisions of this kind may be, those which arise between the respective communities which for certain purposes compose one nation are much more so, for no such nation can long exist without the careful culture of those feelings of confidence and affection which are the effective bonds to union between free and confederated states. Strong as is the tie of interest, it has been often found ineffectual. Men blinded by their passions have been known to adopt measures for their country in direct opposition to all the suggestions of policy. The alternative, then, is to destroy or keep down a bad passion by creating and fostering a good one, and this seems to be the corner stone upon which our American political architects have reared the fabric of our Government. The cement which was to bind it and perpetuate its existence was the affectionate attachment between all its members. To insure the continuance of this feeling, produced at first by a community of dangers, of sufferings, and of interests, the advantages of each were made accessible to all. . . . The lines, too, separating powers to be exercised by the citizens of one State from those of another seem to be so distinctly drawn as to leave no room for misunderstanding. The citizens of each State unite in their persons all the privileges which that character confers and all that they may claim as citizens of the United States, but in no case can the same persons at the same time act as the citizen of two separate States, and he is therefore positively precluded from any interference with the reserved powers of any State but that of which he is for the time being a citizen. . . . Our citizens must be content with the exercise of the powers with which the Constitution clothes them. The attempt of those of one State to control the domestic institutions of another can only result in feelings of distrust and jealousy, the certain harbingers of disunion, violence, and civil war, and the ultimate destruction of our free institutions. Our Confederacy is perfectly illustrated by the terms and principles governing a common copartnership There is a fund of power to be exercised under the direction of the joint councils of the allied members, but that which has been reserved by the individual members is intangible by the common Government or the individual members composing it. To attempt it finds no support in the principles of our Constitution. . . .

When the genuine spirit of liberty animates the body of a people to a thorough examination of their affairs, it leads to the excision of every excrescence which may have fastened itself upon any of the departments of the government, and restores the system to its pristine health and beauty. But the reign of an intolerant spirit of party amongst a free people seldom fails to result in a dangerous accession to the executive power introduced and established amidst unusual professions of devotion to democracy.

The foregoing remarks relate almost exclusively to matters connected with our domestic concerns. It may be proper, however, that I should give some indications to my fellow-citizens of my proposed course of conduct in the management of our foreign relations. . . . Long the defender of my country's rights in the field, I trust that my fellow-citizens will not see in my earnest desire to preserve peace with foreign powers any indication that their rights will ever be sacrificed or the honor of the nation tarnished by any admission on the part of their Chief Magistrate unworthy of their former glory. In our intercourse with our aboriginal neighbors [Native Americans] the same liberality and justice which marked the course prescribed to me by two of my illustrious predecessors when acting under their direction in the discharge of the duties of superintendent and commissioner shall be strictly observed. I can conceive of no more sublime spectacle, none more likely to propitiate an impartial and common Creator, than a rigid adherence to the principles of justice on the part of a powerful nation in its transactions with a weaker and uncivilized people whom circumstances have placed at its disposal. . . .

I deem the present occasion sufficiently important and solemn to justify me in expressing to my fellow-citizens a profound reverence for the Christian religion and a thorough conviction that sound morals, religious liberty, and a just sense of religious responsibility are essentially connected with all true and lasting happiness; and to that good Being who has blessed us by the gifts of civil and religious freedom, who watched over and prospered the labors of our fathers and has hitherto preserved to us institutions far exceeding in excellence those of any other people, let us unite in fervently commending every interest of our beloved country in all future time.

Fellow-citizens, being fully invested with that high office to which the partiality of my countrymen has called me, I now take an affectionate leave of you. You will bear with you to your homes the remembrance of the pledge I have this day given to discharge all the high duties of my exalted station according to the best of my ability, and I shall enter upon their performance with entire confidence in the support of a just and generous people.

JAMES K. POLK

March 4, 1845

Harrison died after only a few months in office, and his successor, John Tyler, was not reelected, so quite a bit of time had elapsed before another president was given occasion to deliver an Inaugural Address. When Polk did so in 1845, the issues of western expansion—particularly the troublesome question of Texas—and sectional agitation over slavery had come to dominate national politics. The new president felt compelled to address these matters at length.

Without solicitation on my part, I have been chosen by the free and voluntary suffrages of my countrymen to the most honorable and most responsible office on earth. I am deeply impressed with gratitude for the confidence reposed in me. Honored with this distinguished consideration at an earlier period of life than any of my predecessors, I can not disguise the diffidence with which I am about to enter on the discharge of my official duties. . . .

It will be my first care to administer the Government in the true spirit of [the Constitution], and to assume no powers not expressly granted or clearly implied in its terms. The Government of the United States is one of delegated and limited powers, and it is by a strict adherence to the clearly granted powers and by abstaining from the exercise of doubtful or unauthorized implied powers that we have the only sure guaranty against the recurrence of those unfortunate collisions between the Federal and State authorities which have occasionally so much disturbed the harmony of our system and even threatened the perpetuity of our glorious Union. . . .

Each State is a complete sovereignty within the sphere of its reserved powers. The Government of the Union, acting within the sphere of its delegated authority, is also a complete sovereignty. While the General Government should abstain from the exercise of authority not clearly delegated to it, the States should be equally careful that in the maintenance of their rights they do not overstep the limits of powers reserved to them. . . . To the Government of the United States has been intrusted the exclusive management of our foreign affairs. Beyond that it wields a few general enumerated powers. It does not force reform on the States. It leaves individuals, over whom it casts its protecting influence, entirely free to improve their own condition by the legitimate exercise of all their mental and physical powers. It is a common protector of each and all the

States; of every man who lives upon our soil, whether of native or foreign birth; of every religious sect, in their worship of the Almighty according to the dictates of their own conscience; of every shade of opinion, and the most free inquiry; of every art, trade, and occupation consistent with the laws of the States. And we rejoice in the general happiness, prosperity, and advancement of our country, which have been the offspring of freedom, and not of power. . . .

It will be my desire to guard against that most fruitful source of danger to the harmonious action of our system which consists in substituting the mere discretion and caprice of the Executive or of majorities in the legislative department of the Government for powers which have been withheld from the Federal Government by the Constitution. By the theory of our Government majorities rule, but this right is not an arbitrary or unlimited one. It is a right to be exercised in subordination to the Constitution and in conformity to it. One great object of the Constitution was to restrain majorities from oppressing minorities or encroaching upon their just rights. Minorities have a right to appeal to the Constitution as a shield against such oppression.

That the blessings of liberty which our Constitution secures may be enjoyed alike by minorities and majorities, the Executive has been wisely invested with a qualified veto upon the acts of the Legislature. It is a negative power, and is conservative in its character. It arrests for the time hasty, inconsiderate, or unconstitutional legislation, invites reconsideration, and transfers questions at issue between the legislative and executive departments to the tribunal of the people. Like all other powers, it is subject to be abused. When judiciously and properly exercised, the Constitution itself may be saved from infraction and the rights of all preserved and protected.

The inestimable value of our Federal Union is felt and acknowledged by all. By this system of united and confederated States our people are permitted collectively and individually to seek their own happiness in their own way, and the consequences have been most auspicious. Since the Union was formed the number of the States has increased from thirteen to twenty-eight; two of these have taken their position as members of the Confederacy within the last week. Our population has increased from three to twenty millions. New communities and States are seeking protection under its aegis, and multitudes from the Old World are flocking to our shores to participate in its blessings. Beneath its benign sway peace and prosperity prevail. Freed from the burdens and miseries of war, our trade and intercourse have extended throughout the world. Mind, no longer tasked in devising means to accomplish or resist schemes of ambition, usurpation, or conquest, is devoting itself to man's true interests in developing his faculties and powers and the capacity of nature to minister to his enjoyments. Genius is free to announce its inventions and discoveries, and the hand is free to accomplish whatever the head conceives not incompatible with the rights of a fellow-being. All distinctions of birth or of rank have been abolished. All citizens, whether native or adopted, are placed upon terms of precise equality. All are entitled to equal rights and equal protection. No union exists between church and state, and perfect freedom of opinion is guaranteed to all sects and creeds.

These are some of the blessings secured to our happy land by our Federal Union. To perpetuate them it is our sacred duty to preserve it. Who shall assign limits to the achievements of free minds and free hands under the protection of this glorious Union? No treason to mankind since the organization of society would be equal in atrocity to that of him who would lift his hand to destroy it. He would overthrow the noblest structure of human wisdom, which protects himself and his fellow-man. He would stop the progress of free government and involve his country either in anarchy or despotism. He would extinguish the fire of liberty, which warms and animates the hearts of happy millions and invites all the nations of the earth to imitate our example. If he say that error and wrong are committed in the administration of the Government, let him remember that nothing human can be perfect, and that under no other system of government revealed by Heaven or devised by man has reason been allowed so free and broad a scope to combat error. Has the sword of despots proved to be a safer or surer instrument of reform in government than enlightened reason? Does he expect to find among the ruins of this Union a happier abode for our swarming millions than they now have under it? Every lover of his country must shudder at the thought of the possibility of its dissolution, and will be ready to adopt the patriotic sentiment, "Our Federal Union—it must be preserved." To preserve it the compromises which alone enabled our fathers to form a common Constitution for the government and protection of so many States and distinct communities, of such diversified habits, interests, and domestic institutions, must be sacredly and religiously observed. Any attempt to disturb or destroy these compromises, being terms of the compact of union, can lead to none other than the most ruinous and disastrous consequences.

It is a source of deep regret that in some sections of our country misguided persons have occasionally indulged in schemes and agitations whose object is the destruction of domestic institutions existing in other sections—institutions which existed at the adoption of the Constitution and were recognized and protected by it. All must see that if it were possible for them to be successful in attaining their object the dissolution of the Union and the consequent destruction of our happy form of government must speedily follow.

I am happy to believe that at every period of our existence as a nation there has existed, and continues to exist, among the great mass of our people a devotion to the Union of the States which will shield and protect it against the moral treason of any who would seriously contemplate its destruction. To secure a continuance of that devotion the compromises of the Constitution must not only be preserved, but sectional jealousies and heartburnings must be discountenanced, and all should remember that they are members of the same political family, having a common destiny. To increase the attachment of our people to the Union, our laws should be just. Any policy which shall tend to favor monopolies or the peculiar interests of sections or classes must operate to the prejudice of the interest of their fellow-citizens, and should be avoided. If the compromises of the Constitution be preserved, if sectional jealousies and heartburnings be discountenanced, if our laws be just and the Government be practically administered strictly within the limits of power prescribed to it, we may discard all apprehensions for the safety of the Union.

With these views of the nature, character, and objects of the Government and the value of the Union, I shall steadily oppose the creation of those institutions and systems which in their nature tend to pervert it from its legitimate purposes and make it the instrument of sections, classes, and individuals. . . .

The Republic of Texas has made known her desire to come into our Union, to form a part of our Confederacy and enjoy with us the blessings of liberty secured and guaranteed by our Constitution. Texas was once a part of our country—was unwisely ceded away to a foreign power—is now independent, and possesses an undoubted right to dispose of a part or the whole of her territory and to merge her sovereignty as a separate and independent state in ours. I congratulate my country that by an act of the late Congress of the United States the assent of this Government has been given to the reunion, and it only remains for the two countries to agree upon the terms to consummate an object so important to both.

I regard the question of annexation as belonging exclusively to the United States and Texas. They are independent powers competent to contract, and foreign nations have no right to interfere with them or to take exceptions to their reunion. Foreign powers do not seem to appreciate the true character of our Government. Our Union is a confederation of independent States, whose policy is peace with each other and all the world. To enlarge its limits is to extend the dominions of peace over additional territories and increasing millions. The world has nothing to fear from military ambition in our Government. While the Chief Magistrate and the popular branch of Congress are elected for short terms by the suffrages of those millions who must in their own persons bear all the burdens and miseries of war, our Government can not be otherwise than pacific. Foreign powers should therefore look on the annexation of Texas to the United States not as the conquest of a nation seeking to extend her dominions by arms and violence, but as the peaceful acquisition of a territory once her own, by adding another member to our confederation, with the consent of that member, thereby diminishing the chances of war and opening to them new and ever-increasing markets for their products.

To Texas the reunion is important, because the strong protecting arm of our Government would be extended over her, and the vast resources of her fertile soil and genial climate would be speedily developed, while the safety of New Orleans and of our whole southwestern frontier against hostile aggression, as well as the interests of the whole Union, would be promoted by it. . . .

None can fail to see the danger to our safety and future peace if Texas remains an independent state or becomes an ally or dependency of some foreign nation more powerful than herself. Is there one among our citizens who would not prefer perpetual peace with Texas to occasional wars, which so often occur between bordering independent nations? Is there one who would not prefer free intercourse with her to high duties on all our products and manufactures which enter her ports or cross her frontiers? Is there one who would not prefer an unrestricted communication with her citizens to the frontier obstructions which must occur if she remains out of the Union? Whatever is good or evil in the local institutions of Texas will remain her own whether annexed to the United States or not. None of the present States will be responsible for them any more than they are for the local institutions of each other. They have confederated together for certain specified objects. Upon the same principle that they would refuse to form a perpetual union with Texas because of her local institutions our forefathers would have been prevented from forming our present Union. Perceiving no valid objection to the measure and many reasons for its adoption vitally affecting the peace, the safety, and the prosperity of both countries, I shall on the broad principle which formed the basis and produced the adoption of our Constitution, and not in any narrow spirit of sectional policy, endeavor by all Constitutional, honorable, and appropriate means to consummate the expressed will of the people and Government of the United States by the re-annexation of Texas to our Union at the earliest practicable period.

Nor will it become in a less degree my duty to assert and maintain by all Constitutional means the right of the United States to that portion of our territory which lies beyond the Rocky Mountains. Our title to the country of the Oregon is "clear and unquestionable," and already are our people preparing to perfect that title by occupying it with their wives and children. But eighty years ago our population was confined on the west by the ridge of the Alleghanies [sic]. Within that period—within the lifetime, I might say, of some of my hearers—our people, increasing to many millions, have filled the eastern valley of the Mississippi, adventurously ascended the Missouri to its headsprings, and are already engaged in establishing the blessings of self-government in valleys of which the rivers flow to the Pacific. The world beholds the peaceful triumphs of the industry of our emigrants. To us belongs the duty of protecting them adequately wherever they may be upon our soil. The jurisdiction of our laws and the benefits of our republican institutions should be extended over them in the distant regions which they have selected for their homes. The increasing facilities of intercourse will easily bring the States, of which the formation in that part of our territory can not be long delayed, within the sphere of our federative Union. In the meantime every obligation imposed by treaty or conventional stipulations should be sacredly respected. . . .

Although in our country the Chief Magistrate must almost of necessity be chosen by a party and stand pledged to its principles and measures, yet in his official action he should not be the President of a part only, but of the whole people of the United States. While he executes the laws with an impartial hand, shrinks from no proper responsibility, and faithfully carries out in the executive department of the Government the principles and policy of those who have chosen him, he should not be unmindful that our fellow-citizens who have differed with him in opinion are entitled to the full and free exercise of their opinions and judgments, and that the rights of all are entitled to respect and regard.

Confidently relying upon the aid and assistance of the coordinate departments of the Government in conducting our public affairs, I enter upon the discharge of the high duties which have been assigned me by the people, again humbly supplicating that Divine Being who has watched over and protected our beloved country from its infancy to the present hour to continue His gracious benedictions upon us, that we may continue to be a prosperous and happy people.

ZACHARY TAYLOR

March 5, 1849

Zachary Taylor was elected president largely on the basis of his record as a military general and hero during the Mexican War; little was known of his politics, and the Whigs preferred to keep it that way, the better to broaden his appeal. Taylor's Inaugural Address reflected this vagueness, and offered few clues concerning how he might go about fashioning solutions to the troubling questions of his time, especially those regarding slavery and western expansion.

Elected by the American people to the highest office known to our laws, I appear here to take the oath prescribed by the Constitution, and, in compliance with a time-honored custom, to address those who are now assembled . . . .

I am conscious that the position which I have been called to fill, though sufficient to satisfy the loftiest ambition, is surrounded by fearful responsibilities. Happily, however, in the performance of my new duties I shall not be without able cooperation. The legislative and judicial branches of the Government present prominent examples of distinguished civil attainments and matured experience, and it shall be my endeavor to call to my assistance in the Executive Departments individuals whose talents, integrity, and purity of character will furnish ample guaranties for the faithful and honorable performance of the trusts to be committed to their charge. With such aids and an honest purpose to do whatever is right, I hope to execute diligently, impartially, and for the best interests of the country the manifold duties devolved upon me . . . .

To command the Army and Navy of the United States; with the advice and consent of the Senate, to make treaties and to appoint ambassadors and other officers; to give to Congress information of the state of the Union and recommend such measures as he shall judge to be necessary; and to take care that the laws shall be faithfully executed— these are the most important functions intrusted to the President by the Constitution, and it may be expected that I shall briefly indicate the principles which will control me in their execution.

Chosen by the body of the people under the assurance that my Administration would be devoted to the welfare of the whole country, and not to the support of any particular section or merely local interest, I this day renew the declarations I have heretofore made and proclaim my fixed determination to maintain to the extent of my ability the Government in its original purity and to adopt as the basis of my public policy those great republican doctrines which constitute the strength of our national existence.

In reference to the Army and Navy, lately employed with so much distinction on active service, care shall be taken to insure the highest condition of efficiency, and in furtherance of that object the military and naval schools, sustained by the liberality of Congress, shall receive the special attention of the Executive.

As American freemen we can not but sympathize in all efforts to extend the blessings of civil and political liberty, but at the same time we are warned by the admonitions of history and the voice of our own beloved Washington to abstain from entangling alliances with foreign nations. In all disputes between conflicting governments it is our interest not less than our duty to remain strictly neutral, while our geographical position, the genius of our institutions and our people, the advancing spirit of civilization, and, above all, the dictates of religion direct us to the cultivation of peaceful and friendly relations with all other powers. It is to be hoped that no international question can now arise which a government confident in its own strength and resolved to protect its own just rights may not settle by wise negotiation; and it eminently becomes a government like our own, founded on the morality and intelligence of its citizens and upheld by their affections, to exhaust every resort of honorable diplomacy before appealing to arms. In the conduct of our foreign relations I shall conform to these views, as I believe them essential to the best interests and the true honor of the country.

The appointing power vested in the President imposes delicate and onerous duties. So far as it is possible to be informed, I shall make honesty, capacity, and fidelity indispensable prerequisites to the bestowal of office, and the absence of either of these qualities shall be deemed sufficient cause for removal.

It shall be my study to recommend such constitutional measures to Congress as may be necessary and proper to secure encouragement and protection to the great interests of agriculture, commerce, and manufactures, to improve our rivers and harbors, to provide for the speedy extinguishment of the public debt, to enforce a strict accountability on the part of all officers of the Government and the utmost economy in all public expenditures; but it is for the wisdom of Congress itself, in which all legislative powers are vested by the Constitution, to regulate these and other matters of domestic policy. I shall look with confidence to the enlightened patriotism of that body to adopt such measures of conciliation as may harmonize conflicting interests and tend to perpetuate that Union which should be the paramount object of our hopes and affections. In any action calculated to promote an object so near the heart of everyone who truly loves his country I will zealously unite with the coordinate branches of the Government.

In conclusion I congratulate you, my fellow-citizens, upon the high state of prosperity to which the goodness of Divine Providence has conducted our common country. Let us invoke a continuance of the same protecting care which has led us from small beginnings to the eminence we this day occupy, and let us seek to deserve that continuance by prudence and moderation in our councils, by well-directed attempts to assuage the bitterness which too often marks unavoidable differences of opinion, by the promulgation and practice of just and liberal principles, and by an enlarged patriotism, which shall acknowledge no limits but those of our own widespread Republic.

FRANKLIN PIERCE

March 4, 1853

Pierce was, in the parlance of the time, a "doughface" president: a bland man who was inoffensive enough and possessed enough northern and southern sympathies to be acceptable to both sections of the Democratic Party. In his address, Pierce offered a typical doughface perspective on slavery and sectionalism. Pierce's enthusiasm for expansion is also evident, as is his rather jingoistic view of Europe.

My Countrymen:

It is a relief to feel that no heart but my own can know the personal regret and bitter sorrow over which I have been borne to a position so suitable for others rather than desirable for myself. . . .

One of the most impressive evidences of [the Founding Fathers'] wisdom is to be found in the fact that the actual working of our system has dispelled a degree of solicitude which at the outset disturbed bold hearts and far-reaching intellects. The apprehension of dangers from extended territory, multiplied States, accumulated wealth, and augmented population has proved to be unfounded. The stars upon your banner have become nearly threefold their original number; your densely populated possessions skirt the shores of the two great oceans; and yet this vast increase of people and territory has not only shown itself compatible with the harmonious action of the States and Federal Government in their respective constitutional spheres, but has afforded an additional guaranty of the strength and integrity of both.

With an experience thus suggestive and cheering, the policy of my Administration will not be controlled by any timid forebodings of evil from expansion. Indeed, it is not to be disguised that our attitude as a nation and our position on the globe render the acquisition of certain possessions not within our jurisdiction eminently important for our protection, if not in the future essential for the preservation of the rights of commerce and the peace of the world. Should they be obtained, it will be through no grasping spirit, but with a view to obvious national interest and security, and in a manner entirely consistent with the strictest observance of national faith. We have nothing in our history or position to invite aggression; we have everything to beckon us to the cultivation of relations of peace and amity with all nations. . . .

The great objects of our pursuit as a people are best to be attained by peace, and are entirely consistent with the tranquillity and interests of the rest of mankind. With the neighboring nations upon our continent we should cultivate kindly and fraternal relations. We can desire nothing in regard to them so much as to see them consolidate their strength and pursue the paths of prosperity and happiness. If in the course of their growth we should open new channels of trade and create additional facilities for friendly intercourse, the benefits realized will be equal and mutual. Of the complicated

European systems of national polity we have heretofore been independent. From their wars, their tumults, and anxieties we have been, happily, almost entirely exempt. Whilst these are confined to the nations which gave them existence, and within their legitimate jurisdiction, they can not affect us except as they appeal to our sympathies in the cause of human freedom and universal advancement. But the vast interests of commerce are common to all mankind, and the advantages of trade and international intercourse must always present a noble field for the moral influence of a great people.

With these views firmly and honestly carried out, we have a right to expect, and shall under all circumstances require, prompt reciprocity. The rights which belong to us as a nation are not alone to be regarded, but those which pertain to every citizen in his individual capacity, at home and abroad, must be sacredly maintained. So long as he can discern every star in its place upon that ensign, without wealth to purchase for him preferment or title to secure for him place, it will be his privilege, and must be his acknowledged right, to stand unabashed even in the presence of princes, with a proud consciousness that he is himself one of a nation of sovereigns and that he can not in legitimate pursuit wander so far from home that the agent whom he shall leave behind in the place which I now occupy will not see that no rude hand of power or tyrannical passion is laid upon him with impunity. He must realize that upon every sea and on every soil where our enterprise may rightfully seek the protection of our flag American citizenship is an inviolable panoply for the security of American rights. And in this connection it can hardly be necessary to reaffirm a principle which should now be regarded as fundamental. The rights, security, and repose of this Confederacy reject the idea of interference or colonization on this side of the ocean by any foreign power beyond present jurisdiction as utterly inadmissible. . . .

Good citizens may well claim the protection of good laws and the benign influence of good government, but a claim for office is what the people of a republic should never recognize. No reasonable man of any party will expect the Administration to be so regardless of its responsibility and of the obvious elements of success as to retain persons known to be under the influence of political hostility and partisan prejudice in positions which will require not only severe labor, but cordial cooperation. Having no implied engagements to ratify, no rewards to bestow, no resentments to remember, and no personal wishes to consult in selections for official station, I shall fulfill this difficult and delicate trust, admitting no motive as worthy either of my character or position which does not contemplate an efficient discharge of duty and the best interests of my country. I acknowledge my obligations to the masses of my countrymen, and to them alone. Higher objects than personal aggrandizement gave direction and energy to their exertions in the late canvass, and they shall not be disappointed. They require at my hands diligence, integrity, and capacity wherever there are duties to be performed. Without these qualities in their public servants, more stringent laws for the prevention or punishment of fraud, negligence, and peculation will be vain. With them they will be unnecessary.

But these are not the only points to which you look for vigilant watchfulness. The dangers of a concentration of all power in the general government of a confederacy so vast as ours are too obvious to be disregarded. You have a right, therefore, to expect your agents in every department to regard strictly the limits imposed upon them by the Constitution of the United States. . . . If the Federal Government will confine itself to the exercise of powers clearly granted by the Constitution, it can hardly happen that its action upon any question should endanger the institutions of the States or interfere with their right to manage matters strictly domestic according to the will of their own people.

In expressing briefly my views upon an important subject which has recently agitated the nation to almost a fearful degree, I am moved by no other impulse than a most earnest desire for the perpetuation of that Union which has made us what we are, showering upon us blessings and conferring a power and influence which our fathers could hardly have anticipated, even with their most sanguine hopes directed to a far-off future. The sentiments I now announce were not unknown before the expression of the voice which called me here. My own position upon this subject was clear and unequivocal, upon the record of my words and my acts, and it is only recurred to at this time because silence might perhaps be misconstrued. With the Union my best and dearest earthly hopes are entwined. Without it what are we individually or collectively? What becomes of the noblest field ever opened for the advancement of our race in religion, in government, in the arts, and in all that dignifies and adorns mankind? From that radiant constellation which both illumines our own way and points out to struggling nations their course, let but a single star be lost, and, if these be not utter darkness, the luster of the whole is dimmed. Do my countrymen need any assurance that such a catastrophe is not to overtake them while I possess the power to stay it? It is with me an earnest and vital belief that as the Union has been the source, under Providence, of our prosperity to this time, so it is the surest pledge of a continuance of the blessings we have enjoyed, and which we are sacredly bound to transmit undiminished to our children. The field of calm and free discussion in our country is open, and will always be so, but never has been and never can be traversed for good in a spirit of sectionalism and uncharitableness. The founders of the Republic dealt with things as they were presented to them, in a spirit of self-sacrificing patriotism, and, as time has proved, with a comprehensive wisdom which it will always be safe for us to consult. Every measure tending to strengthen the fraternal feelings of all the members of our Union has had my heartfelt approbation. To every theory of society or government, whether the offspring of feverish ambition or of morbid enthusiasm, calculated to dissolve the bonds of law and affection which unite us, I shall interpose a ready and stern resistance. I believe that involuntary servitude, as it exists in different States of this Confederacy, is recognized by the Constitution. I believe that it stands like any other admitted right, and that the States where it exists are entitled to efficient remedies to enforce the constitutional provisions. I hold that the laws of 1850, commonly called the "compromise measures," are strictly constitutional and to be unhesitatingly carried into effect. I believe that the constituted authorities of this Republic are bound to regard the rights of the South in this respect as they would view any other legal and constitutional right, and that the laws to enforce them should be respected and obeyed, not with a reluctance encouraged by abstract opinions as to their propriety in a different state of society, but cheerfully and according to the decisions of the tribunal to which their exposition belongs. Such have been, and are, my convictions, and upon them I shall act. I fervently hope that the question is at rest, and that no sectional or ambitious or fanatical excitement may again threaten the durability of our institutions or obscure the light of our prosperity.

But let not the foundation of our hope rest upon man's wisdom. It will not be sufficient that sectional prejudices find no place in the public deliberations. It will not be sufficient that the rash counsels of human passion are rejected. It must be felt that there is no national security but in the nation's humble, acknowledged dependence upon God and His overruling providence. . . .

JAMES BUCHANAN

March 4, 1857

Buchanan was cut from the same cloth as Pierce: a mediocre man with northern and southern connections, he fervently wished the entire slavery controversy would simply disappear. He was particularly worried about the bloodshed in Kansas, as pro- and antislavery forces battled over whether that territory's new state constitution should allow slavery. Buchanan's Inaugural Address is notable in its reference to a pending Supreme Court case, Dred Scott v. Sandford, *which he hoped would finally settle the issue. He also issued a lengthy and passionate appeal for extremists on all sides to value the Union.*

I appear before you this day to take the solemn oath "that I will faithfully execute the office of President of the United States and will to the best of my ability preserve, protect, and defend the Constitution of the United States.". . .

We have recently passed through a Presidential contest in which the passions of our fellow-citizens were excited to the highest degree by questions of deep and vital importance; but when the people proclaimed their will the tempest at once subsided and all was calm.

The voice of the majority, speaking in the manner prescribed by the Constitution, was heard, and instant submission followed. Our own country could alone have exhibited so grand and striking a spectacle of the capacity of man for self-government.

What a happy conception, then, was it for Congress to apply this simple rule, that the will of the majority shall govern, to the settlement of the question of domestic slavery in the Territories. Congress is neither "to legislate slavery into any Territory or State nor to exclude it therefrom, but to leave the people thereof perfectly free to form and regulate their domestic institutions in their own way, subject only to the Constitution of the United States."

As a natural consequence, Congress has also prescribed that when the Territory of Kansas shall be admitted as a State it "shall be received into the Union with or without slavery, as their constitution may prescribe at the time of their admission." A difference of opinion has arisen in regard to the point of time when the people of a Territory shall decide this question for themselves.

This is, happily, a matter of but little practical importance. Besides, it is a judicial question, which legitimately belongs to the Supreme Court of the United States, before whom it is now pending, and will, it is understood, be speedily and finally settled. To their decision, in common with all good citizens, I shall cheerfully submit, whatever this may be. . . . It is the imperative and indispensable duty of the Government of the United States to secure to every resident inhabitant the free and independent expression of his opinion by his vote. This sacred right of each individual must be preserved. That being accomplished, nothing can be fairer than to leave the people of a Territory free from all foreign interference to decide their own destiny for themselves, subject only to the Constitution of the United States.

The whole Territorial question being thus settled upon the principle of popular sovereignty—a principle as ancient as free government itself—everything of a practical nature has been decided. No other question remains for adjustment, because all agree that under the Constitution slavery in the States is beyond the reach of any human power except that of the respective States themselves wherein it exists. May we not, then, hope that the long agitation on this subject is approaching its end, and that the geographical parties to which it has given birth, so much dreaded by the Father of his Country, will speedily become extinct? Most happy will it be for the country when the public mind shall be diverted from this question to others of more pressing and practical importance. Throughout the whole progress of this agitation, which has scarcely known any intermission for more than twenty years, whilst it has been productive of no positive good to any human being it has been the prolific source of great evils to the master, to the slave, and to the whole country. It has alienated and estranged the people of the sister States from each other, and has even seriously endangered the very existence of the Union. Nor has the danger yet entirely ceased. Under our system there is a remedy for all mere political evils in the sound sense and sober judgment of the people. Time is a great corrective. Political subjects which but a few years ago excited and exasperated the public mind have passed away and are now nearly forgotten. But this question of domestic slavery is of far graver importance than any mere political question, because should the agitation continue it may eventually endanger the personal safety of a large portion of our countrymen where the institution exists. In that event no form of government, however admirable in itself and however productive of material benefits, can compensate for the loss of peace and domestic security around the family altar. Let every Union-loving man, therefore, exert his best influence to suppress this agitation, which since the recent legislation of Congress is without any legitimate object.

It is an evil omen of the times that men have undertaken to calculate the mere material value of the Union. Reasoned estimates have been presented of the pecuniary profits and local advantages which would result to different States and sections from its dissolution and of the comparative injuries which such an event would inflict on other States and sections. Even descending to this low and narrow view of the mighty question, all such calculations are at fault. The bare reference to a single consideration will be conclusive on this point. We at present enjoy a free trade throughout our extensive and expanding country such as the world has never witnessed. This trade is conducted on railroads and canals, on noble rivers and arms of the sea, which bind together the North and the South, the East and the West, of our Confederacy. Annihilate this trade, arrest its free progress by the geographical lines of jealous and hostile States, and you destroy the prosperity and onward march of the whole and every part and involve all in one common ruin. But such considerations, important as they are in themselves, sink into insignificance when we reflect on the terrific evils which would result from disunion to every portion of the Confederacy—to the North, not more than to the South, to the East not more than to the West. These I shall not attempt to portray, because I feel an humble confidence that the kind Providence which inspired our fathers with wisdom to frame the most perfect form of government and union ever devised by man will not suffer it to perish until it shall have been peacefully instrumental by its example in the extension of civil and religious liberty throughout the world. . . .

The Federal Constitution is a grant from the States to Congress of certain specific powers, and the question whether this grant should be liberally or strictly construed has more or less divided political parties from the beginning. Without entering into the argument, I desire to state at the commencement of my Administration that long experience and observation have convinced me that a strict construction of the powers of the Government is the only true, as well as the only safe, theory of the Constitution. . . .

I shall now proceed to take the oath prescribed by the Constitution, whilst humbly invoking the blessing of Divine Providence on this great people.

ABRAHAM LINCOLN

First Address: March 4, 1861

No President delivered an Inaugural Address under more difficult circumstances than Lincoln in 1861. As he spoke, the entire Lower South had already seceded, with the Upper South and border states hanging in the Union by a thread. Sharpshooters and cannon were posted nearby to guard Lincoln against a deluge of assassination threats, and he was forced to walk through a covered wooden walkway to the Capitol Building. The speech itself offered both the carrot and the stick to disgruntled white Southerners, making earnest appeals for friendship and camaraderie while insisting that secession was impracticable (and illegal) and asserting Lincoln's desire to retain Federal property located in the South, especially Charleston's Fort Sumter.

In compliance with a custom as old as the Government itself, I appear before you to address you briefly and to take in your presence the oath prescribed by the Constitution of the United States to be taken by the President before he enters on the execution of this office.

I do not consider it necessary at present for me to discuss those matters of administration about which there is no special anxiety or excitement.

Apprehension seems to exist among the people of the Southern States that by the accession of a Republican Administration their property and their peace and personal security are to be endangered. There has never been any reasonable cause for such apprehension. Indeed, the most ample evidence to the contrary has all the while existed and been open to their inspection. It is found in nearly all the published speeches of him who now addresses you. I do but quote from one of those speeches when I declare that—

I have no purpose, directly or indirectly, to interfere with the institution of slavery in the States where it exists. I believe I have no lawful right to do so, and I have no inclination to do so.

Those who nominated and elected me did so with full knowledge that I had made this and many similar declarations and had never recanted them; and more than this, they placed in the platform for my acceptance, and as a law to themselves and to me, the clear and emphatic resolution which I now read:

Resolved, That the maintenance inviolate of the rights of the States, and especially the right of each State to order and control its own domestic institutions according to its own judgment exclusively, is essential to that balance of power on which the perfection and endurance of our political fabric depend; and we denounce the lawless invasion by armed force of the soil of any State or Territory, no matter what pretext, as among the gravest of crimes.

I now reiterate these sentiments, and in doing so I only press upon the public attention the most conclusive evidence of which the case is susceptible that the property, peace, and security of no section are to be in any wise endangered by the now incoming Administration. I add, too, that all the protection which, consistently with the Constitution and the laws, can be given will be cheerfully given to all the States when lawfully demanded, for whatever cause—as cheerfully to one section as to another. . . .

It is seventy-two years since the first inauguration of a President under our National Constitution. During that period fifteen different and greatly distinguished citizens have in succession administered the executive branch of the Government. They have conducted it through many perils, and generally with great success. Yet, with all this scope of precedent, I now enter upon the same task for the brief constitutional term of four years under great and peculiar difficulty. A disruption of the Federal Union, heretofore only menaced, is now formidably attempted.

I hold that in contemplation of universal law and of the Constitution the Union of these States is perpetual. Perpetuity is implied, if not expressed, in the fundamental law of all national governments. It is safe to assert that no government proper ever had a provision in its organic law for its own termination. Continue to execute all the express provisions of our National Constitution, and the Union will endure forever, it being impossible to destroy it except by some action not provided for in the instrument itself.

Again: If the United States be not a government proper, but an association of States in the nature of contract merely, can it, as a contract, be peaceably unmade by less than all the parties who made it? One party to a contract may violate it—break it, so to speak—but does it not require all to lawfully rescind it?

Descending from these general principles, we find the proposition that in legal contemplation the Union is perpetual confirmed by the history of the Union itself. The Union is much older than the Constitution. . . .

But if destruction of the Union by one or by a part only of the States be lawfully possible, the Union is less perfect than before the Constitution, having lost the vital element of perpetuity.

It follows from these views that no State upon its own mere motion can lawfully get out of the Union; that resolves and ordinances to that effect are legally void, and that acts of violence within any State or States against the authority of the United States are insurrectionary or revolutionary, according to circumstances.

I therefore consider that in view of the Constitution and the laws the Union is unbroken, and to the extent of my ability, I shall take care, as the Constitution itself expressly enjoins upon me, that the laws of the Union be faithfully executed in all the States. Doing this I deem to be only a simple duty on my part, and I shall perform it so far as practicable unless my rightful masters, the American people, shall withhold the requisite means or in some authoritative manner direct the contrary. I trust this will not be regarded as a menace, but only as the declared purpose of the Union that it will constitutionally defend and maintain itself.

In doing this there needs to be no bloodshed or violence, and there shall be none unless it be forced upon the national authority. The power confided to me will be used to hold, occupy, and possess the property and places belonging to the Government and to collect the duties and imposts; but beyond what may be necessary for these objects, there will be no invasion, no using of force against or among the people anywhere. Where hostility to the United States in any interior locality shall be so great and universal as to prevent competent resident citizens from holding the Federal offices, there will be no attempt to force obnoxious strangers among the people for that object. While the strict legal right may exist in the Government to enforce the exercise of these offices, the attempt to do so would be so irritating and so nearly impracticable withal that I deem it better to forego for the time the uses of such offices.

The mails, unless repelled, will continue to be furnished in all parts of the Union. So far as possible the people everywhere shall have that sense of perfect security which is most favorable to calm thought and reflection. The course here indicated will be followed unless current events and experience shall show a modification or change to be proper, and in every case and exigency my best discretion will be exercised, according to circumstances actually existing and with a view and a hope of a peaceful solution of the national troubles and the restoration of fraternal sympathies and affections.

That there are persons in one section or another who seek to destroy the Union at all events and are glad of any pretext to do it I will neither affirm nor deny; but if there be such, I need address no word to them. To those, however, who really love the Union may I not speak?

Before entering upon so grave a matter as the destruction of our national fabric, with all its benefits, its memories, and its hopes, would it not be wise to ascertain precisely why we do it? Will you hazard so desperate a step while there is any possibility that any portion of the ills you fly from have no real existence? Will you, while the certain ills you fly to are greater than all the real ones you fly from, will you risk the commission of so fearful a mistake?

All profess to be content in the Union if all constitutional rights can be maintained. Is it true, then, that any right plainly written in the Constitution has been denied? I think not. Happily, the human mind is so constituted that no party can reach to the audacity of doing this. Think, if you can, of a single instance in which a plainly written provision of the Constitution has ever been denied. If by the mere force of numbers a majority should deprive a minority of any clearly written constitutional right, it might in a moral point of view justify revolution; certainly would if such right were a vital one. But such is not our case. All the vital rights of minorities and of individuals are so plainly assured to them by affirmations and negations, guaranties and prohibitions, in the Constitution that controversies never arise concerning them. But no organic law can ever be framed with a provision specifically applicable to every question which may occur in practical administration. No foresight can anticipate nor any document of reasonable length contain express provisions for all possible questions. Shall fugitives from labor be surrendered by national or by State authority? The Constitution does not expressly say. May Congress prohibit slavery in the Territories? The Constitution does not expressly say. Must Congress protect slavery in the Territories? The Constitution does not expressly say.

From questions of this class spring all our constitutional controversies, and we divide upon them into majorities and minorities. If the minority will not acquiesce, the majority must, or the Government must cease. There is no other alternative, for continuing the Government is acquiescence on one side or the other. If a minority in such case will secede rather than acquiesce, they make a precedent which in turn will divide and ruin them, for a minority of their own will secede from them whenever a majority refuses to be controlled by such minority. For instance, why may not any portion of a new confederacy a year or two hence arbitrarily secede again, precisely as portions of the present Union now claim to secede from it? All who cherish disunion sentiments are now being educated to the exact temper of doing this.

Is there such perfect identity of interests among the States to compose a new union as to produce harmony only and prevent renewed secession?

Plainly the central idea of secession is the essence of anarchy. A majority held in restraint by constitutional checks and limitations, and always changing easily with deliberate changes of popular opinions and sentiments, is the only true sovereign of a free people. Whoever rejects it does of necessity fly to anarchy or to despotism. Unanimity is impossible. The rule of a minority, as a permanent arrangement, is wholly inadmissible; so that, rejecting the majority principle, anarchy or despotism in some form is all that is left. . . .

One section of our country believes slavery is right and ought to be extended, while the other believes it is wrong and ought not to be extended. This is the only substantial dispute. . . .

Physically speaking, we can not separate. We can not remove our respective sections from each other nor build an impassable wall between them. A husband and wife may be divorced and go out of the presence and beyond the reach of each other, but the different parts of our country can not do this. They can not but remain face to face, and intercourse, either amicable or hostile, must continue between them. Is it possible, then, to make that intercourse more advantageous or more satisfactory after separation than before? Can aliens make treaties easier than friends can make laws? Can treaties be more faithfully enforced between aliens than laws can among friends? Suppose you go to war, you can not fight always; and when, after much loss on both sides and no gain on either, you cease fighting, the identical old questions, as to terms of intercourse, are again upon you.

This country, with its institutions, belongs to the people who inhabit it. Whenever they shall grow weary of the existing Government, they can exercise their constitutional right of amending it or their revolutionary right to dismember or overthrow it. I can not be ignorant of the fact that many worthy and patriotic citizens are desirous of having the National Constitution amended. While I make no recommendation of amendments, I fully recognize the rightful authority of the people over the whole subject, to be exercised in either of the modes prescribed in the instrument itself; and I should, under existing circumstances, favor rather than oppose a fair opportunity being afforded the people to act upon it. I will venture to add that to me the convention mode seems preferable, in that it allows amendments to originate with the people themselves, instead of only permitting them to take or reject propositions originated by others, not especially chosen for the purpose, and which might not be precisely such as they would wish to either accept or refuse. I understand a proposed amendment to the Constitution—which amendment, however, I have not seen—has passed Congress, to the effect that the Federal Government shall never interfere with the domestic institutions of the States, including that of persons held to service. To avoid misconstruction of what I have said, I depart from my purpose not to speak of particular amendments so far as to say that, holding such a provision to now be implied constitutional law, I have no objection to its being made express and irrevocable. . . .

Why should there not be a patient confidence in the ultimate justice of the people? Is there any better or equal hope in the world? In our present differences, is either party without faith of being in the right? If the Almighty Ruler of Nations, with His eternal truth and justice, be on your side of the North, or on yours of the South, that truth and that justice will surely prevail by the judgment of this great tribunal of the American people.

By the frame of the Government under which we live this same people have wisely given their public servants but little power for mischief, and have with equal wisdom provided for the return of that little to their own hands at very short intervals. While the people retain their virtue and vigilance no Administration by any extreme of wickedness or folly can very seriously injure the Government in the short space of four years.

My countrymen, one and all, think calmly and well upon this whole subject. Nothing valuable can be lost by taking time. If there be an object to hurry any of you in hot haste to a step which you would never take deliberately, that object will be frustrated by taking time; but no good object can be frustrated by it. Such of you as are now dissatisfied still have the old Constitution unimpaired, and, on the sensitive point, the laws of your own framing under it; while the new Administration will have no immediate power, if it would, to change either. If it were admitted that you who are dissatisfied hold the right side in the dispute, there still is no single good reason for precipitate action. Intelligence, patriotism, Christianity, and a firm reliance on Him who has never yet forsaken this favored land are still competent to adjust in the best way all our present difficulty.

In your hands, my dissatisfied fellow-countrymen, and not in mine, is the momentous issue of civil war. The Government will not assail you. You can have no conflict without being yourselves the aggressors. You have no oath registered in heaven to destroy the Government, while I shall have the most solemn one to "preserve, protect, and defend it."

I am loath to close. We are not enemies, but friends. We must not be enemies. Though passion may have strained it must not break our bonds of affection. The mystic chords of memory, stretching from every battlefield and patriot grave to every living heart and hearthstone all over this broad land, will yet swell the chorus of the Union, when again touched, as surely they will be, by the better angels of our nature.

Second Address: March 4, 1865

The circumstances of Lincoln's second inauguration were far different from the first. By 1865 the Confederacy was on its last legs, the North triumphant. Emancipation had become the settled policy of the Union, and millions of white and black Americans were grappling with its consequences. Newly reelected and about to emerge victorious in a horrific civil war, Lincoln felt compelled to speculate on the war's higher meaning. The result was the finest Inaugural Address in American presidential history.

At this second appearing to take the oath of the Presidential office there is less occasion for an extended address than there was at the first. Then a statement somewhat in detail of a course to be pursued seemed fitting and proper. Now, at the expiration of four years, during which public declarations have been constantly called forth on every point and phase of the great contest which still absorbs the attention and engrosses the energies of the nation, little that is new could be presented. The progress of our arms, upon which all else chiefly depends, is as well known to the public as to myself, and it is, I trust, reasonably satisfactory and encouraging to all. With high hope for the future, no prediction in regard to it is ventured.

On the occasion corresponding to this four years ago all thoughts were anxiously directed to an impending civil war. All dreaded it, all sought to avert it. While the inaugural address was being delivered from this place, devoted altogether to saving the Union without war, insurgent agents were in the city seeking to destroy it without war—seeking to dissolve the Union and divide effects by negotiation. Both parties deprecated war, but one of them would make war rather than let the nation survive, and the other would accept war rather than let it perish, and the war came.

One-eighth of the whole population were colored slaves, not distributed generally over the Union, but localized in the southern part of it. These slaves constituted a peculiar and powerful interest. All knew that this interest was somehow the cause of the war. To strengthen, perpetuate, and extend this interest was the object for which the insurgents would rend the Union even by war, while the Government claimed no right to do more than to restrict the territorial enlargement of it. Neither party expected for the war the magnitude or the duration which it has already attained. Neither anticipated that the cause of the conflict might cease with or even before the conflict itself should cease. Each looked for an easier triumph, and a result less fundamental and astounding. Both read the same Bible and pray to the same God, and each invokes His aid against the other. It may seem strange that any men should dare to ask a just God's assistance in wringing their bread from the sweat of other men's faces, but let us judge not, that we be not judged. The prayers of both could not be answered. That of neither has been answered fully. The Almighty has His own purposes. "Woe unto the world because of offenses; for it must needs be that offenses come, but woe to that man by whom the offense cometh." If we shall suppose that American slavery is one of those offenses which, in the providence of God, must needs come, but which, having continued through His appointed time, He now wills to remove, and that He gives to both North and South this terrible war as the woe due to those by whom the offense came, shall we discern therein any departure from those divine attributes which the believers in a living God always ascribe to Him? Fondly do we hope, fervently do we pray, that this mighty scourge of war may speedily pass away. Yet, if God wills that it continue until all the wealth piled by the bondsman's two hundred and fifty years of unrequited toil shall be sunk, and until every drop of blood drawn with the lash shall be paid by another drawn with the sword, as was said three thousand years ago, so still it must be said "the judgments of the Lord are true and righteous altogether."

With malice toward none, with charity for all, with firmness in the right as God gives us to see the right, let us strive on to finish the work we are in, to bind up the nation's wounds, to care for him who shall have borne the battle and for his widow and his orphan, to do all which may achieve and cherish a just and lasting peace among ourselves and with all nations.

Inaugural Addresses
1869–1933

Ulysses S. Grant

First Address: March 4, 1869

Grant came to the presidency with no prior political experience, his political principles and ideology—like many military men turned politicians—vague and ill-defined. His Inaugural Address reflected this, as well as Grant's famously terse personality.

Your suffrages having elected me to the office of President of the United States, I have, in conformity to the Constitution of our country, taken the oath of office prescribed therein. I have taken this oath without mental reservation and with the determination to do to the best of my ability all that is required of me. The responsibilities of the position I feel, but accept them without fear. The office has come to me unsought; I commence its duties untrammeled. I bring to it a conscious desire and determination to fill it to the best of my ability to the satisfaction of the people.

On all leading questions agitating the public mind I will always express my views to Congress and urge them according to my judgment, and when I think it advisable will exercise the constitutional privilege of interposing a veto to defeat measures which I oppose; but all laws will be faithfully executed, whether they meet my approval or not.

I shall on all subjects have a policy to recommend, but none to enforce against the will of the people. Laws are to govern all alike—those opposed as well as those who favor them. I know no method to secure the repeal of bad or obnoxious laws so effective as their stringent execution.

The country having just emerged from a great rebellion, many questions will come before it for settlement in the next four years which preceding Administrations have never had to deal with. In meeting these it is desirable that they should be approached calmly, without prejudice, hate, or sectional pride, remembering that the greatest good to the greatest number is the object to be attained.

This requires security of person, property, and free religious and political opinion in every part of our common country, without regard to local prejudice. All laws to secure these ends will receive my best efforts for their enforcement. . . .

When we compare the paying capacity of the country now, with the ten States in poverty from the effects of war, but soon to emerge, I trust, into greater prosperity than ever before, with its paying capacity twenty-five years ago, and calculate what it probably will be twenty-five years hence, who can doubt the feasibility of paying every dollar then with more ease than we now pay for useless luxuries? Why, it looks as though Providence had bestowed upon us a strong box in the precious metals locked up in the sterile mountains of the far West, and which we are now forging the key to unlock, to meet the very contingency that is now upon us.

Ultimately it may be necessary to insure the facilities to reach these riches and it may be necessary also that the General Government should give its aid to secure this access; but that should only be when a dollar of obligation to pay secures precisely the same sort of dollar to use now, and not before. Whilst the question of specie payments is in abeyance the prudent business man is careful about contracting debts payable in the distant future. The nation should follow the same rule. A prostrate commerce is to be rebuilt and all industries encouraged.

The young men of the country—those who from their age must be its rulers twenty-five years hence—have a peculiar interest in maintaining the national honor. A moment's reflection as to what will be our commanding influence among the nations of the earth in their day, if they are only true to themselves, should inspire them with national pride. All divisions—geographical, political, and religious—can join in this common sentiment. How the public debt is to be paid or specie payments resumed is not so important as that a plan should be adopted and acquiesced in. A united determination to do is worth more than divided counsels upon the method of doing. Legislation upon this subject may not be necessary now, or even advisable, but it will be when the civil law is more fully restored in all parts of the country and trade resumes its wonted channels.

It will be my endeavor to execute all laws in good faith, to collect all revenues assessed, and to have them properly accounted for and economically disbursed. I will to the best of my ability appoint to office those only who will carry out this design. . . .

The proper treatment of the original occupants of this land—the Indians [is] one deserving of careful study. I will favor any course toward them which tends to their civilization and ultimate citizenship.

The question of suffrage is one which is likely to agitate the public so long as a portion of the citizens of the nation are excluded from its privileges in any State. It seems to me very desirable that this question should be settled now, and I entertain the hope and express the desire that it may be by the ratification of the fifteenth article of amendment to the Constitution.

In conclusion I ask patient forbearance one toward another throughout the land, and a determined effort on the part of every citizen to do his share toward cementing a

happy union; and I ask the prayers of the nation to Almighty God in behalf of this consummation.

Second Address: March 4, 1873

*Grant's second term began under a cloud of controversy and scandal, the nation mired
in troubling questions about African American rights and Reconstruction, the administration under investigation for various accusations of wrongdoing and financial
malfeasance. None of the scandals touched Grant personally, who continued to enjoy
widespread popularity as the Union's preeminent Civil War military hero. Still,
Grant's defensiveness over what would become one of the most scandal-plagued presidencies in American history is evident here.*

Under Providence I have been called a second time to act as Executive over this great
nation. It has been my endeavor in the past to maintain all the laws, and, so far as lay
in my power, to act for the best interests of the whole people. My best efforts will be
given in the same direction in the future, aided, I trust, by my four years' experience in
the office.

When my first term of the office of Chief Executive began, the country had not recovered from the effects of a great internal revolution, and three of the former States of the
Union had not been restored to their Federal relations.

It seemed to me wise that no new questions should be raised so long as that condition of affairs existed. Therefore the past four years, so far as I could control events,
have been consumed in the effort to restore harmony, public credit, commerce, and
all the arts of peace and progress. It is my firm conviction that the civilized world is
tending toward republicanism, or government by the people through their chosen representatives, and that our own great Republic is destined to be the guiding star to all
others . . ..

The effects of the late civil strife have been to free the slave and make him a citizen.
Yet he is not possessed of the civil rights which citizenship should carry with it. This
is wrong, and should be corrected. To this correction I stand committed, so far as Executive influence can avail.

Social equality is not a subject to be legislated upon, nor shall I ask that anything be
done to advance the social status of the colored man, except to give him a fair chance
to develop what there is good in him, give him access to the schools, and when he trav-
els let him feel assured that his conduct will regulate the treatment and fare he will receive.

The States lately at war with the General Government are now happily rehabilitated,
and no Executive control is exercised in any one of them that would not be exercised
in any other State under like circumstances . . ..

In future, while I hold my present office, the subject of acquisition of territory must
have the support of the people before I will recommend any proposition looking to such

acquisition. I say here, however, that I do not share in the apprehension held by many as to the danger of governments becoming weakened and destroyed by reason of their extension of territory. Commerce, education, and rapid transit of thought and matter by telegraph and steam have changed all this. Rather do I believe that our Great Maker is preparing the world, in His own good time, to become one nation, speaking one language, and when armies and navies will be no longer required.

My efforts in the future will be directed to the restoration of good feeling between the different sections of our common country; to the restoration of our currency to a fixed value as compared with the world's standard of values—gold—and, if possible, to a par with it; to the construction of cheap routes of transit throughout the land, to the end that the products of all may find a market and leave a living remuneration to the producer; to the maintenance of friendly relations with all our neighbors and with distant nations; to the reestablishment of our commerce and share in the carrying trade upon the ocean; to the encouragement of such manufacturing industries as can be economically pursued in this country, to the end that the exports of home products and industries may pay for our imports—the only sure method of returning to and permanently maintaining a specie basis; to the elevation of labor; and, by a humane course, to bring the aborigines of the country under the benign influences of education and civilization. It is either this or war of extermination: Wars of extermination, engaged in by people pursuing commerce and all industrial pursuits, are expensive even against the weakest people, and are demoralizing and wicked. Our superiority of strength and advantages of civilization should make us lenient toward the Indian. The wrong inflicted upon him should be taken into account and the balance placed to his credit. The moral view of the question should be considered and the question asked, Can not the Indian be made a useful and productive member of society by proper teaching and treatment? If the effort is made in good faith, we will stand better before the civilized nations of the earth and in our own consciences for having made it.

All these things are not to be accomplished by one individual, but they will receive my support and such recommendations to Congress as will in my judgment best serve to carry them into effect. I beg your support and encouragement.

It has been, and is, my earnest desire to correct abuses that have grown up in the civil service of the country. To secure this reformation rules regulating methods of appointment and promotions were established and have been tried. My efforts for such reformation shall be continued to the best of my judgment. The spirit of the rules adopted will be maintained.

I acknowledge before this assemblage, representing, as it does, every section of our country, the obligation I am under to my countrymen for the great honor they have conferred on me by returning me to the highest office within their gift, and the further obligation resting on me to render to them the best services within my power. This I promise, looking forward with the greatest anxiety to the day when I shall be released from responsibilities that at times are almost overwhelming, and from which I have scarcely had a respite since the eventful firing upon Fort Sumter, in April, 1861, to the present day. My services were then tendered and accepted under the first call for troops growing out of that event.

I did not ask for place or position, and was entirely without influence or the acquaintance of persons of influence, but was resolved to perform my part in a struggle threatening the very existence of the nation. I performed a conscientious duty, without asking promotion or command, and without a revengeful feeling toward any section or individual.

Notwithstanding this, throughout the war, and from my candidacy for my present office in 1868 to the close of the last Presidential campaign, I have been the subject of abuse and slander scarcely ever equaled in political history, which to-day I feel that I can afford to disregard in view of your verdict, which I gratefully accept as my vindication.

RUTHERFORD B. HAYES

March 5, 1877

Hayes inherited a presidency that had fallen under a cloud by 1877. This was due to the various scandals that had plagued the Johnson and Grant Administrations, and the fact that the 1876 election had been decided by a special electoral commission, where Hayes had been given Democratic support only upon the condition that he withdraw the last federal troops from the South, thus ending Reconstruction and in effect throwing black Southerners upon the tender mercies of their former Confederate neighbors. Much of Hayes's address was devoted to a lengthy rationalization of that withdrawal, as well as a call for political and civil service reform.

We have assembled to repeat the public ceremonial, begun by Washington, observed by all my predecessors, and now a time-honored custom, which marks the commencement of a new term of the Presidential office. . . .

The permanent pacification of the country upon such principles and by such measures as will secure the complete protection of all its citizens in the free enjoyment of all their constitutional rights is now the one subject in our public affairs which all thoughtful and patriotic citizens regard as of supreme importance.

Many of the calamitous efforts of the tremendous revolution which has passed over the Southern States still remain. The immeasurable benefits which will surely follow, sooner or later, the hearty and generous acceptance of the legitimate results of that revolution have not yet been realized. Difficult and embarrassing questions meet us at the threshold of this subject. The people of those States are still impoverished, and the inestimable blessing of wise, honest, and peaceful local self-government is not fully enjoyed. Whatever difference of opinion may exist as to the cause of this condition of things, the fact is clear that in the progress of events the time has come when such government is the imperative necessity required by all the varied interests, public and private, of those States. But it must not be forgotten that only a local government which recognizes and maintains inviolate the rights of all is a true self-government.

With respect to the two distinct races whose peculiar relations to each other have brought upon us the deplorable complications and perplexities which exist in those States, it must be a government which guards the interests of both races carefully and equally. It must be a government which submits loyally and heartily to the Constitution and the laws—the laws of the nation and the laws of the States themselves—accepting and obeying faithfully the whole Constitution as it is.

Resting upon this sure and substantial foundation, the superstructure of beneficent local governments can be built up, and not otherwise. In furtherance of such obedience to the letter and the spirit of the Constitution, and in behalf of all that its attainment implies, all so-called party interests lose their apparent importance, and party lines may well be permitted to fade into insignificance. The question we have to consider for the immediate welfare of those States of the Union is the question of government or no government; of social order and all the peaceful industries and the happiness that belongs to it, or a return to barbarism. It is a question in which every citizen of the nation is deeply interested, and with respect to which we ought not to be, in a partisan sense, either Republicans or Democrats, but fellow-citizens and fellowmen, to whom the interests of a common country and a common humanity are dear.

The sweeping revolution of the entire labor system of a large portion of our country and the advance of 4,000,000 people from a condition of servitude to that of citizenship, upon an equal footing with their former masters, could not occur without presenting problems of the gravest moment, to be dealt with by the emancipated race, by their former masters, and by the General Government, the author of the act of emancipation. That it was a wise, just, and providential act, fraught with good for all concerned, is not generally conceded throughout the country. That a moral obligation rests upon the National Government to employ its constitutional power and influence to establish the rights of the people it has emancipated, and to protect them in the enjoyment of those rights when they are infringed or assailed, is also generally admitted.

The evils which afflict the Southern States can only be removed or remedied by the united and harmonious efforts of both races, actuated by motives of mutual sympathy and regard; and while in duty bound and fully determined to protect the rights of all by every constitutional means at the disposal of my Administration, I am sincerely anxious to use every legitimate influence in favor of honest and efficient local self-government as the true resource of those States for the promotion of the contentment and prosperity of their citizens. In the effort I shall make to accomplish this purpose I ask the cordial cooperation of all who cherish an interest in the welfare of the country, trusting that party ties and the prejudice of race will be freely surrendered in behalf of the great purpose to be accomplished. In the important work of restoring the South it is not the political situation alone that merits attention. The material development of that section of the country has been arrested by the social and political revolution through which it has passed, and now needs and deserves the considerate care of the

National Government within the just limits prescribed by the Constitution and wise public economy.

But at the basis of all prosperity, for that as well as for every other part of the country, lies the improvement of the intellectual and moral condition of the people. Universal suffrage should rest upon universal education. To this end, liberal and permanent provision should be made for the support of free schools by the State governments, and, if need be, supplemented by legitimate aid from national authority.

Let me assure my countrymen of the Southern States that it is my earnest desire to regard and promote their truest interest—the interests of the white and of the colored people both and equally—and to put forth my best efforts in behalf of a civil policy which will forever wipe out in our political affairs the color line and the distinction between North and South, to the end that we may have not merely a united North or a united South, but a united country.

I ask the attention of the public to the paramount necessity of reform in our civil service—a reform not merely as to certain abuses and practices of so-called official patronage which have come to have the sanction of usage in the several Departments of our Government, but a change in the system of appointment itself; a reform that shall be thorough, radical, and complete; a return to the principles and practices of the founders of the Government. They neither expected nor desired from public officers any partisan service. They meant that public officers should owe their whole service to the Government and to the people . . . .

The President of the United States of necessity owes his election to office to the suffrage and zealous labors of a political party, the members of which cherish with ardor and regard as of essential importance the principles of their party organization; but he should strive to be always mindful of the fact that he serves his party best who serves the country best.

In furtherance of the reform we seek, and in other important respects a change of great importance, I recommend an amendment to the Constitution prescribing a term of six years for the Presidential office and forbidding a reelection. . . .

Fellow-citizens, we have reached the close of a political contest marked by the excitement which usually attends the contests between great political parties whose members espouse and advocate with earnest faith their respective creeds. The circumstances were, perhaps, in no respect extraordinary save in the closeness and the consequent uncertainty of the result.

For the first time in the history of the country it has been deemed best, in view of the peculiar circumstances of the case, that the objections and questions in dispute with reference to the counting of the electoral votes should be referred to the decision of a tribunal appointed for this purpose.

That tribunal—established by law for this sole purpose; its members, all of them, men of long-established reputation for integrity and intelligence, and, with the exception of those who are also members of the supreme judiciary, chosen equally from both political parties; its deliberations enlightened by the research and the arguments of able counsel—was entitled to the fullest confidence of the American people. Its decisions have been patiently waited for, and accepted as legally conclusive by the general judgment of the public. For the present, opinion will widely vary as to the wisdom of the several conclusions announced by that tribunal. This is to be anticipated in every instance where matters of dispute are made the subject of arbitration under the forms of law. Human judgment is never unerring, and is rarely regarded as otherwise than wrong by the unsuccessful party in the contest.

The fact that two great political parties have in this way settled a dispute in regard to which good men differ as to the facts and the law no less than as to the proper course to be pursued in solving the question in controversy is an occasion for general rejoicing.

Upon one point there is entire unanimity in public sentiment—that conflicting claims to the Presidency must be amicably and peaceably adjusted, and that when so adjusted the general acquiescence of the nation ought surely to follow.

It has been reserved for a government of the people, where the right of suffrage is universal, to give to the world the first example in history of a great nation, in the midst of the struggle of opposing parties for power, hushing its party tumults to yield the issue of the contest to adjustment according to the forms of law.

Looking for the guidance of that Divine Hand by which the destinies of nations and individuals are shaped, I call upon you, Senators, Representatives, judges, fellow-citizens, here and everywhere, to unite with me in an earnest effort to secure to our country the blessings, not only of material prosperity, but of justice, peace, and union—a union depending not upon the constraint of force, but upon the loving devotion of a free people; "and that all things may be so ordered and settled upon the best and surest foundations that peace and happiness, truth and justice, religion and piety, may be established among us for all generations."

James A. Garfield

March 4, 1881

The latest in what was becoming a long line of presidents who were Civil War veterans, Garfield offered a passionate defense of African American suffrage in his Inaugural Address, arguing that protection of freedmen's voting rights was an admirable legacy of the Civil War. Unfortunately, the nation was already well on its way to turning its attention to other matters—controversies over the Mormon practice of polygamy, for example, which Garfield also addressed—as he spoke these words.

We stand to-day upon an eminence which overlooks a hundred years of national life—a century crowded with perils, but crowned with the triumphs of liberty and law. . . .

And now, at the close of this first century of growth, with the inspirations of its history in their hearts, our people have lately reviewed the condition of the nation, passed judgment upon the conduct and opinions of political parties, and have registered their will concerning the future administration of the Government. To interpret and to execute that will in accordance with the Constitution is the paramount duty of the Executive.

Even from this brief review it is manifest that the nation is resolutely facing to the front, resolved to employ its best energies in developing the great possibilities of the future. Sacredly preserving whatever has been gained to liberty and good government during the century, our people are determined to leave behind them all those bitter controversies concerning things which have been irrevocably settled, and the further discussion of which can only stir up strife and delay the onward march.

The supremacy of the nation and its laws should be no longer a subject of debate. That discussion, which for half a century threatened the existence of the Union, was closed at last in the high court of war by a decree from which there is no appeal—that the Constitution and the laws made in pursuance thereof are and shall continue to be the supreme law of the land, binding alike upon the States and the people. This decree does not disturb the autonomy of the States nor interfere with any of their necessary rights of local self-government, but it does fix and establish the permanent supremacy of the Union. . . .

The elevation of the negro race from slavery to the full rights of citizenship is the most important political change we have known since the adoption of the Constitution of 1787. No thoughtful man can fail to appreciate its beneficent effect upon our institutions and people. It has freed us from the perpetual danger of war and dissolution. It has added immensely to the moral and industrial forces of our people. It has liberated the master as well as the slave from a relation which wronged and enfeebled both. It has surrendered to their own guardianship the manhood of more than 5,000,000 people, and has opened to each one of them a career of freedom and usefulness. It has given new inspiration to the power of self-help in both races by making labor more honorable to the one and more necessary to the other. The influence of this force will grow greater and bear richer fruit with the coming years.

No doubt this great change has caused serious disturbance to our Southern communities. This is to be deplored, though it was perhaps unavoidable. But those who resisted the change should remember that under our institutions there was no middle ground for the negro race between slavery and equal citizenship. There can be no permanent disfranchised peasantry in the United States. Freedom can never yield its fullness of blessings so long as the law or its administration places the smallest obstacle in the pathway of any virtuous citizen.

The emancipated race has already made remarkable progress. With unquestioning devotion to the Union, with a patience and gentleness not born of fear, they have "followed the light as God gave them to see the light." They are rapidly laying the material foundations of self-support, widening their circle of intelligence, and beginning to enjoy the blessings that gather around the homes of the industrious poor. They deserve the generous encouragement of all good men. So far as my authority can lawfully extend they shall enjoy the full and equal protection of the Constitution and the laws.

The free enjoyment of equal suffrage is still in question, and a frank statement of the issue may aid its solution. It is alleged that in many communities negro citizens are practically denied the freedom of the ballot. In so far as the truth of this allegation is admitted, it is answered that in many places honest local government is impossible if the mass of uneducated negroes are allowed to vote. These are grave allegations. So far as the latter is true, it is the only palliation that can be offered for opposing the freedom of the ballot. Bad local government is certainly a great evil, which ought to be prevented; but to violate the freedom and sanctities of the suffrage is more than an evil. It is a crime which, if persisted in, will destroy the Government itself. Suicide is not a remedy. If in other lands it be high treason to compass the death of the king, it shall be counted no less a crime here to strangle our sovereign power and stifle its voice.

It has been said that unsettled questions have no pity for the repose of nations. It should be said with the utmost emphasis that this question of the suffrage will never give repose or safety to the States or to the nation until each, within its own jurisdiction, makes and keeps the ballot free and pure by the strong sanctions of the law.

But the danger which arises from ignorance in the voter can not be denied. It covers a field far wider than that of negro suffrage and the present condition of the race. It is a danger that lurks and hides in the sources and fountains of power in every state. We have no standard by which to measure the disaster that may be brought upon us by ignorance and vice in the citizens when joined to corruption and fraud in the suffrage.

The voters of the Union, who make and unmake constitutions, and upon whose will hang the destinies of our governments, can transmit their supreme authority to no successors save the coming generation of voters, who are the sole heirs of sovereign power. If that generation comes to its inheritance blinded by ignorance and corrupted by vice, the fall of the Republic will be certain and remediless.

The census has already sounded the alarm in the appalling figures which mark how dangerously high the tide of illiteracy has risen among our voters and their children.

To the South this question is of supreme importance. But the responsibility for the existence of slavery did not rest upon the South alone. The nation itself is responsible for the extension of the suffrage, and is under special obligations to aid in removing the illiteracy which it has added to the voting population. For the North and South alike there is but one remedy. All the constitutional power of the nation and of the States and all the volunteer forces of the people should be surrendered to meet this danger by the savory influence of universal education.

It is the high privilege and sacred duty of those now living to educate their successors and fit them, by intelligence and virtue, for the inheritance which awaits them.

In this beneficent work sections and races should be forgotten and partisanship should be unknown. Let our people find a new meaning in the divine oracle which declares that "a little child shall lead them," for our own little children will soon control the destinies of the Republic.

My countrymen, we do not now differ in our judgment concerning the controversies of past generations, and fifty years hence our children will not be divided in their opinions concerning our controversies. They will surely bless their fathers and their fathers' God that the Union was preserved, that slavery was overthrown, and that both races were made equal before the law. We may hasten or we may retard, but we can not prevent, the final reconciliation. Is it not possible for us now to make a truce with time by anticipating and accepting its inevitable verdict? . . .

The Constitution guarantees absolute religious freedom. Congress is prohibited from making any law respecting an establishment of religion or prohibiting the free exercise thereof. The Territories of the United States are subject to the direct legislative authority of Congress, and hence the General Government is responsible for any violation of the Constitution in any of them. It is therefore a reproach to the Government that in the most populous of the Territories the constitutional guaranty is not enjoyed by the people and the authority of Congress is set at naught. The Mormon Church not only offends the moral sense of manhood by sanctioning polygamy, but prevents the administration of justice through ordinary instrumentalities of law.

In my judgment it is the duty of Congress, while respecting to the uttermost the conscientious convictions and religious scruples of every citizen, to prohibit within its jurisdiction all criminal practices, especially of that class which destroy the family relations and endanger social order. Nor can any ecclesiastical organization be safely permitted to usurp in the smallest degree the functions and powers of the National Government.

The civil service can never be placed on a satisfactory basis until it is regulated by law. For the good of the service itself, for the protection of those who are intrusted with the appointing power against the waste of time and obstruction to the public business caused by the inordinate pressure for place, and for the protection of incumbents against intrigue and wrong, I shall at the proper time ask Congress to fix the tenure of the minor offices of the several Executive Departments and prescribe the grounds upon which removals shall be made during the terms for which incumbents have been appointed. . . .

And now, fellow-citizens, I am about to assume the great trust which you have committed to my hands. I appeal to you for that earnest and thoughtful support which makes this Government in fact, as it is in law, a government of the people.

I shall greatly rely upon the wisdom and patriotism of Congress and of those who may share with me the responsibilities and duties of administration, and, above all, upon our efforts to promote the welfare of this great people and their Government I reverently invoke the support and blessings of Almighty God.

GROVER CLEVELAND

First Address: March 4, 1885

The first Democratic presidential candidate to be elected since before the Civil War, Cleveland offered one of the more bland and nonspecific Inaugural Addresses in presidential history. This reflected perhaps the relative decline of the office's power and prestige, particularly in comparison to Congress, at the end of the nineteenth century. Certain recurring themes are discernible here—the need to set aside partisan strife, neutrality in the affairs of Europe, frugality in government administration, civil service reform—but little in the way of new programs or initiatives.

In the presence of this vast assemblage of my countrymen I am about to supplement and seal by the oath which I shall take the manifestation of the will of a great and free people. In the exercise of their power and right of self-government they have committed to one of their fellow-citizens a supreme and sacred trust, and he here consecrates himself to their service . . ..

Amid the din of party strife the people's choice was made, but its attendant circumstances have demonstrated anew the strength and safety of a government by the people. In each succeeding year it more clearly appears that our democratic principle needs no apology, and that in its fearless and faithful application is to be found the surest guaranty of good government.

But the best results in the operation of a government wherein every citizen has a share largely depend upon a proper limitation of purely partisan zeal and effort and a correct appreciation of the time when the heat of the partisan should be merged in the patriotism of the citizen.

To-day the executive branch of the Government is transferred to new keeping. But this is still the Government of all the people, and it should be none the less an object of their affectionate solicitude. At this hour the animosities of political strife, the bitterness of partisan defeat, and the exultation of partisan triumph should be supplanted by an ungrudging acquiescence in the popular will and a sober, conscientious concern for the general weal. Moreover, if from this hour we cheerfully and honestly abandon all sectional prejudice and distrust, and determine, with manly confidence in one another, to work out harmoniously the achievements of our national destiny, we shall deserve to realize all the benefits which our happy form of government can bestow . . ..

In the discharge of my official duty I shall endeavor to be guided by a just and unstrained construction of the Constitution, a careful observance of the distinction between the powers granted to the Federal Government and those reserved to the States or to the people, and by a cautious appreciation of those functions which by the Constitution and laws have been especially assigned to the executive branch of the Government. . . .

It is the duty of those serving the people in public place to closely limit public expenditures to the actual needs of the Government economically administered, because this bounds the right of the Government to exact tribute from the earnings of labor or the property of the citizen, and because public extravagance begets extravagance among the people. We should never be ashamed of the simplicity and prudential economies which are best suited to the operation of a republican form of government and most compatible with the mission of the American people. Those who are selected for a limited time to manage public affairs are still of the people, and may do much by their example to encourage, consistently with the dignity of their official functions, that plain way of life which among their fellow-citizens aids integrity and promotes thrift and prosperity.

The genius of our institutions, the needs of our people in their home life, and the attention which is demanded for the settlement and development of the resources of our vast territory dictate the scrupulous avoidance of any departure from that foreign policy commended by the history, the traditions, and the prosperity of our Republic. It is the policy of independence, favored by our position and defended by our known love of justice and by our power. It is the policy of peace suitable to our interests. It is the policy of neutrality, rejecting any share in foreign broils and ambitions upon other continents and repelling their intrusion here. . . .

A due regard for the interests and prosperity of all the people demands that our finances shall be established upon such a sound and sensible basis as shall secure the safety and confidence of business interests and make the wage of labor sure and steady, and that our system of revenue shall be so adjusted as to relieve the people of unnecessary taxation, having a due regard to the interests of capital invested and workingmen employed in American industries, and preventing the accumulation of a surplus in the Treasury to tempt extravagance and waste.

Care for the property of the nation and for the needs of future settlers requires that the public domain should be protected from purloining schemes and unlawful occupation.

The conscience of the people demands that the Indians within our boundaries shall be fairly and honestly treated as wards of the Government and their education and civilization promoted with a view to their ultimate citizenship, and that polygamy in the Territories, destructive of the family relation and offensive to the moral sense of the civilized world, shall be repressed.

The laws should be rigidly enforced which prohibit the immigration of a servile class to compete with American labor, with no intention of acquiring citizenship, and bringing with them and retaining habits and customs repugnant to our civilization.

The people demand reform in the administration of the Government and the application of business principles to public affairs. As a means to this end, civil-service reform should be in good faith enforced. Our citizens have the right to protection from the incompetency of public employees who hold their places solely as the reward of partisan service, and from the corrupting influence of those who promise and the vicious methods of those who expect such rewards; and those who worthily seek public employment have the right to insist that merit and competency shall be recognized instead of party subserviency or the surrender of honest political belief. . . .

These topics and the constant and ever-varying wants of an active and enterprising population may well receive the attention and the patriotic endeavor of all who make and execute the Federal law. Our duties are practical and call for industrious application, an intelligent perception of the claims of public office, and, above all, a firm determination, by united action, to secure to all the people of the land the full benefits of the best form of government ever vouchsafed to man. And let us not trust to human effort alone, but humbly acknowledging the power and goodness of Almighty God, who presides over the destiny of nations, and who has at all times been revealed in our country's history, let us invoke His aid and His blessings upon our labors.

BENJAMIN HARRISON

March 4, 1889

Harrison's enthusiasm about the unifying effects of national economic development are evident here, as is his generally optimistic vision of America's urbanizing, industrialized future. He also sounds a warning against what would become a pressing concern of the new century—the growing power of large trusts and corporations—and suggests a tolerant attitude toward the new waves of immigrants entering the nation. On the whole, his address offers a nice little snapshot of the optimism and worries of Gilded Age America.

There is no constitutional or legal requirement that the President shall take the oath of office in the presence of the people, but there is so manifest an appropriateness in the public induction to office of the chief executive officer of the nation that from the beginning of the Government the people, to whose service the official oath consecrates the officer, have been called to witness the solemn ceremonial . . ..

Surely I do not misinterpret the spirit of the occasion when I assume that the whole body of the people covenant with me and with each other to-day to support and defend the Constitution and the Union of the States, to yield willing obedience to all the laws and each to every other citizen his equal civil and political rights. Entering thus solemnly into covenant with each other, we may reverently invoke and confidently expect the favor and help of Almighty God—that He will give to me wisdom, strength, and fidelity, and to our people a spirit of fraternity and a love of righteousness and peace. . . .

The Territory of Dakota has now a population greater than any of the original States (except Virginia) and greater than the aggregate of five of the smaller States in 1790. The center of population when our national capital was located was east of Baltimore, and it was argued by many well-informed persons that it would move eastward rather than westward; yet in 1880 it was found to be near Cincinnati, and the new census about to be taken will show another stride to the westward. That which was the body has come to be only the rich fringe of the nation's robe. But our growth has not been limited to territory, population and aggregate wealth, marvelous as it has been in each of those directions. The masses of our people are better fed, clothed, and housed than their fathers were. The facilities for popular education have been vastly enlarged and more generally diffused.

The virtues of courage and patriotism have given recent proof of their continued presence and increasing power in the hearts and over the lives of our people. The influences of religion have been multiplied and strengthened. The sweet offices of charity have greatly increased. The virtue of temperance is held in higher estimation. We have not attained an ideal condition. Not all of our people are happy and prosperous; not all of them are virtuous and law-abiding. But on the whole the opportunities offered to the individual to secure the comforts of life are better than are found elsewhere and largely better than they were here one hundred years ago . . . .

There was this reason only why the States that divide with Pennsylvania the mineral treasures of the great southeastern and central mountain ranges should have been so tardy in bringing to the smelting furnace and to the mill the coal and iron from their near opposing hillsides. Mill fires were lighted at the funeral pile of slavery. The emancipation proclamation was heard in the depths of the earth as well as in the sky; men were made free, and material things became our better servants.

The sectional element has happily been eliminated from the tariff discussion. We have no longer States that are necessarily only planting States. None are excluded from achieving that diversification of pursuits among the people which brings wealth and contentment. The cotton plantation will not be less valuable when the product is spun in the country town by operatives whose necessities call for diversified crops and create a home demand for garden and agricultural products. Every new mine, furnace, and factory is an extension of the productive capacity of the State more real and valuable than added territory.

Shall the prejudices and paralysis of slavery continue to hang upon the skirts of progress? How long will those who rejoice that slavery no longer exists cherish or tolerate the incapacities it put upon their communities? I look hopefully to the continuance of our protective system and to the consequent development of manufacturing and mining enterprises in the States hitherto wholly given to agriculture as a potent influence in the perfect unification of our people. The men who have invested their capital in these enterprises, the farmers who have felt the benefit of their neighborhood, and the men who work in shop or field will not fail to find and to defend a community of interest.

Is it not quite possible that the farmers and the promoters of the great mining and manufacturing enterprises which have recently been established in the South may yet find that the free ballot of the workingman, without distinction of race, is needed for their defense as well as for his own? I do not doubt that if those men in the South who now accept the tariff views of Clay and the constitutional expositions of Webster would courageously avow and defend their real convictions they would not find it difficult, by friendly instruction and cooperation, to make the black man their efficient and safe ally, not only in establishing correct principles in our national administration, but in preserving for their local communities the benefits of social order and economical and honest government. At least until the good offices of kindness and education have been fairly tried the contrary conclusion can not be plausibly urged.

I have altogether rejected the suggestion of a special Executive policy for any section of our country. It is the duty of the Executive to administer and enforce in the methods and by the instrumentalities pointed out and provided by the Constitution all the laws enacted by Congress. These laws are general and their administration should be uniform and equal. . . . The evil example of permitting individuals, corporations, or communities to nullify the laws because they cross some selfish or local interest or prejudices is full of danger, not only to the nation at large, but much more to those who use this pernicious expedient to escape their just obligations or to obtain an unjust advantage over others. They will presently themselves be compelled to appeal to the law for protection, and those who would use the law as a defense must not deny that use of it to others.

If our great corporations would more scrupulously observe their legal limitations and duties, they would have less cause to complain of the unlawful limitations of their rights or of violent interference with their operations. The community that by concert, open or secret, among its citizens denies to a portion of its members their plain rights under the law has severed the only safe bond of social order and prosperity. The evil works from a bad center both ways. It demoralizes those who practice it and destroys the faith of those who suffer by it in the efficiency of the law as a safe protector. The man in whose breast that faith has been darkened is naturally the subject of dangerous and uncanny suggestions. Those who use unlawful methods, if moved by no higher motive than the selfishness that prompted them, may well stop and inquire what is to be the end of this.

An unlawful expedient can not become a permanent condition of government. If the educated and influential classes in a community either practice or connive at the systematic violation of laws that seem to them to cross their convenience, what can they expect when the lesson that convenience or a supposed class interest is a sufficient cause for lawlessness has been well learned by the ignorant classes? A community where law is the rule of conduct and where courts, not mobs, execute its penalties is the only attractive field for business investments and honest labor.

Our naturalization laws should be so amended as to make the inquiry into the character and good disposition of persons applying for citizenship more careful and searching. Our existing laws have been in their administration an unimpressive and often an unintelligible form. We accept the man as a citizen without any knowledge of his fitness, and he assumes the duties of citizenship without any knowledge as to what they are. The privileges of American citizenship are so great and its duties so grave that we may well insist upon a good knowledge of every person applying for citizenship and a good knowledge by him of our institutions. We should not cease to be hospitable to immigration, but we should cease to be careless as to the character of it. There are men of all races, even the best, whose coming is necessarily a burden upon our public revenues or a threat to social order. These should be identified and excluded.

We have happily maintained a policy of avoiding all interference with European affairs. We have been only interested spectators of their contentions in diplomacy and in war, ready to use our friendly offices to promote peace, but never obtruding our advice and never attempting unfairly to coin the distresses of other powers into commercial advantage to ourselves. We have a just right to expect that our European policy will be the American policy of European courts.

It is so manifestly incompatible with those precautions for our peace and safety which all the great powers habitually observe and enforce in matters affecting them that a shorter waterway between our eastern and western seaboards should be dominated by any European Government that we may confidently expect that such a purpose will not be entertained by any friendly power.

We shall in the future, as in the past, use every endeavor to maintain and enlarge our friendly relations with all the great powers, but they will not expect us to look kindly upon any project that would leave us subject to the dangers of a hostile observation or environment. We have not sought to dominate or to absorb any of our weaker neighbors, but rather to aid and encourage them to establish free and stable governments resting upon the consent of their own people. We have a clear right to expect, therefore, that no European Government will seek to establish colonial dependencies upon the territory of these independent American States. That which a sense of justice restrains us from seeking they may be reasonably expected willingly to forego. . . .

It is a subject of congratulation that there is a near prospect of the admission into the Union of the Dakotas and Montana and Washington Territories. This act of justice has been unreasonably delayed in the case of some of them. The people who have settled these Territories are intelligent, enterprising, and patriotic, and the accession of these new States will add strength to the nation. It is due to the settlers in the Territories who have availed themselves of the invitations of our land laws to make homes upon the public domain that their titles should be speedily adjusted and their honest entries confirmed by patent.

It is very gratifying to observe the general interest now being manifested in the reform of our election laws. Those who have been for years calling attention to the pressing necessity of throwing about the ballot box and about the elector further safeguards, in order that our elections might not only be free and pure, but might clearly appear to be so, will welcome the accession of any who did not so soon discover the need of reform. The National Congress has not as yet taken control of elections in that case over which the Constitution gives it jurisdiction, but has accepted and adopted the election laws of the several States, provided penalties for their violation and a method of supervision. Only the inefficiency of the State laws or an unfair partisan administration of them could suggest a departure from this policy.

It was clearly, however, in the contemplation of the framers of the Constitution that such an exigency might arise, and provision was wisely made for it. The freedom of the ballot is a condition of our national life, and no power vested in Congress or in the Executive to secure or perpetuate it should remain unused upon occasion. The people of all the Congressional districts have an equal interest that the election in each shall truly express the views and wishes of a majority of the qualified electors residing within it. The results of such elections are not local, and the insistence of electors residing in other districts that they shall be pure and free does not savor at all of impertinence.

If in any of the States the public security is thought to be threatened by ignorance among the electors, the obvious remedy is education. The sympathy and help of our people will not be withheld from any community struggling with special embarrassments or difficulties connected with the suffrage if the remedies proposed proceed upon lawful lines and are promoted by just and honorable methods. How shall those who practice election frauds recover that respect for the sanctity of the ballot which is the first condition and obligation of good citizenship? The man who has come to regard the ballot box as a juggler's hat has renounced his allegiance.

Let us exalt patriotism and moderate our party contentions. Let those who would die for the flag on the field of battle give a better proof of their patriotism and a higher glory to their country by promoting fraternity and justice. A party success that is achieved by unfair methods or by practices that partake of revolution is hurtful and evanescent even from a party standpoint. We should hold our differing opinions in mutual respect, and, having submitted them to the arbitrament of the ballot, should accept an adverse judgment with the same respect that we would have demanded of our opponents if the decision had been in our favor. . . .

I do not mistrust the future. Dangers have been in frequent ambush along our path, but we have uncovered and vanquished them all. Passion has swept some of our communities, but only to give us a new demonstration that the great body of our people are stable, patriotic, and law-abiding. No political party can long pursue advantage at the expense of public honor or by rude and indecent methods without protest and fatal disaffection in its own body. The peaceful agencies of commerce are more fully revealing the necessary unity of all our communities, and the increasing intercourse of our people is promoting mutual respect. We shall find unalloyed pleasure in the revelation which our next census will make of the swift development of the great resources of some of the States. Each State will bring its generous contribution to the great aggregate of the nation's increase. And when the harvests from the fields, the cattle from the hills, and the ores of the earth shall have been weighed, counted, and valued, we will turn from them all to crown with the highest honor the State that has most promoted education, virtue, justice, and patriotism among its people.

GROVER CLEVELAND

Second Address: March 4, 1893

When Cleveland was elected president for a second time, he sounded a tone more pessimistic and doubtful than what he had evinced in his first address. Evident in his speech are the pervasive worries about currency and monetary policies that gripped the nation during his time, as well as concerns among some laissez-faire advocates that government had grown too bloated and too intrusive upon the lives of business-minded Americans. Cleveland's presidency reflected the concern for business interests and issues that dominated both parties by 1893.

In obedience of the mandate of my countrymen I am about to dedicate myself to their service under the sanction of a solemn oath. Deeply moved by the expression of confidence and personal attachment which has called me to this service, I am sure my gratitude can make no better return than the pledge I now give before God and these witnesses of unreserved and complete devotion to the interests and welfare of those who have honored me. . . .

While every American citizen must contemplate with the utmost pride and enthusiasm the growth and expansion of our country, the sufficiency of our institutions to stand against the rudest shocks of violence, the wonderful thrift and enterprise of our people, and the demonstrated superiority of our free government, it behooves us to constantly watch for every symptom of insidious infirmity that threatens our national vigor.

The strong man who in the confidence of sturdy health courts the sternest activities of life and rejoices in the hardihood of constant labor may still have lurking near his vitals the unheeded disease that dooms him to sudden collapse.

It can not be doubted that, our stupendous achievements as a people and our country's robust strength have given rise to heedlessness of those laws governing our national health which we can no more evade than human life can escape the laws of God and nature.

Manifestly nothing is more vital to our supremacy as a nation and to the beneficent purposes of our Government than a sound and stable currency. Its exposure to degradation should at once arouse to activity the most enlightened statesmanship, and the danger of depreciation in the purchasing power of the wages paid to toil should furnish the strongest incentive to prompt and conservative precaution.

In dealing with our present embarrassing situation as related to this subject we will be wise if we temper our confidence and faith in our national strength and resources with the frank concession that even these will not permit us to defy with impunity the inexorable laws of finance and trade. At the same time, in our efforts to adjust differences of opinion we should be free from intolerance or passion, and our judgments should be unmoved by alluring phrases and unvexed by selfish interests.

I am confident that such an approach to the subject will result in prudent and effective remedial legislation. In the meantime, so far as the executive branch of the Government can intervene, none of the powers with which it is invested will be withheld when their exercise is deemed necessary to maintain our national credit or avert financial disaster.

Closely related to the exaggerated confidence in our country's greatness which tends to a disregard of the rules of national safety, another danger confronts us not less serious. I refer to the prevalence of a popular disposition to expect from the operation of the Government especial and direct individual advantages.

The verdict of our voters which condemned the injustice of maintaining protection for protection's sake enjoins upon the people's servants the duty of exposing and destroying the brood of kindred evils which are the unwholesome progeny of paternalism. This is the bane of republican institutions and the constant peril of our government by the people. It degrades to the purposes of wily craft the plan of rule our fathers established and bequeathed to us as an object of our love and veneration. It perverts the patriotic sentiments of our countrymen and tempts them to pitiful calculation of the sordid gain to be derived from their Government's maintenance. It undermines the self-reliance of our people and substitutes in its place dependence upon governmental favoritism. It stifles the spirit of true Americanism and stupefies every ennobling trait of American citizenship.

The lessons of paternalism ought to be unlearned and the better lesson taught that while the people should patriotically and cheerfully support their Government its functions do not include the support of the people.

The acceptance of this principle leads to a refusal of bounties and subsidies, which burden the labor and thrift of a portion of our citizens to aid ill-advised or languishing enterprises in which they have no concern. It leads also to a challenge of wild and reckless pension expenditure, which overleaps the bounds of grateful recognition of patriotic service and prostitutes to vicious uses the people's prompt and generous impulse to aid those disabled in their country's defense.

Every thoughtful American must realize the importance of checking at its beginning any tendency in public or private station to regard frugality and economy as virtues which we may safely outgrow. The toleration of this idea results in the waste of the people's money by their chosen servants and encourages prodigality and extravagance in the home life of our countrymen.

Under our scheme of government the waste of public money is a crime against the citizen, and the contempt of our people for economy and frugality in their personal affairs deplorably saps the strength and sturdiness of our national character.

It is a plain dictate of honesty and good government that public expenditures should be limited by public necessity, and that this should be measured by the rules of strict economy; and it is equally clear that frugality among the people is the best guaranty of a contented and strong support of free institutions. . . .

The existence of immense aggregations of kindred enterprises and combinations of business interests formed for the purpose of limiting production and fixing prices is inconsistent with the fair field which ought to be open to every independent activity. Legitimate strife in business should not be superseded by an enforced concession to the demands of combinations that have the power to destroy, nor should the people to be served lose the benefit of cheapness which usually results from wholesome competition. These aggregations and combinations frequently constitute conspiracies against the interests of the people, and in all their phases they are unnatural and opposed to our American sense of fairness. To the extent that they can be reached and restrained by Federal power the General Government should relieve our citizens from their interference and exactions.

Loyalty to the principles upon which our Government rests positively demands that the equality before the law which it guarantees to every citizen should be justly and in good faith conceded in all parts of the land. The enjoyment of this right follows the badge of citizenship wherever found, and, unimpaired by race or color, it appeals for recognition to American manliness and fairness. . . .

Above all, I know there is a Supreme Being who rules the affairs of men and whose goodness and mercy have always followed the American people, and I know He will not turn from us now if we humbly and reverently seek His powerful aid.

WILLIAM MCKINLEY

First Address: March 4, 1897

Currency policy and a raging national debate over the gold standard dominated McKinley's first address, as did the economic downturn that began shortly before he took office. As a result, his speech offered detailed economic arguments that were unusual for such addresses, as was his call for a special session of Congress to deal with the nation's financial woes. McKinley also addressed the ongoing issue of civil service reform and touched briefly on the sobering topic of lynching, particularly directed at African Americans in the South.

In obedience to the will of the people, and in their presence, by the authority vested in me by this oath, I assume the arduous and responsible duties of President of the United States, relying upon the support of my countrymen and invoking the guidance of Almighty God. Our faith teaches that there is no safer reliance than upon the God of our fathers, who has so singularly favored the American people in every national trial, and who will not forsake us so long as we obey His commandments and walk humbly in His footsteps.

The responsibilities of the high trust to which I have been called—always of grave importance—are augmented by the prevailing business conditions entailing idleness upon willing labor and loss to useful enterprises. The country is suffering from industrial disturbances from which speedy relief must be had. Our financial system needs some revision; our money is all good now, but its value must not further be threatened. It should all be put upon an enduring basis, not subject to easy attack, nor its stability to doubt or dispute. Our currency should continue under the supervision of the Government. The several forms of our paper money offer, in my judgment, a constant embarrassment to the Government and a safe balance in the Treasury. Therefore I believe it necessary to devise a system which, without diminishing the circulating medium or offering a premium for its contraction, will present a remedy for those arrangements which, temporary in their nature, might well in the years of our prosperity have been displaced by wiser provisions. With adequate revenue secured, but not until then, we can enter upon such changes in our fiscal laws as will, while insuring safety and volume to our money, no longer impose upon the Government the necessity of maintaining so large a gold reserve, with its attendant and inevitable temptations to speculation. Most of our financial laws are the outgrowth of experience and trial, and should not be amended without investigation and demonstration of the wisdom of the proposed changes. We must be both "sure we are right" and "make haste slowly." If, therefore, Congress, in its wisdom, shall deem it expedient to create a commission to take under early consideration the revision of our coinage, banking and currency laws, and give them that exhaustive, careful and dispassionate examination that their importance demands, I shall cordially concur in such action. If such power is vested in the President, it is my purpose to appoint a commission of prominent, well-informed citizens of different parties, who will command public confidence, both on account of their ability and special fitness for the work. Business experience and public training may thus be combined, and the patriotic zeal of the friends of the country be so directed that such a report will be made as to receive the support of all parties, and our finances cease to be the subject of mere partisan contention. The experiment is, at all events, worth a trial, and, in my opinion, it can but prove beneficial to the entire country. . . .

Economy is demanded in every branch of the Government at all times, but especially in periods, like the present, of depression in business and distress among the people. The severest economy must be observed in all public expenditures, and extravagance stopped wherever it is found, and prevented wherever in the future it may be developed. . . .

The Government should not be permitted to run behind or increase its debt in times like the present. Suitably to provide against this is the mandate of duty—the certain and easy remedy for most of our financial difficulties. A deficiency is inevitable so long as the expenditures of the Government exceed its receipts. It can only be met by loans or an increased revenue. While a large annual surplus of revenue may invite waste and extravagance, inadequate revenue creates distrust and undermines public and private credit. Neither should be encouraged. Between more loans and more revenue there ought to be but one opinion. We should have more revenue, and that without delay, hindrance, or postponement. A surplus in the Treasury created by loans is not a permanent or safe reliance. . . .

The best way for the Government to maintain its credit is to pay as it goes—not by resorting to loans, but by keeping out of debt—through an adequate income secured by a system of taxation, external or internal, or both. It is the settled policy of the Government, pursued from the beginning and practiced by all parties and Administrations, to raise the bulk of our revenue from taxes upon foreign productions entering the United States for sale and consumption, and avoiding, for the most part, every form of direct taxation, except in time of war. . . . It is, therefore, earnestly hoped and expected that Congress will, at the earliest practicable moment, enact revenue legislation that shall be fair, reasonable, conservative, and just, and which, while supplying sufficient revenue for public purposes, will still be signally beneficial and helpful to every section and every enterprise of the people. . . .

Business conditions are not the most promising. It will take time to restore the prosperity of former years. If we cannot promptly attain it, we can resolutely turn our faces in that direction and aid its return by friendly legislation. However troublesome the situation may appear, Congress will not, I am sure, be found lacking in disposition or ability to relieve it as far as legislation can do so. The restoration of confidence and the revival of business, which men of all parties so much desire, depend more largely upon the prompt, energetic, and intelligent action of Congress than upon any other single agency affecting the situation.

It is inspiring, too, to remember that no great emergency in the one hundred and eight years of our eventful national life has ever arisen that has not been met with wisdom and courage by the American people, with fidelity to their best interests and highest destiny, and to the honor of the American name. These years of glorious history have exalted mankind and advanced the cause of freedom throughout the world, and immeasurably strengthened the precious free institutions which we enjoy. The people love and will sustain these institutions. The great essential to our happiness and prosperity is that we adhere to the principles upon which the Government was established and insist upon their faithful observance. Equality of rights must prevail, and our laws be always and everywhere respected and obeyed. We may have failed in the discharge of our full duty as citizens of the great Republic, but it is consoling and encouraging to realize that free speech, a free press, free thought, free schools, the free and unmolested right of religious liberty and worship, and free and fair elections are dearer and more universally enjoyed to-day than ever before. These guaranties must be sacredly preserved and wisely strengthened. The constituted authorities must be cheerfully and vigorously upheld. Lynchings must not be tolerated in a great and civilized country like the United States; courts, not mobs, must execute the penalties of the law. The preservation of public order, the right of discussion, the integrity of courts, and the orderly administration of justice must continue forever the rock of safety upon which our Government securely rests. . . .

Our naturalization and immigration laws should be further improved to the constant promotion of a safer, a better, and a higher citizenship. A grave peril to the Republic would be a citizenship too ignorant to understand or too vicious to appreciate the great value and beneficence of our institutions and laws, and against all who come here to make war upon them our gates must be promptly and tightly closed. Nor must we be unmindful of the need of improvement among our own citizens, but with the zeal of our forefathers encourage the spread of knowledge and free education. Illiteracy must be banished from the land if we shall attain that high destiny as the foremost of the enlightened nations of the world which, under Providence, we ought to achieve.

Reforms in the civil service must go on; but the changes should be real and genuine, not perfunctory, or prompted by a zeal in behalf of any party simply because it happens to be in power. As a member of Congress I voted and spoke in favor of the present law, and I shall attempt its enforcement in the spirit in which it was enacted. The purpose in view was to secure the most efficient service of the best men who would accept appointment under the Government, retaining faithful and devoted public servants in office, but shielding none, under the authority of any rule or custom, who are inefficient, incompetent, or unworthy. The best interests of the country demand this, and the people heartily approve the law wherever and whenever it has been thus administrated. . . .

It has been the policy of the United States since the foundation of the Government to cultivate relations of peace and amity with all the nations of the world, and this accords with my conception of our duty now. We have cherished the policy of non-interference with affairs of foreign governments wisely inaugurated by Washington, keeping ourselves free from entanglement, either as allies or foes, content to leave undisturbed with them the settlement of their own domestic concerns. It will be our aim to pursue a firm and dignified foreign policy, which shall be just, impartial, ever watchful of our national honor, and always insisting upon the enforcement of the lawful rights of American citizens everywhere. . . .

It has been the uniform practice of each President to avoid, as far as possible, the convening of Congress in extraordinary session. It is an example which, under ordinary circumstances and in the absence of a public necessity, is to be commended. But a failure to convene the representatives of the people in Congress in extra session when it involves neglect of a public duty places the responsibility of such neglect upon the Executive himself. The condition of the public Treasury, as has been indicated, demands the immediate consideration of Congress. . . . I shall deem it my duty as President to convene Congress in extraordinary session on Monday, the 15th day of March, 1897.

In conclusion, I congratulate the country upon the fraternal spirit of the people and the manifestations of good will everywhere so apparent. The recent election not only most fortunately demonstrated the obliteration of sectional or geographical lines, but to some extent also the prejudices which for years have distracted our councils and marred our true greatness as a nation. The triumph of the people, whose verdict is carried into effect today, is not the triumph of one section, nor wholly of one party, but of all sections and all the people. The North and the South no longer divide on the old lines, but upon principles and policies; and in this fact surely every lover of the country can find cause for true felicitation. . . .

Second Address: March 4, 1901

McKinley's second speech was more upbeat about the economy, as the problems of 1897 had largely been solved. The biggest news during his first term had been the Spanish-American War, of which President McKinley had been at best a lukewarm supporter. The war was more or less thrust upon him by Congress and an American people hungry for imperial expansion and angry at perceived Spanish wrongdoing.

McKinley's attitude is evident here in his terse reference to the war itself, and his un-derstanding of its consequences is likewise indicated by his lengthy reference to the guerrilla war America was now compelled to wage in the Philippines.

When we assembled here on the 4th of March, 1897, there was great anxiety with regard to our currency and credit. None exists now. Then our Treasury receipts were inadequate to meet the current obligations of the Government. Now they are sufficient for all public needs, and we have a surplus instead of a deficit. Then I felt constrained to convene the Congress in extraordinary session to devise revenues to pay the ordinary expenses of the Government. Now I have the satisfaction to announce that the Congress just closed has reduced taxation in the sum of $41,000,000. Then there was deep solicitude because of the long depression in our manufacturing, mining, agricultural, and mercantile industries and the consequent distress of our laboring population. Now every avenue of production is crowded with activity, labor is well employed, and American products find good markets at home and abroad. . . .

Honesty, capacity, and industry are nowhere more indispensable than in public employment. These should be fundamental requisites to original appointment and the surest guaranties against removal.

Four years ago we stood on the brink of war without the people knowing it and without any preparation or effort at preparation for the impending peril. I did all that in honor could be done to avert the war, but without avail. It became inevitable; and the Congress at its first regular session, without party division, provided money in anticipation of the crisis and in preparation to meet it. It came. The result was signally favorable to American arms and in the highest degree honorable to the Government. It imposed upon us obligations from which we cannot escape and from which it would be dishonorable to seek escape. We are now at peace with the world, and it is my fervent prayer that if differences arise between us and other powers they may be settled by peaceful arbitration and that hereafter we may be spared the horrors of war. . . .

Strong hearts and helpful hands are needed, and, fortunately, we have them in every part of our beloved country. We are reunited. Sectionalism has disappeared. Division on public questions can no longer be traced by the war maps of 1861. These old differences less and less disturb the judgment. Existing problems demand the thought and quicken the conscience of the country, and the responsibility for their presence, as well as for their righteous settlement, rests upon us all—no more upon me than upon you. There are some national questions in the solution of which patriotism should exclude partisanship. Magnifying their difficulties will not take them off our hands nor facilitate their adjustment. Distrust of the capacity, integrity, and high purposes of the American people will not be an inspiring theme for future political contests. Dark pictures and gloomy forebodings are worse than useless. These only becloud, they do not help to point the way of safety and honor. "Hope maketh not ashamed." The prophets of evil were not the builders of the Republic, nor in its crises since have they saved or served it. The faith of the fathers was a mighty force in its creation, and the faith of their descendants has wrought its progress and furnished its defenders. They are obstructionists who despair, and who would destroy confidence in the ability of our people to solve wisely and for civilization the mighty problems resting upon them. The American people, intrenched in freedom at home, take their love for it with them wherever they go, and they reject as mistaken and unworthy the doctrine that we lose our own liberties by securing the enduring foundations of liberty to others. Our institutions will not deteriorate by extension, and our sense of justice will not abate under tropic suns in distant seas. As heretofore, so hereafter will the nation demonstrate its fitness to administer any new estate which events devolve upon it, and in the fear of God will "take occasion by the hand and make the bounds of freedom wider yet." If there are those among us who would make our way more difficult, we must not be disheartened, but the more earnestly dedicate ourselves to the task upon which we have rightly entered. The path of progress is seldom smooth. New things are often found hard to do. Our fathers found them so. We find them so. They are inconvenient. They cost us something. But are we not made better for the effort and sacrifice, and are not those we serve lifted up and blessed?

We will be consoled, to, with the fact that opposition has confronted every onward movement of the Republic from its opening hour until now, but without success. The Republic has marched on and on, and its step has exalted freedom and humanity. We are undergoing the same ordeal as did our predecessors nearly a century ago. We are following the course they blazed. They triumphed. Will their successors falter and plead organic impotency in the nation? Surely after 125 years of achievement for mankind we will not now surrender our equality with other powers on matters fundamental and essential to nationality. With no such purpose was the nation created. In no such spirit has it developed its full and independent sovereignty. We adhere to the principle of equality among ourselves, and by no act of ours will we assign to ourselves a subordinate rank in the family of nations.

My fellow-citizens, the public events of the past four years have gone into history. They are too near to justify recital. Some of them were unforeseen; many of them momentous and far-reaching in their consequences to ourselves and our relations with the rest of the world. The part which the United States bore so honorably in the thrilling scenes in China, while new to American life, has been in harmony with its true spirit and best traditions, and in dealing with the results its policy will be that of moderation and fairness. . . .

While the treaty of peace with Spain was ratified on the 6th of February, 1899, and ratifications were exchanged nearly two years ago, the Congress has indicated no form of government for the Philippine Islands. It has, however, provided an army to enable the Executive to suppress insurrection, restore peace, give security to the inhabitants, and establish the authority of the United States throughout the archipelago. . . . The Government's representatives, civil and military, are doing faithful and noble work in their mission of emancipation and merit the approval and support of their countrymen. The most liberal terms of amnesty have already been communicated to the insurgents, and the way is still open for those who have raised their arms against the Government for honorable submission to its authority. Our countrymen should not be deceived. We are not waging war against the inhabitants of the Philippine Islands. A portion of them are making war against the United States. By far the greater part of the inhabitants recognize American sovereignty and welcome it as a guaranty of order and of security for life, property, liberty, freedom of conscience, and the pursuit of happiness. To them full protection will be given. They shall not be abandoned. We will not leave the destiny of the loyal millions on the islands to the disloyal thousands who are in rebellion against the United States. Order under civil institutions will come as soon as those who now break the peace shall keep it. Force will not be needed or used when those who make war against us shall make it no more. May it end without further bloodshed, and there be ushered in the reign of peace to be made permanent by a government of liberty under law!

THEODORE ROOSEVELT

March 4, 1905

It may seem surprising that a man who dominated his era in so many ways delivered one of the shorter Inaugural Addresses in American presidential history. But packed into its brief phrases are many of the assumptions and principles that would guide TR— and much of America—during the Progressive Era: an embrace of robust and "manly" individualism, an assertion that the United States should become an imperial power- house, and a confident feeling that America was on the cutting edge of history.

My fellow-citizens, no people on earth have more cause to be thankful than ours, and this is said reverently, in no spirit of boastfulness in our own strength, but with gratitude to the Giver of Good who has blessed us with the conditions which have enabled us to achieve so large a measure of well-being and of happiness. To us as a people it has been granted to lay the foundations of our national life in a new continent. We are the heirs of the ages, and yet we have had to pay few of the penalties which in old countries are exacted by the dead hand of a bygone civilization. We have not been obliged to fight for our existence against any alien race; and yet our life has called for the vigor and effort without which the manlier and hardier virtues wither away. Under such conditions it would be our own fault if we failed; and the success which we have had in the past, the success which we confidently believe the future will bring, should cause in us no feeling of vainglory, but rather a deep and abiding realization of all which life has offered us; a full acknowledgment of the responsibility which is ours; and a fixed determination to show that under a free government a mighty people can thrive best, alike as regards the things of the body and the things of the soul.

Much has been given us, and much will rightfully be expected from us. We have duties to others and duties to ourselves; and we can shirk neither. We have become a great nation, forced by the fact of its greatness into relations with the other nations of the earth, and we must behave as beseems a people with such responsibilities. Toward all other nations, large and small, our attitude must be one of cordial and sincere friendship. We must show not only in our words, but in our deeds, that we are earnestly desirous of securing their good will by acting toward them in a spirit of just and generous recognition of all their rights. But justice and generosity in a nation, as in an individual, count most when shown not by the weak but by the strong. While ever careful to refrain from wrongdoing others, we must be no less insistent that we are not wronged ourselves. We wish peace, but we wish the peace of justice, the peace of righteousness. We wish it because we think it is right and not because we are afraid. No weak nation that acts manfully and justly should ever have cause to fear us, and no strong power should ever be able to single us out as a subject for insolent aggression.

Our relations with the other powers of the world are important; but still more important are our relations among ourselves. Such growth in wealth, in population, and in power as this nation has seen during the century and a quarter of its national life is inevitably accompanied by a like growth in the problems which are ever before every nation that rises to greatness. Power invariably means both responsibility and danger. Our forefathers faced certain perils which we have outgrown. We now face other perils, the very existence of which it was impossible that they should foresee. Modern life is both complex and intense, and the tremendous changes wrought by the extraordinary industrial development of the last half century are felt in every fiber of our social and political being. Never before have men tried so vast and formidable an experiment as that of administering the affairs of a continent under the forms of a Democratic republic. The conditions which have told for our marvelous material well-being, which have developed to a very high degree our energy, self-reliance, and individual initiative, have also brought the care and anxiety inseparable from the accumulation of great wealth in industrial centers. Upon the success of our experiment much depends, not only as regards our own welfare, but as regards the welfare of mankind. If we fail, the cause of free self-government throughout the world will rock to its foundations, and therefore our responsibility is heavy, to ourselves, to the world as it is to-day, and to the generations yet unborn. There is no good reason why we should fear the future, but there is every reason why we should face it seriously, neither hiding from ourselves the gravity of the problems before us nor fearing to approach these problems with the unbending, unflinching purpose to solve them aright.

Yet, after all, though the problems are new, though the tasks set before us differ from the tasks set before our fathers who founded and preserved this Republic, the spirit in which these tasks must be undertaken and these problems faced, if our duty is to be well done, remains essentially unchanged. We know that self-government is difficult. We know that no people needs such high traits of character as that people which seeks to govern its affairs aright through the freely expressed will of the freemen who compose it. But we have faith that we shall not prove false to the memories of the men of the mighty past. They did their work, they left us the splendid heritage we now enjoy. We in our turn have an assured confidence that we shall be able to leave this heritage unwasted and enlarged to our children and our children's children. To do so we must show, not merely in great crises, but in the everyday affairs of life, the qualities of practical intelligence, of courage, of hardihood, and endurance, and above all the power of devotion to a lofty ideal, which made great the men who founded this Republic in the days of Washington, which made great the men who preserved this Republic in the days of Abraham Lincoln.

WILLIAM HOWARD TAFT

March 4, 1909

If Teddy Roosevelt's Inaugural Address was a model of powerful brevity, Taft's speech was the quintessential presidential laundry list of concerns great and small. The increased tendency of presidents to attempt directly to influence Congress is evident here, as Taft not only declared his willingness to call Congress into special session, but also tried to specify what sort of business they would undertake. It was also evident that Taft could see the storm clouds of war gathering on the European horizon, and he took the time-honored presidential approach of maintaining that America should stand neutral and above the fray. On the domestic front, Taft sounded a note on race relations typical of the day: vague assertions of African American rights, followed by a call for blacks to promote their own self-sufficiency and an appeal for leaving white Southerners alone for the most part to run their own affairs.

Anyone who has taken the oath I have just taken must feel a heavy weight of responsibility. If not, he has no conception of the powers and duties of the office upon which he is about to enter, or he is lacking in a proper sense of the obligation which the oath imposes. . . .

I have had the honor to be one of the advisers of my distinguished predecessor [Theodore Roosevelt], and, as such, to hold up his hands in the reforms he has initiated. I should be untrue to myself, to my promises, and to the declarations of the party platform upon which I was elected to office, if I did not make the maintenance and enforcement of those reforms a most important feature of my administration. They were directed to the suppression of the lawlessness and abuses of power of the great combinations of capital invested in railroads and in industrial enterprises carrying on interstate commerce. The steps which my predecessor took and the legislation passed on his recommendation have accomplished much, have caused a general halt in the vicious policies which created popular alarm, and have brought about in the business affected a much higher regard for existing law. . . .

It is believed that with the changes to be recommended American business can be assured of that measure of stability and certainty in respect to those things that may be done and those that are prohibited which is essential to the life and growth of all business. Such a plan must include the right of the people to avail themselves of those methods of combining capital and effort deemed necessary to reach the highest degree of economic efficiency, at the same time differentiating between combinations based upon legitimate economic reasons and those formed with the intent of creating monopolies and artificially controlling prices.

The work of formulating into practical shape such changes is creative work of the highest order, and requires all the deliberation possible in the interval. I believe that the amendments to be proposed are just as necessary in the protection of legitimate business as in the clinching of the reforms which properly bear the name of my predecessor.

A matter of most pressing importance is the revision of the tariff. In accordance with the promises of the platform upon which I was elected, I shall call Congress into extra session to meet on the 15th day of March, in order that consideration may be at once given to a bill revising the Dingley Act [an 1897 act imposing high protective tariffs on some imports as a way of protecting American industry]. . . . To secure the needed speed in the passage of the tariff bill, it would seem wise to attempt no other legislation at the extra session. I venture this as a suggestion only, for the course to be taken by Congress, upon the call of the Executive, is wholly within its discretion. . . .

It is imperative that [the federal budget] deficit shall not continue, and the framers of the tariff bill must, of course, have in mind the total revenues likely to be produced by it and so arrange the duties as to secure an adequate income. Should it be impossible to do so by import duties, new kinds of taxation must be adopted, and among these I recommend a graduated inheritance tax as correct in principle and as certain and easy of collection.

The obligation on the part of those responsible for the expenditures made to carry on the Government, to be as economical as possible, and to make the burden of taxation as light as possible, is plain, and should be affirmed in every declaration of government policy. This is especially true when we are face to face with a heavy deficit. But when the desire to win the popular approval leads to the cutting off of expenditures really needed to make the Government effective and to enable it to accomplish its proper objects, the result is as much to be condemned as the waste of government funds in unnecessary expenditure. The scope of a modern government in what it can and ought to accomplish for its people has been widened far beyond the principles laid down by the old "laissez faire" school of political writers, and this widening has met popular approval . . ..

Our international policy is always to promote peace. We shall enter into any war with a full consciousness of the awful consequences that it always entails, whether successful or not, and we, of course, shall make every effort consistent with national honor and the highest national interest to avoid a resort to arms. . . . But we should be blind to existing conditions and should allow ourselves to become foolish idealists if we did not realize that, with all the nations of the world armed and prepared for war, we must be ourselves in a similar condition, in order to prevent other nations from taking advantage of us and of our inability to defend our interests and assert our rights with a strong hand. . . .

The admission of Asiatic immigrants who cannot be amalgamated with our population has been made the subject either of prohibitory clauses in our treaties and statutes or of strict administrative regulation secured by diplomatic negotiation. I sincerely hope that we may continue to minimize the evils likely to arise from such immigration without unnecessary friction and by mutual concessions between self-respecting governments. Meantime we must take every precaution to prevent, or failing that, to punish outbursts of race feeling among our people against foreigners of whatever nationality who have by our grant a treaty right to pursue lawful business here and to be protected against lawless assault or injury. . . .

The incoming Congress should promptly fulfill the promise of the Republican platform and pass a proper postal savings bank bill. . . .

I sincerely hope that the incoming Congress will be alive, as it should be, to the importance of our foreign trade and of encouraging it in every way feasible. . . .

I look forward with hope to increasing the already good feeling between the South and the other sections of the country. My chief purpose is not to effect a change in the electoral vote of the Southern States. That is a secondary consideration. What I look forward to is an increase in the tolerance of political views of all kinds and their advocacy throughout the South, and the existence of a respectable political opposition in every State; even more than this, to an increased feeling on the part of all the people in the South that this Government is their Government, and that its officers in their states are their officers.

The consideration of this question can not, however, be complete and full without reference to the negro race, its progress and its present condition. The thirteenth amendment secured them freedom; the fourteenth amendment due process of law, protection of property, and the pursuit of happiness; and the fifteenth amendment attempted to secure the negro against any deprivation of the privilege to vote because he was a negro. The thirteenth and fourteenth amendments have been generally enforced and have secured the objects for which they are intended. While the fifteenth amendment has not been generally observed in the past, it ought to be observed, and the tendency of Southern legislation today is toward the enactment of electoral qualifications which shall square with that amendment. Of course, the mere adoption of a constitutional law is only one step in the right direction. It must be fairly and justly enforced as well. In time both will come. Hence it is clear to all that the domination of an ignorant, irresponsible element can be prevented by constitutional laws which shall exclude from voting both negroes and whites not having education or other qualifications thought to be necessary for a proper electorate. The danger of the control of an ignorant electorate has therefore passed. With this change, the interest which many of the Southern white citizens take in the welfare of the negroes has increased. The colored men must base their hope on the results of their own industry, self-restraint, thrift, and business success, as well as upon the aid and comfort and sympathy which they may receive from their white neighbors of the South. . . .

If [the Fifteenth Amendment] had not passed, it might be difficult now to adopt it; but with it in our fundamental law, the policy of Southern legislation must and will tend to obey it, and so long as the statutes of the States meet the test of this amendment and are not otherwise in conflict with the Constitution and laws of the United States, it is not the disposition or within the province of the Federal Government to interfere with the regulation by Southern States of their domestic affairs. There is in the South a stronger feeling than ever among the intelligent well-to-do, and influential element in favor of the industrial education of the negro and the encouragement of the race to make themselves useful members of the community. The progress which the negro has made in the last fifty years, from slavery, when its statistics are reviewed, is marvelous, and it furnishes every reason to hope that in the next twenty-five years a still greater improvement in his condition as a productive member of society, on the farm, and in the shop, and in other occupations may come.

The negroes are now Americans. Their ancestors came here years ago against their will, and this is their only country and their only flag. They have shown themselves anxious to live for it and to die for it. Encountering the race feeling against them, subjected at times to cruel injustice growing out of it, they may well have our profound sympathy and aid in the struggle they are making. We are charged with the sacred duty of making their path as smooth and easy as we can. Any recognition of their distinguished men, any appointment to office from among their number, is properly taken as an encouragement and an appreciation of their progress, and this just policy should be pursued when suitable occasion offers.

But it may well admit of doubt whether, in the case of any race, an appointment of one of their number to a local office in a community in which the race feeling is so widespread and acute as to interfere with the ease and facility with which the local government business can be done by the appointee is of sufficient benefit by way of encouragement to the race to outweigh the recurrence and increase of race feeling which such an appointment is likely to engender. Therefore the Executive, in recognizing the negro race by appointments, must exercise a careful discretion not thereby to do it more harm than good. On the other hand, we must be careful not to encourage the mere pretense of race feeling manufactured in the interest of individual political ambition.

Personally, I have not the slightest race prejudice or feeling, and recognition of its existence only awakens in my heart a deeper sympathy for those who have to bear it or suffer from it, and I question the wisdom of a policy which is likely to increase it. Meantime, if nothing is done to prevent it, a better feeling between the negroes and the whites in the South will continue to grow, and more and more of the white people will come to realize that the future of the South is to be much benefited by the industrial and intellectual progress of the negro. The exercise of political franchises by those of this race who are intelligent and well to do will be acquiesced in, and the right to vote will be withheld only from the ignorant and irresponsible of both races. . . .

Having thus reviewed the questions likely to recur during my administration, and having expressed in a summary way the position which I expect to take in recommendations to Congress and in my conduct as an Executive, I invoke the considerate sympathy and support of my fellow-citizens and the aid of the Almighty God in the discharge of my responsible duties.

WOODROW WILSON

First Address: March 4, 1913

Wilson was one of very few presidents who openly discussed party politics in his Inaugural Address; most presidents preferred to follow Washington's example and declare their desire for nonpartisan government. Wilson's openly expressed party loyalties, as well as his academic background, gave his address a lofty, lecturing quality, as he painted in broad brushstrokes a vision for what he believed to be a promising new future for his party and his nation.

There has been a change of government. It began two years ago, when the House of Representatives became Democratic by a decisive majority. It has now been completed. The Senate about to assemble will also be Democratic. The offices of President and Vice-President have been put into the hands of Democrats. What does the change mean? That is the question that is uppermost in our minds to-day. That is the question I am going to try to answer, in order, if I may, to interpret the occasion.

It means much more than the mere success of a party. The success of a party means little except when the Nation is using that party for a large and definite purpose. No one can mistake the purpose for which the Nation now seeks to use the Democratic Party. It seeks to use it to interpret a change in its own plans and point of view. Some old things with which we had grown familiar, and which had begun to creep into the very habit of our thought and of our lives, have altered their aspect as we have latterly looked critically upon them, with fresh, awakened eyes; have dropped their disguises and shown themselves alien and sinister. Some new things, as we look frankly upon them, willing to comprehend their real character, have come to assume the aspect of things long believed in and familiar, stuff of our own convictions. We have been refreshed by a new insight into our own life.

We see that in many things that life is very great. It is incomparably great in its material aspects, in its body of wealth, in the diversity and sweep of its energy, in the industries which have been conceived and built up by the genius of individual men and the limitless enterprise of groups of men. It is great, also, very great, in its moral force. Nowhere else in the world have noble men and women exhibited in more striking forms the beauty and the energy of sympathy and helpfulness and counsel in their efforts to rectify wrong, alleviate suffering, and set the weak in the way of strength and hope. We have built up, moreover, a great system of government, which has stood through a long age as in many respects a model for those who seek to set liberty upon foundations that will endure against fortuitous change, against storm and accident. Our life contains every great thing, and contains it in rich abundance.

But the evil has come with the good, and much fine gold has been corroded. With riches has come inexcusable waste. We have squandered a great part of what we might have used, and have not stopped to conserve the exceeding bounty of nature, without which our genius for enterprise would have been worthless and impotent, scorning to be careful, shamefully prodigal as well as admirably efficient. We have been proud of our industrial achievements, but we have not hitherto stopped thoughtfully enough to count the human cost, the cost of lives snuffed out, of energies overtaxed and broken, the fearful physical and spiritual cost to the men and women and children upon whom the dead weight and burden of it all has fallen pitilessly the years through. The groans and agony of it all had not yet reached our ears, the solemn, moving undertone of our life, coming up out of the mines and factories, and out of every home where the struggle had its intimate and familiar seat. With the great Government went many deep secret things which we too long delayed to look into and scrutinize with candid, fearless eyes. The great Government we loved has too often been made use of for private and selfish purposes, and those who used it had forgotten the people.

At last a vision has been vouchsafed us of our life as a whole. We see the bad with the good, the debased and decadent with the sound and vital. With this vision we approach new affairs. Our duty is to cleanse, to reconsider, to restore, to correct the evil without impairing the good, to purify and humanize every process of our common life without weakening or sentimentalizing it. There has been something crude and heartless and unfeeling in our haste to succeed and be great. Our thought has been "Let every man look out for himself, let every generation look out for itself," while we reared giant machinery which made it impossible that any but those who stood at the levers of control should have a chance to look out for themselves. We had not forgotten our morals. We remembered well enough that we had set up a policy which was meant to serve the humblest as well as the most powerful, with an eye single to the standards of justice and fair play, and remembered it with pride. But we were very heedless and in a hurry to be great.

We have come now to the sober second thought. The scales of heedlessness have fallen from our eyes. We have made up our minds to square every process of our national life again with the standards we so proudly set up at the beginning and have always carried at our hearts. Our work is a work of restoration.

We have itemized with some degree of particularity the things that ought to be altered and here are some of the chief items: A tariff which cuts us off from our proper part in the commerce of the world, violates the just principles of taxation, and makes the Government a facile instrument in the hand of private interests; a banking and currency system based upon the necessity of the Government to sell its bonds fifty years ago and perfectly adapted to concentrating cash and restricting credits; an industrial system which, take it on all its sides, financial as well as administrative, holds capital in leading strings, restricts the liberties and limits the opportunities of labor, and exploits without renewing or conserving the natural resources of the country; a body of agricultural activities never yet given the efficiency of great business undertakings or served as it should be through the instrumentality of science taken directly to the farm, or afforded the facilities of credit best suited to its practical needs; watercourses undeveloped, waste places unreclaimed, forests untended, fast disappearing without plan or prospect of renewal, unregarded waste heaps at every mine. We have studied as perhaps no other nation has the most effective means of production, but we have not studied cost or economy as we should either as organizers of industry, as statesmen, or as individuals.

Nor have we studied and perfected the means by which government may be put at the service of humanity, in safeguarding the health of the Nation, the health of its men and its women and its children, as well as their rights in the struggle for existence. This is no sentimental duty. The firm basis of government is justice, not pity. These are matters of justice. There can be no equality or opportunity, the first essential of justice in the body politic, if men and women and children be not shielded in their lives, their very vitality, from the consequences of great industrial and social processes which they can not alter, control, or singly cope with. Society must see to it that it does not itself crush or weaken or damage its own constituent parts. The first duty of law is to keep sound the society it serves. Sanitary laws, pure food laws, and laws determining conditions of labor which individuals are powerless to determine for themselves are intimate parts of the very business of justice and legal efficiency.

These are some of the things we ought to do, and not leave the others undone, the old-fashioned, never-to-be-neglected, fundamental safeguarding of property and of individual right. This is the high enterprise of the new day: To lift everything that concerns our life as a Nation to the light that shines from the hearthfire of every man's conscience and vision of the right. It is inconceivable that we should do this as partisans; it is inconceivable we should do it in ignorance of the facts as they are or in blind haste. We shall restore, not destroy. We shall deal with our economic system as it is and as it may be modified, not as it might be if we had a clean sheet of paper to write upon; and step by step we shall make it what it should be, in the spirit of those who question their own wisdom and seek counsel and knowledge, not shallow self-satisfaction or the excitement of excursions whither they can not tell. Justice, and only justice, shall always be our motto.

And yet it will be no cool process of mere science. The Nation has been deeply stirred, stirred by a solemn passion, stirred by the knowledge of wrong, of ideals lost, of government too often debauched and made an instrument of evil. The feelings with which we face this new age of right and opportunity sweep across our heartstrings like some air out of God's own presence, where justice and mercy are reconciled and the judge and the brother are one. We know our task to be no mere task of politics but a task which shall search us through and through, whether we be able to understand our time and the need of our people, whether we be indeed their spokesmen and interpreters, whether we have the pure heart to comprehend and the rectified will to choose our high course of action.

This is not a day of triumph; it is a day of dedication. Here muster, not the forces of party, but the forces of humanity. Men's hearts wait upon us; men's lives hang in the balance; men's hopes call upon us to say what we will do. Who shall live up to the great trust? Who dares fail to try? I summon all honest men, all patriotic, all forward-looking men, to my side. God helping me, I will not fail them, if they will but counsel and sustain me!

Second Address: March 5, 1917

Foreign policy barely appeared in Wilson's first address. Four years later, with the world at war and the United States on the cusp of entering the conflict, foreign affairs dominated Wilson's speech. A month later he would travel directly to Congress, an armed cavalry escort at his side, to request a formal declaration of war against Germany and her allies.

The four years which have elapsed since last I stood in this place have been crowded with counsel and action of the most vital interest and consequence. Perhaps no equal period in our history has been so fruitful of important reforms in our economic and industrial life or so full of significant changes in the spirit and purpose of our political action. We have sought very thoughtfully to set our house in order, correct the grosser errors and abuses of our industrial life, liberate and quicken the processes of our national genius and energy, and lift our politics to a broader view of the people's essential interests.

It is a record of singular variety and singular distinction. But I shall not attempt to review it. It speaks for itself and will be of increasing influence as the years go by. This is not the time for retrospect. It is time rather to speak our thoughts and purposes concerning the present and the immediate future.

Although we have centered counsel and action with such unusual concentration and success upon the great problems of domestic legislation to which we addressed ourselves four years ago, other matters have more and more forced themselves upon our attention—matters lying outside our own life as a nation and over which we had no control, but which, despite our wish to keep free of them, have drawn us more and more irresistibly into their own current and influence.

It has been impossible to avoid them. They have affected the life of the whole world. They have shaken men everywhere with a passion and an apprehension they never knew before. It has been hard to preserve calm counsel while the thought of our own people swayed this way and that under their influence. We are a composite and cosmopolitan people. We are of the blood of all the nations that are at war. The currents of our thoughts as well as the currents of our trade run quick at all seasons back and forth between us and them. The war inevitably set its mark from the first alike upon our minds, our industries, our commerce, our politics and our social action. To be indifferent to it, or independent of it, was out of the question.

And yet all the while we have been conscious that we were not part of it. In that consciousness, despite many divisions, we have drawn closer together. We have been deeply wronged upon the seas, but we have not wished to wrong or injure in return; have retained throughout the consciousness of standing in some sort apart, intent upon an interest that transcended the immediate issues of the war itself.

As some of the injuries done us have become intolerable we have still been clear that we wished nothing for ourselves that we were not ready to demand for all mankind—fair dealing, justice, the freedom to live and to be at ease against organized wrong.

It is in this spirit and with this thought that we have grown more and more aware, more and more certain that the part we wished to play was the part of those who mean to vindicate and fortify peace. We have been obliged to arm ourselves to make good our claim to a certain minimum of right and of freedom of action. We stand firm in armed neutrality since it seems that in no other way we can demonstrate what it is we insist upon and cannot forget. We may even be drawn on, by circumstances, not by our own purpose or desire, to a more active assertion of our rights as we see them and a more immediate association with the great struggle itself. But nothing will alter our thought or our purpose. They are too clear to be obscured. They are too deeply rooted in the principles of our national life to be altered. We desire neither conquest nor advantage. We wish nothing that can be had only at the cost of another people. We always professed unselfish purpose and we covet the opportunity to prove our professions are sincere.

There are many things still to be done at home, to clarify our own politics and add new vitality to the industrial processes of our own life, and we shall do them as time and opportunity serve, but we realize that the greatest things that remain to be done must be done with the whole world for stage and in cooperation with the wide and universal forces of mankind, and we are making our spirits ready for those things.

We are provincials no longer. The tragic events of the thirty months of vital turmoil through which we have just passed have made us citizens of the world. There can be no turning back. Our own fortunes as a nation are involved whether we would have it so or not.

And yet we are not the less Americans on that account. We shall be the more American if we but remain true to the principles in which we have been bred. They are not the principles of a province or of a single continent. We have known and boasted all along that they were the principles of a liberated mankind. These, therefore, are the things we shall stand for, whether in war or in peace:

That all nations are equally interested in the peace of the world and in the political stability of free peoples, and equally responsible for their maintenance; that the essential principle of peace is the actual equality of nations in all matters of right or privilege; that peace cannot securely or justly rest upon an armed balance of power; that governments derive all their just powers from the consent of the governed and that no other powers should be supported by the common thought, purpose or power of the family of nations; that the seas should be equally free and safe for the use of all peoples, under rules set up by common agreement and consent, and that, so far as practicable, they should be accessible to all upon equal terms; that national armaments shall be limited to the necessities of national order and domestic safety; that the community of interest and of power upon which peace must henceforth depend imposes upon each nation the duty of seeing to it that all influences proceeding from its own citizens meant to encourage or assist revolution in other states should be sternly and effectually suppressed and prevented.

I need not argue these principles to you, my fellow countrymen; they are your own part and parcel of your own thinking and your own motives in affairs. They spring up native amongst us. Upon this as a platform of purpose and of action we can stand together. And it is imperative that we should stand together. We are being forged into a new unity amidst the fires that now blaze throughout the world. In their ardent heat we shall, in God's Providence, let us hope, be purged of faction and division, purified of the errant humors of party and of private interest, and shall stand forth in the days to come with a new dignity of national pride and spirit. Let each man see to it that the dedication is in his own heart, the high purpose of the nation in his own mind, ruler of his own will and desire.

I stand here and have taken the high and solemn oath to which you have been audience because the people of the United States have chosen me for this august delegation of power and have by their gracious judgment named me their leader in affairs.

I know now what the task means. I realize to the full the responsibility which it involves. I pray God I may be given the wisdom and the prudence to do my duty in the true spirit of this great people. I am their servant and can succeed only as they sustain and guide me by their confidence and their counsel. The thing I shall count upon, the thing without which neither counsel nor action will avail, is the unity of America—an America united in feeling, in purpose and in its vision of duty, of opportunity and of service.

We are to beware of all men who would turn the tasks and the necessities of the nation to their own private profit or use them for the building up of private power.

United alike in the conception of our duty and in the high resolve to perform it in the face of all men, let us dedicate ourselves to the great task to which we must now set our hand. For myself I beg your tolerance, your countenance and your united aid.

The shadows that now lie dark upon our path will soon be dispelled, and we shall walk with the light all about us if we be but true to ourselves—to ourselves as we have wished to be known in the counsels of the world and in the thought of all those who love liberty and justice and the right exalted.

WARREN G. HARDING

March 4, 1921

*America's disillusionment with postwar Europe and resurgent isolationism are promi-
nent themes in Harding's address, as the new president pledged to keep America out
of any future entanglements in European affairs. His disparagement of a new world
"supergovernment" is a reference to the newly formed League of Nations and America's rejection of membership in that organization. Harding also offered a brief word
on women's suffrage, a subject then gaining momentum in the national media and political circles.*

When one surveys the world about him after the great storm, noting the marks of destruction and yet rejoicing in the ruggedness of the things which withstood it, if he is
an American he breathes the clarified atmosphere with a strange mingling of regret and
new hope. We have seen a world passion spend its fury, but we contemplate our Republic unshaken, and hold our civilization secure. Liberty—liberty within the law—and
civilization are inseparable, and though both were threatened we find them now secure;
and there comes to Americans the profound assurance that our representative government is the highest expression and surest guaranty of both. . . .

Confident of our ability to work out our own destiny, and jealously guarding our right
to do so, we seek no part in directing the destinies of the Old World. We do not mean
to be entangled. We will accept no responsibility except as our own conscience and
judgment, in each instance, may determine.

Our eyes never will be blind to a developing menace, our ears never deaf to the call of
civilization. We recognize the new order in the world, with the closer contacts which
progress has wrought. We sense the call of the human heart for fellowship, fraternity, and
cooperation. We crave friendship and harbor no hate. But America, our America, the
America built on the foundation laid by the inspired fathers, can be a party to no permanent military alliance. It can enter into no political commitments, nor assume any economic obligations which will subject our decisions to any other than our own authority.

I am sure our own people will not misunderstand, nor will the world misconstrue.
We have no thought to impede the paths to closer relationship. We wish to promote understanding. We want to do our part in making offensive warfare so hateful that Governments and peoples who resort to it must prove the righteousness of their cause or
stand as outlaws before the bar of civilization.

We are ready to associate ourselves with the nations of the world, great and small, for
conference, for counsel; to seek the expressed views of world opinion; to recommend a
way to approximate disarmament and relieve the crushing burdens of military and
naval establishments. We elect to participate in suggesting plans for mediation, conciliation, and arbitration, and would gladly join in that expressed conscience of progress,

which seeks to clarify and write the laws of international relationship, and establish a world court for the disposition of such justiciable questions as nations are agreed to submit thereto. In expressing aspirations, in seeking practical plans, in translating humanity's new concept of righteousness and justice and its hatred of war into recommended action we are ready most heartily to unite, but every commitment must be made in the exercise of our national sovereignty. Since freedom impelled, and independence inspired, and nationality exalted, a world supergovernment is contrary to everything we cherish and can have no sanction by our Republic. This is not selfishness, it is sanctity. It is not aloofness, it is security. It is not suspicion of others, it is patriotic adherence to the things which made us what we are. . . .

America is ready to encourage, eager to initiate, anxious to participate in any seemly program likely to lessen the probability of war, and promote that brotherhood of mankind which must be God's highest conception of human relationship. Because we cherish ideals of justice and peace, because we appraise international comity and helpful relationship no less highly than any people of the world, we aspire to a high place in the moral leadership of civilization, and we hold a maintained America, the proven Republic, the unshaken temple of representative democracy, to be not only an inspiration and example, but the highest agency of strengthening good will and promoting accord on both continents. . . .

With the nation-wide induction of womanhood into our political life, we may count upon her intuitions, her refinements, her intelligence, and her influence to exalt the social order. We count upon her exercise of the full privileges and the performance of the duties of citizenship to speed the attainment of the highest state. . . .

I have taken the solemn oath of office on that passage of Holy Writ wherein it is asked: "What doth the Lord require of thee but to do justly, and to love mercy, and to walk humbly with thy God?" This I plight to God and country.

CALVIN COOLIDGE

March 4, 1925

For a man renowned for his reticence, Coolidge had much to say in his Inaugural Address. He reiterated America's desire to stay out of Europe's troubles and articulated a laissez-faire approach to government programs that was entirely in keeping with the spirit of the time.

No one can contemplate current conditions without finding much that is satisfying and still more that is encouraging. Our own country is leading the world in the general readjustment to the results of the great conflict. . . . Already we have sufficiently rearranged our domestic affairs so that confidence has returned, business has revived, and we appear to be entering an era of prosperity which is gradually reaching into every part of the Nation. Realizing that we can not live unto ourselves alone, we have contributed of our resources and our counsel to the relief of the suffering and the settlement of the disputes among the European nations. Because of what America is and what America has done, a firmer courage, a higher hope, inspires the heart of all humanity. . . .

If we wish to erect new structures, we must have a definite knowledge of the old foundations. We must realize that human nature is about the most constant thing in the universe and that the essentials of human relationship do not change. We must frequently take our bearings from these fixed stars of our political firmament if we expect to hold a true course. If we examine carefully what we have done, we can determine the more accurately what we can do. . . .

We have never any wish to interfere in the political conditions of any other countries. Especially are we determined not to become implicated in the political controversies of the Old World. With a great deal of hesitation, we have responded to appeals for help to maintain order, protect life and property, and establish responsible government in some of the small countries of the Western Hemisphere. Our private citizens have advanced large sums of money to assist in the necessary financing and relief of the Old World. We have not failed, nor shall we fail to respond, whenever necessary to mitigate human suffering and assist in the rehabilitation of distressed nations. These, too, are requirements which must be met by reason of our vast powers and the place we hold in the world.

Some of the best thought of mankind has long been seeking for a formula for permanent peace. Undoubtedly the clarification of the principles of international law would be helpful, and the efforts of scholars to prepare such a work for adoption by the various nations should have our sympathy and support. Much may be hoped for from the earnest studies of those who advocate the outlawing of aggressive war. But all these plans and preparations, these treaties and covenants, will not of themselves be adequate. One of the greatest dangers to peace lies in the economic pressure to which people find themselves subjected. One of the most practical things to be done in the world is to seek arrangements under which such pressure may be removed, so that opportunity may be renewed and hope may be revived. There must be some assurance that effort and endeavor will be followed by success and prosperity . . . [but] peace will come when there is realization that only under a reign of law, based on righteousness and supported by the religious conviction of the brotherhood of man, can there be any hope of a complete and satisfying life. Parchment will fail, the sword will fail, it is only the spiritual nature of man that can be triumphant.

It seems altogether probable that we can contribute most to these important objects by maintaining our position of political detachment and independence. We are not identified with any Old World interests. This position should be made more and more clear in our relations with all foreign countries. We are at peace with all of them. Our program is never to oppress, but always to assist. . . .

This Administration has come into power with a very clear and definite mandate from the people. The expression of the popular will in favor of maintaining our constitutional guarantees was overwhelming and decisive. There was a manifestation of such faith in the integrity of the courts that we can consider that issue rejected for some time to come. Likewise, the policy of public ownership of railroads and certain electric utilities met with unmistakable defeat. The people declared that they wanted their rights to have not a political but a judicial determination, and their independence and freedom continued and supported by having the ownership and control of their property, not in the Government, but in their own hands. As they always do when they have a fair chance, the people demonstrated that they are sound and are determined to have a sound government.

When we turn from what was rejected to inquire what was accepted, the policy that stands out with the greatest clearness is that of economy in public expenditure with reduction and reform of taxation. The principle involved in this effort is that of conservation. The resources of this country are almost beyond computation. No mind can comprehend them. But the cost of our combined governments is likewise almost beyond definition. Not only those who are now making their tax returns, but those who meet the enhanced cost of existence in their monthly bills, know by hard experience what this great burden is and what it does. No matter what others may want, these people want a drastic economy. They are opposed to waste. They know that extravagance lengthens the hours and diminishes the rewards of their labor. I favor the policy of economy, not because I wish to save money, but because I wish to save people. The men and women of this country who toil are the ones who bear the cost of the Government. Every dollar that we carelessly waste means that their life will be so much the more meager. Every dollar that we prudently save means that their life will be so much the more abundant. Economy is idealism in its most practical form. . . .

We are not without our problems, but our most important problem is not to secure new advantages but to maintain those which we already possess. Our system of government made up of three separate and independent departments, our divided sovereignty composed of Nation and State, the matchless wisdom that is enshrined in our Constitution, all these need constant effort and tireless vigilance for their protection and support. . . .

It is in such contemplations, my fellow countrymen, which are not exhaustive but only representative, that I find ample warrant for satisfaction and encouragement. We should not let the much that is to do obscure the much which has been done. The past and present show faith and hope and courage fully justified. Here stands our country, an example of tranquillity at home, a patron of tranquillity abroad. Here stands its Government, aware of its might but obedient to its conscience. Here it will continue to stand, seeking peace and prosperity, solicitous for the welfare of the wage earner, promoting enterprise, developing waterways and natural resources, attentive to the intuitive counsel of womanhood, encouraging education, desiring the advancement of religion, supporting the cause of justice and honor among the nations. America seeks no earthly empire built on blood and force. No ambition, no temptation, lures her to thought of foreign dominions. The legions which she sends forth are armed, not with the sword, but with the cross. The higher state to which she seeks the allegiance of all mankind is not of human, but of divine origin. She cherishes no purpose save to merit the favor of Almighty God.

HERBERT HOOVER

March 4, 1929

Despite sounding warnings about crime, the failure of Americans to obey the Eighteenth Amendment's alcohol prohibition, and other social ills, Hoover's general optimism about America's future at home and abroad is clear here. His optimism was sadly misplaced; before the year ended, the nation would undergo the worst economic collapse in its history, and Hoover—rightly or wrongly—would shoulder the lion's share of the blame.

This occasion is not alone the administration of the most sacred oath which can be assumed by an American citizen. It is a dedication and consecration under God to the highest office in service of our people. I assume this trust in the humility of knowledge that only through the guidance of Almighty Providence can I hope to discharge its ever-increasing burdens.

It is in keeping with tradition throughout our history that I should express simply and directly the opinions which I hold concerning some of the matters of present importance.

OUR PROGRESS

If we survey the situation of our Nation both at home and abroad, we find many satisfactions; we find some causes for concern. We have emerged from the losses of the Great War and the reconstruction following it with increased virility and strength. From this strength we have contributed to the recovery and progress of the world. . . . In the large view, we have reached a higher degree of comfort and security than ever existed before in the history of the world. Through liberation from widespread poverty we have reached a higher degree of individual freedom than ever before. . . .

Crime is increasing. Confidence in rigid and speedy justice is decreasing. . . .

To reestablish the vigor and effectiveness of law enforcement we must critically consider the entire Federal machinery of justice, the redistribution of its functions, the simplification of its procedure, the provision of additional special tribunals, the better selection of juries, and the more effective organization of our agencies of investigation and prosecution that justice may be sure and that it may be swift. While the authority of the Federal Government extends to but part of our vast system of national, State, and local justice, yet the standards which the Federal Government establishes have the most profound influence upon the whole structure. . . .

Of the undoubted abuses which have grown up under the eighteenth amendment, part are due to the causes I have just mentioned; but part are due to the failure of some States to accept their share of responsibility for concurrent enforcement and to the failure of many State and local officials to accept the obligation under their oath of office zealously to enforce the laws. With the failures from these many causes has come a dangerous expansion in the criminal elements who have found enlarged opportunities in dealing in illegal liquor.

But a large responsibility rests directly upon our citizens. There would be little traffic in illegal liquor if only criminals patronized it. We must awake to the fact that this patronage from large numbers of law-abiding citizens is supplying the rewards and stimulating crime. . . .

I propose to appoint a national commission for a searching investigation of the whole structure of our Federal system of jurisprudence, to include the method of enforcement of the eighteenth amendment and the causes of abuse under it. Its purpose will be to make such recommendations for reorganization of the administration of Federal laws and court procedure as may be found desirable. In the meantime it is essential that a large part of the enforcement activities be transferred from the Treasury Department to the Department of Justice as a beginning of more effective organization. . . .

The election has again confirmed the determination of the American people that regulation of private enterprise and not Government ownership or operation is the course rightly to be pursued in our relation to business. . . .

The larger purpose of our economic thought should be to establish more firmly stability and security of business and employment and thereby remove poverty still further from our borders. Our people have in recent years developed a new-found capacity for cooperation among themselves to effect high purposes in public welfare. It is an advance toward the highest conception of self-government. Self-government does not and should not imply the use of political agencies alone. Progress is born of cooperation in the community—not from governmental restraints. The Government should assist and encourage these movements of collective self-help by itself cooperating with them. . . .

The United States fully accepts the profound truth that our own progress, prosperity, and peace are interlocked with the progress, prosperity, and peace of all humanity. The whole world is at peace. The dangers to a continuation of this peace to-day are largely the fear and suspicion which still haunt the world. No suspicion or fear can be rightly directed toward our country. . . .

Superficial observers seem to find no destiny for our abounding increase in population, in wealth and power except that of imperialism. They fail to see that the American people are engrossed in the building for themselves of a new economic system, a new social system, a new political system all of which are characterized by aspirations of freedom of opportunity and thereby are the negation of imperialism. They fail to realize that because of our abounding prosperity our youth are pressing more and more into our institutions of learning; that our people are seeking a larger vision through art, literature, science, and travel; that they are moving toward stronger moral and spiritual life—that from these things our sympathies are broadening beyond the bounds of our Nation and race toward their true expression in a real brotherhood of man. . . .

Our people have determined that we should make no political engagements such as membership in the League of Nations, which may commit us in advance as a nation to become involved in the settlements of controversies between other countries. They adhere to the belief that the independence of America from such obligations increases its ability and availability for service in all fields of human progress. . . .

It is impossible, my countrymen, to speak of peace without profound emotion. In thousands of homes in America, in millions of homes around the world, there are vacant chairs. It would be a shameful confession of our unworthiness if it should develop that we have abandoned the hope for which all these men died. Surely civilization is old enough, surely mankind is mature enough so that we ought in our own lifetime to find a way to permanent peace. Abroad, to west and east, are nations whose sons mingled their blood with the blood of our sons on the battlefields. Most of these nations have contributed to our race, to our culture, our knowledge, and our progress. From one of them we derive our very language and from many of them much of the genius of our institutions. Their desire for peace is as deep and sincere as our own. . . .

Ours is a progressive people, but with a determination that progress must be based upon the foundation of experience. Ill-considered remedies for our faults bring only penalties after them. But if we hold the faith of the men in our mighty past who created these ideals, we shall leave them heightened and strengthened for our children. . . .

Ours is a land rich in resources; stimulating in its glorious beauty; filled with millions of happy homes; blessed with comfort and opportunity. In no nation are the institutions of progress more advanced. In no nation are the fruits of accomplishment more secure. In no nation is the government more worthy of respect. No country is more loved by its people. I have an abiding faith in their capacity, integrity and high purpose. I have no fears for the future of our country. It is bright with hope.

In the presence of my countrymen, mindful of the solemnity of this occasion, knowing what the task means and the responsibility which it involves, I beg your tolerance, your aid, and your cooperation. I ask the help of Almighty God in this service to my country to which you have called me.

FRANKLIN DELANO ROOSEVELT

First Address: March 4, 1933

Not since 1860 had an American president taken the oath of office under such dire circumstances. FDR was elected to end the Great Depression, and he was well aware that this was so. His first Inaugural Address subsequently lacked much of the jingoism and heady optimism that characterizes most inaugural speeches. Instead, Roosevelt spoke with frank candor and optimism in what was one the best speeches ever given by an American president.

I am certain that my fellow Americans expect that on my induction into the Presidency I will address them with a candor and a decision which the present situation of our Nation impels. This is preeminently the time to speak the truth, the whole truth, frankly and boldly. Nor need we shrink from honestly facing conditions in our country today. This great Nation will endure as it has endured, will revive and will prosper. So, first of all, let me assert my firm belief that the only thing we have to fear is fear itself—nameless, unreasoning, unjustified terror which paralyzes needed efforts to convert retreat into advance. In every dark hour of our national life a leadership of frankness and vigor has met with that understanding and support of the people themselves which is essential to victory. I am convinced that you will again give that support to leadership in these critical days.

In such a spirit on my part and on yours we face our common difficulties. They concern, thank God, only material things. Values have shrunken to fantastic levels; taxes have risen; our ability to pay has fallen; government of all kinds is faced by serious curtailment of income; the means of exchange are frozen in the currents of trade; the withered leaves of industrial enterprise lie on every side; farmers find no markets for their produce; the savings of many years in thousands of families are gone.

More important, a host of unemployed citizens face the grim problem of existence, and an equally great number toil with little return. Only a foolish optimist can deny the dark realities of the moment.

Yet our distress comes from no failure of substance. We are stricken by no plague of locusts. Compared with the perils which our forefathers conquered because they believed and were not afraid, we have still much to be thankful for. Nature still offers her bounty and human efforts have multiplied it. Plenty is at our doorstep, but a generous use of it languishes in the very sight of the supply. Primarily this is because the rulers of the exchange of mankind's goods have failed, through their own stubbornness and their own incompetence, have admitted their failure, and abdicated. . . .

This Nation asks for action, and action now.

Our greatest primary task is to put people to work. This is no unsolvable problem if we face it wisely and courageously. It can be accomplished in part by direct recruiting by the Government itself, treating the task as we would treat the emergency of a war, but at the same time, through this employment, accomplishing greatly needed projects to stimulate and reorganize the use of our natural resources.

Hand in hand with this we must frankly recognize the overbalance of population in our industrial centers and, by engaging on a national scale in a redistribution, endeavor to provide a better use of the land for those best fitted for the land. The task can be helped by definite efforts to raise the values of agricultural products and with this the power to purchase the output of our cities. It can be helped by preventing realistically the tragedy of the growing loss through foreclosure of our small homes and our farms. It can be helped by insistence that the Federal, State, and local governments act forthwith on the demand that their cost be drastically reduced. It can be helped by the unifying of relief activities which today are often scattered, uneconomical, and unequal. It can be helped by national planning for and supervision of all forms of transportation and of communications and other utilities which have a definitely public character. There are many ways in which it can be helped, but it can never be helped merely by talking about it. We must act and act quickly. . . .

The basic thought that guides these specific means of national recovery is not narrowly nationalistic. It is the insistence, as a first consideration, upon the interdependence of the various elements in all parts of the United States—a recognition of the old and permanently important manifestation of the American spirit of the pioneer. It is the way to recovery. It is the immediate way. It is the strongest assurance that the recovery will endure.

In the field of world policy I would dedicate this Nation to the policy of the good neighbor—the neighbor who resolutely respects himself and, because he does so, respects the rights of others—the neighbor who respects his obligations and respects the sanctity of his agreements in and with a world of neighbors.

If I read the temper of our people correctly, we now realize as we have never realized before our interdependence on each other; that we can not merely take but we must give as well; that if we are to go forward, we must move as a trained and loyal army willing to sacrifice for the good of a common discipline, because without such discipline no progress is made, no leadership becomes effective. We are, I know, ready and willing to submit our lives and property to such discipline, because it makes possible a leadership which aims at a larger good. This I propose to offer, pledging that the larger purposes will bind upon us all as a sacred obligation with a unity of duty hitherto evoked only in time of armed strife.

With this pledge taken, I assume unhesitatingly the leadership of this great army of our people dedicated to a disciplined attack upon our common problems. . . .

It is to be hoped that the normal balance of executive and legislative authority may be wholly adequate to meet the unprecedented task before us. But it may be that an unprecedented demand and need for undelayed action may call for temporary departure from that normal balance of public procedure.

I am prepared under my constitutional duty to recommend the measures that a stricken nation in the midst of a stricken world may require. These measures, or such other measures as the Congress may build out of its experience and wisdom, I shall seek, within my constitutional authority, to bring to speedy adoption.

But in the event that the Congress shall fail to take one of these two courses, and in the event that the national emergency is still critical, I shall not evade the clear course of duty that will then confront me. I shall ask the Congress for the one remaining instrument to meet the crisis—broad Executive power to wage a war against the emergency, as great as the power that would be given to me if we were in fact invaded by a foreign foe.

For the trust reposed in me I will return the courage and the devotion that befit the time. I can do no less.

We face the arduous days that lie before us in the warm courage of the national unity; with the clear consciousness of seeking old and precious moral values; with the clean satisfaction that comes from the stern performance of duty by old and young alike. We aim at the assurance of a rounded and permanent national life.

We do not distrust the future of essential democracy. The people of the United States have not failed. In their need they have registered a mandate that they want direct, vigorous action. They have asked for discipline and direction under leadership. They have made me the present instrument of their wishes. In the spirit of the gift I take it.

In this dedication of a Nation we humbly ask the blessing of God. May He protect each and every one of us. May He guide me in the days to come.

Inaugural Addresses
1949–2005

It is interesting to compare post–World War II Inaugural Addresses with those of earlier eras. Where the first presidents made it a point to reiterate George Washington's desire to steer clear of entangling alliances, those who followed in FDR's footsteps made ringing declarations of America's global mission and commitment to worldwide principles of democracy and freedom. Also notable are modern presidents' use of Communism as a rallying force against which to define those American principles.

Harry S. Truman

January 20, 1949

Truman offered a sweeping statement of America's postwar rejection of its traditional isolationism and an assertion of its new sense of global mission. Previous Inaugural Addresses had offered broad statements of America's principles; but here for the first time an American president devoted part of his address to a scathing critique of another nation, the Soviet Union, and its philosophy of Communism. It is a succinct and revealing example of the nation's cold war mentality.

Mr. Vice President, Mr. Chief Justice, and fellow citizens, I accept with humility the honor which the American people have conferred upon me. I accept it with a deep resolve to do all that I can for the welfare of this Nation and for the peace of the world.

In performing the duties of my office, I need the help and prayers of every one of you. I ask for your encouragement and your support. The tasks we face are difficult, and we can accomplish them only if we work together.

Each period of our national history has had its special challenges. Those that confront us now are as momentous as any in the past. Today marks the beginning not only of a new administration, but of a period that will be eventful, perhaps decisive, for us and for the world.

It may be our lot to experience, and in large measure to bring about, a major turning point in the long history of the human race. The first half of this century has been marked by unprecedented and brutal attacks on the rights of man, and by the two most frightful wars in history. The supreme need of our time is for men to learn to live together in peace and harmony.

The peoples of the earth face the future with grave uncertainty, composed almost equally of great hopes and great fears. In this time of doubt, they look to the United States as never before for good will, strength, and wise leadership.

It is fitting, therefore, that we take this occasion to proclaim to the world the essential principles of the faith by which we live, and to declare our aims to all peoples.

The American people stand firm in the faith which has inspired this Nation from the beginning. We believe that all men have a right to equal justice under law and equal opportunity to share in the common good. We believe that all men have the right to freedom of thought and expression. We believe that all men are created equal because they are created in the image of God.

From this faith we will not be moved.

The American people desire, and are determined to work for, a world in which all nations and all peoples are free to govern themselves as they see fit, and to achieve a decent and satisfying life. Above all else, our people desire, and are determined to work for, peace on earth—a just and lasting peace—based on genuine agreement freely arrived at by equals.

In the pursuit of these aims, the United States and other like-minded nations find themselves directly opposed by a regime with contrary aims and a totally different concept of life [the Soviet Union].

That regime adheres to a false philosophy which purports to offer freedom, security, and greater opportunity to mankind. Misled by this philosophy, many peoples have sacrificed their liberties only to learn to their sorrow that deceit and mockery, poverty and tyranny, are their reward.

That false philosophy is communism.

Communism is based on the belief that man is so weak and inadequate that he is unable to govern himself, and therefore requires the rule of strong masters.

Democracy is based on the conviction that man has the moral and intellectual capacity, as well as the inalienable right, to govern himself with reason and justice.

Communism subjects the individual to arrest without lawful cause, punishment without trial, and forced labor as the chattel of the state. It decrees what information he shall receive, what art he shall produce, what leaders he shall follow, and what thoughts he shall think.

Democracy maintains that government is established for the benefit of the individual, and is charged with the responsibility of protecting the rights of the individual and his freedom in the exercise of his abilities.

Communism maintains that social wrongs can be corrected only by violence.

Democracy has proved that social justice can be achieved through peaceful change.

Communism holds that the world is so deeply divided into opposing classes that war is inevitable.

Democracy holds that free nations can settle differences justly and maintain lasting peace.

These differences between communism and democracy do not concern the United States alone. People everywhere are coming to realize that what is involved is material well-being, human dignity, and the right to believe in and worship God.

I state these differences, not to draw issues of belief as such, but because the actions resulting from the Communist philosophy are a threat to the efforts of free nations to bring about world recovery and lasting peace.

Since the end of hostilities, the United States has invested its substance and its energy in a great constructive effort to restore peace, stability, and freedom to the world.

We have sought no territory and we have imposed our will on none. We have asked for no privileges we would not extend to others.

We have constantly and vigorously supported the United Nations and related agencies as a means of applying democratic principles to international relations. We have consistently advocated and relied upon peaceful settlement of disputes among nations.

We have made every effort to secure agreement on effective international control of our most powerful weapon, and we have worked steadily for the limitation and control of all armaments.

We have encouraged, by precept and example, the expansion of world trade on a sound and fair basis. . . .

The initiative is ours. . . .

If we can make it sufficiently clear, in advance, that any armed attack affecting our national security would be met with overwhelming force, the armed attack might never occur. . . .

More than half the people of the world are living in conditions approaching misery. Their food is inadequate. They are victims of disease. Their economic life is primitive and stagnant. Their poverty is a handicap and a threat both to them and to more prosperous areas.

For the first time in history, humanity possesses the knowledge and the skill to relieve the suffering of these people. . . .

Our aim should be to help the free peoples of the world, through their own efforts, to produce more food, more clothing, more materials for housing, and more mechanical power to lighten their burdens. . . .

The old imperialism—exploitation for foreign profit—has no place in our plans. What we envisage is a program of development based on the concepts of democratic fair-dealing. . . .

Democracy alone can supply the vitalizing force to stir the peoples of the world into triumphant action, not only against their human oppressors, but also against their ancient enemies—hunger, misery, and despair. . . .

We are aided by all who wish to live in freedom from fear—even by those who live today in fear under their own governments.

We are aided by all who want relief from the lies of propaganda—who desire truth and sincerity.

We are aided by all who desire self-government and a voice in deciding their own affairs.

We are aided by all who long for economic security—for the security and abundance that men in free societies can enjoy.

We are aided by all who desire freedom of speech, freedom of religion, and freedom to live their own lives for useful ends.

Our allies are the millions who hunger and thirst after righteousness. . . .

Steadfast in our faith in the Almighty, we will advance toward a world where man's freedom is secure.

To that end we will devote our strength, our resources, and our firmness of resolve. With God's help, the future of mankind will be assured in a world of justice, harmony, and peace.

DWIGHT D. EISENHOWER

First Address: January 20, 1953

Nearly all Inaugural Addresses contain references to God; Eisenhower was unique in that he began his address with a prayer. In fact, Ike's speech is heavily laced with religious imagery, setting the familiar goals of cold war diplomacy and politics on an overtly faith-based, spiritual level.

My friends, before I begin the expression of those thoughts that I deem appropriate to this moment, would you permit me the privilege of uttering a little private prayer of my own. And I ask that you bow your heads:

Almighty God, as we stand here at this moment my future associates in the executive branch of government join me in beseeching that Thou will make full and complete our dedication to the service of the people in this throng, and their fellow citizens everywhere.

Give us, we pray, the power to discern clearly right from wrong, and allow all our words and actions to be governed thereby, and by the laws of this land. Especially we pray that our concern shall be for all the people regardless of station, race, or calling.

May cooperation be permitted and be the mutual aim of those who, under the concepts of our Constitution, hold to differing political faiths; so that all may work for the good of our beloved country and Thy glory. Amen.

My fellow citizens:

The world and we have passed the midway point of a century of continuing challenge. We sense with all our faculties that forces of good and evil are massed and armed and opposed as rarely before in history. . . .

For our own country, it has been a time of recurring trial. We have grown in power and in responsibility. We have passed through the anxieties of depression and of war to a summit unmatched in man's history. Seeking to secure peace in the world, we have had to fight through the forests of the Argonne, to the shores of Iwo Jima, and to the cold mountains of Korea.

In the swift rush of great events, we find ourselves groping to know the full sense and meaning of these times in which we live. In our quest of understanding, we beseech God's guidance. We summon all our knowledge of the past and we scan all signs of the future. We bring all our wit and all our will to meet the question:

How far have we come in man's long pilgrimage from darkness toward light? Are we nearing the light—a day of freedom and of peace for all mankind? Or are the shadows of another night closing in upon us? . . .

This trial comes at a moment when man's power to achieve good or to inflict evil surpasses the brightest hopes and the sharpest fears of all ages. We can turn rivers in their courses, level mountains to the plains. Oceans and land and sky are avenues for our colossal commerce. Disease diminishes and life lengthens.

Yet the promise of this life is imperiled by the very genius that has made it possible. Nations amass wealth. Labor sweats to create—and turns out devices to level not only mountains but also cities. Science seems ready to confer upon us, as its final gift, the power to erase human life from this planet.

At such a time in history, we who are free must proclaim anew our faith. This faith is the abiding creed of our fathers. It is our faith in the deathless dignity of man, governed by eternal moral and natural laws.

This faith defines our full view of life. It establishes, beyond debate, those gifts of the Creator that are man's inalienable rights, and that make all men equal in His sight.

In the light of this equality, we know that the virtues most cherished by free people—love of truth, pride of work, devotion to country—all are treasures equally precious in the lives of the most humble and of the most exalted. The men who mine coal and fire furnaces and balance ledgers and turn lathes and pick cotton and heal the sick and plant corn—all serve as proudly, and as profitably, for America as the statesmen who draft treaties and the legislators who enact laws.

This faith rules our whole way of life. It decrees that we, the people, elect leaders not to rule but to serve. It asserts that we have the right to choice of our own work and to the reward of our own toil. It inspires the initiative that makes our productivity the wonder of the world. And it warns that any man who seeks to deny equality among all his brothers betrays the spirit of the free and invites the mockery of the tyrant.

It is because we, all of us, hold to these principles that the political changes accomplished this day do not imply turbulence, upheaval or disorder. Rather this change expresses a purpose of strengthening our dedication and devotion to the precepts of our founding documents, a conscious renewal of faith in our country and in the watchfulness of a Divine Providence.

The enemies of this faith know no god but force, no devotion but its use. They tutor men in treason. They feed upon the hunger of others. Whatever defies them, they torture, especially the truth.

Here, then, is joined no argument between slightly differing philosophies. This conflict strikes directly at the faith of our fathers and the lives of our sons. No principle or treasure that we hold, from the spiritual knowledge of our free schools and churches to the creative magic of free labor and capital, nothing lies safely beyond the reach of this struggle. . . .

So we are persuaded by necessity and by belief that the strength of all free peoples lies in unity; their danger, in discord.

To produce this unity, to meet the challenge of our time, destiny has laid upon our country the responsibility of the free world's leadership.

So it is proper that we assure our friends once again that, in the discharge of this responsibility, we Americans know and we observe the difference between world leadership and imperialism; between firmness and truculence; between a thoughtfully calculated goal and spasmodic reaction to the stimulus of emergencies.

We wish our friends the world over to know this above all: we face the threat—not with dread and confusion—but with confidence and conviction. . . .

These principles are:

(1) Abhorring war as a chosen way to balk the purposes of those who threaten us, we hold it to be the first task of statesmanship to develop the strength that will deter the forces of aggression and promote the conditions of peace. For, as it must be the supreme purpose of all free men, so it must be the dedication of their leaders, to save humanity from preying upon itself. . . .

(2) Realizing that common sense and common decency alike dictate the futility of appeasement, we shall never try to placate an aggressor by the false and wicked bargain of trading honor for security. Americans, indeed all free men, remember that in the final choice a soldier's pack is not so heavy a burden as a prisoner's chains.

(3) Knowing that only a United States that is strong and immensely productive can help defend freedom in our world, we view our Nation's strength and security as a trust upon which rests the hope of free men everywhere. It is the firm duty of each of our free citizens and of every free citizen everywhere to place the cause of his country before the comfort, the convenience of himself.

(4) Honoring the identity and the special heritage of each nation in the world, we shall never use our strength to try to impress upon another people our own cherished political and economic institutions.

(5) Assessing realistically the needs and capacities of proven friends of freedom, we shall strive to help them to achieve their own security and well-being. Likewise, we

shall count upon them to assume, within the limits of their resources, their full and just burdens in the common defense of freedom.

(6) Recognizing economic health as an indispensable basis of military strength and the free world's peace, we shall strive to foster everywhere, and to practice ourselves, policies that encourage productivity and profitable trade. For the impoverishment of any single people in the world means danger to the well-being of all other peoples.

(7) Appreciating that economic need, military security and political wisdom combine to suggest regional groupings of free peoples, we hope, within the framework of the United Nations, to help strengthen such special bonds the world over. The nature of these ties must vary with the different problems of different areas. . . .

(8) Conceiving the defense of freedom, like freedom itself, to be one and indivisible, we hold all continents and peoples in equal regard and honor. We reject any insinuation that one race or another, one people or another, is in any sense inferior or expendable.

(9) Respecting the United Nations as the living sign of all people's hope for peace, we shall strive to make it not merely an eloquent symbol but an effective force. And in our quest for an honorable peace, we shall neither compromise, nor tire, nor ever cease.

By these rules of conduct, we hope to be known to all peoples. . . .

These basic precepts are not lofty abstractions, far removed from matters of daily living. They are laws of spiritual strength that generate and define our material strength. Patriotism means equipped forces and a prepared citizenry. Moral stamina means more energy and more productivity, on the farm and in the factory. Love of liberty means the guarding of every resource that makes freedom possible—from the sanctity of our families and the wealth of our soil to the genius of our scientists. . . .

The peace we seek, then, is nothing less than the practice and fulfillment of our whole faith among ourselves and in our dealings with others. This signifies more than the stilling of guns, easing the sorrow of war. More than escape from death, it is a way of life. More than a haven for the weary, it is a hope for the brave.

This is the hope that beckons us onward in this century of trial. This is the work that awaits us all, to be done with bravery, with charity, and with prayer to Almighty God.

Second Address: January 21, 1957

Ike's second address looked much like the first, reaffirming America's cold war commitments in ringing moralist tones.

THE PRICE OF PEACE

Mr. Chairman, Mr. Vice President, Mr. Chief Justice, Mr. Speaker, members of my family and friends, my countrymen, and the friends of my country, wherever they may be, we meet again, as upon a like moment four years ago, and again you have witnessed my solemn oath of service to you.

I, too, am a witness, today testifying in your name to the principles and purposes to which we, as a people, are pledged.

Before all else, we seek, upon our common labor as a nation, the blessings of Almighty God. And the hopes in our hearts fashion the deepest prayers of our whole people.

May we pursue the right—without self-righteousness.

May we know unity—without conformity.

May we grow in strength—without pride in self.

May we, in our dealings with all peoples of the earth, ever speak truth and serve justice.

And so shall America—in the sight of all men of good will—prove true to the honorable purposes that bind and rule us as a people in all this time of trial through which we pass.

We live in a land of plenty, but rarely has this earth known such peril as today.

In our nation work and wealth abound. Our population grows. Commerce crowds our rivers and rails, our skies, harbors, and highways. Our soil is fertile, our agriculture productive. The air rings with the song of our industry—rolling mills and blast furnaces, dynamos, dams, and assembly lines—the chorus of America the bountiful.

This is our home—yet this is not the whole of our world. For our world is where our full destiny lies—with men, of all people, and all nations, who are or would be free. And for them—and so for us—this is no time of ease or of rest.

In too much of the earth there is want, discord, danger. New forces and new nations stir and strive across the earth, with power to bring, by their fate, great good or great evil to the free world's future. From the deserts of North Africa to the islands of the South Pacific one third of all mankind has entered upon an historic struggle for a new freedom; freedom from grinding poverty. Across all continents, nearly a billion people seek, sometimes almost in desperation, for the skills and knowledge and assistance by which they may satisfy from their own resources, the material wants common to all mankind. . . .

The divisive force is International Communism and the power that it controls.

The designs of that power, dark in purpose, are clear in practice. It strives to seal forever the fate of those it has enslaved. It strives to break the ties that unite the free. And it strives to capture—to exploit for its own greater power—all forces of change in the world, especially the needs of the hungry and the hopes of the oppressed.

Yet the world of International Communism has itself been shaken by a fierce and mighty force: the readiness of men who love freedom to pledge their lives to that love. Through the night of their bondage, the unconquerable will of heroes has struck with the swift, sharp thrust of lightning . . ..

We look upon this shaken earth, and we declare our firm and fixed purpose—the building of a peace with justice in a world where moral law prevails.

The building of such a peace is a bold and solemn purpose. To proclaim it is easy. To serve it will be hard. And to attain it, we must be aware of its full meaning—and ready to pay its full price.

We know clearly what we seek, and why.

We seek peace, knowing that peace is the climate of freedom. And now, as in no other age, we seek it because we have been warned, by the power of modern weapons, that peace may be the only climate possible for human life itself.

Yet this peace we seek cannot be born of fear alone: it must be rooted in the lives of nations. There must be justice, sensed and shared by all peoples, for, without justice the world can know only a tense and unstable truce. There must be law, steadily invoked and respected by all nations, for without law, the world promises only such meager justice as the pity of the strong upon the weak. But the law of which we speak, comprehending the values of freedom, affirms the equality of all nations, great and small.

Splendid as can be the blessings of such a peace, high will be its cost: in toil patiently sustained, in help honorably given, in sacrifice calmly borne.

We are called to meet the price of this peace.

To counter the threat of those who seek to rule by force, we must pay the costs of our own needed military strength, and help to build the security of others.

We must use our skills and knowledge and, at times, our substance, to help others rise from misery, however far the scene of suffering may be from our shores. For wherever in the world a people knows desperate want, there must appear at least the spark of hope, the hope of progress—or there will surely rise at last the flames of conflict.

We recognize and accept our own deep involvement in the destiny of men everywhere. We are accordingly pledged to honor, and to strive to fortify, the authority of the United Nations. For in that body rests the best hope of our age for the assertion of that law by which all nations may live in dignity. . . .

For one truth must rule all we think and all we do. No people can live to itself alone. The unity of all who dwell in freedom is their only sure defense. The economic need of all nations—in mutual dependence—makes isolation an impossibility; not even America's prosperity could long survive if other nations did not also prosper. No nation can longer be a fortress, lone and strong and safe. And any people, seeking such shelter for themselves, can now build only their own prison.

Our pledge to these principles is constant, because we believe in their rightness.

We do not fear this world of change. America is no stranger to much of its spirit. Everywhere we see the seeds of the same growth that America itself has known. The American experiment has, for generations, fired the passion and the courage of millions elsewhere seeking freedom, equality, and opportunity. And the American story of material progress has helped excite the longing of all needy peoples for some satisfaction of their human wants. These hopes that we have helped to inspire, we can help to fulfill.

In this confidence, we speak plainly to all peoples.

We cherish our friendship with all nations that are or would be free. We respect, no less, their independence. And when, in time of want or peril, they ask our help, they may honorably receive it; for we no more seek to buy their sovereignty than we would sell our own. Sovereignty is never bartered among freemen. . . .

We honor, no less in this divided world than in a less tormented time, the people of Russia. We do not dread, rather do we welcome, their progress in education and industry. We wish them success in their demands for more intellectual freedom, greater security before their own laws, fuller enjoyment of the rewards of their own toil. For as such things come to pass, the more certain will be the coming of that day when our peoples may freely meet in friendship.

So we voice our hope and our belief that we can help to heal this divided world. Thus may the nations cease to live in trembling before the menace of force. Thus may the weight of fear and the weight of arms be taken from the burdened shoulders of mankind.

This, nothing less, is the labor to which we are called and our strength dedicated.

And so the prayer of our people carries far beyond our own frontiers, to the wide world of our duty and our destiny.

May the light of freedom, coming to all darkened lands, flame brightly—until at last the darkness is no more.

May the turbulence of our age yield to a true time of peace, when men and nations shall share a life that honors the dignity of each, the brotherhood of all.

JOHN F. KENNEDY

January 20, 1961

Few Inaugural Addresses remained so fixed in the American mind as that delivered by JFK. This was partly due to the circumstances: people would forever remember a young, vibrant Kennedy, delivering the words with ringing authority on a very cold January day during which he hardly seemed affected by the cold. He seemed the very picture of youthful vitality. But the speech was also remembered for its content: an unusually poetic rendering of the principles for a new postwar generation.

Vice President Johnson, Mr. Speaker, Mr. Chief Justice, President Eisenhower, Vice President Nixon, President Truman, reverend clergy, fellow citizens, we observe today not a victory of party, but a celebration of freedom—symbolizing an end, as well as a beginning—signifying renewal, as well as change. For I have sworn before you and Almighty God the same solemn oath our forebears prescribed nearly a century and three quarters ago.

The world is very different now. For man holds in his mortal hands the power to abolish all forms of human poverty and all forms of human life. And yet the same revolutionary beliefs for which our forebears fought are still at issue around the globe—the belief that the rights of man come not from the generosity of the state, but from the hand of God.

We dare not forget today that we are the heirs of that first revolution. Let the word go forth from this time and place, to friend and foe alike, that the torch has been passed to a new generation of Americans—born in this century, tempered by war, disciplined by a hard and bitter peace, proud of our ancient heritage—and unwilling to witness or permit the slow undoing of those human rights to which this Nation has always been committed, and to which we are committed today at home and around the world.

Let every nation know, whether it wishes us well or ill, that we shall pay any price, bear any burden, meet any hardship, support any friend, oppose any foe, in order to assure the survival and the success of liberty.

This much we pledge—and more.

To those old allies whose cultural and spiritual origins we share, we pledge the loyalty of faithful friends. United, there is little we cannot do in a host of cooperative ventures. Divided, there is little we can do—for we dare not meet a powerful challenge at odds and split asunder.

To those new States whom we welcome to the ranks of the free, we pledge our word that one form of colonial control shall not have passed away merely to be replaced by a far more iron tyranny. We shall not always expect to find them supporting our view. But we shall always hope to find them strongly supporting their own freedom—and to remember that, in the past, those who foolishly sought power by riding the back of the tiger ended up inside.

To those peoples in the huts and villages across the globe struggling to break the bonds of mass misery, we pledge our best efforts to help them help themselves, for whatever period is required—not because the Communists may be doing it, not because we seek their votes, but because it is right. If a free society cannot help the many who are poor, it cannot save the few who are rich.

To our sister republics south of our border, we offer a special pledge—to convert our good words into good deeds—in a new alliance for progress—to assist free men and free governments in casting off the chains of poverty. But this peaceful revolution of hope cannot become the prey of hostile powers. Let all our neighbors know that we shall join with them to oppose aggression or subversion anywhere in the Americas. And let every other power know that this Hemisphere intends to remain the master of its own house.

To that world assembly of sovereign states, the United Nations, our last best hope in an age where the instruments of war have far outpaced the instruments of peace, we renew our pledge of support—to prevent it from becoming merely a forum for invective—to strengthen its shield of the new and the weak—and to enlarge the area in which its writ may run.

Finally, to those nations who would make themselves our adversary, we offer not a pledge but a request: that both sides begin anew the quest for peace, before the dark powers of destruction unleashed by science engulf all humanity in planned or accidental self-destruction.

We dare not tempt them with weakness. For only when our arms are sufficient beyond doubt can we be certain beyond doubt that they will never be employed.

But neither can two great and powerful groups of nations take comfort from our present course—both sides overburdened by the cost of modern weapons, both rightly alarmed by the steady spread of the deadly atom, yet both racing to alter that uncertain balance of terror that stays the hand of mankind's final war.

So let us begin anew—remembering on both sides that civility is not a sign of weakness, and sincerity is always subject to proof. Let us never negotiate out of fear. But let us never fear to negotiate.

Let both sides explore what problems unite us instead of belaboring those problems which divide us.

Let both sides, for the first time, formulate serious and precise proposals for the inspection and control of arms—and bring the absolute power to destroy other nations under the absolute control of all nations.

Let both sides seek to invoke the wonders of science instead of its terrors. Together let us explore the stars, conquer the deserts, eradicate disease, tap the ocean depths, and encourage the arts and commerce.

Let both sides unite to heed in all corners of the earth the command of Isaiah—to "undo the heavy burdens . . . and to let the oppressed go free."

And if a beachhead of cooperation may push back the jungle of suspicion, let both sides join in creating a new endeavor, not a new balance of power, but a new world of law, where the strong are just and the weak secure and the peace preserved.

All this will not be finished in the first 100 days. Nor will it be finished in the first 1,000 days, nor in the life of this Administration, nor even perhaps in our lifetime on this planet. But let us begin.

In your hands, my fellow citizens, more than in mine, will rest the final success or failure of our course. Since this country was founded, each generation of Americans has been summoned to give testimony to its national loyalty. The graves of young Americans who answered the call to service surround the globe.

Now the trumpet summons us again—not as a call to bear arms, though arms we need; not as a call to battle, though embattled we are—but a call to bear the burden of a long twilight struggle, year in and year out, "rejoicing in hope, patient in tribulation"—a struggle against the common enemies of man: tyranny, poverty, disease, and war itself.

Can we forge against these enemies a grand and global alliance, North and South, East and West, that can assure a more fruitful life for all mankind? Will you join in that historic effort?

In the long history of the world, only a few generations have been granted the role of defending freedom in its hour of maximum danger. I do not shrink from this responsibility—I welcome it. I do not believe that any of us would exchange places with any other people or any other generation. The energy, the faith, the devotion which we bring to this endeavor will light our country and all who serve it—and the glow from that fire can truly light the world.

And so, my fellow Americans: ask not what your country can do for you—ask what you can do for your country.

My fellow citizens of the world: ask not what America will do for you, but what together we can do for the freedom of man.

Finally, whether you are citizens of America or citizens of the world, ask of us the same high standards of strength and sacrifice which we ask of you. With a good conscience our only sure reward, with history the final judge of our deeds, let us go forth to lead the land we love, asking His blessing and His help, but knowing that here on earth God's work must truly be our own.

LYNDON B. JOHNSON

January 20, 1965

Lyndon Johnson was perhaps the most domestic-minded of modern presidents. While a staunch cold warrior, he would much rather have focused his energies on his Great Society program to end poverty in America. His Inaugural Address revealed LBJ's optimistic, even utopian vision of America's future as a place where hunger and want had finally vanished.

My fellow countrymen, on this occasion, the oath I have taken before you and before God is not mine alone, but ours together. We are one nation and one people. Our fate as a nation and our future as a people rest not upon one citizen, but upon all citizens.

This is the majesty and the meaning of this moment.

For every generation, there is a destiny. For some, history decides. For this generation, the choice must be our own.

Even now, a rocket moves toward Mars [a reference to Mariner IV, the first successful mission to Mars, launched on November 28, 1964]. It reminds us that the world will not be the same for our children, or even for ourselves in a short span of years. The next man to stand here will look out on a scene different from our own, because ours is a time of change—rapid and fantastic change bearing the secrets of nature, multiplying the nations, placing in uncertain hands new weapons for mastery and destruction, shaking old values, and uprooting old ways. . . .

Our destiny in the midst of change will rest on the unchanged character of our people, and on their faith.

THE AMERICAN COVENANT

They came here—the exile and the stranger, brave but frightened—to find a place where a man could be his own man. They made a covenant with this land. Conceived in justice, written in liberty, bound in union, it was meant one day to inspire the hopes of all mankind; and it binds us still. If we keep its terms, we shall flourish.

JUSTICE AND CHANGE

First, justice was the promise that all who made the journey would share in the fruits of the land.

In a land of great wealth, families must not live in hopeless poverty. In a land rich in harvest, children just must not go hungry. In a land of healing miracles, neighbors must not suffer and die unattended. In a great land of learning and scholars, young people must be taught to read and write.

For the more than 30 years that I have served this Nation, I have believed that this injustice to our people, this waste of our resources, was our real enemy. For 30 years or more, with the resources I have had, I have vigilantly fought against it. I have learned, and I know, that it will not surrender easily.

But change has given us new weapons. Before this generation of Americans is finished, this enemy will not only retreat—it will be conquered.

Justice requires us to remember that when any citizen denies his fellow, saying, "His color is not mine," or "His beliefs are strange and different," in that moment he betrays America, though his forebears created this Nation.

LIBERTY AND CHANGE

Liberty was the second article of our covenant. It was self-government. It was our Bill of Rights. But it was more. America would be a place where each man could be proud to be himself: stretching his talents, rejoicing in his work, important in the life of his neighbors and his nation.

This has become more difficult in a world where change and growth seem to tower beyond the control and even the judgment of men. We must work to provide the knowledge and the surroundings which can enlarge the possibilities of every citizen.

The American covenant called on us to help show the way for the liberation of man. And that is today our goal. Thus, if as a nation there is much outside our control, as a people no stranger is outside our hope.

Change has brought new meaning to that old mission. We can never again stand aside, prideful in isolation. Terrific dangers and troubles that we once called "foreign" now constantly live among us. If American lives must end, and American treasure be spilled, in countries we barely know, that is the price that change has demanded of conviction and of our enduring covenant.

Think of our world as it looks from the rocket that is heading toward Mars. It is like a child's globe, hanging in space, the continents stuck to its side like colored maps. We are all fellow passengers on a dot of earth. And each of us, in the span of time, has really only a moment among our companions.

How incredible it is that in this fragile existence, we should hate and destroy one another. There are possibilities enough for all who will abandon mastery over others to pursue mastery over nature. There is world enough for all to seek their happiness in their own way.

Our Nation's course is abundantly clear. We aspire to nothing that belongs to others. We seek no dominion over our fellow man but man's dominion over tyranny and misery.

But more is required. Men want to be a part of a common enterprise—a cause greater than themselves. Each of us must find a way to advance the purpose of the Nation, thus finding new purpose for ourselves. Without this, we shall become a nation of strangers.

UNION AND CHANGE

The third article was union. To those who were small and few against the wilderness, the success of liberty demanded the strength of union. Two centuries of change have made this true again.

No longer need capitalist and worker, farmer and clerk, city and countryside, struggle to divide our bounty. By working shoulder to shoulder, together we can increase the bounty of all. We have discovered that every child who learns, every man who finds work, every sick body that is made whole—like a candle added to an altar—brightens the hope of all the faithful.

So let us reject any among us who seek to reopen old wounds and to rekindle old hatreds. They stand in the way of a seeking nation.

Let us now join reason to faith and action to experience, to transform our unity of interest into a unity of purpose. For the hour and the day and the time are here to achieve progress without strife, to achieve change without hatred—not without difference of opinion, but without the deep and abiding divisions which scar the union for generations.

THE AMERICAN BELIEF

Under this covenant of justice, liberty, and union we have become a nation—prosperous, great, and mighty. And we have kept our freedom. But we have no promise from God that our greatness will endure. We have been allowed by Him to seek greatness with the sweat of our hands and the strength of our spirit.

I do not believe that the Great Society is the ordered, changeless, and sterile battalion of the ants. It is the excitement of becoming—always becoming, trying, probing, falling, resting, and trying again—but always trying and always gaining.

In each generation, with toil and tears, we have had to earn our heritage again.

If we fail now, we shall have forgotten in abundance what we learned in hardship: that democracy rests on faith, that freedom asks more than it gives, and that the judgment of God is harshest on those who are most favored.

If we succeed, it will not be because of what we have, but it will be because of what we are; not because of what we own, but, rather because of what we believe.

For we are a nation of believers. Underneath the clamor of building and the rush of our day's pursuits, we are believers in justice and liberty and union, and in our own Union. We believe that every man must someday be free. And we believe in ourselves.

. . .

For myself, I ask only, in the words of an ancient leader: "Give me now wisdom and knowledge, that I may go out and come in before this people: for who can judge this thy people, that is so great?"

RICHARD M. NIXON

First Address: January 20, 1969

In contrast with Johnson, Richard Nixon's foremost concern lay in the realm of foreign affairs, a concern that is likewise evident in his speech. But also notable are Nixon's worries about what had been a decade of turmoil, with demonstrations, assassinations, and violence roiling America's college campuses and cities. Thus did Nixon appeal to unity and an end to discord and division.

Senator [Everett] Dirksen, Mr. Chief Justice [Earl Warren], Mr. Vice President [Spiro Agnew], President [Lyndon] Johnson, Vice President [Hubert] Humphrey, my fellow Americans—and my fellow citizens of the world community:

I ask you to share with me today the majesty of this moment. In the orderly transfer of power, we celebrate the unity that keeps us free.

Each moment in history is a fleeting time, precious and unique. But some stand out as moments of beginning, in which courses are set that shape decades or centuries.

This can be such a moment.

Forces now are converging that make possible, for the first time, the hope that many of man's deepest aspirations can at last be realized. The spiraling pace of change allows us to contemplate, within our own lifetime, advances that once would have taken centuries.

In throwing wide the horizons of space, we have discovered new horizons on earth.

For the first time, because the people of the world want peace, and the leaders of the world are afraid of war, the times are on the side of peace. . . .

The greatest honor history can bestow is the title of peacemaker. This honor now beckons America—the chance to help lead the world at last out of the valley of turmoil, and onto that high ground of peace that man has dreamed of since the dawn of civilization. . . .

The second third of this century has been a time of proud achievement. We have made enormous strides in science and industry and agriculture. We have shared our wealth more broadly than ever. We have learned at last to manage a modern economy to assure its continued growth.

We have given freedom new reach, and we have begun to make its promise real for black as well as for white.

We see the hope of tomorrow in the youth of today. I know America's youth. I believe in them. We can be proud that they are better educated, more committed, more passionately driven by conscience than any generation in our history.

No people has ever been so close to the achievement of a just and abundant society, or so possessed of the will to achieve it. Because our strengths are so great, we can afford to appraise our weaknesses with candor and to approach them with hope.

Standing in this same place a third of a century ago, Franklin Delano Roosevelt addressed a Nation ravaged by depression and gripped in fear. He could say in surveying the Nation's troubles: "They concern, thank God, only material things."

Our crisis today is the reverse.

We have found ourselves rich in goods, but ragged in spirit; reaching with magnificent precision for the moon, but falling into raucous discord on earth.

We are caught in war, wanting peace. We are torn by division, wanting unity. We see around us empty lives, wanting fulfillment. We see tasks that need doing, waiting for hands to do them.

To a crisis of the spirit, we need an answer of the spirit. . . .

The simple things are the ones most needed today if we are to surmount what divides us, and cement what unites us.

To lower our voices would be a simple thing.

In these difficult years, America has suffered from a fever of words; from inflated rhetoric that promises more than it can deliver; from angry rhetoric that fans discontents into hatreds; from bombastic rhetoric that postures instead of persuading.

We cannot learn from one another until we stop shouting at one another—until we speak quietly enough so that our words can be heard as well as our voices.

For its part, government will listen. We will strive to listen in new ways—to the voices of quiet anguish, the voices that speak without words, the voices of the heart—to the injured voices, the anxious voices, the voices that have despaired of being heard.

Those who have been left out, we will try to bring in.

Those left behind, we will help to catch up.

For all of our people, we will set as our goal the decent order that makes progress possible and our lives secure.

As we reach toward our hopes, our task is to build on what has gone before—not turning away from the old, but turning toward the new.

In this past third of a century, government has passed more laws, spent more money, initiated more programs, than in all our previous history.

In pursuing our goals of full employment, better housing, excellence in education; in rebuilding our cities and improving our rural areas; in protecting our environment and enhancing the quality of life—in all these and more, we will and must press urgently forward.

We shall plan now for the day when our wealth can be transferred from the destruction of war abroad to the urgent needs of our people at home.

The American dream does not come to those who fall asleep.

But we are approaching the limits of what government alone can do.

Our greatest need now is to reach beyond government, and to enlist the legions of the concerned and the committed.

What has to be done, has to be done by government and people together or it will not be done at all. The lesson of past agony is that without the people we can do nothing; with the people we can do everything.

To match the magnitude of our tasks, we need the energies of our people—enlisted not only in grand enterprises, but more importantly in those small, splendid efforts that make headlines in the neighborhood newspaper instead of the national journal.

With these, we can build a great cathedral of the spirit—each of us raising it one stone at a time, as he reaches out to his neighbor, helping, caring, doing. . . .

No man can be fully free while his neighbor is not. To go forward at all is to go forward together.

This means black and white together, as one nation, not two. The laws have caught up with our conscience. What remains is to give life to what is in the law: to ensure at last that as all are born equal in dignity before God, all are born equal in dignity before man.

As we learn to go forward together at home, let us also seek to go forward together with all mankind.

Let us take as our goal: where peace is unknown, make it welcome; where peace is fragile, make it strong; where peace is temporary, make it permanent.

After a period of confrontation, we are entering an era of negotiation.

Let all nations know that during this administration our lines of communication will be open.

We seek an open world—open to ideas, open to the exchange of goods and people—a world in which no people, great or small, will live in angry isolation.

We cannot expect to make everyone our friend, but we can try to make no one our enemy.

Those who would be our adversaries, we invite to a peaceful competition—not in conquering territory or extending dominion, but in enriching the life of man.

As we explore the reaches of space, let us go to the new worlds together—not as new worlds to be conquered, but as a new adventure to be shared.

With those who are willing to join, let us cooperate to reduce the burden of arms, to strengthen the structure of peace, to lift up the poor and the hungry.

But to all those who would be tempted by weakness, let us leave no doubt that we will be as strong as we need to be for as long as we need to be. . . .

I speak from my own heart, and the heart of my country, the deep concern we have for those who suffer, and those who sorrow.

I have taken an oath today in the presence of God and my countrymen to uphold and defend the Constitution of the United States. To that oath I now add this sacred commitment: I shall consecrate my office, my energies, and all the wisdom I can summon, to the cause of peace among nations.

Let this message be heard by strong and weak alike:

The peace we seek to win is not victory over any other people, but the peace that comes "with healing in its wings"; with compassion for those who have suffered; with understanding for those who have opposed us; with the opportunity for all the peoples of this earth to choose their own destiny. . . .

We have endured a long night of the American spirit. But as our eyes catch the dimness of the first rays of dawn, let us not curse the remaining dark. Let us gather the light.

Our destiny offers, not the cup of despair, but the chalice of opportunity. So let us seize it, not in fear, but in gladness—and, "riders on the earth together," let us go forward, firm in our faith, steadfast in our purpose, cautious of the dangers; but sustained by our confidence in the will of God and the promise of man.

Second Address: January 20, 1973

Various foreign policy issues—negotiations with China, détente with Russia, the impending end of America's controversial involvement in Vietnam—preoccupied Nixon during his second address. The president was generally optimistic, little realizing that what seemed a "second-rate burglary" at the Watergate building would soon destroy his administration.

Mr. Vice President [Spiro Agnew], Mr. Speaker [Carl Albert], Mr. Chief Justice [Warren Burger], Senator [Marlin W.] Cook, Mrs. [Mamie] Eisenhower, and my fellow citizens of this great and good country we share together:

When we met here four years ago, America was bleak in spirit, depressed by the prospect of seemingly endless war abroad and of destructive conflict at home.

As we meet here today, we stand on the threshold of a new era of peace in the world.

The central question before us is: How shall we use that peace? Let us resolve that this era we are about to enter will not be what other postwar periods have so often been: a time of retreat and isolation that leads to stagnation at home and invites new danger abroad.

Let us resolve that this will be what it can become: a time of great responsibilities greatly borne, in which we renew the spirit and the promise of America as we enter our third century as a nation.

This past year saw far-reaching results from our new policies for peace. By continuing to revitalize our traditional friendships, and by our missions to Peking and to Moscow, we were able to establish the base for a new and more durable pattern of relationships among the nations of the world. Because of America's bold initiatives, 1972 will be long remembered as the year of the greatest progress since the end of World War II toward a lasting peace in the world.

The peace we seek in the world is not the flimsy peace which is merely an interlude between wars, but a peace which can endure for generations to come.

It is important that we understand both the necessity and the limitations of America's role in maintaining that peace.

Unless we in America work to preserve the peace, there will be no peace.

Unless we in America work to preserve freedom, there will be no freedom.

But let us clearly understand the new nature of America's role, as a result of the new policies we have adopted over these past four years.

We shall respect our treaty commitments.

We shall support vigorously the principle that no country has the right to impose its will or rule on another by force.

We shall continue, in this era of negotiation, to work for the limitation of nuclear arms, and to reduce the danger of confrontation between the great powers.

We shall do our share in defending peace and freedom in the world. But we shall expect others to do their share.

The time has passed when America will make every other nation's conflict our own, or make every other nation's future our responsibility, or presume to tell the people of other nations how to manage their own affairs.

Just as we respect the right of each nation to determine its own future, we also recognize the responsibility of each nation to secure its own future.

Just as America's role is indispensable in preserving the world's peace, so is each nation's role indispensable in preserving its own peace. . . .

We have the chance today to do more than ever before in our history to make life better in America—to ensure better education, better health, better housing, better transportation, a cleaner environment—to restore respect for law, to make our communities more livable—and to insure the God-given right of every American to full and equal opportunity.

Because the range of our needs is so great—because the reach of our opportunities is so great—let us be bold in our determination to meet those needs in new ways.

Just as building a structure of peace abroad has required turning away from old policies that failed, so building a new era of progress at home requires turning away from old policies that have failed.

Abroad, the shift from old policies to new has not been a retreat from our responsibilities, but a better way to peace.

And at home, the shift from old policies to new will not be a retreat from our responsibilities, but a better way to progress.

Abroad and at home, the key to those new responsibilities lies in the placing and the division of responsibility. We have lived too long with the consequences of attempting to gather all power and responsibility in Washington.

Abroad and at home, the time has come to turn away from the condescending policies of paternalism—of "Washington knows best."

A person can be expected to act responsibly only if he has responsibility. This is human nature. So let us encourage individuals at home and nations abroad to do more for themselves, to decide more for themselves. Let us locate responsibility in more places. Let us measure what we will do for others by what they will do for themselves.

That is why today I offer no promise of a purely governmental solution for every problem. We have lived too long with that false promise. In trusting too much in government, we have asked of it more than it can deliver. This leads only to inflated expectations, to reduced individual effort, and to a disappointment and frustration that erode confidence both in what government can do and in what people can do . . ..

In our own lives, let each of us ask—not just what will government do for me, but what can I do for myself?

In the challenges we face together, let each of us ask—not just how can government help, but how can I help? . . .

As America's longest and most difficult war [Vietnam] comes to an end, let us again learn to debate our differences with civility and decency. And let each of us reach out for that one precious quality government cannot provide—a new level of respect for the rights and feelings of one another, a new level of respect for the individual human dignity which is the cherished birthright of every American.

Above all else, the time has come for us to renew our faith in ourselves and in America.

In recent years, that faith has been challenged.

Our children have been taught to be ashamed of their country, ashamed of their parents, ashamed of America's record at home and of its role in the world.

At every turn, we have been beset by those who find everything wrong with America and little that is right. But I am confident that this will not be the judgment of history on these remarkable times in which we are privileged to live.

America's record in this century has been unparalleled in the world's history for its responsibility, for its generosity, for its creativity and for its progress.

Let us be proud that our system has produced and provided more freedom and more abundance, more widely shared, than any other system in the history of the world.

Let us be proud that in each of the four wars in which we have been engaged in this century, including the one we are now bringing to an end, we have fought not for our selfish advantage, but to help others resist aggression.

Let us be proud that by our bold, new initiatives, and by our steadfastness for peace with honor, we have made a break-through toward creating in the world what the world has not known before—a structure of peace that can last, not merely for our time, but for generations to come.

We are embarking here today on an era that presents challenges great as those any nation, or any generation, has ever faced.

We shall answer to God, to history, and to our conscience for the way in which we use these years.

As I stand in this place, so hallowed by history, I think of others who have stood here before me. I think of the dreams they had for America, and I think of how each recognized that he needed help far beyond himself in order to make those dreams come true.

Today, I ask your prayers that in the years ahead I may have God's help in making decisions that are right for America, and I pray for your help so that together we may be worthy of our challenge.

Let us pledge together to make these next four years the best four years in America's history, so that on its 200th birthday America will be as young and as vital as when it began, and as bright a beacon of hope for all the world.

Let us go forward from here confident in hope, strong in our faith in one another, sustained by our faith in God who created us, and striving always to serve His purpose.

JIMMY CARTER

January 20, 1977

President Carter's Inaugural Address fit both the man and the times perfectly: subdued, imbued with a strong sense of religious faith, and quietly optimistic. The stain of Watergate and the Vietnam debacle was evident in Carter's reference to "recent mistakes."

For myself and for our Nation, I want to thank my predecessor for all he has done to heal our land.

In this outward and physical ceremony we attest once again to the inner and spiritual strength of our Nation. As my high school teacher, Miss Julia Coleman, used to say: "We must adjust to changing times and still hold to unchanging principles."

Here before me is the Bible used in the inauguration of our first President, in 1789, and I have just taken the oath of office on the Bible my mother gave me a few years ago, opened to a timeless admonition from the ancient prophet Micah:

"He hath showed thee, O man, what is good; and what doth the Lord require of thee, but to do justly, and to love mercy, and to walk humbly with thy God." (Micah 6: 8)

This inauguration ceremony marks a new beginning, a new dedication within our Government, and a new spirit among us all. A President may sense and proclaim that new spirit, but only a people can provide it . . ..

You have given me a great responsibility—to stay close to you, to be worthy of you, and to exemplify what you are. Let us create together a new national spirit of unity and trust. Your strength can compensate for my weakness, and your wisdom can help to minimize my mistakes.

Let us learn together and laugh together and work together and pray together, confident that in the end we will triumph together in the right.

The American dream endures. We must once again have full faith in our country—and in one another. I believe America can be better. We can be even stronger than before.

Let our recent mistakes bring a resurgent commitment to the basic principles of our Nation, for we know that if we despise our own government we have no future. We recall in special times when we have stood briefly, but magnificently, united. In those times no prize was beyond our grasp.

But we cannot dwell upon remembered glory. We cannot afford to drift. We reject the prospect of failure or mediocrity or an inferior quality of life for any person. Our Government must at the same time be both competent and compassionate.

We have already found a high degree of personal liberty, and we are now struggling to enhance equality of opportunity. Our commitment to human rights must be absolute, our laws fair, our natural beauty preserved; the powerful must not persecute the weak, and human dignity must be enhanced.

We have learned that "more" is not necessarily "better," that even our great Nation has its recognized limits, and that we can neither answer all questions nor solve all problems. We cannot afford to do everything, nor can we afford to lack boldness as we meet the future. So, together, in a spirit of individual sacrifice for the common good, we must simply do our best.

Our Nation can be strong abroad only if it is strong at home. And we know that the best way to enhance freedom in other lands is to demonstrate here that our democratic system is worthy of emulation. . . .

The passion for freedom is on the rise. Tapping this new spirit, there can be no nobler nor more ambitious task for America to undertake on this day of a new beginning than to help shape a just and peaceful world that is truly humane.

We are a strong nation, and we will maintain strength so sufficient that it need not be proven in combat—a quiet strength based not merely on the size of an arsenal, but on the nobility of ideas.

We will be ever vigilant and never vulnerable, and we will fight our wars against poverty, ignorance, and injustice—for those are the enemies against which our forces can be honorably marshaled.

We are a purely idealistic Nation, but let no one confuse our idealism with weakness.

Because we are free we can never be indifferent to the fate of freedom elsewhere. Our moral sense dictates a clearcut preference for these societies which share with us an abiding respect for individual human rights. We do not seek to intimidate, but it is clear that a world which others can dominate with impunity would be inhospitable to decency and a threat to the well-being of all people. . . .

Within us, the people of the United States, there is evident a serious and purposeful rekindling of confidence. And I join in the hope that when my time as your President has ended, people might say this about our Nation:

- that we had remembered the words of Micah and renewed our search for humility, mercy, and justice;
- that we had torn down the barriers that separated those of different race and region and religion, and where there had been mistrust, built unity, with a respect for diversity;
- that we had found productive work for those able to perform it;
- that we had strengthened the American family, which is the basis of our society;

- that we had ensured respect for the law, and equal treatment under the law, for the weak and the powerful, for the rich and the poor;

- and that we had enabled our people to be proud of their own Government once again.

I would hope that the nations of the world might say that we had built a lasting peace, built not on weapons of war but on international policies which reflect our own most precious values.

These are not just my goals, and they will not be my accomplishments, but the affirmation of our Nation's continuing moral strength and our belief in an undiminished, ever-expanding American dream.

RONALD REAGAN

First Address: January 20, 1981

Reagan promised "morning again in America" during the 1980 campaign and explicitly contrasted this sunny disposition with President Carter's talk of an American "malaise." It won him the election, and in his address Reagan felt the need to continue the theme of optimism about America's future. At the same time, he expounded the themes that would lay the foundation for a conservative resurgence: faith in free market capitalism, limited government, and a belief in America's unique mission in the world.

Senator [Mark] Hatfield, Mr. Chief Justice [Warren E. Burger], Mr. President [Jimmy Carter], Vice President [George H. W.] Bush, Vice President [Walter] Mondale, Senator [Howard] Baker, Speaker [Thomas "Tip"] O'Neill, Reverend [Donn] Moomaw, and my fellow citizens: To a few of us here today, this is a solemn and most momentous occasion; and yet, in the history of our Nation, it is a commonplace occurrence. The orderly transfer of authority as called for in the Constitution routinely takes place as it has for almost two centuries and few of us stop to think how unique we really are. In the eyes of many in the world, this every–4-year ceremony we accept as normal is nothing less than a miracle. . . .

The business of our nation goes forward. These United States are confronted with an economic affliction of great proportions. We suffer from the longest and one of the worst sustained inflations in our national history. It distorts our economic decisions, penalizes thrift, and crushes the struggling young and the fixed-income elderly alike. It threatens to shatter the lives of millions of our people.

Idle industries have cast workers into unemployment, causing human misery and personal indignity. Those who do work are denied a fair return for their labor by a tax system which penalizes successful achievement and keeps us from maintaining full productivity.

But great as our tax burden is, it has not kept pace with public spending. For decades, we have piled deficit upon deficit, mortgaging our future and our children's future for the temporary convenience of the present. To continue this long trend is to guarantee tremendous social, cultural, political, and economic upheavals.

You and I, as individuals, can, by borrowing, live beyond our means, but for only a limited period of time. Why, then, should we think that collectively, as a nation, we are not bound by that same limitation?

We must act today in order to preserve tomorrow. And let there be no misunderstanding—we are going to begin to act, beginning today.

The economic ills we suffer have come upon us over several decades. They will not go away in days, weeks, or months, but they will go away. They will go away because we, as Americans, have the capacity now, as we have had in the past, to do whatever needs to be done to preserve this last and greatest bastion of freedom.

In this present crisis, government is not the solution to our problem.

From time to time, we have been tempted to believe that society has become too complex to be managed by self-rule, that government by an elite group is superior to government for, by, and of the people. But if no one among us is capable of governing himself, then who among us has the capacity to govern someone else? All of us together, in and out of government, must bear the burden. The solutions we seek must be equitable, with no one group singled out to pay a higher price. . . .

Well, this administration's objective will be a healthy, vigorous, growing economy that provides equal opportunity for all Americans, with no barriers born of bigotry or discrimination. Putting America back to work means putting all Americans back to work. Ending inflation means freeing all Americans from the terror of runaway living costs. All must share in the productive work of this "new beginning" and all must share in the bounty of a revived economy. With the idealism and fair play which are the core of our system and our strength, we can have a strong and prosperous America at peace with itself and the world.

So, as we begin, let us take inventory. We are a nation that has a government—not the other way around. And this makes us special among the nations of the Earth. Our Government has no power except that granted it by the people. It is time to check and reverse the growth of government which shows signs of having grown beyond the consent of the governed.

It is my intention to curb the size and influence of the Federal establishment and to demand recognition of the distinction between the powers granted to the Federal Government and those reserved to the States or to the people. All of us need to be reminded that the Federal Government did not create the States; the States created the Federal Government.

Now, so there will be no misunderstanding, it is not my intention to do away with government. It is, rather, to make it work—work with us, not over us; to stand by our side, not ride on our back. Government can and must provide opportunity, not smother it; foster productivity, not stifle it. . . .

It is no coincidence that our present troubles parallel and are proportionate to the intervention and intrusion in our lives that result from unnecessary and excessive growth of government. It is time for us to realize that we are too great a nation to limit ourselves to small dreams. We are not, as some would have us believe, doomed to an inevitable decline. I do not believe that fate will fall on us no matter what we do. I do believe in a fate that will fall on us if we do nothing. So, with all the creative energy at our command, let us begin an era of national renewal. Let us renew our determination, our courage, and our strength. And let us renew; our faith and our hope. . . .

Can we solve the problems confronting us? Well, the answer is an unequivocal and emphatic "yes." To paraphrase Winston Churchill, I did not take the oath I have just taken with the intention of presiding over the dissolution of the world's strongest economy.

In the days ahead I will propose removing the roadblocks that have slowed our economy and reduced productivity. Steps will be taken aimed at restoring the balance between the various levels of government. Progress may be slow—measured in inches and feet, not miles—but we will progress. It is time to reawaken this industrial giant, to get government back within its means, and to lighten our punitive tax burden. And these will be our first priorities, and on these principles, there will be no compromise. . . .

To those neighbors and allies who share our freedom, we will strengthen our historic ties and assure them of our support and firm commitment. We will match loyalty with loyalty. We will strive for mutually beneficial relations. We will not use our friendship to impose on their sovereignty, for our own sovereignty is not for sale.

As for the enemies of freedom, those who are potential adversaries, they will be reminded that peace is the highest aspiration of the American people. We will negotiate for it, sacrifice for it; we will not surrender for it—now or ever.

Our forbearance should never be misunderstood. Our reluctance for conflict should not be misjudged as a failure of will. When action is required to preserve our national security, we will act. We will maintain sufficient strength to prevail if need be, knowing that if we do so we have the best chance of never having to use that strength.

Above all, we must realize that no arsenal, or no weapon in the arsenals of the world, is so formidable as the will and moral courage of free men and women. It is a weapon our adversaries in today's world do not have. It is a weapon that we as Americans do have. Let that be understood by those who practice terrorism and prey upon their neighbors.

I am told that tens of thousands of prayer meetings are being held on this day, and for that I am deeply grateful. We are a nation under God, and I believe God intended for us to be free. It would be fitting and good, I think, if on each Inauguration Day in future years it should be declared a day of prayer. . . .

We are Americans. God bless you, and thank you.

Second Address: January 21, 1985

President Reagan's second address was much like the first, sounding themes of limited government, American progress, and a robust foreign policy dedicated to eventual victory over the Soviet Union.

Senator [Charles] Mathias, Chief Justice [Warren] Burger, Vice President [George H. W.] Bush, Speaker [Thomas "Tip"] O'Neill, Senator [Robert] Dole, Reverend Clergy, members of my family and friends, and my fellow citizens. . . .

There are no words adequate to express my thanks for the great honor that you have bestowed on me. I will do my utmost to be deserving of your trust. . . .

When I took this oath four years ago, I did so in a time of economic stress. Voices were raised saying we had to look to our past for the greatness and glory. But we, the present-day Americans, are not given to looking backward. In this blessed land, there is always a better tomorrow.

Four years ago, I spoke to you of a new beginning and we have accomplished that. But in another sense, our new beginning is a continuation of that beginning created two centuries ago when, for the first time in history, government, the people said, was not our master, it is our servant; its only power that which we the people allow it to have.

That system has never failed us, but, for a time, we failed the system. We asked things of government that government was not equipped to give. We yielded authority to the National Government that properly belonged to States or to local governments or to the people themselves. We allowed taxes and inflation to rob us of our earnings and savings and watched the great industrial machine that had made us the most productive people on Earth slow down and the number of unemployed increase.

By 1980, we knew it was time to renew our faith, to strive with all our strength toward the ultimate in individual freedom consistent with an orderly society.

We believed then and now there are no limits to growth and human progress when men and women are free to follow their dreams. . . .

My fellow citizens, our Nation is poised for greatness. We must do what we know is right and do it with all our might. Let history say of us, "These were golden years— when the American Revolution was reborn, when freedom gained new life, when America reached for her best.". . .

At the heart of our efforts is one idea vindicated by 25 straight months of economic growth: Freedom and incentives unleash the drive and entrepreneurial genius that are the core of human progress. We have begun to increase the rewards for work, savings, and investment; reduce the increase in the cost and size of government and its interference in people's lives.

We must simplify our tax system, make it more fair, and bring the rates down for all who work and earn. We must think anew and move with a new boldness, so every American who seeks work can find work; so the least among us shall have an equal chance to achieve the greatest things—to be heroes who heal our sick, feed the hungry, protect peace among nations, and leave this world a better place. . . .

We have already started returning to the people and to State and local governments responsibilities better handled by them. Now, there is a place for the Federal Government in matters of social compassion. But our fundamental goals must be to reduce dependency and upgrade the dignity of those who are infirm or disadvantaged. And here a growing economy and support from family and community offer our best chance for a society where compassion is a way of life, where the old and infirm are cared for, the young and, yes, the unborn protected, and the unfortunate looked after and made self.

And there is another area where the Federal Government can play a part. As an older American, I remember a time when people of different race, creed, or ethnic origin in our land found hatred and prejudice installed in social custom and, yes, in law. There is no story more heartening in our history than the progress that we have made toward the "brotherhood of man" that God intended for us. Let us resolve there will be no turning back or hesitation on the road to an America rich in dignity and abundant with opportunity for all our citizens.

Let us resolve that we the people will build an American opportunity society in which all of us—white and black, rich and poor, young and old—will go forward together arm in arm. Again, let us remember that though our heritage is one of blood lines from every corner of the Earth, we are all Americans pledged to carry on this last, best hope of man on Earth. . . .

Today, we utter no prayer more fervently than the ancient prayer for peace on Earth. Yet history has shown that peace will not come, nor will our freedom be preserved, by good will alone. There are those in the world who scorn our vision of human dignity and freedom. One nation, the Soviet Union, has conducted the greatest military buildup in the history of man, building arsenals of awesome offensive weapons.

We have made progress in restoring our defense capability. But much remains to be done. There must be no wavering by us, nor any doubts by others, that America will meet her responsibilities to remain free, secure, and at peace.

There is only one way safely and legitimately to reduce the cost of national security, and that is to reduce the need for it. And this we are trying to do in negotiations with the Soviet Union. We are not just discussing limits on a further increase of nuclear weapons. We seek, instead, to reduce their number. We seek the total elimination one day of nuclear weapons from the face of the Earth . . ..

America must remain freedom's staunchest friend, for freedom is our best ally.

And it is the world's only hope, to conquer poverty and preserve peace. Every blow we inflict against poverty will be a blow against its dark allies of oppression and war. Every victory for human freedom will be a victory for world peace.

So we go forward today, a nation still mighty in its youth and powerful in its purpose. With our alliances strengthened, with our economy leading the world to a new age of economic expansion, we look forward to a world rich in possibilities. And all this because we have worked and acted together, not as members of political parties, but as Americans.

My friends, we live in a world that is lit by lightning. So much is changing and will change, but so much endures, and transcends time.

History is a ribbon, always unfurling; history is a journey. And as we continue our journey, we think of those who traveled before us. We stand together again at the steps of this symbol of our democracy—or we would have been standing at the steps if it hadn't gotten so cold. Now we are standing inside this symbol of our democracy. Now we hear again the echoes of our past: a general falls to his knees in the hard snow of Valley Forge; a lonely President paces the darkened halls, and ponders his struggle to preserve the Union; the men of the Alamo call out encouragement to each other; a settler pushes west and sings a song, and the song echoes out forever and fills the unknowing air.

It is the American sound. It is hopeful, big-hearted, idealistic, daring, decent, and fair. That's our heritage; that is our song. We sing it still. For all our problems, our differences, we are together as of old, as we raise our voices to the God who is the Author of this most tender music. And may He continue to hold us close as we fill the world with our sound—sound in unity, affection, and love—one people under God, dedicated to the dream of freedom that He has placed in the human heart, called upon now to pass that dream on to a waiting and hopeful world.

God bless you and may God bless America.

George Bush Sr.

January 20, 1989

In many ways, George Bush Sr. tried to emulate his highly successful predecessor, carrying on the ideas and principles that had defined the Reagan Revolution for the previous eight years. Like Reagan, Bush called for a powerful American foreign policy and defense establishment, limits to federal spending, a sense of public service (hence his trademark reference to "a thousand points of light"), and a moral core of American values that transcended materialism. Note also his reference to the passing of totalitarianism, as the Soviet Union was crumbling even as Bush took the oath of office, ending the cold war and the legitimacy of a brand of Communism that had been used by presidents to define their foreign policies since the end of World War II.

Mr. Chief Justice [William Rehnquist], Mr. President [Ronald Reagan], Vice President [Dan] Quayle, Senator [George] Mitchell, Speaker [Jim] Wright, Senator [Robert] Dole, Congressman [Robert] Michel, and fellow citizens, neighbors, and friends. . . .

I come before you and assume the Presidency at a moment rich with promise. We live in a peaceful, prosperous time, but we can make it better. For a new breeze is blowing, and a world refreshed by freedom seems reborn; for in man's heart, if not in fact, the day of the dictator is over. The totalitarian era is passing, its old ideas blown away like leaves from an ancient, lifeless tree. A new breeze is blowing, and a nation refreshed by freedom stands ready to push on. There is new ground to be broken, and new action to be taken. There are times when the future seems thick as a fog; you sit and wait, hoping the mists will lift and reveal the right path. But this is a time when the future seems a door you can walk right through into a room called tomorrow.

Great nations of the world are moving toward democracy through the door to freedom. Men and women of the world move toward free markets through the door to prosperity. The people of the world agitate for free expression and free thought through the door to the moral and intellectual satisfactions that only liberty allows.

We know what works: Freedom works. We know what's right: Freedom is right. We know how to secure a more just and prosperous life for man on Earth: through free markets, free speech, free elections, and the exercise of free will unhampered by the state.

For the first time in this century, for the first time in perhaps all history, man does not have to invent a system by which to live. We don't have to talk late into the night about which form of government is better. We don't have to wrest justice from the kings. We only have to summon it from within ourselves. We must act on what we know. I take as my guide the hope of a saint: In crucial things, unity; in important things, diversity; in all things, generosity.

America today is a proud, free nation, decent and civil, a place we cannot help but love. We know in our hearts, not loudly and proudly, but as a simple fact, that this country has meaning beyond what we see, and that our strength is a force for good. But have we changed as a nation even in our time? Are we enthralled with material things, less appreciative of the nobility of work and sacrifice?

My friends, we are not the sum of our possessions. They are not the measure of our lives. In our hearts we know what matters. We cannot hope only to leave our children a bigger car, a bigger bank account. We must hope to give them a sense of what it means to be a loyal friend, a loving parent, a citizen who leaves his home, his neighborhood and town better than he found it. What do we want the men and women who work with us to say when we are no longer there? That we were more driven to succeed than anyone around us? Or that we stopped to ask if a sick child had gotten better, and stayed a moment there to trade a word of friendship?

No President, no government, can teach us to remember what is best in what we are. But if the man you have chosen to lead this government can help make a difference; if he can celebrate the quieter, deeper successes that are made not of gold and silk, but of better hearts and finer souls; if he can do these things, then he must.

America is never wholly herself unless she is engaged in high moral principle. We as a people have such a purpose today. It is to make kinder the face of the Nation and gentler the face of the world. My friends, we have work to do. There are the homeless, lost and roaming. There are the children who have nothing, no love, no normalcy. There are those who cannot free themselves of enslavement to whatever addiction—drugs, welfare, the demoralization that rules the slums. There is crime to be conquered, the rough crime of the streets. There are young women to be helped who are about to become mothers of children they can't care for and might not love. They need our care, our guidance, and our education, though we bless them for choosing life.

The old solution, the old way, was to think that public money alone could end these problems. But we have learned that is not so. And in any case, our funds are low. We have a deficit to bring down. We have more will than wallet; but will is what we need. We will make the hard choices, looking at what we have and perhaps allocating it differently, making our decisions based on honest need and prudent safety. And then we will do the wisest thing of all: We will turn to the only resource we have that in times of need always grows—the goodness and the courage of the American people. . . .

I have spoken of a thousand points of light, of all the community organizations that are spread like stars throughout the Nation, doing good. We will work hand in hand, encouraging, sometimes leading, sometimes being led, rewarding. We will work on this in the White House, in the Cabinet agencies. I will go to the people and the programs that are the brighter points of light, and I will ask every member of my government to become involved. The old ideas are new again because they are not old, they are timeless: duty, sacrifice, commitment, and a patriotism that finds its expression in taking part and pitching in. . . .

To the world, too, we offer new engagement and a renewed vow: We will stay strong to protect the peace. The "offered hand" is a reluctant fist; but once made, strong, and can be used with great effect. There are today Americans who are held against their will in foreign lands, and Americans who are unaccounted for. Assistance can be shown here, and will be long remembered. Good will begets good will. Good faith can be a spiral that endlessly moves on.

Great nations like great men must keep their word. When America says something, America means it, whether a treaty or an agreement or a vow made on marble steps. We will always try to speak clearly, for candor is a compliment, but subtlety, too, is good and has its place. While keeping our alliances and friendships around the world strong, ever strong, we will continue the new closeness with the Soviet Union, consistent both with our security and with progress. One might say that our new relationship in part reflects the triumph of hope and strength over experience. But hope is good, and so are strength and vigilance. . . .

A President is neither prince nor pope, and I don't seek a window on men's souls. In fact, I yearn for a greater tolerance, an easy-goingness about each other's attitudes and way of life. . . .

And so, there is much to do; and tomorrow the work begins. I do not mistrust the future; I do not fear what is ahead. For our problems are large, but our heart is larger. Our challenges are great, but our will is greater. And if our flaws are endless, God's love is truly boundless.

Some see leadership as high drama, and the sound of trumpets calling, and sometimes it is that. But I see history as a book with many pages, and each day we fill a page with acts of hopefulness and meaning. The new breeze blows, a page turns, the story unfolds. And so today a chapter begins, a small and stately story of unity, diversity, and generosity—shared, and written, together.

Thank you. God bless you and God bless the United States of America.

WILLIAM JEFFERSON "BILL" CLINTON

First Address: January 20, 1993

During the 1992 election, a photograph circulated of a teenaged Bill Clinton shaking hands with President Kennedy during the 1960s. It was an apt image for Clinton; JFK's legacy loomed large over Clinton, and his influence on Clinton is evident here, particularly in Mr. Clinton's talk of generational change and renewal. The first "baby boomer" president, Clinton hoped to usher in a new era of change and revival reminiscent of Kennedy's Camelot days.

Today we celebrate the mystery of American renewal.

This ceremony is held in the depth of winter. But, by the words we speak and the faces we show the world, we force the spring. A spring reborn in the world's oldest democracy, that brings forth the vision and courage to reinvent America . . ..

On behalf of our nation, I salute my predecessor, President Bush, for his half-century of service to America. And I thank the millions of men and women whose steadfastness and sacrifice triumphed over Depression, fascism and Communism.

Today, a generation raised in the shadows of the Cold War assumes new responsibilities in a world warmed by the sunshine of freedom but threatened still by ancient hatreds and new plagues.

Raised in unrivaled prosperity, we inherit an economy that is still the world's strongest, but is weakened by business failures, stagnant wages, increasing inequality, and deep divisions among our people. . . .

Profound and powerful forces are shaking and remaking our world, and the urgent question of our time is whether we can make change our friend and not our enemy.

This new world has already enriched the lives of millions of Americans who are able to compete and win in it. But when most people are working harder for less; when others cannot work at all; when the cost of health care devastates families and threatens to bankrupt many of our enterprises, great and small; when fear of crime robs law-abiding citizens of their freedom; and when millions of poor children cannot even imagine the lives we are calling them to lead, we have not made change our friend. . . .

Though our challenges are fearsome, so are our strengths. And Americans have ever been a restless, questing, hopeful people. We must bring to our task today the vision and will of those who came before us. . . .

And so today, we pledge an end to the era of deadlock and drift; a new season of American renewal has begun. To renew America, we must be bold. We must do what no generation has had to do before. We must invest more in our own people, in their jobs, in their future, and at the same time cut our massive debt. And we must do so in a world in which we must compete for every opportunity. It will not be easy; it will require sacrifice. But it can be done, and done fairly, not choosing sacrifice for its own sake, but for our own sake. We must provide for our nation the way a family provides for its children. . . .

It is time to break the bad habit of expecting something for nothing, from our government or from each other. Let us all take more responsibility, not only for ourselves and our families but for our communities and our country. To renew America, we must revitalize our democracy. . . .

To renew America, we must meet challenges abroad as well at home. There is no longer division between what is foreign and what is domestic; the world economy, the world environment, the world AIDS crisis, the world arms race; they affect us all.

Today, as an old order passes, the new world is more free but less stable. Communism's collapse has called forth old animosities and new dangers. Clearly America must continue to lead the world we did so much to make.

While America rebuilds at home, we will not shrink from the challenges, nor fail to seize the opportunities, of this new world. Together with our friends and allies, we will work to shape change, lest it engulf us. . . .

To that work I now turn, with all the authority of my office. I ask the Congress to join with me. But no president, no Congress, no government, can undertake this mission alone. My fellow Americans, you, too, must play your part in our renewal. I challenge a new generation of young Americans to a season of service; to act on your idealism by helping troubled children, keeping company with those in need, reconnecting our torn communities. There is so much to be done; enough indeed for millions of others who are still young in spirit to give of themselves in service, too.

In serving, we recognize a simple but powerful truth, we need each other. And we must care for one another. Today, we do more than celebrate America; we rededicate ourselves to the very idea of America. . . .

And so, my fellow Americans, at the edge of the 21st century, let us begin with energy and hope, with faith and discipline, and let us work until our work is done. The scripture says, "And let us not be weary in well-doing, for in due season, we shall reap, if we faint not."

From this joyful mountaintop of celebration, we hear a call to service in the valley. We have heard the trumpets. We have changed the guard. And now, each in our way, and with God's help, we must answer the call.

Thank you, and God bless you all.

Second Address: January 20, 1997

The coming of a new century provided the background theme for Clinton's second address. A key issue for the twenty-first century was the proper role of government, the balance of federal-state relations, and the extent to which government should interfere in the daily lives of American citizens. During his first term, Clinton was confronted by a resurgent Republican Party whose answer was to limit government activity as much as possible. The president tried to offer a more moderate response here, suggesting a balance between government and private activity. Mr. Clinton also felt compelled to address racial and ethnic divisions—manifested in the Rodney King riots in Los Angeles and the terror bombing of a federal building in Oklahoma City in 1995—which he feared were rending the nation's sense of unity.

My fellow citizens:

At this last presidential inauguration of the 20th century, let us lift our eyes toward the challenges that await us in the next century. It is our great good fortune that time and chance have put us not only at the edge of a new century, in a new millennium, but on the edge of a bright new prospect in human affairs, a moment that will define our course, and our character, for decades to come. We must keep our old democracy forever young. Guided by the ancient vision of a promised land, let us set our sights upon a land of new promise. . . .

At the dawn of the 21st century a free people must now choose to shape the forces of the Information Age and the global society, to unleash the limitless potential of all our people, and, yes, to form a more perfect union.

When last we gathered, our march to this new future seemed less certain than it does today. We vowed then to set a clear course to renew our nation.

In these four years, we have been touched by tragedy, exhilarated by challenge, strengthened by achievement. America stands alone as the world's indispensable nation. Once again, our economy is the strongest on Earth. Once again, we are building stronger families, thriving communities, better educational opportunities, a cleaner environment. Problems that once seemed destined to deepen now bend to our efforts: our streets are safer and record numbers of our fellow citizens have moved from welfare to work.

And once again, we have resolved for our time a great debate over the role of government. Today we can declare: Government is not the problem, and government is not the solution. We,—the American people, we are the solution. Our founders understood that well and gave us a democracy strong enough to endure for centuries, flexible enough to face our common challenges and advance our common dreams in each new day.

As times change, so government must change. We need a new government for a new century—humble enough not to try to solve all our problems for us, but strong enough to give us the tools to solve our problems for ourselves; a government that is smaller, lives within its means, and does more with less. Yet where it can stand up for our values and interests in the world, and where it can give Americans the power to make a real difference in their everyday lives, government should do more, not less. The preeminent mission of our new government is to give all Americans an opportunity,—not a guarantee, but a real opportunity to build better lives.

Beyond that, my fellow citizens, the future is up to us. Our founders taught us that the preservation of our liberty and our union depends upon responsible citizenship. And we need a new sense of responsibility for a new century. There is work to do, work that government alone cannot do: teaching children to read; hiring people off welfare rolls; coming out from behind locked doors and shuttered windows to help reclaim our streets from drugs and gangs and crime; taking time out of our own lives to serve others.

Each and every one of us, in our own way, must assume personal responsibility, not only for ourselves and our families, but for our neighbors and our nation. Our greatest responsibility is to embrace a new spirit of community for a new century. For any one of us to succeed, we must succeed as one America. . . .

The divide of race has been America's constant curse. And each new wave of immigrants gives new targets to old prejudices. Prejudice and contempt, cloaked in the pretense of religious or political conviction are no different. These forces have nearly destroyed our nation in the past. They plague us still. They fuel the fanaticism of terror. And they torment the lives of millions in fractured nations all around the world.

These obsessions cripple both those who hate and, of course, those who are hated, robbing both of what they might become. We cannot, we will not, succumb to the dark impulses that lurk in the far regions of the soul everywhere. We shall overcome them. And we shall replace them with the generous spirit of a people who feel at home with one another.

Our rich texture of racial, religious and political diversity will be a Godsend in the 21st century. Great rewards will come to those who can live together, learn together, work together, forge new ties that bind together. . . .

My fellow Americans, as we look back at this remarkable century, we may ask, can we hope not just to follow, but even to surpass the achievements of the 20th century in America and to avoid the awful bloodshed that stained its legacy? To that question, every American here and every American in our land today must answer a resounding "Yes."

This is the heart of our task. With a new vision of government, a new sense of responsibility, a new spirit of community, we will sustain America's journey. The promise we sought in a new land we will find again in a land of new promise . . . .

We will stand mighty for peace and freedom, and maintain a strong defense against terror and destruction. Our children will sleep free from the threat of nuclear, chemical or biological weapons. Ports and airports, farms and factories will thrive with trade and innovation and ideas. And the world's greatest democracy will lead a whole world of democracies. . . .

Fellow citizens, let us build that America, a nation ever moving forward toward realizing the full potential of all its citizens. Prosperity and power, yes, they are important, and we must maintain them. But let us never forget: The greatest progress we have made, and the greatest progress we have yet to make, is in the human heart. In the end, all the world's wealth and a thousand armies are no match for the strength and decency of the human spirit . . ..

To that effort I pledge all my strength and every power of my office. I ask the members of Congress here to join in that pledge. The American people returned to office a President of one party and a Congress of another. Surely, they did not do this to advance the politics of petty bickering and extreme partisanship they plainly deplore. No, they call on us instead to be repairers of the breach, and to move on with America's mission.
. . .

And so, my fellow Americans, we must be strong, for there is much to dare. The demands of our time are great and they are different. Let us meet them with faith and courage, with patience and a grateful and happy heart. Let us shape the hope of this day into the noblest chapter in our history. Yes, let us build our bridge. A bridge wide enough and strong enough for every American to cross over to a blessed land of new promise.

May those generations whose faces we cannot yet see, whose names we may never know, say of us here that we led our beloved land into a new century with the American Dream alive for all her children; with the American promise of a more perfect union a reality for all her people; with America's bright flame of freedom spreading throughout all the world.

From the height of this place and the summit of this century, let us go forth. May God strengthen our hands for the good work ahead, and always, always bless our America.

GEORGE BUSH JR.

First Address: January 20, 2001

Few presidents entered office under a cloud of controversy as dark as that which hung over President Bush. A bitterly contested election was followed by deadlock and crisis over disputed voting counts in Florida; in the end, the Supreme Court in effect declared Bush the winner over his rival, Democrat Al Gore. This was a solution that fully satisfied no one and left a bitter legacy of rancor on all sides—hence Mr. Bush's references to the need for a new sense of civility and harmony among Americans. The president also returned to his campaign theme of promoting "compassionate conservatism" in domestic policies, balancing a conservative desire to curb government growth with a need to repair the nation's ailing education and welfare systems.

President [William] Clinton, distinguished guests and my fellow citizens:

The peaceful transfer of authority is rare in history, yet common in our country. With a simple oath, we affirm old traditions and make new beginnings.

As I begin, I thank President Clinton for his service to our nation; and I thank Vice President [Al] Gore for a contest conducted with spirit and ended with grace. . . .

Through much of the last century, America's faith in freedom and democracy was a rock in a raging sea. Now it is a seed upon the wind, taking root in many nations. Our democratic faith is more than the creed of our country, it is the inborn hope of our humanity, an ideal we carry but do not own, a trust we bear and pass along; and even after nearly 225 years, we have a long way yet to travel. . . .

Today, we affirm a new commitment to live out our nation's promise through civility, courage, compassion and character. America, at its best, matches a commitment to principle with a concern for civility. A civil society demands from each of us good will and respect, fair dealing and forgiveness. Some seem to believe that our politics can afford to be petty because, in a time of peace, the stakes of our debates appear small. But the stakes for America are never small. If our country does not lead the cause of freedom, it will not be led. If we do not turn the hearts of children toward knowledge and character, we will lose their gifts and undermine their idealism. If we permit our economy to drift and decline, the vulnerable will suffer most. We must live up to the calling we share. Civility is not a tactic or a sentiment. It is the determined choice of trust over cynicism, of community over chaos. This commitment, if we keep it, is a way to shared accomplishment. . . .

The enemies of liberty and our country should make no mistake, America remains engaged in the world by history and by choice, shaping a balance of power that favors freedom. We will defend our allies and our interests; we will show purpose without arrogance; we will meet aggression and bad faith with resolve and strength; and to all nations, we will speak for the values that gave our nation birth.

America, at its best, is compassionate. In the quiet of American conscience, we know that deep, persistent poverty is unworthy of our nation's promise. Whatever our views of its cause, we can agree that children at risk are not at fault. Abandonment and abuse are not acts of God, they are failures of love. The proliferation of prisons, however necessary, is no substitute for hope and order in our souls. Where there is suffering, there is duty. Americans in need are not strangers, they are citizens, not problems, but priorities, and all of us are diminished when any are hopeless. Government has great responsibilities for public safety and public health, for civil rights and common schools. Yet compassion is the work of a nation, not just a government. Some needs and hurts are so deep they will only respond to a mentor's touch or a pastor's prayer. Church and charity, synagogue and mosque lend our communities their humanity, and they will have an honored place in our plans and in our laws. Many in our country do not know the pain of poverty, but we can listen to those who do. I can pledge our nation to a goal, "When we see that wounded traveler on the road to Jericho, we will not pass to the other side."

America, at its best, is a place where personal responsibility is valued and expected. Encouraging responsibility is not a search for scapegoats, it is a call to conscience. Though it requires sacrifice, it brings a deeper fulfillment. We find the fullness of life not only in options, but in commitments. . . .

Americans are generous and strong and decent, not because we believe in ourselves, but because we hold beliefs beyond ourselves. When this spirit of citizenship is missing, no government program can replace it. When this spirit is present, no wrong can stand against it. . . .

God bless you all, and God bless America.

Second Address: January 20, 2005

Note: The text is taken from www.whitehouse.gov/news/releases/2005/01/20050120–1 .html.

Foreign policy issues barely registered in Mr. Bush's first address; four years later, in the wake of the World Trade Center and Pentagon bombings on September 11, 2001, and subsequent wars in Afghanistan and Iraq, foreign policy had taken center stage in Bush's thinking. Whereas during the 2000 election Bush had frowned upon "nation building" and other attempts to effect democratic change abroad, by 2004 he had come to see such programs as essential to the survival of American democracy. Thus did his second Inaugural Address possess a tone of global triumphalism rarely seen since the days of the cold war.

Vice President Cheney, Mr. Chief Justice, President Carter, President Bush, President Clinton, reverend clergy, distinguished guests, fellow citizens:

On this day, prescribed by law and marked by ceremony, we celebrate the durable wisdom of our Constitution, and recall the deep commitments that unite our country. I am grateful for the honor of this hour, mindful of the consequential times in which we live, and determined to fulfill the oath that I have sworn and you have witnessed.

At this second gathering, our duties are defined not by the words I use, but by the history we have seen together. For a half century, America defended our own freedom by standing watch on distant borders. After the shipwreck of communism came years of relative quiet, years of repose, years of sabbatical—and then there came a day of fire.

We have seen our vulnerability—and we have seen its deepest source. For as long as whole regions of the world simmer in resentment and tyranny—prone to ideologies that feed hatred and excuse murder—violence will gather, and multiply in destructive power, and cross the most defended borders, and raise a mortal threat. There is only one force of history that can break the reign of hatred and resentment, and expose the pretensions of tyrants, and reward the hopes of the decent and tolerant, and that is the force of human freedom.

We are led, by events and common sense, to one conclusion: The survival of liberty in our land increasingly depends on the success of liberty in other lands. The best hope for peace in our world is the expansion of freedom in all the world. . . .

So it is the policy of the United States to seek and support the growth of democratic movements and institutions in every nation and culture, with the ultimate goal of ending tyranny in our world.

This is not primarily the task of arms, though we will defend ourselves and our friends by force of arms when necessary. Freedom, by its nature, must be chosen, and defended by citizens, and sustained by the rule of law and the protection of minorities. And when the soul of a nation finally speaks, the institutions that arise may reflect customs and traditions very different from our own. America will not impose our own style of government on the unwilling. Our goal instead is to help others find their own voice, attain their own freedom, and make their own way.

The great objective of ending tyranny is the concentrated work of generations. The difficulty of the task is no excuse for avoiding it. America's influence is not unlimited, but fortunately for the oppressed, America's influence is considerable, and we will use it confidently in freedom's cause.

My most solemn duty is to protect this nation and its people against further attacks and emerging threats. Some have unwisely chosen to test America's resolve, and have found it firm.

We will persistently clarify the choice before every ruler and every nation: The moral choice between oppression, which is always wrong, and freedom, which is eternally right. America will not pretend that jailed dissidents prefer their chains, or that women welcome humiliation and servitude, or that any human being aspires to live at the mercy of bullies. . . .

Some, I know, have questioned the global appeal of liberty—though this time in history, four decades defined by the swiftest advance of freedom ever seen, is an odd time for doubt. Americans, of all people, should never be surprised by the power of our ideals. Eventually, the call of freedom comes to every mind and every soul. We do not accept the existence of permanent tyranny because we do not accept the possibility of permanent slavery. Liberty will come to those who love it.

Today, America speaks anew to the peoples of the world:

All who live in tyranny and hopelessness can know: the United States will not ignore your oppression, or excuse your oppressors. When you stand for your liberty, we will stand with you.

Democratic reformers facing repression, prison, or exile can know: America sees you for who you are: the future leaders of your free country.

The rulers of outlaw regimes can know that we still believe as Abraham Lincoln did: "Those who deny freedom to others deserve it not for themselves; and, under the rule of a just God, cannot long retain it."

The leaders of governments with long habits of control need to know: To serve your people you must learn to trust them. Start on this journey of progress and justice, and America will walk at your side.

And all the allies of the United States can know: we honor your friendship, we rely on your counsel, and we depend on your help. Division among free nations is a primary goal of freedom's enemies. The concerted effort of free nations to promote democracy is a prelude to our enemies' defeat.

Today, I also speak anew to my fellow citizens:

From all of you, I have asked patience in the hard task of securing America, which you have granted in good measure. Our country has accepted obligations that are difficult to fulfill, and would be dishonorable to abandon. Yet because we have acted in the great liberating tradition of this nation, tens of millions have achieved their freedom. And as hope kindles hope, millions more will find it. By our efforts, we have lit a fire as well—a fire in the minds of men. It warms those who feel its power, it burns those who fight its progress, and one day this untamed fire of freedom will reach the darkest corners of our world . . ..

America has need of idealism and courage, because we have essential work at home— the unfinished work of American freedom. In a world moving toward liberty, we are determined to show the meaning and promise of liberty.

In America's ideal of freedom, citizens find the dignity and security of economic independence, instead of laboring on the edge of subsistence. . . . By making every citizen an agent of his or her own destiny, we will give our fellow Americans greater freedom from want and fear, and make our society more prosperous and just and equal.

In America's ideal of freedom, the public interest depends on private character—on integrity, and tolerance toward others, and the rule of conscience in our own lives. Self-government relies, in the end, on the governing of the self. That edifice of character is built in families, supported by communities with standards, and sustained in our national life by the truths of Sinai, the Sermon on the Mount, the words of the Koran, and the varied faiths of our people. Americans move forward in every generation by reaffirming all that is good and true that came before—ideals of justice and conduct that are the same yesterday, today, and forever.

In America's ideal of freedom, the exercise of rights is ennobled by service, and mercy, and a heart for the weak. Liberty for all does not mean independence from one another. Our nation relies on men and women who look after a neighbor and surround the lost with love. Americans, at our best, value the life we see in one another, and must always remember that even the unwanted have worth. And our country must abandon all the habits of racism, because we cannot carry the message of freedom and the baggage of bigotry at the same time.

From the perspective of a single day, including this day of dedication, the issues and questions before our country are many. From the viewpoint of centuries, the questions that come to us are narrowed and few. Did our generation advance the cause of freedom? And did our character bring credit to that cause? . . .

We go forward with complete confidence in the eventual triumph of freedom. Not because history runs on the wheels of inevitability; it is human choices that move events. Not because we consider ourselves a chosen nation; God moves and chooses as He wills. We have confidence because freedom is the permanent hope of mankind, the hunger in dark places, the longing of the soul. When our Founders declared a new order of the ages; when soldiers died in wave upon wave for a union based on liberty; when citizens marched in peaceful outrage under the banner "Freedom Now"—they were acting on an ancient hope that is meant to be fulfilled. History has an ebb and flow of justice, but history also has a visible direction, set by liberty and the Author of Liberty. . . .

May God bless you, and may He watch over the United States of America.

STATE OF THE UNION ADDRESSES

(Edited Highlights)

The presidents' State of the Union Addresses tend to be more specific and immediate than their inauguration day speeches. In editing these addresses, I have focused on the bigger themes and more revealing statements a given president made about his policies and his times, while excising those passages that seemed excessively archaic or detailed. In most cases, I have chosen one representative State of the Union Address for each president. Unless otherwise noted, the texts were obtained from the American Presidency Project at http://www.presidency.ucsb.edu/sou.php.

STATE OF THE UNION ADDRESSES 1790–1862

GEORGE WASHINGTON

George Washington's State of the Union Addresses focused on the sort of problems one might expect for the fledgling government of a new nation. He discussed admittance of new states, the various problems endemic to creating an army and navy from scratch, and the United States' ongoing border troubles with the Indians. His later addresses also indicate a growing concern over the turmoil in Europe.

First Address: January 18, 1790

I embrace with great satisfaction the opportunity which now presents itself of congratulating you on the present favorable prospects of our public affairs. The recent accession of the important state of north Carolina to the Constitution of the United States (of which official information has been received), the rising credit and respectability of our country, the general and increasing good will toward the government of the Union, and the concord, peace, and plenty with which we are blessed are circumstances auspicious in an eminent degree to our national prosperity. . . .

Among the many interesting objects which will engage your attention that of providing for the common defense will merit particular regard. To be prepared for war is one of the most effectual means of preserving peace.

A free people ought not only to be armed, but disciplined; to which end a uniform and well-digested plan is requisite; and their safety and interest require that they should promote such manufactories as tend to render them independent of others for essential, particularly military, supplies. . . .

There was reason to hope that the pacific measures adopted with regard to certain hostile tribes of Indians would have relieved the inhabitants of our southern and western frontiers from their depredations, but you will perceive from the information contained in the papers which I shall direct to be laid before you (comprehending a communication from the Commonwealth of Virginia) that we ought to be prepared to afford protection to those parts of the Union, and, if necessary, to punish aggressors. . . .

The advancement of agriculture, commerce, and manufactures by all proper means will not, I trust, need recommendation; but I can not forbear intimating to you the expediency of giving effectual encouragement as well to the introduction of new and useful inventions from abroad as to the exertions of skill and genius in producing them at home, and of facilitating the intercourse between the distant parts of our country by a due attention to the post-office and post-roads.

Nor am I less persuaded that you will agree with me in opinion that there is nothing which can better deserve your patronage than the promotion of science and literature. Knowledge is in every country the surest basis of public happiness. In one in which the measures of government receive their impressions so immediately from the sense of the community as in ours it is proportionably essential. . . .

JOHN ADAMS

For Adams, the presidency was a rather unhappy period. Forced to choose sides between England and France in what was rapidly becoming a European-wide war, Adams chose to do neither, adhering to a careful policy of neutrality. Historians have judged him wise in this regard, but his contemporaries were not quite so generous.

First Address: November 22, 1797

I was for some time apprehensive that it would be necessary, on account of the contagious sickness which afflicted the city of Philadelphia, to convene the National Legislature at some other place. This measure it was desirable to avoid. . . . [Therefore] I postponed my determination, having hopes, now happily realized, that, without hazard to the lives or health of the members, Congress might assemble at this place, where it was next by law to meet. . . .

Although I can not yet congratulate you on the reestablishment of peace in Europe and the restoration of security to the persons and properties of our citizens from injustice and violence at sea, we have, nevertheless, abundant cause of gratitude to the source of benevolence and influence for interior tranquillity and personal security, for propitious seasons, prosperous agriculture, productive fisheries, and general improvements, and, above all, for a rational spirit of civil and religious liberty and a calm but steady determination to support our sovereignty, as well as our moral and our religious principles, against all open and secret attacks. . . .

Indeed, whatever may be the issue of the negotiation with France, and whether the war in Europe is or is not to continue, I hold it most certain that permanent tranquility and order will not soon be obtained. The state of society has so long been disturbed, the sense of moral and religious obligations so much weakened, public faith and national honor have been so impaired, respect to treaties has been so diminished, and the law of nations has lost so much of its force, while pride, ambition, avarice and violence have been so long unrestrained, there remains no reasonable ground on which to raise an expectation that a commerce without protection or defense will not be plundered. . . .

We are met together at a most interesting period. The situation of the principal powers of Europe are singular and portentous. Connected with some by treaties and with all by commerce, no important event there can be indifferent to us. Such circumstances call with peculiar importunity not less for a disposition to unite in all those measures on which the honor, safety, and prosperity of our country depend than for all the exertions of wisdom and firmness.

In all such measures you may rely on my zealous and hearty concurrence.

THOMAS JEFFERSON

Thomas Jefferson was a cautious supporter of the Constitution when it was drafted, worrying that the Framers had created a new national government that could potentially become much too powerful, especially at the expense of the states. Accordingly, as president, Jefferson sought to cut federal expenditures in defense and administration and was proud of his frugality. One exception to this, however, was the purchase of the Louisiana Territory from France.

First Address: December 18, 1801

It is a circumstance of sincere gratification to me that on meeting the great council of our nation I am able to announce to them on grounds of reasonable certainty that the wars and troubles which have for so many years afflicted our sister nations have at length come to an end, and that the communications of peace and commerce are once more opening among them. . . .

To this state of general peace with which we have been blessed, one only exception exists. Tripoli, the least considerable of the Barbary States, had come forward with demands unfounded either in right or in compact, and had permitted itself to denounce war on our failure to comply before a given day. The style of the demand admitted but one answer.

I sent a small squadron of frigates into the Mediterranean, with assurances to that power of our sincere desire to remain in peace, but with orders to protect our commerce against the threatened attack. The measure was seasonable and salutary. The Bey had already declared war. His cruisers were out. Two had arrived at Gibraltar. Our commerce in the Mediterranean was blockaded and that of the Atlantic in peril.

The arrival of our squadron dispelled the danger. One of the Tripolitan cruisers having fallen in with and engaged the small schooner Enterprise, commanded by Lieutenant Sterret, which had gone as a tender to our larger vessels, was captured, after a heavy slaughter of her men, without the loss of a single 1 on our part. The bravery exhibited by our citizens on that element will, I trust, be a testimony to the world that it is not the want of that virtue which makes us seek their peace, but a conscientious desire to direct the energies of our nation to the multiplication of the human race, and not to its destruction. Unauthorized by the Constitution, without the sanction of Congress, to go beyond the line of defense, the vessel, being disabled from committing further hostilities, was liberated with its crew. . . .

I wish I could say that our situation with all the other Barbary States was entirely satisfactory. Discovering that some delays had taken place in the performance of certain articles stipulated by us, I thought it my duty, by immediate measures for fulfilling them, to vindicate to ourselves the right of considering the effect of departure from stipulation on their side. From the papers which will be laid before you you will be enabled to judge whether our treaties are regarded by them as fixing at all the measure of their demands or as guarding from the exercise of force our vessels within their power, and to consider how far it will be safe and expedient to leave our affairs with them in their present posture. . . .

When we consider that this Government is charged with the external and mutual relations only of these States; that the States themselves have principal care of our persons, our property, and our reputation, constituting the great field of human concerns, we may well doubt whether our organization is not too complicated, too expensive; whether offices and officers have not been multiplied unnecessarily and sometimes injuriously to the service they were meant to promote. . . .

Among those who are dependent on Executive discretion I have begun the reduction of what was deemed unnecessary. . . .

Considering the general tendency to multiply offices and dependencies and to increase expense to the ultimate term of burthen which the citizen can bear, it behooves us to avail ourselves of every occasion which presents itself for taking off the surcharge, that it never may be seen here that after leaving to labor the smallest portion of its earnings on which it can subsist, Government shall itself consume the whole residue of what it was instituted to guard. . . .

JAMES MADISON

Foreign policy issues, particularly America's deteriorating relationship with Britain and eventual war, dominated the Madison Administration. Through his annual addresses to Congress, one can trace the precipitous decline of Anglo-American relations. This also furnishes the first (but certainly not final) example of how a president could use the forum of his office to justify and sustain a national war effort.

Fifth Address: December 7, 1813

In meeting you at the present interesting conjuncture it would have been highly satisfactory if I could have communicated a favorable result to the mission charged with negotiations for restoring peace. It was a just expectation, from the respect due to the distinguished Sovereign who had invited them by his offer of mediation, from the readiness with which the invitation was accepted on the part of the United States, and from the pledge to be found in an act of their Legislature for the liberality which their plenipotentiaries would carry into the negotiations, that no time would be lost by the British Government in embracing the experiment for hastening a stop to the effusion of blood. A prompt and cordial acceptance of the mediation on that side was the less to be doubted, as it was of a nature not to submit rights or pretensions on either side to the decision of an umpire, but to afford merely an opportunity, honorable and desirable to both, for discussing and, if possible, adjusting them for the interest of both.

The British cabinet, either mistaking our desire of peace for a dread of British power or misled by other fallacious calculations, has disappointed this reasonable anticipation. No communications from our envoys having reached us, no information on the subject has been received from that source; but it is known that the mediation was declined in the 1st instance, and there is no evidence, notwithstanding the lapse of time, that a change of disposition in the British councils has taken place or is to be expected.

Under such circumstances a nation proud of its rights and conscious of its strength has no choice but an exertion of the one in support of the other.

To this determination the best encouragement is derived from the success with which it has pleased the Almighty to bless our arms both on the land and on the water. . . .

In violation both of consistency and of humanity, American officers and non-commissioned officers in double the number of the British soldiers confined here were ordered into close confinement, with formal notice that in the event of a retaliation for the death which might be inflicted on the prisoners of war sent to Great Britain for trial the officers so confined would be put to death also. It was notified at the same time that the commanders of the British fleets and armies on our coasts are instructed in the same event to proceed with a destructive severity against our towns and their inhabitants.

That no doubt might be left with the enemy of our adherence to the retaliatory resort imposed on us, a correspondent number of British officers, prisoners of war in our hands, were immediately put into close confinement to abide the fate of those confined by the enemy, and the British Government was apprised of the determination of this Government to retaliate any other proceedings against us contrary to the legitimate modes of warfare.

It is fortunate for the United States that they have it in their power to meet the enemy in this deplorable contest as it is honorable to them that they do not join in it but under the most imperious obligations, and with the humane purpose of effectuating a return to the established usages of war. . . .

With all good citizens the justice and necessity of resisting wrongs and usurpations no longer to be borne will sufficiently outweigh the privations and sacrifices inseparable from a state of war. But it is a reflection, moreover, peculiarly consoling, that, whilst wars are generally aggravated by their baneful effects on the internal improvements and permanent prosperity of the nations engaged in them, such is the favored situation of the United States that the calamities of the contest into which they have been compelled to enter are mitigated by improvements and advantages of which the contest itself is the source. . . .

The war has proved moreover that our free Government, like other free governments, though slow in its early movements, acquires in its progress a force proportioned to its freedom, and that the union of these States, the guardian of the freedom and safety of all and of each, is strengthened by every occasion that puts it to the test.

In fine, the war, with all its vicissitudes, is illustrating the capacity and the destiny of the United States to be a great, a flourishing, and a powerful nation, worthy of the friendship which it is disposed to cultivate with all others, and authorized by its own example to require from all an observance of the laws of justice and reciprocity. Beyond these their claims have never extended, and in contending for these we behold a subject for our congratulations in the daily testimonies of increasing harmony throughout the nation, and may humbly repose our trust in the smiles of Heaven on so righteous a cause.

JAMES MONROE

President Monroe inherited a peaceful nation, albeit one beset with economic difficulties (the Panic of 1819), the growing pains of a new national market economy, and ongoing issues with Native American tribes. His lasting contribution to American foreign policy, however, came in the form of his seventh State of the Union Address, which set out the principle of European noninterference with affairs in the Western Hemisphere—thereafter known as the Monroe Doctrine.

Seventh Address: December 2, 1823

Many important subjects will claim your attention during the present session, of which I shall endeavor to give, in aid of your deliberations, a just idea in this communication. I undertake this duty with diffidence, from the vast extent of the interests on which I have to treat and of their great importance to every portion of our Union. I enter on it with zeal from a thorough conviction that there never was a period since the establishment of our Revolution when, regarding the condition of the civilized world and its bearing on us, there was greater necessity for devotion in the public servants to their respective duties, or for virtue, patriotism, and union in our constituents. . . .

A precise knowledge of our relations with foreign powers as respects our negotiations and transactions with each is thought to be particularly necessary. Equally necessary is it that we should for a just estimate of our resources, revenue, and progress in every kind of improvement connected with the national prosperity and public defense. It is by rendering justice to other nations that we may expect it from them. It is by our ability to resent injuries and redress wrongs that we may avoid them. . . .

The citizens of the United States cherish sentiments the most friendly in favor of the liberty and happiness of their fellow men on that side of the Atlantic. In the wars of the European powers in matters relating to themselves we have never taken any part, nor does it comport with our policy so to do.

It is only when our rights are invaded or seriously menaced that we resent injuries or make preparation for our defense. With the movements in this hemisphere we are of necessity more immediately connected, and by causes which must be obvious to all enlightened and impartial observers.

The political system of the allied powers is essentially different in this respect from that of America. This difference proceeds from that which exists in their respective Governments; and to the defense of our own, which has been achieved by the loss of so much blood and treasure, and matured by the wisdom of their most enlightened citizens, and under which we have enjoyed unexampled felicity, this whole nation is devoted.

We owe it, therefore, to candor and to the amicable relations existing between the United States and those powers to declare that we should consider any attempt on their part to extend their system to any portion of this hemisphere as dangerous to our peace and safety. With the existing colonies or dependencies of any European power we have not interfered and shall not interfere, but with the Governments who have declared their independence and maintained it, and whose independence we have, on great consideration and on just principles, acknowledged, we could not view any interposition for the purpose of oppressing them, or controlling in any other manner their destiny, by any European power in any other light than as the manifestation of an unfriendly disposition toward the United States.

In the war between those new Governments and Spain we declared our neutrality at the time of their recognition, and to this we have adhered, and shall continue to adhere, provided no change shall occur which, in the judgment of the competent authorities of this Government, shall make a corresponding change on the part of the United States indispensable to their security. . . .

Our policy in regard to Europe, which was adopted at an early stage of the wars which have so long agitated that quarter of the globe, nevertheless remains the same, which is, not to interfere in the internal concerns of any of its powers; to consider the government de facto as the legitimate government for us; to cultivate friendly relations with it, and to preserve those relations by a frank, firm, and manly policy, meeting in all instances the just claims of every power, submitting to injuries from none.

But in regard to those continents circumstances are eminently and conspicuously different. It is impossible that the allied powers should extend their political system to any portion of either continent without endangering our peace and happiness; nor can anyone believe that our southern brethren, if left to themselves, would adopt it of their own accord. It is equally impossible, therefore, that we should behold such interposition in any form with indifference. If we look to the comparative strength and resources of Spain and those new Governments, and their distance from each other, it must be obvious that she can never subdue them. It is still the true policy of the United States to leave the parties to themselves, in the hope that other powers will pursue the same course. . . .

JOHN QUINCY ADAMS

In many ways, John Quincy Adams's presidency was as unhappy for him as it had been for his father. The elder Adams had experienced grief over his conduct of foreign affairs; the younger Adams was heavily criticized for his proposals to expand vastly the national economy via an ambitious, federally funded program of road construction and navigational improvements and through federal support for the arts, science, higher education, and so forth. His first State of the Union Address laid out his plans. With prosperity at home and peace in Europe for the first time in years, Adams felt the nation had a moral obligation to improve itself and work for the betterment of mankind.

First Address: December 6, 1825

In taking a general survey of the concerns of our beloved country, with reference to subjects interesting to the common welfare, the first sentiment which impresses itself upon the mind is of gratitude to the Omnipotent Disposer of All Good for the continuance of the signal blessings of His providence, and especially for that health which to an unusual extent has prevailed within our borders, and for that abundance which in the vicissitudes of the seasons has been scattered with profusion over our land. Nor ought we less to ascribe to Him the glory that we are permitted to enjoy the bounties of His hand in peace and tranquillity—in peace with all the other nations of the earth, in tranquillity among our selves. There has, indeed, rarely been a period in the history of civilized man in which the general condition of the Christian nations has been marked so extensively by peace and prosperity.

Europe, with a few partial and unhappy exceptions, has enjoyed 10 years of peace, during which all her Governments, what ever the theory of their constitutions may have been, are successively taught to feel that the end of their institution is the happiness of the people, and that the exercise of power among men can be justified only by the blessings it confers upon those over whom it is extended.

During the same period our intercourse with all those nations has been pacific and friendly; it so continues. Since the close of your last session no material variation has occurred in our relations with any one of them. . . .

Among the unequivocal indications of our national prosperity is the flourishing state of our finances. The revenues of the present year, from all their principal sources, will exceed the anticipations of the last. . . .

Upon this first occasion of addressing the Legislature of the Union, with which I have been honored, in presenting to their view the execution so far as it has been effected of the measures sanctioned by them for promoting the internal improvement of our country, I can not close the communication without recommending to their calm and persevering consideration the general principle in a more enlarged extent. The great object of the institution of civil government is the improvement of the condition of those who are parties to the social compact, and no government, in what ever form constituted, can accomplish the lawful ends of its institution but in proportion as it improves the condition of those over whom it is established. Roads and canals, by multiplying and facilitating the communications and intercourse between distant regions and multitudes of men, are among the most important means of improvement. But moral, political, intellectual improvement are duties assigned by the Author of Our Existence to social no less than to individual man.

For the fulfillment of those duties governments are invested with power, and to the attainment of the end—the progressive improvement of the condition of the governed—the exercise of delegated powers is a duty as sacred and indispensable as the usurpation of powers not granted is criminal and odious.

Among the first, perhaps the very first, instrument for the improvement of the condition of men is knowledge, and to the acquisition of much of the knowledge adapted to the wants, the comforts, and enjoyments of human life public institutions and seminaries of learning are essential. So convinced of this was the first of my predecessors in this office, now first in the memory, as, living, he was first in the hearts, of our country-men, that once and again in his addresses to the Congresses with whom he cooperated in the public service he earnestly recommended the establishment of seminaries of learning, to prepare for all the emergencies of peace and war—a national university and a military academy. With respect to the latter, had he lived to the present day, in turning his eyes to the institution at West Point he would have enjoyed the gratification of his most earnest wishes; but in surveying the city which has been honored with his name he would have seen the spot of earth which he had destined and bequeathed to the use and benefit of his country as the site for a university still bare and barren.

In assuming her station among the civilized nations of the earth it would seem that our country had contracted the engagement to contribute her share of mind, of labor, and of expense to the improvement of those parts of knowledge which lie beyond the reach of individual acquisition, and particularly to geographical and astronomical science. . . . Is it not incumbent upon us to inquire whether we are not bound by obligations of a high and honorable character to contribute our portion of energy and exertion to the common stock? . . .

We have been partakers of that improvement and owe for it a sacred debt, not only of gratitude, but of equal or proportional exertion in the same common cause. Of the cost of these undertakings, if the mere expenditures of outfit, equipment, and completion of the expeditions were to be considered the only charges, it would be unworthy of a great and generous nation to take a second thought. . . . If we take into account the lives of those benefactors of man-kind of which their services in the cause of their species were the purchase, how shall the cost of those heroic enterprises be estimated, and what compensation can be made to them or to their countries for them? Is it not by bearing them in affectionate remembrance? Is it not still more by imitating their example—by enabling country-men of our own to pursue the same career and to hazard their lives in the same cause?

In inviting the attention of Congress to the subject of internal improvements upon a view thus enlarged it is not my desire to recommend the equipment of an expedition for circumnavigating the globe for purposes of scientific research and inquiry. We have objects of useful investigation nearer home, and to which our cares may be more beneficially applied. The interior of our own territories has yet been very imperfectly explored. . . .

Connected with the establishment of [a national] university, or separate from it, might be undertaken the erection of an astronomical observatory, with provision for the support of an astronomer, to be in constant attendance of observation upon the phenomena of the heavens, and for the periodical publication of his observances. It is with no feeling of pride as an American that the remark may be made that on the comparatively small territorial surface of Europe there are existing upward of 130 of these lighthouses of the skies, while throughout the whole American hemisphere there is not one. . . .

Our commerce, our wealth, and the extent of our territories have increased. . . . But the executive and, still more, the judiciary departments are yet in a great measure confined to their primitive organization, and are now not adequate to the urgent wants of a still growing community. . . .

The Constitution under which you are assembled is a charter of limited powers. After full and solemn deliberation upon all or any of the objects which, urged by an irresistible sense of my own duty, I have recommended to your attention should you come to the conclusion that, however desirable in themselves, the enactment of laws for effecting them would transcend the powers committed to you by that venerable instrument which we are all bound to support, let no consideration induce you to assume the exercise of powers not granted to you by the people.

But if . . . these powers and others enumerated in the Constitution may be effectually brought into action by laws promoting the improvement of agriculture, commerce, and manufactures, the cultivation and encouragement of the mechanic and of the elegant arts, the advancement of literature, and the progress of the sciences, ornamental and profound, to refrain from exercising them for the benefit of the people themselves would be to hide in the earth the talent committed to our charge—would be treachery to the most sacred of trusts.

The spirit of improvement is abroad upon the earth. It stimulates the hearts and sharpens the faculties not of our fellow citizens alone, but of the nations of Europe and of their rulers. While dwelling with pleasing satisfaction upon the superior excellence of our political institutions, let us not be unmindful that liberty is power; that the nation blessed with the largest portion of liberty must in proportion to its numbers be the most powerful nation upon earth, and that the tenure of power by man is, in the moral purposes of his Creator, upon condition that it shall be exercised to ends of beneficence, to improve the condition of himself and his fellow men.

While foreign nations less blessed with that freedom which is power than ourselves are advancing with gigantic strides in the career of public improvement, were we to slumber in indolence or fold up our arms and proclaim to the world that we are palsied by the will of our constituents, would it not be to cast away the bounties of Providence and doom ourselves to perpetual inferiority? . . .

ANDREW JACKSON

Jackson was a new breed of president, a product of the brash new popular democracy that was driving the engine of political, social, and economic change in early-nineteenth-century America. As president, he hammered at the theme of popular rule, and in his State of the Union Addresses he argued for putting the government in a more direct relationship with the people by abolishing the Electoral College. He also suggested that the Bank of the United States had become dangerous to American liberties and explained his reasons for vetoing its charter. In a similar vein, he articulated a states' rights–based philosophy of government, which became the foundation for many of his administration's policies, including even his highly controversial actions toward the Cherokee Indians.

First Address: December 8, 1829

It affords me pleasure to tender my friendly greetings to you on the occasion of your assembling at the seat of Government to enter upon the important duties to which you have been called by the voice of our country-men. The task devolves on me, under a provision of the Constitution, to present to you, as the Federal Legislature of 24 sovereign States and 12,000,000 happy people, a view of our affairs, and to propose such measures as in the discharge of my official functions have suggested themselves as necessary to promote the objects of our Union. . . .

Blessed as our country is with every thing which constitutes national strength, she is fully adequate to the maintenance of all her interests. In discharging the responsible trust confided to the Executive in this respect it is my settled purpose to ask nothing that is not clearly right and to submit to nothing that is wrong; and I flatter myself that, supported by the other branches of the Government and by the intelligence and patriotism of the people, we shall be able, under the protection of Providence, to cause all our just rights to be respected. . . .

I consider it one of the most urgent of my duties to bring to your attention the propriety of amending that part of the Constitution which relates to the election of President and Vice-President. Our system of government was by its framers deemed an experiment, and they therefore consistently provided a mode of remedying its defects.

To the people belongs the right of electing their Chief Magistrate; it was never designed that their choice should in any case be defeated, either by the intervention of electoral colleges or by the agency confided, under certain contingencies, to the House of Representatives. Experience proves that in proportion as agents to execute the will of the people are multiplied there is danger of their wishes being frustrated. Some may be unfaithful; all are liable to err. So far, therefore, as the people can with convenience speak, it is safer for them to express their own will. . . .

In this as in all other matters of public concern policy requires that as few impediments as possible should exist to the free operation of the public will. Let us, then, endeavor so to amend our system that the office of Chief Magistrate may not be conferred upon any citizen but in pursuance of a fair expression of the will of the majority.

I would therefore recommend such an amendment of the Constitution as may remove all intermediate agency in the election of the President and Vice-President. . . .

[Political] Office is considered as a species of property, and government rather as a means of promoting individual interests than as an instrument created solely for the service of the people. Corruption in some and in others a perversion of correct feelings and principles divert government from its legitimate ends and make it an engine for the support of the few at the expense of the many. . . . I submit, therefore, to your consideration whether the efficiency of the Government would not be promoted and official industry and integrity better secured by a general extension of the law which limits appointments to four years.

In a country where offices are created solely for the benefit of the people no one man has any more intrinsic right to official station than another. Offices were not established to give support to particular men at the public expense. No individual wrong is, therefore, done by removal, since neither appointment to nor continuance in office is a matter of right. . . . The proposed limitation would destroy the idea of property now so generally connected with official station, and although individual distress may be some times produced, it would, by promoting that rotation which constitutes a leading principle in the republican creed, give healthful action to the system. . . .

The great mass of legislation relating to our internal affairs was intended to be left where the Federal Convention found it—in the State governments. Nothing is clearer, in my view, than that we are chiefly indebted for the success of the Constitution under which we are now acting to the watchful and auxiliary operation of the State authorities. This is not the reflection of a day, but belongs to the most deeply rooted convictions of my mind. I can not, therefore, too strongly or too earnestly, for my own sense of its importance, warn you against all encroachments upon the legitimate sphere of State sovereignty. Sustained by its healthful and invigorating influence the federal system can never fall. . . .

A portion, however, of the Southern tribes [the Cherokees], having mingled much with the whites and made some progress in the arts of civilized life, have lately attempted to erect an independent government within the limits of Georgia and Alabama. These States, claiming to be the only sovereigns within their territories, extended their laws over the Indians, which induced the latter to call upon the United States for protection.

Under these circumstances the question presented was whether the General Government had a right to sustain those people in their pretensions. The Constitution declares that "no new State shall be formed or erected within the jurisdiction of any other State" without the consent of its legislature. If the General Government is not permitted to tolerate the erection of a confederate State within the territory of one of the members of this Union against her consent, much less could it allow a foreign and independent government to establish itself there. . . .

Actuated by this view of the subject, I informed the [Cherokee] Indians inhabiting parts of Georgia and Alabama that their attempt to establish an independent government would not be countenanced by the Executive of the United States, and advised them to emigrate beyond the Mississippi or submit to the laws of those States. . . .

Our conduct toward these people is deeply interesting to our national character. . . . Surrounded by the whites with their arts of civilization, which by destroying the resources of the savage doom him to weakness and decay, the fate of the Mohegan, the Narragansett, and the Delaware is fast over-taking the Choctaw, the Cherokee, and the Creek. That this fate surely awaits them if they remain within the limits of the States does not admit of a doubt. Humanity and national honor demand that every effort should be made to avert so great a calamity. It is too late to inquire whether it was just in the United States to include them and their territory within the bounds of new States, whose limits they could control. That step can not be retraced. A State can not be dismembered by Congress or restricted in the exercise of her constitutional power. But the people of those States and of every State, actuated by feelings of justice and a regard for our national honor, submit to you the interesting question whether something can not be done, consistently with the rights of the States, to preserve this much-injured race.

As a means of effecting this end I suggest for your consideration the propriety of setting apart an ample district west of the Mississippi, and without the limits of any State or Territory now formed, to be guaranteed to the Indian tribes as long as they shall occupy it, each tribe having a distinct control over the portion designated for its use. . . .

This emigration should be voluntary, for it would be as cruel as unjust to compel the aborigines to abandon the graves of their fathers and seek a home in a distant land. But they should be distinctly informed that if they remain within the limits of the States they must be subject to their laws. . . .

MARTIN VAN BUREN

Van Buren ascended to the White House with two unenviable tasks at hand: succeeding the enormously popular Andrew Jackson and guiding the nation through the economic downturn of 1837. The Little Magician tried to meet these challenges by maintaining a strict adherence to his predecessor's policies: no National Bank; limited federal funding of internal improvements; and keeping federal deposits in the hands of specially appointed federal officers rather than putting the funds in state (or "pet") banks or recreating a national bank. It is interesting to note here how worried Van Buren had become concerning the influence of banks and financial institutions of power on the nation's political discourse.

First Address: December 5, 1837

We have reason to renew the expression of our devout gratitude to the Giver of All Good for His benign protection. Our country presents on every side the evidences of that continued favor under whose auspices it, has gradually risen from a few feeble and dependent colonies to a prosperous and powerful confederacy. We are blessed with domestic tranquility and all the elements of national prosperity. . . .

Your attention was at the last session invited to the necessity of additional legislative provisions in respect to the collection, safe-keeping, and transfer of the public money. . . .

On that occasion three modes of performing this branch of the public service were presented for consideration. These were, the creation of a national bank; the revival, with modifications, of the deposit system established by the act of the 23d of June, 1836, permitting the use of the public moneys by the banks; and the discontinuance of the use of such institutions for the purposes referred to, with suitable provisions for their accomplishment through the agency of public officers. Considering the opinions of both Houses of Congress on the first two propositions as expressed in the negative, in which I entirely concur, it is unnecessary for me again to recur to them. In respect to the last, you have had an opportunity since your adjournment not only to test still further the expediency of the measure by the continued practical operation of such parts of it as are now in force, but also to discover what should ever be sought for and regarded with the utmost deference—the opinions and wishes of the people. . . .

I have found no reason to change my own opinion as to the expediency of adopting the system proposed [discontinuance of reliance upon either state or national banks], being perfectly satisfied that there will be neither stability nor safety either in the fiscal affairs of the Government or in the pecuniary transactions of individuals and corporations so long as a connection exists between them which, like the past, offers such strong inducements to make them the subjects of political agitation. Indeed, I am more than ever convinced of the dangers to which the free and unbiased exercise of political opinion—the only sure foundation and safeguard of republican government—would be exposed by any further increase of the already overgrown influence of corporate authorities. I can not, therefore, consistently with my views of duty, advise a renewal of a connection which circumstances have dissolved.

The discontinuance of the use of State banks for fiscal purposes ought not to be regarded as a measure of hostility toward those institutions. Banks properly established and conducted are highly useful to the business of the country. . . . The object of the measure under consideration is to avoid for the future a compulsory connection of this kind. It proposes to place the General Government, in regard to the essential points of the collection, safe-keeping, and transfer of the public money, in a situation which shall relieve it from all dependence on the will of irresponsible individuals or corporations; to withdraw those moneys from the uses of private trade and confide them to agents constitutionally selected and controlled by law; to abstain from improper interference with the industry of the people and withhold inducements to improvident dealings on the part of individuals; to give stability to the concerns of the Treasury; to preserve the measures of the Government from the unavoidable reproaches that flow from such a connection, and the banks themselves from the injurious effects of a supposed participation in the political conflicts of the day, from which they will otherwise find it difficult to escape.

These are my views upon this important subject, formed after careful reflection and with no desire but to arrive at what is most likely to promote the public interest. . . .

JOHN TYLER

Tyler was the first vice president to ascend to the presidency upon the death of his predecessor (in this case, William Henry Harrison). Tyler became president at a time when the nation was trying to decide how to settle peacefully a territorial dispute with Britain concerning Oregon, how to address differences between the two nations concerning the international slave trade, and whether or not the Lone Star Republic of Texas should be annexed to the Union. Northerners worried about the problems involved in adding such a large slave-owning state to the Union, and heavy pressure was placed upon Tyler to avoid annexation. He chose annexation anyway, angering so many people within his own party that he became one of the very few presidents in American history who failed to be renominated for another term.

Fourth Address: December 3, 1844

We have continued cause for expressing our gratitude to the Supreme Ruler of the Universe for the benefits and blessings which our country, under His kind providence, has enjoyed during the past year. Notwithstanding the exciting scenes through which we have passed, nothing has occurred to disturb the general peace or to derange the harmony of our political system. . . .

In my last annual message I felt it to be my duty to make known to Congress, in terms both plain and emphatic, my opinion in regard to the war which has so long existed between Mexico and Texas which since the battle of San Jacinto has consisted altogether of predatory incursions, attended by circumstances revolting to humanity. I repeat now what I then said, that after eight years of feeble and ineffectual efforts to reconquer Texas it was time that the war should have ceased. The United States have a direct interest in the question. The contiguity of the two nations to our territory was but too well calculated to involve our peace. Unjust suspicions were engendered in the mind of one or the other of the belligerents against us, and as a necessary consequence American interests were made to suffer and our peace became daily endangered; in addition to which it must have been obvious to all that the exhaustion produced by the war subjected both Mexico and Texas to the interference of other powers, which, without the interposition of this Government, might eventuate in the most serious injury to the United States. This Government from time to time exerted its friendly offices to bring about a termination of hostilities upon terms honorable alike to both the belligerents. Its efforts in this behalf proved unavailing. Mexico seemed almost without an object to persevere in the war, and no other alternative was left the Executive but to take advantage of the well-known dispositions of Texas and to invite her to enter into a treaty for annexing her territory to that of the United States.

Since your last session Mexico has threatened to renew the war, and has either made or proposes to make formidable preparations for invading Texas. She has issued decrees and proclamations, preparatory to the commencement of hostilities, full of threats revolting to humanity, and which if carried into effect would arouse the attention of all Christendom. This new demonstration of feeling, there is too much reason to believe, has been produced in consequence of the negotiation of the late treaty of annexation with Texas. The Executive, therefore, could not be indifferent to such proceedings, and it felt it to be due as well to itself as to the honor of the country that a strong representation should be made to the Mexican Government upon the subject. This was accordingly done. . . . [Texas] is settled by emigrants from the United States under invitations held out to them by Spain and Mexico. Those emigrants have left behind them friends and relatives, who would not fail to sympathize with them in their difficulties, and who would be led by those sympathies to participate in their struggles, however energetic the action of the Government to prevent it. . . .

Mexico had no just ground of displeasure against this Government or people for negotiating the treaty. What interest of hers was affected by the treaty? She was despoiled of nothing, since Texas was forever lost to her. The independence of Texas was recognized by several of the leading powers of the earth. She was free to treat, free to adopt her own line of policy, free to take the course which she believed was best calculated to secure her happiness.

Her Government and people decided on annexation to the United States, and the Executive saw in the acquisition of such a territory the means of advancing their permanent happiness and glory. What principle of good faith, then, was violated? What rule of political morals trampled under foot? So far as Mexico herself was concerned, the measure should have been regarded by her as highly beneficial. Her inability to reconquer Texas had been exhibited, I repeat, by eight (now nine) years of fruitless and ruinous contest. In the meantime Texas has been growing in population and resources. Emigration has flowed into her territory from all parts of the world in a current which continues to increase in strength. Mexico requires a permanent boundary between that young Republic and herself. . . . The interests of Mexico, therefore, could in nothing be better consulted than in a peace with her neighbors which would result in the establishment of a permanent boundary. Upon the ratification of the treaty the Executive was prepared to treat with her on the most liberal basis. Hence the boundaries of Texas were left undefined by the treaty. The Executive proposed to settle these upon terms that all the world should have pronounced just and reasonable. . . .

The great popular election which has just terminated afforded the best opportunity of ascertaining the will of the States and the people upon it. Pending that issue it became the imperative duty of the Executive to inform Mexico that the question of annexation was still before the American people, and that until their decision was pronounced any serious invasion of Texas would be regarded as an attempt to forestall their judgment and could not be looked upon with indifference. I am most happy to inform you that no such invasion has taken place; and I trust that whatever your action may be upon it Mexico will see the importance of deciding the matter by a resort to peaceful expedients in preference to those of arms. The decision of the people and the States on this great and interesting subject has been decisively manifested. The question of annexation has been presented nakedly to their consideration. . . . A controlling majority of the people and a large majority of the States have declared in favor of immediate annexation. Instructions have thus come up to both branches of Congress from their respective constituents in terms the most emphatic. It is the will of both the people and the States that Texas shall be annexed to the Union promptly and immediately. . . . We seek no conquest made by war. No intrigue will have been resorted to or acts of diplomacy essayed to accomplish the annexation of Texas. Free and independent herself, she asks to be received into our Union. It is a question for our own decision whether she shall be received or not. . . .

JAMES K. POLK

Expansion dominated Polk's presidency, even more so than previous chief executives. In the 1844 campaign, he pledged to resolve both the Oregon dispute with Britain and the Texas dispute with Mexico to the gratification of the Manifest Destiny expansionists who dominated his Democratic Party. He kept his campaign promises, but not without a great deal of controversy, particularly where Texas was concerned.

Second Address: December 8, 1846

In resuming your labors in the service of the people it is a subject of congratulation that there has been no period in our past history when all the elements of national prosperity have been so fully developed. Since your last session no afflicting dispensation has visited our country. . . .

The existing war with Mexico was neither desired nor provoked by the United States. On the contrary, all honorable means were resorted to avert it. After years of endurance of aggravated and unredressed wrongs on our part, Mexico, in violation of solemn treaty stipulations and of every principle of justice recognized by civilized nations, commenced hostilities, and thus by her own act forced the war upon us. Long before the advance of our Army to the left bank of the Rio Grande we had ample cause of war against Mexico, and had the United States resorted to this extremity we might have appealed to the whole civilized world for the justice of our cause. . . . The war has been represented as unjust and unnecessary and as one of aggression on our part upon a weak and injured enemy. Such erroneous views, though entertained by but few, have been widely and extensively circulated, not only at home, but have been spread throughout Mexico and the whole world. A more effectual means could not have been devised to encourage the enemy and protract the war than to advocate and adhere to their cause, and thus give them "aid and comfort." It is a source of national pride and exultation that the great body of our people have thrown no such obstacles in the way of the Government in prosecuting the war successfully, but have shown themselves to be eminently patriotic and ready to vindicate their country's honor and interests at any sacrifice. The alacrity and promptness with which our volunteer forces rushed to the field on their country's call prove not only their patriotism, but their deep conviction that our cause is just.

The wrongs which we have suffered from Mexico almost ever since she became an independent power and the patient endurance with which we have borne them are without a parallel in the history of modern civilized nations. There is reason to believe that if these wrongs had been resented and resisted in the first instance the present war might have been avoided. One outrage, however, permitted to pass with impunity almost necessarily encouraged the perpetration of another, until at last Mexico seemed to attribute to weakness and indecision on our part a forbearance which was the offspring of magnanimity and of a sincere desire to preserve friendly relations with a sister republic.

Scarcely had Mexico achieved her independence, which the United States were the first among the nations to acknowledge, when she commenced the system of insult and spoliation which she has ever since pursued. Our citizens engaged in lawful commerce were imprisoned, their vessels seized, and our flag insulted in her ports. If money was wanted, the lawless seizure and confiscation of our merchant vessels and their cargoes was a ready resource, and if to accomplish their purposes it became necessary to imprison the owners, captains, and crews, it was done. Rulers superseded rulers in Mexico in rapid succession, but still there was no change in this system of depredation. The Government of the United States made repeated reclamations on behalf of its citizens, but these were answered by the perpetration of new outrages. Promises of redress made by Mexico in the most solemn forms were postponed or evaded. . . .

So far from affording reasonable satisfaction for the injuries and insults we had borne, a great aggravation of them consists in the fact that while the United States, anxious to preserve a good understanding with Mexico, have been constantly but vainly employed in seeking redress for past wrongs, new outrages were constantly occurring, which have continued to increase our causes of complaint and to swell the amount of our demands. While the citizens of the United States were conducting a lawful commerce with Mexico under the guaranty of a treaty of "amity, commerce, and navigation," many of them have suffered all the injuries which would have resulted from open war. . . . We had ample cause of war against Mexico long before the breaking out of hostilities; but even then we forbore to take redress into our own hands until Mexico herself became the aggressor by invading our soil in hostile array and shedding the blood of our citizens.

Such are the grave causes of complaint on the part of the United States against Mexico—causes which existed long before the annexation of Texas to the American Union; and yet, animated by the love of peace and a magnanimous moderation, we did not adopt those measures of redress which under such circumstances are the justified resort of injured nations.

The annexation of Texas to the United States constituted no just cause of offense to Mexico. The pretext that it did so is wholly inconsistent and irreconcilable with well-authenticated facts connected with the revolution by which Texas became independent of Mexico. . . .

The United States never attempted to acquire Texas by conquest. On the contrary, at an early period after the people of Texas had achieved their independence they sought to be annexed to the United States. . . .

Every honorable effort has been used by me to avoid the war which followed, but all have proved vain. All our attempts to preserve peace have been met by insult and resistance on the part of Mexico. . . .

Upon the commencement of hostilities by Mexico against the United States the indignant spirit of the nation was at once aroused. Congress promptly responded to the expectations of the country, and by the act of the 13th of May last recognized the fact that war existed, by the act of Mexico, between the United States and that Republic, and granted the means necessary for its vigorous prosecution. Being involved in a war thus commenced by Mexico, and for the justice of which on our part we may confidently appeal to the whole world, I resolved to prosecute it with the utmost vigor. . . .

The war will continue to be prosecuted with vigor as the best means of securing peace. It is hoped that the decision of the Mexican Congress, to which our last overture has been referred, may result in a speedy and honorable peace. With our experience, however, of the unreasonable course of the Mexican authorities, it is the part of wisdom not to relax in the energy of our military operations until the result is made known. In this view it is deemed important to hold military possession of all the Provinces which have been taken until a definitive treaty of peace shall have been concluded and ratified by the two countries.

The war has not been waged with a view to conquest, but, having been commenced by Mexico, it has been carried into the enemy's country and will be vigorously prosecuted there with a view to obtain an honorable peace, and thereby secure ample indemnity for the expenses of the war, as well as to our much-injured citizens, who hold large pecuniary demands against Mexico. . . .

ZACHARY TAYLOR

Taylor's untimely death in office allowed him the opportunity to make only one State of the Union Address. In that message we see the lingering issues that resulted from the victorious war with Mexico.

December 4, 1849

Sixty years have elapsed since the establishment of this Government, and the Congress of the United States again assembles to legislate for an empire of freemen. The predictions of evil prophets, who formerly pretended to foretell the downfall of our institutions, are now remembered only to be derided, and the United States of America at this moment present to the world the most stable and permanent Government on earth. . . .

In the adjustment of the claims of American citizens on Mexico, provided for by the late treaty, the employment of counsel on the part of the Government may become important for the purpose of assisting the commissioners in protecting the interests of the United States. I recommend this subject to the early and favorable consideration of Congress. . . .

The extension of the coast of the United States on the Pacific and the unexampled rapidity with which the inhabitants of California especially are increasing in numbers have imparted new consequence to our relations with the other countries whose territories border upon that ocean. It is probable that the intercourse between those countries and our possessions in that quarter, particularly with the Republic of Chile, will become extensive and mutually advantageous in proportion as California and Oregon shall increase in population and wealth. It is desirable, therefore, that this Government should do everything in its power to foster and strengthen its relations with those States, and that the spirit of amity between us should be mutual and cordial.

I recommend the observance of the same course toward all other American States. The United States stand as the great American power, to which, as their natural ally and friend, they will always be disposed first to look for mediation and assistance in the event of any collision between them and any European nation. As such we may often kindly mediate in their behalf without entangling ourselves in foreign wars or unnecessary controversies. Whenever the faith of our treaties with any of them shall require our interference, we must necessarily interpose. . . .

No civil government having been provided by Congress for California, the people of that Territory, impelled by the necessities of their political condition, recently met in convention for the purpose of forming a constitution and State government, which the latest advices give me reason to suppose has been accomplished; and it is believed they will shortly apply for the admission of California into the Union as a sovereign State. Should such be the case, and should their constitution be conformable to the requisitions of the Constitution of the United States, I recommend their application to the favorable consideration of Congress. The people of New Mexico will also, it is believed, at no very distant period present themselves for admission into the Union. Preparatory to the admission of California and New Mexico the people of each will have instituted for themselves a republican form of government, "laying its foundation in such principles and organizing its powers in such form as to them shall seem most likely to effect their safety and happiness." By awaiting their action all causes of uneasiness may be avoided and confidence and kind feeling preserved. With a view of maintaining the harmony and tranquillity so dear to all, we should abstain from the introduction of those exciting topics of a sectional character which have hitherto produced painful apprehensions in the public mind; and I repeat the solemn warning of the first and most illustrious of my predecessors against furnishing "any ground for characterizing parties by geographical discriminations. . . ."

The cession of territory made by the late treaty with Mexico has greatly extended our exposed frontier and rendered its defense more difficult. That treaty has also brought us under obligations to Mexico, to comply with which a military force is requisite. But our military establishment is not materially changed as to its efficiency from the condition in which it stood before the commencement of the Mexican War. Some addition to it will therefore be necessary, and I recommend to the favorable consideration of Congress an increase of the several corps of the Army at our distant Western posts, as proposed in the accompanying report of the Secretary of War. . . .

MILLARD FILLMORE

Fillmore inherited the presidency when the Whigs' run of bad luck continued as Zachary Taylor died soon after taking office. Fillmore also inherited a nation that had started to show the cracks of sectional strife, as Southerners and Northerners argued over the disposition of the lands acquired during the Mexican War, the growing trickle of fugitive slaves into the North, and other matters. Congress's Compromise of 1850 seemed to have forestalled a civil war over these matters, and in his State of the Union Address of 1850, President Fillmore breathed a palpable sigh of relief.

First Address: December 2, 1850

The act [the Compromise of 1850], passed at your last session, making certain propositions to Texas for settling the disputed boundary between that State and the Territory of New Mexico was, immediately on its passage, transmitted by express to the governor of Texas, to be laid by him before the general assembly for its agreement thereto. Its receipt was duly acknowledged, but no official information has yet been received of the action of the general assembly thereon. It may, however, be very soon expected, as, by the terms of the propositions submitted they were to have been acted upon on or before the first day of the present month.

It was hardly to have been expected that the series of measures passed at your last session with the view of healing the sectional differences which had sprung from the slavery and territorial questions should at once have realized their beneficent purpose. All mutual concession in the nature of a compromise must necessarily be unwelcome to men of extreme opinions. And though without such concessions our Constitution could not have been formed, and can not be permanently sustained, yet we have seen them made the subject of bitter controversy in both sections of the Republic. It required many months of discussion and deliberation to secure the concurrence of a majority of Congress in their favor. It would be strange if they had been received with immediate approbation by people and States prejudiced and heated by the exciting controversies of their representatives. I believe those measures to have been required by the circumstances and condition of the country. I believe they were necessary to allay asperities and animosities that were rapidly alienating one section of the country from another and destroying those fraternal sentiments which are the strongest supports of the Constitution. They were adopted in the spirit of conciliation and for the purpose of conciliation. I believe that a great majority of our fellow citizens sympathize in that spirit and that purpose, and in the main approve and are prepared in all respects to sustain these enactments. I can not doubt that the American people, bound together by kindred blood and common traditions, still cherish a paramount regard for the Union of their fathers, and that they are ready to rebuke any attempt to violate its integrity, to disturb the compromises on which it is based, or to resist the laws which have been enacted under its authority.

The series of measures to which I have alluded are regarded by me as a settlement in principle and substance—a final settlement of the dangerous and exciting subjects which they embraced. Most of these subjects, indeed, are beyond your reach, as the legislation which disposed of them was in its character final and irrevocable. It may be presumed from the opposition which they all encountered that none of those measures was free from imperfections, but in their mutual dependence and connection they formed a system of compromise the most conciliatory and best for the entire country that could be obtained from conflicting sectional interests and opinions.

For this reason I recommend your adherence to the adjustment established by those measures until time and experience shall demonstrate the necessity of further legislation to guard against evasion or abuse.

By that adjustment we have been rescued from the wide and boundless agitation that surrounded us, and have a firm, distinct, and legal ground to rest upon. And the occasion, I trust, will justify me in exhorting my countrymen to rally upon and maintain that ground as the best, if not the only, means of restoring peace and quiet to the country and maintaining inviolate the integrity of the Union. . . .

FRANKLIN PIERCE

Pierce was one of a series of what were termed by the press "doughface" presidents; that is, northern men with southern sympathies who exuded a certain blandness and who tried to steer a middling way between the sections by, in effect, doing nothing at all. Elected by an increasingly divided Democratic Party, Pierce wanted at all costs to avoid making slavery a national question that might someday rend the Union. Events in Bleeding Kansas, where proslavery and antislavery forces had resorted to armed force, seemed to presage the impossibility of this goal.

Third Address: December 31, 1855

In the Territory of Kansas there have been acts prejudicial to good order, but as yet none have occurred under circumstances to justify the interposition of the Federal Executive. That could only be in case of obstruction to Federal law or of organized resistance to Territorial law, assuming the character of insurrection, which, if it should occur, it would be my duty promptly to overcome and suppress. I cherish the hope, however, that the occurrence of any such untoward event will be prevented by the sound sense of the people of the Territory, who by its organic law, possessing the right to determine their own domestic institutions, are entitled while deporting themselves peacefully to the free exercise of that right, and must be protected in the enjoyment of it without interference on the part of the citizens of any of the States. . . .

I have thus passed in review the general state of the Union, including such particular concerns of the Federal Government, whether of domestic or foreign relation, as it appeared to me desirable and useful to bring to the special notice of Congress. Unlike the great States of Europe and Asia and many of those of America, these United States are wasting their strength neither in foreign war nor domestic strife. Whatever of discontent or public dissatisfaction exists is attributable to the imperfections of human nature or is incident to all governments, however perfect, which human wisdom can devise. Such subjects of political agitation as occupy the public mind consist to a great extent of exaggeration of inevitable evils, or over zeal in social improvement, or mere imagination of grievance, having but remote connection with any of the constitutional functions or duties of the Federal Government. To whatever extent these questions exhibit a tendency menacing to the stability of the Constitution or the integrity of the Union, and no further, they demand the consideration of the Executive and require to be presented by him to Congress. . . .

Before the thirteen colonies became a confederation of independent States they were associated only by community of transatlantic origin, by geographical position, and by the mutual tie of common dependence on Great Britain. When that tie was sundered they severally assumed the powers and rights of absolute self-government. . . . As for the subject races, whether Indian or African, the wise and brave statesmen of that day, being engaged in no extravagant scheme of social change, left them as they were, and thus preserved themselves and their posterity from the anarchy and the ever-recurring civil wars which have prevailed in other revolutionized European colonies of America.

It is necessary to speak thus plainly of projects the offspring of that sectional agitation now prevailing in some of the States, which are as impracticable as they are unconstitutional, and which if persevered in must and will end calamitously. It is either disunion and civil war or it is mere angry, idle, aimless disturbance of public peace and tranquillity. Disunion for what? If the passionate rage of fanaticism and partisan spirit did not force the fact upon our attention, it would be difficult to believe that any considerable portion of the people of this enlightened country could have so surrendered themselves to a fanatical devotion to the supposed interests of the relatively few Africans in the United States as totally to abandon and disregard the interests of the 25,000,000 Americans; to trample under foot the injunctions of moral and constitutional obligation, and to engage in plans of vindictive hostility against those who are associated with them in the enjoyment of the common heritage of our national institutions.

Nor is it hostility against their fellow-citizens of one section of the Union alone. The interests, the honor, the duty, the peace, and the prosperity of the people of all sections are equally involved and imperiled in this question. And are patriotic men in any part of the Union prepared on such issue thus madly to invite all the consequences of the forfeiture of their constitutional engagements? It is impossible. The storm of frenzy and faction must inevitably dash itself in vain against the unshaken rock of the Constitution. I shall never doubt it. I know that the Union is stronger a thousand times than all the wild and chimerical schemes of social change which are generated one after another in the unstable minds of visionary sophists and interested agitators. I rely confidently on the patriotism of the people, on the dignity and self-respect of the States, on the wisdom of Congress, and, above all, on the continued gracious favor of Almighty God to maintain against all enemies, whether at home or abroad, the sanctity of the Constitution and the integrity of the Union.

JAMES BUCHANAN

Buchanan was a personally decent enough man, but he proved to be a weak leader during a time of extraordinary crisis. As the South prepared to leave the Union, Buchanan delivered a rather tepid State of the Union Address that at once decried secession but also announced his helplessness in addressing the matter. The message also betrayed his pro-southern sympathies, as he blamed Northerners for creating the mess by agitating the subject of slavery.

Fourth Address: December 3, 1860

Throughout the year since our last meeting the country has been eminently prosperous in all its material interests. The general health has been excellent, our harvests have been abundant, and plenty smiles throughout the laud. Our commerce and manufactures have been prosecuted with energy and industry, and have yielded fair and ample returns. In short, no nation in the tide of time has ever presented a spectacle of greater material prosperity than we have done until within a very recent period.

Why is it, then, that discontent now so extensively prevails, and the Union of the States, which is the source of all these blessings, is threatened with destruction?

The long-continued and intemperate interference of the Northern people with the question of slavery in the Southern States has at length produced its natural effects. The different sections of the Union are now arrayed against each other, and the time has arrived, so much dreaded by the Father of his Country, when hostile geographical parties have been formed. . . .

The immediate peril arises . . . from the fact that the incessant and violent agitation of the slavery question throughout the North for the last quarter of a century has at length produced its malign influence on the slaves and inspired them with vague notions of freedom. Hence a sense of security no longer exists around the family altar. This feeling of peace at home has given place to apprehensions of servile insurrections. Many a matron throughout the South retires at night in dread of what may befall herself and children before the morning. Should this apprehension of domestic danger, whether real or imaginary, extend and intensify itself until it shall pervade the masses of the Southern people, then disunion will become inevitable. . . . Sooner or later the bonds of such a union must be severed. It is my conviction that this fatal period has not yet arrived, and my prayer to God is that He would preserve the Constitution and the Union throughout all generations.

But let us take warning in time and remove the cause of danger. It can not be denied that for five and twenty years the agitation at the North against slavery has been incessant. . . .

How easy would it be for the American people to settle the slavery question forever and to restore peace and harmony to this distracted country! They, and they alone, can do it. All that is necessary to accomplish the object, and all for which the slave States have ever contended, is to be let alone and permitted to manage their domestic institutions in their own way. . . .

And this brings me to observe that the election of any one of our fellow-citizens to the office of President does not of itself afford just cause for dissolving the Union. This is more especially true if his election has been effected by a mere plurality, and not a majority of the people, and has resulted from transient and temporary causes, which may probably never again occur. In order to justify a resort to revolutionary resistance, the Federal Government must be guilty of "a deliberate, palpable, and dangerous exercise" of powers not granted by the Constitution.

The late Presidential election, however, has been held in strict conformity with its express provisions. How, then, can the result justify a revolution to destroy this very Constitution? Reason, justice, a regard for the Constitution, all require that we shall wait for some overt and dangerous act on the part of the President elect before resorting to such a remedy. . . .

In order to justify secession as a constitutional remedy, it must be on the principle that the Federal Government is a mere voluntary association of States, to be dissolved at pleasure by any one of the contracting parties. If this be so, the Confederacy is a rope of sand, to be penetrated and dissolved by the first adverse wave of public opinion in any of the States. In this manner our thirty-three States may resolve themselves into as many petty, jarring, and hostile republics, each one retiring from the Union without responsibility whenever any sudden excitement might impel them to such a course. By this process a Union might be entirely broken into fragments in a few weeks which cost our forefathers many years of toil, privation, and blood to establish.

Such a principle is wholly inconsistent with the history as well as the character of the Federal Constitution. . . .

The right of the people of a single State to absolve themselves at will and without the consent of the other States from their most solemn obligations, and hazard the liberties and happiness of the millions composing this Union, can not be acknowledged. Such authority is believed to be utterly repugnant both to the principles upon which the General Government is constituted and to the objects which it is expressly formed to attain. . . .

What, in the meantime, is the responsibility and true position of the Executive? He is bound by solemn oath, before God and the country, "to take care that the laws be faithfully executed," and from this obligation he can not be absolved by any human power. But what if the performance of this duty, in whole or in part, has been rendered impracticable by events over which he could have exercised no control? Such at the present moment is the case throughout the State of South Carolina so far as the laws of the United States to secure the administration of justice by means of the Federal judiciary are concerned. . . .

Apart from the execution of the laws, so far as this may be practicable, the Executive has no authority to decide what shall be the relations between the Federal Government and South Carolina. He has been invested with no such discretion. He possesses no power to change the relations heretofore existing between them, much less to acknowledge the independence of that State. . . .

The fact is that our Union rests upon public opinion, and can never be cemented by the blood of its citizens shed in civil war. If it can not live in the affections of the people, it must one day perish. Congress possesses many means of preserving it by conciliation, but the sword was not placed in their hand to preserve it by force. . . .

ABRAHAM LINCOLN

Lincoln's various State of the Union Addresses usually lacked the ringing grandeur of his famous speeches, like the Gettysburg Address or his Second Inaugural Address. This was due to the circumstances: Lincoln used his annual addresses to Congress to report on the state of the war and its myriad details rather than to articulate the war's highest ideals. Nevertheless, his State of the Union Addresses do offer interesting examples of the ways in which Lincoln's policies and thought developed, particularly on the issue of emancipation and race. Note in particular his recommendations for a complex compensated emancipation and colonization plan in 1862—as emancipation was about to become the Union's official policy—contrasted with later declarations to Congress that emancipation was an unalterable part of his administration's legacy.

Second Address: December 1, 1862

Since your last annual assembling another year of health and bountiful harvests has passed, and while it has not pleased the Almighty to bless us with a return of peace, we can but press on, guided by the best light He gives us, trusting that in His own good time and wise way all will yet be well. . . .

On the 22d day of September last a proclamation was issued by the Executive, a copy of which is herewith submitted. In accordance with the purpose expressed in the second paragraph of that paper, I now respectfully recall your attention to what may be called "compensated emancipation. . . ."

In this view I recommend the adoption of the following resolution and articles amendatory to the Constitution of the United States:

ART.—. Every State wherein slavery now exists which shall abolish the same therein at any time or times before the 1st day of January, A. D. 1900, shall receive compensation from the United States [federal government]. . . .

ART—All slaves who shall have enjoyed actual freedom by the chances of the war at any time before the end of the rebellion shall be forever free; but all owners of such who shall not have been disloyal shall be compensated for them at the same rates as is provided for States adopting abolishment of slavery, but in such way that no slave shall be twice accounted for.

ART.—Congress may appropriate money and otherwise provide for colonizing free colored persons with their own consent at any place or places without the United States.

I beg indulgence to discuss these proposed articles at some length. Without slavery the rebellion could never have existed; without slavery it could not continue.

Among the friends of the Union there is great diversity of sentiment and of policy in regard to slavery and the African race amongst us. Some would perpetuate slavery; some would abolish it suddenly and without compensation; some would abolish it gradually and with compensation: some would remove the freed people from us, and some would retain them with us; and there are yet other minor diversities. Because of these diversities we waste much strength in struggles among ourselves. By mutual concession we should harmonize and act together. This would be compromise, but it would be compromise among the friends and not with the enemies of the Union. These articles are intended to embody a plan of such mutual concessions. If the plan shall be adopted, it is assumed that emancipation will follow, at least in several of the States. . . .

The emancipation will be unsatisfactory to the advocates of perpetual slavery, but the length of time should greatly mitigate their dissatisfaction. The time spares both races from the evils of sudden derangement—in fact, from the necessity of any derangement—while most of those whose habitual course of thought will be disturbed by the measure will have passed away before its consummation. They will never see it. Another class will hail the prospect of emancipation, but will deprecate the length of time. They will feel that it gives too little to the now living slaves. But it really gives them much. It saves them from the vagrant destitution which must largely attend immediate emancipation in localities where their numbers are very great, and it gives the inspiring assurance that their posterity shall be free forever. The plan leaves to each State choosing to act under it to abolish slavery now or at the end of the century, or at any intermediate time, or by degrees extending over the whole or any part of the period, and it obliges no two States to proceed alike. It also provides for compensation, and generally the mode of making it. This, it would seem, must further mitigate the dissatisfaction of those who favor perpetual slavery, and especially of those who are to receive the compensation. Doubtless some of those who are to pay and not to receive will object. Yet the measure is both just and economical. In a certain sense the liberation of slaves is the destruction of property—property acquired by descent or by purchase, the same as any other property. It is no less true for having been often said that the people of the South are not more responsible for the original introduction of this property than are the people of the North; and when it is remembered how unhesitatingly we all use cotton and sugar and share the profits of dealing in them, it may not be quite safe to say that the South has been more responsible than the North for its continuance. If, then, for a common object this property is to be sacrificed, is it not just that it be done at a common charge?

And if with less money, or money more easily paid, we can preserve the benefits of the Union by this means than we can by the war alone, is it not also economical to do it? . . .

The proposed emancipation would shorten the war, perpetuate peace, insure this increase of population, and proportionately the wealth of the country. With these we should pay all the emancipation would cost, together with our other debt, easier than we should pay our other debt without it. . . .

But it is dreaded that the freed people will swarm forth and cover the whole land. Are they not already in the land? Will liberation make them any more numerous? Equally distributed among the whites of the whole country, and there would be but one colored to seven whites. Could the one in any way greatly disturb the seven? . . . People of any color seldom run unless there be something to run from. Heretofore colored people to some extent have fled North from bondage, and now, perhaps, from both bondage and destitution. But if gradual emancipation and deportation be adopted, they will have neither to flee from. . . .

We can succeed only by concert. It is not "Can any of us imagine better?" but "Can we all do better?" Object whatsoever is possible, still the question recurs, "Can we do better?" The dogmas of the quiet past are inadequate to the stormy present. The occasion is piled high with difficulty, and we must rise with the occasion. As our case is new, so we must think anew and act anew. We must disenthrall ourselves, and then we shall save our country.

Fellow-citizens, we can not escape history. We of this Congress and this Administration will be remembered in spite of ourselves. No personal significance or insignificance can spare one or another of us. The fiery trial through which we pass will light us down in honor or dishonor to the latest generation. We say we are for the Union. The world will not forget that we say this. We know how to save the Union. The world knows we do know how to save it. We, even we here, hold the power and bear the responsibility. In giving freedom to the slave we assure freedom to the free—honorable alike in what we give and what we preserve. We shall nobly save or meanly lose the last best hope of earth. Other means may succeed; this could not fail. The way is plain, peaceful, generous, just—a way which if followed the world will forever applaud and God must forever bless.

STATE OF THE UNION ADDRESSES
1865–1930

ANDREW JOHNSON

Johnson's stormy presidency began with an address to Congress that spelled out his state-oriented constitutionalism and his aversion to long-term Union military rule in the conquered South. While this was discouraging news for Americans who hoped that army bayonets might afford freed slaves some measure of protection, it offered hope to those who believed the president would not go very far in protecting black rights or inflicting a punishing form of Reconstruction on former Confederates.

First Address: December 4, 1865

To express gratitude to God in the name of the people for the preservation of the United States is my first duty in addressing you. Our thoughts next revert to the death of the late President [Abraham Lincoln] by an act of parricidal treason. The grief of the nation is still fresh. . . . His removal cast upon me a heavier weight of cares than ever devolved upon any one of his predecessors. To fulfill my trust I need the support and confidence of all who are associated with me in the various departments of Government and the support and confidence of the people. There is but one way in which I can hope to gain their necessary aid. It is to state with frankness the principles which guide my conduct, and their application to the present state of affairs, well aware that the efficiency of my labors will in a great measure depend on your and their undivided approbation.

The Union of the United States of America was intended by its authors to last as long as the States themselves shall last. "The Union shall be perpetual" are the words of the Confederation. "To form a more perfect Union," by an ordinance of the people of the United States, is the declared purpose of the Constitution. The hand of Divine Providence was never more plainly visible in the affairs of men than in the framing and the adopting of that instrument. . . .

The maintenance of the Union brings with it "the support of the State governments in all their rights," but it is not one of the rights of any State government to renounce its own place in the Union or to nullify the laws of the Union. . . . The largest liberty is to be maintained in the discussion of the acts of the Federal Government, but there is no appeal from its laws except to the various branches of that Government itself, or to the people, who grant to the members of the legislative and of the executive depart-ments no tenure but a limited one, and in that manner always retain the powers of re-dress.

"The sovereignty of the States" is the language of the Confederacy, and not the lan-guage of the Constitution. . . .

States, with proper limitations of power, are essential to the existence of the Consti-tution of the United States. . . . So long as the Constitution of the United States en-dures, the States will endure. The destruction of the one is the destruction of the other; the preservation of the one is the preservation of the other.

I have thus explained my views of the mutual relations of the Constitution and the States, because they unfold the principles on which I have sought to solve the momen-tous questions and overcome the appalling difficulties that met me at the very com-mencement of my Administration. It has been my steadfast object to escape from the sway of momentary passions and to derive a healing policy from the fundamental and unchanging principles of the Constitution.

I found the States suffering from the effects of a civil war. Resistance to the General Government appeared to have exhausted itself. The United States had recovered pos-session of their forts and arsenals, and their armies were in the occupation of every State which had attempted to secede. . . .

Now military governments, established for an indefinite period, would have offered no security for the early suppression of discontent, would have divided the people into the vanquishers and the vanquished, and would have envenomed hatred rather than have restored affection. Once established, no precise limit to their continuance was conceivable. . . .

The relations of the General Government toward the 4,000,000 inhabitants whom the war has called into freedom have engaged my most serious consideration. On the propriety of attempting to make the freedmen electors by the proclamation of the Ex-ecutive I took for my counsel the Constitution itself, the interpretations of that instru-ment by its authors and their contemporaries, and recent legislation by Congress. When, at the first movement toward independence, the Congress of the United States instructed the several States to institute governments of their own, they left each State to decide for itself the conditions for the enjoyment of the elective franchise. . . .

Every danger of conflict is avoided when the settlement of the question is referred to the several States. They can, each for itself, decide on the measure, and whether it is to be adopted at once and absolutely or introduced gradually and with conditions. In my judgment the freedmen, if they show patience and manly virtues, will sooner obtain a participation in the elective franchise through the States than through the General Government, even if it had power to intervene. When the tumult of emotions that have been raised by the suddenness of the social change shall have subsided, it may prove that they will receive the kindest usage from some of those on whom they have hereto-fore most closely depended.

But while I have no doubt that now, after the close of the war, it is not competent for the General Government to extend the elective franchise in the several States, it is equally clear that good faith requires the security of the freedmen in their liberty and their property, their right to labor, and their right to claim the just return of their labor. I can not too strongly urge a dispassionate treatment of this subject, which should be carefully kept aloof from all party strife. We must equally avoid hasty assumptions of any natural impossibility for the two races to live side by side in a state of mutual benefit and good will. The experiment involves us in no inconsistency; let us, then, go on and make that experiment in good faith, and not be too easily disheartened. The country is in need of labor, and the freedmen are in need of employment, culture, and protection. While their right of voluntary migration and expatriation is not to be questioned, I would not advise their forced removal and colonization. Let us rather encourage them to honorable and useful industry, where it may be beneficial to themselves and to the country; and, instead of hasty anticipations of the certainty of failure, let there be nothing wanting to the fair trial of the experiment. The change in their condition is the substitution of labor by contract for the status of slavery. The freedman can not fairly be accused of unwillingness to work so long as a doubt remains about his freedom of choice in his pursuits and the certainty of his recovering his stipulated wages. In this the interests of the employer and the employed coincide. . . .

I know that sincere philanthropy is earnest for the immediate realization of its remotest aims; but time is always an element in reform. It is one of the greatest acts on record to have brought 4,000,000 people into freedom. The career of free industry must be fairly opened to them, and then their future prosperity and condition must, after all, rest mainly on themselves. If they fail, and so perish away, let us be careful that the failure shall not be attributable to any denial of justice. In all that relates to the destiny of the freedmen we need not be too anxious to read the future; many incidents which, from a speculative point of view, might raise alarm will quietly settle themselves. . . .

Who will not join with me in the prayer that the Invisible Hand which has led us through the clouds that gloomed around our path will so guide us onward to a perfect restoration of fraternal affection that we of this day may be able to transmit our great inheritance of State governments in all their rights, of the General Government in its whole constitutional vigor, to our posterity, and they to theirs through countless generations?

ULYSSES S. GRANT

Grant's presidency was a time of distraction, as the nation was steadily drawn away from addressing the ever-present problems of race and Reconstruction to address various scandals that plagued the White House and the wars with the Plains Indians. Grant's last State of the Union Address provides a succinct summary of the issues facing the nation as it entered the Gilded Age.

Eighth Address: December 5, 1876

In submitting my eighth and last annual message to Congress it seems proper that I should refer to and in some degree recapitulate the events and official acts of the past eight years.

It was my fortune, or misfortune, to be called to the office of Chief Executive without any previous political training. From the age of 17 I had never even witnessed the excitement attending a Presidential campaign but twice antecedent to my own candidacy, and at but one of them was I eligible as a voter.

Under such circumstances it is but reasonable to suppose that errors of judgment must have occurred. Even had they not, differences of opinion between the Executive, bound by an oath to the strict performance of his duties, and writers and debaters must have arisen. It is not necessarily evidence of blunder on the part of the Executive because there are these differences of views. Mistakes have been made, as all can see and I admit, but it seems to me oftener in the selections made of the assistants appointed to aid in carrying out the various duties of administering the Government—in nearly every case selected without a personal acquaintance with the appointee, but upon recommendations of the representatives chosen directly by the people. It is impossible, where so many trusts are to be allotted, that the right parties should be chosen in every instance. History shows that no Administration from the time of Washington to the present has been free from these mistakes. But I leave comparisons to history, claiming only that I have acted in every instance from a conscientious desire to do what was right, constitutional, within the law, and for the very best interests of the whole people. Failures have been errors of judgment, not of intent.

My civil career commenced, too, at a most critical and difficult time. Less than four years before, the country had emerged from a conflict such as no other nation had ever survived. Nearly one-half of the States had revolted against the Government, and of those remaining faithful to the Union a large percentage of the population sympathized with the rebellion and made an "enemy in the rear" almost as dangerous as the more honorable enemy in the front. The latter committed errors of judgment, but they maintained them openly and courageously; the former received the protection of the Government they would see destroyed, and reaped all the pecuniary advantage to be gained out of the then existing state of affairs, many of them by obtaining contracts and by swindling the Government in the delivery of their goods.

Immediately on the cessation of hostilities the then noble President [Lincoln], who had carried the country so far through its perils, fell a martyr to his patriotism at the hands of an assassin.

The intervening time to my first inauguration was filled up with wranglings between Congress and the new Executive as to the best mode of "reconstruction," or, to speak plainly, as to whether the control of the Government should be thrown immediately into the hands of those who had so recently and persistently tried to destroy it, or whether the victors should continue to have an equal voice with them in this control. Reconstruction, as finally agreed upon, means this and only this, except that the late slave was enfranchised, giving an increase, as was supposed, to the Union-loving and Union-supporting votes. If free in the full sense of the word, they would not disappoint this expectation. Hence at the beginning of my first Administration the work of reconstruction, much embarrassed by the long delay, virtually commenced. It was the work of the legislative branch of the Government. My province was wholly in approving their acts, which I did most heartily, urging the legislatures of States that had not yet done so to ratify the fifteenth amendment to the Constitution. . . .

A policy has been adopted toward the Indian tribes inhabiting a large portion of the territory of the United States which has been humane and has substantially ended Indian hostilities in the whole land except in a portion of Nebraska, and Dakota, Wyoming, and Montana Territories—the Black Hills region and approaches thereto. Hostilities there have grown out of the avarice of the white man, who has violated our treaty stipulations in his search for gold. The question might be asked why the Government has not enforced obedience to the terms of the treaty prohibiting the occupation of the Black Hills region by whites. The answer is simple: The first immigrants to the Black Hills were removed by troops, but rumors of rich discoveries of gold took into that region increased numbers. Gold has actually been found in paying quantity, and an effort to remove the miners would only result in the desertion of the bulk of the troops that might be sent there to remove them. All difficulty in this matter has, however, been removed—subject to the approval of Congress—by a treaty ceding the Black Hills and approaches to settlement by citizens. . . .

RUTHERFORD B. HAYES

Hayes became president upon an understanding that he would usher an end to Reconstruction by withdrawing the army from the former Confederate states. His State of the Union Address for 1877 suggests that his rationale in doing so was essentially returning control of the South to its white leaders and abandoning the freedmen in the region to Jim Crow.

First Address: December 3, 1877

To complete and make permanent the pacification of the country continues to be, and until it is fully accomplished must remain, the most important of all our national interests. The earnest purpose of good citizens generally to unite their efforts in this endeavor is evident. . . . There was a widespread apprehension that the momentous results in our progress as a nation marked by the recent amendments [the Thirteenth, Fourteenth, and Fifteenth Amendments] to the Constitution were in imminent jeopardy; that the good understanding which prompted their adoption, in the interest of a loyal devotion to the general welfare, might prove a barren truce, and that the two sections of the country, once engaged in civil strife, might be again almost as widely severed and disunited as they were when arrayed in arms against each other.

The course to be pursued, which, in my judgment, seemed wisest in the presence of this emergency, was plainly indicated in my inaugural address. It pointed to the time, which all our people desire to see, when a genuine love of our whole country and of all that concerns its true welfare shall supplant the destructive forces of the mutual animosity of races and of sectional hostility. . . . Any course whatever which might have been entered upon would certainly have encountered distrust and opposition. These measures were, in my judgment, such as were most in harmony with the Constitution and with the genius of our people, and best adapted, under all the circumstances, to attain the end in view. . . . The discontinuance of the use of the Army for the purpose of upholding local governments in two States of the Union was no less a constitutional duty and requirement, under the circumstances existing at the time, than it was a much-needed measure for the restoration of local self-government and the promotion of national harmony. The withdrawal of the troops from such employment was effected deliberately, and with solicitous care for the peace and good order of society and the protection of the property and persons and every right of all classes of citizens.

The results that have followed are indeed significant and encouraging. All apprehension of danger from remitting those States to local self-government is dispelled, and a most salutary change in the minds of the people has begun and is in progress in every part of that section of the country once the theater of unhappy civil strife, substituting for suspicion, distrust, and aversion, concord, friendship, and patriotic attachment to the Union. No unprejudiced mind will deny that the terrible and often fatal collisions which for several years have been of frequent occurrence and have agitated and alarmed the public mind have almost entirely ceased, and that a spirit of mutual forbearance and hearty national interest has succeeded. There has been a general reestablishment of order and of the orderly administration of justice. Instances of remaining lawlessness have become of rare occurrence; political turmoil and turbulence have disappeared; useful industries have been resumed; public credit in the Southern States has been greatly strengthened, and the encouraging benefits of a revival of commerce between the sections of the country lately embroiled in civil war are fully enjoyed. Such are some of the results already attained, upon which the country is to be congratulated. They are of such importance that we may with confidence patiently await the desired consummation that will surely come with the natural progress of events.

It may not be improper here to say that it should be our fixed and unalterable determination to protect by all available and proper means under the Constitution and the laws the lately emancipated race in the enjoyment of their rights and privileges; and I urge upon those to whom heretofore the colored people have sustained the relation of bondmen the wisdom and justice of humane and liberal local legislation with respect to their education and general welfare. A firm adherence to the laws, both national and

State, as to the civil and political rights of the colored people, now advanced to full and equal citizenship; the immediate repression and sure punishment by the national and local authorities, within their respective jurisdictions, of every instance of lawlessness and violence toward them, is required for the security alike of both races, and is justly demanded by the public opinion of the country and the age. In this way the restoration of harmony and good will and the complete protection of every citizen in the full enjoyment of every constitutional right will surely be attained. Whatever authority rests with me to this end I shall not hesitate to put forth. . . .

CHESTER A. ARTHUR

When Arthur inherited the president's chair following the assassination of James Garfield (who died before he could deliver a State of the Union Address), the nation was moving steadily forward from the problems of sectional strife and Reconstruction to the issues that confronted it during the industrializing age. These included civil service reform, labor relations, attempts by Congress to begin regulating the American workplace, and the circumstances created by the cresting wave of a great tide of immigration. Arthur's State of the Union Addresses therefore tended to be filled with meticulous economic details about tariff policies, tax rates, trade balances, and so on. An excerpt from his last Address offers an example of the myriad economic details that preoccupied the nation during his time.

Fourth Address: December 1, 1884

Our existing naturalization laws also need revision. Those sections relating to persons residing within the limits of the United States in 1795 and 1798 have now only a historical interest. . . . There are special provisions of law favoring the naturalization of those who serve in the Army or in merchant vessels, while no similar privileges are granted those who serve in the Navy or the Marine Corps.

"An uniform rule of naturalization" such as the Constitution contemplates should, among other things, clearly define the status of persons born within the United States subject to a foreign power (section 1992) and of minor children of fathers who have declared their intention to become citizens but have failed to perfect their naturalization. It might be wise to provide for a central bureau of registry, wherein should be filed authenticated transcripts of every record of naturalization in the several Federal and State courts, and to make provision also for the vacation or cancellation of such record in cases where fraud had been practiced upon the court by the applicant himself or where he had renounced or forfeited his acquired citizenship. A just and uniform law in this respect would strengthen the hands of the Government in protecting its citizens abroad and would pave the way for the conclusion of treaties of naturalization with foreign countries. . . .

In my annual message of 1882 I recommended the abolition of all excise taxes except those relating to distilled spirits. This recommendation is now renewed. In case these taxes shall be abolished the revenues that will still remain to the Government will, in my opinion, not only suffice to meet its reasonable expenditures, but will afford a surplus large enough to permit such tariff reduction as may seem to be advisable when the results of recent revenue laws and commercial treaties shall have shown in what quarters those reductions can be most judiciously effected. . . .

On the 29th of February last I transmitted to the Congress the first annual report of the Civil Service Commission, together with communications from the heads of the several Executive Departments of the Government respecting the practical workings of the law under which the Commission had been acting. The good results therein foreshadowed have been more than realized.

The system has fully answered the expectations of its friends in securing competent and faithful public servants and in protecting the appointing officers of the Government from the pressure of personal importunity and from the labor of examining the claims and pretensions of rival candidates for public employment.

The law has had the unqualified support of the President and of the heads of the several Departments, and the members of the Commission have performed their duties with zeal and fidelity. Their report will shortly be submitted, and will be accompanied by such recommendations for enlarging the scope of the existing statute as shall commend themselves to the Executive and the Commissioners charged with its administration.

In view of the general and persistent demand throughout the commercial community for a national bankrupt law, I hope that the differences of sentiment which have hitherto prevented its enactment may not outlast the present session. . . .

GROVER CLEVELAND

Monetary policies dominated political debates during the latter part of the nineteenth century. Commercial- and business-minded Americans from the big market money centers of the Northeast wanted America's money to be coined on the basis of the nation's gold reserves alone, seeing this as a safe, fiscally conservative way to create a sound dollar and relatively risk-free economy. Supporters of silver, on the other hand, wanted a silver-based system that would provide more flexibility in the economy, increase the money supply, and help debt-ridden farmers and other working-class Americans hard-pressed in what had become a sluggish economy. Cleveland represented the gold wing of the Democratic Party, and the fiscal conservatism that system implied.

First Address: December 8, 1885

Nothing more important than the present condition of our currency and coinage can claim your attention. . . .

A reasonable appreciation of a delegation of power to the General Government would limit its exercise, without express restrictive words, to the people's needs and the requirements of the public welfare. . . .

Upon this theory the authority to "coin money" given to Congress by the Constitution, if it permits the purchase by the Government of bullion for coinage in any event, does not justify such purchase and coinage to an extent beyond the amount needed for a sufficient circulating medium. . . .

The desire to utilize the silver product of the country should not lead to a misuse or the perversion of this power. . . .

If continued long enough, this operation will result in the substitution of silver for all the gold the Government owns applicable to its general purposes. . . . The proportion of silver and its certificates received by the Government will probably increase as time goes on, for the reason that the nearer the period approaches when it will be obliged to offer silver in payment of its obligations the greater inducement there will be to hoard gold against depreciation in the value of silver or for the purpose of speculating.

This hoarding of gold has already begun.

When the time comes that gold has been withdrawn from circulation, then will be apparent the difference between the real value of the silver dollar and a dollar in gold, and the two coins will part company. Gold, still the standard of value and necessary in our dealings with other countries, will be at a premium over silver; banks which have substituted gold for the deposits of their customers may pay them with silver bought with such gold, thus making a handsome profit; rich speculators will sell their hoarded gold to their neighbors who need it to liquidate their foreign debts, at a ruinous premium over silver, and the laboring men and women of the land, most defenseless of all, will find that the dollar received for the wage of their toil has sadly shrunk in its purchasing power. . . .

We are accumulating silver coin, based upon our own peculiar ratio, to such an extent, and assuming so heavy a burden to be provided for in any international negotiations, as will render us an undesirable party to any future monetary conference of nations. . . .

The so-called debtor class, for whose benefit the continued compulsory coinage of silver is insisted upon, are not dishonest because they are in debt, and they should not be suspected of a desire to jeopardize the financial safety of the country in order that they may cancel their present debts by paying the same in depreciated dollars. Nor should it be forgotten that it is not the rich nor the money lender alone that must submit to such a readjustment, enforced by the Government and their debtors. The pittance of the widow and the orphan and the incomes of helpless beneficiaries of all kinds would be disastrously reduced. The depositors in savings banks and in other institutions which hold in trust the savings of the poor, when their little accumulations are scaled down to meet the new order of things, would in their distress painfully realize the delusion of the promise made to them that plentiful money would improve their condition. . . .

BENJAMIN HARRISON

President Harrison was a hard-working, no-nonsense Indiana lawyer who came to the presidency at a time when the federal government had begun to involve itself deeply in the workings of the nation's economy. Harrison was a details-oriented chief executive on such matters, as this excerpt from his second State of the Union Address indicates.

Second Address: December 1, 1890

The report of the Secretary of Agriculture deserves especial attention in view of the fact that the year has been marked in a very unusual degree by agitation and organization among the farmers looking to an increase in the profits of their business. It will be found that the efforts of the Department have been intelligently and zealously devoted to the promotion of the interests entrusted to its care.

A very substantial improvement in the market prices of the leading farm products during the year is noticed. The price of wheat advanced from 81 cents in October, 1889, to $1.00 3/4 in October, 1890; corn from 31 cents to 50 1/4 cents; oats from 19 1/4 cents to 43 cents, and barley from 63 cents to 78 cents. Meats showed a substantial but not so large an increase. The export trade in live animals and fowls shows a very large increase. The total value of such exports for the year ending June 30, 1890, was $33,000,000, and the increase over the preceding year was over $15,000,000. Nearly 200,000 more cattle and over 45,000 more hogs were exported than in the preceding year. The export trade in beef and pork products and in dairy products was very largely increased, the increase in the article of butter alone being from 15,504,978 pounds to 29,748,042 pounds, and the total increase in the value of meat and dairy products exported being $34,000,000. This trade, so directly helpful to the farmer, it is believed, will be yet further and very largely increased when the system of inspection and sanitary supervision now provided by law is brought fully into operation.

The efforts of the Secretary to establish the healthfulness of our meats against the disparaging imputations that have been put upon them abroad have resulted in substantial progress. . . .

The information given by the Secretary of the progress and prospects of the beet-sugar industry is full of interest. It has already passed the experimental stage and is a commercial success. The area over which the sugar beet can be successfully cultivated is very large, and another field crop of great value is offered to the choice of the farmer. . . .

I congratulate the Congress and the country upon the passage at the first session of the Fifty-first Congress of an unusual number of laws of very high importance. That the results of this legislation will be the quickening and enlargement of our manufacturing industries, larger and better markets for our breadstuffs and provisions both at home and abroad, more constant employment and better wages for our working people, and an increased supply of a safe currency for the transaction of business, I do not doubt. Some of these measures were enacted at so late a period that the beneficial effects upon commerce which were in the contemplation of Congress have as yet but partially manifested themselves. . . .

WILLIAM McKINLEY

By the turn of the century, the United States had embarked upon a program of robust naval construction, which in turn created the need for new bases overseas. Added to this was the ambition of many Americans to compete on the world stage and assume the nation's place as an imperial power. These motives were behind America's war with Spain. McKinley was a reluctant imperialist in many ways, and his justifications and descriptions of the war in his third State of the Union Address lack the bellicosity that has characterized other presidents during war.

Third Address: December 5, 1899

Notwithstanding the added burdens rendered necessary by the war, our people rejoice in a very satisfactory and steadily increasing degree of prosperity, evidenced by the largest volume of business ever recorded. . . . Military service under a common flag and for a righteous cause has strengthened the national spirit and served to cement more closely than ever the fraternal bonds between every section of the country.

A review of the relation of the United States to other powers, always appropriate, is this year of primary importance in view of the momentous issues which have arisen, demanding in one instance the ultimate determination by arms and involving far-reaching consequences which will require the earnest attention of the Congress.

In my last annual message very full consideration was given to the question of the duty of the Government of the United States toward Spain. . . . I concluded it was honestly due to our friendly relations with Spain that she should be given a reasonable chance to realize her expectations of reform to which she had become irrevocably committed. Within a few weeks previously she had announced comprehensive plans which it was confidently asserted would be efficacious to remedy the evils so deeply affecting our own country, so injurious to the true interests of the mother country as well as to those of Cuba, and so repugnant to the universal sentiment of humanity.

All these things carried conviction to the most thoughtful . . . that a crisis in our relations with Spain and toward Cuba was at hand. So strong was this belief that it needed but a brief Executive suggestion to the Congress to receive immediate answer to the duty of making instant provision for the possible and perhaps speedily probable emergency of war. . . . It is sufficient to say that the outbreak of war when it did come found our nation not unprepared to meet the conflict.

I felt it my duty to remit the whole question to the Congress. In the message of April 11, 1898, I announced that with this last overture in the direction of immediate peace in Cuba and its disappointing reception by Spain the effort of the Executive was brought to an end. . . .

Spain having thus . . . initiated that complete form of rupture of relations which attends a state of war, the executive powers authorized by the resolution were at once used by me to meet the enlarged contingency of actual war between sovereign states. . . . Due notification of the existence of war as aforesaid was given April 25 by telegraph to all the governments with which the United States maintain relations, in order that their neutrality might be assured during the war. . . .

Our country thus, after an interval of half a century of peace with all nations, found itself engaged in deadly conflict with a foreign enemy. Every nerve was strained to meet the emergency. . . .

[McKinley here offered a detailed description of the war's major campaigns and Spain's acceptance of the terms of surrender, what the president called the "protocols" that terminated the war.] In tracing these events we are constantly reminded of our obligations to the Divine Master for His watchful care over us and His safe guidance, for which the nation makes reverent acknowledgment and offers humble prayer for the continuance of His favor. . . .

Immediately upon the conclusion of the protocol I issued a proclamation, of August 12, suspending hostilities on the part of the United States. The necessary orders to that end were at once given by telegraph. The blockade of the ports of Cuba and San Juan de Puerto Rico was in like manner raised. On the 18th of August the muster out of 100,000 volunteers, or as near that number as was found to be practicable, was ordered. . . .

I do not discuss at this time the government or the future of the new possessions which will come to us as the result of the war with Spain. Such discussion will be appropriate after the treaty of peace shall be ratified. In the meantime and until the Congress has legislated otherwise it will be my duty to continue the military governments which have existed since our occupation and give to the people security in life and property and encouragement under a just and beneficent rule. . . .

THEODORE ROOSEVELT

Teddy Roosevelt was nothing if not energetic, pursuing both the nation's growing imperialist ambitions abroad and a complex domestic agenda of social and economic reform, all in the name of a robust, even jingoistic patriotism. His State of the Union Addresses tended to be more than laundry lists of departmental appropriations, expenditures, and the like: TR also used the annual addresses to Congress to enunciate his broad philosophical outlook on all things foreign and domestic.

Second Address: December 2, 1902

We still continue in a period of unbounded prosperity. This prosperity is not the creature of law, but undoubtedly the laws under which we work have been instrumental in creating the conditions which made it possible, and by unwise legislation it would be easy enough to destroy it. There will undoubtedly be periods of depression. The wave will recede; but the tide will advance. This Nation is seated on a continent flanked by two great oceans. It is composed of men the descendants of pioneers, or, in a sense, pioneers themselves; of men winnowed out from among the nations of the Old World by the energy, boldness, and love of adventure found in their own eager hearts. Such a Nation, so placed, will surely wrest success from fortune.

As a people we have played a large part in the world, and we are bent upon making our future even larger than the past. In particular, the events of the last four years have definitely decided that, for woe or for weal, our place must be great among the nations. We may either fall greatly or succeed greatly; but we can not avoid the endeavor from which either great failure or great success must come. Even if we would, we can not play a small part. If we should try, all that would follow would be that we should play a large part ignobly and shamefully.

But our people, the sons of the men of the Civil War, the sons of the men who had iron in their blood, rejoice in the present and face the future high of heart and resolute of will. Ours is not the creed of the weakling and the coward; ours is the gospel of hope and of triumphant endeavor. We do not shrink from the struggle before us. There are many problems for us to face at the outset of the twentieth century—grave problems abroad and still graver at home; but we know that we can solve them and solve them well, provided only that we bring to the solution the qualities of head and heart which were shown by the men who, in the days of Washington, rounded this Government, and, in the days of Lincoln, preserved it. . . .

In my Message to the present Congress at its first session I discussed at length the question of the regulation of those big corporations commonly doing an interstate business, often with some tendency to monopoly, which are popularly known as trusts. The experience of the past year has emphasized, in my opinion, the desirability of the steps I then proposed. A fundamental requisite of social efficiency is a high standard of individual energy and excellence; but this is in no wise inconsistent with power to act in combination for aims which can not so well be achieved by the individual acting alone. A fundamental base of civilization is the inviolability of property; but this is in no wise inconsistent with the right of society to regulate the exercise of the artificial powers which it confers upon the owners of property, under the name of corporate franchises, in such a way as to prevent the misuse of these powers. Corporations, and especially combinations of corporations, should be managed under public regulation. Experience has shown that under our system of government the necessary supervision can not be obtained by State action. It must therefore be achieved by national action. Our aim is not to do away with corporations; on the contrary, these big aggregations are an inevitable development of modern industrialism, and the effort to destroy them would be futile unless accomplished in ways that would work the utmost mischief to the entire body politic. We can do nothing of good in the way of regulating and supervising these corporations until we fix clearly in our minds that we are not attacking the corporations, but endeavoring to do away with any evil in them. We are not hostile to them; we are merely determined that they shall be so handled as to subserve the public good. We draw the line against misconduct, not against wealth. The capitalist who, alone or in conjunction with his fellows, performs some great industrial feat by which he wins money is a welldoer, not a wrongdoer, provided only he works in proper and legitimate lines. We wish to favor such a man when he does well. We wish to supervise and control his actions only to prevent him from doing ill. Publicity can do no harm to the honest corporation; and we need not be over tender about sparing the dishonest corporation.

In curbing and regulating the combinations of capital which are, or may become, injurious to the public we must be careful not to stop the great enterprises which have legitimately reduced the cost of production, not to abandon the place which our country has won in the leadership of the international industrial world, not to strike down wealth with the result of closing factories and mines, of turning the wage-worker idle in the streets and leaving the farmer without a market for what he grows. Insistence upon the impossible means delay in achieving the possible, exactly as, on the other hand, the stubborn defense alike of what is good and what is bad in the existing system, the resolute effort to obstruct any attempt at betterment, betrays blindness to the historic truth that wise evolution is the sure safeguard against revolution. . . .

I believe that monopolies, unjust discriminations, which prevent or cripple competition, fraudulent overcapitalization, and other evils in trust organizations and practices which injuriously affect interstate trade can be prevented under the power of the Congress to "regulate commerce with foreign nations and among the several States" through regulations and requirements operating directly upon such commerce, the instrumentalities thereof, and those engaged therein. . . .

The Congress has wisely provided that we shall build at once an isthmian canal, if possible at Panama. The Attorney-General reports that we can undoubtedly acquire good title from the French Panama Canal Company. Negotiations are now pending with Colombia to secure her assent to our building the canal. This canal will be one of the greatest engineering feats of the twentieth century; a greater engineering feat than has yet been accomplished during the history of mankind. The work should be carried out as a continuing policy without regard to change of Administration; and it should be begun under circumstances which will make it a matter of pride for all Administrations to continue the policy.

The canal will be of great benefit to America, and of importance to all the world. It will be of advantage to us industrially and also as improving our military position. It will be of advantage to the countries of tropical America. It is earnestly to be hoped that all of these countries will do as some of them have already done with signal success, and will invite to their shores commerce and improve their material conditions by recognizing that stability and order are the prerequisites of successful development. No independent nation in America need have the slightest fear of aggression from the United States. It behooves each one to maintain order within its own borders and to discharge its just obligations to foreigners. When this is done, they can rest assured that, be they strong or weak, they have nothing to dread from outside interference. More and more the increasing interdependence and complexity of international political and economic relations render it incumbent on all civilized and orderly powers to insist on the proper policing of the world. . . .

WILLIAM HOWARD TAFT

If Roosevelt liked to insert ideas and philosophy in his State of the Union Addresses, then his successor liked details. Taft's messages returned to the detail-packed laundry list format characteristic of so many other chief executives' Inaugural Addresses. An effective manager, Taft lacked TR's skills at painting with broad brushstrokes the political ideology that animated his policies. His State of the Union Addresses reflected this. The following excerpt, addressing issues related to the Panama Canal, aptly illustrates both his grasp of detail and the relative lack here of Roosevelt's big-idea framing of that detail.

Second Address: December 6, 1910

PANAMA CANAL

At the instance of Colonel Goethals, the Army Engineer officer in charge of the work on the Panama Canal, I have just made a visit to the Isthmus to inspect the work done and to consult with him on the ground as to certain problems which are likely to arise in the near future. The progress of the work is most satisfactory. If no unexpected obstacle presents itself, the canal will be completed well within the time fixed by Colonel Goethals, to wit, January 1, 1915, and within the estimate of cost, $375,000,000.

Press reports have reached the United States from time to time giving accounts of slides of earth of very large yardage in the Culebra Cut and elsewhere along the line, from which it might be inferred that the work has been much retarded and that the time of completion has been necessarily postponed.

The report of Doctor Hayes, of the Geological Survey, whom I sent within the last month to the Isthmus to make an investigation, shows that this section of the Canal Zone is composed of sedimentary rocks of rather weak structure and subject to almost immediate disintegration when exposed to the air. Subsequent to the deposition of these sediments, igneous rocks, harder and more durable, have been thrust into them, and being cold at the time of their intrusion united but indifferently with the sedimentary rock at the contacts. The result of these conditions is that as the cut is

deepened, causing unbalanced pressures, slides from the sides of the cut have occurred. These are in part due to the flowing of surface soil and decomposed sedimentary rocks upon inclined surfaces of the underlying undecomposed rock and in part
by the crushing of structurally weak beds under excessive pressure. These slides
occur on one side or the other of the cut through a distance of 4 or 5 miles, and now
that their character is understood, allowance has been made in the calculations of
yardage for the amount of slides which will have to be removed and the greater slope
that will have to be given to the bank in many places in order to prevent their recurrence. Such allowance does not exceed ten millions of yards. Considering that the
number of yards removed from this cut on an average of each month through the year
is 1,300,000, and that the total remaining to be excavated, including slides, is about
30,000,000 yards, it is seen that this addition to the excavation does not offer any
great reason for delay.

While this feature of the material to be excavated in the cut will not seriously delay
or obstruct the construction of a canal of the lock type, the increase of excavation due
to such slides in the cut made 85 feet deeper for a sea-level canal would certainly have
been so great as to delay its completion to a time beyond the patience of the American
people. . . .

WOODROW WILSON

*Woodrow Wilson was an idealist. When he led the nation to war with Germany in
1917, he did so on what he believed were the highest possible principles of global
peace, freedom, and democracy.*

Fifth Address: December 4, 1917

I shall not go back to debate the causes of the war. The intolerable wrongs done and
planned against us by the sinister masters of Germany have long since become too
grossly obvious and odious to every true American to need to be rehearsed. But I shall
ask you to consider again and with a very grave scrutiny our objectives and the measures by which we mean to attain them; for the purpose of discussion here in this place
is action, and our action must move straight toward definite ends. Our object is, of
course, to win the war; and we shall not slacken or suffer ourselves to he diverted until
it is won. But it is worth while asking and answering the question, When shall we consider the war won? . . .

Let there be no misunderstanding. Our present and immediate task is to win the
war and nothing shall turn us aside from it until it is accomplished. Every power and
resource we possess, whether of men, of money, or of materials, is being devoted and
will continue to be devoted to that purpose until it is achieved. Those who desire to
bring peace about before that purpose is achieved I counsel to carry their advice else-

where. We will not entertain it. We shall regard the war as won only when the German people say to us, through properly accredited representatives, that they are ready to agree to a settlement based upon justice and reparation of the wrongs their rulers have done. . . .

The wrongs, the very deep wrongs, committed in this war will have to be righted. That, of course. But they cannot and must not be righted by the commission of similar wrongs against Germany and her allies. The world will not permit the commission of similar wrongs as a means of reparation and settlement. Statesmen must by this time have learned that the opinion of the world is everywhere wide awake and fully comprehends the issues involved. . . . The thought of the plain people here and everywhere throughout the world, the people who enjoy no privilege and have very simple and unsophisticated standards of right and wrong, is the air all governments must henceforth breathe if they would live. . . .

Justice and equality of rights can be had only at a great price. We are seeking permanent, not temporary, foundations for the peace of the world, and must seek them candidly and fearlessly. As always, the right will prove to be the expedient. . . .

WARREN G. HARDING

Warren Harding's presidency ushered in a long period of peace and prosperity for the United States. America turned its back on the crusading Progressivism of the Roosevelt and Wilson eras and found itself overcome with war weariness following the unprecedented bloodletting of World War I. Harding's first State of the Union Address reflects a national consensus that good times, isolationism, and social complacency should rule the day. It also reflects a desire on the part of many Americans to restore harmony between Congress and the White House following the often-rancorous clashes that had recently occurred between the two branches.

First Address: December 6, 1921

It is a very gratifying privilege to come to the Congress with the Republic at peace with all the nations of the world. More, it is equally gratifying to report that our country is not only free from every impending, menace of war, but there are growing assurances of the permanency of the peace which we so deeply cherish.

For approximately ten years we have dwelt amid menaces of war or as participants in war's actualities, and the inevitable aftermath, with its disordered conditions, bits added to the difficulties of government which adequately can not be appraised except by, those who are in immediate contact and know the responsibilities. Our tasks would be less difficult if we had only ourselves to consider, but so much of the world was involved, the disordered conditions are so well-nigh universal, even among nations not engaged in actual warfare, that no permanent readjustments can be effected without consideration of our inescapable relationship to world affairs in finance and trade. Indeed, we should be unworthy of our best traditions if we were unmindful of social, moral, and political conditions which are not of direct concern to us, but which do appeal to the human sympathies and the very becoming interest of a people blest with our national good fortune.

It is not my purpose to bring to you a program of world restoration. In the main such a program must be worked out by the nations more directly concerned. They must themselves turn to the heroic remedies for the menacing conditions under which they are struggling, then we can help, and we mean to help. We shall do so unselfishly because there is compensation in the consciousness of assisting, selfishly because the commerce and international exchanges in trade, which marked our high tide of fortunate advancement, are possible only when the nations of all continents are restored to stable order and normal relationship. . . .

I am very sure we shall have no conflict of opinion about constitutional duties or authority. During the anxieties of war, when necessity seemed compelling there were excessive grants of authority and all extraordinary concentration of powers in the Chief Executive. The repeal of war-time legislation and the automatic expirations which attended the peace proclamations have put an end to these emergency excesses but I have the wish to go further than that. I want to join you in restoring, in the most cordial way, the spirit of coordination and cooperation, and that mutuality of confidence and respect which is necessary ill representative popular government.

Encroachment upon the functions of Congress or attempted dictation of its policy are not to be thought of, much less attempted, but there is all insistent call for harmony of purpose and concord of action to speed the solution of the difficult problems confronting both the legislative and executive branches of the Government. . . .

CALVIN COOLIDGE

Americans during the Roaring Twenties did not want activist presidents. Times were good, the nation was largely uninvolved with troubles overseas, and most people did not want a president who might try to rock what seemed to be a very stable national boat. Calvin Coolidge exemplified the limited sort of chief executive the nation desired.

Fourth Address: December 26, 1926

In reporting to the Congress the state of the Union, I find it impossible to characterize it other than one of general peace and prosperity. In some quarters our diplomacy is vexed with difficult and as yet unsolved problems, but nowhere are we met with armed conflict. If some occupations and areas are not flourishing, in none does there remain any acute chronic depression. What the country requires is not so much new policies as a steady continuation of those which are already being crowned with such abundant success. It can not be too often repeated that in common with all the world we are engaged in liquidating the war.

In the present short session no great amount of new legislation is possible, but in order to comprehend what is most desirable some survey of our general situation is necessary. A large amount of time is consumed in the passage of appropriation bills. If each Congress in its opening session would make appropriations to continue for two years, very much time would be saved which could either be devoted to a consideration of the general needs of the country or would result in decreasing the work of legislation. . . .

Nothing is easier than the expenditure of public money. It does not appear to belong to anybody. The temptation is overwhelming to bestow it on somebody. But the results of extravagance are ruinous. The property of the country, like the freedom of the country, belongs to the people of the country. They have not empowered their Government to take a dollar of it except for a necessary public purpose. But if the Constitution conferred such right, sound economics would forbid it. Nothing is more, destructive of the progress of the Nation than government extravagance. It means an increase in the burden of taxation, dissipation of the returns from enterprise, a decrease in the real value of wages, with ultimate stagnation and decay. The whole theory of our institutions is based on the liberty and independence of the individual. He is dependent on himself for support and therefore entitled to the rewards of his own industry. He is not to be deprived of what he earns that others may be benefited by what they do not earn. What [he] saves through his private effort is not to be wasted by Government extravagance. . . .

America is not and must not be a country without ideals. They are useless if they are only visionary; they are only valuable if they are practical. A nation can not dwell constantly on the mountain tops. It has to be replenished and sustained through the ceaseless toil of the less inspiring valleys. But its face ought always to be turned upward, its vision ought always to be fixed on high.

We need ideals that can be followed in daily life, that can be translated into terms of the home. We can not expect to be relieved from toil, but we do expect to divest it of degrading conditions. Work is honorable; it is entitled to an honorable recompense. We must strive mightily, but having striven there is a defect in our political and social system if we are not in general rewarded with success. To relieve the land of the burdens that came from the war, to release to the individual more of the fruits of his own industry, to increase his earning capacity and decrease his hours of labor, to enlarge the circle of his vision through good roads and better transportation, to lace before him the opportunity for education both in science and in art, to leave him free to receive the inspiration of religion, all these are ideals which deliver him from the servitude of the body and exalt him to the service of the soul. Through this emancipation from the things that are material, we broaden our dominion over the things that are spiritual.

Herbert Hoover

The last of the laissez-faire Roaring Twenties presidents, Herbert Hoover was in many ways a tragic figure. A genial and compassionate man, he was nonplussed by the onset of the Great Depression in 1929 and was ill-equipped to deal with its staggering problems. His second State of the Union Address occurred in the immediate wake of the economy's crash and reflects a president and a nation groping for answers to the crisis.

Second Address: December 2, 1930

I have the honor to comply with the requirement of the Constitution that I should lay before the Congress information as to the state of the Union, and recommend consideration of such measures as are necessary and expedient.

Substantial progress has been made during the year in national peace and security; the fundamental strength of the Nation' economic life is unimpaired; education and scientific discovery have made advances; our country is more alive to its problems of moral and spiritual welfare. . . .

During the past 12 months we have suffered with other Nations from economic depression.

The origins of this depression lie to some extent within our own borders through a speculative period which diverted capital and energy into speculation rather than constructive enterprise. Had overspeculation in securities been the only force operating, we should have seen recovery many months ago, as these particular dislocations have generally readjusted themselves.

Other deep-seated causes have been in action, however, chiefly the world-wide overproduction beyond even the demand of prosperous times for such important basic commodities as wheat, rubber, coffee, sugar, copper, silver, zinc, to some extent cotton, and other raw materials. The cumulative effects of demoralizing price falls of these important commodities in the process of adjustment of production to world consumption have produced financial crises in many countries and have diminished the buying power of these countries for imported goods to a degree which extended the difficulties farther afield by creating unemployment in all the industrial nations. The political agitation in Asia; revolutions in South America and political unrest in some European States; the methods of sale by Russia of her increasing agricultural exports to European markets; and our own drought—have all contributed to prolong and deepen the depression.

In the larger view the major forces of the depression now lie outside of the United States, and our recuperation has been retarded by the unwarranted degree of fear and apprehension created by these outside forces. . . .

We should remember that these occasions have been met many times before, that they are but temporary, that our country is to-day stronger and richer in resources, in equipment, in skill, than ever in its history. We are in an extraordinary degree self-sustaining, we will overcome world influences and will lead the march of prosperity as we have always done hitherto.

Economic depression can not be cured by legislative action or executive pronouncement. Economic wounds must be healed by the action of the cells of the economic body—the producers and consumers themselves. Recovery can be expedited and its effects mitigated by cooperative action. That cooperation requires that every individual should sustain faith and courage; that each should maintain his self-reliance; that each and every one should search for methods of improving his business or service; that the vast majority whose income is unimpaired should not hoard out of fear but should pursue their normal living and recreations; that each should seek to assist his neighbors who may be less fortunate; that each industry should assist its own employees; that each community and each State should assume its full responsibilities for organization of employment and relief of distress with that sturdiness and independence which built a great Nation.

Our people are responding to these impulses in remarkable degree. The best contribution of government lies in encouragement of this voluntary cooperation in the community. The Government, National, State, and local, can join with the community in such programs and do its part. A year ago I, together with other officers of the Government, initiated extensive cooperative measures throughout the country. . . .

It is my belief that after the passing of this depression, when we can examine it in retrospect, we shall need to consider a number of other questions as to what action may be taken by the Government to remove Possible governmental influences which make for instability and to better organize mitigation of the effect of depression. It is as yet too soon to constructively formulate such measures. . . .

STATE OF THE UNION ADDRESSES
1934–2002

FRANKLIN D. ROOSEVELT

FDR was arguably the most influential chief executive in modern American history. He was elected to an unprecedented four terms in office, and he successfully shepherded the nation through two terrible, traumatic events: the Great Depression and World War II. He also oversaw a significant increase in federal authority, in particular the growing scope of his office. The following excerpts from his State of the Union Addresses (he delivered twelve, by far the most of any president) capture the flavor of the man and his extraordinary times.

First Address: January 3, 1934

I COME before you at the opening of the Regular Session of the 73d Congress, not to make requests for special or detailed items of legislation; I come, rather, to counsel with you, who, like myself, have been selected to carry out a mandate of the whole people, in order that without partisanship you and I may cooperate to continue the restoration of our national wellbeing and, equally important, to build on the ruins of the past a new structure designed better to meet the present problems of modern civilization.

Such a structure includes not only the relations of industry and agriculture and finance to each other but also the effect which all of these three have on our individual citizens and on the whole people as a Nation.

Now that we are definitely in the process of recovery, lines have been rightly drawn between those to whom this recovery means a return to old methods—and the number of these people is small—and those for whom recovery means a reform of many old methods, a permanent readjustment of many of our ways of thinking and therefore of many of our social and economic arrangements. . . .

Civilization cannot go back; civilization must not stand still. We have undertaken new methods. It is our task to perfect, to improve, to alter when necessary, but in all cases to go forward. To consolidate what we are doing, to make our economic and social structure capable of dealing with modern life is the joint task of the legislative, the judicial, and the executive branches of the national Government.

Without regard to party, the overwhelming majority of our people seek a greater opportunity for humanity to prosper and find happiness. They recognize that human welfare has not increased and does not increase through mere materialism and luxury, but that it does progress through integrity, unselfishness, responsibility and justice.

In the past few months, as a result of our action, we have demanded of many citizens that they surrender certain licenses to do as they please, in their business relationships; but we have asked this in exchange for the protection which the State can give against exploitation by their fellow men or by combinations of their fellow men. . . .

I cannot, unfortunately, present to you a picture of complete optimism regarding world affairs. . . .

Fear of immediate or future aggression and with it the spending of vast sums on armament and the continued building up of defensive trade barriers prevent any great progress in peace or trade agreements. I have made it clear that the United States cannot take part in political arrangements in Europe but that we stand ready to cooperate at any time in practicable measures on a world basis looking to immediate reduction of armaments and the lowering of the barriers against commerce. . . .

I shall continue to regard it as my duty to use whatever means may be necessary to supplement State, local and private agencies for the relief of suffering caused by unemployment. With respect to this question, I have recognized the dangers inherent in the direct giving of relief and have sought the means to provide not mere relief, but the opportunity for useful and remunerative work. We shall, in the process of recovery, seek to move as rapidly as possible from direct relief to publicly supported work and from that to the rapid restoration of private employment.

It is to the eternal credit of the American people that this tremendous readjustment of our national life is being accomplished peacefully, without serious dislocation, with only a minimum of injustice and with a great, willing spirit of cooperation throughout the country.

Disorder is not an American habit. Self-help and self-control are the essence of the American tradition—not of necessity the form of that tradition, but its spirit. The program itself comes from the American people.

It is an integrated program, national in scope. Viewed in the large, it is designed to save from destruction and to keep for the future the genuinely important values created by modern society. The vicious and wasteful parts of that society we could not save if we wished; they have chosen the way of self-destruction. We would save useful mechanical invention, machine production, industrial efficiency, modern means of communication, broad education. We would save and encourage the slowly growing impulse among consumers to enter the industrial market place equipped with sufficient organization to insist upon fair prices and honest sales.

But the unnecessary expansion of industrial plants, the waste of natural resources, the exploitation of the consumers of natural monopolies, the accumulation of stagnant surpluses, child labor, and the ruthless exploitation of all labor, the encouragement of speculation with other people's money, these were consumed in the fires that they themselves kindled; we must make sure that as we reconstruct our life there be no soil in which such weeds can grow again.

We have plowed the furrow and planted the good seed; the hard beginning is over. If we would reap the full harvest, we must cultivate the soil where this good seed is sprouting and the plant is reaching up to mature growth.

A final personal word. I know that each of you will appreciate that. I am speaking no mere politeness when I assure you how much I value the fine relationship that we have shared during these months of hard and incessant work. Out of these friendly contacts we are, fortunately, building a strong and permanent tie between the legislative and executive branches of the Government. The letter of the Constitution wisely declared a separation, but the impulse of common purpose declares a union. In this spirit we join once more in serving the American people.

HARRY S. TRUMAN

Truman had big shoes to fill upon FDR's death in 1945; additionally, he faced a dangerous new cold war with the Soviet Union. This new kind of war involved an extensive arms race and a policy of containment aimed at hemming in the Communist regimes of the Soviet Union and China when they were perceived to have sponsored revolutions overseas. This included an attempted Communist takeover of Korea in 1950, to which Truman responded by deploying troops. In his fourth address Truman explained America's entry into the Korean war, and his philosophy toward Communism in general.

Fourth Address: January 8, 1951

Mr. President, Mr. Speaker, Members of the Congress: . . .

At this critical time, I am glad to say that our country is in a healthy condition. Our democratic institutions are sound and strong. We have more men and women at work than ever before. We are able to produce more than ever before—in fact, far more than any country ever produced in the history of the world. . . .

As we meet here today, American soldiers are fighting a bitter campaign in Korea. We pay tribute to their courage, devotion, and gallantry.

Our men are fighting, alongside their United Nations allies, because they know, as we do, that the aggression in Korea is part of the attempt of the Russian Communist dictatorship to take over the world, step by step.

Our men are fighting a long way from home, but they are fighting for our lives and our liberties. They are fighting to protect our right to meet here today—our right to govern ourselves as a free nation.

The threat of world conquest by Soviet Russia endangers our liberty and endangers the kind of world in which the free spirit of man can survive. This threat is aimed at all peoples who strive to win or defend their own freedom and national independence.

Indeed, the state of our Nation is in great part the state of our friends and allies throughout the world. The gun that points at them points at us, also. The threat is a total threat and the danger is a common danger.

All free nations are exposed and all are in peril. Their only security lies in banding together. No one nation can find protection in a selfish search for a safe haven from the storm.

The free nations do not have any aggressive purpose. We want only peace in the world—peace for all countries. No threat to the security of any nation is concealed in our plans and programs.

We had hoped that the Soviet Union, with its security assured by the Charter of the United Nations, would be willing to live and let live. But I am sorry to say that has not been the case.

The imperialism of the czars has been replaced by the even more ambitious, more crafty, and more menacing imperialism of the rulers of the Soviet Union.

This new imperialism has powerful military forces. It is keeping millions of men under arms. It has a large air force and a strong submarine force. It has complete control of the men and equipment of its satellites. It has kept its subject peoples and its economy in a state of perpetual mobilization.

The present rulers of the Soviet Union have shown that they are willing to use this power to destroy the free nations and win domination over the whole world.

The Soviet imperialists have two ways of going about their destructive work. They use the method of subversion and internal revolution, and they use the method of external aggression. In preparation for either of these methods of attack, they stir up class strife and disorder. They encourage sabotage. They put out poisonous propaganda. They deliberately try to prevent economic improvement.

If their efforts are successful, they foment a revolution, as they did in Czechoslovakia and China, and as they tried, unsuccessfully, to do in Greece. If their methods of subversion are blocked, and if they think they can get away with outright warfare, they resort to external aggression. This is what they did when they loosed the armies of their puppet states against the Republic of Korea, in an evil war by proxy.

We of the free world must be ready to meet both of these methods of Soviet action. We must not neglect one or the other.

The free world has power and resources to meet these two forms of aggression—resources that are far greater than those of the Soviet dictatorship. We have skilled and vigorous peoples, great industrial strength, and abundant sources of raw materials. And above all, we cherish liberty. Our common ideals are a great part of our strength. These ideals are the driving force of human progress.

The free nations believe in the dignity and the worth of man.

We believe in independence for all nations.

We believe that free and independent nations can band together into a world order based on law. We have laid the cornerstone of such a peaceful world in the United Nations.

We believe that such a world order can and should spread the benefits of modern science and industry, better health and education, more food and rising standards of living—throughout the world.

These ideals give our cause a power and vitality that Russian communism can never command.

The free nations, however, are bound together by more than ideals. They are a real community bound together also by the ties of self-interest and self-preservation. If they should fall apart, the results would be fatal to human freedom.

Our own national security is deeply involved with that of the other free nations. While they need our support, we equally need theirs. Our national safety would be gravely prejudiced if the Soviet Union were to succeed in harnessing to its war machine the resources and the manpower of the free nations on the borders of its empire.

If Western Europe were to fall to Soviet Russia, it would double the Soviet supply of coal and triple the Soviet supply of steel. If the free countries of Asia and Africa should fall to Soviet Russia, we would lose the sources of many of our most vital raw materials, including uranium, which is the basis of our atomic power. And Soviet command of the manpower of the free nations of Europe and Asia would confront us with military forces which we could never hope to equal.

In such a situation, the Soviet Union could impose its demands on the world, without resort to conflict, simply through the preponderance of its economic and military power. The Soviet Union does not have to attack the United States to secure domination of the world. It can achieve its ends by isolating us and swallowing up all our allies. Therefore, even if we were craven enough I do not believe we could be—but, I say, even if we were craven enough to abandon our ideals, it would be disastrous for us to withdraw from the community of free nations.

We are the most powerful single member of this community, and we have a special responsibility. We must take the leadership in meeting the challenge to freedom and in helping to protect the rights of independent nations.

This country has a practical, realistic program of action for meeting this challenge.

First, we shall have to extend economic assistance, where it can be effective. The best way to stop subversion by the Kremlin is to strike at the roots of social injustice and economic disorder. People who have jobs, homes, and hopes for the future will defend themselves against the underground agents of the Kremlin. Our programs of economic aid have done much to turn back Communism. . . .

Second, we shall need to continue our military assistance to countries which want to defend themselves. . . .

The principles for which we are fighting in Korea are right and just. They are the foundations of collective security and of the future of free nations. Korea is not only a country undergoing the torment of aggression; it is also a symbol. It stands for right and justice in the world against oppression and slavery. The free world must always stand for these principles—and we will stand with the free world.

As the third part of our program, we will continue to work for peaceful settlements in international disputes. We will support the United Nations and remain loyal to the great principles of international cooperation laid down in its charter.

We are willing, as we have always been, to negotiate honorable settlements with the Soviet Union. But we will not engage in appeasement.

The Soviet rulers have made it clear that we must have strength as well as right on our side. If we build our strength—and we are building it—the Soviet rulers may face the facts and lay aside their plans to take over the world.

That is what we hope will happen, and that is what we are trying to bring about. That is the only realistic road to peace.

These are the main elements of the course our Nation must follow as a member of the community of free nations. These are the things we must do to preserve our security and help create a peaceful world. But they will be successful only if we increase the strength of our own country. . . .

Let us keep our eyes on the issues and work for the things we all believe in.

Let each of us put our country ahead of our party, and ahead of our own personal interests. . . .

Peace is precious to us. It is the way of life we strive for with all the strength and wisdom we possess. But more precious than peace are freedom and justice. We will fight, if fight we must, to keep our freedom and to prevent justice from being destroyed.

These are the things that give meaning to our lives, and which we acknowledge to be greater than ourselves.

This is our cause—peace, freedom, justice. We will pursue this cause with determination and humility, asking divine guidance that in all we do we may follow the will of God.

DWIGHT D. EISENHOWER

Eisenhower inherited leadership of a nation that was at once complacent and nervous. The complacency came from a booming postwar economy that made the 1950s a decade of growth and prosperity for many Americans. The nervousness grew from ongoing concerns about Communism and the cold war, concerns that had led the United States into a difficult war in Korea and pursuit of domestic Communist enemies—real and imagined—at home.

Second Address: January 7, 1954

It is a high honor again to present to the Congress my views on the state of the Union and to recommend measures to advance the security, prosperity, and well-being of the American people.

All branches of this Government—and I venture to say both of our great parties—can support the general objective of the recommendations I make today, for that objective is the building of a stronger America. A nation whose every citizen has good reason for bold hope; where effort is rewarded and prosperity is shared; where freedom expands and peace is secure—that is what I mean by a stronger America . . ..

First of all we are deeply grateful that our sons no longer die on the distant mountains of Korea. Although they are still called from our homes to military service, they are no longer called to the field of battle. [The United States had recently concluded an agreement to keep Korea divided into a Communist northern half and a democratic southern half.]

The nation has just completed the most prosperous year in its history. The damaging effect of inflation on the wages, pensions, salaries and savings of us all has been brought under control. Taxes have begun to go down. The cost of our government has been reduced and its work proceeds with some 183,000 fewer employees; thus the discouraging trend of modern governments toward their own limitless expansion has in our case been reversed. The cost of armaments becomes less oppressive as we near our defense goals; yet we are militarily stronger every day. During the year, creation of the new Cabinet Department of Health, Education, and Welfare symbolized the government's permanent concern with the human problems of our citizens.

Segregation in the armed forces and other Federal activities is on the way out. We have also made progress toward its elimination in the District of Columbia. These are steps in the continuing effort to eliminate inter-racial difficulty. . . .

There has been in fact a great strategic change in the world during the past year. That precious intangible, the initiative, is becoming ours. Our policy, not limited to mere reaction against crises provoked by others, is free to develop along lines of our choice not only abroad, but also at home. As a major theme for American policy during the coming year, let our joint determination be to hold this new initiative and to use it. . . .

American freedom is threatened so long as the world Communist conspiracy exists in its present scope, power and hostility. More closely than ever before, American freedom is interlocked with the freedom of other people. In the unity of the free world lies our best chance to reduce the Communist threat without war. In the task of maintaining this unity and strengthening all its parts, the greatest responsibility falls naturally on those who, like ourselves, retain the most freedom and strength.

We shall, therefore, continue to advance the cause of freedom on foreign fronts.

In the Far East, we retain our vital interest in Korea. We have negotiated with the Republic of Korea a mutual security pact, which develops our security system for the Pacific and which I shall promptly submit to the Senate for its consent to ratification. We are prepared to meet any renewal of armed aggression in Korea. . . .

As we enter this new year, our military power continues to grow. This power is for our own defense and to deter aggression. We shall not be aggressors, but we and our allies have and will maintain a massive capability to strike back. . . .

From the special employment standards of the Federal government I turn now to a matter relating to American citizenship. The subversive character of the Communist Party in the United States has been clearly demonstrated in many ways, including court proceedings. We should recognize by law a fact that is plain to all thoughtful citizens—that we are dealing here with actions akin to treason—that when a citizen knowingly participates in the Communist conspiracy he no longer holds allegiance to the United States.

I recommend that Congress enact legislation to provide that a citizen of the United States who is convicted in the courts of hereafter conspiring to advocate the overthrow of this government by force or violence be treated as having, by such act, renounced his allegiance to the United States and forfeited his United States citizenship.

In addition, the Attorney General will soon appear before your Committees to present his recommendations for needed additional legal weapons with which to combat subversion in our country and to deal with the question of claimed immunity. . . .

I want to add one final word about the general purport of these many recommendations.

Our government's powers are wisely limited by the Constitution; but quite apart from those limitations, there are things which no government can do or should try to do.

A government can strive, as ours is striving, to maintain an economic system whose doors are open to enterprise and ambition—those personal qualities on which economic growth largely depends. But enterprise and ambition are qualities which no government can supply. Fortunately no American government need concern itself on this score; our people have these qualities in good measure.

A government can sincerely strive for peace, as ours is striving, and ask its people to make sacrifices for the sake of peace. But no government can place peace in the hearts of foreign rulers. It is our duty then to ourselves and to freedom itself to remain strong in all those ways—spiritual, economic, military—that will give us maximum safety against the possibility of aggressive action by others.

No government can inoculate its people against the fatal materialism that plagues our age. Happily, our people, though blessed with more material goods than any people in history, have always reserved their first allegiance to the kingdom of the spirit, which is the true source of that freedom we value above all material things.

But a government can try, as ours tries, to sense the deepest aspirations of the people, and to express them in political action at home and abroad. So long as action and aspiration humbly and earnestly seek favor in the sight of the Almighty, there is no end to America's forward road; there is no obstacle on it she will not surmount in her march toward a lasting peace in a free and prosperous world.

JOHN F. KENNEDY

Kennedy brought a reformer's spirit to the White House that had been largely absent during the previous decade, when President Eisenhower had taken a laid-back approach to presidential power, shades of the 1920s. JFK replaced Ike's genial, grandfatherly demeanor with energy and enthusiasm.

First Address: January 30, 1961

I speak today in an hour of national peril and national opportunity. Before my term has ended, we shall have to test anew whether a nation organized and governed such as ours can endure. The outcome is by no means certain. The answers are by no means clear. All of us together—this Administration, this Congress, this nation—must forge those answers. . . .

Our national household is cluttered with unfinished and neglected tasks. Our cities are being engulfed in squalor. Twelve long years after Congress declared our goal to be "a decent home and a suitable environment for every American family," we still have 25 million Americans living in substandard homes. A new housing program under a new Housing and Urban Affairs Department will be needed this year.

Our classrooms contain 2 million more children than they can properly have room for, taught by 90,000 teachers not properly qualified to teach. One third of our most promising high school graduates are financially unable to continue the development of their talents. The war babies of the 1940's, who overcrowded our schools in the 1950's, are now descending in 1960 upon our colleges—with two college students for every one, ten years from now—and our colleges are ill prepared. We lack the scientists, the engineers and the teachers our world obligations require. We have neglected oceanography, saline water conversion, and the basic research that lies at the root of all progress. Federal grants for both higher and public school education can no longer be delayed.

Medical research has achieved new wonders—but these wonders are too often beyond the reach of too many people, owing to a lack of income (particularly among the aged), a lack of hospital beds, a lack of nursing homes and a lack of doctors and dentists. Measures to provide health care for the aged under Social Security, and to increase the supply of both facilities and personnel, must be undertaken this year.

Our supply of clean water is dwindling. Organized and juvenile crimes cost the taxpayers millions of dollars each year, making it essential that we have improved enforcement and new legislative safeguards. The denial of constitutional rights to some of our fellow Americans on account of race—at the ballot box and elsewhere—disturbs the national conscience, and subjects us to the charge of world opinion that our democracy is not equal to the high promise of our heritage. Morality in private business has not been sufficiently spurred by morality in public business. . . .

But all these problems pale when placed beside those which confront us around the world. No man entering upon this office, regardless of his party, regardless of his previous service in Washington, could fail to be staggered upon learning—even in this brief 10 day period—the harsh enormity of the trials through which we must pass in the next four years. Each day the crises multiply. Each day their solution grows more difficult. Each day we draw nearer the hour of maximum danger, as weapons spread and hostile forces grow stronger. I feel I must inform the Congress that our analyses over the last ten days make it clear that—in each of the principal areas of crisis—the tide of events has been running out and time has not been our friend. . . .

Our greatest challenge is still the world that lies beyond the Cold War—but the first great obstacle is still our relations with the Soviet Union and Communist China. We must never be lulled into believing that either power has yielded its ambitions for world domination—ambitions which they forcefully restated only a short time ago. On the contrary, our task is to convince them that aggression and subversion will not be profitable routes to pursue these ends. Open and peaceful competition—for prestige, for markets, for scientific achievement, even for men's minds—is something else again. For if Freedom and Communism were to compete for man's allegiance in a world at peace, I would look to the future with ever increasing confidence.

To meet this array of challenges—to fulfill the role we cannot avoid on the world scene—we must reexamine and revise our whole arsenal of tools: military, economic and political.

One must not overshadow the other: On the Presidential Coat of Arms, the American eagle holds in his right talon the olive branch, while in his left he holds a bundle of arrows. We intend to give equal attention to both. . . .

I would like to conclude with a few remarks about the state of the Executive branch. We have found it full of honest and useful public servants—but their capacity to act decisively at the exact time action is needed has too often been muffled in the morass of committees, timidities and fictitious theories which have created a growing gap between decision and execution, between planning and reality. In a time of rapidly deteriorating situations at home and abroad, this is bad for the public service and particularly bad for the country; and we mean to make a change.

I have pledged myself and my colleagues in the cabinet to a continuous encouragement of initiative, responsibility and energy in serving the public interest. Let every public servant know, whether his post is high or low, that a man's rank and reputation in this Administration will be determined by the size of the job he does, and not by the size of his staff, his office or his budget. Let it be clear that this Administration recognizes the value of dissent and daring—that we greet healthy controversy as the hallmark of healthy change. Let the public service be a proud and lively career. And let every man and woman who works in any area of our national government, in any branch, at any level, be able to say with pride and with honor in future years: "I served the United States government in that hour of our nation's need."

For only with complete dedication by us all to the national interest can we bring our country through the troubled years that lie ahead. Our problems are critical. The tide is unfavorable. The news will be worse before it is better. And while hoping and working for the best, we should prepare ourselves now for the worst.

We cannot escape our dangers—neither must we let them drive us into panic or narrow isolation. In many areas of the world where the balance of power already rests with our adversaries, the forces of freedom are sharply divided. It is one of the ironies of our time that the techniques of a harsh and repressive system should be able to instill discipline and ardor in its servants—while the blessings of liberty have too often stood for privilege, materialism and a life of ease.

But I have a different view of liberty.

Life in 1961 will not be easy. Wishing it, predicting it, even asking for it, will not make it so. There will be further setbacks before the tide is turned. But turn it we must. The hopes of all mankind rest upon us—not simply upon those of us in this chamber, but upon the peasant in Laos, the fisherman in Nigeria, the exile from Cuba, the spirit that moves every man and Nation who shares our hopes for freedom and the future. And in the final analysis, they rest most of all upon the pride and perseverance of our fellow citizens of the great Republic.

In the words of a great President, whose birthday we honor today, closing his final State of the Union Message sixteen years ago, "We pray that we may be worthy of the unlimited opportunities that God has given us."

LYNDON B. JOHNSON

If anything, Johnson was even more dedicated to reform than his predecessor. Early in his presidency, LBJ announced the creation of his Great Society initiative, designed to end poverty in America through massive federal spending. His third State of the Union Address offered a good idea of what Johnson meant by this and the outlines of a program that he hoped would be his signature achievement in the White House. But that same address also contained words concerning the war in Vietnam, an American tragedy that would unfortunately overshadow all else in the Johnson era. In fact, one can almost feel the two major issues of LBJ's presidency—the Great Society and Vietnam—warring with one another in this speech.

Third Address: January 12, 1966

Our Nation tonight is engaged in a brutal and bitter conflict in Vietnam. Later on I want to discuss that struggle in some detail with you. It just must be the center of our concerns.

But we will not permit those who fire upon us in Vietnam to win a victory over the desires and the intentions of all the American people. This Nation is mighty enough, its society is healthy enough, its people are strong enough, to pursue our goals in the rest of the world while still building a Great Society here at home.

And that is what I have come here to ask of you tonight.

I recommend that you provide the resources to carry forward, with full vigor, the great health and education programs that you enacted into law last year.

I recommend that we prosecute with vigor and determination our war on poverty.

I recommend that you give a new and daring direction to our foreign aid program, designed to make a maximum attack on hunger and disease and ignorance in those countries that are determined to help themselves, and to help those nations that are trying to control population growth.

I recommend that you make it possible to expand trade between the United States and Eastern Europe and the Soviet Union.

I recommend to you a program to rebuild completely, on a scale never before attempted, entire central and slum areas of several of our cities in America.

I recommend that you attack the wasteful and degrading poisoning of our rivers, and, as the cornerstone of this effort, clean completely entire large river basins.

I recommend that you meet the growing menace of crime in the streets by building up law enforcement and by revitalizing the entire Federal system from prevention to probation.

I recommend that you take additional steps to insure equal justice to all of our people by effectively enforcing nondiscrimination in Federal and State jury selection, by making it a serious Federal crime to obstruct public and private efforts to secure civil rights, and by outlawing discrimination in the sale and rental of housing.

I recommend that you help me modernize and streamline the Federal Government by creating a new Cabinet level Department of Transportation and reorganizing several existing agencies. In turn, I will restructure our civil service in the top grades so that men and women can easily be assigned to jobs where they are most needed, and ability will be both required as well as rewarded.

I will ask you to make it possible for Members of the House of Representatives to work more effectively in the service of the Nation through a constitutional amendment extending the term of a Congressman to 4 years, concurrent with that of the President. . . .

Because of Vietnam we cannot do all that we should, or all that we would like to do. We will ruthlessly attack waste and inefficiency. We will make sure that every dollar is spent with the thrift and with the commonsense which recognizes how hard the taxpayer worked in order to earn it.

We will continue to meet the needs of our people by continuing to develop the Great Society. . . .

I have not come here tonight to ask for pleasant luxuries or for idle pleasures. I have come here to recommend that you, the representatives of the richest Nation on earth, you, the elected servants of a people who live in abundance unmatched on this globe, you bring the most urgent decencies of life to all of your fellow Americans.

There are men who cry out: We must sacrifice. Well, let us rather ask them: Who will they sacrifice? Are they going to sacrifice the children who seek the learning, or the sick who need medical care, or the families who dwell in squalor now brightened by the hope of home? Will they sacrifice opportunity for the distressed, the beauty of our land, the hope of our poor?

Time may require further sacrifices. And if it does, then we will make them.

But we will not heed those who wring it from the hopes of the unfortunate here in a land of plenty.

I believe that we can continue the Great Society while we fight in Vietnam. But if there are some who do not believe this, then, in the name of justice, let them call for the contribution of those who live in the fullness of our blessing, rather than try to strip it from the hands of those that are most in need.

And let no one think that the unfortunate and the oppressed of this land sit stifled and alone in their hope tonight. . . .

A great nation is one which breeds a great people. A great people flower not from wealth and power, but from a society which spurs them to the fullness of their genius. That alone is a Great Society.

Yet, slowly, painfully, on the edge of victory, has come the knowledge that shared prosperity is not enough. In the midst of abundance modern man walks oppressed by forces which menace and confine the quality of his life, and which individual abundance alone will not overcome.

We can subdue and we can master these forces—bring increased meaning to our lives—if all of us, Government and citizens, are bold enough to change old ways, daring enough to assault new dangers, and if the dream is dear enough to call forth the limitless capacities of this great people. . . .

Tonight the cup of peril is full in Vietnam. That conflict is not an isolated episode, but another great event in the policy that we have followed with strong consistency since World War II.

The touchstone of that policy is the interest of the United States—the welfare and the freedom of the people of the United States. But nations sink when they see that interest only through a narrow glass.

In a world that has grown small and dangerous, pursuit of narrow aims could bring decay and even disaster.

An America that is mighty beyond description—yet living in a hostile or despairing world—would be neither safe nor free to build a civilization to liberate the spirit of man. . . .

History is on the side of freedom and is on the side of societies shaped from the genius of each people. History does not favor a single system or belief—unless force is used to make it so.

That is why it has been necessary for us to defend this basic principle of our policy, to defend it in Berlin, in Korea, in Cuba—and tonight in Vietnam.

For tonight, as so many nights before, young Americans struggle and young Americans die in a distant land.

Tonight, as so many nights before, the American Nation is asked to sacrifice the blood of its children and the fruits of its labor for the love of its freedom.

How many times—in my lifetime and in yours—have the American people gathered, as they do now, to hear their President tell them of conflict and tell them of danger?

Each time they have answered. They have answered with all the effort that the security and the freedom of this Nation required.

And they do again tonight in Vietnam. . . .

We could leave, abandoning South Vietnam to its attackers and to certain conquest, or we could stay and fight beside the people of South Vietnam. We stayed.

And we will stay until aggression has stopped. . . .

The enemy is no longer close to victory. Time is no longer on his side. There is no cause to doubt the American commitment.

Our decision to stand firm has been matched by our desire for peace. . . .

This is the State of the Union.

But over it all—wealth, and promise, and expectation—lies our troubling awareness of American men at war tonight.

How many men who listen to me tonight have served their Nation in other wars? How very many are not here to listen?

The war in Vietnam is not like these other wars. Yet, finally, war is always the same. It is young men dying in the fullness of their promise. It is trying to kill a man that you do not even know well enough to hate.

Therefore, to know war is to know that there is still madness in this world.

Many of you share the burden of this knowledge tonight with me. But there is a difference. For finally I must be the one to order our guns to fire, against all the most inward pulls of my desire. For we have children to teach, and we have sick to be cured, and we have men to be freed. There are poor to be lifted up, and there are cities to be built, and there is a world to be helped.

Yet we do what we must.

I am hopeful, and I will try as best I can, with everything I have got, to end this battle and to return our sons to their desires.

Yet as long as others will challenge America's security and test the clearness of our beliefs with fire and steel, then we must stand or see the promise of two centuries tremble. I believe tonight that you do not want me to try that risk. And from that belief your President summons his strength for the trials that lie ahead in the days to come.

The work must be our work now. Scarred by the weaknesses of man, with whatever guidance God may offer us, we must nevertheless and alone with our mortality, strive.

RICHARD M. NIXON

Richard Nixon brought to the White House both extraordinary talent and extraordinary faults. Among the latter was his penchant for secrecy. His State of the Union Addresses reflect this fact, as he offered Congress comparatively little detailed information concerning his foreign policy initiatives in Vietnam, China, and elsewhere. On the domestic front, Nixon's messages suggest his understanding of problems that preoccupied America of the 1970s: economic inflation, intractable poverty, and other issues, along with the worry among many Americans that the federal government was steadily growing too large and unwieldy.

Fourth Address: February 2, 1973

The role of the Federal Government as we approach our third century of independence should not be to dominate any facet of American life, but rather to aid and encourage people, communities and institutions to deal with as many of the difficulties and challenges facing them as possible, and to help see to it that every American has a full and equal opportunity to realize his or her potential.

If we were to continue to expand the Federal Government at the rate of the past several decades, it soon would consume us entirely. The time has come when we must make clear choices—choices between old programs that set worthy goals but failed to reach them and new programs that provide a better way to realize those goals; and choices, too, between competing programs—all of which may be desirable in themselves but only some of which we can afford with the finite resources at our command.

Because our resources are not infinite, we also face a critical choice in 1973 between holding the line in Government spending and adopting expensive programs which will surely force up taxes and refuel inflation.

Finally, it is vital at this time that we restore a greater sense of responsibility at the State and local level, and among individual Americans. . . .

The basic state of our Union today is sound, and full of promise.

We enter 1973 economically strong, militarily secure and, most important of all, at peace after a long and trying war.

America continues to provide a better and more abundant life for more of its people than any other nation in the world. We have passed through one of the most difficult periods in our history without surrendering to despair and without dishonoring our ideals as a people.

Looking back, there is a lesson in all this for all of us. The lesson is one that we sometimes had to learn the hard way over the past few years. But we did learn it. That lesson is that even potentially destructive forces can be converted into positive forces when we know how to channel them, and when we use common sense and common decency to create a climate of mutual respect and goodwill.

By working together and harnessing the forces of nature, Americans have unlocked some of the great mysteries of the universe.

Men have walked the surface of the moon and soared to new heights of discovery.

This same spirit of discovery is helping us to conquer disease and suffering that have plagued our own planet since the dawn of time.

By working together with the leaders of other nations, we have been able to build a new hope for lasting peace—for a structure of world order in which common interest outweighs old animosities, and in which a new generation of the human family can grow up at peace in a changing world.

At home, we have learned that by working together we can create prosperity without fanning inflation; we can restore order without weakening freedom. . . .

In the field of foreign policy, we must remember that a strong America—an America whose word is believed and whose strength is respected—is essential to continued peace and understanding in the world. The peace with honor we have achieved in Vietnam has strengthened this basic American credibility. We must act in such a way in coming years that this credibility will remain intact, and with it, the world stability of which it is so indispensable a part.

At home, we must reject the mistaken notion—a notion that has dominated too much of the public dialogue for too long—that ever bigger Government is the answer to every problem.

We have learned only too well that heavy taxation and excessive Government spending are not a cure-all. In too many cases, instead of solving the problems they were aimed at, they have merely placed an ever heavier burden on the shoulders of the American taxpayer, in the form of higher taxes and a higher cost of living. At the same time they have deceived our people because many of the intended beneficiaries received far less than was promised, thus undermining public faith in the effectiveness of Government as a whole.

The time has come for us to draw the line. The time has come for the responsible leaders of both political parties to take a stand against overgrown Government and for the American taxpayer. We are not spending the Federal Government's money, we are spending the taxpayer's money, and it must be spent in a way which guarantees his money's worth and yields the fullest possible benefit to the people being helped.

The answer to many of the domestic problems we face is not higher taxes and more spending. It is less waste, more results and greater freedom for the individual American to earn a rightful place in his own community—and for States and localities to address their own needs in their own ways, in the light of their own priorities.

By giving the people and their locally elected leaders a greater voice through changes such as revenue sharing, and by saying "no" to excessive Federal spending and higher taxes, we can help achieve this goal. . . .

GERALD R. FORD

Few presidents have assumed the job under more difficult circumstances than Ford. Following in the footsteps of the Watergate scandal and President Nixon's resignation, Ford was also forced to address problems related to an increasingly stagnant economy and a growing energy shortage. In his speeches, he tried to put the best possible face on matters.

Second Address: January 19, 1976

As we begin our Bicentennial, America is still one of the youngest nations in recorded history. Long before our forefathers came to these shores, men and women had been struggling on this planet to forge a better life for themselves and their families. . . .

One peak stands highest in the ranges of human history. One example shines forth of a people uniting to produce abundance and to share the good life fairly and with freedom. One union holds out the promise of justice and opportunity for every citizen: That union is the United States of America.

We have not remade paradise on Earth. We know perfection will not be found here. But think for a minute how far we have come in 200 years.

We came from many roots, and we have many branches. Yet all Americans across the eight generations that separate us from the stirring deeds of 1776, those who know no other homeland and those who just found refuge among our shores, say in unison:

I am proud of America, and I am proud to be an American. Life will be a little better here for my children than for me. I believe this not because I am told to believe it, but because life has been better for me than it was for my father and my mother. I know it will be better for my children because my hands, my brains, my voice, and my vote can help make it happen.

It has happened here in America. It has happened to you and to me. Government exists to create and preserve conditions in which people can translate their ideas into practical reality. In the best of times, much is lost in translation. But we try. Sometimes we have tried and failed. Always we have had the best of intentions.

But in the recent past, we sometimes forgot the sound principles that guided us through most of our history. We wanted to accomplish great things and solve age-old problems. And we became overconfident of our abilities. We tried to be a policeman abroad and the indulgent parent here at home.

We thought we could transform the country through massive national programs, but often the programs did not work. Too often they only made things worse. In our rush to accomplish great deeds quickly, we trampled on sound principles of restraint and endangered the rights of individuals. We unbalanced our economic system by the huge and unprecedented growth of Federal expenditures and borrowing. And we were not totally honest with ourselves about how much these programs would cost and how we would pay for them. Finally, we shifted our emphasis from defense to domestic problems while our adversaries continued a massive buildup of arms.

The time has now come for a fundamentally different approach for a new realism that is true to the great principles upon which this Nation was founded.

We must introduce a new balance to our economy—a balance that favors not only sound, active government but also a much more vigorous, healthy economy that can create new jobs and hold down prices.

We must introduce a new balance in the relationship between the individual and the government—a balance that favors greater individual freedom and self-reliance.

We must strike a new balance in our system of federalism—a balance that favors greater responsibility and freedom for the leaders of our State and local governments.

We must introduce a new balance between the spending on domestic programs and spending on defense—a balance that ensures we will fully meet our obligation to the needy while also protecting our security in a world that is still hostile to freedom.

And in all that we do, we must be more honest with the American people, promising them no more than we can deliver and delivering all that we promise.

The genius of America has been its incredible ability to improve the lives of its citizens through a unique combination of governmental and free citizen activity.

History and experience tells us that moral progress cannot come in comfortable and in complacent times, but out of trial and out of confusion. Tom Paine aroused the troubled Americans of 1776 to stand up to the times that try men's souls because the harder the conflict, the more glorious the triumph.

Just a year ago I reported that the state of the Union was not good. Tonight, I report that the state of our Union is better—in many ways a lot better—but still not good enough.

To paraphrase Tom Paine, 1975 was not a year for summer soldiers and [sun] shine patriots. It was a year of fears and alarms and of dire forecasts—most of which never happened and won't happen.

As you recall, the year 1975 opened with rancor and with bitterness. Political misdeeds of the past had neither been forgotten nor forgiven. The longest, most divisive war in our history was winding toward an unhappy conclusion. Many feared that the end of that foreign war of men and machines meant the beginning of a domestic war of recrimination and reprisal. Friends and adversaries abroad were asking whether America had lost its nerve. Finally, our economy was ravaged by inflation—inflation that was plunging us into the [worst] recession in four decades. At the same time, Americans became increasingly alienated from big institutions. They were steadily losing confidence, not just in big government but in big business, big labor, and big education, among others. Ours was a troubled land.

And so, 1975 was a year of hard decisions, difficult compromises, and a new realism that taught us something important about America. It brought back a needed measure of common sense, steadfastness, and self-discipline.

Americans did not panic or demand instant but useless cures. In all sectors, people met their difficult problems with the restraint and with responsibility worthy of their great heritage. . . .

The worst recession since World War II turned around in April. The best cost-of-living news of the past year is that double-digit inflation of 12 percent or higher was cut almost in half. The worst—unemployment remains far too high.

Today, nearly 1,700,000 more Americans are working than at the bottom of the recession. At year's end, people were again being hired much faster than they were being laid off.

Yet, let's be honest. Many Americans have not yet felt these changes in their daily lives. They still see prices going up far too fast, and they still know the fear of unemployment.

We are also a growing nation. We need more and more jobs every year. Today's economy has produced over 85 million jobs for Americans, but we need a lot more jobs, especially for the young.

My first objective is to have sound economic growth without inflation.

We all know from recent experience what runaway inflation does to ruin every other worthy purpose. We are slowing it. We must stop it cold. . . .

Taking a longer look at America's future, there can be neither sustained growth nor more jobs unless we continue to have an assured supply of energy to run our economy. Domestic production of oil and gas is still declining. Our dependence on foreign oil at high prices is still too great, draining jobs and dollars away from our own economy at the rate of $125 per year for every American.

Last month, I signed a compromise national energy bill which enacts a part of my comprehensive energy independence program. This legislation was late, not the complete answer to energy independence, but still a start in the right direction. . . .

I see America today crossing a threshold, not just because it is our Bicentennial but because we have been tested in adversity. We have taken a new look at what we want to be and what we want our Nation to become.

I see America resurgent, certain once again that life will be better for our children than it is for us, seeking strength that cannot be counted in megatons and riches that cannot be eroded by inflation.

I see these United States of America moving forward as before toward a more perfect Union where the government serves and the people rule.

We will not make this happen simply by making speeches, good or bad, yours or mine, but by hard work and hard decisions made with courage and with common sense. . . .

JIMMY CARTER

Carter was elected to be a breath of fresh air for a nation weary of scandal in the White House. Personally honest and lacking strong ties to Washington's political culture, Carter seemed to bring to his job a blue-collar sensibility and integrity. But the problems of the 1970s shadowed his White House no less than his predecessor: economic and energy difficulties; difficult social issues; and the painful hostage crisis in Iran that threatened to swamp Carter's presidency and sap the nation's self-confidence. As with other presidents, Carter wanted an optimistic note in State of the Union Addresses.

Fourth Address: January 16, 1981

The State of the Union is sound. Our economy is recovering from a recession. A national energy plan is in place and our dependence on foreign oil is decreasing. We have been at peace for four uninterrupted years.

But, our Nation has serious problems. Inflation and unemployment are unacceptably high. The world oil market is increasingly tight. There are trouble spots throughout the world, and 53 American hostages are being held in Iran against international law and against every precept of human affairs.

However, I firmly believe that, as a result of the progress made in so many domestic and international areas over the past four years, our Nation is stronger, wealthier, more compassionate and freer than it was four years ago. I am proud of that fact. And I believe the Congress should be proud as well, for so much of what has been accomplished over the past four years has been due to the hard work, insights and cooperation of Congress. I applaud the Congress for its efforts and its achievements. . . .

During the last decade our Nation has withstood a series of economic shocks unprecedented in peacetime. The most dramatic of these has been the explosive increases of OPEC oil prices. But we have also faced world commodity shortages, natural disasters, agricultural shortages and major challenges to world peace and security. Our ability to deal with these shocks has been impaired because of a decrease in the growth of productivity and the persistence of underlying inflationary forces built up over the past 15 years.

Nevertheless, the economy has proved to be remarkably resilient. Real output has grown at an average rate of 3 percent per year since I took office, and employment has grown by 10 percent. We have added about 8 million productive private sector jobs to the economy. However, unacceptably high inflation—the most difficult economic problem I have faced—persists.

This inflation—which threatens the growth, productivity, and stability of our economy—requires that we restrain the growth of the budget to the maximum extent consistent with national security and human compassion. I have done so in my earlier budgets, and in my FY '82 budget. However, while restraint is essential to any appropriate economic policy, high inflation cannot be attributed solely to government spending. The growth in budget outlays has been more the result of economic factors than the cause of them.

We are now in the early stages of economic recovery following a short recession. Typically, a post-recessionary period has been marked by vigorous economic growth aided by anti-recessionary policy measures such as large tax cuts or big, stimulation spending programs. I have declined to recommend such actions to stimulate economic activity, because the persistent inflationary pressures that beset our economy today dictate a restrained fiscal policy. . . .

For too long prior to my Administration, many of our Nation's basic human and social needs were being ignored or handled insensitively by the Federal government. Over the last four years, we have significantly increased funding for many of the vital programs in these areas; developed new programs where needs were unaddressed; targeted Federal support to those individuals and areas most in need of our assistance; and removed barriers that have unnecessarily kept many disadvantaged citizens from obtaining aid for their most basic needs.

Our record has produced clear progress in the effort to solve some of the country's fundamental human and social problems. My Administration and the Congress, working together, have demonstrated that government must and can meet our citizens' basic human and social needs in a responsible and compassionate way. . . .

From the time I assumed office four years ago this month, I have stressed the need for this country to assert a leading role in a world undergoing the most extensive and intensive change in human history. . . .

One very immediate and pressing objective that is uppermost on our minds and those of the American people is the release of our hostages in Iran.

We have no basic quarrel with the nation, the revolution or the people of Iran. The threat to them comes not from American policy but from Soviet actions in the region. We are prepared to work with the government of Iran to develop a new and mutually beneficial relationship.

But that will not be possible so long as Iran continues to hold Americans hostages, in defiance of the world community and civilized behavior. They must be released unharmed. We have thus far pursued a measured program of peaceful diplomatic and economic steps in an attempt to resolve this issue without resorting to other remedies available to us under international law. This reflects the deep respect of our nation for the rule of law and for the safety of our people being held, and our belief that a great power bears a responsibility to use its strength in a measured and judicious manner. But our patience is not unlimited and our concern for the well-being of our fellow citizens grows each day. . . .

RONALD REAGAN

Ronald Reagan came to the White House promising to restore America's honor abroad and shrink the ballooning size of the federal government at home. His first State of the Union Address spelled out these twin goals in some detail.

First Address: January 26, 1982

It's my duty to report to you tonight on the progress that we have made in our relations with other nations, on the foundation we've carefully laid for our economic recovery, and finally, on a bold and spirited initiative that I believe can change the face of American government and make it again the servant of the people.

Seldom have the stakes been higher for America. What we do and say here will make all the difference to autoworkers in Detroit, lumberjacks in the Northwest, steelworkers in Steubenville who are in the unemployment lines; to black teenagers in Newark and Chicago; to hard-pressed farmers and small businessmen; and to millions of everyday Americans who harbor the simple wish of a safe and financially secure future for their children. To understand the state of the Union, we must look not only at where we are and where we're going but where we've been. The situation at this time last year was truly ominous.

The last decade has seen a series of recessions. There was a recession in 1970, in 1974, and again in the spring of 1980. Each time, unemployment increased and inflation soon turned up again. We coined the word "stagflation" to describe this.

Government's response to these recessions was to pump up the money supply and increase spending. In the last 6 months of 1980, as an example, the money supply increased at the fastest rate in postwar history—13 percent. Inflation remained in double digits, and government spending increased at an annual rate of 17 percent. Interest rates reached a staggering 21.5 percent. There were 8 million unemployed.

Late in 1981 we sank into the present recession, largely because continued high interest rates hurt the auto industry and construction. And there was a drop in productivity, and the already high unemployment increased.

This time, however, things are different. We have an economic program in place, completely different from the artificial quick fixes of the past. . . .

Together, we not only cut the increase in government spending nearly in half, we brought about the largest tax reductions and the most sweeping changes in our tax structure since the beginning of this century. And because we indexed future taxes to the rate of inflation, we took away government's built-in profit on inflation and its hidden incentive to grow larger at the expense of American workers.

Together, after 50 years of taking power away from the hands of the people in their States and local communities, we have started returning power and resources to them.

Together, we have cut the growth of new Federal regulations nearly in half. In 1981 there were 23,000 fewer pages in the Federal Register, which lists new regulations, than there were in 1980. By deregulating oil we've come closer to achieving energy independence and helped bring down the cost of gasoline and heating fuel.

Together, we have created an effective Federal strike force to combat waste and fraud in government. In just 6 months it has saved the taxpayers more than $2 billion, and it's only getting started. . . .

Together we've begun to restore that margin of military safety that ensures peace. Our country's uniform is being worn once again with pride.

Together we have made a New Beginning, but we have only begun. . . .

I will seek no tax increases this year, and I have no intention of retreating from our basic program of tax relief. I promise to bring the American people—to bring their tax rates down and to keep them down, to provide them incentives to rebuild our economy, to save, to invest in America's future. I will stand by my word. Tonight I'm urging the American people: Seize these new opportunities to produce, to save, to invest, and together we'll make this economy a mighty engine of freedom, hope, and prosperity again. . . .

Our foreign policy is a policy of strength, fairness, and balance. By restoring America's military credibility, by pursuing peace at the negotiating table wherever both sides are willing to sit down in good faith, and by regaining the respect of America's allies and adversaries alike, we have strengthened our country's position as a force for peace and progress in the world.

When action is called for, we're taking it. Our sanctions against the military dictatorship that has attempted to crush human rights in Poland—and against the Soviet regime behind that military dictatorship—clearly demonstrated to the world that America will not conduct "business as usual" with the forces of oppression. . . .

In the last decade, while we sought the moderation of Soviet power through a process of restraint and accommodation, the Soviets engaged in an unrelenting buildup of their military forces. The protection of our national security has required that we undertake a substantial program to enhance our military forces. . . .

We have made pledges of a new frankness in our public statements and worldwide broadcasts. In the face of a climate of falsehood and misinformation, we've promised the world a season of truth—the truth of our great civilized ideas: individual liberty, representative government, the rule of law under God. We've never needed walls or minefields or barbed wire to keep our people in. Nor do we declare martial law to keep our people from voting for the kind of government they want.

Yes, we have our problems; yes, we're in a time of recession. And it's true, there's no quick fix, as I said, to instantly end the tragic pain of unemployment. But we will end it. The process has already begun, and we'll see its effect as the year goes on.

We speak with pride and admiration of that little band of Americans who overcame insuperable odds to set this nation on course 200 years ago. But our glory didn't end with them. Americans ever since have emulated their deeds. . . .

GEORGE BUSH SR.

War with Saddam Hussein's Iraq and the end of the Soviet Union were the defining events of George Bush Sr.'s presidency. In his third State of the Union Address, he explained the reasons behind his commitment of American forces to the Persian Gulf and his administration's elation at the turn of events in Russia.

Third Address: January 29, 1991

I come to this House of the people to speak to you and all Americans, certain that we stand at a defining hour. Halfway around the world, we are engaged in a great struggle in the skies and on the seas and sands. We know why we're there: We are Americans, part of something larger than ourselves. For two centuries, we've done the hard work of freedom. And tonight, we lead the world in facing down a threat to decency and humanity.

What is at stake is more than one small country; it is a big idea: a new world order, where diverse nations are drawn together in common cause to achieve the universal aspirations of mankind—peace and security, freedom, and the rule of law. Such is a world worthy of our struggle and worthy of our children's future.

The community of nations has resolutely gathered to condemn and repel lawless aggression. Saddam Hussein's unprovoked invasion—his ruthless, systematic rape of a peaceful neighbor—violated everything the community of nations holds dear. The world has said this aggression would not stand, and it will not stand. Together, we have resisted the trap of appeasement, cynicism, and isolation that gives temptation to tyrants. The world has answered Saddam's invasion with 12 United Nations resolutions, starting with a demand for Iraq's immediate and unconditional withdrawal, and backed up by forces from 28 countries of 6 continents. With few exceptions, the world now stands as one. . . .

The end of the cold war has been a victory for all humanity. A year and a half ago, in Germany, I said that our goal was a Europe whole and free. Tonight, Germany is united. Europe has become whole and free, and America's leadership was instrumental in making it possible. . . .

We will watch carefully as the situation develops. And we will maintain our contact with the Soviet leadership to encourage continued commitment to democratization and reform. If it is possible, I want to continue to build a lasting basis for U.S.-Soviet cooperation—for a more peaceful future for all mankind.

The triumph of democratic ideas in Eastern Europe and Latin America and the continuing struggle for freedom elsewhere all around the world all confirm the wisdom of our nation's founders. Tonight, we work to achieve another victory, a victory over tyranny and savage aggression.

We in this Union enter the last decade of the 20th century thankful for our blessings, steadfast in our purpose, aware of our difficulties, and responsive to our duties at home and around the world. For two centuries, America has served the world as an inspiring example of freedom and democracy. For generations, America has led the struggle to preserve and extend the blessings of liberty. And today, in a rapidly changing world, American leadership is indispensable. Americans know that leadership brings burdens and sacrifices. But we also know why the hopes of humanity turn to us. We are Americans; we have a unique responsibility to do the hard work of freedom. And when we do, freedom works.

The conviction and courage we see in the Persian Gulf today is simply the American character in action. The indomitable spirit that is contributing to this victory for world peace and justice is the same spirit that gives us the power and the potential to meet our toughest challenges at home. We are resolute and resourceful. If we can selflessly confront the evil for the sake of good in a land so far away, then surely we can make this land all that it should be. If anyone tells you that America's best days are behind her, they're looking the wrong way. . . .

The war in the Gulf is not a war we wanted. We worked hard to avoid war. For more than 5 months we . . . all worked for a solution. But time and again, Saddam Hussein flatly rejected the path of diplomacy and peace. . . .

Tonight I am pleased to report that we are on course. Iraq's capacity to sustain war is being destroyed. Our investment, our training, our planning—all are paying off. Time will not be Saddam's salvation. . . .

Let me make clear what I mean by the region's stability and security. We do not seek the destruction of Iraq, its culture, or its people. Rather, we seek an Iraq that uses its great resources not to destroy, not to serve the ambitions of a tyrant, but to build a better life for itself and its neighbors. We seek a Persian Gulf where conflict is no longer the rule, where the strong are neither tempted nor able to intimidate the weak.

Most Americans know instinctively why we are in the Gulf. They know we had to stop Saddam now, not later. They know that this brutal dictator will do anything, will use any weapon, will commit any outrage, no matter how many innocents suffer.

They know we must make sure that control of the world's oil resources does not fall into his hands, only to finance further aggression. They know that we need to build a new, enduring peace, based not on arms races and confrontation but on shared principles and the rule of law.

And we all realize that our responsibility to be the catalyst for peace in the region does not end with the successful conclusion of this war.

Democracy brings the undeniable value of thoughtful dissent, and we've heard some dissenting voices here at home—some, a handful, reckless; most responsible. But the fact that all voices have the right to speak out is one of the reasons we've been united in purpose and principle for 200 years. . . .

We will succeed in the Gulf. And when we do, the world community will have sent an enduring warning to any dictator or despot, present or future, who contemplates outlaw aggression.

The world can, therefore, seize this opportunity to fulfill the long-held promise of a new world order, where brutality will go unrewarded and aggression will meet collective resistance.

Yes, the United States bears a major share of leadership in this effort. Among the nations of the world, only the United States of America has both the moral standing and the means to back it up. We're the only nation on this Earth that could assemble the forces of peace. This is the burden of leadership and the strength that has made America the beacon of freedom in a searching world.

This nation has never found glory in war. Our people have never wanted to abandon the blessings of home and work for distant lands and deadly conflict. If we fight in anger, it is only because we have to fight at all. And all of us yearn for a world where we will never have to fight again.

Each of us will measure within ourselves the value of this great struggle. Any cost in lives—any cost—is beyond our power to measure. But the cost of closing our eyes to aggression is beyond mankind's power to imagine. This we do know: Our cause is just; our cause is moral; our cause is right.

Let future generations understand the burden and the blessings of freedom. Let them say we stood where duty required us to stand. Let them know that, together, we affirmed America and the world as a community of conscience.

The winds of change are with us now. The forces of freedom are together, united. We move toward the next century more confident than ever that we have the will at home and abroad to do what must be done—the hard work of freedom. . . .

WILLIAM JEFFERSON "BILL" CLINTON

Where George Bush's primary consideration was foreign policy, Clinton wanted to focus on domestic issues: health care, social security and welfare reform, budget deficit reduction, and so on. His relations with a Republican-controlled Congress in these endeavors were often contentious, particularly following the scandals that plagued his administration and Congress's aggressive investigation of the president's behavior. His State of the Union Address in 1999—his seventh—was a long list of domestic initiatives, coupled with calls for bipartisan cooperation.

Seventh Address: January 19, 1999

Mr. Speaker, at your swearing-in, you asked us all to work together in a spirit of civility and bipartisanship. Mr. Speaker, let's do exactly that . . .

Now, America is working again. The promise of our future is limitless. But we cannot realize that promise if we allow the hum of our prosperity to lull us into complacency. How we fare as a nation far into the 21st century depends upon what we do as a nation today. So with our budget surplus growing, our economy expanding, our confidence rising, now is the moment for this generation to meet our historic responsibility to the 21st century.

Our fiscal discipline gives us an unsurpassed opportunity to address a remarkable new challenge, the aging of America. With the number of elderly Americans set to double by 2030, the baby boom will become a senior boom. So first, and above all, we must save Social Security for the 21st century. . . .

We should put Social Security on a sound footing for the next 75 years. We should reduce poverty among elderly women, who are nearly twice as likely to be poor as our other seniors. And we should eliminate the limits on what seniors on Social Security can earn.

Now, these changes will require difficult but fully achievable choices over and above the dedication of the surplus. They must be made on a bipartisan basis. They should be made this year. So let me say to you tonight, I reach out my hand to all of you in both Houses, in both parties, and ask that we join together in saying to the American people: We will save Social Security now.

Now, last year we wisely reserved all of the surplus until we knew what it would take to save Social Security. Again, I say, we shouldn't spend any of it, not any of it, until after Social Security is truly saved. First things first. . . .

We must be willing to work in a bipartisan way and look at new ideas, including the upcoming report of the bipartisan Medicare Commission. If we work together, we can secure Medicare for the next two decades and cover the greatest growing need of seniors, affordable prescription drugs. . . .

Today we can say something we couldn't say 6 years ago: With tax credits and more affordable student loans, with more work-study grants and more Pell grants, with education IRA's and the new HOPE scholarship tax cut that more than 5 million Americans will receive this year, we have finally opened the doors of college to all Americans. . . .

Last fall, you passed our proposal to start hiring 100,000 new teachers to reduce class size in the early grades. Now I ask you to finish the job. . . .

If we do these things—end social promotion; turn around failing schools; build modern ones; support qualified teachers; promote innovation, competition and discipline—then we will begin to meet our generation's historic responsibility to create 21st century schools. . . .

America's families deserve the world's best medical care. Thanks to bipartisan Federal support for medical research, we are now on the verge of new treatments to prevent or delay diseases from Parkinson's to Alzheimer's, to arthritis to cancer. But as we continue our advances in medical science, we can't let our medical system lag behind. Managed care has literally transformed medicine in America, driving down costs but threatening to drive down quality as well.

I think we ought to say to every American: You should have the right to know all your medical options, not just the cheapest. If you need a specialist, you should have a right to see one. You have a right to the nearest emergency care if you're in an accident. These are things that we ought to say. And I think we ought to say: You should have a right to keep your doctor during a period of treatment, whether it's a pregnancy or a chemotherapy treatment, or anything else. I believe this. . . .

Today, America is the most dynamic, competitive, job-creating economy in history. But we can do even better in building a 21st century economy that embraces all Americans.

Today's income gap is largely a skills gap. Last year, the Congress passed a law enabling workers to get a skills grant to choose the training they need. And I applaud all of you here who were part of that. This year, I recommend a 5-year commitment to the new system so that we can provide, over the next 5 years, appropriate training opportunities for all Americans who lose their jobs and expand rapid response teams to help all towns which have been really hurt when businesses close. I hope you will support this. . . .

You know, no nation in history has had the opportunity and the responsibility we now have to shape a world that is more peaceful, more secure, more free. All Americans can be proud that our leadership helped to bring peace in Northern Ireland. All Americans can be proud that our leadership has put Bosnia on the path to peace. And with our NATO allies, we are pressing the Serbian Government to stop its brutal repression in Kosovo, to bring those responsible to justice, and to give the people of Kosovo the self-government they deserve. . . .

As we work for peace, we must also meet threats to our Nation's security, including increased dangers from outlaw nations and terrorism. We will defend our security wherever we are threatened, as we did this summer when we struck at Usama bin Ladin's network of terror. The bombing of our Embassies in Kenya and Tanzania reminds us again of the risks faced every day by those who represent America to the world. So let's give them the support they need, the safest possible workplaces, and the resources they must have so America can continue to lead.

We must work to keep terrorists from disrupting computer networks. We must work to prepare local communities for biological and chemical [emergencies], to support research into vaccines and treatments. . . .

Six years ago, I came to office in a time of doubt for America, with our economy troubled, our deficit high, our people divided. Some even wondered whether our best days were behind us. But across this country, in a thousand neighborhoods, I have seen, even amidst the pain and uncertainty of recession, the real heart and character of America. I knew then that we Americans could renew this country.

Tonight, as I deliver the last State of the Union Address of the 20th century, no one anywhere in the world can doubt the enduring resolve and boundless capacity of the American people to work toward that "more perfect Union" of our Founders' dream.

We're now at the end of a century when generation after generation of Americans answered the call to greatness, overcoming depression, lifting up the disposed, bringing down barriers to racial prejudice, building the largest middle class in history, winning two World Wars and the long twilight struggle of the cold war. We must all be profoundly grateful for the magnificent achievement of our forebears in this century. Yet, perhaps, in the daily press of events, in the clash of controversy, we don't see our own time for what it truly is, a new dawn for America. . . .

GEORGE BUSH JR.

In Clinton's seventh State of the Union Address (see above), he inserted a brief warning concerning the dangers of international terrorism and the threat posed by a then-obscure Islamic extremist named Osama bin Laden. Two years later that threat became palpably evident with the attack on the World Trade Center. Fighting terrorism became the centerpiece of George Bush Jr.'s presidency, as his second State of the Union Address shows. In this speech he coined the famous phrase "axis of evil" to describe nations that sponsored terrorism, and he laid out a post 9/11 theory of just warfare.

Second Address: January 29, 2002

Thank you very much. Mr. Speaker, Vice President Cheney, Members of Congress, distinguished guests, fellow citizens: As we gather tonight, our Nation is at war; our economy is in recession; and the civilized world faces unprecedented dangers. Yet, the state of our Union has never been stronger.

We last met in an hour of shock and suffering. In 4 short months, our Nation has comforted the victims, begun to rebuild New York and the Pentagon, rallied a great coalition, captured, arrested, and rid the world of thousands of terrorists, destroyed Afghanistan's terrorist training camps, saved a people from starvation, and freed a country from brutal oppression.

The American flag flies again over our Embassy in Kabul. Terrorists who once occupied Afghanistan now occupy cells at Guantanamo Bay. And terrorist leaders who urged followers to sacrifice their lives are running for their own.

America and Afghanistan are now allies against terror. We'll be partners in rebuilding that country. . . .

Our progress is a tribute to the spirit of the Afghan people, to the resolve of our coalition, and to the might of the United States military. When I called our troops into action, I did so with complete confidence in their courage and skill. And tonight, thanks to them, we are winning the war on terror. The men and women of our Armed Forces have delivered a message now clear to every enemy of the United States: Even 7,000 miles away, across oceans and continents, on mountaintops and in caves, you will not escape the justice of this Nation.

For many Americans, these 4 months have brought sorrow and pain that will never completely go away. . . .

Our cause is just, and it continues. Our discoveries in Afghanistan confirmed our worst fears and showed us the true scope of the task ahead. We have seen the depth of our enemies' hatred in videos where they laugh about the loss of innocent life. And the depth of their hatred is equaled by the madness of the destruction they design. . . .

Thanks to the work of our law enforcement officials and coalition partners, hundreds of terrorists have been arrested. Yet, tens of thousands of trained terrorists are still at large. These enemies view the entire world as a battlefield, and we must pursue them wherever they are. So long as training camps operate, so long as nations harbor terrorists, freedom is at risk. And America and our allies must not and will not allow it.

Our Nation will continue to be steadfast and patient and persistent in the pursuit of two great objectives. First, we will shut down terrorist camps, disrupt terrorist plans, and bring terrorists to justice. And second, we must prevent the terrorists and regimes who seek chemical, biological, or nuclear weapons from threatening the United States and the world. . . .

My hope is that all nations will heed our call and eliminate the terrorist parasites who threaten their countries and our own. . . . And make no mistake about it: If they do not act, America will.

States like these [Iran, Iraq, and North Korea] and their terrorist allies constitute an axis of evil, arming to threaten the peace of the world. By seeking weapons of mass destruction, these regimes pose a grave and growing danger. They could provide these arms to terrorists, giving them the means to match their hatred. They could attack our allies or attempt to blackmail the United States. In any of these cases, the price of indifference would be catastrophic.

We will work closely with our coalition to deny terrorists and their state sponsors the materials, technology, and expertise to make and deliver weapons of mass destruction. We will develop and deploy effective missile defenses to protect America and our allies from sudden attack. And all nations should know: America will do what is necessary to ensure our Nation's security.

We'll be deliberate; yet, time is not on our side. I will not wait on events while dangers gather. I will not stand by as peril draws closer and closer. The United States of America will not permit the world's most dangerous regimes to threaten us with the world's most destructive weapons.

Our war on terror is well begun, but it is only begun. This campaign may not be finished on our watch; yet, it must be and it will be waged on our watch. We can't stop short. If we stop now, leaving terror camps intact and terrorist states unchecked, our sense of security would be false and temporary. History has called America and our allies to action, and it is both our responsibility and our privilege to fight freedom's fight.

Our first priority must always be the security of our Nation, and that will be reflected in the budget I send to Congress. My budget supports three great goals for America: We will win this war; we will protect our homeland; and we will revive our economy.

September the 11th brought out the best in America and the best in this Congress. And I join the American people in applauding your unity and resolve. Now Americans deserve to have this same spirit directed toward addressing problems here at home. I'm a proud member of my party. Yet as we act to win the war, protect our people, and create jobs in America, we must act, first and foremost, not as Republicans, not as Democrats but as Americans. . . .

None of us would ever wish the evil that was done on September the 11th. Yet, after America was attacked, it was as if our entire country looked into a mirror and saw our better selves. We were reminded that we are citizens with obligations to each other, to our country, and to history. We began to think less of the goods we can accumulate and more about the good we can do.

For too long our culture has said, "If it feels good, do it." Now America is embracing a new ethic and a new creed, "Let's roll." In the sacrifice of soldiers, the fierce brotherhood of firefighters, and the bravery and generosity of ordinary citizens, we have glimpsed what a new culture of responsibility could look like. We want to be a nation that serves goals larger than self. We've been offered a unique opportunity, and we must not let this moment pass. . . .

No nation owns these aspirations, and no nation is exempt from them. We have no intention of imposing our culture. But America will always stand firm for the nonnegotiable demands of human dignity: the rule of law; limits on the power of the state; respect for women; private property; free speech; equal justice; and religious tolerance.

America will take the side of brave men and women who advocate these values around the world, including the Islamic world, because we have a greater objective than eliminating threats and containing resentment. We seek a just and peaceful world beyond the war on terror. . . .

In a single instant, we realized that this will be a decisive decade in the history of liberty, that we've been called to a unique role in human events. Rarely has the world faced a choice more clear or consequential.

Our enemies send other people's children on missions of suicide and murder. They embrace tyranny and death as a cause and a creed. We stand for a different choice, made long ago on the day of our founding. We affirm it again today. We choose freedom and the dignity of every life.

Steadfast in our purpose, we now press on. We have known freedom's price. We have shown freedom's power. And in this great conflict, my fellow Americans, we will see freedom's victory. . . .

ANNOTATED BIBLIOGRAPHY

Please note that this is a selective discussion of the more noteworthy and important books that have been written about the American presidency. I have focused on general historical studies that may introduce the reader to these men and their times. I have also focused primarily on works of history rather on than the large literature on the theory and political science of the executive branch. I have chosen not to include the almost innumerable tangential studies that are related to presidents and their lives without focusing on the men and the office itself—works addressing George Washington's generalship, for example. There are many worthy studies that fall within this category, but their inclusion would make this bibliography of sources impossibly large and unwieldy.

GENERAL SOURCES

Perhaps surprisingly, there are remarkably few modern studies that cover the entire breadth of the presidency's two-hundred-plus-year history. Leonard Levy and Louis Fisher edited an exhaustive four-volume reference work, *The Encyclopedia of the American Presidency* (New York: Simon and Schuster, 1994). Forrest McDonald, *The American Presidency: An Intellectual History* (Lawrence: University Press of Kansas, 1994), addresses the office from the Founding era through the late twentieth century; it is, however, heavily weighted toward discussion of the Constitution and the Founding Fathers.

There are a number of good one-volume studies covering broad areas of presidential history. Lewis J. Gould's *The Modern American Presidency* (Lawrence: University Press of Kansas, 2003) addresses the office from McKinley through Clinton. At the other end of the chronological spectrum, Ralph Ketchum, *Presidents above Party: The First American Presidency, 1789–1829* (Chapel Hill: University of North Carolina Press, 1987), addresses the presidents of the Founding era. It offers a particularly thorough overview of the presidency's intellectual roots in Western thought. Richard Neustadt, *Presidential Power and the Modern Presidents: The Politics of Leadership from Roosevelt to Reagan*, 4th ed. (New York: Free Press, 1991), is an oft-reprinted classic that addresses the relationship between the White House and democratic politics during the modern era. So does Stephen Skowronek, *The Politics Presidents Make: Leadership from John Adams to Bill Clinton*, 2nd ed. (New York: Belknap Press, 1997). Leadership and greatness is likewise the organizing theme for Marc K. Landis's *Presidential Greatness* (Lawrence: University Press of Kansas, 2000). The reader may or may not find Landis' arguments about greatness (and the recent lack thereof in the White House) convincing, but it is an intriguing book, with interesting chapters on Washington, Jefferson, Lincoln, and FDR in particular.

There are also many useful thematic studies focusing on the history of specific aspects of the office. Thomas Cronin, ed., *Inventing the American Presidency* (Lawrence: University Press of Kansas, 1989), offers essays from leading scholars that mix history with theory in addressing the roots of presidential powers in war making, vetoes, pardons, and so on. Donald Young, *American Roulette: The History and Dilemma of the Vice Presidency* (New York: Holt, Rinehart and Winston, 1972), is a bit dated, but nevertheless is an essential guide to the history of the often-overlooked vice-presidential component of the executive branch. Fred I. Greenstein, *The Presidential Difference: Leadership Style from FDR to George W. Bush*, 2nd ed. (Princeton, NJ: Princeton University Press, 2004), is particularly useful in studying the effect of mass media on the presidency's modern development. So is Jeffrey K. Tullis, *The Rhetorical Presidency*, 2nd ed. (Princeton, NJ: Princeton University Press, 1988), which is heavily theoretical but also does a good job of addressing historical issues from Theodore Roosevelt through Ronald Reagan.

The University Press of Kansas's American Presidency Series deserves special mention here. Kansas is perhaps the leading scholarly press on the presidency. In addition to numerous fine general works, the press has created an outstanding series that focuses upon each individual president. The series includes well-written, manageable, one-volume studies written by leading scholars in their respective time periods and fields. I have referenced these volumes in the sections devoted to individual presidents (see below), but the reader should be aware that the series, as a body of work itself, represents the best historical writing we currently have on the presidency.

The Internet offers a number of valuable resources on the presidency's history. The Web site www.whitehouse.gov has nice thumbnail biographies of the presidents and is a good resource for quick facts and basic information on individual White House occupants. The American Presidency Project's Web site, www.presidency.ucsb.edu, is a treasure trove of presidential data, including State of the Union Addresses, Inaugural Addresses, election data, executive orders, and a variety of miscellaneous documents. The Avalon Project at www.yale.edu/lawweb/avalon/avalon.htm is perhaps the best place for any primary source documents related to American history and hosts many sources on the presidency from George Washington to the present day.

GEORGE WASHINGTON

Forrest McDonald's contribution to the American Presidency Series, *George Washington* (Lawrence: University Press of Kansas, 1974), is a fine, brief study of Washington's presidential years. Readers interested in studying Washington's entire life and career would do well to consult James Flexner's older *George Washington* (Boston: Little, Brown, 1965). Douglas Southall Freeman's much more extensive seven-volume *George Washington* (New York: Austin M. Kelley, 1949–1957) is a Pulitzer Prize–winning classic of American historical literature. Joseph J. Ellis's recent study, *His Excellency, George Washington* (New York: Knopf, 2004), updates these classics in Ellis's readable style. Richard Brookhiser offers an interesting interpretive study of Washington as the nation's preeminent political and cultural father figure in *Founding Father* (New York: Free Press, 1996). The Library of America Series includes an excellent edited sampling of Washington's papers, *George Washington: Writings* (New York: Library of America, 1997), edited by John Rhodehamel.

THE FOUNDING ERA PRESIDENTS: JOHN ADAMS THROUGH JOHN QUINCY ADAMS

While John Adams has inspired a number of talented scholars and writers to address his remarkable life, there are still relatively few that focus on his years as president. Mary W. M. Hargreaves, *The Presidency of John Adams* (Lawrence: University Press of Kansas, 1985), is just about the only readily available work that places his presidency at the center of its narrative. David McCullough's popular and enjoyable *John Adams* (New York: Simon and Schuster, 2001) is a nice general biography. Joseph J. Ellis's *Passionate Sage: The Character and Legacy of John Adams* (New York: W.W. Norton, 1993) is a creative interpretation of Adams's entire career and includes several cogently written and argued chapters on Adams as the nation's chief executive.

Thomas Jefferson's career is of course the subject of an expansive and ever-expanding historical literature. Forrest McDonald brought his expertise in the Founding era to Jefferson's presidential years in *The Presidency of Thomas Jefferson* (Lawrence: University Press of Kansas, 1976). Joseph J. Ellis wrote the standard modern biography in *American Sphinx: The Character of Thomas Jefferson* (New York: Vintage, 1998). R. B. Burnstein, *Thomas Jefferson* (New York: Oxford University Press, 2003), is likewise a good single-volume work, with particularly keen insight into Jefferson's psychology and character. James F. Simon, *What Kind of Nation: Thomas Jefferson, John Marshall, and the Epic Struggle to Create a United States* (New York: Simon and Schuster, 2003), examines the debates over federal authority that dominated early thinking about the presidency and the new American government in general. The Library of America's edited edition of Jefferson's writings, Merrill D. Peterson, ed., *Thomas Jefferson: Writings* (New York: Library of America, 1984), is a wonderful sampling of Jefferson's thought.

As with Adams, James Madison's brilliant career in other arenas of American life has generally attracted more attention than his presidency. Jack Rakove's biography, *James Madison and the Creation of the American Republic* (New York: Longman, 2001), is useful, as is Drew McCoy's *The Last of the Fathers: James Madison and the Republican Legacy* (New York: Cambridge University Press, 1991). Robert Rutland produced a serviceable installment on Madison for the American Presidency Series in *The Presidency of James Madison* (Lawrence: University Press of Kansas, 1990).

James Monroe's presidency is a relatively neglected topic. The best study available is Noble E. Cunningham's *The Presidency of James Monroe* (Lawrence: University Press of Kansas, 1996). Harry Ammon's *James Monroe: The Quest for National Identity* (Charlottesville: University of Virginia Press, 1990) is strong on foreign policy issues.

John Quincy Adams has attracted much scholarly attention as a result not only of his presidency, but also his career as a U.S. representative and his life as a member of one of America's most famous families. Paul C. Nagel, *John Quincy Adams: A Public Life, a Private Life* (New York: Alfred A. Knopf, 1997), is a fine general biography with a useful overview of his presidency. Mary W. M. Hargreaves, *The Presidency of John Quincy Adams* (Lawrence: University Press of Kansas, 1985), is a serviceable study.

THE JACKSONIAN-ERA PRESIDENTS: JACKSON THROUGH POLK

Andrew Jackson's colorful career has attracted a great deal of attention from scholars. Robert V. Remini made Jackson his lifelong subject and produced a classic multi-volume biography; Jackson's presidency is exhaustively covered in the last two volumes: *Andrew Jackson and the Course of American Empire* (New York: Harper and Row, 1977) and *Andrew Jackson and the Course of American Democracy, 1833–1845* (New York: Harper and Row, 1984). Remini's single-volume biography of Jackson, *Andrew Jackson* (New York: Twayne, 1966), is also quite useful. Donald Cole wrote the Andrew Jackson installment in the American Presidency Series, *The Presidency of Andrew Jackson* (Lawrence: University Press of Kansas, 1993), which updates Remini's earlier work and is a bit more critical of Jackson's policies. Also of more recent vintage is John F. Marszalek's readable overview of the Margaret Eaton scandal in the Jackson administration, *The Petticoat Affair: Manners, Mutiny, and Sex in Andrew Jackson's White House* (Baton Rouge: Louisiana State University Press, 1997). Anthony F. C. Wallace and Eric Foner penned a useful overview of Jackson's Indian policies in *The Long, Bitter Trail: Andrew Jackson and the Indians* (New York: Hill and Wang, 1993).

Remini likewise has produced a very good study of Jackson's successor, Martin Van Buren, that focuses particularly on his impact on the party system; see *Martin Van Buren and the Making of the Democratic Party* (New York: Columbia University Press, 1959). Joel Silby likewise focuses on the Little Magician's political acumen in *Martin Van Buren and the Emergence of American Popular Politics* (Boston: Rowman and Littlefield, 2002). Major L. Wilson's *The Presidency of Martin Van Buren* (Lawrence: University Press of Kansas, 1984) is a solid addition to the American Presidency Series.

William Henry Harrison's election ("Tippecanoe and Tyler, Too") was widely seen as a watershed in American popular politics. Freeman Cleaves chronicled this, along with Harrison's colorful military career, in his *Old Tippecanoe: William Henry Harrison and His Time* (Newtown, CT: American Political Biography Series, 1990). Norma Louise Peterson understandably combined Harrison's and Tyler's presidencies for the American Presidency Series in her *The Presidencies of William Henry Harrison and John Tyler* (Lawrence: University Press of Kansas, 1989). *John Tyler: Champion of the Old South* (New York: American Political Biography Series, 1990), by Oliver P. Chitwood, emphasizes Tyler's actions—particularly the annexation of Texas—as seminal to the simmering sectional crisis of the 1840s.

James K. Polk has attracted attention in recent years, and not always for positive reasons. He is seen by many modern scholars as a defender of slavery and slaveholding interests, an argument proffered most forcefully in William Dusinberre, *Slavemaster President: The Double Career of James Polk* (New York: Oxford University Press, 2003). Sam W. Haynes offers a similar but more balanced approach in his *James Polk and the Expansionist Impulse* (New York: Longman, 2005). Paul Bergeron's *The Presidency of James K. Polk* (Lawrence: University Press of Kansas, 1987) is likewise a balanced treatment of Polk's policies.

THE SECTIONAL ERA: TAYLOR THROUGH BUCHANAN

The literature on Zachary Taylor's presidency is quite sparse, reflecting both his brief tenure in the White House and the fact that there is little available primary source material. K. Jack Bauer wrote a serviceable biography for the Southern Biography Series, *Zachary Taylor: Soldier, Planter, Statesman of the Old Southwest* (Baton Rouge: Louisiana State University Press, 1985), that does much with Taylor's military career but (understandably) little with his politics. Elbert B. Smith is a bit more thorough in his combined study of Taylor and Fillmore for the American Presidency Series, *The Presidencies of Zachary Taylor and Millard Fillmore* (Lawrence: University Press of Kansas, 1988). On Fillmore, Smith's book is quite useful; one would also do well to consult Robert J. Scarry's more recent biography, *Millard Fillmore* (New York: MacFarland and Co., 2001).

Pierce and Buchanan have received remarkably little attention, given the fact that they occupied the White House during some of the most tumultuous years in American history. There are of course the ubiquitous and typically solid entries in the American Presidency Series, Larry Gara's *The Presidency of Franklin Pierce* (Lawrence: University Press of Kansas, 1991), and Jean H. Baker's *The Presidency of James Buchanan* (Lawrence: University Press of Kansas, 2004). Philip S. Klein's older *President James Buchanan: A Biography* (University Park: Pennsylvania State University Press, 1962) is also useful.

ABRAHAM LINCOLN

Where to start? The historical literature on America's sixteenth president is vast, rich, and still growing. For a basic biography, David Donald's *Lincoln* (New York: Simon and Schuster, 1995) is thorough and magnificently written. Stephen B. Oates's *With Malice toward None: The Life of Abraham Lincoln* (New York: Harper and Row, 1977), is a fine older work. William Gienapp penned a briefer but excellent biography, *Abraham Lincoln and Civil War America* (New York: Oxford University Press, 2002).

On Lincoln's presidency in general, Philip S. Paludan wrote a fine overview in *The Presidency of Abraham Lincoln* (Lawrence: University Press of Kansas, 1994); this book is a logical starting point for any investigation of Lincoln's political and constitutional policies. Doris Kearns Goodwin's very popular and readable *Team of Rivals: The Political Genius of Abraham Lincoln* (New York: Simon and Schuster, 2005) is an excellent investigation of the various personalities within the Lincoln Administration. While Richard Carwardine's *Lincoln: A Life of Purpose and Power* (New York: Alfred Knopf, 2006) is a general biography, its author devotes much of his attention to the presidential years. So does Allan Guelzo's *Abraham Lincoln: Redeemer President* (Grand Rapids, MI: W.B. Eerdman's, 1999). Both Carwardine and Guelzo are especially strong on the influence of religion on Lincoln's life and policies.

Specific facets of the Lincoln presidency have been the focus of much scholarly literature. Emancipation receives the best recent treatment in Allan Guelzo's *Lincoln's Emancipation Proclamation: The End of Slavery in America* (New York: Simon and Schuster, 2004), though LaWanda Cox's *Lincoln and Black Freedom: A Study in Presidential Leadership*, 2nd ed. (Columbia: University of South Carolina Press, 1994), is still valuable. William C. Davis, *Lincoln's Men: How President Lincoln Became Father to an Army and a Nation* (New York: Free Press, 1999), details Lincoln's relationship with ordinary Union soldiers. T. Harry Williams's older *Lincoln and His Generals* (New York: Alfred A. Knopf, 1952) is still the standard study of his relationship with his commanding officers. Mark Neely's *The Fate of Liberty: Abraham Lincoln and Civil Liberties* (New York: Oxford University Press, 1991) is an excellent examination of the administration's record on wartime dissent. Jean H. Baker's *Mary Todd Lincoln: A Biography* (New York: W.W. Norton, 1987) is the standard biography of the First Lady. Edward Steers's *Blood on the Moon: The Assassination of Abraham Lincoln* (Lexington: University Press of Kentucky, 2001) is the best modern treatment of that oft-studied subject.

There are almost innumerable anthologies of Lincoln's speeches and letters. The Library of America's two-volume collection, *Lincoln: Speeches and Writings* (New York: Library of America, 1989), is a wonderful resource. All such collections start with Roy P. Basler's seminal *Collected Works of Abraham Lincoln*, 9 vols. (New Brunswick, NJ: Rutgers University Press, 1953–1955). Harold Holzer, ed., *Dear Mr. Lincoln: Letters to the President* (Carbondale: Southern Illinois University Press, 2006), is an entertaining sampling of the thousands of letters Lincoln received. Deep studies of famous Lincoln speeches have become fashionable, beginning with Garry Wills's highly regarded *Lincoln at Gettysburg: The Words that Remade America* (New York: Simon and Schuster, 1992). In a similar vein is Ronald C. White's thoughtful *Lincoln's Greatest Speech: The Second Inaugural* (New York: Simon and Schuster, 2003).

THE RECONSTRUCTION AND GILDED AGE PRESIDENTS:
JOHNSON THROUGH MCKINLEY

Andrew Johnson's rather ignominious presidential career has been the focus of several scholars who are critical of Lincoln's successor. The best book here is the somewhat older but quite thorough *Andrew Johnson and Reconstruction* (Chicago: University of Chicago Press, 1960), by Eric L. McKitrick. As the title suggests, McKitrick's work focuses primarily on Johnson's battles with Congress over Reconstruction policies. For a more general overview of Johnson's life and career, look at Albert E. Castel's *The Presidency of Andrew Johnson* (Lawrence: University Press of Kansas, 1979). Howard Means, *The Avenger Takes His Place: Andrew Johnson and the 45 Days That Changed the Nation* (New York: Harcourt, 2006), is a study of Johnson's first weeks in office that is geared toward a popular readership.

The large literature on Ulysses S. Grant understandably emphasizes his brilliant military career, but two general biographies, William S. McFeely's *Grant: A Biography* (New York: W.W. Norton, 1981) and Jean Edward Smith's *Grant* (New York: Simon and Schuster, 2002) cover the presidential years. The Gilded Age presidents from Grant through McKinley have (perhaps) understandably generated a comparatively thin historical literature. Ari Arthur Hoogenboom penned two solid biographies of Rutherford B. Hayes: *The Presidency of Rutherford B. Hayes* (Lawrence: University Press of Kansas, 1988) and a later biography, *Rutherford B. Hayes: Warrior and President* (Lawrence: University Press of Kansas, 1995). James A. Garfield's brief White House tenure prior to his assassination has made for little in the way of book-length studies. Allan Peskin's *Garfield: A Biography* (Kent, OH: Kent State University Press, 1978) is useful, as is the Garfield section of *The Presidencies of James A. Garfield and Chester A. Arthur* (Lawrence: University Press of Kansas, 1981), by Justus D. Doenecke. Doenecke also did solid work on Arthur in that volume; the reader would also do well to consult Thomas C. Reeves's earlier and generally laudatory biography, *Gentleman Boss: The Life of Chester Alan Arthur* (New York: Alfred A. Knopf, 1975). Richard Welch offered the only recent scholarly study of note on Grover Cleveland in *The Presidencies of Grover Cleveland* (Lawrence: University Press of Kansas, 1988). In a similar vein, Benjamin Harrison's presidency has its best modern treatment in Homer E. Socolofsky's *The Presidency of Benjamin Harrison* (Lawrence: University Press of Kansas, 1987).

William McKinley's longer tenure of office prior to his assassination means that scholars have examined his legacy more often than is the case with Garfield. Lewis Gould is a fine scholar of the presidency who wrote the McKinley installment for the American Presidency Series, *The Presidency of William McKinley* (Lawrence: University Press of Kansas, 1980). H. Wayne Morgan wrote a solid older study that is particularly strong on McKinley's foreign policy, *William McKinley and His America* (Syracuse, NY: Syracuse University Press, 1963). For a unique perspective on the ways in which the Civil War influenced the lives and policies of five Civil War veterans who occupied the White House—Grant, Hayes, Garfield, Harrison, and McKinley—see James M. Perry's *Touched with Fire: Five Presidents and the Civil War Battles That Made Them* (New York: Public Affairs, 2003).

THE PROGRESSIVES AND THEIR CRITICS: THEODORE ROOSEVELT THROUGH HOOVER

Teddy Roosevelt's status as an American cultural icon, on a par with Lincoln and Washington, has produced a rich literature on his life and presidency. Perhaps the best recent biographical treatment is Edmund Morris's two volume, prize-winning *The Rise of Theodore Roosevelt* (New York: Modern Library, 2001) and *Theodore Rex* (New York: Modern Library, 2002). A more succinct treatment of his career may be found in Kathleen Dalton's biography, *Theodore Roosevelt: A Strenuous Life* (New York: Alfred A. Knopf, 2002). Henry F. Pringle, *Theodore Roosevelt* (New York: Smithmark, 1995), is a useful older biography. Arthur M. Schlesinger Jr. and Louis Auchinloss wrote a good political overview, *Theodore Roosevelt* (New York: Times Books, 2002). Lewis L. Gould wrote a similarly solid treatment for the American Presidency Series, *The Presidency of Theodore Roosevelt* (Lawrence: University Press of Kansas, 1991). H. Collin wrote a good scholarly study of Roosevelt's Panama Canal adventures, *Theodore Roosevelt's Caribbean: The Panama Canal, the Monroe Doctrine, and the Latin American Context* (Baton Rouge: Louisiana State University Press, 1993). John Gable's *The Bull Moose Years: Theodore Roosevelt and the Progressive Party* (Port Washington, NY: Kennikat Press, 1978) focuses on TR's later political career.

William Howard Taft's distinguished political career included more than the presidency; he was a talented administrator, a key member of the Republican Party during the first decades of the twentieth century, and a U.S. Supreme Court justice. Yet for all that, he has garnered surprisingly little attention among modern historians. The best studies of his presidency are arguably Donald F. Anderson's *William Howard Taft: A Conservative's Road to the Presidency* (Ithaca, NY: Cornell University Press, 1973), which is especially good on Taft's relationship with Teddy Roosevelt, and Paolo E. Coletta's *The Presidency of William Howard Taft* (Lawrence: University Press of Kansas, 1973). Taft's own book on the executive branch, *The President and His Powers* (New York: Columbia University Press, 1967), offers a lucid overview of his conservative conception of the presidency. James Chace's recent study of the 1912 election has some useful information on Taft's politics and personality; see Chace, *1912: Wilson, Roosevelt, Taft, and Debs—the Election that Changed the Country* (New York: Simon and Schuster, 2004).

Woodrow Wilson has received more attention for his foreign policy ideas and his leadership during World War I than anything else. Several studies chronicle his idealist vision of the world and his failed quest to enact his Fourteen Points: see Lloyd E. Ambrosius, *Woodrow Wilson and His Legacy in American Foreign Relations* (New York: Palgrave MacMillan, 2002), which is generally sympathetic to Wilson; Thomas J.

Knock, *To End All Wars: Woodrow Wilson and the Quest for a New World Order* (Princeton, NJ: Princeton University Press, 1995), which is also generally sympathetic but suggests that Wilson's failings as a politician at home doomed his foreign policy efforts abroad; and Kendrick A. Clements, *Woodrow Wilson: World Statesman* (New York: Ivan R. Dee, 1999), which is brief but balanced. John Milton Cooper, *Breaking the Heart of the World* (Cambridge: Cambridge University Press, 2001), focuses on the battle over the League of Nations and is generally sympathetic to Wilson's cause. For a good general overview of the Wilson presidency, see Clements's installment in the American Presidency Series, *The Presidency of Woodrow Wilson* (Lawrence: University Press of Kansas, 1992). Also useful—and a good read—is Cooper's comparative biography of Wilson and Theodore Roosevelt, *The Warrior and the Priest: Woodrow Wilson and Theodore Roosevelt* (Cambridge, MA: Harvard University Press, 1983).

The presidents of the Roaring Twenties were conservative, low-key types, and the historical literature on them reflects this. Eugene P. Trani and David L. Wilson's *The Presidency of Warren G. Harding* (Lawrence: University Press of Kansas, 1977) is the best study of the man; but also look at Francis Russell's older *President Harding: His Life and Times, 1865–1923* (London: Eyre and Spottiswoode, 1969) for good personal information on him. Robert H. Ferrell, *The Presidency of Calvin Coolidge* (Lawrence: University Press of Kansas, 1998), is good on Coolidge's politics and ideology, while Donald McCoy's *Calvin Coolidge: The Quiet President* (New York: Macmillan, 1967) is better on Coolidge's personality. Herbert Hoover has received the most attention from scholars among the 1920s presidents, given his pivotal role in the Great Depression. Most believe history has treated him too harshly. See Martin L. Fausold, *The Presidency of Herbert Hoover* (Lawrence: University Press of Kansas, 1985); David Burner, *Herbert Hoover: A Public Life* (New York: Knopf, 1979); Joan Hoff, *Herbert Hoover: Forgotten Progressive* (Boston: Little, Brown, 1975); and Eugene Lyons, *Herbert Hoover: A Biography* (Garden City, NY: Doubleday, 1964).

FRANKLIN ROOSEVELT

FDR has garnered a great deal of attention from historians—understandably so, given his long tenure in the White House. There are several fine general studies of the man and his career. Ted Morgan's *FDR: A Biography* (New York: Simon and Schuster, 1985) is a solid one-volume biography. Kenneth S. Davis authored an exhaustive multivolume biography from birth through the middle of the Second World War: *FDR: The Beckoning of Destiny, 1882–1928: A History* (New York: Putnam, 1972; *FDR, The New York Years, 1928–1933: A History* (New York: Random House, 1994); *FDR, The New Deal Years, 1933–1937* (New York: Random House, 1986); *FDR, Into the Storm, 1937–1940: A History* (New York: Random House, 1993); and *FDR, The War President, 1940–1943: A History* (New York: Random House, 2000). George T. McJimsey, *The Presidency of Franklin Delano Roosevelt* (Lawrence: University Press of Kansas, 2000), is a worthy entry in the American Presidency Series.

FDR's domestic and New Deal policies, and in particular his sometimes stormy relationship with Congress, are addressed in Albert U. Romasco, *The Politics of Recovery: Roosevelt's New Deal* (New York: Oxford University Press, 1983). Paul Conkin's older *The New Deal* (Arlington Heights: AHM, 1975) is useful. Geoffrey Ward tackled Roosevelt's early life and political career in *Before the Trumpet: Young Franklin Roosevelt, 1882–1905* (New York: Harper and Row, 1985) and *A First-Class Temperament: The Emergence of Franklin Roosevelt* (New York: Harper and Row, 1989). Davis W. Houck, *FDR and Fear Itself: The First Inaugural Address* (College Station: Texas A&M Press, 2002), analyzed the background and impact of FDR's greatest speech. In a similar vein, Halford Ryan, *Franklin Roosevelt's Rhetorical Presidency* (New York: Greenwood Press, 1988), is especially strong on FDR's media innovations such as the fireside chats. George Wolfskill's *All but the People: Franklin D. Roosevelt and His Critics, 1933–1939* (New York: Macmillan, 1969) is a useful compendium of conservative Republican responses to FDR's New Deal programs.

Foreign policy and wartime issues have been the focus of a number of book-length studies. Versatile presidential historian Robert Dallek surveyed FDR's entire foreign policy approach in his *Franklin D. Roosevelt and American Foreign Policy, 1932–1945* (New York: Oxford University Press, 1981). Geared for a general audience, Doris Kearns Goodwin's *No Ordinary Time: Franklin and Eleanor Roosevelt: The Homefront during World War II* (New York: Simon and Schuster, 1994) is a readable, if not terribly original, narrative. David Reynolds's *From Munich to Pearl Harbor: Roosevelt's America and the Origins of the Second World War* (Chicago: Ivan R. Dee, 2000) is excellent on the context of FDR's movements toward war, as is Waldo H. Heinrichs, *Threshold of War: Franklin D. Roosevelt and America's Entry into World War II* (New York: Oxford University Press, 1988). Amos Perlmutter, *FDR and Stalin: A Not So Grand Alliance, 1943–1945* (Columbia: University of Missouri Press, 1993), argues that Roosevelt's declining health, among other factors, caused him to compromise excessively with the Russian dictator. Edward M. Bennett addressed the neglected topic of FDR's prewar relations with the Soviets in *Franklin D. Roosevelt and the Search for Security: American-Soviet Relations, 1933–1939* (Wilmington, DE: Scholarly Resources, 1985). Roosevelt's military decision making is well covered in Eric Larrabee, *Commander in Chief: Franklin Delano Roosevelt, His Lieutenants, and Their War* (New York: Harper and Row, 1987).

COLD WAR PRESIDENTS: TRUMAN THROUGH NIXON

David McCullough's prize-winning biography, *Truman* (New York: Simon and Schuster, 1992), sparked renewed popular interest in Harry Truman. McCullough's fine work unfortunately overshadowed the release, at about the same time, of an equally fine—if less flashy—biography of Truman, Robert H. Ferrell's, *Truman: A Life* (Columbia: University of Missouri Press, 1994). Also useful is Robert J. Donovan's two-volume study of the Truman presidency, *Conflict and Crisis: The Presidency of Harry S. Truman,*

1945–1948 (Columbia: University of Missouri Press, 1996), and *Tumultuous Years: The Presidency of Harry S. Truman, 1949–1953* (New York: W.W. Norton, 1983). Truman's *The Autobiography of Harry S. Truman* (Columbia: University of Missouri Press, 1997), is an interesting if somewhat spotty collection of Truman's ruminations on his life and career.

As with Ulysses S. Grant, Dwight D. Eisenhower's historical literature is dominated by studies that focus on his illustrious military career at the expense of his presidency. Popular historian Stephen Ambrose penned a good general overview of Ike's life, *Eisenhower* (New York: Simon and Schuster, 1990). Fred I. Greenstein, *The Hidden-Hand Presidency: Eisenhower as Leader* (Baltimore: Johns Hopkins University Press, 1982), offers an interesting interpretation of Eisenhower's leadership style. The Eisenhower installment in the American Presidency Series, *The Presidency of Dwight D. Eisenhower*, by Chester J. Pach (Lawrence: University Press of Kansas, 1991), is, as usual in this series, a solid and useful study. Steven Wagner, *Eisenhower Republicanism: Pursuing the Middle Way* (DeKalb: Northern Illinois University Press, 2006), presents a version of Ike as GOP moderate.

John F. Kennedy has sparked a tremendous professional and popular historical literature. For a good recent biography, see Robert Dallek's thorough and well-written *An Unfinished Life: John F. Kennedy, 1917–1963* (Boston: Little, Brown, 2003). The standard account of the Cuban missile crisis is *High Noon in the Cold War: Kennedy, Khrushchev, and the Cuban Missile Crisis* (New York: Ballantine Books, 2004). John Hellman, *The Kennedy Obsession: The American Myth of JFK* (New York: Columbia University Press, 1997), is a critical assessment of Kennedy's place in American memory. Likewise on a critical note is Richard Reeves, *President Kennedy: Profile of Power* (New York: Simon and Schuster, 1994). More laudatory are Thurston Clarke, *Ask Not: The Inauguration of John F. Kennedy and the Speech That Changed America* (New York: Henry Holt and Co., 2004), and Richard J. Tofel, *Sounding the Trumpet: The Making of John F. Kennedy's Inaugural Address* (New York: Ivan R. Dee, 2005), which offer interesting studies of the process by which JFK delivered one the most famous speeches in American history.

Lyndon Johnson has attracted some first-rate biographers. Robert A. Caro is writing a multivolume biography of Johnson that has garnered a great deal of praise and several book awards. As of 2006, he has completed three volumes: *The Path to Power* (New York: Vintage, 1990), *Means of Ascent* (New York: Vintage, 1991), and *Master of the Senate* (New York: Vintage, 2002). These volumes collectively take the reader from LBJ's birth to his acceptance of the vice-presidential nomination in 1960; a fourth and final volume will cover the years of his presidency. Presidential historian Robert Dallek has authored a more succinct (but still quite comprehensive) two-volume biography: *Lone Star Rising: Lyndon Johnson and His Times, 1908–1960* (New York: Oxford University Press, 1990) and *Flawed Giant: Lyndon Johnson and His Times, 1961–1973* (New York: Oxford University Press, 1998). Also useful is Randall Woods's one-volume treatment of LBJ's career, *LBJ: Architect of American Ambition* (New York: Free Press, 2006).

Richard Nixon's almost Shakespearian rise and fall is an irresistible story for many historians. Stephen Ambrose was Nixon's first major biographer; his three-volume biography, *Nixon: The Education of a Politician, 1913–1962* (New York: Simon and Schuster, 1987), *Nixon: The Triumph of a Politician, 1963–1972* (New York: Simon and Schuster, 1989), and *Nixon: Ruin and Recovery, 1973–1990* (New York: Simon and Schuster, 1991), is still the best multivolume treatment available. Richard Reeves, *President Nixon: Alone in the White House* (New York: Simon and Schuster, 2001), offers a riveting account of Nixon's psychological struggles during his presidency but is rather thin on Watergate and its attendant issues. On that complicated subject, consult Stanley Cutler's thorough *Wars of Watergate: The Last Crisis of Richard Nixon* (New York: Simon and Schuster, 1992). Nixon's autobiography, *RN: The Memoirs of Richard Nixon* (New York: Simon and Schuster, 1978), is useful, if only to understand how Nixon himself justified his actions.

BEYOND WATERGATE: FORD THROUGH GEORGE BUSH JR.

John R. Greene's *The Presidency of Gerald Ford* (Lawrence: University Press of Kansas, 1995) is the best study of Ford's White House years. For general biographical information, the reader would be best served by consulting Ford's own memoirs, *A Time to Heal: The Autobiography of Gerald Ford* (New York: Harper and Row, 1979), though an older biography, Clark R. Mollenhoff, *The Man Who Pardoned Nixon* (New York: St. Martin's Press, 1976), is useful as well.

Jimmy Carter has inspired a broader literature, due in part to his post-presidential career as a humanitarian and commentator on national and world affairs. Burton I. Kauffman, *The Presidency of James Earl Carter* (Lawrence: University Press of Kansas, 1993), is the best study of his presidency. Gary M. Fink, ed., *The Carter Presidency: Policy Choices in the Post–New Deal Era* (Lawrence: University Press of Kansas, 1998), offers a wide-ranging collection of essays on everything from Carter's economics to his relationship with the feminist movement. Gaddis Smith, *Morality, Reason, and Power: American Diplomacy in the Carter Years* (New York: Hill and Wang, 1987), is a balanced look at Carter's foreign policies. Of his own voluminous writings, Carter's autobiography, *Keeping Faith: Memoirs of a President* (New York: Bantam Books, 1982), is the most useful for the general student of his presidency.

Studies of Ronald Reagan have proliferated in recent years as his reputation as one of America's better presidents has grown. Lou Cannon's *President Reagan: Role of a Lifetime* (New York: Simon and Schuster, 1991) is the best of the early biographies. Former speechwriter Peggy Noonan penned a laudatory account of Reagan in *When Character Was King: A Memoir of Ronald Reagan* (New York: Penguin Books, 2002), as did conservative intellectual Dinesh D'Souza in *Ronald Reagan: How an Ordinary Man Became an Extraordinary Leader* (New York: Free Press, 1999). Also generally positive in its portrayal of Reagan is Richard Reeves's *President Reagan: The Triumph of Imagination* (New York: Simon and Schuster, 2004).

The administrations of the post-Reagan presidents are still a bit too recent to have created much in the way of serious historical literature. So far, the best book-length resource on George Bush Sr. is his own *All the Best, George Bush: My Life and Other Writings* (New York: Scribner, 1999). Bill Clinton's *My Life* (New York: Knopf, 2004) is turgid and self-serving, but probably no more so than other presidential memoirs. The literature on George Bush Jr. is contentious and colored by the animosity that has characterized much of early twenty-first-century political writing; but the reader will find useful Bush speechwriter David Frum's inside account of the early Bush presidency in *The Right Man: The Surprise Presidency of George W. Bush* (New York: Random House, 2003).

Index

Note: italic page numbers indicate photos.

Adams, John, 29, 49–50, *139*
  attitude toward speeches, 83
  on the Constitution, 252
  and diplomacy, 81, 82
  distrust of political parties, 139–140
  on factionalism, 252–253
  grooming of son for presidency, 150
  and Hamilton, 141
  Inaugural Address, 251–254
  and Jefferson, 139, 141
  as member of Revolutionary generation,
    80
  neutrality between France and England,
    140–141, 398–399
  on pressures of presidency, 1
  relations with Congress, 194
  State of the Union Address (1797),
    398–399
  as successful Federalist candidate, 139
  on vice presidency, 135
  on Washington, 252–253
  as writer, 79
Adams, John Quincy, 40, 50, *150*
  as diplomat, 81–82, 150
  and election of 1824, 148–149
  on factionalism, 271–273
  on federal support for roads, navigation,
    arts, sciences, education, etc., 404–407
  Inaugural Address, 270–273
  as member of Revolutionary generation,
    80
  on Polk, 205
  public image, 149–150
  State of the Union Address (1825),
    404–407
  on westward expansion, 270

Adams, Sam, 135
Afghanistan War, 74
African Americans
  and A. Johnson, 103, 104, 105
  abandonment by Republican Party, 166
  and ending of segregation in armed
    forces, 455
  Garfield on voting rights, 313–315
  Hayes on, 310
  Lincoln on suffrage for, 102
  McKinley on intolerance for lynchings,
    327
  and presidential politics, 42–43, 58
  Taft on, 335–337
  See also Slavery
Afro-American National League, 166
Ames, Fisher, 133–134
Anderson, John, 184
Arthur, Chester, 55
  and civil service reform, 106
  comments upon veto of appropriations
    bill, 226
  on economic issues, 434
  as member of Civil War generation, 98
  on naturalization laws, 433
  State of the Union Address (1884),
    433–434
Ashmun, George, 210
Assassinations, and conspiracy theories,
    40–41

Baker, Edward, 217
Bank of the United States. *See* National
    Bank issue
Barbary pirates. *See* Tripolitan affair
Bas, John, 200

Bas v. Tingy, 200–202
Battle of Ball's Bluff, 217–218
Battle of Buena Vista, 210, *211*
Bedford, Gunning, 18, 20
Bernstein, Carl, 71
Bonaparte, Charles, 33
Brandeis, Louis D., 230
Brokaw, Tom, 115
Brown, Edmund G., 69
Browning, Orville, 216
Bryan, William Jennings, 167–168
Buchanan, James, 51, 190
    Inaugural Address, 95, 295–297
    on Kansas and slavery, 295–296
    as member of Doughface generation, 95
    request of loan from Congress, 214
    and secession of southern states, 98,
        420–422
    and sectional crisis, 95–96
    State of the Union Address (1860),
        420–422
    on value of Union, 296–297
Bureaucracy. *See* Federal bureaucracy
Burnside, Ambrose, 157
Burr, Aaron, 142–143
Bush, Barbara, 40
Bush, George, Jr.
    and Afghanistan War, 74, 234
    and African American cabinet members,
        42
    on "axis of evil," 477
    and Card, 36
    on "compassionate conservatism," 389
    first Inaugural Address, 388–390
    and Iraq War, 40, 74, 234
    on security and nation building, 390–393
    second Inaugural Address, 390–393
    State of the Union Address (2002),
        476–479
    story-reading at time of 9/11 attacks,
        127
    and 2000 election, 7, 388
    and 2004 election, 133
    unflattering description of, 40
    and war on terror, 40, 234, 390–393,
        476–479
Bush, George, Sr.
    and broccoli, 40

    on decline of Soviet Unon, 382, 472
    and Gulf War (1991), 74, 471–473
    Inaugural Address, 381–384
    on "new world order," 473
    State of the Union Address (1991),
        471–474
    "thousand points of light," 383
    at time of assassination attempt on
        Reagan, 23–24
Butler, Pierce, 31

Cabinet, 35
Calhoun, John C., 85, 91, 92, 204
California, 416–417
Cameron, Simon, 122, 165, 203, 216
Card, Andrew, 36
Carter, Jimmy, *183*
    and brown-bag lunches, 127
    on the economy, 467–469
    on eliminating electoral college, 17
    Inaugural Address, 374–376
    and Iran hostage crisis, 179–180, 184,
        469
    pardon issued by, 34
    State of the Union Address (1981),
        467–469
    style as president, 178–180, 182–183
    See also Election of 1980
Central Intelligence Agency, 27
Chandler, Zachariah, 218, 219
Chase, Salmon, 156, 159–160, 216
Cherokee removal, 408–409
Chief of staff, 4, 36–37
    deputies, 37
Chisholm, Shirley, 43
Churchill, Winston, 120, *121*
CIA. *See* Central Intelligence Agency
Civil Rights Act of 1866, 104
Civil service reform
    Garfield on, 315
    Hayes on, 311
    McKinley on, 327–328
Civil War
    Battle of Ball's Bluff, 217–218
    Grant on his service in, 308–309
    and growth of army, 216
    and growth of federal bureaucracy, 216
    and Lincoln, 53–54, 66, 96, 98–102

Wilson and reconciliation ceremony, 165
  See also Election of 1864; Secession;
    Sectional crisis (1840s–1850s); Slavery
Civil War generation, 97–106
  and constitutional challenge of war and
    Reconstruction, 98–99
  and dominance of Congress, 5, 55, 58,
    106, 166
  passing of, 106–107
  presidents of, 98
  See also Johnson, Andrew; Lincoln,
    Abraham
Clay, Henry
  and election of 1824, 148–149
  and election of 1828, 151
  and Jackson, 85, 92, 148–149, 152, 210
Cleveland, Grover
  on business trusts, 324
  on currency, 323, 434–435
  as first filmed president, 60
  first Inaugural Address, 315–318
  as member of Civil War generation, 98
  nonconsecutive terms, 167
  and pension fraud issue, 106
  on public expenditues, 323–324
  removal of cancerous growth, 22
  second Inaugural Address, 322–325
  State of the Union Address (1885),
    434–435
Clinton, Bill
  and common touch, 127
  domestic policy proposals, 30
  on education, 475
  on entering twenty-first century,
    386–387
  first Inaugural Address, 384–385
  and health care plan, 28–29
  humor regarding sexual peccadilloes, 40
  impeachment of, 21
  Lewinsky and "travelgate" scandals, 74
  on Medicare and health care, 474–475
  on peacekeeping efforts, 475
  and pressures of presidency, 1
  on racial tensions, 387
  second Inaugural Address, 386–388
  on Social Security, 474
  State of the Union Address (1999),
    474–476

  as talented communicator, 7
  on terrorism, 476
Clinton, Hillary Rodham
  emulation of Eleanor Roosevelt, 42
  and health care plan, 28
Cold War
  Eisenhower on, 357–362
  Kennedy on, 363–364
  L. Johnson on, 366
  Truman on, 354–356
Commander in chief, 2, 3, 24–25
  as administrative title, 26
  and concerns about standing army, 25
  as possible direct commander, 25–26
Compromise of 1850, 94
  Fillmore on, 417–418
Conkling, Roscoe, 165
The Conscience of a Conservative, 177
Constellation, 201
Constitution, 195–196
Coolidge, Calvin, 59, 171
  Inaugural Address, 344–347
  on laissez-faire capitalism, 345–346,
    444–445
  as member of Progressive generation,
    114
  on post–World War I Europe, 344–345
  State of the Union Address (1926),
    444–445
Copperheads, 157–158, 160
Corporations and trusts
  B. Harrison on, 320
  Cleveland on, 324
  T. Roosevelt on, 439–440
Cortelyou, George, 222
Council of Economic Advisers, 4
Crawford, William, 148
Currency issue
  Cleveland on, 323, 434–435
  McKinley on, 325–326

Davis, David, 129–130, 155
Davis, Jefferson, 93–94, 106
De Gaulle, Charles, 176
Defense
  Monroe on, 266–267
  Washington on, 397
Defense Department, 4

Democratic Party
  and elections of 1860 and 1864, 157, 158,
    160–161
  formation around Jackson, 154
  Gold and Silver wings, 167
  and government activism, 176–177
  Jacksonian-era, 205
  and Kansas-Nebraska Act, 156
  mid-twentieth century dominance,
    173–174
  post–Civil War experience, 166–168
Depression of 1890s, 325–326. *See also*
    Great Depression
Dewey, Tom, 173
Diplomatic function, 26–28
Director (czar) of national intelligence, 33
Domestic policy, 28
  and limits on presidential influence,
    28–29
  and relations with legislative branch,
    30–31
  and State of the Union Addresses, 29–30
Doughface generation
  as nonactivists, 96
  and sectional crisis (slavery and western
    expansion), 92–98
  See also Buchanan, James; Fillmore,
    Millard; Pierce, Franklin; Taylor,
    Zachary
Douglas, Stephen, 156, 157
Douglass, Frederick, 42, 157
Dred Scott v. Sandford, 95–96, 190

Eaton, John Henry and Margaret, 85, 122
Economic issues
  and Arthur, 434
  and B. Harrison, 318–319, 436–437
  and Carter, 467–469
  and F. D. Roosevelt, 228
  and Ford, 464–467
  and Grant, 305–306
  and Reagan, 469–470
  and Wilson, 111, 338–339
  See also Depression of 1890s; Great
    Depression
Eisenhower, Dwight, 65, 77, 121–122, 173
  and chief of staff, 37
  on Cold War, 357–362

  on communism, 455–456
  on ending segregation in armed forces,
    455
  first Inaugural Address, 356–359
  and increased executive power, 175, 176,
    177
  on Korean War, 455
  on military-industrial complex, 122
  and Office of Congressional Relations, 4
  on perquisites of presidency, 1
  second Inaugural Address, 359–362
  State of the Union Address (1954),
    454–456
  and Vietnam War, 67
Election of 1796, 139
Election of 1800, 133
  contest between Adams and Jefferson,
    141–143
  faultlines exposed by, 143–144
  as showdown between Federalists and
    Republicans, 141–143
  victory of Jefferson, 143
Election of 1824, 148
Election of 1828
  and campaign paraphernalia, 147
  divisions among Republicans, 147–148
  effects on antebellum politics, 154
  and grass roots democracy, 145–146,
    152
  and J. Q. Adams, 149–151, 153
  and Jackson, 145, 150–152
  Jackson poster, *147*
  and the press, 146
  victory of Jackson, 153
  and young political operatives, 146–147
  See also Jackson, Andrew
Election of 1860, 155–157
Election of 1864, 157–158
  and Democrats, 160–161, *162*, 164–165
  and emancipation, 155–156, 158,
    162–163
  Lincoln-Johnson campaign banner, *160*
  Lincoln's middle-ground position, 160
  as referendum on Lincoln's war policies,
    158–159, 163–164
  Republican platform, 162
  and Republicans against Lincoln,
    159–160

and subsequent Republican dominance, 164–166

and uniqueness of election during civil war, 165

See also Civil War

Election of 1876, 309, 311–312

Election of 1932, 169–172

Roosevelt's landslide victory, 172

Election of 1980, 180–184

Reagan's landslide victory, 184

Election of 2000, 7

Election of 2004, 133

Elections

campaign process, 6

founders' differing preferences for, 14–15

See also Electoral college

Electoral college, 15–16

and founders' considerations, 14–16

and possibility of nonmajority electee, 16–17

and reform movements, 17

Eliza, 200

Ellsberg, Daniel, 71

Emancipation Proclamaton, *101, 102*

and Election of 1864, 155–156, 158, 162–163

political effects for Republicans, 132

Enterprise, 195

EOP. *See* Executive Office of the President

Era of Good Feelings, 144–145, 205

Ex parte Merryman, 99–100

Ex parte Milligan, 224

Ex parte Vallandigham, 224

Executive branch, 3–4

congressional control of salaries, 4, 12–14

expansion under F. D. Roosevelt, 117–119

president's direct advisers and support staff, 3–4

See also Federal bureaucracy

Executive Office of the President, 4

Fairbanks, Charles, 187–188

Federal Bureau of Investigation (FBI), 33

Federal bureaucracy, 31–32. *See also* Executive branch

Federalist Party

and Adams, 139–140

decline of, 144–145

and election of 1800, 141–143

favoring of England (1790s), 140

and Hamilton, 136–139

merger with Republicans to form Whigs, 153–154

Fifteenth Amendment, 306

Fillmore, Millard

on Compromise of 1850, 417–418

as member of Doughface generation, *93*

State of the Union Address (1850), 417–418

First Ladies, influence of, 41–42

Ford, Gerald

and bicentennial, 66–67

on the economy, 464–467

and negative legacy of Nixon, 178–179

pardons of Tokyo Rose and Nixon, 34–35

State of the Union Address (1976), 464–467

and Vietnam War, 73–74

Fort Pillow, Tennessee, 220

Fourteenth Amendment, 105

Franklin, Benjamin, *13*

biographical sketch, 13

on impeachment, 20

on presidential salary, 12

on presidential veto, 30

Freedmen's Bureau Act, 104

Fremont, John C., 159

French-American Quasi-War, 200–202, *201*

Ganges, 200

Garfield, James, 55, 167

on African American suffrage, 313–315

Inaugural Address, 312–315

as member of Civil War generation, 98, 312

on Mormon polygamy, 315

Garner, John Nance, 171, 187

Garrison, William Lloyd, 100–101, 157

Generations. *See* Presidential generations

Gerry, Elbridge, 189

Goldwater, Barry, 177–178

Gonzalez, Henry B., 21

Gore, Al, 7, 28

Grant, Ulysses S., 55, 65
  on A. Johnson, 105
  death of, 106
  on Fifteenth Amendment, 306
  first Inaugural Address, 305–307
  on his service in Civil War, 308–309
  as member of Civil War generation, 98
  on Native Americans, 306, 431
  on post-war economics, 305–306
  on Reconstruction, 307–308, 430–431
  scandals in administration, 122, 166
  second Inaugural Address, 307–309
  State of the Union Address (1876),
    429–431
Grayson, William, 95
Great Depression
  and F. D. Roosevelt, 61–62, 227–229,
    349–352, 449–451
  and Hoover, 61, 62, 169, 170–171,
    446–447
Greatest generation, 115, 121–122. *See also*
    Roosevelt, Franklin D.
Greeley, Horace, 156, 163
Green, Duff, 87
Gulf War (1991), 74

Habeas corpus, 99–100, 161
Haig, Alexander, 23–24
Haldeman, H. R. (Bob), 124, 125
Hamilton, Alexander, 20, *137*
  attack on Adams, 141
  biographical sketch, 137
  on commander in chief, 24–25
  death in duel with Burr, 142
  and Federalist Party, 138–139, 142
  and Jefferson, 49, 136–138
  on law enforcement function, 32
  and neutrality between France and
    England, 193–194
  on pardoning power, 34
  on presidential standards, 5, 10, 11
  on Roman democracy and tyranny, 18
  on Supreme Court, 198
  and Tripolitan affair, 197
Hamlin, Hannibal, 160
Hancock, John, 135
Hancock, Winfield Scott, 167
Harding, Warren G., 21–22

  on aftermath of World War I, 343,
    443–444
  Inaugural Address, 343–344
  on League of Nations, 343–344
  as member of Progressive generation,
    114
  State of the Union Address (1921),
    443–444
  on women's suffrage, 344
Harper, Robert, 144
Harrison, Benjamin, 43
  on civil service and party affiliation, 225
  on corporations and trusts, 320
  on economic issues, 436–437
  on election reform, 321–322
  as first audio-recorded president, 60
  on immigration, 320
  Inaugural Address, 318–322
  as member of Civil War generation, 98
  on westward expansion and economic
    growth, 318–319
  State of the Union Address (1890),
    436–437
Harrison, William Henry, 21–22, 39, 44,
    155
  death of, 207
  as first photographed president, 60
  on freedom of press, 283
  Inaugural Address, 280–285
  on limiting himself to single term, 282
  on Native Americans, 284
  presidential campaign, 203–204
  on separation of powers, 281–282, 283
  on states' rights, 282
  on veto power, 282
Hay, John, 3, 214, *214*
Hay, Milton, 3
Hayes, Rutherford B., 55
  on African Americans, 310
  on civil service reform, 311
  on 1876 election, 311–312
  and end of Reconstruction, 309–311,
    431–433
  Inaugural Address, 309–312
  as member of Civil War generation, 98
  State of the Union Address (1877),
    431–433
Health care, 474–475

Hearst, Patricia, 34
Hinckley, John, 23
The Hireling and the Slave, 95
Hitler, Adolf, 119
Hobbes, Thomas, 79
Holmes, Oliver Wendell Jr., 98
  in Battle of Ball's Bluff, 217
Hoover, Herbert, 40, *168*
  continuing opposition to Roosevelt, 173
  and Depression, 61, 62, 169, 170–171,
    446–447
  Inaugural Address, 347–349
  on League of Nations, 349
  as president, 168–169
  on private enterprise, 166
  on Prohibition, 348
  State of the Union Address (1930),
    446–447
  See also Election of 1932
Hopkins, Harry, 229
Hume, David, 79
Humphrey, Hubert, 70

Immigration and naturalization policy
  Arthur on, 433
  B. Harrison on, 320
  McKinley on, 327
  Taft on Asians, 335
Impeachment
  founders' deliberations concerning,
    19–21
  as legal proceeding with political
    implications, 21
  and limit on pardoning power, 33–34
The Imperial Presidency, 174–175
Imperialism, 56, 107, 227
  and T. Roosevelt, 108–109, 227, 332
Iran hostage crisis, 179–180, 184, 469
Iraq War, 40, 74

Jackson, Andrew, 22, 40, 50, *86,* 122
  on abolishing Electoral College, 407–408
  and Battle of New Orleans, 145, 149, *151*
  on Cherokee removal, 408–409
  and Clay, 85, 92, 148–149, 152, 210
  Congressional censure of, 209, 210
  and election of 1824, 148–149
  and exercise of power, *89,* 90–91

extreme reactions to, 145
extremist personality of, 85–86
first Inaugural Address, 273–275
and formation of Democratic Party, 154
humble background and subsequent
  prosperity, 43
inauguration ceremony and celebrations,
  153
on management of public revenue, 274
on Native Americans, 275, 408–409
on nature of executive power, 274
as populist, 89–90, 145
public image, 150–151
Revolutionary War experience, 85
rumors about marriage, 151–152
on standing armies, 274–275
State of the Union Address (1829),
  407–409
on states' rights and federal
  responsibilities, 274, 275, 276–277
on threat of disunion, 90–91, 92, 97
See also Election of 1828
Jackson, Jesse, 43
Jackson, Rachel, 151–152
Jackson, Stonewall, 65
Jacksonian generation
  expanding suffrage and democratization,
    87
  and interpretation of Constitution, 86–87
  Jackson's influence, 85–87
  and patronage, 88–89
  relation to Revolutionary generation, 91
  and slavery, 92
  and view of Revolution, 86
  See also Jackson, Andrew; Van Buren,
    Martin
Jefferson, Thomas, *36, 39,* 49–50, *136*
  and Adams, 139, 141
  as diplomat, 81
  on factionalism, 255–256
  on governmental restraint, 256–257
  first Inaugural Address, 254–257
  and Hamilton, 49, 136–138
  and Louisiana Purchase, 207, 258
  as member of Revolutionary generation,
    80
  and the military, 192–193
  on Native Americans, 258–259

Jefferson, Thomas *(cont.)*
  and neutrality between France and
    England, 193–194, 199–200
  on patronage, 88–89
  on political parties, 144–145
  on presidential powers, 192
  on the press, 259–260
  on pressures of presidency, 37
  relations with Congress, 194–195, 197
  and Republican Party, 138
  second Inaugural Address, 258–261
  State of the Union Address (1801),
    399–400
  as states' rights advocate, 192
  support staff, 3
  on Tripolitan Affair, 399–400
  on Washington, 22, 257
  as writer, 79
  See also Election of 1800; Tripolitan
    affair
Johnson, Andrew, 39, *103, 160*
  and African Americans, 42, 55, 103, 104,
    105
  impeachment of, 21, 55, 106
  as inept communicator, 55
  and legacy of Lincoln, 103–104
  as member of Civil War generation, 98
  and Reconstruction, 103–106, 427–429
  State of the Union Address (1865),
    427–429
  and subsequent dominance of Congress,
    5, 55, 58, 106, 166
  "swing around the circle," 105
Johnson, Junior, 34
Johnson, Lyndon, 173
  on Cold War, 366
  and first African American cabinet
    member, 42
  and Great Society, 67–68, 175–176,
    365–366, 367, 459–461
  Inaugural Address, 365–367
  on Kennedy, 176
  mixed public image, 123–124
  and pressures of presidency, 1
  State of the Union Address (1966),
    459–462
  and taping of presidential conversations,
    71–72

and Vietnam War, 67–68, *69*, 123–124,
    234, 459, 460, 461–462
  as vice president, 188
Joint Chiefs of Staff, 2, 26
Julian, George, 219

Kansas-Nebraska Act of 1854, 155–156
Kennedy, John F., 65, 173
  "ask not . . .," 364–365
  and assassination conspiracy theories,
    40–41, 71
  and Catholicism, 40
  on Cold War, 363–364
  domestic agenda, 457
  on executive branch, 458
  and generational change, 77–78
  health problems, 123
  and "Ich bin ein Berliner," 39
  Inaugural Address, 362–365
  and increased executive power, 175
  and the media, 64, 122–123
  and Nixon, 69
  sense of world crisis, 457, 458–459
  State of the Union Address (1961),
    456–459
  and Vietnam War, 67
Kennedy, Ted, 182
Kerry, John, 133
Knox, Henry, *36, 135*
Korean War
  Eisenhower on, 455
  Truman on, 451
Ku Klux Klan, 104

Law enforcement function, 32–33
  federal agencies, 3, 33
  pardoning power, 33–34
League of Nations
  Harding on, 343–344
  Hoover on, 349
  and Wilson, 112, 223–224, *223*
Legal Tender Act, 158
Lewinsky, Monica, 74
Lewis, Meriwether, 3, 192
Lincoln, Abraham, 22, 40, *52*, 65, *101, 160*
  acceptance of visitors, 214–215
  and African Americans, 42, 102
  and assassination conspiracy theories, 40

and Civil War, 53–54, 66, 96, 98–102,
    303
communication methods, 53–55
and Emancipation Proclamation, *101*,
    102, 422–425
extent of writing on, 39
first Inaugural Address, 100, 297–302
folksy campaign speech, 146
Gettysburg Address, 54
humble background and subsequent
    prosperity, 43, 50–51
and lack of popular majority, 16, 52
"malice toward none . . . ," 304
and McClellan, 26, 216–217, 219–221,
    221
on Mexican-American War, 210–212
as moral spokesman, 51, 53
nomination of, 129–131
as one of best presidents, 4–5
political effects of emancipation
    position, 132
on Revolution, 86
on saving the Union, 53–54
on secession, 298–302
second Inaugural Address, 54–55,
    302–304
and secretaries, 214, *214*
and slavery, 42, 51–54, 100–102,
    155–156, 298, 301, 303
soldiers' feelings for, 163–164
State of the Union Address (1862),
    422–425
support staff, 3
suspension of habeas corpus, 99–100, 161
on Vallandigham incident, 157
vilification by opponents, 155, 156
See also Election of 1860; Election of
    1864
Lincoln, Benjamin, 135
Lincoln, Mary Todd
    friendship with Sumner, 215
    influence on husband, 41
Livingston, Robert R., 48
Locke, John, 79
Lovejoy, Elijah, 51

MacArthur, Douglas, 65
Madison, James, *16*, 49–50

activation of New York militia in War of
    1812, 202
as diplomat, 81
biographical sketch, 16
on election format, 15–16
first Inaugural Address, 261–262
on legislative power, 18–19, 29
and *Marbury v. Madison*, 198
as member of Revolutionary generation,
    80
on nation's prosperity, 261
on Native Americans, 264
on need to remove bad presidents, 19
on neutrality regarding European wars,
    261–262
on president's diplomatic function, 27
second Inaugural Address, 262–265
on separation of powers, 30
State of the Union Address (1813),
    400–402
on War of 1812, 263–265, 400–402
Marbury v. Madison, 198
Marcy, William, 204
Marine Corps, and Tripolitan affair, 195
Marshall, George, 61
Marshall, John, 65, 198
Martin v. Mott, 202
Mason, George, 11, 14, 18, 20, *20*, 30
    on presidential veto, 31
    on vice president as president of Senate,
        189
McAlpin, Harry S., 42–43
McClellan, George B., 26, 161, *162*, 163
    with Lincoln, *221*
    management of Civil War, 216–217,
        219–221
    See also Election of 1864
McCulloch v. Maryland, 65
McKinley, William, 167–168
    and business, 56, 106
    on civil service reform, 327–328
    on currency, 325–326
    on depression of 1890s, 325–326
    first Inaugural Address, 325–328
    on immigration, 327
    on intolerance for lynchings, 327
    as member of Civil War generation, 98,
        107

McKinley, William *(cont.)*
  on Philippines, 330–331
  second Inaugural Address, 328–333
  and Spanish-American War, 56, 107, 222,
    328–329, 437–438
  State of the Union Address (1899),
    437–438
  on T. Roosevelt, 56, 107
McNamara, Robert, *69*
Merryman, John, 99
Mexican-American War, 92–93, 208–209
  and annexation of Texas, 207–208
  and proposed Congressional censure of
    Polk, 209–211
  See also Texas annexation
Monroe, James, 50
  on defense, 266–267
  and diplomacy, 81, 82
  first Inaugural Address, 265–267
  Jackson on, 85
  as member of Revolutionary generation,
    80
  on nation's positive conditions, 265–266
  on Native Americans, 267, 268–269
  on neutrality regarding European wars,
    268, 269
  on political factions, 134–135, 267
  second Inaugural Address, 268–270
  State of the Union Address (1823),
    402–403
  on War of 1812, 268
  on westward expansion, 269–270
Monroe Doctrine
  introduction of, 402–403
  Roosevelt Corollary, 110
Morgenthau, Henry, Jr., *63*
Morris, Gouverneur, 15, 20
Mott, Jacob, 202

Nast, Thomas, 167
National Bank issue, 209–210, 407
  Van Buren on, 409–411
National Industrial Recovery Act, 117, 230
National Security Adviser, 2
National Security Council, 2
Native Americans
  Grant on, 306, 431
  Jackson on, 275

Jackson on Cherokee removal, 408–409
  Jefferson on, 258–259
  Madison on, 264
  Monroe on, 267, 268–269
  W. H. Harrison on, 284
  Washington on, 397
New Mexico, 416–417
Nicolay, John, 3, 214, *214*
Nixon, Richard, *125*
  background, 68–69
  on dissension of 1960s, 369, 371
  on domestic policy role, 28
  on eliminating electoral college, 17
  farewell speech, 72
  first Inaugural Address, 368–371
  Ford's pardon of, 34–35
  on foreign affairs, 370–372
  on government paternalism, 372–373
  on growth of federal government,
    462–464
  and his dog, 124
  and increased executive power, 176, 177
  and the media, 8
  paranoia, hatreds, and secrecy of, 68–69,
    70–71, 124, 125, 127
  and public distrust of presidency, 5–6,
    66–67, 73, 124–126
  resignation of, 72–73
  resiliency of, 68, 69–70, 74
  second Inaugural Address, 371–374
  and "silent majority," 178
  State of the Union Address (1973),
    462–464
  and taping of presidential conversations,
    71–72, 125
  threatened impeachment of, 21, 72
  and Vietnam War, 70, 71, 73
  and Watergate scandal, 71–73, 124–126
North Carolina, 397
Nullification Crisis, 90–91, 92

Obama, Barack, 43
Office of Congressional Relations, 4
Office of Homeland Security, 26, 33
Office of Management and Budget, 4
Office of National AIDS Policy, 36
Office of Science and Technology Policy, 36
O'Neill, Tip, 88

Oregon
   and Polk, 289, 413
   Taylor on, 416
   and Tyler, 411
Overman Act of 1918, 113

Paine, Thomas, 79
Panama Canal, 109, 227, 440–441
Patton, George, 65
Pearl Harbor attack, 119
Pendleton, George H., 161, *162*
Philadelphia, 195–196
Pierce, Franklin
   Inaugural Address, 292–295
   as member of Doughface generation,
      93–94
   on perpetuation of Union, 294
   on sectional crisis, 419–420
   and slavery, 94–95, 294–295
   State of the Union Address (1855), 418–420
   on Union, 96
   on westward expansion, 292
Pinckney, Charles Cotesworth, 14, 141–142
Political parties
   Adams on, 139–140
   founders' views on, 133–135
   and ideology, 132, 177
   Jacksonian-era, 203–204
   Jefferson on, 144–145
   roots of, 49
   Washington on, 49, 135
   See also Election of 1796; Election of
      1800; Election of 1824; Election of
      1828; Election of 1860; Election of
      1864; Election of 1932; Election of
      1980; Election of 2000; Election of
      2004; Elections
Polk, James K., 50–51, 93, *206*
   as expansionist, 205–207
   Inaugural Address, 285–290
   and Mexican-American War, 92,
      132–133, 208–209
   and Oregon, 289, 413
   proposed Congressional censure of,
      209–211
   relations with Congress, 206–207
   State of the Union Address (1846),
      413–415

   as states' rights advocate, 206, 285–288
   on Texas annexation, 288–289, 413–415
   on value of Union, 286–288
Polly, 193
Powell, Colin, 42, 43
Presidency
   endurance of, 65
   F. D. Roosevelt's effect on shaping of,
      59–64
   increased power of, 174–177
   and legislative and judicial branches,
      189–191
   as life in fishbowl, 122–123
   Lincoln's effect on shaping of, 50–55
   Nixon's effect on shaping of, 65–74
   post-FDR power of, 233–234
   presidents' effects on shaping of, 43–44
   and Supreme Court, 197–198
   T. Roosevelt's effect on shaping of,
      56–59
   Washington's effect on shaping of, 44–50
   as white-men-only club, 42
Presidential generations, 78–79
   Civil War generation, 97–106
   Doughface generation, 92–96
   generations as defined by shared
      experiences, 79
   Greatest generation, 115–121
   Jacksonian generation, 85–91
   Progressive generation, 106–114
   Revolutionary generation, 79–85
   Watergate generation, 121–126
   World War II veterans, 77
Presidential power
   and balance of powers, 8–9
   and Constitution, 2–3
   as derived from the people, 6–7
   and executive branch employees, 3–4
   and federal bureaucracy, 31–32
   founders' differing views on how much
      to grant, 9–11
   and the media, 7–8
   and military. *See* Commander in chief
   and presidential legitimacy, 4–6
   and restraint, 45–46, 49, 65–66
   and salary, 12–14
   See also Commander in Chief; Veto
      power

Presidents
    and African Americans, 42–43
    and benefit of the doubt, 122
    and fascination with personalities of,
        39–41, 43–44
    low profile among early presidents,
        50–51, 59–60
    nicknames, 40
    and political parties, 129–133, 156–157
    and public expectation to be above
        politics, 131–132
    as rich white men, 42, 43
    as shapers of presidency, 43–44
    as something larger than ordinary
        people, 39
President's Critical Infrastructure
    Protection Board, 36
Prize Cases, 224
Progressive generation, 107
    presidents of, 113–114
    and shaping of modern presidency,
        114–115
    See also Roosevelt, Theodore; Wilson,
        Woodrow
Prohibition, 348

Radd, Victoria, 37
Randolph, Edmund, 8–9, 8, 20, 36
    biographical sketch, 8
    and Virginia Plan, 14–15
Reagan, Ronald, 181
    as the anti-Carter, 180
    assassination attempt against, 23–24
    and conservative coalition, 181–182
    on the economy, 469–470
    first Inaugural Address, 376–378
    on foreign policy, 470–471
    and the media, 64
    on neoconservative principles, 376–381
    optimistic style, 183–184
    pardon issued by, 34
    on pressures of presidency, 1, 37
    rejection of New Deal, 180
    second Inaugural Address, 379–381
    southern strategy, 180–181
    State of the Union Address (1982),
        469–471
    as staunch conservative, 180, 184
    as talented communicator, 7
    on two-party system, 131
    See also Election of 1980
Reconstruction
    and A. Johnson, 103–106, 427–429
    and Civil War generation, 98–99
    Grant on, 307–308, 430–431
    Hayes and end of, 309–311, 431–433
Removal from office, 17–18
    fixed term of office, 18–19
    illness and vice presidential succession,
        21–24
    impeachment, 19–22
Republican Party (1790s ff)
    favoring of France, 140, 141
    and Jefferson, 136–138
    merger with Federalists to form Whigs,
        153–154
Republican Party (1854 ff)
    abandonment of African Americans, 166
    and conservative coalition, 181–182
    and 1862 elections, 158
    dominance from Civil War to Great
        Depression, 164–166, 174
    formation of, 155, 156
    as party of big business, 165–166,
        168–169
    post-Hoover decline, 173
Requirements for office, 12, 14
    character, 9–10
    and oath of office, 11–12
    and presidential salary, 12–14
Revolutionary generation
    attitude toward speeches and
        communications, 82–84
    and diplomacy, 81–82
    and implementation of Constitution, 80
    intellectual influence, 79
    and presidential protocol and demeanor,
        80–81
    presidents of, 80
    quest for balance between dignity and
        democracy, 84
    shared events, 79
    See also Adams, John; Adams, John
        Quincy; Jefferson, Thomas; Madison,
        James; Monroe, James; Washington,
        George
Rice, Condoleezza, 42
Robards, Lewis, 151

Roosevelt, Anna, *172*
Roosevelt, Eleanor, *172*
　as public and political figure, 41–42
Roosevelt, Franklin D., *63, 65, 116, 121,*
　　172
　as activist president, 115–117, 118–119,
　　172–173
　background and personality, 60, 170
　and Congress, 117, 118, 227–229, 231
　death of, 120–121
　and Depression, 61–62, 227–229,
　　349–352, 449–451
　on Depression as war, 229
　on economic and political reform, 228
　emergence of, 170
　and EOP, 4
　expansion of executive branch,
　　117–119
　fireside chats, 62–63, 123
　first Inaugural Address, 349–352
　as grandfather figure, 77
　illness of, 22
　and the media, 60–64, 115
　and New Deal, 117, 171
　One Hundred Days, 228
　as one of best presidents, 4–5
　as only president to exceed two terms,
　　19, 120–121, 234
　pardons issued, 34
　physical disability, 60–61
　State of the Union Address (1934),
　　449–451
　and Supreme Court, 117, 229–231,
　　232–233
　as teacher, 115
　travel abroad, 120
　on world affairs in 1930s, 450
　and World War II, 63–64, 119–120,
　　231–232
　See also Election of 1932
Roosevelt, Theodore, 22, *109*
　as activist president, 108–110, 166,
　　226–227
　and African Americans, 58
　and bully pulpit, 107–108
　and Cabinet room, 36
　as communicator, 58
　and Congress, 226–227
　on corporations, 439–440

　and expansion of presidential power,
　　58–59
　foreign policy, 108–110
　imperialist ambitions, 332, 439
　Inaugural Address, 331–333
　as McKinley's VP and successor, 56, 107
　and the media, 108, 122–123
　as member of Progressive generation,
　　107–108
　and Panama Canal, 109, 227, 440–441
　personality traits, 56–58
　policy priorities, 58–59
　Roosevelt Corollary (to Monroe
　　Doctrine), 110
　and Spanish-American War, 56, *57*
　and Square Deal, 108
　State of the Union Address (1902),
　　438–441
　and the teddy bear, 39–40
Ross, James, 144
Rusk, Dean, *69*

Sand Creek Massacre, 220
Schechter v. United States, 230
Schlesinger, Arthur Jr., 174–175, 176
Scott, Winfield, 216
Secession
　and Buchanan, 98, 420–422
　Lincoln on, 298–302
　See also Civil War; Slavery
Secret Service, 33
Secretary of defense, 2, 26
Sectional crisis (1840s–1850s), 92–98
　Pierce on, 419–420
　See also Civil War; Compromise of
　　1850
Separation of powers
　between Civil War and 1930s, 222,
　　225–226
　and Civil War, 212–222, 224–225
　and F. D. Roosevelt, 227–234
　and League of Nations, 223–224, 223 223
　Madison on, 30, 190–191
　as slight misnomer, 190–191
　and T. Roosevelt, 226–227
　W. H. Harrison on, 281–282, 283
　and World War I, 222
　See also Mexican-American War;
　　Tripolitan affair

Seward, William, 96, 129, 130, 190
    on Lincoln's acceptance of visitors,
        214–215
Shays, Daniel, and rebellion, 9–10
Sherman, William Tecumseh, 106–107
Slavery, 51
    B. Harrison on legacy of, 319
    Buchanan on, 295–296
    1840s–1850s, 92–93, 94–95
    and Jackson, 43
    and Jacksonian generation, 92
    and Lincoln, 42, 51–54, 100–102
    Pierce on, 294–295
    and Polk, 132–133
    Van Buren on, 279
    and Washington, 46
    See also African Americans; Civil War;
        Compromise of 1850; Secession
Social Security, 474
Spanish-American War, 56, 57, 107, 222,
    328–329, 437–438
Stalin, Joseph, 120, 121
State Department, 27, 35
State of the Union Addresses, 29–30. See
    also under individual presidents
States' rights
    Jackson on, 274, 275, 276–277
    and Jefferson, 192
    and Polk, 206, 285–288
    W. H. Harrison on, 282
Stevens, Thaddeus, 104
Stone, Charles, 217
Story, Joseph, 202
Stowe, Harriet Beecher, 95
Suffrage
    and African Americans, 102
    expansion in Jacksonian era, 87
Sumner, Charles, 215

Taft, William Howard, 40
    on African Americans, 335–337
    on Asian immigration, 335
    on imminence of World War I, 334–335
    Inaugural Address, 333–337
    as member of Progressive generation,
        113–114
    on Panama Canal, 441–442
    State of the Union Address (1910),
        441–442

    on tariffs and taxation, 334
Taney, Roger, 99–100, 190
Tappan, Benjamin, 209
Taylor, Zachary, 21–22, 44, 155
    and aftermath of Mexican-American
        War, 416–417
    Inaugural Address, 290–291
    as member of Doughface generation, 93
    and Mexican-American War, 208, 210,
        211
    State of the Union Address (1849),
        416–417
Terrorism
    and Bush Jr., 40, 234, 390–393,
        476–479
    Clinton on, 476
Texas annexation
    and Polk, 288–289
    and Tyler, 207–208, 209
    See also Mexican-American War
Tingy, Captain. See Bas v. Tingy
"Touched by Fire" generation. See Civil
    War generation
Treasury Department, 33, 35
Tripolitan affair, 195–197, 196
    background, 191–195
    Jefferson on, 399–400
    and presidential war powers, 198–202
Truman, Bess, 42
Truman, Harry, 77, 121, 173
    changing views of, 5
    communication gaffes, 64
    on communism and Cold War, 354–356,
        451–454
    and Fair Deal, 175
    Inaugural Address, 353–356
    on Korean War, 451
    on respect for office, 5
    State of the Union Address (1951),
        451–454
    and Vietnam War, 67
Tweed, William, 165
Twenty-fifth Amendment, 23
Twenty-second Amendment, 19, 234
Tyler, John, 39, 92, 203
    and annexation of Texas, 207–208, 209,
        411–413
    State of the Union Address (1844),
        411–413

Uncle Tom's Cabin, 95
United States Marshal's Service, 33
United States Military Academy, 192
U.S. Congress
    dominance following A. Johnson
        presidency, 5, 55, 58, 106
    Joint Committee on the Conduct of the
        [Civil] War, 217–222
    payment of executive branch salaries, 4,
        12–14
    and Spanish-American War, 222
    and T. Roosevelt, 59
U.S. Constitution
    Adams on, 252
    Article II, 2
    endurance of, 65
    signing of, 3
U.S. Supreme Court
    and Civil War, 224–225
    and F. D. Roosevelt, 117, 229–233
    Hamilton on, 198
    national responsibility, 6–7
    and presidency, 197–198
    and 2000 election, 7
USA Freedom Corps, 36
U-2 incident, 122

Vallandigham, Clement, 157–158, 161,
    224
Van Buren, Martin, 39, 51, 59, *88*, 203
    on balance of state and federal powers,
        279
    Inaugural Address, 278–280
    as Jackson's vice president, 91, 204
    as member of Jacksonian generation,
        87–88
    on National Bank, 409–411
    on national expansion, 279
    on nation's prosperity, 278–279
    relations with Congress, 204–205
    on slavery, 279
    State of the Union Address (1837),
        409–411
Veto power, 30–31
    and A. Johnson, 104, 105
    and Jackson, 90
    Jefferson's urging of Washington to use,
        90
    W. H. Harrison on, 282

Vice presidency, 187–189
    Adams on, 135, 187
    Garner on, 187
    succession in case of president's
        incapacitation, 23–24
Vietnam War, 67
    and Ford, 73–74
    and L. Johnson, 67–68, *69*, 123–124, 234,
        459, 460, 461–462
    and Nixon, 70, 71, 73
    and subsequent wars, 74
Villa, Pancho, 111
Virginia Dynasty, 80, 86
Virginia Plan, 14–15

Wade, Benjamin, 159, 219
War
    American attitude toward, 65, 66, 67, 73
    and Bush Jr. policies, 40
    McKinley on, 56, 107
    See also Afghanistan War; Civil War;
        Gulf War (1991); Iraq War; Korean
        War; Mexican-American War; Spanish-
        American War; Tripolitan affair;
        Vietnam War; World War I; World
        War II
War Department, 35
War Industries Board, 113
War powers, 191
    and Civil War, 212–222
    and Mexican-American War, 209–212
    and possibility of despotism, 234
    and Tripolitan affair, 198–202
War Powers Act of 1973, 126
Warren, Mercy Otis and James, 79
Washington, Booker T., 58
Washington, Bushrod, 201–202
Washington, George, 39, *44, 47*, 65
    Adams on, 252–253
    adaptations on Constitution, 84–85
    and Cabinet, 35–36, *36*
    decision not to seek third term, 49
    deference to legislature, 48–49
    election by acclamation, 135
    energetic nature, 47–48
    on factionalism, 250–251
    and factions centered around Jefferson
        and Hamilton, 138
    Farewell Address, 82

Washington, George *(cont.)*
  first Inaugural Address, 249–251
  health of, 21, 22
  inauguration ceremony, 48
  Jefferson on, 257
  as member of Revolutionary generation, 80
  as model for the presidency, 44–45, 49–50
  on Native Americans, 29–30, 397
  as one of best presidents, 4–5
  on openness to the public, 80
  pardons issued, 34
  on patronage, 88
  on political parties, 49, 135
  and precedents for presidency, 19, 24, 35–36
  on preparedness for war, 397
  relations with Congress, 194
  restrained exercise of power, 45–46, 49
  and salary, 12, 13
  and self-discipline, 46–47
  on Shays' Rebellion, 9–10
  State of the Union Address (1790), 397–398
  on threat of disunion, 97
  and virtue of balance, 48–49
  on visit to Senate, 83
  and Whiskey Rebellion, 26, 91
Watergate generation
  and erosion of trust, 122, 124–127
  See also Johnson, Lyndon; Kennedy, John F.; Nixon, Richard
Watergate scandal, 71–73
  and subsequent "-gate" scandal descriptions, 74
Weaver, Robert Clifton, 42
Weed, Thurlow, 129, 156, 164, 203

Whigs, 153–154, 155, 205
Williamson, Hugh, 9
Wilmot, David, 93
Wilson, James, 11, *11*
  biographical sketch, 11
  on presidential salary, 12–13
Wilson, Woodrow, 59, *111*
  background and personality, 110, 111
  on Democratic party's regaining presidency, 131–132
  and economic issues, 111, 338–339
  first Inaugural Address, 337–340
  foreign policy, 111–113
  Gettysburg anniversary and reconciliation, 165
  illness of, and wife's management of White House, 22, 23
  and League of Nations, 112, 223–224, 223 223
  as member of Progressive generation, 113
  and New Freedom, 111
  second Inaugural Address, 340–342
  State of the Union Address (1917), 442–443
  views on roles of Congress and executive branch, 110–111
  and World War I, 111–113, 222, 340–342, 442–443
Women's suffrage, 344
Woodbury, Levi, 146–147
Woodward, Bob, 71
World War I
  Harding on aftermath of, 343, 443–444
  Taft on imminence of, 334–335
  and Wilson, 111–113, 222, 340–342, 442–443
World War II, 63–64 119–120, 231– 232

ABOUT THE AUTHOR

Brian Dirck is associate professor of history at Anderson University in Anderson, Indiana. He specializes in the American Civil War era, particularly the life and career of Abraham Lincoln. He is the author of *Lincoln and Davis: Imagining America, 1809–1865* (Lawrence: University Press of Kansas, 2001) and *Lincoln the Lawyer* (Urbana: University of Illinois Press, 2007). He is currently working on a study of Lincoln and American race relations.